W9-BWO-722

International Encyclopedia of Communications

THE UNIVERSITY OF PENNSYLVANIA

The *International Encyclopedia of Communications* was conceived, developed, and edited at The Annenberg School of Communications, University of Pennsylvania.

International Encyclopedia of Communications

ERIK BARNOUW
Editor in Chief

GEORGE GERBNER
Chair, Editorial Board

WILBUR SCHRAMM
Consulting Editor

TOBIA L. WORTH
Editorial Director

LARRY GROSS
Associate Editor

Volume 4

Published jointly with
THE ANNENBERG SCHOOL OF COMMUNICATIONS,
University of Pennsylvania

OXFORD UNIVERSITY PRESS
New York Oxford

Oxford University Press

Oxford New York Toronto
Delhi Bombay Calcutta Madras Karachi
Petaling Jaya Singapore Hong Kong Tokyo
Nairobi Dar es Salaam Cape Town
Melbourne Auckland

and associated companies in
Berlin Ibadan

Published jointly by
The Annenberg School of Communications,
University of Pennsylvania,
and Oxford University Press, Inc.,
200 Madison Avenue, New York, New York 10016

Library of Congress Cataloging-in-Publication Data

International encyclopedia of communications / Erik Barnouw, editor-in-chief . . . [et al.].
p. cm.
Bibliography: p.
Includes index.
1. Communication—Dictionaries. I. Barnouw, Erik, 1908–
P87.5.I5 1989 001.51'0321—dc19 88-18132 CIP
ISBN 0-19-504994-2 (set)
ISBN 0-19-505802-X (vol. 1)
ISBN 0-19-505803-8 (vol. 2)
ISBN 0-19-505804-6 (vol. 3)
ISBN 0-19-505805-4 (vol. 4)

Acknowledgments of sources of illustrative materials appear in captions throughout this work. Conscientious efforts have been made to locate owners of copyrights on illustrative materials and to secure their permission to use them herein. If any illustration has been inadvertently used without proper acknowledgment of its source, the publishers invite notification by copyright owners so that a correction can be made in future printings.

2 4 6 8 9 7 5 3 1

Printed in the United States of America
on acid-free paper

Editorial Board

(es), the nineteenth letter of the English and other modern alphabets, and the eighteenth of the ancient Roman alphabet, derives its form (through the 𐌔 and Σ, Ʃ of early Latin and Greek inscriptions) from the Phœnician W (Hebrew שׁ *shīn*), which represented a voiceless sibilant: in some of the Semitic languages (s), in others (ʃ). . . . In ancient Greek and Latin the value of the letter is believed to have been always (s).

SAPIR, EDWARD (1884–1939)

U.S. anthropologist and linguist. Edward Sapir was born in Lauenburg, Pomerania, but his family emigrated to the United States five years later. He grew up on New York's Lower East Side, where his father was a cantor. Winning a prestigious Pulitzer scholarship to Columbia University, Sapir obtained a B.A. in 1904, an M.A. in 1905, and a Ph.D. in 1909. His first two degrees were in Germanic philology, but FRANZ BOAS persuaded him to switch to anthropology, initiating a lifelong commitment to the salvage recording of American Indian linguistic and cultural data. Sapir became the preeminent linguist of Boasian anthropology and later a seminal figure in the emergence of LINGUISTICS as an autonomous discipline in North America.

Sapir began American Indian fieldwork in 1905, held positions at the University of California (1907–1908) and the University of Pennsylvania (1908–1910), and in 1910 (at the age of twenty-six) became head of the new Division of Anthropology of the Geological Survey of Canada. Sapir moved to the University of Chicago in 1925 and to Yale University in 1931; he held joint appointments in anthropology and linguistics at both institutions.

Sapir was an intuitive and eclectic thinker, acknowledged for his genius by his contemporaries and intellectual progeny. His numerous publications include many that are revolutionary in American Indian linguistics. Virtually alone among his generation, Sapir had a verbal artistry and an intellectual incisiveness that allowed him to present complex technical ideas about LANGUAGE and CULTURE to a wider audience. Thus his early linguistic and ethnological publications gave way, in emphasis at least, to more general orientations.

During the mid-Ottawa years Sapir turned to the writing of POETRY and LITERARY CRITICISM as an escape from the rigidity of scientific writing. He became intrigued by psychological literature and moved into the emerging interdisciplinary field of culture and personality. After his return to academic life Sapir became the primary spokesman for the interdisciplinary study of personality, at Chicago mediating effectively between sociology and psychiatry, particularly in the interactional paradigm of HARRY STACK SULLIVAN. Much of this work was abortive, because of Sapir's premature death in 1939 at the age of fifty-five and the advent of World War II, but it set the stage for investigations by other scholars.

Sapir's only full-length book, *Language,* appeared in 1921 and was directed at a popular audience. It remains the classic text for the nontechnical view of language, tracing language through human history and geographical variation as a means of symbolic communication whose internal form characterizes the thought patterns and lifeways of its speakers. In the generation after Sapir linguistics became much narrower in its definition of language, stressing internal form in isolation from MEANING, ignoring cultural context, and excluding the aesthetic dimensions of language. Sapir's view is again in ascendancy, however, and his delineation of the legitimate scope of linguistics—not denying linguistic form but placing it in a context of everyday human life—is a manifesto for all disciplines focusing on communication, not solely for anthropology and linguistics.

Sapir attempted to tie the concerns of his disciplines to understanding of his own society, arguing that a "genuine culture" was one in which the individual member experienced a sense of security and integration of his or her worldview. He berated his colleagues for reifying the notion of "superorganic" culture and thus overshadowing the individual as the locus of culture; he even argued that there are as many cultures as there are individuals.

A series of articles published in the *Encyclopedia of the Social Sciences* between 1931 and 1934 provides the best manifesto of Sapir's mature thought. Topics include communication, custom, dialect, fashion, group, language, personality, and SYMBOLISM. Sapir argued that linguistic form is the core of the human ability to define culture and provide a satisfying context for individual fulfillment. His emphases on culturally constituted meaning, variability within a culture based on individual creativity, and symbolic thought as the essence of being human have been elaborated in disciplines as diverse as anthropology, sociology, FOLKLORE, linguistics, psychology and psychiatry, and belles lettres.

Sapir himself easily crossed disciplinary boundaries. For example, he used native-speaker intuitions of linguistic form to define the "psychological reality" of the phoneme (the smallest meaningful unit of sound), thereby revolutionizing the way in which grammars were written (*see* GRAMMAR). He used linguistic labels to approach the complexity of ethnographic cultures. He experimented with poetry and essays as literary genres to present anthropological content. And he argued that the task of the anthropologist was to take the exotic out of the primitive, thereby revealing the humanness of all members of culture. He speculated on the relationship between linguistic categories and human thought, a hypothesis more systematically elaborated by his student BENJAMIN LEE WHORF. Then, of course, he trained a generation of American Indian linguists and students of culture and personality. There is no single disciplinary label or intellectual paradigm within which the richness of Sapir's thought can be contained or its repercussions traced through subsequent scholarship.

Bibliography. Regna Darnell, *Edward Sapir: Linguist, Anthropologist, and Humanist,* Berkeley, Calif., forthcoming; Edward Sapir, *Selected Writings of Edward Sapir in Language, Culture and Personality,* ed. by David G. Mandelbaum, Berkeley, Calif., 1949, reprint (with a new epilogue) 1985.

REGNA DARNELL

SARNOFF, DAVID (1891–1971)

U.S. broadcasting executive whose meteoric career was closely interwoven with the history of the Radio Corporation of America (RCA). David Sarnoff played a key role in the company's creation in 1919 (a reorganization of British-controlled American Marconi), its long domination of RADIO manufacturing and broadcasting, its shaping of an electronic television industry (*see* TELEVISION HISTORY), and its eventual evolution into what President Lyndon B. Johnson called "a key element in our defense structure," specializing not only in military communications but in a range of electronic weaponry.

Born in the bleak village of Uzlian, Russia (in the province of Minsk), Sarnoff emigrated to the United States at age nine. On New York's Lower East Side he attended school while helping support his immigrant family by working as a newsboy and at other jobs. Having joined American Marconi as an errand boy, he learned TELEGRAPHY and became a junior telegraph operator. During the 1912 *Titanic* disaster he gained public recognition by staying at his post long hours to relay news of survivors telegraphed by rescue vessels. In 1917 he moved to American Marconi's newly formed Commercial Department, a response to the government's stepped-up orders for military communications equipment. Sarnoff, still in his twenties, gained valuable experience in negotiating with military contractors.

The military importance of electronics led to the Americanization of the company as RCA in a takeover engineered by General Electric (GE) under prodding from the U.S. Navy. By 1921 Sarnoff was RCA's general manager. The sudden eruption of the broadcasting boom made radio the company's principal field of action. Sarnoff, who had for some time urged manufacture and sale of "radio music boxes"—along lines long promoted by LEE DE FOREST—took up the challenge.

RCA was at this point controlled by GE, Westinghouse, AT&T, and United Fruit, which had jointly taken over the majority holdings formerly in British hands. This had created a patent pool that included virtually all major U.S. electronic patents. But RCA was not in control of its own affairs: under the RCA trademark it sold radio sets that were manufactured (in agreed-on proportions) by GE and Westinghouse.

Figure 1. *(Sarnoff, David)* David Sarnoff *(left)* and Guglielmo Marconi at RCA facilities, ca. 1930. The National Portrait Gallery, Smithsonian Institution, Washington, D.C. Gift of Erik Barnouw.

As the MONOPOLY implications of the arrangement began to alert antitrust officials in Washington, Sarnoff used the threat skillfully to win independence for RCA. He urged its corporate owners to support unification of manufacturing and marketing under RCA. Eventually GE and Westinghouse relinquished their ownership in exchange for RCA debentures and other inducements. RCA, emerging from its role as sales agent, became a powerful entity in its own right. Its purchase of the Victor Talking Machine Company in 1929 broadened its power. In 1930 Sarnoff became president.

By this time television had moved to the top of Sarnoff's agenda. Inauguration of an electronic television era became his overwhelming ambition. VLADIMIR K. ZWORYKIN, who had conducted television experiments in czarist Russia and later at Westinghouse, became leader of the RCA televison research staff. Sarnoff set a rigid schedule and drove his cohorts relentlessly. Although he engaged in bitter patent struggles with two independent inventors, EDWIN H. ARMSTRONG and PHILO FARNSWORTH, Sarnoff succeeded in introducing television at the 1939

New York World's Fair. He also won an enthusiastic reception for an improved system following World War II and for RCA color television soon afterward. From 1947 to 1970 he was chairman of the board; within RCA his power was unchallenged.

The thin immigrant boy had by now become a remote, imperious executive, impeccably dressed and speaking flawless executive English. At RCA he was called "the General" in recognition of his brief service in uniform during World War II, which had made him a brigadier general. RCA officialdom now communicated with him through memorandums, on which he penciled "yes," "no," or "PSM" ("please see me"). Few knew him intimately, but world leaders were ready to listen to him. After the war he was constantly back and forth to Washington, proposing new and more heinous weapons of mass destruction. Anti-Russian strategies became an obsession. Some associates deplored the trend, but few opposed him. He had made RCA one of the great corporations of the modern era and was virtually the corporation's embodiment. So closely was RCA identified with him and controlled by him that his retirement in 1970 brought a period of internal conflict and declining fortune. In 1985, after a series of disastrous decisions and dwindling revenue, the corporation was ready to be absorbed by GE, which had led in its creation.

Bibliography. Kenneth Bilby, *The General: David Sarnoff and the Rise of the Communications Industry,* New York, 1986; Carl Dreher, *Sarnoff: An American Success,* New York, 1977.

JEANNE THOMAS ALLEN

SATELLITE

Space vehicle designed to follow a predetermined route, usually orbiting the earth, for the purpose of collecting and transmitting information. Located at the intersection of space and communications technologies, satellites are central to the revolution in communications that has characterized the second half of the twentieth century. While satellites play an important role in space exploration, this article will address their communications function—the collection and transmission of information via earth-orbiting satellites.

There are many types of satellites. While the U.S. space agency, the National Aeronautics and Space Administration (NASA), used to divide them into four general categories (communication and navigation, meteorology, remote sensing, and geology), eighteen types of satellites have been identified for the purposes of international technical regulation. However, in terms of the services performed by satellites, they can be divided into two broad categories: observation satellites used for the collection, processing, and transmission of data about earth and its environment; and communication satellites used for the transmission of information from one location on earth to another.

Observation satellites. The potential value of using satellites for monitoring the earth's environment was recognized at an early stage of space activities. However, it took almost a decade to appreciate the wealth of information available by these means and to develop techniques for using the new data. Satellite technology has several advantages over traditional techniques such as ground observation and aerial photography. A satellite circling the earth at an altitude of several hundred kilometers or more, or in a geostationary orbit at thirty-six thousand kilometers, can cover a large portion of the terrestrial landscape in a single photograph and can survey areas of the earth that are virtually inaccessible for continuous observation by any other means. Even after fifty years of aerial surveys, only about 30 percent of the earth was considered adequately mapped, while photographs from high-altitude satellites have provided extensive maps with very little distortion.

A number of technical innovations were developed to assist the observation satellites. New methods for the collection of images and data have included multispectral cameras and sensors capable of measuring even minute differences in the amounts of energy reflection, so that it is possible to distinguish between salt and pure water or clear and polluted air, and to identify the composition of soil, air, and water. The large amount of information that is generated by these technologies makes the processing of data and their translation into usable forms one of the most important and difficult challenges of satellite use. As a result, the use of digital data processing and interactive and automated data analysis has increased rapidly in order to optimize or enhance images for visual interpretation and to develop a variety of specific applications.

The new technology and the equipment developed for satellites during the early stages of space exploration have been applied to the global observation of the earth in three main areas: meteorology, remote sensing, and military surveillance. In meteorology, which by definition is an international science, there has been extensive cooperation between countries. National satellites play a key role in the international programs established under the aegis of the World Meteorological Organization (WMO). For the space-based subsystem of the Global Observing System geostationary satellites were launched by the United States, Japan, and the European Space Agency, and polar-orbiting satellites were launched by the United States and the Soviet Union. Data received from these satellites are used to determine profiles of atmosphere

Figure 1. *(Satellite)* Drawing of the French satellite SPOT 1, which records images in orbit 517 miles from earth. Courtesy of Spot Image Corporation.

temperatures, cloud cover and height, snowmelt, surface water boundaries, and water-vapor sensing. Such information is also provided by the Global Atmospheric Research Programme (GARP). In addition, meteorological satellites are used by the World Weather Watch to monitor and trace typhoons and monsoons and to observe the effects of droughts, particularly in the Sahel region of Africa. Not only scientists but also the general public have become acquainted with this space technology through the satellite weather pictures displayed on TELEVISION NEWS programs.

Remote sensing of the environment was pioneered by special earth-exploration satellites such as the U.S. Landsat series, the Soviet Soyuz 5 and 6, and experimental space platforms such as Skylab. Remote sensing data collected via satellites have applications in agriculture, forestry and range management, hydrology, geology, oceanography, energy resource identification, flood and disaster warnings, and land-use charting (*see* CARTOGRAPHY). Despite the great promises of this technology, it was long considered experimental or preoperational because of the lack of the necessary institutional setting to ensure continuity of service, as well as the absence of international agreements on costs and legal principles. It is expected, however, that data from remote sensing via satellites will be available to growing numbers of diverse users, particularly in developing countries.

Satellites have also been used for meteorological and remote sensing activities by the military. These techniques have found a more controversial use in military reconnaissance and surveillance, conducted particularly by the two major space powers to observe ballistic missile sites, weapons testing and deployment, military exercises, and wars. While controversial, these activities have also been viewed as a potentially stabilizing factor, since they could be used as part of the verification clauses in arms agreements such as the SALT treaties.

Communications satellite systems. By the time the first Sputnik was launched in 1957, communications technology was ready for outer space. In fact, space communication had already begun during the previous decade through the use of the moon as a reflector for signals from earth. The same principle was used in the U.S. Echo project in which signals were bounced off a large, aluminized, space-borne balloon. Subsequent developments focused on active satellites, which receive signals from earth, shift their frequencies as required, and amplify and retransmit the signals to earth.

The primary uses of communications satellites have been for long-distance, point-to-point, two-way telecommunication links carrying TELEPHONE and other traditional telecommunications messages; for providing live transoceanic television transmissions; and, increasingly, for data traffic between large and costly earth stations linked to TELECOMMUNICATIONS NETWORKS. Advances in rocket technology have made possible the use of heavier, more powerful satellites, which, together with the introduction of new communication techniques such as digital transmission, have permitted reductions in the size of the earth stations. Satellite systems in use and under development provide a wide range of services: satellite networks with earth stations situated at each branch or local office of large organizations; facilities for communication with mobile entities such as ships, aircraft, trucks, or patrol units; general telecommunication services with earth stations close to or within each large city in a country; and the opportunity for remote and isolated communities to establish reliable access to global communication networks.

In the early years of satellite communication it was generally thought that this new technology would be organized in the form of a few major systems providing all required services in all parts of the world. Contrary to these expectations, there has been a proliferation of specialized systems at the international, regional, and national levels for the purposes of general telecommunications, navigation, direct broadcast, and military activities.

Two organizations have provided services at the international level for general telecommunications such as telephone, telex, data, and television transmissions: INTELSAT (International Telecommunications Satellite Consortium), first established in 1964 at the initiative of the United States and including more than one hundred member countries by 1985; and Intersputnik, established in 1968 at the initiative of the Soviet Union and including eastern European countries and some countries in Asia, Africa, and Central America. Concurrently, a number of systems were established or planned at the regional level (western Europe, the Arab region, Africa) and the national level (Canada, the United States, the Soviet Union, Indonesia, India, Japan, Brazil, France, the Federal Republic of Germany, the People's Republic of China, etc.).

The first satellites to provide navigation services were developed for military purposes, but such systems have now also found civilian uses. In 1978 the international agency INMARSAT was established to provide worldwide maritime communications. The use of satellites for aircraft navigation has remained in an exploratory stage.

Much attention has been devoted to direct broadcast satellites (DBS), which are capable of providing a signal strong enough to be received by individual sets equipped with small antennas and are, therefore, independent of the telecommunications networks linking earth stations. The American ATS-6 satellite was an example of an experimental satellite used for early trials of this service in the United States, India (the famous Satellite Instructional Television Experiment, SITE, in 1975–1976), and other countries (*see* EDUCATIONAL TELEVISION). A number of operational DBS systems have been or will be deployed in various countries, including the United States, Canada, the Soviet Union, Japan, India, and various European countries. A clear distinction was once made between the fixed-satellite service for point-to-point telecommunications and the broadcasting-satellite service for direct reception, but developing technology has blurred it. Signals from certain fixed satellites can be received on individual sets, and satellite systems with direct broadcast capacity can also be used for two-way services.

As with all other communication technologies, satellites have military applications. Though satellites are used by the military for many so-called nonaggressive purposes (the three Cs: control, command, communications), they inevitably made outer space a major strategic frontier. Thus, military communication satellites became such an integral part of modern arms systems that they were added to the long list of potential military targets, and technologies whose functions were directly aggressive were developed and tested. These have included antisatellite weapons in the form of interceptor/destructor satellites and other systems such as high-energy laser and particle-beam weapons.

Future technological developments. Technically, the development of satellite communications depends on advances in launcher, satellite, and ground equipment technology. The rapid advances in these technologies were reflected in the approximately 150 civilian communications satellites in orbit by the mid-1980s, with the prospect of further rapid growth.

Figure 2. *(Satellite)* A GOES satellite photograph of Hurricane Allen taken on August 8, 1980. Courtesy of NOAA/NESDIS.

Satellite communications were a multimillion-dollar business, mainly in the hands of a few countries. In a very short time the problem of overcrowding in space developed for satellites in geostationary orbit. The use of this space must be determined in reference to the problems of interference in the frequency bands, which, according to international agreements, are supposed to be available for space communications (*see* SPECTRUM). Consequently, new satellite communication concepts were developed by various space organizations and by industry. These include multimission satellites that could combine the payloads of different operations and locate them on one large, multipurpose satellite; clusters of jointly operated satellites located at the same longitude; and geostationary platforms consisting of diverse elements that are launched separately into space and then assembled, or making up what in another design version is called an orbital antenna farm. The implementation of such concepts will demand new and imaginative legal, organizational, and financial arrangements.

International regulation. Communication satellite operations were organized in a variety of ways at the international, regional, and national levels. From the beginning, though, international regulation has been a crucial aspect of the development of satellite communication. This is particularly true with regard to agreements on the use of radio frequencies, since the regulations for the new technology had to be compatible with international rules governing the allocation and use of frequencies for earthbound radio services. The complicated technical and administrative work in this field is managed by the International Telecommunication Union (ITU), the specialized agency within the United Nations system responsible for the international ordering and regulation of telecommunications. Through a series of international conferences starting in 1963, an increasing number of frequency ranges were allocated to the different kinds of space communication, primarily to satellite services. In addition, a series of detailed rules was agreed upon for advance notification about projected satellite services and other administrative procedures.

Other international aspects of this area have been the concern of the United Nations Committee on the Peaceful Uses of Outer Space as part of its work on the development of space law. In this context two issues have proved to be important and controversial: international legal principles to govern remote sensing via satellites, particularly in respect to rules concerning the use of information about one country collected by another; and international legal principles governing direct satellite broadcasting from one country to another (in addition to the technical-administrative rules agreed upon within the context of the ITU). The continuing negotiations show clearly the complex issues associated with the use of communications satellites and their growing importance in the communications systems of the world.

See also INTERNATIONAL ORGANIZATIONS.

Bibliography. Centre for Research of Air and Space Law, *Space Activities and Implications: Where From and Where To at the Threshold of the 80's,* Toronto and Montreal, 1981; Ralph Chipman, ed., *The World in Space: A Survey of Space Activities and Issues* (prepared for UNISPACE 82, United Nations), Englewood Cliffs, N.J., 1982; Arthur C. Clarke, ed., *The Coming of the Space Age,* New York, 1967; Bhupendra Jasani, ed., *Outer Space: A New Dimension of the Arms Race,* London, 1982; Kiran Karnik, ed., *Alternative Space Futures and the Human Condition* (prepared for UNISPACE 82, United Nations), Oxford and New York, 1982; Edward W. Ploman, *Space, Earth, and Communication,* Westport, Conn., 1984; Delbert D. Smith, *Communication via Satellite: A Vision in Retrospect,* Leyden and Boston, 1976.

EDWARD W. PLOMAN

SAUSSURE, FERDINAND DE (1857–1913)

Swiss linguist. Born in Geneva into a prominent Huguenot family, Ferdinand de Saussure studied Indo-European LINGUISTICS at the Universities of Leipzig and Berlin (1876–1880), then taught in Paris at the École des Hautes Études (1881–1891). His publications, particularly *Memoire sur le système primitif des voyelles dans les langues indo-européennes* (1879), brought him international attention at a very young age. In 1891 he was called to the University of Geneva, where he was the first professor of Sanskrit and Indo-European languages and later professor of general linguistics (1906–1913). Between 1907 and 1911 he gave three courses on general linguistics, a subject that had interested him for many years but about which he published nothing during his lifetime. After his death two younger colleagues, Albert Sechehaye and Charles Bally, compiled a book appropriately entitled *Cours de linguistique générale* (1916), based on the students' notes, in which they attempted to offer a synthesis of the essential ideas that Saussure had developed in the three courses.

Scholarly acquaintance with Saussure's ideas was initially based entirely on the *Cours*. It was not until 1957 that Robert Godel published a monograph, *Les sources manuscrits du Cours de linguistique générale de F. de Saussure,* in which the lecture notes themselves and Saussure's own notes were for the first time examined and extensively analyzed. In 1968 Rudolf Engler published a critical edition of the *Cours de linguistique générale,* in which each paragraph of the text is flanked by the student notes relating to it. Another milestone in the study of Saussure's thought was the publication in 1967 of an Italian translation of, and careful commentary on, the *Cours* by Tullio de Mauro (the commentary has since been published in a French version). These contributions have enabled scholars to gain a more intimate acquaintance with Saussure's ideas as they were unfolded in his Geneva lectures and thus to correct and refine earlier analyses of the *Cours*.

Saussure's posthumous fame has largely rested on two notions: first, his conception of LANGUAGE as a system of interrelated elements, and, second, his conviction that language is a set of signs, one of a number of "semiological" institutions characteristic of the human species. As regards the first, the systematicity of language precludes any atomistic approach to words or their meanings; both facets of language can only be defined and identified relationally. Linguistic units exist insofar as they contrast with, that is, are not identical to, other units similar to them. For example, the MEANING of the English word *dog* is definable only negatively, as not the same as the meanings of other words associated with it, such as *wolf* and *fox*. One language, for instance, may have verbs that distinguish between locomotion on foot and locomotion in a vehicle (e.g., German *gehen* and *fahren*), and another language may lump them together (e.g., Italian *andare* and English *go*). Every language is, therefore, a vast system of multiply interrelated sets of associated units. Moreover, each of these units is a SIGN, namely, the conjunction of a *signified* (roughly, a meaning) and a *signifier* (roughly, a word). The relationship between signified and signifier is arbitrary, as is the relationship among signifiers. *See also* SEMIOTICS; SIGN SYSTEM.

Saussure was the first linguist to impress on his colleagues the need to achieve terminological and conceptual clarity. Regarding the nature of the object that linguists analyze, he insisted that three things be distinguished clearly, namely, (1) language (*langue*), (2) SPEECH (*parole*), and (3) the linguistic faculty (*faculté de langage*). *Langue,* for Saussure, is the set of conventions prevalent in a speech community that makes it possible for individual speakers to utilize their *faculté de langage.* Hence, the linguistic faculty is something entirely distinct from language, but the former cannot be exercised without the latter.

By the term *parole* Saussure denotes the acts of individual speakers utilizing their linguistic faculties by means of the particular social conventions observed in the speech community of which they are members. The result of *parole,* thus, is the concrete speech act. Within this conceptual system, *langue* occupies a position of priority; it should be the focus of the linguist's preoccupations, according to Saussure. Clearly, in such a "semiological" perspective, *langue* is eminently social in character: any complex system of signs owes its very existence to the community that uses it. However, compared with other cultural institutions, *langue* is something over which the members of society can exercise little freedom of choice, if only because it is inherited by the social group in toto from preceding generations. This accounts for the stability of linguistic systems over relatively long periods of time.

As for the discipline of linguistics, Saussure recommended that a radical distinction be observed between studying a language current at a particular point in time and viewing a language as an ever-changing object. From the first perspective, the language is seen as a system of contemporaneously functioning signs. This Saussure called the synchronic or static viewpoint. Adopting the other perspective, which he called the diachronic or dynamic viewpoint, the linguist follows the historical development of a language such as French. In his opinion these two perspectives should never be mixed, as they often were in the "historical" grammars of the late nineteenth century. But neither should one of them be neglected in favor of the other. Thus Saussure disapproved of the one-sided preoccupation of the linguists of his own day with historical research, and the publication of the *Cours* contributed to the shift of interest that has occurred in linguistic research over the past half-century toward descriptive (i.e., synchronic) work.

The influence of the *Cours* among twentieth-century linguists has been considerable, especially since World War II. Though it cannot be said that Saussure ignited the spark that gave rise to the various structuralist schools (e.g., the so-called Copenhagen and Prague circles), theoretical linguists certainly found inspiration in the pages of the *Cours.* Saussure's ideas have also enjoyed great popularity among certain philosophers, anthropologists, and literary theorists, particularly in French-speaking countries. *See also* LITERARY CRITICISM; POETICS; STRUCTURALISM.

Bibliography. Rudolf Engler, *Lexique de la terminologie saussurienne,* Utrecht, 1968; Ferdinand de Saussure, *Cours de linguistique générale,* critical ed., ed. by Tullio de Mauro, Paris, 1972; idem, *Course in General Linguistics,* ed. by Charles Bally and Albert Sechehaye, trans. from the French by Wade Baskin, New York, 1959; idem, *Course in General Linguistics,* ed. by Charles Bally and Albert Sechehaye, trans. from the French by Roy Harris, La Salle, Ill., and London, 1983.

W. KEITH PERCIVAL

SCHOOL

An institution for preparing the younger generation to participate in the life of society. Not usually thought of as a medium of mass communication, the school is nevertheless a complex communications network that provides the basis for much of the future communication in society. Essentially the school trains students as receivers and senders of messages.

Like the LIBRARY, MUSEUM, and ARCHIVES, the school is a repository of CULTURE, which encompasses the history and achievements of the society. But the school has a special mission to transmit this culture to the younger generation: it disseminates information, inculcates values, and develops tastes. It also trains students in the use of signs and symbols, beginning with READING, WRITING, and MATHEMATICS. Finally, at a deeper level the school transmits the structures of society, habits of PERCEPTION, and view of reality implicit in the culture and sign systems. *See* SIGN SYSTEM; STRUCTURALISM.

Figure 1. *(School)* An exercise tablet belonging to a Babylonian schoolchild. The elementary sign for "dish" has been impressed again and again on both sides of the clay tablet. Nippur, ca. 1700 B.C.E. The University Museum, Philadelphia. Neg. 133371.

Yet the school does not merely aim to transmit the accumulated knowledge to the younger generation. It also hopes to prepare the younger generation to hand on the knowledge to its successors and, in more open societies, to add something in the process. The process necessarily rests on a number of optimistic assumptions, the most important being that the human race—or at least a significant portion—is capable of learning. It also assumes that knowledge is infinite and that the human race is capable of managing the knowledge accumulated even though the burden becomes greater with each generation. Within this context modern communications techniques are essential, becoming what MARSHALL MCLUHAN called "extensions" of humankind.

The history of the school reflects, in part, its close links to communications techniques. Even amid modern technology the school's basic technique is still INTERPERSONAL COMMUNICATION, centered on the student-teacher relationship (*see also* INTERACTION, FACE-TO-FACE). A vital remnant of ORAL CULTURE and perhaps RITUAL, the student-teacher relationship is an outgrowth of the young person's relationships to parents, peers, priests, and storytellers that sufficed for instruction in earlier nonliterate societies. The beginning of schools is associated with the invention of writing: schools were established to train priests and scribes. Writing and scribal education first developed in Egypt, Sumer, and China during the third millennium B.C.E.; a parallel development occurred during the first millennium B.C.E. in Mesoamerica (*see* AMERICAS, PRE-COLUMBIAN). The next radical change in the school did not occur until the invention of PRINTING in the mid-fifteenth century (*see* GUTENBERG, JOHANNES). The printed BOOK affected the school in two ways: through the far-reaching changes in society that resulted from this invention—including the extension of schooling to a wider populace—and directly through shifts in curricula and methods of TEACHING.

A similar revolution is occurring as the school adapts to the electronic communications media developed during the second half of the twentieth century, the main ones being television and the computer. Both of these, like the printing press before them, have brought about a change in all aspects of the school. Objectives considered in the past to be desirable but unattainable are now within reach because of the new media. Teaching methods that utilize the new technology no longer resemble those traditionally used in schools, and teaching how to use the new communications media occupies a growing part of the curriculum.

The factors most important in molding the school's method of operation are, however, political and economic. The school is a social institution, and its history mainly reflects that of the societies—their ambitions, biases, and limitations—within which it has functioned. Historical changes in the school have included three dimensions:

1. the organizational dimension, which determines *who* will benefit from the school's services (and also who will be teachers);
2. the dimension of the curriculum, which reflects *what* is considered appropriate to teach in different societies and eras; and
3. the didactic dimension, which determines *how* the appropriate curriculum will be taught.

Organizational decisions incorporate political assumptions about society (in an aristocratic society the population of school pupils differs from that in a democratic society). Curricular decisions incorporate the accepted cultural view (in traditional societies the learnings that are considered important, such as classical literature, differ from those in technological societies, such as mathematics or science). Didactic decisions incorporate prevailing concepts about human nature (rote learning as a learning method reflects a view of human nature different from that of a more creative method).

The way these three dimensions are affected by the interplay of communications, politics, and economics is illustrated by the history of the school in Western culture. As the history shows, the aims of EDUCATION depend largely on the particular society managing it. *See also* EAST ASIA, ANCIENT; ISLAM, CLASSICAL AND MEDIEVAL ERAS; SOUTH ASIA, ANCIENT.

An Illustrative History

In European languages the word for school is derived from the Greek *scholē,* meaning "spare time." The etymology suggests that the first Western schools taught older children, for whom it was more significant to distinguish between spare and nonspare time. The etymology also supports the hypothesis that schools were established when social differentiation began. The appearance of schools marks that stage in the division of labor when physical labor is separated from spiritual labor and the social roles are so diversified that the FAMILY no longer reflects social life in its entirety. Various regulations in the form of written laws or accepted practices indicate the social interest that accompanied the school from its very beginning.

Ancient Greece and Rome. The school first became institutionalized in ancient Greece (*see* HELLENIC WORLD). In Athens the schools were not compulsory, but only the sons of free citizens could receive education (girls were trained by their mothers at home). From ages seven to fourteen the Athenian boy studied reading, writing, music, and gymnastics. The state did not support education, but it did supervise and regulate by law all elementary education.

Roman education during the empire period absorbed the Greek educational ideals (*see* ROMAN EMPIRE). The various schools sprang up without governmental regulation, but the state later came to regulate them. The educational system of Rome, which influenced Europe until modern times, assumed the following forms:

1. the *ludus* or elementary school (from about ages seven to twelve)
2. the grammar school (from ages twelve to sixteen)
3. the school of rhetoric (equivalent to contemporary college, from ages sixteen to twenty)

The Middle Ages. During the MIDDLE AGES, after the educational patterns established in classical times were practically destroyed, the church adopted the school as an educational framework, first as a tool for preparing the various levels of the priesthood and later for disseminating its influence among the faithful. The church school imitated the classical curriculum, which included the seven liberal arts (the trivium, consisting of GRAMMAR, RHETORIC, and dialectics; and the quadrivium, consisting of music, arithmetic, geometry, and astronomy), but it eliminated pagan values and focused on the Christian faith. After the twelfth century cities began developing their own institutions of education, including universities (*see* UNIVERSITY). They were centers of freethinking at that time, and the research undertaken within them led to the crystallization of attitudes that were eventually manifested in humanism, the RENAISSANCE, and the Reformation. *See also* RELIGION.

During the Middle Ages schools were not yet important to most social classes. The aristocracy did not need their services, as the exchange of sons between the various courts was sufficient for its purposes. In villages there were a few church schools, which undertook religious indoctrination, but most craftsmen in the towns educated their sons through apprenticeship arrangements.

The Renaissance and Reformation. There was a decisive change during the Renaissance, and particularly at the time of the Reformation. The Renaissance, which reflected the antifeudal spirit of urban society, shifted the emphasis from *divina studia* to *humana studia* (principally at the universities). Vittorino da Feltre (1378–1446) established the House of Joy (*Casa giocosa*) at Mantua. This was a school that, in the spirit of humanism and Greek general education, aimed at developing aesthetic taste and moral values, provided physical education, and encouraged pupils' motor and constructive impulses. Most Renaissance thinkers, however, were satisfied to undermine the validity of the educational features accepted at the time. Juan Luis Vives (1492–1540) in Spain, François Rabelais (ca. 1483–1553) in France, Desiderius Erasmus (ca. 1465–1536) in the Netherlands, Jacob Wimpfeling (1450–1528) in Germany, and many others condemned scholastic teaching methods and curricula, demanding that educational processes be based on sense perception and educational content on ancient classics.

In comparison with the Renaissance, whose character was individual and aristocratic, the Reformation was imbued with the spirit of religion and was more of a mass movement. Whereas during the Renaissance considerable interest centered on the universities, during the Reformation elementary and secondary schools were developed. MARTIN LUTHER (1483–1546), one of the leaders of the Reformation, regarded education as a precondition for a religious revival, and in contrast to the Catholic doctrine that saw the church as sole legitimate intermediary between individuals and their creator, he relied on individuals to address God directly and understand God's messages in the Holy Scriptures (*see* SCRIPTURE). This accounts for the great importance he attached to the elementary school as an institution that taught reading and writing in the vernacular and for his demand that free schools be established for all children of both sexes under the supervision of the state (and whose curriculum would include physical education and musical instruction). Philipp Melanchthon (1497–1560) and Johannes Sturm (1507–1589) were among the planners of the secondary school, using Latin rather than the vernacular and using methods of education based on the pupils' activities (debates, dramatization, LETTER writing, recitation, etc.). Luther and Melanchthon also influenced the universities of their time by stressing the

Figure 2. *(School)* A Roman school. The Bettmann Archive, Inc.

need for critical thought freed from the authority of the church (even though they themselves limited it by emphasizing the authority of the Holy Scriptures).

The Catholic Reformation. In the sixteenth and seventeenth centuries the Catholic church adopted the educational methods that had been developed during the Reformation and directed them against it. The Jesuit order established an educational system (primarily for secondary and higher education) that was designed to strengthen the Catholic church by training religious and secular leaders imbued with faith and loyal to the church. Their schools preserved the content of church education and added content taken from humanist education (the ancient literature of Greece and Rome) but meanwhile neutralized those influences that could undermine the foundations of Catholicism. The Jesuits' principal innovations were to rigidly centralize the entire educational system, permitting close supervision of each pupil, but at the same time to grant individual care and encourage pupils' talents (which were intended to serve the church). They fostered competition between pupils (by organizing them into competing pairs), awarded prizes (instead of administering corporal punishment), and frequently repeated the material studied. The teachers were selected from among the best pupils and were specially trained for their task. Eventually the Jesuits added the residential school to the regular school, thereby extending their educational influence over their pupils. These schools evinced the basic elements of the modern school that developed later in Europe: close contact between teacher and pupil, as a precondition for influencing the latter's character and intelligence, and the organization of pupils into groups or classes.

During the seventeenth century the method of the Jesuits was opposed from within the Catholic camp by the Jansenists in France. They sought to base faith primarily on religious experience and not necessarily on ritual. In 1637 they founded the Little Port Royal Schools, whose object was to provide the pupils with individual attention. The focus of education was the person, not the role the student was destined to fulfill. They were also interested in younger children and opened elementary schools. Characterized by an educational atmosphere free of fear, coercion, and competition, their schools contained small classes and used group methods of teaching. Despite the fact that the Jansenists' educational enterprise continued for only seventeen years and was limited in its extent, their attempts constituted a step toward the crystallization of the modern school.

Toward the new school. Johann Amos Comenius (1592–1670), a teacher and one of the leaders of the Moravian Brothers sect, provided the most comprehensive theoretical basis for education in the spirit of the age. In his book *Didactica Magna* (1657) he laid the foundations of the new education and outlined a scientific approach to the problems of education. He wanted to prove that it was possible "to teach everyone everything," relying on "the laws of nature," and proposed a new structure for the educational system (for boys and girls) at four levels:

- the mother school, for young children (up to six years old)

- the elementary school, in which subjects would be taught in the vernacular (for ages six to twelve)
- the Latin school, or gymnasium (for ages twelve to eighteen)
- the university and study tours (for ages eighteen to twenty-four)

Among the many books Comenius wrote, his innovative *Orbis Pictus* (1658) was the first to contain didactic illustrations and to be arranged according to methodical considerations. Comenius both outlined his theories and taught in many parts of Europe, trying to implement his theories practically.

During and after the eighteenth century the rate of change in the organization of schools and in teaching methods accelerated. The ideas of Jean-Jacques Rousseau (1712–1778) and the enterprises of Johann Bernhard Basedow (1724–1790), Johann Heinrich Pestalozzi (1746–1827), Andrew Bell (1753–1832), Joseph Lancaster (1778–1838), and many others provided a theoretical and practical basis for the development of the new school. Two trends are evident in their activities:

1. Attempts to organize and fund education in such a way that wide sections of the population would benefit from its services. For example, in the "monitorial schools" of Bell and Lancaster the older pupils taught the younger ones; one teacher supervised hundreds of pupils through "monitors" who dealt with groups of pupils. In the institutions established by Robert Owen (1771–1858) and Pestalozzi at the beginning of the nineteenth century an attempt was made to combine study with the students' labor (by Owen in industry, by Pestalozzi in agriculture), thereby solving the problem of funding schools at a time when the state had not yet taken over.

2. Attempts to extend teaching methods and adapt them to the needs of pupils from the various social classes. Of primary importance in this area were Rousseau's ideas concerning the intrinsic value of childhood, the autonomy of the personality, education through activity and contact with objects, natural punishment, and so forth. The outstanding representative of this approach was Pestalozzi, who based the teaching process on "sense perception and observation" and utilized psychological considerations. He regarded the harmonious development of all the child's "powers" as his objective, perceiving the teacher's love for the pupil as a precondition for this. Pestalozzi contended that education was the principal way by which society could be improved and was called the father of the elementary school for his contribution to laying its organizational and educational foundations. His disciples—Friedrich Diesterweg (1790–1866); Friedrich Froebel (1782–1852), the founder of the modern kindergarten; Johann Friedrich Herbart (1776–1841), who laid the foundation of teaching theory; and many others—disseminated his ideas throughout Europe. As a result of their efforts schools ceased to be the precinct of pioneering innovators alone and became a central concern of society, a basic part of the network of social, cultural, economic, and political activities of the modern state.

Schools in Modern Industrial Society

Schools in modern society are constantly changing in their structure, curriculum, and aims, so that change itself is one of their fundamental values. They have switched their emphasis from the past—when, according to the view that prevailed formerly, all ideals had been fulfilled (the younger generation was therefore supposed to emulate these ideals)—to the future, which bears within it the chance of fulfilling the ideals of today. The orientation toward the future has given rise to reforms and changes, in contrast to the orientation toward the past, which reinforced conservative trends.

Another fundamental change has been the expansion of educational opportunity through the rise of state-run schools that are compulsory and free. State schools arose from the recognition that education is one of every individual's basic rights that it is the state's duty to ensure. In nineteenth-century Europe the rise of state schools was intertwined with political struggle, first of the middle class and later of the working class. Yet the trend of sociopolitical pressure has not always been to make education generally available and compulsory. In the United States and England, even among groups influenced by liberal ideas, reservations concerning state schooling continued for a long time because of fear that the state would dominate the education of children and the consciences of their parents. In the end, however, compulsory education became the official policy of the modern state, although its implementation varies from one country to another and illiteracy is still prevalent in the world (*see* LITERACY).

The state replaced the church as the chief agent of education and took over supervision of schools during the course of the nineteenth and twentieth centuries. The transition was smoother in Protestant than in Catholic countries and in countries with several religions rather than predominantly one. At the end of the process the state assumed actual (though not always formal) control of the schools either by separating church from state, sometimes leaving a certain sphere of influence within state-controlled schools to the church, or by recognizing church schools after they had accepted the supervision of the state. The place formerly held by religion was now occupied by the national IDEOLOGY, which dominated the school and was a main influence on the content

Figure 3. *(School)* Johann Heinrich Pestalozzi (1746–1827), Swiss educational reformer. The Bettmann Archive, Inc.

and trends of educational activity. The classics of the ancient world were superseded by national literature, and the history of Greece and Rome by national history. Geography focused primarily on the pupils' native land, and the vernacular became one of the most important subjects. The demand for physical education was reinforced by emphasizing "defending the homeland," and premilitary education became part of the general curriculum in many countries. Countries receiving immigrants gave the schools the additional task of absorbing them into the dominant culture.

Hence the state's supervision of schools in modern society is threefold:

1. determining the extent of compulsory education (at what age it should begin and can end);
2. funding the education budget; and
3. determining the curriculum.

The state may determine the curriculum either through government or public committees for preparing curricula or by selecting teachers, determining official or administrative procedures, and appointing supervisory bodies.

A final change, resulting from the processes of industrialization and accelerated technological development, is that education has acquired a utilitarian character. The previous concept of education as a way of bringing the individual closer to human perfection has been replaced increasingly by the view that education is a means by which the individual can climb the social scale and one country can compete with another. This approach has contributed greatly to the expansion of educational processes and the democratization of schools.

Schools in New States

The colonial and semicolonial countries of the past were influenced while under foreign rule by the educational patterns of the European powers, which established schools for their own purposes—namely, to prepare local personnel for minor administrative positions and to crystallize an intelligentsia that would identify with the culture of the rulers. Most of the countries also had schools that had been founded by various religious sects. In some countries modern schools and traditional institutions of education existed side by side, but most of the population remained uneducated in a formal sense. At the final stages of the colonial period many countries had a thin stratum of intellectuals who, imbued with the spirit of nationalism, led the struggle for independence and fought for education in the spirit of the native culture. *See* DEVELOPMENT COMMUNICATION.

When they achieved independence, most of these countries imitated the organizational forms, educational methods, and curricula of European education, combining them with the values of their own culture. Many made education compulsory for five to ten years but encountered considerable problems in implementing this, primarily because of the dearth of teachers and the high rate of illiteracy as well as the large financial investment required to build the appropriate structures. Complex cultural and religious problems—such as tribal and linguistic differences—

Figure 4. *(School)* Jacob A. Riis, *Talmud School on Hester Street,* ca. 1890. Jacob A. Riis Collection, Museum of the City of New York.

led some states to decide that the language of instruction would be the language of their former rulers because it was the only one the different tribes shared. These countries are trying to prepare cadres of academically trained professionals (by sending them to developed countries for further education) who will be able to run research and teaching institutions in their countries later on. *See also* LANGUAGE IDEOLOGY.

The Critique of the School

Few would dispute the claim that since the Industrial Revolution schools have supported the various national cultures and trained people for the different economic tasks prevalent in modern societies. Since World War I, however, radical criticism has been directed against the activities of schools. The principal contentions have been that schools isolate children from society, occupying them with activities not relevant for their lives, and that schools are designed to compel children to accept the authority of society and its ruling bodies—that the schools, in short, are mechanisms for controlling citizens' thoughts. The values transmitted by the schools, some critics claim, are those of the ruling classes, and in modern mass societies they are those of the middle class. As a result children from other classes fail at school. Thus schools are a mechanism for perpetuating the existing structure of society and for giving preferential treatment to children from certain social classes.

These criticisms have led to several proposals that are being tested to a limited extent in various parts of the world. The most extreme is the idea of deschooling society. That is, education should return to its original form, with children educated by direct participation in the activities of adults, within the framework of their informal age groups, and through the cultural institutions of society, such as museums and libraries.

A less extreme idea is the open school, in which children learn primarily because of their own motivation and not according to a preordained curriculum. In these schools learning is meant to be a function of the children's lives in the present and not a process designed to prepare them for the future on the basis of fixed models of social needs.

Technological changes, the democratization of societies, and changes in values—which have occurred primarily in the mass societies of the West—are reflected in the frequent reforms in schools since the beginning of the twentieth century. They indicate that schools are in a process of change that will undoubtedly be extensive, encompassing organization, curriculum, and teaching methods.

Bibliography. Martin Ballard, *The Story of Teaching,* New York, 1971; James Bowen, *A History of Western Education,* 3 vols., New York, 1975; Lawrence A. Cremin, *The Transformation of the School,* New York, 1964; Paulo Freire, *Pedagogy of the Oppressed* (Pedagogía del oprimido), trans. by Myra Bergman Ramos, New York, 1970; Dennis Gardner, *Developments in Communications: Their Implications for Education,* London, 1974; Ronald Gross and Beatrice Gross, eds., *Radical School Reform,* New York, 1969; Ivan Illich, *Deschooling Society,* New York, 1970, reprint 1983; Ithiel de Sola Pool, Hiroshe Inose, Nozumu Takasaki, and Roger Hurwitz, *Communications Flows: A Census in the United States and Japan,* Amsterdam, 1984; Wilbur L. Schramm, *Men, Women, Messages, and Media: Understanding Human Communication,* 2d ed., New York, 1982; Charles Silberman, *Crisis in the Classroom,* New York, 1970; Robert Ulich, ed., *Three Thousand Years of Educational Wisdom,* 2d ed., enl., Cambridge, Mass., 1954; Michael F. D. Young, ed., *Knowledge and Control,* London, 1971.

ZVI LAMM

SCHRAMM, WILBUR (1907–1987)

U.S. scholar and researcher who helped establish communications as a recognized field of academic study. Wilbur Lang Schramm grew up in Marietta, Ohio, where he attended Marietta College. Later he studied simultaneously at Harvard University and, on a music scholarship, at the New England Conservatory. But his experience as a newspaper reporter and correspondent while at Harvard steered him toward journalistic interests.

Schramm is often credited with the creation of the field of communication. Schramm himself constantly paid tribute to those he called the "Four Fathers" of the field: HAROLD D. LASSWELL, PAUL F. LAZARSFELD, KURT LEWIN, and CARL HOVLAND. The work of these four, each from a different discipline—political science, sociology, group dynamics, and experimental social psychology—represented Schramm's interdisciplinary approach to communications and his view that communication plays a central role in society at all levels, from the intrapersonal to the group to the social to the international. Schramm attempted to synthesize relevant ideas from different areas into a new, separate but related field of study devoted principally to the clarification of processes of information dissemination, PERSUASION, and social pressure. *See* COMMUNICATIONS RESEARCH: ORIGINS AND DEVELOPMENT.

Schramm had a substantial influence on the field in two principal ways: first, through his creation of the Institute for Communication Research at the University of Illinois (1948) and a similar research center at Stanford University (1955); and second, through his many books and articles touching on a wide variety of research areas. Schramm contributed to the institutionalization of communications as an academic discipline, gaining for it the recognition of universities and funding agencies. His early writings and compilations helped attract students from such fields as journalism, English, sociology, psychology, and political science to concentrate on communications problems. The unprecedented DIFFUSION of television (*see* TELEVISION HISTORY) may have helped convince administrators that this new medium, along with the press, MOTION PICTURES, and RADIO, required people specially trained not only for its operation but also for the study and analysis of its impact on society. *See also* COMMUNICATIONS, STUDY OF.

Lasswell's studies of World War I PROPAGANDA probably contributed to Schramm's interest in POLITICAL COMMUNICATION. Communist press theory was the subject of a chapter in *Four Theories of the Press* (with Fred S. Siebert and Theodore Peterson, 1956). Developments in the United States after World War II, particularly the 1947 report of the Hutchins Commission on a Free and Responsible Press, spurred him to focus on the U.S. scene. His book *Responsibility in Mass Communication* was first published in 1957 (a revised edition with coauthor William L. Rivers appeared in 1969) and contributed further to the view that journalism and the mass media in general carry a major responsibility to society, qualifying the libertarian ideal of media freedom.

From the late 1950s on Schramm's work focused increasingly on the unrealized potential of the mass media in two areas: The first was their meaning for children, as discussed in *Television in the Lives of Our Children* (1961), written with Jack Lyle and Edwin Parker. The second was the role of the media in national development, as surveyed in *Mass Media and National Development* (1964) and other works. In 1963 Schramm wrote: "As nations move from the patterns of traditional society toward the patterns of modern industrial society, spectacular developments take place in their communication. From one point of view, developments in communication are brought about by the economic, social, and political evolution which is part of the national growth. From another point, however, they are among the chief makers and movers of that evolution." Results in some cases seemed to justify his enthusiasm, but Schramm himself saw the long-term results as mixed or disappointing (*see* DEVELOPMENT COMMUNICATION).

Communication programs in many countries carry the Schramm imprint and continue to influence training, practice, and research. Schramm always emphasized the need for scientific rigor in communications research because of his real interest, as Lyle Nelson has written, in the media's "potential to better the lives of people everywhere."

Bibliography. Godwin C. Chu and Wilbur Schramm, *Learning from Television: What the Research Says*, Washington, D.C., 1967; Daniel Lerner and Wilbur Schramm, *Communication and Change in the Developing Countries*, Honolulu, Hawaii, 1967; John W. Riley, Jr., and Wilbur Schramm, *The Reds Take a City: The Communist Occupation of Seoul, with Eyewitness Accounts*, New Brunswick, N.J., 1951; William L. Rivers, Wilbur Schramm, and Clifford C. Christians, *Responsibility in Mass Communication*, 3d ed., New York, 1980; Wilbur Schramm, *Mass Media and National Development*, Stanford, Calif., 1964; Wilbur Schramm, Jack Lyle, and Edwin B. Parker, *Television in the Lives of Our Children*, Stanford, Calif., 1961; Wilbur Schramm, ed., *The Impact of Educational Television*, Urbana, Ill., 1960; Wilbur Schramm and Daniel Lerner, eds., *Communication and Change: The Last Ten Years—And the Next*, Honolulu, Hawaii, 1976; Frederick S. Siebert, Theodore Peterson, and Wilbur Schramm, *Four Theories of the Press*, Urbana, Ill., 1946, reprint Freeport, N.Y., 1973.

GODWIN C. CHU

SCHUTZ, ALFRED (1899–1959)

Austrian-U.S. philosopher. Since his death Alfred Schutz has been recognized as one of the leading philosophers of the social sciences in the twentieth century. His major contributions to communications theory derive from his interest in how people know and interpret their everyday experiences as they interact in the social world.

Schutz was born in Vienna, where he received his early education and later studied law and social science at the University of Vienna. He drew heavily on the writings of German sociologist MAX WEBER, whose influence was extensive in western Europe when Schutz was a student. He also turned to the work of European philosophers Edmund Husserl and Henri Bergson for inspiration and material to develop his phenomenological theories and to arrive at a consistent theory of MEANING. By applying Husserl's concept of meaning to interpersonal and social action, Schutz was able to give interpretive sociology a sounder footing in phenomenology. This methodological footing enabled interpretive sociology to penetrate to the subjective phenomena at the heart of social experience.

Schutz left Austria during the unrest in the 1930s before it fell to the Nazis, and he spent a year in Paris. In 1939 he came to the United States, where he settled in New York City and joined the faculty of the New School for Social Research. Here Schutz came in contact with the writings of pragmatic philosopher and social psychologist GEORGE HERBERT MEAD, who had also focused on the analysis of meaning in social interaction in work that paralleled Schutz's. Mead's perspective stimulated Schutz and broadened his analysis and interpretation of the meanings of human interactions.

Schutz's best-known work, *Der sinnhafte Aufbau der sozialen Welt* (The Phenomenology of the Social World, 1932), was not translated and published in English until 1967; before then his work was little known to U.S. social scientists and philosophers. In this book he devoted extensive consideration to intersubjective understanding, meaning establishment, and meaning interpretation, as well as to the meaning context of communication.

Schutz theorized that communicative acts can consist of gestures, words, or artifacts (*see* ARTIFACT; GESTURE; LANGUAGE), all of which employ signs and a SIGN SYSTEM in evoking understanding (*see* SIGN). He wrote that the sign system is present to the person who understands it as a meaning context of a higher order between previously experienced signs. For example, Schutz notes that the German language is the meaning context of each of its component words. Or, for another example, the sign system of a map is the meaning context of every symbol on that map (*see* CARTOGRAPHY; MAP PROJECTION). He points out that even though someone may not know how to play a game of cards, that person can still recognize the cards as "playing cards." The placing of a sign within its sign system is something we do by putting it within the total context of experience. Further, one does not have to understand the meaning of the individual signs or be fully conversant with the sign system. (For instance, a Westerner can ascertain that certain characters are Chinese without understanding their meaning.) Therefore, an established sign is meaningful and, in principle, is intelligible.

Schutz was aware that merely focusing on the establishment and interpretation of meaning was too limited. To him these aspects were the content of communication, but the actual communication is itself a meaningful act that calls for interpretation in its own right. Once the interpreter has determined both the objective and subjective meanings of the content of any communication, he or she may proceed to ask why the communication was made in the first place. Writing in *The Phenomenology of the Social World,* Schutz states:

> For it is essential to every act of communication that it have an extrinsic goal. When I say something to you, I do so for a reason, whether to evoke a particular attitude on your part or simply to explain something to you. Every act of communication has, therefore, as its in-order-to [purposeful] motive the aim that the person being addressed take cognizance of it in one way or another.
>
> The person who is the object or recipient of the communication is frequently the one who makes this kind of interpretation. Having settled what are the objective and subjective meanings of the content of the communication by finding the corresponding interpretive or expressive schemes, he proceeds to inquire into the reason why the other person said this in the first place. In short, he seeks the "plan" behind the communication.

Schutz stressed that every communication has both objective and subjective meanings. He believed that the tendency to look for these meanings in everything in existence is deeply rooted in the human mind. Schutz died in 1959 just as he was working on a fuller statement of his theories on the meanings of signs, symbols, and their role in communication.

See also COGNITION; COMMUNICATION, PHILOSOPHIES OF; INTERACTION, FACE-TO-FACE; INTERPERSONAL COMMUNICATION; NONVERBAL COMMUNICATION; SYMBOLISM.

Bibliography. Alfred Schutz, *The Phenomenology of the Social World* (Der sinnhafte Aufbau der sozialen Welt), trans. by George Walsh and Frederick Lehnert, Evanston, Ill., 1967.

EDITH W. KING AND R. P. CUZZORT

SCIENCE FICTION

The fantastic GENRE of romantic literature (*see* ROMANTICISM) that both warns against and applauds the advance of science and technology. Through its heritage of utopian speculation (*see* UTOPIAS) and social satire, science fiction can claim a lineage almost as old as recorded history. Its modern efflorescence parallels the increasing rate at which technological innovation has changed our world. In 1818 English novelist Mary Shelley provided a name and an image for the modern fear of science gone awry: Frankenstein's monster. Later that century the enthusiastic imaginary voyages of Frenchman Jules Verne taught that the exploring mind could tame time and space (Figure 1). In its popular forms science fiction often assuages the widespread unease in our ever-changing world by offering blatant wish fulfillment. While some have therefore dismissed science fiction as merely escapist, in our era of rocket travel (first proposed in 1657 by French soldier-writer Cyrano de Bergerac) and the planetary communication SATELLITE (first proposed in 1945 by English science-fiction writer Arthur C. Clarke) only science fiction consistently considers the problems and possibilities posed by meeting the new, the unexpected, the alien. Science fiction draws its considerable entertainment value from deep mythic or social wells. In the 1980s the single best-selling author in the Communist world was Stanisław Lem, a Pole who slyly sets his social speculations on other worlds or, frequently, in a putative United States. Clearly science fiction has grown well beyond the central zone of fantastic, romantic literature, indeed beyond literature itself. Just as a mushroom cloud and a single footprint on the moon are this era's linked icons of despair and hope, so science fiction in both warning against arrogance and proselytizing for perpetual discovery embraces our deep ambivalence toward the institutions of science and technology, their products, and their effects on humanity.

History and Themes

Frankenstein is the earliest work today called science fiction. While it is Victor Frankenstein who endues dead flesh with life, the name Frankenstein is popularly misused to refer to the monster rather than its creator, probably because of the strong visual impact of the creature's image in the longest series of films (beginning with the Edison Company's 1910 version) based on any single work. These mostly HOLLYWOOD productions—of which the most admirable may be the 1931 version starring Boris Karloff and directed by James Whale (*see* HORROR FILM)—distort the book by calling the creator "Doctor" or "Baron," tarring the scientist with the popular mistrust in the United States of aloof, privileged power (Figure 2).

Shelley's novel is subtitled *The Modern Prometheus.* Victor Frankenstein seeks the divine fire of life, but as happens with so many figures in the tradition of Prometheus and the medieval Faust, the stock figure of the science-fiction scientist is often punished for hubris. The prideful search for knowledge and power leads to a social isolation that rejects ordinary community restraints. Sometimes the scientist does succeed, like Prospero in Shakespeare's *The Tempest* (1611), but in so doing typically must abjure science, or, as Prospero promises, "drown" his books and return to society. Occasionally scientists rightly rule their worlds. Notable heirs to PLATO's philosopher-kings (called Guardians) are the scientists imagined in *The New Atlantis* (1626), by Englishman Francis Bacon, the man who, in *Novum Organum* (1620), first expounded what has since

Figure 1. *(Science Fiction)* "At the idea that *L'Épouvante* could rival the eagles . . ." Illustration by George Roux for *Maître du monde* (Master of the World), by Jules Verne. From Jules Verne, *Voyages extraordinaires,* Paris (1866): Hachette, 1979, p. 351.

come to be called the scientific method. Popular literature (*see* LITERATURE, POPULAR) has sometimes adulated the scientist hero or, more commonly, the engineer-technician hero, but often scientists are portrayed as myopically overeducated clowns, like Professor Aronnax in Verne's *Twenty Thousand Leagues under the Sea* (1869), who always reasons carefully to wrong conclusions, or evil geniuses like Rotwang in *Metropolis* (1926), by German novelist and screenwriter Thea von Harbou. In those cases the day—and usually the world and the human race—is typically saved not by the scientist but by a jack-of-all-trades. From Captain John Carter in the *Mars* books (1912–1943) of U.S. writer Edgar Rice Burroughs to adolescents with special talents such as telepathy or teleportation to young adults with less spectacular talents, science fiction typically applauds not the specialized knowledge of the scientist but the adaptability, resourcefulness, and faith of the young. The dominant myth of modern popular science fiction offers an adolescent power fantasy not gone awry, as it did for Victor Frankenstein, but crowned with success, as in the wildly popular *Dune* books (1967–1985) of U.S. writer Frank Herbert.

In "literary" science fiction, too, Guardian scientists occasionally recur, as in the later works of Englishman H. G. Wells, including *The Shape of Things to Come* (1933; Figure 3). More typically, however, the scientist, even if viewed kindly, is isolated by his or her intellectual acts, as with the title characters in such early Wells novels as *The Island of Dr. Moreau* (1896) and *The Invisible Man* (1897). When scientists take on socially dominant roles, they are typically exposed as foolish, like the rulers of Laputa in *Gulliver's Travels* (1726), by Englishman Jonathan Swift, or ruthless, like the figureheads of totalitarianism in such important dystopian works as *We* (1920), by the Russian Yevgeny Zamyatin, English novelist Aldous Huxley's *Brave New World* (1932), and *1984* (1949), by Englishman George Orwell. While popular science fiction displays a range of ideologies, literary science fiction is almost exclusively monitory.

Science fiction's heritage of social imagination and commentary runs from Plato's *Republic* through *Utopia* (1516), by Englishman Thomas More, to the scientifically perfect world of *Walden Two* (1948), by U.S. psychologist B. F. Skinner, and the transcendentally perfect world of Clarke's *Childhood's End* (1953). When LITERARY CRITICISM has viewed science fiction favorably, as with the chilling projections of *A Clockwork Orange* (1962), by English novelist Anthony Burgess, it typically does not label the works as science fiction at all. This critical prejudice arises from ideological conflicts both within and outside science fiction.

Directions in Contemporary Science Fiction

One can point to three major tendencies in science fiction: "hard" science fiction, "escape" science fiction, and "soft" science fiction. Hard science fiction, exemplified by U.S. writer Isaac Asimov's *I, Robot* (1950) or Clarke's *A Fall of Moondust* (1961), offers the reader a concrete puzzle to solve using science, MATHEMATICS, and specific rules and conditions (often of the author's own invention). In hard science fiction, science usually saves the day. When Hugo Gernsback, an enormously influential editor, began producing the first "pulp" science-fiction magazines (*Modern Electrics* in 1911, *Amazing Stories* in 1926), he played up the U.S. faith in technological progress, publishing new works and reprinting such nineteenth-century classics as Edgar Allan Poe's "tales of ratiocination." Gernsback also began developing what has come to be called fandom, the loose but highly active association of readers, writers, editors, and critics who communicate through magazine letters columns and a network of fan conventions.

Figure 2. *(Science Fiction)* James Whale, *Frankenstein*, 1931. Poster from the Universal rerelease. National Film Archive, London. Copyright © by Universal Pictures, a Division of Universal City Studios, Inc. Courtesy of MCA Publishing Rights, a Division of MCA, Inc.

There are more than two hundred such conventions each year in the United States. Gernsback's early efforts eventually led to the establishment of an annual world science-fiction convention that bestows fan-chosen awards called Hugos, in his honor, and the Science Fiction Writers of America, which confers annual Nebula awards. The fan movement is worldwide. Japan, for example, home of writer Kobo Abe, held its twenty-fifth national science-fiction convention in 1986. Active fandom has made scientific accuracy—and the discovery of scientific errors—a perpetual game in hard science fiction.

Escape science fiction reveals most clearly the fairy-tale roots of much science fiction. Children—and childlike adults—save the universe repeatedly. In the so-called sword-and-sorcery works such as those featuring Conan the Barbarian, and in wish-fulfillment fantasies such as the dragon books of U.S. writer Anne McCaffrey, science fiction offers in full measure admittedly simple psychological pleasures. Because these pleasures are usually deemed trivial by critics and because the puzzle-solving pleasures also enjoyed by fandom often require a technical background foreign to many reviewers, science fiction has historically been dismissed as trash.

Soft science fiction concerns itself not with the relatively deterministic sciences like physics and chemistry but with the social sciences, including anthropology, sociology, and political science. Works like *The Left Hand of Darkness* (1969), by U.S. writer Ursula K. LeGuin, try to explore our social systems and the meaning of being human. While this subgenre clearly reflects descent from both the quasi-gothic *Frankenstein* and Western utopian literature, it typically rejects science as the answer to problems and points instead to the need to rethink human behavior and relationships with the social and natural environment. In the twentieth century such thoughtfulness has been prized by literary critics, who admire it in works like Wells's *The Time Machine* (1895) and *War with the Newts* (1936), by Czech writer Karel Čapek (whose 1921 play, *R.U.R.*, added the word *robot* to the English language). While appreciating these works, critics historically refused to see them as science fiction. Beginning in the 1970s, however, with a new refinement of soft science fiction, particularly through the works of U.S. feminist writers like LeGuin and Joanna Russ, critics began to see that not all science fiction is technical and have begun therefore to accord the genre as a whole more respect.

Although science fiction is a phenomenon that arises wherever modern science and technology make people aware of new problems or cause them to view old problems in new ways, science fiction worldwide has a distinctly U.S. flavor. Western European science fiction tends to be bleaker, eastern European science fiction tends to be more politically subtle, and Asian science fiction tends to be more philosophical; but all have been influenced by U.S. technological leadership and by early U.S. domination of the popular science-fiction market (*see* PUBLISHING—PUBLISHING INDUSTRY). With the international influence of Hollywood, even such xenophobic works as *Invasion of the Body Snatchers* (1955) have had international impact. Most famous science-fiction works have

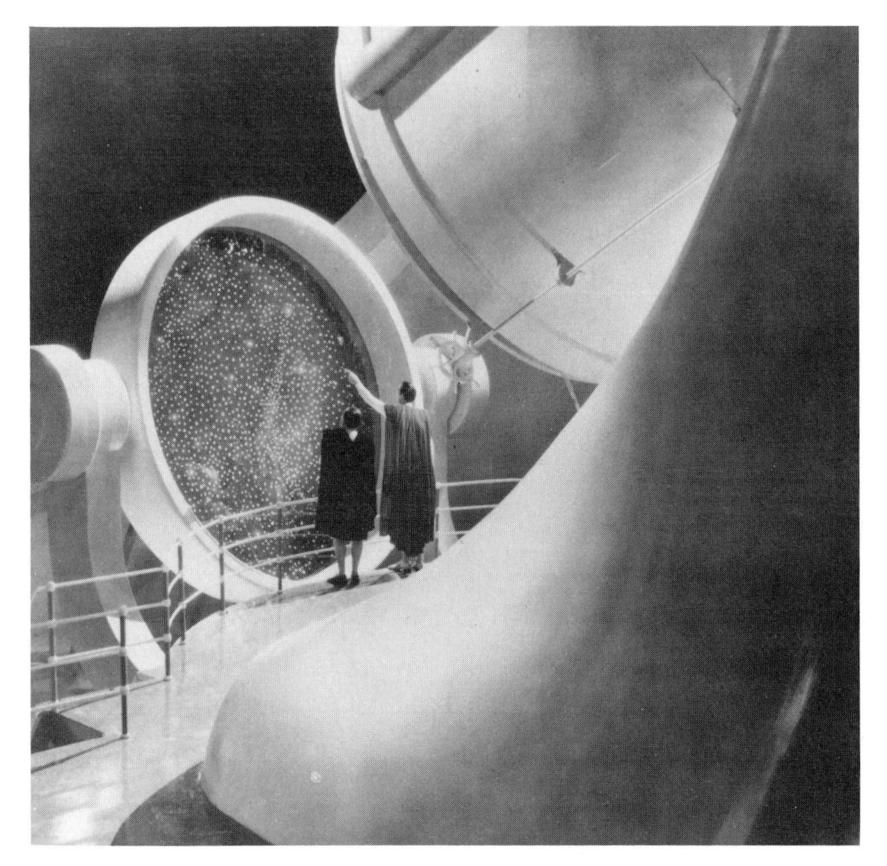

Figure 3. *(Science Fiction)* H. G. Wells's men of tomorrow confront the universe in *The Shape of Things to Come,* 1933, directed by Alexander Korda. National Film Archive, London/London Films.

Figure 4. *(Science Fiction)* Tom Baker as Dr. Who and Lalla Ward as Romana, in the BBC-1 series "Dr. Who." Copyright BBC (Enterprises) 1980.

Figure 5. *(Science Fiction)* "Star Trek" souvenirs for sale at the Trekkies convention held in Hollywood on October 12, 1985, to celebrate the twentieth anniversary of the television series. UPI/Bettmann Newsphotos.

reached larger audiences as films than as books, and many, like *Alien* (1979), are now written directly for the screen or, like "Star Trek" (1966–1968) in the United States and Britain's "Dr. Who" (1963–), for television (Figure 4). As film and television viewership increases, and as the problems created by science and technology grow in world consciousness, science fiction will become ever more the popular and high-culture art of our age (Figure 5).

See also MOTION PICTURES; SPECIAL EFFECTS; TELEVISION HISTORY.

Bibliography. Brian W. Aldiss, *Billion Year Spree: The True History of Science Fiction,* New York, 1973; William Sims Bainbridge, *Dimensions of Science Fiction,* Cambridge, Mass., 1986; John Brosnan, *Future Tense: The Cinema of Science Fiction,* New York, 1978; Paul A. Carter, *The Creation of Tomorrow: Fifty Years of Magazine Science Fiction,* New York, 1977; James E. Gunn, *Alternate Worlds: The Illustrated History of Science Fiction,* Englewood Cliffs, N.J., 1975; Mark Rose, *Alien Encounters: Anatomy of Science Fiction,* Cambridge, Mass., 1981; Robert Scholes and Eric S. Rabkin, *Science Fiction: History, Science, Vision,* New York, 1977; Darko Suvin, *Metamorphoses of Science Fiction,* New Haven, Conn., 1979.

ERIC RABKIN

SCRIPPS, E. W. (1854–1926)

U.S. newspaper publisher. Edward Wyllis Scripps, who called himself "the damned old crank," did not invent the idea of a newspaper chain (or "group"), but he was the first U.S. publisher to make it work. It worked so well that when Scripps died he left behind the most formidable collection of chain operations then in existence. They included the Booth Newspapers of Michigan; the Scripps League of Newspapers in the Northwest; the John P. Scripps papers on the Pacific Coast; and the Scripps-Howard chain, with its allied United Press International, besides three feature syndicates.

All this came from a man who was once known around Rushville, Illinois, near where he was born, as "the laziest boy in Schuyler County." The youngest of thirteen children, Scripps found himself in charge of the family farm when his father grew ill. He hired town boys at twenty-five cents a day to do the work while he watched from under a tree. ("Never do anything yourself that you can get someone else to do for you," he wrote in 1925 in one of his "disquisitions.") Most of Scripps's education came from his older half-sister, Ellen Browning Scripps, until he left the farm at eighteen to join his half-brother James, a Detroit newspaper editor. In 1873 James launched the Detroit *Evening News,* employing young Scripps in circulation. Ellen and another half-brother, George, also joined the *News,* which became the foundation of the Scripps empire.

In 1878, with ten thousand dollars from the family, E. W. Scripps founded the Cleveland *Penny Press,* at the same time proclaiming himself the enemy of power and privilege. Ellen Scripps's contributions to this paper, short paragraphs under the heading "Miscellany," in time grew into the Newspaper Enterprise Association, which distributed syndicated features. From this Cleveland beginning, E. W. Scripps acquired the Cincinnati *Penny Paper* in 1883, changed its name to the *Cincinnati Post,* and declared war on municipal corruption. A disruptive family quarrel in 1887 led to the firing of Scripps as president of the Detroit News Association and the Scripps Publishing Company. The break was never mended.

Joining forces then with Milton McRae, a prospering entrepreneur, Scripps made an arrangement by which he could "retire" in 1890 at the age of thirty-six and let his properties develop. Wanting to avoid the rest of humanity as much as possible, Scripps settled with his wife and three children at Miramar Ranch near San Diego, and from there he managed his enterprises and built his chains, summoning employees to him when needed. The papers Scripps established were often catchpenny affairs, but they had the advantage of Scripps's managerial genius, and some of them attracted highly talented editors and writers whom he controlled with a tight hand. He became a striking figure with bushy red beard, balding head beneath a skullcap, trousers tucked into white kid boots—hated by the rich as a renegade and by the poor for being rich.

Like fellow publishers JAMES GORDON BENNETT and JOSEPH PULITZER, Scripps loved his yacht, on which he spent much of his last six years. He died on it, of apoplexy, as it lay anchored in Monrovia Bay off Liberia, and was buried at sea. He had trained his three sons to succeed him, but only one, Robert, survived. In 1922 the name of Scripps's combined operations had been changed from Scripps-McRae to Scripps-Howard. After Scripps's death Roy Howard, a genius in his own right who had been business manager, gradually took over, beginning a new era and a new dynasty of his own.

See also NEWS AGENCIES; NEWSPAPER: HISTORY; NEWSPAPER: TRENDS—TRENDS IN NORTH AMERICA; SYNDICATION.

Bibliography. Negley D. Cochran, *E. W. Scripps,* New York, 1933; Gilson Gardner, *Lusty Scripps,* New York, 1932; Oliver Knight, ed., *I Protest: Selected Disquisitions of E. W. Scripps,* Madison, Wis., 1966; Charles R. McCabe, ed., *Damned Old Crank: A Self-Portrait of E. W. Scripps,* New York, 1951; Kenneth Stewart and John Tebbel, *Makers of Modern Journalism,* New York, 1952.

JOHN TEBBEL

SCRIPTURE

Holy or sacred writings (holy writ); that is, books, shorter texts, or collections of texts considered to have a sacred origin and to possess religious authority, especially when they are held by believers to have been divinely revealed (*see* RELIGION). The manner and mechanisms of this revelation are differently conceived in different religious cultures and are generally connected with beliefs and theories concerning inspiration, prophecy, or the special circumstances in which the texts were found or "discovered" (in mysterious caves, distant mountains, etc.). The transition to LITERACY in societies is considered a revolutionary cultural change decisively affecting all areas of social life including the very nature of tradition, which is no longer only orally transmitted (*see* ORAL CULTURE). In the history of religions the difference between religions with or without writings is similarly crucial. Every religion is a system of communication between the gods (or God, or the "divine") and humans. In most literate societies this communication takes place—in addition to occurring through other modes (*see* MODE) such as RITUAL—by means of holy writings that may contain elements from earlier oral mythological traditions.

Not all WRITING arose as a secular and practical method of interhuman communication that was subsequently extended or applied to the religious sphere. There are indications that writing was sometimes primarily of a religious nature, written signs of communication between gods and humans. This seems to be true of ancient China, where these religious beginnings subsequently developed into an all-purpose script (*see* EAST ASIA, ANCIENT), and of some pre-Columbian American cultures, where writing retained its magical, cosmogonic, and symbolic character and bore no relation to practical needs (*see* AMERICAS, PRE-COLUMBIAN).

Figure 1. *(Scripture)* Arñao Guillen de Brocar, page from the Polyglot Bible, 1514–1517. PML 812–817, The Pierpont Morgan Library, New York.

Scriptural texts are literature and as such exhibit every kind of literary form and GENRE: epic, legend, mythological accounts, DRAMA (often as the script for ritual representations of mythological events), historical NARRATIVE, preaching and doctrinal and moral instruction (e.g., Buddha's sermons, the Epistles of St. Paul; *see also* HOMILETICS), philosophical TEACHING (e.g., the Indian Upanishads), liturgical texts, hymns of prayer and praise and adoration (e.g., the Psalms), legal codes, and magical formulas. Some texts originate as magic incantations, whereas others exhibit the reverse development. Texts of such different character as the Bible, the Qur'an, and Buddhist sutras, because of their holiness and the cosmic power inherent in that holiness, can be used as magic formulas or as means of divination and oracle. Even a highly "philosophical" text such as the Mahayana Buddhist Sutra of the Perfection of Wisdom specifically calls its climactic message a mantra (namely, *dharani*), an incantation charged with magical power.

In religious worship holy scriptures do not always have to be read or even understood. It is enough to physically display or handle them—for example, by turning them in so-called prayer wheels. Scriptures are always treated with extreme reverence, carried in procession (e.g., the Torah-like scroll in Jewish services or the Granth in the daily Sikh ritual at the Golden Temple) or sprinkled with incense (like the New Testament during the Catholic Mass). But as literature they can also be subjected to philological and literary analysis. Although such methods are often accepted by contemporary theologians, holy writ has historically been held—and is still in some orthodox fundamentalist circles—to be different and not analyzable by secular methods, especially when such analysis looks at holy texts as human, cultural products and comes to unorthodox conclusions regarding their AUTHORSHIP, date of composition, and dependence on various influences and sources.

The term *holy scriptures* is often used in a loose way because of its range of possible definitions. Which texts, considered to be classical, authoritative, and sanctified by age or eminence, are scripture in the narrow, technical sense? Perhaps the Qur'an comes closest to the precise definition of a holy book: it is uncreated and eternal, it was revealed to the Prophet Muhammad, and every terrestrial copy of the book is regarded as a kind of photocopy of the heavenly master copy (*see* ISLAM, CLASSICAL AND MEDIEVAL ERAS). Orthodox Jews consider the Five Books of Moses (the Torah) not only as verbally inspired but also as a replica of a heavenly book dictated by God to Moses (despite its historiographical and legal contents), whereas the rest of the Old Testament is believed to have been written by human beings under divine inspiration and guidance (*see* JUDAISM). But should the Talmud, important and authoritative as it is, be considered holy writ in the strict sense? The Confucian classics are certainly not divine revelation, but the roles of the sage CONFUCIUS and of the literature ascribed to him and his disciples qualify these texts as Chinese holy scriptures although their character is very different from the canon of Chinese Taoist or Buddhist scriptures.

Few scriptures originated as written documents. The Muslim Qur'an and the Jewish Torah are (at least theoretically) exceptions to this, as are the Sikh Granth or the Book of Mormon, "rediscovered" in the United States in the nineteenth century by Joseph Smith and engraved in a mysterious script on golden tablets. More often than not the holy teachings or revelations were communicated orally and committed to writing much later. The Old Testament tells how Barukh wrote down the utterances of his master, the prophet Jeremiah. The Gospels are an account of the life and teachings of Jesus, based on diverse oral traditions and committed to writing much later by the early Christian church. The Epistles of Paul, however, are his own exhortations and instructions

Figure 2. *(Scripture)* Qur'an stand *(rahla)*, 1360. Carved wood. The Metropolitan Museum of Art, New York, Rogers Fund, 1910. (10.218)

to various churches, elevated to the rank of holy scripture. The Buddha's oral preaching (the suttas) as well as the rules (the vinaya) he laid down for the order of monks he founded were written down at a later date. In fact, Manes, the Persian founder of a gnostic-type religion in the third century, was clearly aware of this when he prefaced his writings with the remark that he was the first religious founder to put his revelations in written form. Muhammad's conception of the Islamic Holy Book may have been influenced by the Manichaean precedent.

A most interesting case concerns the most ancient, fundamental, and sacred of all Indian holy scriptures, the Vedas (*see* SOUTH ASIA, ANCIENT). For a long period the four canonical collections of Vedic hymns and texts were not meant to be written down: transmission from master to disciple was strictly oral. The technical term describing the Vedas is sruti (literally "thing heard"). Only later were these hymns committed to writing.

Sacred writings require INTERPRETATION and commentary, in part because of their often archaic style but mainly because they are considered to be of eternal validity, applicability, and relevance. Often the commentaries become so authoritative that they themselves approach the status of holy writ. In most cases the sanctity of the holy writ is connected with its age or with its attribution to venerable or sacred ancient personalities (prophets, sages, rishis). Hence many late-biblical Scriptures (called Apocrypha but more accurately termed pseudepigrapha) were fictitiously ascribed by their usually anonymous authors to well-known ancient authorities. Many biblical books (mainly extracanonical), Mahayana sutras, Buddho-Taoist texts, and so on are therefore called apocryphal (meaning pseudepigraphic). The aesthetic and literary evaluation of holy scriptures can vary. Islamic doctrine teaches that the perfection and inim-

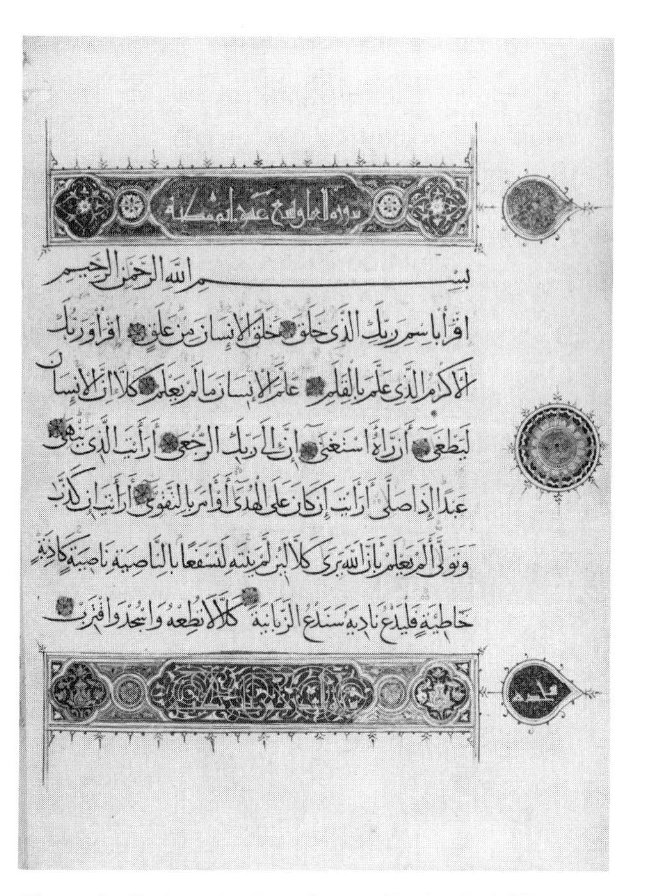

بسم الله الرحمن الرحيم
اقرأ باسم ربك الذي خلق خلق الإنسان من علق اقرأ وربك
الأكرم الذي علم بالقلم علم الإنسان ما لم يعلم كلا إن الإنسان
ليطغى أن رآه استغنى إن إلى ربك الرجعى أرأيت الذي ينهى
عبدا إذا صلى أرأيت إن كان على الهدى أو أمر بالتقوى أرأيت إن كذب
وتولى ألم يعلم بأن الله يرى كلا لئن لم ينته لنسفعا بالناصية ناصية كاذبة
خاطئة فليدع ناديه سندع الزبانية كلا لا تطعه واسجد واقترب

Figure 3. *(Scripture)* Page from a Qur'an in Jalil script, Mamluk, thirteenth century. By permission of the British Library.

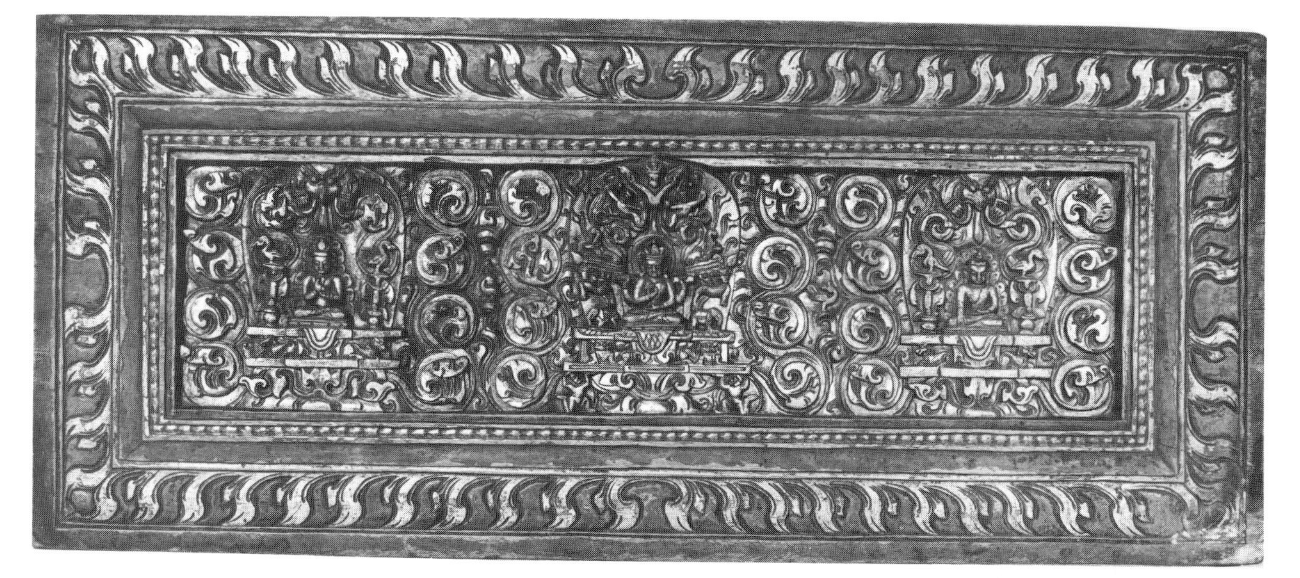

Figure 4. *(Scripture)* Sutra cover from Tibet, nineteenth century. Painted wood. The University Museum, Philadelphia. Neg. 2162.

itability of the Qur'an are proof of its divine origin. Conversely, many Greek philosophers argued that the religious writings of the "barbarians" were more divine precisely because they were less refined, less polished, and therefore less "artificial" than the products of more advanced literary cultures.

No holy scripture necessarily convinces the reader of its sacred nature or divine origin. No scripture is self-authenticating and self-validating; it is regarded as holy because, from a sociological point of view, it has been previously accepted as such by those who hold authority in a given society. Thus every holy scripture presents a paradox. Theologically a text may be considered the foundation and source of tradition and of all religious authority, but it is actually the socially recognized bearers of religious authority who legitimate and validate the sacredness of holy scripture.

Bibliography. F. F. Bruce and E. G. Rupp, eds., *Holy Book and Holy Tradition,* Manchester, Eng., 1968; Gunter Lanczkowski, *Sacred Writings: A Guide to the Literature of Religions* (Heilige Schriften), trans. by Stanley Godman, New York, 1961; Johannes Leipoldt and Siegfried Morenz, *Heilige Schriften,* Leipzig, 1953; "Schriften," *Die Religion in Geschichte und Gegenwart,* Vol. 5, Stuttgart, 1961 ed.; "Scripture," *Encyclopaedia of Religion and Ethics,* Vol. 11–12, New York, 1951 ed.

R. J. ZWI WERBLOWSKY

SCULPTURE

What do works of sculpture communicate, and how do they do it? There are at least two good ways of answering these questions. One could proceed historically and show how under varying conditions and for various purposes sculptors supply social groups, institutions, and individuals with the images of gods, saints, heroes, ideal types, or the portraits of valued persons. Another way of exploring these conditions will be taken in the following analysis of sculpture as a medium of ART. By describing somewhat systematically the physical and psychological properties of the medium, one can arrive at an understanding of the functions to be fulfilled by this particular social instrument, as distinguished from others.

All media of art have their place in space, but not all of them operate also within the dimension of time. Music and dance, theater and film accompany the happenings of life by actions of their own and thereby report, interpret, and comment in response to the human ways of handling events as they occur in time. They reflect processes of becoming and undoing. Not so the media of painting, sculpture, and ARCHITECTURE. Once made, their works display a permanent state of being. Buildings provide protective security against the vicissitudes of time and guarantee an existence continued under established and congenial circumstances of living. Paintings and sculpture extrapolate from the ever-changing spectacle of experience certain frozen states, esteemed for their validity, significance, and enlightenment (Figure 1). Outside the dimension of time, these immobile objects connect the past with the future through a permanent presence. They supply us with stable sets of images by which to orient ourselves as we navigate the stream of protean events.

Since all works of sculpture, although at different

Figure 1. *(Sculpture)* Seated Buddha, Burma, nineteenth century. Wood, heavily gilded and decorated with paste jewels. The University Museum, Philadelphia. Neg. 29-96-791.

levels of abstractness, reflect the human condition, our attitude toward them is curiously ambiguous. On the one hand, they are of our own kind, to an extent that can create close intimacy. On the other hand, they tend to lack the most material quality of life, namely motion. This chill is somewhat relieved in so-called kinetic sculpture (Figure 2). But sculptures rotating on turntables or mobiles animated by wind or water are limited to rondo patterns that keep returning in an endless, timeless state. If they were programmed to act out goal-directed plots, they would shift to the performing arts of puppet play and dance; that is, they would serve a function other than the one that distinguishes the atemporal media.

Sculptures like to be tied to permanent locations—an observation that turns our analysis to the relations of sculpture to space. Much more than framed paintings, although less radically than architecture, sculpture is rooted in the ground. A statue is more like a tree than like a star. It transmits the experience of stable grounding and is particularly suited to symbolize such foundation. The subservience of life on earth to the force of gravity is much more compellingly expressed in sculpted figures than it is in painted objects. Therefore, when sculptures do float suspended in the air, they display their anchorless freedom all the more convincingly. Examples are Ernst Barlach's soaring figure originally designed as a war memorial for the cathedral of Güstrow in Germany or the candelabralike metal clusters of the American sculptor Richard Lippold, which brighten the atriums of banks and theaters.

But when sculptures are moved around in museums and art galleries, they are being disturbed in their venerable function of holding the fort for what is immutable; and when in the pilgrimage chapel of Ronchamp the architect Le Corbusier placed the figure of the Virgin on a swiveling base, enabling her to officiate at outdoor and indoor services alike, he aroused some feeling of religious and aesthetic sacrilege.

At their most effective, then, sculptures are not handled as mobile objects but are tied to a place to which they convey meaning and which, in turn, determines theirs. Michelangelo's David loses much of its impact when today's visitors to Florence see the colossal marble figure confined to the empty rotunda of the Accademia Delle Belle Arti (Figure 3). For the past century only a copy of the statue (Figure 4) indicates its original position at the entrance of the town hall, the Palazzo Vecchio, where it had been placed in 1504 to represent, as Charles de Tolnay tells us, "the incarnation of the two principal republican civic virtues: he is a *cittadino guerriero.*"

The example of Michelangelo's David demonstrates also that sculpture lives up most fully to its nature when it is monumental. Monuments are places of pilgrimage, to be sought out like the great sights

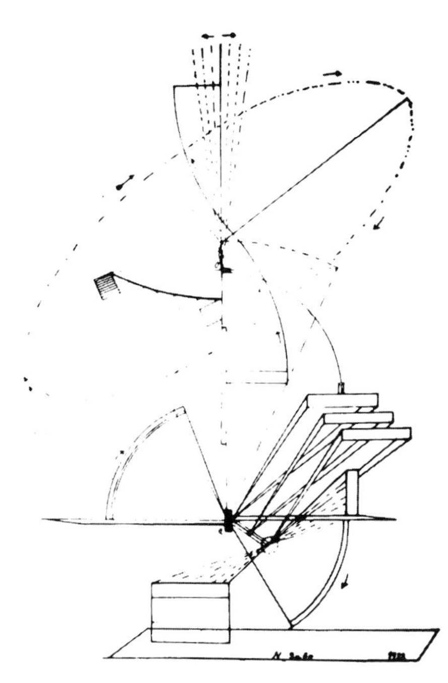

Figure 2. *(Sculpture)* Naum Gabo, design for *Kinetic Construction,* 1922. From *Two Kinetic Sculptors: Nicholas Schöffer and Jean Tinguely,* New York: October House, 1965, fig. 23. Exhibition catalog. Jewish Museum/Art Resource, New York.

of nature. To exert their power, they need space. They stand on public squares, in front of buildings, on the top of hills, where they concentrate the meaning of a diffuse cityscape or landscape in an articulate focus (Figure 5). This is why sculpture calls for the outdoors. Within the four walls of an interior, the compositional theme of the room's purpose organizes the architectural design and the arrangement of the furniture so compellingly that the self-centered power of a sculptural bust or figure can come as a disturbance. Tucked away in a corner or impeding the traffic as an object without practical function, it may state its message in vain.

By the same token, however, sculpture plays an essential role when it is incorporated in the architectural plan as an intermediary between the abstractness of the building and the living bodies of its inhabitants. The Parthenon was designed around the statue of Athena in the central cella, just as the Lincoln Memorial in Washington is the shell for the marble portrait of the seated president. The altar figures of saints or the Virgin Mary are focal points of chapels and churches, and in a more subordinate position the rows of religious figures in the porches of medieval cathedrals introduce the faithful to the spirit of their visit.

All these properties derive from the basic fact that sculptures are, like us, physical objects and occupy our own physical space. Whereas pictures are images detached from our world, dwelling in a space of their

Figure 3. *(Sculpture)* Michelangelo, *David,* 1502–1504. Marble. Galleria dell'Accademia, Florence. Alinari/Art Resource, New York.

Figure 4. *(Sculpture)* Copy of Michelangelo's *David.* Marble. Near the main entrance to the Palazzo Vecchio, Florence. The Bettmann Archive, Inc.

own, into which we can look but which we cannot enter, sculptures must cope with the double function of sharing our life space as fellow inhabitants and at the same time reflecting it as an observer's interpretation. Their substantial presence invites bodily intercourse, which interferes with their appearance as images. In culture periods in which the value of the wisdom acquired through visual symbols gives way to a careless indulgence in the company of congenial bodies there are instances of disturbing intermingling, as when on the steps of the Hellenistic altar at Pergamon the marble gods fighting the Titans scramble up the steps of the sanctuary (Figure 6). Similarly, two thousand years later, Auguste Rodin proposed to place his bronze figures of the Burghers of Calais directly on the pavement in front of the town hall as though they were actually on their way to meet the conqueror. The sculptor Pygmalion's desire to make his figure come to life is, of course, the classic example of art perverted into the duplication of physical reality.

The ambiguous relation between sculpture and the visitor expresses itself also in the varying degrees of isolation manifest in their compositional form. Abstract sculpture, such as obelisks or the triumphal columns of Rome, tends to be self-contained and without any gesture indicating an invitation to the viewer. The same is true for some modern abstractions, such as the stabiles of Alexander Calder. Other works, however, acknowledge their function by exposing themselves to the visitors or even addressing them. Frontality is the most effective way of showing such a response. Religious icons face the worshipper and petitioner explicitly. But even in styles that develop the body's action fully in the round, an artist like Bernini prefers to offer the essence of the message in a principal view.

In painting, the physical material of the pigments characterizes the medium but not the objects represented in the pictures. Sculptured objects possess the nature of their materials and derive effective symbolical connotations from them. Pliny reports that bowls of clay were often used to offer libations to the gods, because clay reveals to thoughtful persons "the indescribable kindness of the Earth." Through the ages, there remains a significant difference of meaning between materials manifesting the texture of natural growth and structure, such as wood or stone, and amorphous substances, such as plaster or poured metal. A carver like Henry Moore stresses the affinity between humanity and its natural origin and habitat by giving prominence to the strains of the wood grain and representing the human figure through shapes that derive from the growth patterns of trees (Figure 7).

The preciousness of materials, such as gold, ebony, or bronze, used to reflect the social importance of the monument. Durability or the lack of it is often distinctly symbolical. A whole range of meaning leads from the porphyry and granite of Egyptian tomb sculptures in quest of immortality to the deliberately flimsy stuffs employed by some modern artists, who denounce permanence. The least tangible works of three-dimensional visual art are plays of light in space created by neon or laser beams or the fugitive spectacles of fireworks and colored searchlights.

Another decisive character trait of sculpture derives from its way of representing its subjects without their context. Comparisons with literature or painting reveal the difference. G. E. Lessing, in his classic essay on the *Laocoön*, compares the Hellenistic marble figures of the Trojan priest and his sons attacked by serpents (Figure 8) with the same episode recounted in Virgil's *Aeneid*. In a verbal narration the story is embedded in time and space: it ties the event to a chain of cause and effect by explaining how human destinies come about and what consequences they lead to. It presents the life of the individual in its physical and social setting. Something similar is the case when paintings show human actions in a landscape or city, in a palace or stable. In contrast, the marble group of Laocoön and his sons is extracted from space and time. It limits its statement to the struggle between the attacking beasts and the suffering of their victims. Devoid of the time dimension of action, it displays a state of affairs rather than a happening.

Even so, the Laocoön group is of considerable

Figure 5. *(Sculpture)* Mark di Suvero, *Mother Peace,* 1970. Steel painted orange. Courtesy of Storm King Art Center, Mountainville, N.Y.

Figure 6. *(Sculpture)* Altar of Zeus and Athena, Pergamon: *The Gods Fighting the Giants* (detail), ca. 170 B.C.E. Marble. Pergamon Museum, East Berlin. Marburg/Art Resource, New York.

Figure 7. *(Sculpture)* Henry Moore, *Reclining Figure,* 1939. Elm wood. The Detroit Institute of Arts. Gift of the Dexter M. Ferry Jr. Trustee Corporation.

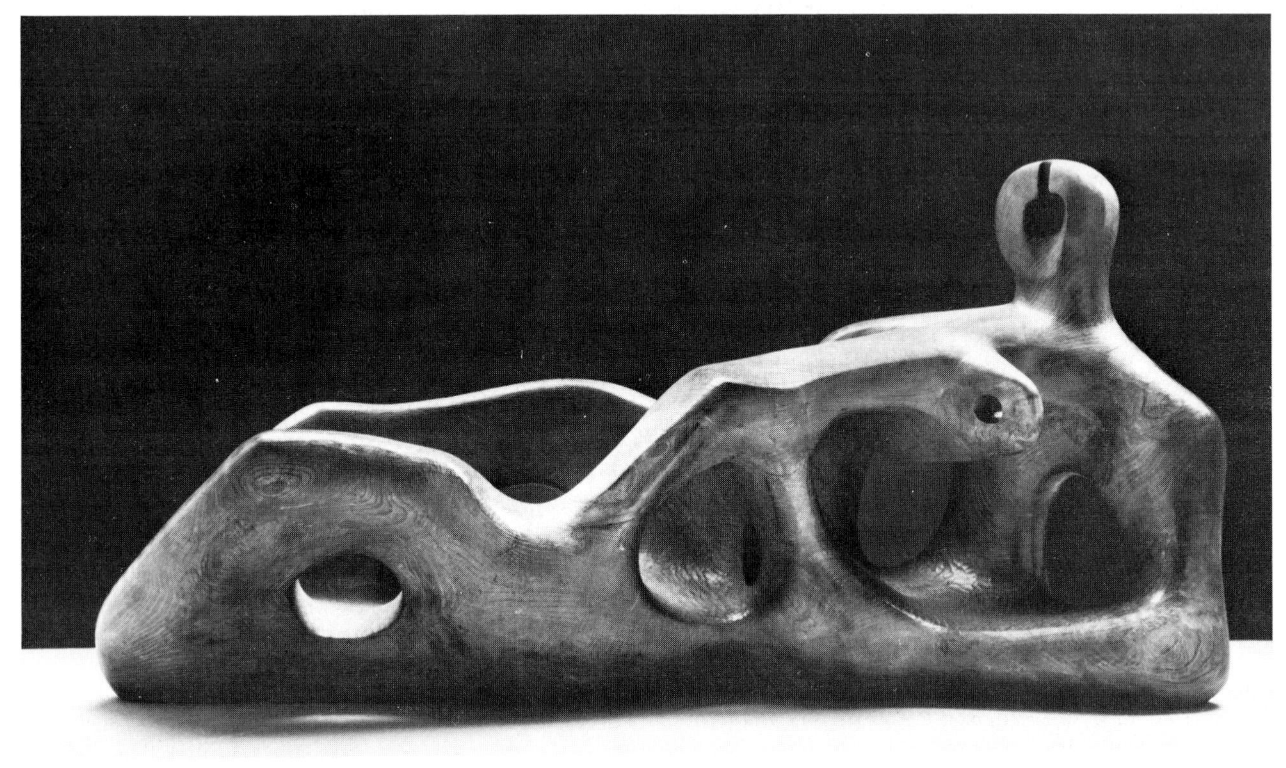

complexity by presenting more than one figure. When limited to a single shape, such as a single human body, sculpture often compensates the viewer for this limitation by symbolically presenting within its own orbit significant themes such as parallelism and contrast, expansion and contraction, resistance and yielding, rising and falling. In this manner, the interplay between the spatial gestures of torso, head, and limbs in a figure such as Wilhelm Lehmbruck's *Kneeling Woman* (Figure 9) adds up to a symphonic image of moves and countermoves, which reflects a whole world in a single body. Remember here that in the philosophy of the RENAISSANCE the proportions of the human body were considered a microcosmic image of the universe, whose macrocosmic structure was beyond the reach of our senses.

More radically than the other arts, sculpture is monopolized by the subject matter of the human figure. Just as the first man in the Garden of Eden was formed as a piece of sculpture from a lump of clay, human beings, once created, make their likenesses most readily from lumps of physical matter. This material affinity between the signifier and the signified expresses itself at all levels of abstraction, from the purely nonrepresentational shapes of a David Smith or the highly stylized fetishes and totem poles of early cultures to the life-sized trompe l'oeil casts of a Duane Hanson or George Segal (Figure 10) and the less ambitious portraits of notable contemporaries in the wax museums. The highly emotional responses to deceptively faithful duplications of the human figure are twofold. On the one hand, the public welcomes the familiar look of the figures, which may seem taken directly from the daily life of the streets. This response derives from the age-old appreciation of skillful imitations of nature. On the other hand, there is clearly discernible in the modern products the specifically surrealist shock caused by creatures that look alive but reveal the iciness of dead bodies and an absence of feeling. These dwellers in the no-man's-land between life and death descend from the wraiths and ghosts of the folk traditions, the golems and the Frankenstein robots. They symbolize the awesome ability of the creative mind to conceive artifacts that display telling attributes of life while lacking life itself.

The existential twilight in which art and life meet provides an emotional affinity that encourages identification with the graven images. Sculpted likenesses serve to pay homage to gods and heroes, they embody ideals of physical beauty, and they preserve the memory of cherished individuals. The curiously am-

Figure 8. *(Sculpture)* *Laocoön,* ca. first century B.C.E. Marble. Vatican Museum, Rome. Lauros-Giraudon/Art Resource, New York.

Figure 9. *(Sculpture)* Wilhelm Lehmbruck, *Kneeling Woman,* 1911. Cast stone. 69½ in. high, at base 56 by 27 in. Collection, The Museum of Modern Art, New York. Abby Aldrich Rockefeller Fund.

Figure 10. *(Sculpture)* George Segal, *To All Gates,* 1971. Plaster, wood, plastic, lights, metal. Des Moines Art Center. Coffin Fine Arts Trust Fund, 1972.

biguous reality status of such images is of psychological interest. It may seem hard to understand that, for example, in voodoo rites a physical attack on a distant enemy is thought possible by means of a mere image. Nor is it obvious that faithful believers address the portraits of gods and saints so directly as though they were appealing to a present power while knowing that the figures are made of wood or plaster. To be sure, the medium of sculpture favors such identification. The church fathers who objected to the veneration of icons worried mostly about the compelling presence of three-dimensional figures while they tended to accept paintings as nonverbal means of spreading the word of God.

But even realistic sculpture fails to deceive the common sense of the viewer. The psychological paradox inherent in the attitude toward images remains puzzling as long as one defines identity as depending upon physical uniqueness. The logic of the excluded middle seems to insist that a thing is either alive or dead, either in one place or in another, either a person or the person's image; but the human mind deals with the task of identification more interestingly. It is involved with essences or ways of being rather than with their individual material carriers. The essences of power or courage or charity or evil are the targets of human concern, and such essences can make their appearance in any number of different manifestations. They can be projected on unworthy vehicles, such as the broomstick that serves as a hobbyhorse; they may be embodied in the countenance of expressive icons fashioned by artists; or they may present themselves most authentically "in person." Whatever the medium of incarnation, however, it is the particular spiritual quality coming across from its carrier that transmits the message and matters to the receiver.

See also VISUAL IMAGE.

Bibliography. Hans Joachim Albrecht, *Skulptur im 20. Jahrhundert,* Cologne, 1977; Kenneth Clark, *The Nude, A Study in Ideal Form,* Princeton, N.J., 1956, reprint 1972; F. David Martin, *Sculpture and Enlivened Space,* Lexington, Ky., 1981; Charles De Tolnay, *Michelangelo, Sculptor, Painter, Architect,* Princeton, N.J., 1975; Rudolf Wittkower, *Sculpture: Processes and Principles,* New York, 1977.

RUDOLF ARNHEIM

SECRECY

The deliberate concealment of information that may be private or public. Secrecy implies that the holder of the information has reasons to keep something (the secret) from the knowledge or observation of others. Secrecy is applied to and not embodied in information, and it is usually the actual or expected added value of such information in the eyes of the holder that leads to secrecy. When individuals or private entities conceal information, they may be within their rights to PRIVACY. However, the added value of such information can be entirely subjective and may never materialize in an actual communication exchange. There are many unresolved questions about the ethics of private secrecy (which may be linked to DECEPTION) and about issues of confidentiality in relationships with, for example, doctors, lawyers, psychologists, and journalists. When the holder of information is a public entity such as a government, however, an entirely new set of issues arises. Government secrecy is a deliberate act on the part of those who govern to conceal information from the governed at a given time. The assumption is that secrecy will preserve or add to the value of the concealed information. Such secrecy can be employed by government as a whole (state secrets) or by specific public institutions, bureaus, political leaders, and administrators.

Government privilege to conceal. There is no such thing in government as complete openness—that is, a transparent governing process—but there are fundamental differences between democratic and nondemocratic systems with respect to questions of secrecy and openness. In nondemocratic regimes the government privilege to practice secrecy is usually absolute; there is no need for justification because the ruler controls the flow of public information. In a democracy, however, openness is regarded as desirable; only special circumstances are felt to justify tampering with the free flow of information. Hence the government's privilege to conceal is accepted only grudgingly—both in theory and practice—as a temporary measure that will, it is hoped, wither away with international peace and enlightened democracy.

In democratic regimes the government privilege to conceal information is defended as a means of protecting a public interest that, on balance, is judged to be more important than other public interests. In external affairs the public interest to be protected may be national security and the effective conduct of international relations. In domestic affairs the public interests requiring protection include the efficiency of the governing process; the privacy of individuals, groups, and organizations; and official information pertaining to crime prevention, prison security, commercial secrets, currency, and related financial matters. In all democratic countries there are axioms or laws or established practices legitimizing government's privilege to conceal information from the public. This privilege is applied in many ways and appears under different names—crown, state, or executive privilege; confidentiality; discretionary power; classification rights; CENSORSHIP; rules of nondiscovery in courts; and others.

The right to know. In democracies there are other axioms or constitutional provisions or laws that express the principle of citizens' sovereignty. These support the right of individuals and groups to demand and obtain information about public affairs. In order for citizens to exercise their right of autonomous participation, they need information about what the government is in fact doing. In other words, they have a right to know.

Nondemocratic regimes also have secrecy problems; otherwise there would be no need to employ a secret police. Their constitutions sometimes provide for citizens' access to information that is necessary for certain types of participation (Hungary, for instance, has such a constitutional provision). Yet regimes that do not emphasize human and civil rights are not usually concerned with freedom of information. Government secrecy is the rule in such regimes.

The people's right to know in a democracy is a prerequisite for citizens' participation. It enables them to secure information in order to formulate their preferences and choose wisely and also to ensure government accountability. The right to know is therefore part of democratic freedom, related to yet distinct from freedoms of expression, association, movement, and the press. Knowing is a prerequisite, not a guarantee, for enlightened participation. Citizens may form their preferences with or without information. Moreover, available information can be easily distorted and be in fact a shroud for secrecy.

The dilemma of secrecy. The dilemma of secrecy in democracies is a result of the contradiction between the government's privilege to conceal and the people's right to know. Secrecy is justified as a deliberate act to protect the public by withholding official information, yet one important public interest is the ability of citizens to find out what government is doing. Publicity is required to find out whether secrecy is justified. Furthermore, in exercising their privilege to conceal, those who govern may be motivated by selfish reasons that have nothing to do with protecting the public interest. Conversely, people may want information for reasons other than their desire to participate in democratic processes—for example, GOSSIP or revealing commercial secrets.

The advocates of the people's right to know do not demand complete openness. They are trying to change the existing rules so that disclosure becomes the prevailing norm and the withholding of public information must be specifically justified. The advocates of maintaining or strengthening the government's privilege to conceal do not demand complete secrecy. They argue instead that some secrecy is a necessary evil that must be borne by free citizens in a democracy because of imperfections in international relations, human nature, or the governing process. Secrecy is therefore required for security, for the further perfection of democracy, and to enable officials to say in closed meetings what they dare not say publicly. As a result certain measures are required: classification of documents, closed sessions, civil servants' oaths of allegiance, single spokespersons for releasing information, censorship, and other restrictions on publicity and the press.

The Watergate fiasco in the United States revealed most aspects of the secrecy dilemma in modern democracies. President Richard M. Nixon claimed that no court could require him to produce his White House tapes. He argued for absolute executive privilege, that is, for the final authority of the president to decide whether government privilege applies. The Supreme Court rejected this claim; it recognized executive privilege for maintaining military and diplomatic secrecy but insisted that the applicability of the privilege is a judicial decision, not an executive one. This ruling established two important principles. First, the executive has no monopoly on determining what the public interest is and on deciding when secrecy is needed to preserve it. Second, the inherent conflict in government secrecy is between two legitimate public interests, and the delicate balance between them must be reexamined from time to time.

The way different systems deal with the secrecy dilemma is influenced by specific historical and cultural backgrounds. These backgrounds determine attitudes toward the concept of secrecy, the configuration of communication networks in society, traditions of critical or deferential attitudes toward government, the social legitimacy of secrecy, and the role played by various channels, including the mass media. The practice of secrecy is also determined by the political marketplace in which transactions of public information occur and in which information is a scarce resource. In this setting, secrecy and publicity are the result of exchanges between actors, and access to information becomes a means of power and influence.

In addition, constitutional and legal provisions provide formal rules for government secrecy and publicity and for solving conflicts between holders and requesters of information. Here, in a legal sense, information is defined as a tangible commodity: documents, memorandums, tapes, transcripts, exhibits, and so on. Access rights are consequently formulated in terms of property rights and are to be found in laws defining state or official secrets, executive privilege, document classification procedures, codes of behavior for civil servants, disclosure of evidence before the courts, censorship, and laws affecting freedom of expression and publication.

Freedom of information laws. The legal issues of freedom of information generally center around the conflict between the legal right or "privilege" of the custodian (the government) to conceal information versus the legal right or "freedom" of the claimant (the citizen) to obtain it. In support of the former, the laws attempt to guarantee government secrecy, primarily by establishing state secrets and rules on how to prevent disclosures to unauthorized persons. In this context the burden of proof is on the citizen who tries to gain access despite specific laws and regulations aimed at protecting official secrets. A primary example of such a law is the British Official Secrets Act of 1911, which provided that all government information is secret unless specifically exempted.

The legal right of the citizen to obtain information is a much more recent principle and attempts to establish that disclosure is the rule, not the exception, and that whatever government does is in the public domain unless legally restricted. Its purpose is to legislate the people's right to know and to compel the government to justify secrecy. The first such law was passed in Sweden in 1766 and established the principle—within the framework of the freedom of the press—that every citizen shall have access to all official documents, unless specifically restricted. Subsequently it became a constitutional law specifying the types of documents to be restricted. Finland inherited from Sweden this tradition of openness, but a specific law permitting access to official documents was enacted only in 1951.

The U.S. Freedom of Information Act (1966) was more ambitious because it attempted to establish the general principle of the people's right to know and provided a legal channel for appeals to the courts when information requests were denied. The law went into effect in 1967, and it soon became obvious that there were many practical obstacles to the free flow of information: the exemptions were very broadly defined, actual access was technically impossible, and the fees were high. The law was amended in 1974, again mainly as a result of public pressure and congressional initiative, with no assistance from the executive branch (President Gerald Ford vetoed the 1974 amendments, and both houses overrode the veto). The amended law facilitated access, enabled federal judges to review classification decisions of government, restricted the language of some exemptions, and required agencies to report to Congress the number of cases and the reasons for decisions to withhold information. The Federal Advisory Committee Act of 1972, together with the Sunshine Act of 1976, further enhanced openness by prescribing open meetings of advisory bodies, congressional committees, federal regulatory agencies, and other statutory authorities. The opening of such meetings and their minutes (even though they can be closed through certain procedures) signified a real change.

A number of other democratic countries followed the Swedish and U.S. examples and enacted various freedom of information or public access laws: Denmark and Norway (1970); Austria (1973); the Netherlands and France (1978); Australia, New Zealand, and Canada (1982–1983). Other democracies were still without such laws. Closely related are the recently enacted privacy laws in many countries that allow citizens to inspect personal files being held on them in government agencies.

The secrecy dilemma cannot be solved by statute alone. Withholding of information is still practiced in the corridors of power despite all the legal changes. Holders of information will always find ways to exclude certain groups and individuals, particularly the weaker ones in society. Moreover, government PROPAGANDA is in many ways another form of secrecy, and no law can solve this kind of tampering with the free flow of information. The controversy continues also in democracies that have freedom of information laws, because those who oppose them argue that these laws, as practiced, cause serious damage to vital national interests, the security of the country, and the efficient conduct of government activities.

The secrecy dilemma is peculiar to democracies precisely because they aspire to be open. The details of government secrecy in a particular country are the combined result of the general social context of human communication, the constitutional and legal provisions, and the practice of politics. Changes in one or more of these attributes will also affect government secrecy. In practice government secrecy will continue to be a complex balance between the government's privilege to conceal and the people's right to know. Nevertheless, maintaining a balance that safeguards the right to know is essential for preserving democracy.

See also COMPUTER: IMPACT—IMPACT ON GOVERNMENT; GOVERNMENT REGULATION.

Bibliography. Sissela Bok, *Secrets: On the Ethics of Concealment and Revelation,* New York, 1983; T. N. Chaturvedi, ed., *Secrecy in Government,* New Delhi, 1980; Thomas M. Franck and Edward Weisband, eds., *Secrecy and Foreign Policy,* New York, 1974; Carl J. Friedrich, *The Pathology of Politics,* New York, 1972; Itzhak Galnoor, ed., *Government Secrecy in Democracies,* New York, 1977; James Michael, *The Politics of Secrecy,* London and New York, 1982; Donald C. Rowat, ed., *Administrative Secrecy in Developed Countries,* New York, 1979; Edward A. Shils, *The Torment of Secrecy,* Glencoe, Ill., 1956; David Wise, *The Politics of Lying,* New York, 1973.

ITZHAK GALNOOR

SELECTIVE RECEPTION

Selective reception subsumes two related but distinct classes of audience behavior: selective exposure and selective PERCEPTION. What they have in common is that both behaviors change and individualize the media-use experience. When an individual elects to expose himself or herself to one medium or type of content and not another, or when an individual perceives something in a message that others do not, the media-use experience becomes less uniform.

At the heart of the issue of selective exposure and selective perception are questions and assumptions about the extent to which receivers of communication messages are active participants with some control over the process. At one extreme is the "straw man" position that receivers are completely passive, accepting messages based entirely on habit and availability and interpreting these messages in a uniform manner such that shared MEANING is universal. It is well established, however, that not everyone interprets a given message the same way, and we clearly exercise some control over what we read in newspapers or watch on television. The issues are instead questions of degree and kind of selectivity. How much control do we exercise over exposure and perception, and how often do we exercise it? Why and how are we selective? And what difference does selectivity make in the uses and effects of communication messages?

Selective Exposure

In the early 1960s a central explanation for apparently minimal effects of mass communication was that people consistently avoided messages that might change their ATTITUDES. But several years later U.S. scholars David Sears and Jonathan Freedman pointed out that people sometimes seem to prefer messages contradicting their views and other times seem to have no preference at all—in other words, the need for supportive information is not constant. Sears and Freedman substituted the more general idea of utility to argue that people select messages that will be useful to them, although specifying just what an individual will find useful is often difficult.

What is selected? Although people do not always seek supportive messages, the attitudinal character of messages is clearly one reason people select some messages over others. Those who have recently purchased a car often prefer to read or see ads about that car than ones about its competitors. Similarly, political partisans often report receiving more messages about their preferred candidate than about the opponent, or reading more about positions they favor than about those they oppose. One reason suggested for this is that because taking in messages that conflict with one's attitudes produces uncomfortable mental dissonance, such messages are avoided (*see* COGNITIVE CONSISTENCY THEORIES). However, selection based on attitudes seems much more likely to be selection of supportive messages rather than attempts to avoid conflicting information.

Such selection of supportive messages requires an explanation other than simple dissonance reduction. It may be that genuine uncertainty about the correct position can also lead individuals to seek information to elaborate their attitude positions—a cognitive rather than defensive motivation. In addition, although the evidence is less direct, supportive information probably requires less cognitive effort to process than less familiar conflicting messages.

Obviously, for receivers to select messages based on attitude or IDEOLOGY, they must have an attitude toward the particular subject. This is not a trivial point, since people probably have many opportunities to receive messages on topics about which they have no prior opinion, and thus selection or avoidance for attitudinal reasons is irrelevant. Furthermore, a number of intervening or conditional variables determine whether and how much selection occurs, even for those with attitudes on a given issue. Selection seems more likely for issues more important to the individual, and there is also evidence that selectivity is complexly related to certainty about or commitment to one's attitude position. Those with little commitment to a position have no reason to be selective, and those firmly committed can afford to be liberal with their attention. However, those only moderately committed are most likely to be selective, whether to defend their position or to solidify it.

A number of other conditions and variables may make selecting supportive information more or less likely. Some personality traits may make defensiveness or ease of processing a more important instrumental goal in communication than others. Those who prefer high levels of stimulation may deliberately seek messages to conflict with their own attitudes. And any of these variables might interact with such situational factors as stress, mood, goals, and social setting.

In contrast to selective exposure based on attitudes expressed in the message, selection of a level of stimulation or of a type or genre of content seems to be more directly dependent on situational factors. Experiments by U.S. scholar Dolf Zillmann and his colleagues have shown that people bored by a monotonous task will be much more likely to choose exciting, action-packed television programs than people who have just worked at demanding tasks under time pressure. In other words, if one's level of stress or boredom is outside acceptable limits, selecting a compensating level of media stimulation seems satisfying. There is evidence that such selection works, but compensation alone does not fully explain why an individual chooses a particular level of media stimulation, since, for example, watching any kind of television program lowers the heart rate of stressed subjects. Apparently television viewing also affects arousal by absorbing people and distracting them from their current state.

Some sort of behavioral affinity between current affective state and the content of specific programs also influences content choices independent of program pace. Manipulating subjects' moods by having them succeed or fail at a task or by praising or criticizing their performance causes variation in program selection among comedies, action dramas, and game shows. Because these variations are often among programs that seem equally arousing and because selection differences in some cases do not occur until after several minutes have passed, compensation for arousal is clearly not the process involved. Unfortunately, behavioral affinity can predict both selection and avoidance, and it is often hard to tell whether differences occur because people seek programs that contain cues reminding them of their present happy state or avoid programs reminding them of unhappy states.

Similar considerations probably influence selection of mass communication use over other activities or selection of a particular medium of communication, but the evidence so far contains some contradictions. Time-sampling studies, for example, have found that television viewing is a much more likely evening activity after a rough day at work. But some experiments have found that annoyed individuals are less inclined to select television viewing than are praised individuals. It may be that the annoyance leads to short-lived avoidance of television but that after several hours the annoyances of the workday are less immediately felt, and television viewing is then regarded as well suited to an accompanying fatigued state.

Just as attitude-based selection requires that the receiver have an attitude in the first place, selection for a level of stimulation or behavioral affinity presumes that the receiver has a learned store of knowledge or expectations about the characteristics of different media and content, particularly about their ability to arouse and their particular behavioral affinities. This store of knowledge and expectations, when available to consciousness, is often studied under the rubric "uses and gratifications" (*see also* MASS MEDIA EFFECTS). Finally, these momentary, situational selections seem to be associated with moderate levels of internal states. Extreme conditions, such as extreme fear or very strong dissonance, may simply not be resolvable by selectivity in one's communication behaviors.

What happens in selective exposure? People can deliberately select messages through conscious examination of internal states and motives or by applying well-developed expectations of media and messages to a present situation. However, much selective exposure may be carried out with little or no awareness by the person being selective. Although some researchers limit selective exposure to "deliberate behaviors to attain and sustain perceptual control," attribution theory and research make it clear that humans are quite limited in their propensity (and perhaps even ability) for accurate introspection.

Various reflexive and automatic processes are thus likely to impinge on selection as well. Social science has learned quite a bit about the "orienting reflex," "attentional inertia," and other basic sensory constituents of the human organism. In addition, it appears that even very young children develop scanning and monitoring strategies that build on these basic reflexes with learned cue associations. Such perceptual monitoring processes quickly become highly automatic, complex, and efficient but are probably themselves influenced by moods and needs as important motivators. Thus the relatively conscious aspects of selective exposure do not occur in a vacuum; rather, they are part of a continuum that includes many simultaneously operating processes.

Selection versus habit. The idea of a continuum from reflexive to conscious action in selectivity raises the issue of activity versus passivity in audience behavior. This issue is most often viewed as a dichotomy between active and passive audiences rather than as a continuum of individuals or, better yet, of behaviors. When focused on selective exposure the debate centers on whether audiences are active and selective or passive and habitual in their communication reception.

There is much evidence to support both views. Instead of emphasizing selection, one can as easily conclude that people read or view habitually according to the time of day or the availability of messages. A more fruitful approach to such divisions is to view selection and habit as a continuum and to ask questions such as the following: What is the balance of selection and habit? When are we selective and when habitual? How do we shift along the continuum between them?

We tend to treat selective exposure as decisions about individual messages or about the choice between media at a particular moment of time. Thus the issue is always first whether or not people are selective at a given moment in their choice of messages or media. Often we discover that they are not—that the decision of the moment is no decision at all but merely habit.

Examined over a longer time frame, however, the meaning of selective exposure and its prevalence may broaden. Habits can be quite selective in effect, and selectivity, applied once or twice to the same problem, can then become habitual. Looked at this way, one research issue becomes the balance of the individual versus the social system in the initial formation of a selective habit.

Consequences of selective exposure. The original motivation for studying selective exposure was its expected power to predict and explain a wide variety of effects of communication (e.g., PERSUASION, aggression). The perception that Sears and Freedman's conclusions cast doubt on that power probably contributed to the period of relative neglect of selective exposure studies. This changed only when selective exposure was examined as a phenomenon of interest in its own right.

When selection of supportive information occurs, either at a particular instant or as a long-term habit, reinforcement effects are of course much more likely than change effects. But the broadening look at selective exposure suggests two broader hypotheses. First, selecting to expose oneself to mass media apparently leads to absorption in the media and distraction from one's current state, which can change arousal levels and cognitive sets and thus can change traditional effects in a variety of ways. Second, messages attended to for relatively conscious reasons or behavioral affinity may be used under conditions of greater cognitive activity and effort, which should also produce large differences in the effects of those messages.

Selective Perception

Fundamentally, selective perception is simply the recognition that individuals can form different interpretations of the same message. Although selective perception is often invoked as an explanation after the fact for supposed ineffectiveness of purposive communication, meaning probably is not infinitely malleable. Most of the time most people will construct at least similar meanings from the same message. Selective perception has become a research question primarily when variation seems more likely and predictable. Thus many studies have attempted to demonstrate (some successfully) that liberals and conservatives form opposite perceptions to humor about racial or ethnic stereotypes, or that partisans of a candidate or football team see a quite different result of a debate or game than partisans on the opposing side or those with no ostensible predisposition.

The mechanism by which selective perception occurs is open to question. The fact that it seems to require strongly held attitudes or beliefs makes selective perception different from selective exposure, in which message selection is practiced mainly by those moderately committed to an issue or attitude and is not necessary for strong partisans. Nevertheless, one possible explanation for selective perception relies on dissonance theory, suggesting that interpreting situations and messages in ways congruent with one's beliefs minimizes dissonant cognitions.

A more cognitive explanation starts with a model of memory or mental representation as a kind of associative network. Within such a network, any experience "primes" some nodes directly, and this activation will spread to other memory nodes associated (for whatever reason) with those nodes. The relevance of priming theories to selective perception is that different experiences and attitudes will lead to differences in how the associative network is structured and which nodes are primed by particular experiences. Thus the perception by a partisan that the preferred candidate won the debate may simply result from a mental structure in which the points that that candidate raised are all closely associated in memory and primed other, favorable cognitions, whereas the opponent's points were less related to the individual's own cognitive structure—another way of saying that the opponent's remarks made less sense.

Priming could be involved in subliminal perception (to the extent it occurs) as well. If images can be received without our being conscious of them, the real effects may occur through the activation of neighboring nodes in the associative network.

Another point is that selective perception probably occurs in many more situations than the political, athletic, or ideological arenas in which it is usually studied. In limited ways, audience members perceive selectively all the time, and some of these individual selective perceptions probably differ dramatically. But such selective perceptions are probably too subtle or unique to be easily registered by researchers. Research on selective perception is thus largely limited to situations in which substantial portions of the audience share a predisposition that will lead them to also share a perception of the message that is different from that of the rest of the audience.

Bibliography. Charles Atkin, "Instrumental Utilities and Information Seeking," in *New Models for Mass Communication Research,* ed. by Peter Clarke, Beverly Hills, Calif., 1973; Leonard Berkowitz and Karen H. Rogers, "A Priming Effect Analysis of Media Influences," in *Perspectives on Media Effects,* ed. by Jennings Bryant and Dolf Zillmann, Hillsdale, N.J., 1986; David O. Sears and Jonathan L. Freedman, "Selective Exposure to Information: A Critical Review," *Public Opinion Quarterly* 31 (1967): 194–213; Dolf Zillmann and Jennings Bryant, eds., *Selective Exposure to Communication,* Hillsdale, N.J., 1985.

ROBERT P. HAWKINS

SEMANTIC DIFFERENTIAL

One of the tools that make human communication possible is LANGUAGE, which allows people to share the MEANING of words and concepts. The semantic differential is a measurement technique developed by CHARLES OSGOOD and associates in the 1950s to assess the connotative (i.e., contextual, affective) meaning for individuals of verbal concepts and of nonverbal signs like colors, figures, or sounds.

The technique assumes that the meaning of concepts can be "mapped" as points in what Osgood and associates called "semantic space." This analogy has proved quite useful in different applications, for it makes possible conceptualizations of psychological objects as unidimensional or multidimensional semantic entities. The availability of sophisticated statistical analysis techniques (e.g., factor analysis) in turn permitted the identification of salient dimensions consistent across different cultural settings.

Procedure

There are two general steps to follow when using the semantic differential: (1) choosing the concept or concepts to be rated and (2) selection of the adjective pairs used for rating.

Although the first step seems self-evident, two things must be kept in mind. First, the concept or object under consideration should not elicit uniform responses from different individuals (i.e., some variance is required); second, the concepts or objects chosen must cover, even if only to a limited extent, the semantic space. The method proceeds by presenting individuals with pairs of descriptive adjectives, usually opposites, and asks them to indicate the direction and the intensity of association between the given sign and the qualifiers defining each scale. A typical semantic differential form is shown in Figure 1.

Research studies by Osgood and many others have reported three main factors of meaning, regarded as the primary dimensions that seem to organize semantic space. The three factors are commonly la-

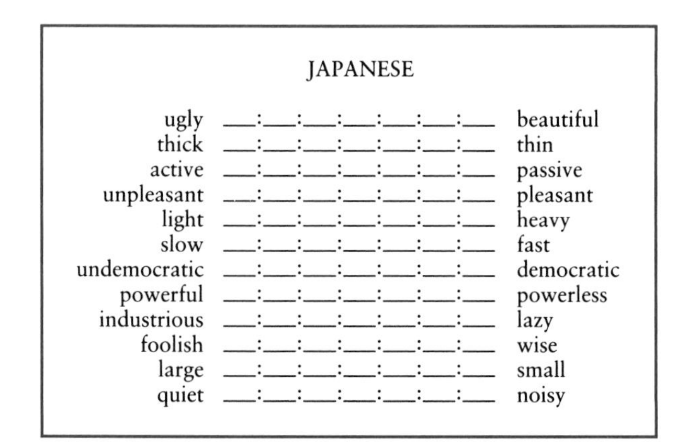

Figure 1. *(Semantic Differential)* Example of a semantic differential scale. Respondents are to check only the space on each scale that best represents their view of the concept (here "Japanese"). Data can later be analyzed both graphically and numerically.

beled "evaluation" (e.g., good-bad), "potency" (e.g., strong-weak), and "activity" (e.g., active-passive). When a group of subjects judges a set of concepts such as "mother," the color "red," or a line form, using adjective pairs such as ugly-beautiful, thick-thin, and slow-fast (i.e., one or more pairs from each of the three dimensions), a cube of data is generated. The rows are defined by scales, the columns by the concepts being judged, and the "slices" from front to back by the subjects doing the judging. Each cell represents with a single value how a specific individual judged a particular concept using a particular scale (see Figure 2). Factor analysis and other data-reduction techniques are thus logical tools for analysis. It is possible to conduct separate analyses for single objects (e.g., to examine generality across subjects), for single concepts (e.g., to examine generality across concepts), or to collapse either the subject dimension (when the interest lies in cultural meanings) or the concept dimension (when one is interested in concept-class characteristics).

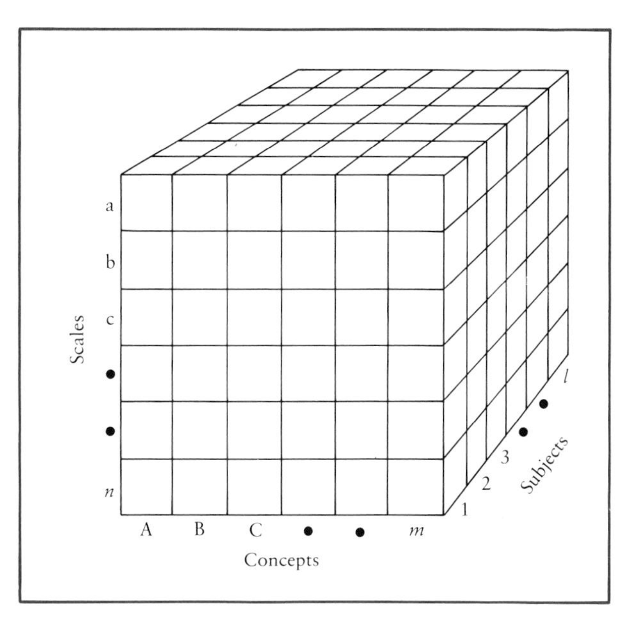

Figure 2. *(Semantic Differential)* The cube of data generated when *l* subjects judge *m* concepts using *n* scales.

As a result of extensive cross-cultural research, covering more than thirty different language/culture communities, Osgood and associates have found that the evaluation, potency, and activity factors constantly appear, despite differences in language and CULTURE. However, it has become evident that the scale composition of semantic spaces can be modified to some extent depending on the object of judgment. Thus the relative importance of, and relationship among, semantic factors may vary with the concept class being judged. Using auditory stimuli in a cross-cultural investigation of phonetic symbolism, Murray Miron found in the early 1960s that the potency factor is most salient across both culturally and linguistically different subject groups. In another cross-cultural study Yasumasa Tanaka and others found that the affective meaning of several scales varies among concept classes, causing changes in the structure of various semantic spaces but behaving consistently across subject groups differing in both language and culture. In general, there is evidence to support the view that there is generality across cultures among affective meaning systems operating in the cognitive processes of humans.

Allocation of Affective Meanings

In order to locate the cultural meaning of a particular concept, one may proceed by asking a series of questions, each corresponding to the three main factors identified: Is this concept good or bad (evaluation)? Is it strong or weak (potency)? Is it active or passive (activity)? Thus with only three binary questions it is possible to assign a concept to one of eight octants in semantic space. If each straight "cut" representing a factor dimension is scaled into seven discriminable steps (assuming a seven-point scale), then each decision reduces uncertainty by six-sevenths, and the three cuts produce a semantic space having 343 discrete regions. The cultural meaning of any concept can be represented with just one of these 343 discrete regions.

Multilingual Semantic Differentials

The multilingual semantic differential is a special form of the semantic differential used in cross-cultural research, in which the affective meaning of the scales used in the analysis must be semantically equivalent—if not identical—across different linguistic or cultural communities. Multilingual semantic differentials may be constructed either by using translated pairs of adjectives or by eliciting indigenous pairs of adjectives to define the scales.

In the 1970s Osgood and associates developed what they called "pan-cultural" semantic differentials, consisting of indigenously elicited pairs of adjectives from a common set of one hundred substantives translated into the indigenous language. Indigenous qualifier forms were collected in more than twenty-five language/culture communities, and the affective meaning equivalence of each indigenous scale was tested mathematically (through factor analysis) to compare the factor structures across communities. The semantic differential has proved to be a reliable cross-cultural research tool in disciplines such as psychology, political science, ADVERTISING, and communications research.

Evaluation in the Cognitive Process

In the general mediation theory of meaning—to which semantic differential operations belong—evaluative meanings of concepts are implicit reactions to given, learned signs. The general consensus regarding the psychological nature of the evaluative process is that (1) it is learned and implicit, (2) it is a predisposition to respond evaluatively to certain attitude objects, and (3) the evaluative predisposition may fall anywhere along a scale ranging from "extremely desirable" through "neutral" to "extremely undesirable." From this perspective, multilingual semantic differentials may tap the general but implicit evaluative framework through which people differing in language and culture experience, perceive, and judge various kinds of cognitive events. Thus the method seems to constitute a useful tool for gathering information on the cross-cultural generality and the cultural uniqueness of values and/or ATTITUDES that are part of human cognitive processes.

Incompatible value or attitude systems could become critical obstacles for INTERCULTURAL COMMUNICATION, reducing the opportunities for mutual understanding and even resulting in hostility among different language/culture communities. To the ex-

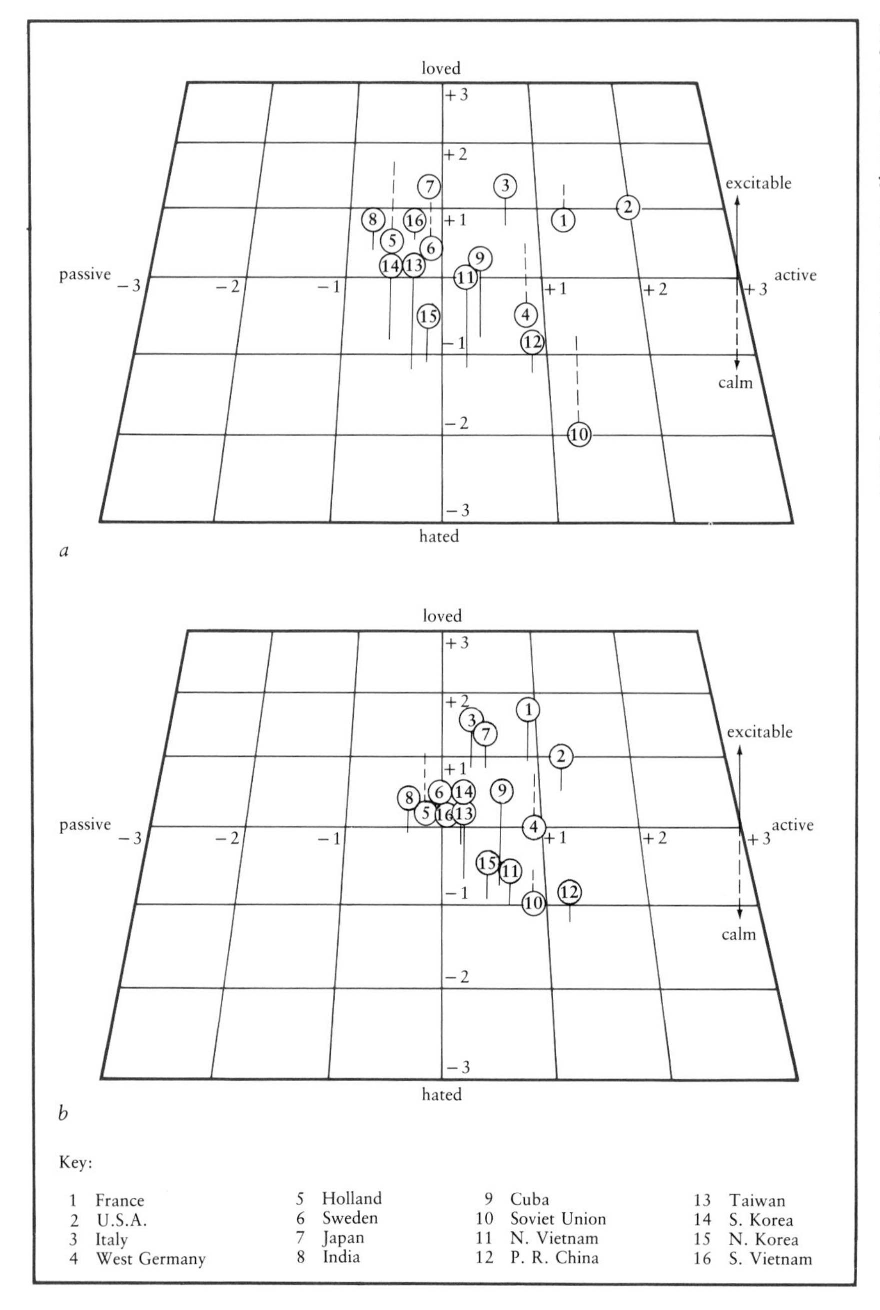

Figure 3. *(Semantic Differential)* Three-dimensional model of semantic space in a cross-cultural study of national stereotypes. Respondents were *(a)* Japanese college students and *(b)* Japanese specialists in foreign affairs. The scales are "loved-hated" ("top" to "bottom"), "passive-active" ("left" to "right"), and "excitable-calm" ("above" and "below" the imaginary plane). A solid projection indicates a rating toward the "excitable" end of the scale and a broken projection a rating toward "calm." From Yasumasa Tanaka, *Cross-Cultural Generality of Psychologic Operating in Perceiving National Stereotypes,* Tokyo, 1970.

tent that language is a major vehicle of human thought and beliefs, peoples with incompatible value or attitude systems would soon find that, for example, the values held by one group as "good" and "moral" may be considered "bad" and "immoral" by another group, possibly leading to misunderstandings and mutual incomprehension.

Applications

From a few scattered uses in the early 1950s the semantic differential has come to play an important role in almost all areas of the behavioral sciences and many other applied fields. In communications research in particular, Percy Tannenbaum early on devised an experimental situation in which cognitive interaction between sources and messages was tested through the use of semantic differentials in a before-after experimental design. Psychologist Harry Triandis studied cognitive similarity and interpersonal communications in organizations (*see* ORGANIZATIONAL COMMUNICATION) and also developed the "behavioral differential," which he claims taps the behavioral component of attitudes. Triandis was able to provide cross-cultural evidence supporting the correspondence between the affective and behavioral components of attitude in complex interpersonal perception. William Mindak applied the semantic differential to marketing problems, especially the analysis of product images (*see* CONSUMER RESEARCH). Tanaka used the method for predicting the effects of a televised national ELECTION campaign on voting behavior, in a cross-cultural study on perception of national stereotypes (see Figure 3), and for the analysis of the negative psychological responses to anything associated with "nuclear" among Japanese people. And Patrice French, Leon Jakobovits, Hartmut Espe, and others have been active in the development of the "graphic differential," a variation on the semantic differential that attempts to make the method more "language-free."

Although the semantic differential as an analytical tool is aging, the method continues to be used extensively and still captures the imagination of many behavioral scientists and researchers in various applied areas, whose basic interest continues to be the search for answers to the age-old questions "What is meaning?" and "How can we measure it?"

Bibliography. William A. Mindak, "Fitting the Semantic Differential to the Marketing Problem," *Journal of Marketing* 25 (1961): 28–33; Murray S. Miron, "A Cross-Linguistic Investigation of Phonetic Symbolism," *Journal of Abnormal and Social Psychology* 62 (1961): 623–630; Charles E. Osgood, William H. May, and Murray S. Miron, *Cross-Cultural Universals of Affective Meaning,* Urbana, Ill., 1975; Charles E. Osgood, George J. Suci, and Percy H. Tannenbaum, *The Measurement of Meaning,* Urbana, Ill., 1957; Yasumasa Tanaka, "A Case Study of Effectiveness of Communication: A Televised Election Campaign," in *Readings in Cross-Cultural Psychology* (proceedings, International Association for Cross-Cultural Psychology, Hong Kong, 1972), ed. by John L. M. Dawson and Walter J. Lonner, Hong Kong, 1974; idem, "Subjective Culture and Technology: A Social Psychological Examination of 'Nuclear Allergy' in the Japanese," *Annals of the New York Academy of Sciences* 285 (1977): 516–538; Percy H. Tannenbaum, *Attitudes toward Source and Concept as Factors in Attitude Change through Communications,* Urbana, Ill., 1953; Harry C. Triandis, "Cognitive Similarity and Interpersonal Communication in Industry," *Journal of Applied Psychology* 43 (1959): 321–326; Harry C. Triandis, Varso Varsilian, et al., *The Analysis of Subjective Culture,* New York, 1972.

YASUMASA TANAKA

SEMANTICS

The study of linguistic MEANING: the meaning of the expressions of a LANGUAGE and the understanding that can be derived from their communicative use. The term covers a variety of approaches to the study of the meaning, INTERPRETATION, and understanding of language that differ in focus and methodology. In contrast with SEMIOTICS, semantics focuses on languages, both natural and artificial, rather than treating linguistic meaning within a general theory of symbolic systems.

Semantics broadly construed seeks answers to three related questions: how to account for the meaningfulness of linguistic expressions, how meaning is related to grammatical structure, and how the meaning of an expression determines its use. Within this broad construal of semantics, a distinction is usually drawn between semantics in a narrow sense and pragmatics. In the terminology of CHARLES MORRIS (in *Foundations of the Theory of Signs,* 1938), semantics is the study of reference (the relation between language and the world it is used to talk about), and pragmatics deals with language use.

Approaches to the study of meaning differ in the aspect of linguistic communication that is taken as the focus: the part that varies from communicative act to communicative act or the part that remains constant. To illustrate, consider a situation in which A says to B:

(1) The book is on the table.

By saying (1), A may inform B of the location of a particular book. A's act of speaking is a communicative act of informing. The location of the book is communicated when A exploits their common knowledge of English to utter (1). A's utterance is a sentence token, a use of a sentence. Another token of (1) might be uttered on another occasion by C to D. On such an occasion, a different book and table might be referred to, but the meaning of the sentence itself would be the same. Shared knowledge of the language determines the meaning of the sentence, which is constant from use to use, though the understandings of tokens of (1) will vary.

Semantic theory may begin with the fact that A is doing something, that communication arises through actions of the individuals involved, and work from utterance situations toward an answer to how the meaning of the sentence enables speakers of a language to use it correctly. In this view the meaning of a sentence is whatever governs its use on particular occasions.

In two utterances of (1), different books and different tables can be referred to, but at each utterance some table and some book must be referred to. The meaning of the sentence guarantees it. A speaks truthfully only if the book is on the table. What stays constant from utterance to utterance is the condition that (1) places on the world, a condition that must be satisfied for it to be used truthfully. The meaning of a sentence requires an account of the relation between language and the world, reference and truth. Principles of use must include a theory of truth conditions.

Some semantic analysis concentrates on stating principles that govern the correct use of certain constructions (e.g., John R. Searle's account of how to promise, in *Speech Acts*). Logical semantic analysis gives a theory of truth conditions abstracted away from aspects of the situation of use (e.g., Richard Montague's treatment of quantification in English, in *Formal Philosophy*). A complete account of language use also considers the psychological dimension of understanding and how principles that are peculiar to language interact with other cognitive abilities such as reasoning and general knowledge (*see* COGNITION).

No semantic theory gives equal consideration to all of these points, and they are not mutually exclusive. But every semantic theory should have a notion of meaning that can satisfy some general requirements.

First, it must be general enough to account for every meaningful expression in a language. It must make sense not only for declarative sentences (for acts of asserting and denying) but also for interrogative and imperative sentences (for acts of questioning and ordering). Second, it should explain how a competent user of a language is able to determine the meaning of novel utterances from the infinite range of expressions in a language. The meaning of a sentence must be related to the meanings of its constituent parts (the compositionality property of linguistic meaning). The connection between the basic linguistic units and their meanings is arbitrary, but the connection between syntactically complex expressions and their meanings is not. Lexical semantics studies relations among the meanings of words of a language. Compositional semantics provides a theory of what type of thing the meanings for various expressions are and the principles for assigning meanings to complex expressions based on the meanings of their components. Finally, a semantic theory should support an account of the semantic intuitions that the users of a language have about its sentences, including intuitions of synonymy and paraphrase, inconsistency, contradiction, redundancy, and entailment, on which a theory of reasoning can be based.

Semantic questions are among the first philosophical questions, and so the history of semantics can be traced back to ancient Greek philosophy. The development of modern semantics was influenced greatly by the work in logic and the foundations of MATHEMATICS that began in the late nineteenth century, particularly the work of German philosopher Gottlob Frege and English philosopher Bertrand Russell. They explored the advantages and problems of reference-based theories of meaning. One of Frege's most important contributions ("Über Sinn und Bedeutung," 1892) is the distinction between the sense of an expression and its reference. A name has an object as its reference, but its sense is the "mode of presentation," the guise under which the object is picked out. Two names might have the same reference but different senses, though names with the same sense cannot have different reference. This point can be illustrated with a puzzle about (2) and (3):

(2) The morning star is the morning star.
(3) The morning star is the evening star.

The terms *morning star* and *evening star* refer to the same object, the planet Venus. If the meaning of a term were its referent, these two terms would have the same meaning. But if these two terms are synonymous, substituting one for the other should not change the meaning of the whole sentence, and (2) and (3) should have the same meaning. But they do not: (3) is informative, but (2) is not. Frege argued that the truth value of a sentence should be considered its reference and that the sense of the sentence is the thought it expresses. Sentences (2) and (3) have different senses because their constituent terms have different senses. The distinction between sense and reference is similar to distinctions drawn by others, such as intension versus extension and connotation versus denotation (though the term *connotation* has come to be used for associations of an expression that are not considered part of its meaning).

Russell rejected Frege's distinction and in "On Denoting" (1905) considered a puzzle about (4), which seems to be about the present king of France.

(4) The present king of France is bald.

Both the truth of (4) and its negation require that there be a king of France. Yet if no such individual exists, the subject does not have a denotation, and the whole sentence fails to have a denotation (truth value). Russell proposed that the subject-predicate form of (4) is misleadingly unlike its "logical form," which is better represented by (5):

(5) There is exactly one king of France, and he is bald.

Someone who utters (5) does two things: asserts that there is a king of France and also that he is bald. In this analysis (4) can be false for one of two reasons: either that there is no king of France or that there is, but he is not bald.

The formal approach to the analysis of language and the concentration on reference and truth continued in the logical positivist approach to language (e.g., that of Rudolf Carnap). The logical positivists attempted, unsuccessfully, to reduce sentence meaning to methods for verification. This work also sought the construction of an ideal language for philosophical discourse, one that would not incorporate the ambiguities of natural language.

The later work of LUDWIG WITTGENSTEIN (*Philosophical Investigations,* 1953) rejects the reference-based approach and suggests that the meaning of an expression is the principles that govern its use. This idea is continued in the reaction by the "ordinary language" philosophers (e.g., John L. Austin) to the logical positivist search for an ideal language.

The importance of taking both the use of an expression and its meaning into account is demonstrated in philosopher P. F. Strawson's reply ("On Referring," 1950) to Russell's theory of definite descriptions. He argued that meaningfulness is a property of sentences, but truth is a property of uses of sentences. He claimed that "mentioning or referring is not something an expression does, it is something that someone can use an expression to do." In Strawson's view sentence (4) is true or false only if there is a king of France, but its failure to be true or false in a particular use is not a question of meaninglessness. Rather the use of the definite description presupposes that there is a king of France and asserts that he is bald. If there is no king of France, the presupposition fails, and the sentence, still meaningful, cannot be used to make a statement.

Presupposition has been given two different analyses: logical (or semantic) presupposition and speaker (or pragmatic) presupposition. Semantic presupposition is defined in a logic that allows some sentences to be neither true nor false. A formula ϕ presupposes ψ if and only if in order for ϕ or $\neg\phi$ to be true, ψ must be true. In this view presupposition is a relation that holds between sentences and contrasts with entailment. Pragmatic presupposition views presupposing not as something sentences do but as something people do when they use sentences. What is presupposed by the utterance of (4) is not that there is a king of France but that the speaker believes that there is a king of France. In this view presupposition contrasts with assertion. Some distinction between presupposition and assertion is generally accepted.

The investigation of meaning from the point of view of use in speech act theory views every speech act on three levels: (i) what sentence is uttered and what its propositional content is (the locutionary act), (ii) the act the utterer performs in speaking (e.g., to assert, command, promise, or apologize; the illocutionary force), and (iii) the effect on the hearer (e.g., to persuade, frighten, disgust, or inform; the perlocutionary effect). Presuppositional and assertional meaning is conventionally associated with linguistic expressions; that is, it must be learned and is undetachable from a use of the expression. There are, however, aspects of meaning that can be derived from general, nonlinguistic principles. The work of British philosopher H. P. Grice ("Logic and Conversation," 1975) has been influential as an analysis of "implicative meaning." According to Grice, an utterance conveys more than the truth-conditional meaning of the sentence uttered. He distinguishes what is said from what is implicated, dividing implicatures into two types: conventional and conversational. Conventional implicatures are "backgrounded" conditions that are conventionally associated with expressions. Conversational implicatures are conclusions that a hearer can draw based on what is said and the assumption that the conversation is proceeding under a "cooperative principle" that is assumed to govern human interaction generally. This principle subsumes several "maxims of conversation" (e.g., Make your contribution as informative as is required, Do not say what you believe to be false, Be brief, and Be relevant). For example, consider (6):

(6) A: My car is out of gas.
B: There is a garage around the corner.

B's utterance is irrelevant unless he thinks that the garage is open and can sell gas. B does not say that the garage is open, but he conversationally implies it.

Semantics is an increasingly important part of linguistic theory. The question of how the meaning of a sentence is related to its grammatical structure is given much attention when attempts are made to integrate a semantic theory with grammatical theory. LINGUISTICS has contributed to the development of semantics by broadening the range of languages and phenomena that have been analyzed and by attempting to integrate theories of meaning from philosophical traditions with the psychological orientation of its subject matter.

Bibliography. David R. Dowty, Robert E. Wall, and Stanley Peters, *Introduction to Montague Semantics,* Dordrecht, Holland, and Boston, 1981; Norman Kretzmann, "Semantics, History of," *The Encyclopedia of Philosophy,* Vol. 7, New York, 1967 ed.; Steven C. Levinson, *Pragmatics,* Cambridge, 1983; John Lyons, *Semantics,* Cambridge, 1977; Richard Montague, *Formal Philosophy: Selected Papers of Richard Montague,* ed. with an intro. by Richard H. Thomason, New Haven, Conn., 1974; John R. Searle, *Speech Acts,* Cambridge, 1969; Dan Sperber and Deirdre Wilson, *Relevance: Communication and Cognition,* Cambridge, Mass., 1986.

WILLIAM A. LADUSAW

SEMANTICS, GENERAL

A discipline proposing that the scientific method and its assumptions be applied to everyday language habits. Named and promulgated by Alfred Korzybski (1879–1950), general semantics concerns not only the relationship between words and what they stand for (conventional SEMANTICS) but also the ways in which people respond to symbols.

Korzybski, born in Poland, had studied engineering and was later an interpreter at the League of Nations. He was struck by the contrast between the scientist's use of language and that of politicians, many philosophers, and most people most of the time. Along with contemporaries such as JOHN DEWEY who were disillusioned in the aftermath of World War I, Korzybski called for a change in thought and behavior based on changes in fundamental language habits. Believing that meaningful knowledge of the world should be grounded in sense data, Korzybski felt that most people speak "non-sense." He reasoned that if a measure of sanity is one's ability to recognize and symbolically talk about reality, most people act "un-sane" and are guided by "false maps" of reality. He was one of the first to wed the twentieth-century concern over psychological health to empiricism and language behavior. Being "normal," he argued, should be determined by how closely one adheres to the communication norms of the scientist, not the traditional norms of society. Korzybski believed that most people confuse words and the "realities" they symbolize and that what causes this confusion is an internalization of classical Aristotelian deductive logic. People use words in ways that might be consistent logically but do not necessarily correspond to reality. General semantics values induction ("the natural order of abstracting"), distrusts high-level abstractions, and shows other features now associated with the school of logical positivism.

Korzybski offered a radical critique of the way people talked and thought, but his own ideas were presented in a style that was eccentric and difficult. His interpreters, in contrast, were extraordinarily successful in disseminating his concerns and in the process influencing the study of communication for decades. Stuart Chase, one of President Franklin D. Roosevelt's "Brain Trust," wrote the influential *Tyranny of Words,* and S. I. Hayakawa wrote a textbook, *Language in Action,* which helped to introduce general semantics into courses in INTERPERSONAL COMMUNICATION, counseling, speech pathology, and professional fields such as journalism. Its influence was greatest from about 1940 until the mid-1960s. During this development, theories from other disciplines that explored the possible influence of language on thought and behavior, including much of social psychology and anthropological linguistics (especially the "linguistic relativity" writings of EDWARD SAPIR and BENJAMIN LEE WHORF), were incorporated into general semantics teaching.

North American empiricism and pragmatism proved receptive to the principles of general semantics but also may have blunted the more radical goals articulated by Korzybski. His vision of a language-focused therapy called for no less than the "restructuring of human nervous systems." Thus general semantics might be identified as neurolinguistic psychotherapy as much as a practical aid to everyday communication.

In many respects general semantics follows the history of radical political and economic proposals in the United States of the 1920s and 1930s: its influence became so much a part of communication theory that it now seems unexceptional, while the system it challenged remains virtually unchanged.

See also MEANING; PSYCHOANALYSIS.

Bibliography. S. I. Hayakawa, *Language in Thought and Action,* 4th ed., New York, 1978; Alfred Korzybski, *Science and Sanity* (1933), 4th ed., with a new pref. by Russell Meyers, 1958; Anatol Rapoport, *Semantics,* New York, 1975.

JOHN CONDON

SEMIOTICS

The modern usage of the term *semiotics* can be traced to the British philosopher JOHN LOCKE, who in *An Essay concerning Human Understanding* (1690) appropriated the Greek word *semeiotiké* to designate the *doctrine of signs,* "the business whereof is to consider the nature of signs, the mind makes use of *for the understanding of things,* or conveying its knowledge to others." Though the notion of the SIGN has preoccupied many thinkers from early antiquity to modern times, the idea of semiotics as an interdisciplinary matrix for a multitude of intellectual endeavors did not emerge before the late nineteenth century and was institutionalized on an international scale only in the 1960s. Semioticians do not yet agree on the definition of their enterprise, on its scope or limitations, or on a shared historical canon.

In light of such fluidity the only feature that can be said to differentiate semiotic from other scholarly discourses is the prominence within it of the concept of the sign. Yet as Locke's discussion of *semeiotiké* indicates, this concept has more than one INTERPRETATION. The various notions of the sign have led to three general, interlocking fields of semiotics.

First, a sign is a conjunction of two heterogeneous planes: a sensorily perceptible or material vehicle and an intelligible or mental MEANING. Thus *formal semiotics* (the space traditionally occupied by phonetics, etymology, or logic) is concerned with the kinds of relations between vehicle and meaning (natural versus conventional, literal versus figurative) from which it derives various sign typologies. Second, a sign is a representation, that is, an entity that stands for something else. *Cognitive semiotics* (extending over the domain of such cognitive sciences as epistemology, psychology, or AESTHETICS) studies the character of this representation and its influence on our interaction with the surrounding world. Finally, *communication semiotics* treats the sign as an instrument of exchange among its users, subsuming all the social sciences concerned with intersubjective transactions, whether anthropology, economics, or LINGUISTICS. This branch of semiotics deals with other media of communication previously neglected (GESTURE, BODY MOVEMENT, SPEECH surrogates) or of recent origin (film [*see* FILM THEORY], television) and with other modes of information transmission (ANIMAL COMMUNICATION, genetic codes, ARTIFICIAL INTELLIGENCE).

The study of signs has very ancient origins. In speculating on the origins of LANGUAGE the Socratic dialogue *Cratylus,* attributed to PLATO, describes the linkage between linguistic sound and meaning as either naturally or conventionally motivated (*physei* versus *thesei*), thus establishing one of the basic dichotomies for all subsequent discussions. ARISTOTLE's *On Interpretation* and *Rhetoric* and St. Augustine's *On Christian Doctrine* and *The Teacher* are other crucial ancient sign treatises, and philosophers Roger Bacon, Thomas of Erfurt, and William of Ockham continued the line of inquiry in medieval times. The major modern figures, besides Locke, are the philosophers and linguists Gottfried Wilhelm Leibniz, Johann Heinrich Lambert, Étienne Bonnot de Condillac, Wilhelm von Humboldt, and Bernhard Bolzano. However, two twentieth-century traditions lie behind the rich field of contemporary semiotics: Anglo-American pragmatism and Continental structuralist linguistics.

Anglo-American Pragmatism

The most comprehensive program for the general science of signs was charted by U.S. philosopher CHARLES S. PEIRCE. His brilliant work was enormous in scope and was characterized by ever-multiplying typologies and neologisms that only recently have come under systematic study. According to Peirce, "a sign or *representamen* is something which stands to somebody for something in some respect or capacity." Hence every sign-process (or semiosis) is the correlation of three components: the sign itself, the object represented, and the interpretant. The relationship between the sign and its object (as the above definition suggests) implies a certain inadequacy between the two. The sign does not stand for the object in its entirety but merely in relation to some of its aspects. There are three basic modes, Peirce claimed, in which the sign can represent something else, and hence three types of signs: (1) A sign that resembles its object (such as a model or a map) is an *icon;* (2) A sign that is factually linked to its object (such as a weathercock or a pointer) is an *index;* or (3) A sign conventionally associated with its object (such as words or traffic signals) is a *symbol.*

The relationship between the sign and the interpretant is determined, Peirce maintains, by the sign's relation to its object, because the interpretant is supposed to stand to the object in the same relation as the sign. In fact, the interpretant of a sign is yet another sign that the original sign has evoked in the interpreter. To explain this seeming paradox one need only point out that the process of interpretation is nothing but the substitution of some signs for others. To interpret the word *table* one can resort to an icon (by drawing its picture), an index (by pointing to an actual table), or a symbol (by supplying a synonym). From this perspective, then, thought or knowledge is a web of interconnected signs capable of unlimited self-generation.

The seminal nature of Peirce's contribution to the general theory of signs was fully recognized by subsequent generations of semioticians. Among these a prominent position belongs to two British scholars, C. K. Ogden (1889–1957) and I. A. RICHARDS (1893–1979), whose *The Meaning of Meaning* (1923) provided not only a broad historical survey of various sign theories but also new insights into the structure of the sign and its functioning in different contexts (scientific, aesthetic, etc.). The Peircean legacy was most systematically developed by the Chicago philosopher CHARLES MORRIS. As he declared in his widely acclaimed *Foundations of the Theory of Signs* (1938), "Human civilization is dependent upon the sign and systems of signs, and the human mind is inseparable from the functioning of signs—if indeed mentality is not to be identified with such functioning."

Following the Peircean path, Morris conceived of the sign as a tripartite entity consisting of (1) a *sign vehicle,* (2) a *designatum* or referent of the sign (or *denotatum* if the referent is an actual object), and (3) an *interpretant*—the effect of the sign on someone (the *interpreter*). The relations among these components yield the following dimensions of semiosis, each governed by its own rules: *syntactic* (the sign vehicle vis-à-vis other sign vehicles), *semantic* (the sign vehicle vis-à-vis its designatum/denotatum), and *pragmatic* (the sign vehicle vis-à-vis the interpretant). It must be stressed that Morris considered this division a mere heuristic device and maintained that semiotics must be concerned with the totality. In his subsequent writings Morris remolded his semiotics according to the specifications of behaviorist psychology and treated the sign in terms of the stimulus-response sequence. Perhaps because of this limited perspective the impact of his later work has not matched that of the earlier *Foundations.*

Continental Structuralist Linguistics

In the European context the rise of contemporary semiotics is linked to the teaching of Swiss linguist FERDINAND DE SAUSSURE, whose lectures, compiled and published by his students in 1916 as the *Course in General Linguistics,* heralded the arrival of STRUCTURALISM on the intellectual scene. "*A science that studies the life of signs within society* is conceivable," Saussure informed his pupils. "I shall call it semiology (from the Greek *sēmeîon,* 'sign'). Semiology would show what constitutes signs, what laws govern them. Since this science does not yet exist, no one can say what it would be; but it has a right to existence, a place staked out in advance." Within this general science the study of language would be the branch concerned with "the most important . . . system of signs that express ideas."

Because of his linguistic orientation Saussure perceived the nature of signs differently from Peirce and his followers. Since words are the prime example of conventional signs, he focused exclusively on the system of linguistic conventions (*langue*) that makes actual utterances (*parole*) understandable to language users. He considered *langue* a purely formal set of relations that, in the absence of other motivations, conjoins the two components of the linguistic sign arbitrarily—the sensory *signifier* and the intelligible *signified.* Accordingly, the study of the signifier was to yield a set of oppositions (the phonological system) that provides sonorous substance with linguistic form by articulating it into a limited inventory of *phonemes,* the minimal sound units capable of differentiating words of unlike meaning in a given language (e.g., the voiceless *p* and voiced *b* in *pit* and *bit*). The study of the signified, on the other hand, would be concerned with the semantic grid that segments extralinguistic reality into meaningful linguistic units (words). The semantic value of every particular signified would be derived solely from its opposition to other signifieds coexisting within the grid. Thus English *mutton* differs from French *mouton* precisely because the meaning of the former is circumscribed by the word *sheep,* which has no equivalent in the French vocabulary.

Saussure's fundamental insight, that behind every utterance is a linguistic CODE shared by speakers, was disseminated throughout Europe shortly after his death and provided semiotic studies with a theoretical focus. Brought to Moscow in 1917 by Saussure's pupil Sergej Karcevskij (1884–1955), it instantly captivated the minds of young Russian linguists, partially because of its overlap with local inquiries into the phonic stratum of language. It also inspired the Russian formalists, a loose-knit group of young literary scholars, who in the 1920s applied some of Saussure's ideas about language to POETICS. Crucial to the future development of sign theory was the critical reaction to Saussure and formalism by the Marxist followers of critic MIKHAIL BAKHTIN (1895–1975). The Bakhtinians claimed that the dichotomy between *langue* and *parole* and the privileging of the abstract system over actual speech failed to account for the communicative nature of language as a medium of exchange. For them every sign (utterance) was an ideological product, a direct or oblique reply to other signs (utterances) from alien ideological milieus in an ongoing dialogic process that is the culture of a given collectivity. Thus, the Bakhtinians argued, rather than focusing on the abstract identity of signs within a formal system, semiotics should instead study their actual changeability in concrete social contexts.

The ascendancy of Stalinism in the 1930s led to the official suppression of semiotics in the USSR. But meanwhile the Saussurian legacy had taken root elsewhere. The Prague Linguistic Circle (1926–1948) was the most important center of semiotic studies in interwar Europe. The formation of this group was stimulated to some extent by the migration of Russian scholars pursuing semiotic research. Along with Karcevskij and Petr Bogatyrev (1893–1971) was ROMAN JAKOBSON (1896–1982), vice-chairman of the circle and the most influential figure within it. Prague semiotics fused Saussure and the Russian tradition with the sign theories of contemporary German thinkers, in particular the phenomenological philosophy of Edmund Husserl (1859–1938) and the *Sematologie* of psychologist Karl Bühler (1879–1963).

Despite the name of their association the members of the Prague Linguistic Circle did not limit their semiotic inquiries to language. This was especially true of the Czech aesthetician Jan Mukařovský (1891–1975) and his pupils, who focused on the general theory of ART, literature, THEATER, music, and FOLKLORE.

Partially in opposition to the Prague school a similar group was founded in Copenhagen in the late 1930s. While the Prague structuralists insisted on sociological and historical analyses of semiotic phenomena, the Danish glossematicians (from the Greek *glossema,* "language") strove for an algebraic formalization of semiotic codes as sets of logical functions. *The Prolegomena to a Theory of Language* (1943), by Louis Hjelmslev, the leader of this school, provides a comprehensive account of the Danish theory of signs.

World War II and Postwar Influences

The advent of World War II affected the development of semiotics in two important ways. First, this cataclysmic event shattered the borders among nations, intellectual traditions, and scholarly disciplines. The exodus of European thinkers to the United States led in 1943 to the creation of the New York Linguistic Circle, under whose aegis a most impressive theoretical cross-pollination took place. Important within this was the German neo-Kantian Ernst Cassirer (1874–1945), who directed the attention of U.S. philosophers to the suggestive semiotic category of the symbol. At the same time, the European exiles profited from their exposure to the local heritage of sign study. Jakobson, for example, incorporated some key concepts of Peircean semiotics into his structuralist linguistics. The war also changed the course of semiotics through the rapid development of new sciences and technologies. CYBERNETICS and its spin-off, the General Theory of Information (*see* INFORMATION THEORY), approached communication from a perspective not previously offered by the traditional disciplines and provided quantifiable methods for dealing with the sign.

The 1950s were a period of gestation. Characteristic of this decade was, first of all, concentrated research in logical syntax and SEMANTICS. Second, structuralist linguistics expanded steadily and extended its tenets to related disciplines. Most significant in this respect was the work of another former member of the New York Linguistic Circle, CLAUDE LÉVI-STRAUSS, whose *Structural Anthropology* (1958) inaugurated the subsequent structuralist revolution in France. Finally, at this time semiotics branched out into various behavioral sciences, and new fields of inquiry began to be charted: KINESICS, concerned with gestures and body movements as conduits of information; PROXEMICS, dealing with the meaning of the SPATIAL ORGANIZATION of the human environment; and animal communication, for which the label *zoosemiotics* was later coined.

But it was the next decade that gave semiotics its intellectual respectability. From 1960 on, new centers of semiotic study began to appear around the world. The most influential in eastern Europe was the Moscow-Tartu School built around the linguist Vjačeslav Ivanov and the critic Jurij Lotman. It approached cultural phenomena as manifestations of "secondary modeling systems," sign systems superimposed upon the primary system of language (*see* SIGN SYSTEM). In western Europe the spectacular rise of French structuralism extended the principles of Saussurian *sémiologie* far beyond linguistics and emphasized the analyses of semiotic codes governing such disparate phenomena as mythological thought (Lévi-Strauss), the literary process (the *Tel Quel* group, Gérard Genette, Tzvetan Todorov), fashion (ROLAND BARTHES), or the subconscious (Jacques Lacan). Elsewhere, stimulating research into the domain of signs was undertaken by the Stuttgart group headed by aesthetician Max Bense, Cesare Segre (a literary scholar from Pavia), and the chair of semiotics in Bologna, Umberto Eco. In the United States, where sign studies had been maximally diversified, an important role in the institutionalization of semiotics was performed by Thomas A. Sebeok, under whose leadership the Research Center for Language and Semiotic Studies at Indiana University (established in 1956) provided a necessary clearinghouse for the ideas emanating from so many different fields. To encourage collaboration among semioticians around the world, the International Association for Semiotic Studies was founded in Paris in January 1969 with the quarterly *Semiotica* as its official publication.

Bibliography. Henryk Baran, ed., *Semiotics and Structuralism: Readings from the Soviet Union,* trans. by H. Baran, William Mandel, and A. J. Hollander, White Plains, N.Y., 1974; Eric Buyssens, *Les langages et le discours: Essai de linguistique fonctionelle dans le cadre de la sémiologie,* Brussels, 1943; Ernst Cassirer, *An Essay on Man: An Introduction to a Philosophy of Human Culture,* New Haven, Conn., 1944; Jonathan Culler, *Structuralist Poetics: Structuralism, Linguistics and the Study of Literature,* Ithaca, N.Y., 1975; Umberto Eco, *A Theory of Semiotics,* Bloomington, Ind., 1976; André Helbo, ed., *Le champ sémiologique,* Brussels, 1979; Roman Jakobson, *Main Trends in the Science of Language,* London, 1973; Thomas A. Sebeok, ed., *Current Trends in Linguistics,* Vol. 12, Pt. 2, The Hague, 1974; Peter Steiner, ed., *The Prague School: Selected Writings, 1929–1946* (Pražský linguistický Kroužek), trans. by John Burbank, Olga Hasty, Manfred Jacobson, Bruce Kochis, and Wendy Steiner, Austin, Tex., 1982; V. N. Vološinov, *Marxism and the Philosophy of*

Language (Marksizm i filosofi͡a i͡azyka), trans. by Ladislaw Matejka and I. R. Titunik, New York, 1973.

PETER STEINER

SERIAL

At its most technical, *serial* is a library term, referring to any publication that appears in short installments at regular intervals. By extension it refers to individual works published in MAGAZINE form, like the novels of Charles Dickens or William Makepeace Thackeray during the nineteenth century. By amplification it can be made to take in RADIO and television SOAP OPERA, Saturday matinee film sagas, comic strips (*see* COMICS), Victorian novels, and medieval chansons de geste. And by association with *sequel* it may refer to any group of works in which there are recurring characters and an unfolding story that appears to last beyond the usual confines of the form. Here "serial" begins to touch on GENRE, as that term is used in the discussion of films that share common elements of plot, characters, motifs, or even directorial style. At this degree of generalization, where "serial" becomes "seriality," one might talk about the western (*see* WESTERN, THE) or the films of ALFRED HITCHCOCK as sharing aspects of seriality with Giovanni Boccaccio's *Decameron, A Thousand*

Figure 1. *(Serial)* Hablot Browne ("Phiz"), *The Shadow in the little parlor.* Etching. From Charles Dickens, *Dombey and Son,* London: The Encyclopaedia Brittanica Company, ca. 1870, p. 586.

and One Nights, and the adventures of Li'l Abner.

For the purposes of literary analysis, the importance of the separate episodes of a serial is in their common links of plot and character. The term generally implies a story that continues in time, usually forward but sometimes backward. Unhampered by a theory of progress, HOLLYWOOD has invented the "prequel" to open up space on both sides of the original story—although one might argue a noble precedent in the way the New Testament presents itself as a sequel to the Old and at the same time redefines its predecessor as a mere prelude to the real story. When serial episodes become less distinctive, on the other hand, seriality shades into repetition and thereby into RITUAL—that is, a story that does not continue so much as it exists outside chronological time and is restaged again and again, with different players and in different costumes, but with the same plot, the same roles, and perhaps even the same lines.

These affinities between the serial and the ritual emphasize the difference between the potentially unending pattern of the serial story and the typically end-stopped plot of the work whose aesthetic claim is to be unique and original. When originality became an essential criterion in the evaluation of artistic work, the shaped quality of those works, whether visual or literary, along with the artistic willfulness behind that shaping, became a prime focus. In contrast the serial or repetitive work came to be considered as belonging to a more primitive era or, by association, to a more primitive level of taste. Hence, seriality and genre repetition became a hallmark of popular art, and uniqueness and irreproducibility the consequent indication of high artistic intention and achievement that scorned the easy invocation of past successes in order to invent anew.

But even in the earliest days of the romantic assertion of originality and individual artistic power, writers such as William Wordsworth, Samuel Taylor Coleridge, and Lord Byron combined their commitment to what was new in their art with a return to what was deeply rooted and ancient (*see* ROMANTICISM). The ambiguity, if such it is, derived from the double meaning of *original:* not only never before seen but also (or because of this) a return to the beginning. At worst, then, the audience for serial works desired only debased or commercially successful "formula" art. At best, it was a folk audience, weaned on ballads, grown up with rituals, and thus more temperamentally attuned to the rhythms of familiarity than the jarring notes of the modern.

By the end of the nineteenth century this separation between popular and high culture had become more codified. With the entrance of literary and artistic study into the university, the gap widened, and the establishment of such maxims of critical modernism as the self-contained work and the genius-artist seemed forever to banish serial form and its often anonymous creators from any serious consideration.

Serial form as an actuality, however, continued to thrive, and the energy it drew from the new media of communication was apparent because they were themselves constantly telling their unfolding story of what was happening in the world. The individual episodes told in film, on the radio, or in the comic strips pulled the reader along through a larger story whose end was never necessarily reached. For the real narrative investment was in the succession of frames themselves, which would be always present every time you looked into the newspaper, turned on the radio, or went to the movies.

The rise of television after World War II (*see* TELEVISION HISTORY) further consolidated the importance of serial form, if only in sheer numbers, as the dominant style of storytelling NARRATIVE. Watched primarily in private homes, often in living rooms, television programming grew to occupy virtually every hour of the day, usually with shows of predictable format and local variation—in short, the perfect serial. In such shows the basic unit of narrative construction was less the plot of the immediate episode than the relations between regular characters. In the early days of U.S. television two styles of such shows predominated: those in which the characters had a family relation (presumably like that among those who watched them) and those focusing on a single character at large in the world. Thus, as in most popular art, an identification was made between the situation of the audience (a family or an unattached person) and the situation of the continuing character or characters.

With its inclusive envelope of constant programming, television proved to be a formidable hothouse for developing its audience's awareness of conventions of serial storytelling and its desire for more elaborate forms. The family shows had a long life. But the more adventure-oriented shows that featured a lone individual—with their roots in the literary picaresque—gradually gave way to stories that focused on two or more characters without blood connection whose relationship was that of an extended family, each member representing a different character type available for the empathy of an increasingly diverse audience. Similarly, the exclusively domestic setting of the family situation comedies expanded into "workplace" shows such as "M*A*S*H," in which an army medical unit served as a surrogate family, and "Barney Miller" with its police precinct staff representing virtually every racial, religious, and ethnic type. Whether set in the present or the past, whether urban crime was tinged with sentiment or upper-class luxury with skullduggery, the common thread was the connection the

Figure 2. *(Serial)* Poster for *Le maître du mystère* (The Master of Mystery), a fifteen-part Pathé serial, ca. 1910. Courtesy of the Library of Congress.

Figure 3. *(Serial)* Wendy Richard and Bill Treacher in "EastEnders," a biweekly drama set in an imaginary borough in London's East End. Copyright BBC (Enterprises) 1985.

audience had with the characters, those it detested as much as those it loved.

Formally, the development of television plots was based on the realization that, since character was the prime connection with the show, the older episodic structure was unnecessary. Daytime television, following the lead of daytime radio, had long assumed that its audience tuned in to the same show every day and that therefore no particular show had to have a plot shape of its own. Nighttime television, like nighttime radio, had in contrast been on a weekly structure and therefore tended to present a complete story in each episode. With their large casts of continuing characters, the workplace shows especially pioneered stories that ran simultaneously, although each might be stretched over a varying number of individual episodes. The episode itself might have a general theme, but there was no fit required between the theme and the beginning, middle, and end of the episode's plot. With the success of the British Broadcasting Corporation's serial dramatizations of lengthy novelistic works, the miniseries pattern, which in principle required a commitment of several consecutive days or weeks to watch, became a strong influence on the structure of the weekly shows as well. Thus, a formal evolution might be sketched in the history of television from "I Love Lucy" and "The Fugitive," with their self-contained episodes, through "Dallas" and "Hill Street Blues," with their stories that unwind unmindful of episodic structure, to "Upstairs, Downstairs" and "The Jewel in the Crown," in which formal closure of any conventional sort is no longer a major objective.

In a world of commercial media looking for ways to lure and especially to keep an audience, serials, sequels, and genres equally offer the possibility of replicating and extending familiar emotions and satisfactions. They are therefore prime ways to protect an investment that might disappear if spent on some theme or characters less presold and formulaic. But mere repetition does not guarantee the same audience appeal, as countless failed Hollywood genre films, sequels, and remakes show. From one point of view, seriality may be the ultimate example of the power of commercial considerations to dictate what films or television shows get made. But from another, it invokes the ability of the audience to step back and become aesthetically self-conscious. Because all innovations in serial form embody a shift of emphasis from the framework of plot to the armature of character, there must be something in the unfolding story that continues to keep the audience's attention, something new in the development of the characters who are at the core of the work's appeal. Knowing the forms, audience members are more in a position to distinguish and judge the success of each particular example.

As television created an environment within which the serial or soap opera form (to pay tribute to its origins) became the common mode of experiencing stories, more critical attention was given to their special characteristics. Of particular interest here were terms drawn from the study of LINGUISTICS and the study of anthropology, both areas in which the unique was less interesting than the common. The linguistics of FERDINAND DE SAUSSURE, the structural anthro-

Figure 4. *(Serial)* Joan Collins, John Forsythe, and Linda Evans, "Dynasty," 1986. Courtesy of Richard and Esther Shapiro Productions in association with Aaron Spelling Productions.

pology of CLAUDE LÉVI-STRAUSS, and the SEMIOTICS of Umberto Eco all emphasized the continuity as well as the repetition of forms and motifs, thereby helping to fashion a critical vocabulary more attuned to the connections between works than to their differences. Similarly, Vladimir Propp's *Morphology of the Folktale* (1928; translated into English, 1968) explored the basic motifs of character types, while Northrop Frye's *Anatomy of Criticism* distinguished the genre myths that have shaped literary forms since the classical period. At its most extreme such study promoted an intertextual approach that attempted to do away with the concept of AUTHORSHIP as an originating concept, replacing it with a literary self-generation reminiscent of the "folk process" in song composition first argued in the eighteenth century by Joseph Ritson against those who believed all songs were created by some single bard.

As part of the defense of the vitality of popular culture and an effort to dethrone the canon of great works as the only true entry to literary value (*see* LITERARY CANON), the critical study of seriality is a crucial element in the effort to see works of art as elements without special privilege in an entire world of communication and discourse. By focusing on character as the binder of stories rather than on stories as the shapers of character, serial forms imply an account of the scope of human will less hedged by fate (in the shape of the divine or artistic plotter) and potentially more free to explore and establish less premeditated shapes of its own (*see* FICTION, PORTRAYAL OF CHARACTER IN). With their equal allegiance to stories in the past as well as to character in the present, serial forms can thus raise questions of the interaction between individuality and context that are difficult to consider within the confines of more intricately plotted works. At least as much as the works of original creation to which they have been so often contrasted, they are a crucial part of the way we tell stories to each other about the connections between ourselves and the world.

Bibliography. Umberto Eco, *The Role of the Reader,* Bloomington, Ind., 1976; idem, *Semiotics and the Philosophy of Language,* Bloomington, Ind., 1984; Northrop Frye, *Anatomy of Criticism,* Princeton, N.J., 1957; Gérard Genette, *Narrative Discourse: An Essay in Method,* trans. by Jane E. Lewin, Ithaca, N.Y., 1980; Claude Lévi-Strauss, *Structural Anthropology,* 2 vols., New York, 1963–1976; Vladimir Propp, *Morphology of the Folktale,* 2d ed., rev., trans. by Laurence Scott, Austin, Tex., 1968; idem, *Theory and History of Folklore,* ed. by Anatoly Liberman, trans. by Ariadna Y. Martin and Richard P. Martin, Minneapolis, Minn., 1984; Ferdinand de Saussure, *Course in General Linguistics,* ed. by Charles Bally and Albert Sechehaye, London, 1974, reprint 1983.

LEO BRAUDY

SEXISM

This entry consists of two articles:
1. **Overview**
2. **Sexism in Interpersonal Communication**

1. OVERVIEW

The degree to which males and females are socially unequal has varied, both cross-culturally and historically, from near equality to radical female disadvantage. Such variation is linked to the type of technology and economy (e.g., industrial, agrarian, horticultural, foraging) and to women's role in the economy. Women's status relative to men's in a given society is closely related to that society's dominant, gender-related IDEOLOGY, whether secular, religious, or both (*see* GENDER). Dominant, gender-related ideology refers to the manner in which a society defines appropriate behavior, personality, interests, and so on for each sex and justifies any differences in their rights, duties, and rewards. When women are disadvantaged relative to men in their access to socially valued resources and the dominant ideology explains and justifies such disadvantage, we use the term *sexism*. Sexism in some degree is universal in contemporary societies.

There is disagreement among social scientists concerning the relative causal power of economic versus ideological factors in producing sexism. U.S. anthropologist Peggy Sanday has examined a large number of tribal societies and argues that each society produces a "sex-role plan" specifying how relationships between the sexes are to be structured. Such plans are rooted in an overarching cultural orientation manifested in creation myths. Such myths may include deities of both sexes or only one sex as original creators. When mythical creative power is attributed to males only, that sex is dominant in the secular as well as the sacred realm. The more central female figures are in such myths, the more equitable the sex-role plan and the statuses of the two sexes. Sociologists such as Rae Lesser Blumberg and Janet Saltzman Chafetz in the United States have theorized that the degree of sexism is a function primarily of the relative control each sex exercises over the economic resources of that society. When such control is vested exclusively in males, sexism is at its height. In turn, males are led to develop an ideology that legitimates their control and social advantages, which further reinforces those socioeconomic advantages.

In technologically simple, non-surplus-producing societies (horticultural and hunting-gathering) women's productive roles are usually central to the collectivity inasmuch as they typically provide from 40 to 80 percent of the food. In such societies sexism is minimal to nonexistent, and their religious imagery typically incorporates a female principle. As the technology becomes more complex the production of surplus commodities for trade and familial aggrandizement becomes a primary goal. When this happens males come increasingly to control economic resources, and RELIGION increasingly stresses the male principle.

The most extreme female socioeconomic disadvantage is found generally in agrarian and pastoral societies. Virtually all the great world religions, namely, those that spread beyond the tribal level, developed in agrarian or mixed agrarian and pastoral societies. Those that became monotheistic (e.g., Judaism, Christianity, Islam) dropped the female element entirely from their concept of the deity and original creation. They came to view the sexes in an invidious fashion. Women were barred from formal religious roles such as the clergy, were defined as polluted or as temptresses, and were made subject to the secular as well as sacred authority of male kin. Even when monotheism did not develop (e.g., Hinduism, Confucianism), the same types of controls over women came to be justified by religion on the basis of women's supposed innate inferiority.

Such religions constitute the cultural heritage of most modern societies. With the changes wrought by advanced industrialization, women have regained some economic power. This has been reflected in ideological change, both religious and secular. Reform Judaism and many branches of Protestantism, for instance, have altered LANGUAGE and practice in their services in an attempt to reduce sexism, and they even ordain women. Secular authorities in India, China, and the Soviet Union, among many other nations, have created legal documents embodying the principle of sexual equality in their secular ideologies. Nonetheless, centuries of religious heritage constitute a powerful force shaping often unconscious images of the sexes.

One very common practice in extremely sexist societies has been much stricter control over women's sexuality than over men's sexuality. This has been done in order to ensure "proper" paternity, which in turn is linked to the intergenerational transmission of property from father to son. It takes an extreme form such as purdah (the total seclusion of women in Hindu and Islamic tradition) or milder forms such as chaperoning unmarried women, covering women's bodies and faces almost entirely, or simply a double standard that punishes women (either alone or more harshly than men) who lose their virginity premaritally or commit adultery. The ideological justification often stresses women's extreme sexuality and the diversion from duty this supposedly creates for men. Left unchecked, female sexuality would presumably constitute a danger to the social collectivity. In such cases the image of females is sharply bifurcated: the pure, virginal, or chaste woman who conforms to religious and social strictures (the "lady") versus the polluted, whorelike temptress, the fallen woman who has rebelled against God and society. There is no counterpart bifurcation of males on the basis of sexuality. Language often reflects this phenomenon by producing a vast terminology of "dirty words" to refer to women who step out of bounds and more generally to specific parts of the female anatomy. Women are thus defined essentially on the basis of their sexuality and sexual conduct, resulting in the irony that in attempting to repress female sexuality women are made into sexual objects. Moreover, when the repressive aspect is removed the objectification does not quickly disappear, as manifested by contemporary ADVERTISING and PORNOGRAPHY.

Extensive control over women by men may result for many women in traits of passivity, childlike dependence, and the inability to function as responsible adults. At the very least, women come to be stereotyped in this manner. In turn, such traits and/or stereotypes further suggest the "need" for male domination. Denied the opportunity to become responsible and independent, women come to be defined as fit only for the domestic role, which is relatively devalued in surplus-producing societies. On this basis women become objectified in a second way. To the extent that they conform to their domestic role and behave in a proper manner sexually, they may be admired, even worshiped, but only as idealized mothers, a role nature has ostensibly created them for.

In the more sexist societies, masculinity and femininity are typically defined as opposites: that which is masculine is nonfeminine. If females are passive, dependent, immature, and incapable of playing societal roles outside the family, then males must be active, independent, mature people who can and should guide and control not only women but the social collectivity. U.S. anthropologist Sherry Ortner has argued that this split between masculinity/public roles and femininity/domestic roles results in an association of males with "culture" and females with "nature." The reasoning is that women play domestic roles because they bear children; they bear children because that is what they are biologically fit to do. Men do those things that involve use of their intellect and creativity; they function in the literally manmade world of ART, government, commerce, and so on. Many cultures, especially in the West, have defined the human species as superior to all others precisely because it presumably escapes from the purely natural by creating the cultural. If only half the species is perceived as producing the cultural, it will appear obvious that that is the superior, fully human half.

In controlling the cultural, public aspects of their societies, including the very institutions that produce the ideology legitimating such control, men in sexist societies become the gatekeepers who decide what is to be defined as valuable, worthy, and proper. It is their imagery of females that becomes the official, societal definition. Men define that which constitutes humanness, and, in the words of French existentialist Simone de Beauvoir, women become simply "the other." Substantial research suggests that conceptions of "human" and "masculine" tend to coincide, but they differ from those of "feminine." If a woman manages to produce a painting, a musical composition, a poem, or a scientific paper, it will be judged by the standards men have set, if indeed male gatekeepers deem a woman's production worthy of being judged at all. Such standards are taken to be universal and unbiased, not as the products of specific people with vested interests. They assume a reality of their own that transcends their social origins and are seen as applicable across time and space. Women who would produce cultural artifacts in a sexist society are thus caught in a double bind: they can attempt to meet male standards that are defined as universal, but since they are not male they compete for recognition at a disadvantage; or they can produce according to their own experience and ideas of quality, and their products will typically be defined as inferior by societal gatekeepers. Thus, for instance, women's art in basketry, weaving, and needlework constitute only "crafts," whereas men's in paint, stone, and bronze are "fine arts."

Besides standards of judgment, male assumptions about the world, male definitions, and male perceptions of what constitute problems all become synonymous with "reality." Western science has provided numerous examples of how sexism intrudes to shape even the ostensibly most objective type of cultural production. For example, in the seventeenth century European scientists defined sperm as carrying a miniature fetus; the female provided only the environment for its growth. The resulting child "obviously" belonged to the father. As (male) medical doctors took over childbirth from (female) midwives in the nineteenth century, pregnancy and parturition became increasingly defined as a problem, even a kind of illness; after all, physicians do not treat "normal" events. Until about 1970 anthropologists largely ignored women's extensive contributions to the food supplies of preliterate societies, developing theories based on the centrality of male hunting to the survival of families and societies, and even to the evolution of the species. SIGMUND FREUD and his followers defined masochism, passivity, and narcissism as normal female traits and developed a theory to explain women's innately inferior conscience (superego). Psychologist Carol Gilligan has demonstrated that males and females employ basically different notions of moral behavior. The former tend to base morality on abstract principles, the latter on a concern with concrete relationships. Yet the field of psychology has assumed that the masculine approach is synonymous with the general concept of moral behavior and that therefore females are less moral. Work has been defined by economists and sociologists in terms of the labor force, ignoring the domestic labor of homemakers and implying that they do not "work."

The power to define the world and to define standards of judgment constitutes the power to shape the sociocultural world to one's own image and interests. Sexism, rooted in economic phenomena, legitimated and extended by ideologies, vests such power in males. In turn, definitional power reinforces sexism.

Figure 1. *(Sexism—Overview)* Billboard with graffito. Farringdon, London, 1979. From J. Posener, *Spray It Loud,* London: Routledge & Kegan Paul Plc, 1982, p. 13.

When extensive sexism exists, women are not simply denied all manner of rights, resources, and opportunities but are denied the ability to define themselves, their experiences, and their works as worthy and valuable, sometimes even as real.

Bibliography. Rae Lesser Blumberg, *Stratification: Socioeconomic and Sexual Inequality,* Dubuque, Iowa, 1978; Janet Saltzman Chafetz, *Sex and Advantage: A Comparative, Macro-Structural Theory of Sex Stratification,* Totowa, N.J., 1984; Carol Gilligan, *In a Different Voice: Psychological Theory and Women's Development,* Cambridge, Mass., 1982; Erving Goffman, *Gender Advertisements* (*Studies in Visual Communication,* Vol. 3, no. 2, Washington, D.C., 1976), New York and Cambridge, Mass., 1979; Nancy M. Henley, *Body Politics: Power, Sex, and Nonverbal Communications,* Englewood Cliffs, N.J., 1977; Charlotte O'Kelly and Larry Carney, *Women and Men in Society,* 2d ed., Belmont, Calif., 1986; Michelle Zimbalist Rosaldo and Louise Lamphere, eds., *Women, Culture, and Society,* Stanford, Calif., 1974; Peggy Sanday, *Female Power and Male Dominance,* Cambridge and New York, 1981; Edwin Schur, *Labeling Women Deviant: Gender, Stigma, and Social Control,* New York, 1984.

JANET SALTZMAN CHAFETZ

2. SEXISM IN INTERPERSONAL COMMUNICATION

Sexism is reflected and reinforced by GENDER differences and inequities in LANGUAGE, language use, and NONVERBAL COMMUNICATION. Sexist elements in INTERPERSONAL COMMUNICATION vary according to CULTURE and language. Although most of the research in this area has been conducted in the West, primarily in the United States, its findings have functional counterparts in languages and cultures around the world.

Vocabulary. The most obvious and frequently noted manifestation of sexism in communication is contained in the basic vocabulary typical of ordinary usage. Most languages conceptualize God as male and refer to the deity as *He.* The generic term most commonly employed for our species is *man.* When the sex of an individual is unknown or irrelevant, we use masculine singular pronouns and possessives: *he, him, his.* This creates a subtle mind-set that assumes maleness is the norm and femaleness deviant or invisible.

Many traditional occupational titles still widely employed convey the expectation that their incumbents will be male: *businessman, policeman, garbageman.* In contemporary bureaucratized society, leadership is commonly vested in *chairmen.* Nor are polite titles free of sexist assumptions. The proper title for almost all men is *Mr.* Exceptions convey occupation: *Doctor, Coach, Judge.* However, attachment to men has been considered the most salient attribute for women, and the common titles *Miss* and *Mrs.* convey marital status. At its extreme, a married woman loses her identity totally and becomes Mrs. *husband's first name, husband's last name. Ms.,* the direct feminine counterpart of *Mr.,* is uncommon usage.

Many words take on very different connotations depending on the sex of the person to whom they refer. These differences reflect social stereotypes of the two sexes. To say that a man is "aggressive," "competitive," or "handsome" is complimentary; to attribute those characteristics to a woman is derogatory. Similarly, to say that a man is "sensitive" or "beautiful" is to belittle him, but for a woman these constitute compliments.

Many ostensibly sex-neutral, high-prestige occupational titles are simply assumed to refer to men. This is clear by the way we modify these words when a woman is the role incumbent: *lady doctor, woman lawyer, female professor.*

We also attach different meanings to supposedly parallel sex-related terms. A boy is a juvenile male. Adult males are usually insulted when called "boy," a term commonly used for black men until the 1960s. *Girl,* however, is commonly used to refer to adult females. *Gentleman* refers to men who behave politely and/or have high status; it is used relatively infrequently. *Lady* is a virtual synonym for *woman* and, given its formal definition, is often used in patently ridiculous contexts: "ladies of the night," "cleaning lady" (imagine "gentleman janitor"), "ladies' basketball team." The fact that adult males are almost always "men" but adult females are equally or more likely to be "girls" or "ladies" than "women" has been attributed to the sexual double standard. Girls are presexual, ladies are asexual, but women, like men, are sexually mature and presumably active. The terms *father* and *mother* are also parallel, but to say someone "fathered" a child is to convey a biological fact; when someone "mothers" a child, it is assumed to refer to a long-term, social relationship of a special, nurturant kind. This distinction reflects different societal expectations of the two parental roles. Bachelors and spinsters are both single, never married, but the latter term is clearly derogatory, whereas the former often connotes an envied status, reflecting the social injunction that women should be attached to men but not necessarily the opposite. "Tomboy" is often a badge of pride, "sissy" always one of shame, manifesting the greater prestige of maleness, even when exhibited by a female. *See also* LANGUAGE IDEOLOGY; LANGUAGE VARIETIES.

Speech. Early investigations focused on hypothesized inequities between female and male language usage: in the extent and emphasis of vocabulary, use of euphemism and hyperbole, and reliance on devices that preface assertions with apologies or pleas for attention (e.g., "Listen, this is interesting . . .") or, as with the tag question, that turn a statement into a request for permission (e.g., "Dinner will be ready at six, okay?"). Many of these hypotheses were based on assumptions about the ways in which women, encouraged from childhood to be ladylike and to defer to men, tend to reduce the forcefulness and assertiveness of their SPEECH. However, most such assumptions have not been borne out by empirical research. No differences have been established between the sexes in terms of type or range of vocabulary or with respect to patterns of question asking.

What has been discovered is that speech style or language use varies for both women and men according to situational or social context, thus opening a fruitful new field for study. In addition, researchers have found that similar speech patterns may be interpreted differently by listeners depending on the sex of the speaker—in other words, that bias may be in the ear of the hearer. Studies also indicate that although women do much of the conversational work in male-female interactions—initiating talk, asking questions, providing verbal support—men tend to control interaction by such tactics as withholding response to topics initiated by women and minimizing self-disclosure.

Substantial research suggests that when men and women converse, women support and encourage the speech of men with sounds ("uh-huh," "mmmm") and words conveying agreement and/or interest ("right," "really?"). Generally, this is not reciprocated by men, however. Research by U.S. sociologists Candace West and Donald Zimmerman demonstrates that men are more likely to interrupt women than vice versa, manifesting their superior power by "grabbing the floor."

Nonverbal behavior. While people speak, their bodies are communicating as well. Women establish more eye contact with conversational partners, whereas men are more apt to look away from their partner entirely. Women are therefore more apt to perceive (even if not consciously) their partner's body language, which may contradict the verbal message (*see* KINESICS). The information provided by this greater attentiveness to nonverbal cues may be at least part of the basis for women's supposedly greater intuition. Those with less power must be more attentive to their superiors than vice versa, since their well-being is more contingent on the actions of the more powerful person.

Women also smile and nod more during conversation, a nonverbal form of conversational support that goes largely unreciprocated by men. The fact that women are, in a variety of both verbal and nonverbal ways, more attentive to and supportive of their conversational partner than are men reflects a fundamental gender-role difference, in addition to their differential social power. A basic component of the feminine role is nurturance and concern for human relationships. The masculine role is more instrumental or task-oriented. Through their different styles of communicating, women demonstrate a primary concern for their interactional partner, men for the actual content of the specific interactional situation.

The ways in which people arrange and move their bodies while they speak affect the forcefulness of their communication, reflecting and reinforcing power differences. Men tend to have greater "presence" and are therefore more forceful than women, not only because they tend to be larger but also because appropriate feminine behavior entails keeping the limbs and the trunk of the body compressed. Men's arms move more when they speak; their legs splay out from their bodies when they sit (compare the way men and women typically cross their legs). Added to this is both the naturally deeper male voice and the systematic encouragement of men to "speak up" but of women to use a soft, polite tone of voice.

TOUCH constitutes a very direct form of communication, manifesting a powerful relationship when it involves people who are not intimate. According to U.S. psychologist Nancy Henley, people who initiate touch with nonintimates are demonstrating their power over the recipient. For example, adults feel few compunctions about casually touching even unfamiliar children. Men initiate most touching that occurs between nonintimate members of the sexes (e.g., a casual arm around the shoulder). Women typically shrink at such a touch, indicating acquiescence to power. *See also* INTERACTION, FACE-TO-FACE.

Communication and social change. Both verbal and nonverbal modes of communication grow out of the physical and social reality in which a group of individuals is embedded (*see* MODE). In turn, communication modes shape the ways in which people perceive, define, and react to phenomena. As the behaviors and values of women and men change, along with their relations to one another, modes of communication within each gender and between the two genders do tend to change. In formal, written language sexist modes of communication are disappearing. However, to communicate with and understand others comfortably and quickly, ordinary modes of communication must be based in habit. They are thus also relatively resistant to change.

In order to succeed in masculine contexts, women have increasingly adopted a male vocabulary and communication mode as they move into roles formerly monopolized by males in the economy, politics, SPORTS, and RELIGION, becoming, as U.S. linguist Robin Lakoff argues, bilingual. Similarly, as fathers become more involved in parental duties, they adopt a vocabulary and speech style long associated with mothering. Whereas gender differences in communication are declining, women's language is changing more rapidly than men's, inasmuch as women's social roles have been changing more rapidly. Moreover, given the lesser power and prestige associated with femaleness, males are far less motivated to learn or use feminine means of communication and are often ridiculed when they do so.

The continued use of sexist modes of communication helps to retard social change because language shapes our perceptions of the world. As CHILDREN learn sexist means of communication, they learn to assume a reality that is increasingly obsolete. It is these very assumptions that help to perpetuate at least remnants of the old structure.

See also FEMINIST THEORIES OF COMMUNICATION.

Bibliography. Max K. Adler, *Sex Differences in Human Speech: A Socio-Linguistic Study,* Hamburg, 1978; Robin T. Lakoff, *Language and Woman's Place,* New York, 1975; Clara Mayo and Nancy M. Henley, eds., *Gender and Nonverbal Behavior,* New York, 1981; Alleen Pace Nilsen, *Sexism and Language,* Urbana, Ill., 1977; Barrie Thorne, Cheris Kramarae, and Nancy Henley, eds., *Language, Gender and Society,* Rowley, Mass., 1983.

JANET SALTZMAN CHAFETZ

SHANNON, CLAUDE (1916–)

U.S. mathematician and educator, in the field of communication known largely for his INFORMATION THEORY, which profoundly changed scientific perspectives on human communication and facilitated the concurrent development of new communication technology for the efficient transmission and processing of information. Claude Elwood Shannon's *Mathematical Theory of Communication,* first published as a Bell System Monograph in 1948 and a year later, after insightful review in *Scientific American,* as a book with commentary by WARREN WEAVER, was still in print forty years later. No single book on communication theory has so far surpassed its publication record.

Shannon's ideas did not originate in a vacuum, but none of his predecessors (e.g., Ludwig Boltzmann, Karl Küpfmüller, Harry Nyquist, Ralph V. L. Hartley, Leo Szilard, or Ronald A. Fisher) or contemporaries (e.g., NORBERT WIENER and the independently working Andrei Nikolaevich Kolmogoroff) presented such a large body of coherent concepts, abstract propositions, and theorems, along with a research agenda that could be applied to virtually any discipline concerned with knowledge, and none had the benefit of working at a time or in places so pregnant with intellectual and technological developments in communication. The completeness of Shannon's work (not a single proposition has had to be retracted) and the opportunities it promised for conceptualizing and quantifying a process so basic to human existence surprised many. Within a few years of its publication the theory provided the scientific justification for academic programs in human communication (which sprang up largely in U.S. universities), expanded communication research to new media, created novel areas of inquiry as well as two new journals, and stimulated the development of new communication technology for handling knowledge, including in computers. The theory became a milestone in communication research and marked the transition from an industrial to an information society.

Figure 1. *(Shannon, Claude)* Claude Shannon demonstrating his maze-solving electrical mouse at Bell Laboratories in 1952 in an experiment to study telephone switching systems and the logical powers of computers. Courtesy of AT&T Bell Laboratories.

Born in Gaylord, Michigan, Shannon received a B.S. in electrical engineering from the University of Michigan and an M.S. and a Ph.D. in MATHEMATICS from the Massachussetts Institute of Technology (MIT), where he held the Bowles Fellowship. In 1940, the year he received both graduate degrees, he won a National Research Fellowship at Princeton University. In 1941 he joined Bell Telephone Laboratories as a research mathematician and later became executive consultant to Bell's mathematics and statistics research center. In 1956 he was appointed professor of communication at MIT, where he was given the Donner Chair of Science two years later. He remained a consultant to Bell Laboratories until 1972 and became a professor emeritus in 1979. He has received numerous awards and honorary degrees.

In a nutshell, Shannon's work established novel connections between symbolic and physical forms: Boolean algebra of switching nets, automata theory, cryptography (*see* CRYPTOLOGY), theory of coding (*see* CODE), and, above all, his communication theory (or information theory, as it is now called). Shannon's master's thesis, completed when he was twenty-one, was entitled "A Symbolic Analysis of Relay and Switching Circuits" and was published in 1938. Reputed to be the most important master's thesis of this century, it established an isomorphism between the Boolean logic of propositions and the kind of switching networks then beginning to be used in electronic machines and showed that any logical operation that could be described in a finite number of steps could also be carried out by an appropriate switching circuit. It also suggested that the programming of computers ought to be thought of not as an arithmetical problem (then the dominant view) but as a problem in formal logic. Simultaneously Shannon provided not only a powerful tool for synthesis, analysis, and optimization of relay circuits but also the crucial link between logic—the crown of human reasoning and symbolism—and the newly emerging computing machines. He continued to explore this new synthesis, designing an electronic mouse that could learn from mistakes and find its way through a maze, editing *Automata Studies* with John McCarthy (who became a leading figure in the field of ARTIFICIAL INTELLIGENCE), and pursuing his interest in reliable machines built from unreliable components in work on chess-playing computers, for example.

Shannon's interest in cryptography began as a hobby but took on great significance during World War II, when he became associated with Bell Laboratories, where work on pulse-code modulation was in progress. His confidential monograph *Communication Theory of Secrecy Systems,* circulated in 1945 and cleared for publication in 1949, discussed cryptographic ideals—variable coding transformations that are easy to do and undo and that make the enciphered text seem random—and furnished proofs of the conditions under which cryptograms should in principle be decipherable. The work contained many of the ideas that became central to his information theory. He described communication as "the fundamental problem . . . of reproducing at one point either exactly or approximately a message selected at another point." He showed coding to be central to any communication—a message must be encoded into a medium suitable for transmission and the received signal decoded by applying the inverse of the encoding transformation—and became aware of the need for a statistical characterization of message sources and channels, including transmission errors or noise. Coding problems suddenly came to be recognized as central in research ranging from communication engineering to LINGUISTICS (e.g., in the form of LANGUAGE translation) and resulted in the notion of information processing in humans, machines, or social organizations.

By his own account, Shannon started work on his mathematical theory of communication as early as 1940 while a fellow at Princeton. Subsequent work, especially on coding problems, must have shaped its direction. One of the theory's crucial innovations was its linking of communication to the freedom of choice a sender has in selecting a message, and the constraints this imposes on the receiver. What a message is or contains, why it is selected, or how it is coded became secondary to the choices exhausted in a communication relationship. Realizing that the very idea of communication implies that one cannot know in advance the messages chosen, Shannon decided to regard sending and receiving as a stochastic process, that is, as a process of selecting among sets of alternatives whose probabilities are somewhat dependent and knowable, at least in the long run. For this idea he acknowledged the influence of Wiener's work on statistical prediction and filtering of time series and made use of the Russian mathematician Andrey Andreyevich Markov's 1913 theory of chains of symbols in literature. However, his most consequential invention was the now famous logarithmic measuring function $-\Sigma p_i \log_2 p_i$, for quantifying the volume of choices available, uncertain about, consumed, or channeled. He had misgivings about assigning uncommon meanings to the word *information* and took JOHN VON NEUMANN's suggestion that this function be called *entropy* because its mathematical form resembled one known by that name in quantum physics and interpreted in that field as lack of information. The mathematical properties of this function proved to be unique and enabled Shannon to develop the theory into a full-fledged calculus for information quantities. Shannon avoided the term *information theory* in his own work, suggesting that communication across time and space was always his primary concern.

Although terms such as *freedom of choice, uncertainty, information, information transmission, channel capacity, (en-, de-, re-)coding, redundancy, equivocation,* and *noise* quickly spread into many disciplines, they also stimulated wild claims by unqualified enthusiasts who thought they had found a philosophers' stone, and harsh condemnations by equally unqualified critics who supposed an engineering bias, especially in the diagram Shannon used to depict communication processes paradigmatically.

After the early enthusiasm the limitations of Shannon's contribution can now be seen in perspective. First of all, it should be stressed that Shannon contributed a *mathematical theory.* It has a few axioms and an ever-growing number of proven theorems whose rich concepts afford many real-world applications. Like counting, in which it does not matter what one counts as long as the entities concerned are countable, information theory is applicable to any situation in which its axioms can be shown not to be violated. However, applicability does not guarantee meaningful or complete explanations of the phenomena of interest. Because of its content-independent character, information theory has been applied to many areas not directly related to communication: statistics, complexity, memory, intelligence, decision making, uncertainty analysis, self-organization.

Like the concept of energy in physics, which is defined as the capacity for doing mechanical work, information is neither MEANING nor matter but *what a message does* in the context of what is conceived as possible. The theory shifts attention from static attributes of isolated objects to processes of doing logical work in particular contexts—whether these are provided by machines, biological beings, or social organizations.

Like the laws of thermodynamics, the theorems of information theory *assert limits* on what can be done; they do not spell out how to communicate or what to design. Rather, they divide the world into two parts—that which is possible (communicable, controllable, knowable, constructable, etc.) and that which is condemned to remain fiction (like the perpetuum mobile in the physical world). Often these parts are separated by a gap of impracticality.

Like all measurement in science, the information calculus of the theory does not assert facts but enables social scientists to make heretofore unknown *quantitative comparisons* and to pursue research questions posed by the theory's new conceptual apparatus; it also shows engineers where communication resources might be used more efficiently in combating noise with redundancy, designing adaptive computers from unreliable parts, or conceiving simple controllers of complex systems.

After positing his mathematical theory of communication, Shannon worked out missing details, sampling theorems, coding theorems, and the like; invented interesting applications such as his guessing experiments with strings of text, showing that the English language is about 50 percent (later upgraded to 70 percent) redundant; and saw his theory proliferate into numerous disciplines. Despite limitations, which can be found in any theory, Shannon's theory has been neither disproved nor surpassed but has profoundly changed the world of communication.

See also CYBERNETICS; MODELS OF COMMUNICATION.

Bibliography. Colin Cherry, "A History of Information Theory," *Proceedings of the Institute of Electrical Engineers* 98 (1951): 383–393; Howard Gardner, *The Mind's New Science: A History of the Cognitive Revolution,* New York, 1985; John R. Pierce, "The Early Days of Information Theory," *IEEE Transactions on Information Theory* 19 (1973): 3–8; Claude E. Shannon and Warren Weaver, *The Mathematical Theory of Communication,* Urbana, Ill., 1949, reprint 1964.

KLAUS KRIPPENDORFF

SHIHUANG DI (ca. 259–210 B.C.E.)

Creator of the first unified Chinese empire; also known as Shih Huang Ti. After eight hundred years

Figure 1. *(Shihuang Di)* Figure from the terra-cotta army of Shihuang Di, excavated at his tomb in Mount Li, Xian. From *The Great Bronze Age of China,* a loan exhibition from the People's Republic of China. The Metropolitan Museum of Art, New York/Cultural Relics Bureau, Beijing.

of strife, the numerous feudal states that composed China had been reduced to eight by the fourth century B.C.E. The state of Qin on the strategic northwestern frontier, toughened in alternating struggle and trade with the northern nomad barbarians, strengthened by adoption of their cavalry tactics, and using chariots and steel for weapons, crushed all its rivals and brought the country under unified military rule. Its third-century ruler, taking the title Qin Shihuang Di, "First Emperor of the Qin Dynasty" (221–207 B.C.E.), ended the power of the hereditary landed aristocracy by replacing its feudal fiefs with thirty-six provinces under his direct imperial administration and laws based on the principles of the Legalist school of philosophy. He expanded the borders of his centralized empire to the northern steppes and across the Yangtze River to the south sea. He promoted economic integration and fostered trade and traders by standardizing weights and measures, coinage, taxes, and axle widths to facilitate road transport.

The building of the Great Wall emphasized the unity of China under Qin Shihuang's pervasive imperial bureaucracy and armed might. It protected the vast empire from the one great external threat, that of the northern barbarians. But the first emperor exacerbated the danger from within. He conscripted millions of peasants for his armies and for forced labor to aggrandize imperial power and to build roads and other massive public works, palaces, and even his imperial tomb at enormous cost in human life and treasure. He attempted to enforce conformity of thought by draconian methods: the massacre of Confucianists and other dissidents and the burning of their books (213 B.C.E.).

The positive impact of Qin Shihuang was massive and long lasting. He brought about a revolution in communications in a country in which the speediest means of transmitting information or things had been the signal bonfire and the horse. He set a model for all future dynasties with his express roads, post stations, canals, and other public works, and his support of the simplification and standardization of the written characters. These were powerful unifying factors. It is still not uncommon to see someone who speaks the Cantonese dialect communicating with a person from northern China by tracing characters on the palm of the hand.

Qin Shihuang's dynasty lasted a scant fifteen years, but it created a unified feudal empire that lasted over two thousand years and gave the country its name: China.

See also CONFUCIUS; EAST ASIA, ANCIENT.

Bibliography. Jack Chen, *The Sinkiang Story,* New York, 1977; René Grousset, *The Rise and Splendor of the Chinese Empire* (Histoire de la Chine), Berkeley, Calif., 1953; Edwin O. Reischauer and John K. Fairbank, *East Asia: The Great Tradition,* Boston, 1958.

JACK CHEN

SIGN

The process of communication consists in transmitting or exchanging messages with the use of signs, and for this reason the notions of sign and SIGN SYSTEM play an essential role in the theory of information. In discussing sign several terms come to mind: indication, index, symptom, syndrome, icon, signal, symbol (*see* MEANING; STRUCTURALISM; SYMBOLISM). Each of these words is polysemous. To CHARLES S. PEIRCE, for example, a sign is "something which stands to somebody for something in some respect or capacity." Signs for him are the *index* (a sign with an objective relationship to its object, e.g., footprints), the *icon* (a sign that in some way is like its object, e.g., image, diagram, and METAPHOR), and the *symbol* (a sign that is a sign because it is used as such, e.g., word, sentence, concept). The sign in Peirce's theory is a generic notion of very wide scope; feeling, image, conception, thought, and even a person are signs. On the other hand, in philosopher Susanne Langer's theory, image, diagram, word, sentence, and proposition are not signs but symbols. Of all the above examples only the footprints are for Langer a sign, and the notions of sign and symbol are mutually exclusive in this theory. Langer's concept of sign is similar to Peirce's concept of index and not Peirce's concept of sign.

Indication, symptom, and syndrome are often placed in opposition to signs because the former are allegedly natural, unlike signs; or because the former are supposedly events, states of affairs, phenomena, or processes, and signs are things; or because the former are claimed to be wholes having signs as their essential part.

Another opposition is between signals as concrete tools produced by humans in order to transmit a message and semiotic units that do not have a human sender and are not intentional and teleologic. The sign is in this approach an element of *seme,* which is an abstract unit composed of the signifiant (i.e., a class of signals) and of the signifié (i.e., a class of messages admissible for the given signal). An entirely different notion of signal is found in the works of CHARLES MORRIS, in which it is contrasted with the notion of symbol: pulse is a signal, but the word *pulse* is a symbol. Both the signal and the symbol are signs, but the former, unlike the latter, is not produced by its interpreter and is not a substitute for some other sign with which it is synonymous. Thus the signal in Morris's treatment is neither conventional nor intentional, being related to the notion of natural indication or symptom. Yet another notion of signal occurs in Russian physiologist Ivan Pavlov's stimulus-response theory, in which every conditioned stimulus is a signal of one of the relatively few unconditioned stimuli.

Signs, indications, indexes, symptoms, syndromes, icons, signals, symbols, and also allegories, coats of arms (*see* HERALDRY), insignia, emblems, medals, badges—all those may occur in the process of communication (*see* GRAPHICS; VISUAL IMAGE). Hence the notion of sign system to be constructed should be maximally comprehensive, using the broadest possible generic concept of sign embracing all the kinds of signs listed above. Because a given occurrence of a sign is always of mixed character—that is, it symbolizes and at the same time indicates something—it would be more convenient to speak of gradable properties of the given use of something by someone at a given time as a sign of something else than to introduce kinds of signs. Each of these properties should be defined, with the definitions being adapted to the research task at hand. Next, instead of distinguishing symbols from icons or signals, the given sign use could be qualified, as, for example, symbolic to a certain degree and also as iconic to a certain degree. This would be in accord with suggestions by Peirce, Karl Bühler, and ROMAN JAKOBSON. Peirce assigned several simultaneously performed functions to the sign, and the other two authors did so with regard to the linguistic text (*see* LINGUISTICS).

Token-type. A token is a particular instance of a sign, whereas a type is the overall class to which all instances of this sign belong. The distinction of token-type as applied to signs may be explained with the following example: *1 x 1 = 1.* We have here three tokens of the sign *1.* However, when asked about the number of numerals present in this sentence, the answer is that there is only one numeral, namely, *1.* This latter case no longer concerns the so-called sign event but the sign design: a certain abstract pattern—a class, in the set-theoretic sense—of all the past, present, and future separate occurrences of *1.* The distinction is thus reduced to the opposition between individual object and class, which, accordingly, shares with this distinction the polysemy connected with the expression *individual object.* This object may be real and concrete, occurring in a certain time and place and being used as a sign, but its role may also be performed by an individual unreal object, one not perceptible through the senses (e.g., an intentional object).

Peirce distinguished three kinds of signs in themselves, that is, with regard to their own nature: the *qualisign,* the *sinsign,* and the *legisign.* The difference between a sinsign (an individual object or event) and a legisign (a general type) is the same as that between a token and a type. For example, the sinsigns "+," "plus," and the sound of saying *plus*—that is, all such inscriptions and their utterings—combine to form the class termed the "plus" legisign. A qualisign is a quality that is a sign, such as the redness of the "stop" signal, the nature of its appearance—that is, the subclass composed of all the equiformal sinsigns comprising the given legisign. For instance, the sinsigns "+" and "+" do not differ as to qualisign, but the sinsigns "+" and "plus" belong to different qualisigns, being a subclass in the "plus" legisign class.

If the word *system* is used in its broad sense, the legisign can be seen as a system in which one rule distinguishes subsystems termed qualisigns and another rule distinguishes elements called sinsigns. The legisigns (i.e., types) or the qualisigns (i.e., formal types) are used as units of sign systems more often than sinsigns (i.e., tokens).

Sign vehicle—sign functions—sign. This distinction, stemming from Stoic SEMIOTICS, is in modern times linked with the theory of FERDINAND DE SAUSSURE, who characterized the linguistic sign as an arbitrary functional combination of sound-image with concept. He referred to the former as *signifiant* (signifier) and to the latter as *signifié* (signified). The signifier and the signified are inseparably bonded to each other, as are two sides of a single page, but the relation in their case is conventional. This is indicated by polysemous expressions in a given LANGUAGE and by the symbolization of the same notion by different sounds among various languages. In this theory the sign, the signifier, and the signified are all abstract entities, with the two last-mentioned having no independent existence outside their combination within the sign. For although a concrete sound such as "bay" exists independently as a material object, it is not an element of the class called the signifiant of the sign "bay" until it is joined: in some cases with the concept of *laurel,* in other cases with the concept of *compartment,* in some cases with the concept of *bodies of water,* and in still others with the concept of *barking.* And although in every instance this will be a class of identical sounds, there will appear four different signifiants and four different signifieds assigned to them. It is thus clear that the sign vehicle understood in this manner is not identical with either the token or the qualisign.

Saussure's distinction was developed and elaborated in Danish linguist Louis Hjelmslev's glossematics, in which sign is used as "the name for the unit consisting of content-form and the expression-form and established by the solidarity that we have called sign-function." The expression-form and the expression-substance together constitute the expression-plane, and the content-form and the content-substance form the content-plane. The expression-forms are abstract phonological units, namely, cenemes and taxemes treated as a system of relations between the given phoneme and other units of the phonological system determining the place of the phoneme in this system. As for the content-form, it is a system of relations between semantic elements. The sign vehicle understood as expression-form is an element of a whole that is also composed of expression-substance and that is relativized to expression-planes of the remaining signs of the given language. The problem of content-plane as sign function is analogous. On the other hand, the sign as a described structure may be regarded as a kind of system. In such a case the sign system would be a system composed of subsystems. Also possible are systems of sign vehicles or signifiers or expression-planes separate from the content, such as an ALPHABET of an unknown writing system composed of ordered graphic signs—small and capital letters—that, however, remain uninterpreted, meaning that no sound is ascribed to each letter. Aside from these, we may also have systems of signified units or content-planes, such as the combination-theory *ars universalis* outlined by Ramon Llull (ca. 1235–1316) in his *Ars Magna,* composed of elementary concepts and intended for proofs of the veracity of the Christian faith.

Sign versus sign use. The formulation that a sign is composed of the sign vehicle and the sign function is metaphorical. The statement that a sign means contains a personification. In reality, both in communication with the use of signs and in COGNITION of reality through them, there must be an interpreter—person, animal, or appropriately built apparatus—that at time t will use the given object, event, state of affairs or phenomenon, or, in general, a given A actually existing or only imagined as a sign of the conjectural B. This use consists in the interpreter performing the following reasoning. First premise: A takes place—or at least so the interpreter believes; second premise: there is, or at least the interpreter believes there is, a natural or conventional relation between A and B such that it may be surmised that B takes place; conclusion: B is the case. This reasoning deserves the term *semiosic inference.* In fact, the interpreter usually does not realize that he or she is performing this reasoning; it is nearly always enthymematical (i.e., it tacitly assumes premises obvious to the interpreter); and it is spontaneous and automatic, so to speak. When the interpreter is an animal, this process is not verbalized. Thanks to such semiosic inference, A—that is, any kind of entity—becomes, according to Edmund Husserl, semantically transparent for the interpreter. In other words, the interpreter sees B through it, as through a glass screen, at the same time ceasing to pay attention to A. At this moment A begins—for the interpreter—to play the role of a sign of the entity B, different from A. This conjectural B may be of both semantic (the sign's meaning, its extension, referent, truth value) and pragmatic character (e.g., thoughts, feelings, and wishes of the sign's sender). This is the essential part of semiosis (sign process), consisting in decoding, deciphering, interpreting, or simply understanding the sign. According to one opinion, every inference is of sign character, because the premise(s) is the sign of the conclusion, and even—as Peirce believed—every thought in general is of such character. In Peirce's view we think only with the use of signs. In certain very numerous cases this part of semiosis is preceded by the phase in which the sender transmits the sign, performing at the same time an analogous semiosic inference; namely, the sender reconstructs in his or her mind the semiosic reasoning that—according to the sender's intentions—ought to be performed by the supposed interpreter of sign A. However, the occurrence of a sender in the process of semiosis is not necessary for something to become at some time a sign of something else for someone; not every sign was sent by someone. On the other hand, in order for something to become a sign, it must be interpreted by someone. There is no sign outside the use of something as a sign.

The semiosis acts are always realized in a broadly understood context; in the situational one, that is, the circumstances of time, place, and persons of sign users, amid social relations, cultural ties, and the like; and in a sign context. With respect to the last, an isolated sign must be distinguished from a sign as an element of a set of signs, of a sign sequence, or of a sign system. Both kinds of context modify the meaning of the sign. In every use of the sign its meaning is a result of, on the one hand, rules of the given sign system determining the so-called dictionary meaning of each sign and, on the other, the circumstances accompanying the given use of each of these signs. For this reason one should always view a given sign as an element of sign system, and the use of the sign should be considered in the concrete situational and sign context (e.g., a language context).

See also LITERARY CRITICISM; POETICS.

Bibliography. Karl Bühler, *Sprachtheorie: Die Darstellungsfunktion der Sprache,* 2d ed., Stuttgart, 1965; Louis Hjelmslev, *Prologomena to a Theory of Language* (Omkring sprogteoriens grundlaeggelse), 2d ed., Madison, Wis., 1961; Susanne K. Langer, *Philosophy in a New Key: A Study in the Symbolism of Reason, Rite, and Art,* 3d ed., Cambridge, Mass., 1967; Charles Morris, *Writings on the General Theory of Signs,* The Hague and Paris, 1971; Charles Sanders Peirce, *Collected Papers of Charles Sanders Peirce,* Vols. 1–6 ed. by Charles Hartshorne and Paul Weiss, Vols. 7–8 ed. by Arthur W. Burks, Cambridge, Mass., 1931–1960; Ferdinand de Saussure, *Cours de linguistique générale* (Course in General Linguistics, ed. by Charles Bally and Albert Sechehaye, London, 1959, reprint 1974), Paris, 1916.

JERZY PELC

SIGN LANGUAGE

This topic is discussed in four sections:

1. OVERVIEW

This term may be applied to any of several different types of communicative code in which the code elements are highly conventionalized bodily gestures, used in more or less complex organized sequences serving the same functions as spoken LANGUAGE. The best-known sign languages are those developed among the deaf, although sign languages have developed occasionally in speaker-hearer communities.

The ability of persons born deaf to develop the use of complex systems of GESTURE has been recorded since classical times. In a community with a high proportion of deaf persons, a shared system of gestures may become established as a system of communication in the group. This may be termed a primary sign language insofar as it has been developed by those who have never had direct access to a spoken language. An example of a primary sign language is American sign language (see section 4, below).

An alternate sign language is one that has been developed in a community of speaker-hearers as an alternate to spoken language, as when SPEECH is avoided for social or religious reasons. Unlike primary sign languages, alternate sign languages show direct structural relationships with the spoken languages of the communities in which they have developed (see section 2, below). Examples here are those developed by the Aborigines of central and northern Australia or in certain monasteries in Europe. The Plains Indians of North America also used sign languages, in part as a form of intertribal communication. These sign languages appear to have been autonomous and not structurally related to any specific spoken language.

Occupational sign language is a term that sometimes has been applied to systems of gesture that develop within specific occupational settings. They have been recorded in such places as sawmills, among members of SPORTS teams, and in auction rooms. Occupational sign languages are restricted in scope and function only in the task situation.

All of these systems are to be distinguished from manual language codes, which are used in deaf education to convey a specific spoken language, such as English or French, in manual form, either by fingerspelling or by establishing distinct gestures for the words or word components (morphemes) of the language (see section 3, below).

Linguistic analysis of sign languages has been in progress since 1960, with most attention being paid to primary sign languages. This work has shown (a) a high degree of systematicity in the way signs are formed; (b) systematic features to variations in sign performance that are comparable to the morphological processes of inflection of lexical forms in spoken languages; and (c) considerable systematicity in syntax. It is also clear that although primary sign languages may not differ from one another in grammatical organization as radically as spoken languages do, they differ sharply in their lexical organization, and sign languages developed separately are mutually unintelligible. There is no universal sign language, as

Figure 1. *(Sign Language—Overview)* A child learning sign language. Courtesy of the Laboratory for Language and Cognitive Studies, The Salk Institute, San Diego, Calif.

some have thought. In short, primary sign languages exhibit the same general properties of organization as spoken languages, although they differ markedly in the actual modes of expression employed because they are organized in the three dimensions of space as well as in time.

ADAM KENDON

2. ALTERNATE SIGN LANGUAGES

Sign languages developed by speaker-hearers for use on special occasions, during periods when SPEECH is not permitted for reasons of RITUAL, or when circumstances make speech difficult. Such sign languages have been described for the Plains Indians of North America, the Australian Aborigines, and certain European monastic orders. The sign languages used by these groups have large vocabularies, show some degree of grammatical organization, and may thus be said to be complex. Sign languages of a more restricted nature (i.e., with small vocabularies and little in the way of grammar) sometimes develop in occupational circumstances in which speech is impossible. We may also include here specialized PERFORMANCE sign languages found in certain kinds of narrative DANCE, as, for example, in India.

North American Indian sign languages. European explorers from the sixteenth century onward frequently reported that Indians from northern Mexico and the southern Plains made extensive use of conventionalized gestures, often using them to communicate with the explorers themselves (*see* EXPLORATION). The idea that there was a universal sign language throughout North America gained wide currency. Without doubt, many tribes of North American Indians, especially those of the Plains, made considerable use of complex sign languages (Figure 1). Some tribes, notably the Kiowas of the south central Plains, were considered especially adept. Sign language was used in formal ORATORY, storytelling, public performances, and dances, as well as in everyday interactions. Comparisons of the descriptions of signs provided by many different writers show great diversity in these sign languages.

However, following the introduction of the horse in the seventeenth century, groups of Indians previously not in contact with one another came to be so. Existing sign languages appear to have been adapted for intertribal communication, resulting in a convergence of sign languages in the Plains region. A survey carried out in 1956 showed that one form of sign language was widely shared in the northern Plains, although in the more northerly reaches of this area (in Alberta and Saskatchewan) a different form prevailed. The widely shared form appears not to have been structured in relation to any specific Indian language, and it showed properties in many ways quite similar to those found in primary sign languages. See section 3, below.

Australian Aboriginal sign languages. Complex sign languages in Aboriginal Australia have been reported from southern, central, and western desert regions, from Arnhem Land, the western side of Cape York, and the islands of the north coast and the Torres Strait, but not from the eastern and southeastern regions. In the far northwest (the Kimberleys) only a simple sign language is evident. The complex sign languages of central Australia probably developed in association with the custom of women remaining silent as a sign of mourning. A woman bereaved of spouse or child, her immediate sisters, and certain other female relatives of the deceased sustain periods of silence—in the case of the bereaved spouse or mother, for as long as two years. Study of the sign languages of central desert Aborigines (such as the Warlpiri and the Warumungu) shows that they are structurally very dependent on the spoken language. Signs match words, and signed sentences are close manual renditions of spoken sentences, although tense and grammatical markers are not transposed to SIGN and some use is made of expressive processes found in primary sign languages (e.g., spatial inflection of verbal signs to "incorporate" subject and object of the sentence and the modification of verbal sign performance to express aspect). Among the Warlpiri only women use sign language, but in other parts of Australia sign languages are or were used by men—for example, during male initiation ceremonies or in hunting. Comparison of sign language vocabularies shows that there are considerable differences from one group to the next, although these differences are not always coordinate with differences in spoken languages.

Monastic sign languages. Several monastic orders, including the Cistercian and Trappist orders, follow a rule of silence and use speech sparingly or not at all during most parts of the day because they believe that speech distracts from religious devotion. To meet essential communication requirements, a limited official list of signs is sanctioned, but additional vocabularies of signs have come to be established so that in some monasteries quite complex communication can be carried out by means of signs (Figure 2). There is no single monastic sign language. Each monastery tends to have its own system. A linguistic study of the sign system in a Cistercian monastery in the United States, published in 1975, showed that, apart from the official signs, the sign language in use there is structurally highly dependent on English. Because its vocabulary is fairly limited, however, many things are expressed by means of combinations of signs. For example, the sign for "freeze" may be made up of the signs for "arrange," "hard," and "water." Some signs also make direct reference to the sounds of English words, as in the sign for

Figure 1. *(Sign Language—Alternate Sign Languages)* Tce-caq-a-daq-a-qic (Lean Wolf), chief of the Hidatsa Indians of Dakota Territory, who visited Washington, D.C., in 1880. From Garrick Mallery, *Sign Language among North American Indians,* The Hague and Paris, 1972, pp. 282, 284. Copyright 1972 Mouton Publishers. Reprinted by permission of Mouton de Gruyter, a division of Walter de Gruyter & Co., Berlin, Amsterdam, New York.

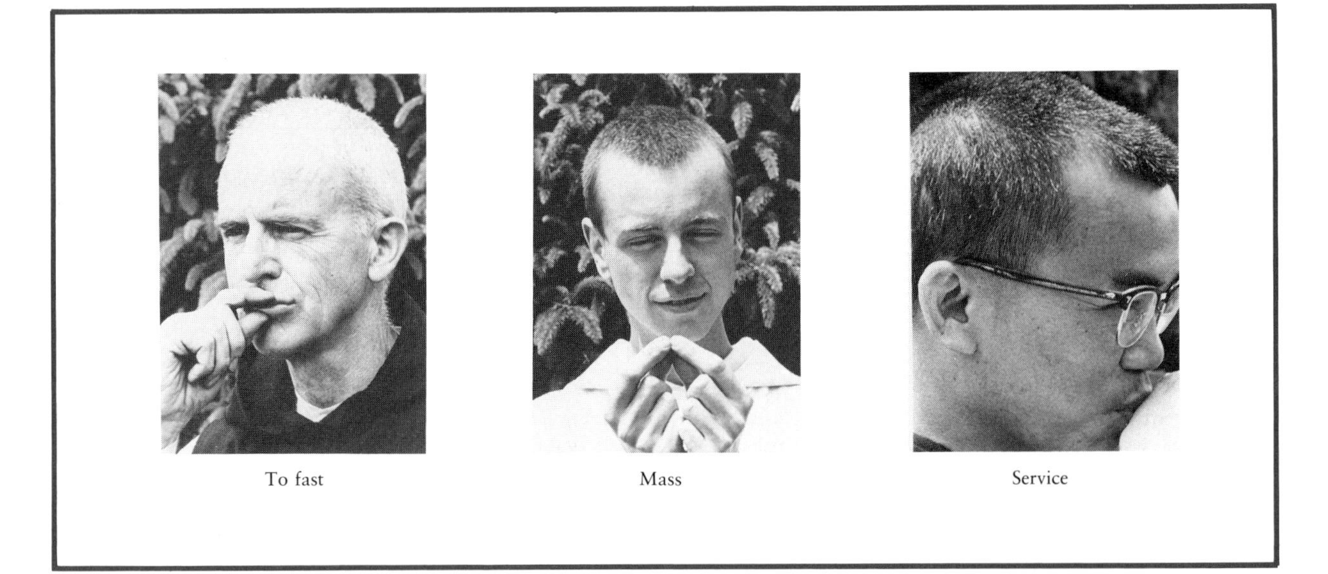

Figure 2.. *(Sign Language—Alternate Sign Languages)* Cistercian Order: examples of basic signs. From Robert A. Barakat, *The Cistercian Sign Language: A Study in Non-Verbal Communication,* Kalamazoo, Mich., 1975, pp. 104, 111, 120. Copyright Cistercian Publications, Kalamazoo, Mich.

"Cincinnati," which is reported to be signed as "sin sin A T"; the sign for "cookie" is reported to be the sign for "cook" followed by the sign for "key."

Performance sign languages. The most complex performance sign language is the one developed in the classical Hindu dance tradition of southern India, in which stories are told with the use of an extremely detailed vocabulary of gestures. Treatises dating from the fifth century C.E. present a gesture system with the systematicity of the early Sanskrit grammarians. Gestures were constructed with actions using all articulable body parts, often with complex forms being

Figure 3. *(Sign Language—Alternate Sign Languages)* Auxiliary policewoman halting traffic to let schoolchildren cross the street, New York, ca. 1910. The Bettmann Archive, Inc.

built up out of elaborate combinations of hand, arm, FACE, eye, neck, and foot action. Less complex systems of GESTURE have been developed in the classical ballet tradition of Europe, perhaps from a tradition that can be traced back to the theatrical pantomime of classical Rome. *See also* DRAMA—PERFORMANCE.

Occupational sign languages. Occasionally these develop in task situations in which communication by speech is difficult or impossible because of distance or noise level. The most complex system described is that developed by sawmill workers in the northwest United States and western Canada. In some cases these sawmill sign languages expanded to allow communication beyond the narrow requirements of the task. Other examples of occupational sign languages are those used by traffic police (see Figure 3), orchestra conductors, topographers, and baseball players. Most occupational sign languages are quite restricted in the functions they serve, however, and usually have quite small vocabularies.

See also LANGUAGE; SIGN SYSTEM.

Bibliography. Robert Barakat, *Cistercian Sign Language,* Kalamazoo, Mich., 1976; Russell M. Hughes [La Meri], *Gesture Language of the Hindu Dance,* New York, 1941, reprint 1964; Garrick Mallery, *Sign Language among North American Indians Compared with that among Other Peoples and Deaf-Mutes,* Washington, D.C., 1881, reprint The Hague, 1972; Nandikeśvara, *Nandikeśvara's Abinaya-darpaṇam: A Manual of Gesture and Posture Used in Indian Dance and Drama,* 3d ed., trans. and ed. by Manomohan Ghosh, Calcutta, 1975; D. Jean Umiker-Sebeok and Thomas A. Sebeok, eds., *Aboriginal Sign Languages of the Americas and Australia,* 2 vols., New York, 1978.

ADAM KENDON

3. MANUAL LANGUAGE CODES

An invented system of manual gestures by which a spoken LANGUAGE may be transmitted. Such a CODE is to be distinguished from a primary sign language (such as American Sign Language), which is a language transmitted gesturally by deaf people and which is not a representation of a surrounding spoken language (see section 4, below). A manual language code is also to be distinguished from an alternate sign language, which is a gestural system developed by speaker-hearers for use as an alternative to SPEECH when speech cannot be used, either for environmental or RITUAL reasons (see section 2, above). Alternate sign languages may or may not represent a spoken language. Manual language codes have been devised specifically for such representation.

There are two different types of manual language codes: fingerspelling and a signed form of the spoken language.

Fingerspelling. Fingerspelling is a procedure whereby each letter in the spelling of a word is represented on the hand(s). In order to use the fingerspelling ALPHABET, both the sender and the receiver must know the spoken language and how each word is spelled. In the United States, the fingerspelling alphabet is one-handed and consists of twenty-six different handshapes (see Figure 1), one for each letter of the written alphabet. In England, although the spoken language is also English, the fingerspelling alphabet is two-handed (see Figure 2). Related two-handed forms are also used in Australia, Scotland, and Indonesia. The fingerspelling alphabets used in France, Italy, and other European countries are similar to that used in the United States. This similarity led to the adoption of the International Fingerspelling Alphabet by the Fourth Congress of the World Federation of the Deaf in Stockholm in 1963. The International Fingerspelling Alphabet, although not truly international, has gained some small acceptance in Europe, with its use at congresses of the World Federation of the Deaf and at the Deaf Olympics. In China a fingerspelling procedure consisting of thirty hand configurations has been developed; it corresponds roughly to the recently developed pinyin, a phonetic alphabet using roman letters (*see* WRITING). A book of charts of forty-three fingerspelling alphabets used in forty-six countries has been published.

Skilled fingerspelling can provide very rapid transmission of a message. In natural conversation between deaf people using fingerspelling, familiarity with the context allows some letters/handshapes to be slurred or omitted (in some respects similar to shorthand, abbreviations, or rapid speech) without loss of intelligibility. In the United States, fingerspelling and speaking at the same time is sometimes used in the education of deaf children and is referred to as the Rochester Method.

Signed form of a spoken language. Signed forms of spoken languages have been developed primarily for educational purposes. Speaking and signing at the same time is often called *simultaneous communication.* To use the signed form of a spoken language, the sender and the receiver must know both the spoken language being transmitted and the signs being used to do the transmission. Signs may be borrowed from the sign languages used by deaf people or they may be invented; or, most frequently, a combination of both may be used. Occasionally invented signs are in turn adopted by the deaf community and become part of the sign language itself.

Signs used in natural sign languages differ from fingerspelling in a number of respects. Each fingerspelled letter consists of a handshape and, in some alphabets, a small movement. Signs are composed of handshape, place of formation, movement, point of contact, orientation of the palm and fingers, direction

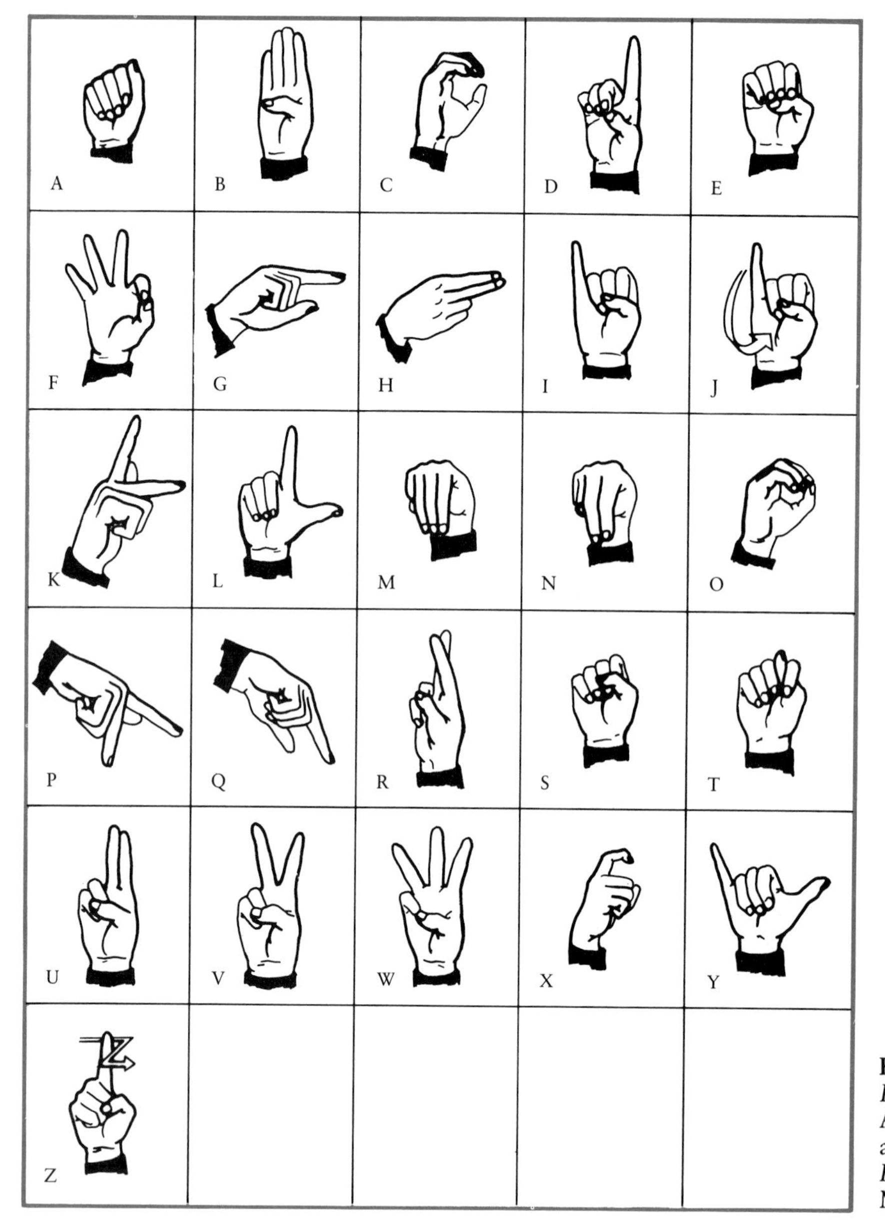

Figure 1. *(Sign Language—Manual Language Codes)* United States: American hand alphabet. Redrawn after S. J. Carmel, *International Hand Alphabet Charts,* Rockville, Md.: Studio Printing, 1982, p. 77.

of movement, and other dynamic and spatial characteristics. Each fingerspelled *letter* refers to one written letter; to represent a whole word, all of the letters must be fingerspelled in the proper order. A *sign* used in a natural sign language represents a meaning or concept. When signs from a natural sign language are chosen to represent spoken words for educational purposes, a problem of translation may arise (*see* TRANSLATION, THEORIES OF). A single spoken word may require more than one sign to translate it; a single sign may require more than one spoken word to translate it. This translation problem is no different from the problem of translating from one spoken language to another. Because of the mismatch problems, educators have sometimes chosen to invent new signs to improve the match between the spoken language and its signed representation and, in some cases, new rules for deciding how to match signs with spoken words.

Extensive use of invented signs and rules for matching signs to spoken words results in a signed form known as a SIGN SYSTEM. The use of sign systems is generally restricted to educational settings; they are not considered to be languages in their own right because their grammar is that of the spoken language being transmitted. In the late 1700s, Abbé de l'Épée constructed a system of "methodical signs" that were meant to make sign structure more parallel

Figure 2. *(Sign Language—Manual Language Codes)* Great Britain: British hand alphabet. Redrawn after S. J. Carmel, *International Hand Alphabet Charts,* Rockville, Md.: Studio Printing, 1982, p. 27.

to that of spoken French. In England a system called the Paget Gorman Systematic Sign (PGSS) was constructed for educational purposes independently from British Sign Language. In the United States, signed representations of English are called signed English or manually coded English (MCE). Within this generic category are several sign systems: Seeing Essential English (SEE I), Signing Exact English (SEE II), Linguistics of Visual English (LOVE), Manual English, and Signed English. These systems differ in (1) their rules for representing English words and inflectional endings (e.g., past tense, plural, progressive), (2) their use of signs from American Sign Language as opposed to invented signs, and (3) the amount of fingerspelling used in addition to signs. Two systems, Signing Exact English and Signed English, are more widely used than the others. The degree of success in teaching the grammar of English to deaf students through manual codes is controversial and not well researched.

Bibliography. Simon J. Carmel, *International Hand Alphabet Charts,* 2d ed., Rockville, Md., 1982; Harlan Lane, ed., and Franklin Philip, trans., *The Deaf Experience: Classics in Language and Education,* Cambridge, Mass., 1984; Ronnie B. Wilbur, *American Sign Language: Linguistic and Educational Dimensions,* 2d ed., San Diego, Calif., 1986.

RONNIE B. WILBUR

4. PRIMARY SIGN LANGUAGES

Primary sign languages differ from spoken languages in that gestural instead of vocal activity is their primary mode of expression (*see* GESTURE). They are like spoken languages in almost all other linguistic respects: phonological, morphological, and syntactic; that is, the elementary gestural signals obey rules for selection and combination just as do sounds in spoken languages. For example, *blick* is not a word in English though its pronunciation follows English rules, but *bnick,* another nonword, breaks those rules; just so, a user of a primary sign language can produce well-formed signs that are not words of the LANGUAGE but are possible by its rules, and other signs that break the rules (*see* SIGN).

Signs and Combination Rules

The nonvocal material on which the rules of primary sign languages operate is certain activity, especially of the EYES, FACE, head, arms, and hands. This order reflects the importance of the signaling source for communication, but because hand gestures appear most salient to nonsigners and are the easiest of sign language phenomena to study, much research on sign languages has concentrated on what the hands do; in fact, both students and opponents of primary sign languages sometimes refer to them erroneously as manual languages (see section 3, above).

Like spoken languages, primary sign languages have rules for making the products of element selection and combination into higher-level forms. For example, if *blick* should be adopted as an English verb, the rules of English ensure that whatever it is *to blick,* doing it will be *blicking.* Similarly, certain semantic features are signed in primary sign languages by regular formal changes in a sign, that is, by inflections or modulations. In American Sign Language (ASL), perhaps the most studied of primary sign languages, such features as negation are expressed with many verbs not by adding an adverbial sign to a sign verb but by changing one of the elements of the sign verb's formation; the inflection is more akin to English *think-thought* than to *link-linked.*

From the perspective of a user of a spoken language the syntactic as well as the morphological rules of primary sign languages appear to generate fewer signs than spoken words to express the same proposition, but much of this apparent economy may simply be due to difference in the human visual and auditory systems. Early in the study of ASL, researchers reported that subject and object pronouns were often "omitted" in ordinary CONVERSATION; a performance of the verb sign *look,* for example, would be all that the researcher could find when one signer of ASL was saying to another, "He kept on looking at me." Later research showed that all the elements of this meaning were indeed signaled: the particular position and direction of the hand making *look* in this performance indicated a third person (already identified) as agent of looking and the speaker as the one looked at; the slight circling action of the hand (not used for simple *look*) and possibly the backward inclination of the head indicated that looking was sustained and continuous; the FACIAL EXPRESSION of the signer also may have indicated some of the affect. In short, the whole picture made by the signer in the addressee's field of vision constitutes the carrier of information in a primary sign language, not a single stream of sequentially produced sounds.

Besides compression, poverty in vocabulary has been charged against some primary sign languages. For instance, it has been claimed that in Spanish Sign Language there is but one (manual) sign to mean *brother* and *sister.* To understand what is being signed here, one must look at the signer's face as well as the hands. While signing *sister* the Spanish deaf signer also is shaping the mouth into the position for pronouncing "ah" (the end of the word *hermana*), and for *brother* the mouth takes the shape for pronouncing "oh" (*hermano*).

This, of course, reveals that primary sign languages can be affected by contact with spoken languages, but at the same time it indicates how small and subtle such influences may be. On the other hand, the effect of primary sign languages on each other is likely to be as great as the actual contact of their users allows. For example, since the 1950s the sign names for nations and peoples in ASL have changed as more and more ASL users have traveled abroad and discovered the signs that deaf people use for themselves and their countries.

Relationships among Sign Languages

Are all primary sign languages varieties of one universal sign language, or are the similarities found in them due to cultural contact? If the former, then psychophysiological constraints must make all sign language basically alike; if the latter, then primary sign languages are related, as are other languages, because of MIGRATION and cultural contact. It is too early for a definitive answer to these questions, but so far research seems to show some truth in both answers. It is certainly true that for deaf participants to understand the proceedings of international conferences each national group needs its own sign language interpreter. For example, in Rome in 1983, Italian, U.S., British, French, Danish, Swedish, Norwegian, Finnish, Dutch, German, and Thai sign interpreters worked simultaneously. Research by Robbin M. Battison and I. King Jordan has shown that there is little mutual intelligibility among primary sign languages of national deaf groups and also that deaf persons nevertheless show remarkable ability to communicate with deaf persons from other nations. Thus it appears that unlike speakers, who usually are hampered severely when they try to communicate without a common spoken language, deaf signers can much more easily set aside temporarily the rules of their primary languages and communicate gesturally because they are both familiar with the multichannel visual cues and highly skilled in gestural production. Again, this is not to say that sign language is universal; everything discovered in research points to the structural similarity of spoken language and primary sign language. The Battison and Jordan findings do affirm, however, that persons skilled in gesture by virtue of their competence in a primary sign language are often able to communicate effectively across language barriers. It should also be noted that the informal communication within groups of deaf persons meeting at an international conference allows for improvisation and ad hoc signing, while those attending formal sessions on research demand skilled interpreters' services so that the presenters' spoken messages can be fully comprehended.

Semiotic Issues

The semiotic differences between signing and speaking as between seeing and hearing also need to be considered; that is, there is a fundamental difference between signs to be heard and signs to be seen (*see* SEMIOTICS). From the action of actual drinking, for example, to a miming of that action to a conventionalized sign for drinking is a direct and seemingly simple progression in a primary sign language. The path from actions to representation in words is not so clear. Psycholinguists since FERDINAND DE SAUSSURE have made much of the completely arbitrary relationship between a MEANING and a spoken word, sometimes even arguing that unless the relationship is arbitrary a sign cannot be a linguistic sign. But this ignores the semiotic difference. To distinguish in a primary sign language the signs designating the action of drinking, a drink, and a drinking vessel calls upon not the resemblance of gesture to act but the rules of that language. In ASL, as Ted Supalla, a linguist and a native ASL signer, has pointed out, the gestural difference between noun and verb is regular and unmistakable. The same kind of signing action that separates *to drink* from *a drink* also separates *sit* from *chair* and *fly* from *airplane* (which except for this difference look alike).

Individual signs of a primary sign language, like individual words of a spoken language, permit all kinds of testing and speculation, some of which may draw attention from the fact that a language is a system. Undeniably many more words of a primary sign language than of a spoken language are iconic (with meanings easily guessed when the sign is seen) or translucent (with meaning and form obviously related once the relationship has been pointed out). This does not mean, however, that phrases and sentences in a primary sign language are by any means translucent or transparent; it means simply that the difference between vision and hearing distributes iconicity unequally in spoken and signed languages. However iconic an individual word of a primary sign language may be, there is no predicting its morphological features or how it can or cannot be combined with other words in that language.

See also MIME.

Bibliography. Charlotte Baker and Dennis Cokley, *American Sign Language: A Teacher's Resource Text on Grammar and Culture,* Silver Spring, Md., 1980; Robbin M. Battison and I. King Jordan, "Cross-cultural Communication with Foreign Signers: Fact and Fancy," *Sign Language Studies* 10 (1976): 53–68; William C. Stokoe, Dorothy Casterline, and Carl G. Croneberg, *A Dictionary of American Sign Language on Linguistic Principles,* 2d rev. ed., Silver Spring, Md., 1976; William C. Stokoe and Virginia Volterra, eds., *SLR '83: Proceedings of the III International Symposium on Sign Language Research,* Silver Spring, Md., and Rome, 1985.

WILLIAM C. STOKOE

SIGN SYSTEM

The expression *sign system* may refer not only to a system of signs but also to SIGN as a system, and not only to a system of sign uses or a system of SPEECH acts but also to sign use as a system or speech act as a system. The notion of system has diverse applications in the analysis of the notion of sign, as well as of the notions of CODE, GRAMMAR, and LANGUAGE. *See also* SEMIOTICS.

In what follows, the term *system* will mean an ordered set composed of at least two elements. The relations binding these elements are such that the structure of which the elements are a part has different properties from these elements themselves. In addition to elements and relations between them, the states and/or modifications determined by these relations are also seen as parts of the system. The system is usually a closed whole, isolated from other sets but functionally connected with them by the tasks set up for the entire system.

Sign as System

Most of the theories treating the sign as a kind of system are theories of natural language signs, especially theories of terms included in referential SEMANTICS.

Early writings. Thinking about signs as sign systems has a long history. In the *Cratylus* PLATO said that corresponding to every name (common noun) is an ideal name that is a concept of the form of the named object. According to ARISTOTLE (*On Interpretation*), the written word is a conventional sign—a symbol—of the spoken word, and the latter is a natural sign—a symptom—of a presence of mental modification in the speaker's mind and at the same time a symbol of this modification. The relationship between the written word as a symbol and the spoken word is analogous to that between the spoken word and the modification corresponding to it, which in turn is an iconic sign or likeness of a thing outside language. Hence in this conception the sign was treated as a system having as its elements the graphic symbol, the acoustic symptom (and symbol at the same time), and the mental iconic sign, all bound by antisymmetric relations of three kinds: the referring, the indicating, and the representing.

The Stoics distinguished two corporal entities within the sign as a system: the speech sound and, at the opposite end of the sign relation, a real object or real event. Intermediate stages were two immaterial entities; the sign's subjective content in the mind and the *lekton,* a MEANING objectivized as a result of rational justification of the nature of the denoted object. When the sign is a word, the *lekton* corresponding to it is incomplete; when it is a sentence, the *lekton* is complete. The same sentence may perform various pragmatic functions, such as question, predication, or command.

In Chinese logic of the third century B.C.E. (*Moist Canons*) the name refers to one of its standards, that is, patterns, either in the mind of the speaker or in the speaker's surroundings. If some extralinguistic object satisfies this pattern, it may be named with this name.

In the early and late MIDDLE AGES in the West ideas about signs were found in the works of religious thinkers. Important writings by St. Augustine were *Principia dialecticae, De Trinitate, De doctrina Christiana,* and *The Teacher*. St. Augustine saw the word as a four-element system: *verbum,* "word," is an articulated sound; *dicibile* or *locutio* is the word of mental speech corresponding to a given *verbum; dictio* is the use of the word that includes joining *verbum* and *dicibile* and furnishing them with *vis,* "force," that is, pragmatic function; finally, *res,* "thing," is a concrete or abstract object to which this word refers. A similar sign-meaning-referent scheme is found in the writings of St. Anselm, who maintained that the name per se signifies a property and *per aliud* a person or thing. The medieval doctrine of properties of terms, and especially of their suppositions, is an example of sign use as a system. It dealt with subjects and predicates of proposition. Each term of this kind has a broadly understood meaning called *significatio,* which—together with the verbal context (especially the verb or copula in a given proposition), the speaker's intention, and other pragmatic circumstances—determines what the given categorematic expression refers to in each separate case. Depending on these factors governing referential use, the noun or pronoun has a certain *suppositio* and *appellatio* and the verb or adjective a certain *copulatio*.

With the exception of those used metaphorically, terms had proper supposition, in which material supposition (i.e., metalinguistic use), for instance of the word *man* in the sentence "Man is a noun," was distinguished from formal supposition, for instance of the word *man* in "Man is a rational being" (simple formal supposition) or "This man is writing" (personal formal supposition). In turn, the so-called *appellatio* of a noun consisted in a limitation of its applications to objects occurring in the time indicated by the tense of the verb in the sentence. The doctrine of term properties may be treated either as a theory of referential uses of a term, elaborated to form a system, or as a system of semantic categories and thus a system of signs.

Modern theories. The most elaborate modern semiotic system is the so-called pragmaticism of CHARLES S. PEIRCE. This theory may be regarded in two ways, either as one treating sign use as a dynamic system or as a most comprehensive system of signs occurring within the process of semiosis. Unlike the medieval doctrine of supposition, Peirce's theory does not confine itself to terms but deals with all kinds of signs, giving special prominence to the use of propositions. Peirce said:

> A *sign,* or *representamen,* is a First which stands in such a genuine triadic relation to a Second, called its *object,* as to be capable of determining a Third, called its *interpretant,* to assume the same triadic relation to its object in which it stands itself to the same object. The triadic relation is *genuine,* that is its three members are bound together by it in a way that does not consist in any complexus of dyadic relations. . . . The Third . . . must have a second triadic relation in which the representamen, or rather the relation thereof to its object, shall be its own (the Third's) object and must be capable of determining a Third to this relation. All this must equally be true of the Third's Third and so on endlessly.
> . . . [S]igns require at least two *quasi-minds,* a *quasi-utterer* and a *quasi-interpreter;* and although these two are in one (i.e. *are* one mind) in the sign itself, they must nevertheless be distinct. In the sign they are, so to say, *welded.* Accordingly, it is not merely a fact of human psychology but a necessity of logic, that every logical evolution of thought should be dialogic. . . . [B]eing dialogical it [thought] is essentially composed of signs.
> . . . [T]he purpose of signs—which is the purpose of

thought—is to bring truth to expression. The law under which a sign must be true is the law of inference. . . .

As we see, Peirce's sign-as-a-system is a logical reconstruction of the process of semiosis consisting of a series of hierarchical triads. In reality the scheme of each of these triads has additional branches, because the representamen is relativized not only to its object and interpretant but also to its ground, namely, the idea with regard to which this representamen stands for its object. Moreover, the representamen stands for two kinds of objects: the immediate object, that is, as it is represented by a given sign, and the dynamic object, occurring outside the sign and determining the immediate object, which in its turn determines the sign. There are also three kinds of interpretant: the immediate interpretant (the effect "the sign . . . may produce upon a mind, without any reflection upon it"), the dynamic interpretant ("that which is experienced in each act of interpretation and is different from that of any other"), and the final interpretant ("the effect the sign would produce upon any mind upon which circumstances should permit it to work out its full effect"). This is merely a skeleton of the system, a system not so much of a static sign as of the possible activity of an abstract mind in an idealized process of semiosis that consists in drawing consequences from subsequent abstract thoughts by means of gradually self-correcting possible conditional predictions. Because the interpretant of a given sign triad becomes a sign in the next triad, and so on, we may speak of both the sign-as-a-system and a system of signs in discussing Peirce's doctrine.

Systems of Signs

The expression *system of signs* is polysemous not only because of the polysemy of its words. In addition, there is disagreement about whether it is a system of instruments of intentional communication only or whether it is also a system of, among others, natural means for cognizing reality.

Classification of signs as systems of signs. Peirce's doctrine features a classification of signs arising from the intersection of three trichotomies: the one regarding the nature of the sign itself divides signs into the qualisign, the sinsign, and the legisign; the one regarding the sign's relation to its object distinguishes the icon, the index, and the symbol; and the one regarding the sign's relation to its interpretant distinguishes the rheme (or predicate), the dicent (or proposition), and the argument. There is ordering within each of these trichotomies according to the triad of ontological categories: of firstness, "the being of positive qualitative possibility"; of secondness, "the being of actual fact"; and of thirdness, "the being of law that will govern facts in the future." There is also ordering according to the triads of the gnoseological categories and kinds of relations corresponding to them. Thus qualisign, icon, and rheme belong to firstness; sinsign, index, and dicent to secondness; and legisign, symbol, and argument to thirdness. In the resultant system the description of each sign is composed of three parts; for example, the sentence as a type is at once a legisign, a symbol, and a dicent. In this way the place of a sign in a system is settled. This is an important determinant of the sign's communication function. Signs of like form may perform different functions depending on their place in the system. This principle is exemplified by the localization of the same musical note in various places on the staff, by the same rendering of a person in different parts of a medieval altar, by the same emblem in different fields on a coat of arms (*see* HERALDRY), and by the same words in different contexts.

Examples of systems of signs. Systems of signs are exemplified by natural languages; artificial formal languages; writing systems composed of pictograms, ideograms, hieroglyphs, or ALPHABET signs (*see* AMERICAS, PRE-COLUMBIAN—WRITING SYSTEMS; EGYPTIAN HIEROGLYPHS; SYMBOLIC LOGIC); systems of phonograms; the International Phonetic Alphabet; systems of phonemes (*see* PHONOLOGY); systems of road signs and clock chimes (*see* SIGNAGE); systems of etiquette composed of human behaviors; systems of different culture units; medieval systems of gestures such as St. Bede's counting on fingers or the *Indicia monasteralia* of Cotton Tiberius devised to enable monks who took vows of silence to communicate with gestures (*see* SIGN LANGUAGE—ALTERNATE SIGN LANGUAGES); the sign language of deaf-mutes (*see* SIGN LANGUAGE—PRIMARY SIGN LANGUAGES); the so-called flower language created in 1819 by Charlotte de Latour (Louise Cortambert); Peirce's existential graphs; the system of goods in economic exchange; the Morse code (*see* MORSE, SAMUEL F. B.) and that of flag signaling; the system of symptoms or syndromes of illness or meteorological situations; the system of information transmitted by genes; systems of ANIMAL COMMUNICATION; and so on.

Some see codes and languages as distinct among the systems of signs. Others regard all systems of signs, including languages, as codes. Still others consider every system of signs to be a language. These categorizations depend on the definition of the terms *code* and *language,* and the selection of a definition depends on the research task and discipline of study or on the individual preferences of the selector.

Code. The word *code* serves either as a name of some system of signs in which all the separate signifiers were assigned their values or as a set of rules determining this assignment. More important than this difference is whether uninterpreted signs of another system are also among those regarded as values of signifiers. If so, then, for example, the mutual assignment of signs of two alphabets, or what is often called a cipher (*see* CRYPTOLOGY), will be recognized as a code despite the fact that the phonetic value of each of these signs remains unknown; that is, we cannot read any one of them aloud.

Most often, however, code is regarded as a system in which to every signifier—treated as a type (or, in INFORMATION THEORY terminology, a signal type)—is assigned its signification, that is, the signified (known in information theory as the message or, strictly speaking, as a class of messages). This assignment is a semantic relation between the signifier and its signified. The domain of this relation is the set of all signifiers of the given code, and its counterdomain is the set of all its signifieds. Two subsets may be distinguished in the domain of a given code: the set containing one element only—the given signifier—and the complementary set. The code's rules assign to the division of this domain a suitable division of its counterdomain, namely, into the subset with the signified of the signifier from the previous subset as the sole element and into the complementary set. The ordered signifier-signified couple constitutes a sign, termed *seme* by some authors.

Some signs consist of components. For example, the NUMBER *91* consists of two components, *9* and *1,* and each one is a correlation of its signifier with the signified corresponding to it. Both the signifier and the signified of a composite sign are logical products of, respectively, the signifiers and the signifieds of all the components of this sign. The relation between the signifier and the signified of every component of the composite sign is of the same type as the relation between the signifier and the signified of the entire sign built up of these components.

The code embracing signs thus composed is subject to the first articulation. On the other hand, the code belongs to the second articulation if it is one having the first articulation in which signifiers of the components of a given sign can be decomposed into so-called *figurae,* that is, second-order members that have no signifieds. The codes subject to both articulations must be distinguished from so-called two-class systems of signs, for instance, ones including expressions belonging to such separate semiotic categories as words and sentences.

Codes can be classified from several viewpoints:

1. Codes in which the signifieds of the separate signs are mutually exclusive (e.g., the code of railway signals) and all the others;
2. Codes consisting of only one sign (e.g., the code of the white cane carried by the blind) and all the others;
3. Codes in which the absence of a sign is a sign (e.g., the code of automobile turn signals) and all the others;
4. With regard to articulation, codes are divided into
   (a) those devoid of articulation (e.g., the code of traffic lights at road intersections),
   (b) those with second articulation only (e.g., the code of naval flag signaling),
   (c) those with first articulation only (e.g., decimal numeration),
   (d) those with double articulation (e.g., some systems of telephone numeration), and
   (e) digital and at the same time discrete codes (i.e., ones with a finite number of signs, for example, *4a,* as distinguished from analog codes, such as the code of the potentiometer in a radio).

Language. In discussing language as a system of signs one has to decide whether to deal with a general notion of language or with any of the special notions, such as the notion of natural language.

In a general notion of language encountered, for example, in information theory, language is being defined as any system of information conveyance between people or between parts of a biological organism or between fragments of a machine, the system being an infinite set of sounds or inscriptions, each of which is a combination of a finite number of symbols of a fixed alphabet. A set of rules called the grammar of this language serves to distinguish well-formed from badly formed sentences of the given language. Such a notion of language is used, for example, in constructing the intermediate language for machine translation.

The description of a formal system, namely, an idealized abstract artificial language, and especially of a deductive system, reveals significant structural properties of a language. A formal deductive system is constructed by giving a list of symbols (variables, logical constants, individual constants, predicates, brackets), rules of sentence formation (i.e., the system's grammar), and axioms selected from among the logically correct sentences, as well as the rules of their transformation (i.e., the deductive apparatus of the system). The system's grammar (its syntactic part) is interpreted with the use of the model (its semantic part). It consists of a universe of discourse, that is, an arbitrary, nonempty set of objects of any kind and of distinguished elements of the model denoted by individual constants according to a specific function. The notions of logical validity and logical consequence are defined using the notion of satisfaction relativized to the given model. Every sentence of the given system that is formally deducible from the set of its hypotheses is also a consequence of this set.

This framework is constructed in abstraction from the peculiarities of the various languages.

A similar idea of that which is common to all languages and hence also common to thought guided the medieval *modistae* as authors of speculative grammar based on Aristotle's distinction of ontological categories—especially of substance, matter, form, quality, and quantity—and on the Arabic commentaries of Aristotle's work, in particular on the *Philosophia Prima* and *Logica* of Ibn Sīnā (Avicenna). The speculative grammarians and philosophers, such as Roger Bacon, John of Salisbury, Petrus Helias, Robert Kilwardby, and Siger de Courtrai, aspired to formulate a science of *modi significandi,* or modes of meaning, in both verbal and mental speech. They held that the relation of grammar to ordinary speech is analogous to that between logic and internal speech. Grammar is thus an indirect reflection of thought structure.

The speculative grammar system was continued in different variants of universal grammar constructed as a system of words representing the system of ideas in the mind. For example, according to *Grammaire générale et raisonnée* (1660), by French theologians Antoine Arnauld and Claude Lancelot, grammar gives a primary division of the art of thinking; and according to French philosopher Étienne Bonnot de Condillac (*Essai sur l'origine des connaissances humaines,* 1746), the use of signs reveals the source of all our ideas, and the analysis of thoughts becomes complete in discourse. Finally, U.S. linguist Noam Chomsky believes that universal grammar determines the essential nature of human language because it is a system of principles to which any grammar must conform as a matter of biological necessity.

The present-day categorial grammars formulated by logicians and philosophers may be regarded as a variant of universal grammar. Similarly, as speculative grammar these grammars, such as the system of Stanisław Leśniewski (1930), go back to Aristotle's conception of categories, and as universal grammar they go back to the concept of part of speech or, as in Edmund Husserl, to the medieval distinction of categorematic and syncategorematic expressions. Both the conception of categorical grammar and the distinction between categorematic and syncategorematic expression occur in Kazimierz Ajdukiewicz's system of categorical grammar, which employs a special notation that makes possible the checking of the syntactic connection of a sentence and a compound expression.

The idea of symbolic notation is already present in the Middle Ages, for example, in scholasticism in the logical square and names of syllogistical moods as a system of iconic-symbolic signs intended for classificational and mnemotechnical purposes. In modern times the idea of symbolic notation is connected mainly with Gottfried Wilhelm Leibniz. In the nineteenth century it was realized by George Boole in his book *An Investigation of the Laws of Thought* (1854), which contained an exposition of a symbolic algebra formally representing the necessary operations of thought. Continuations of this idea were William S. Jevons's tables, John Venn's diagrams, Peirce's existential graphs, and the so-called Polish notation in logic devised by Jan Łukasiewicz.

Most of the universal grammars and systems of symbolism are generative, as are, among others, phrase structure grammars (e.g., that of U.S. linguist Paul Postal) and the generative grammars superimposed on the former (e.g., that of Chomsky), and finite-state grammars such as the ones of Yehoshua Bar-Hillel and E. Shamir. They are composed of a vocabulary (a finite set of initial strings) and a set of grammatical rules, usually of substitution. Despite being grammars of individual natural languages, they share with universal grammar the assumption that the so-called deep structure of a sentence reflects the structure of thought.

A distinction must be made between universal grammar on the one hand and universal language—or, rather, according to French philosopher René Descartes's distinction, two of its kinds—on the other. These two kinds are the a priori universal language (i.e., the philosophical), which is to serve clarity of thinking, and the a posteriori universal language based on greatly simplified vocabulary and syntax of natural languages intended for facile international communication. An example of an a posteriori language is Esperanto. An a priori language—a schematic language—is the so-called Real Character of Bishop John Wilkins (*An Essay towards a Real Character and a Philosophical Language,* 1668), allegedly reflecting the arrangement of the world and hence based on the differentiation of ontological categories. Francis Bacon (*Advancement of Learning* and *De Augmentis Scientiarum*) postulated that the universal language contain as many arbitrary real characters as there are real words and that these radical characters denote notions and things without the mediation of words.

A similar desire guided Leibniz as the author of *characteristica universalis,* akin to an alphabet of human thoughts, an artificial ideal language patterned after the mathematical symbolic notation in which ideas are unequivocally and mechanically represented logically and things are not represented figuratively. The language was to serve as a pattern against which theorems of all sciences would be measured. Leibniz's artificial language was not intended for recording and communicating knowledge, as was Descartes's a priori language; it was to serve heuristic purposes. It was to mirror the operations of the mind as well as the structure of the world, both of the empirical world and of the possible worlds. Leibniz wrote that although characters are arbitrary, the relations between characters are not; they reflect relations occurring between things denoted by these characters, and this in fact is the foundation of truth. Just as an integer is uniquely decomposable into its prime factors, Leibniz maintained that a composite concept is analyzable into simple concepts that may be denoted with prime numbers. In order to determine if a given sentence is true, it is enough to calculate whether the product of prime factors connected with the predicate divides the product connected with the subject. In devising his universal language Leibniz anticipated categorial grammar and the idea of semantic universals, and by regarding the verb as a representation of the proposition, he outlined the concept of propositional function.

All artificial languages stem from verbal human language, often called natural language. According to FERDINAND DE SAUSSURE (1916), language is a system of signs expressing ideas and thus is comparable to WRITING, the alphabet of deaf-mutes, ceremonies, etiquette, military signals, and so forth. It is only the most important of these systems. Saussure distinguished *langue* (language system), *parole* (individual concrete act of speaking), and *langage* (speech as a set of acts of speaking).

There is agreement that natural language is a system serving broadly understood communication. The following functions of language are mentioned (by Karl Bühler) in this context: the expressive, the impressive, and the representative, all performed by every utterance. According to ROMAN JAKOBSON, on the other hand, an utterance performs one or a combination of the following functions: referential, emotive, imperative, phatic, metalinguistic, and/or poetic. Some of these functions, especially the representative (i.e., referential) in combination with the expressive, consist not only in reflecting reality but also in treating it in a way peculiar to the given language.

According to Wilhelm von Humboldt, each natural language is an "*energeia,*" that is, a dynamic system furnished with an inner form unique for it, namely, a set of grammatical categories analogous to Immanuel Kant's a priori forms and categories of mind. A reference to this is the hypothesis of EDWARD SAPIR and BENJAMIN LEE WHORF that every language is not only a means of communicating experiences but also (to a certain degree) a determiner and shaper of the experiences of people using the language. Ideas in a sense similar to those of von Humboldt may be found in Condillac's *Essai sur l'origine des connaissances humaines,* a conception of innate language, "language of actions"; according to Condillac, the elements of this language are natural and spontaneous organs serving the expression of emotions and are capable of being transformed by analogy into conventional signs or "signs of institution."

Most of the enumerated functions and features of natural languages are shared by all systems of signs as communication systems, or at least they are common to all human systems of communication including artificial systems of signs created and used by humans. This may also be said of such structural properties of natural language as the fact that the language systems consist of vocabulary and grammar; that the constant units of the vocabulary are combinable into compound units; that natural language is context dependent and that, for example, the situational or verbal context turns a general symbol into an individual symbol; and that natural language is linear and hence successively and discoursively understood. Some of these structural properties belong either to all other systems of signs or at least to those used by humans and not only to natural language.

According to Chomsky, the characteristic features of natural language include, among others, an infinite number of functionally distinct expressions and a finite number of grammatical rules. It is thus a system for the infinite use of finite means. Speakers of natural language make use of modality, propositional attitude, description, presupposition, aspect, anaphora, and quantification. Natural language serves to tell a story, to express an opinion, to enhance understanding. Finally, natural language is acquired effortlessly.

The distinction of natural language from code, especially when the latter is regarded as a human system of signs, has aroused controversy. According to one distinction, code is a communication system with a finite number of signal types or a finite number of ways of interpreting them; language, on the other hand, is a communication system containing jointly an infinite number of signal types and an infinite number of ways of interpreting them. Thus, in addition to natural language, the following are included among languages: the artificial or partly artificial languages of the various sciences, the so-called analog systems of signs belonging to the same syntactic-semantic category, and systems of composite signs being logical products of an infinite number of sign factors belonging to the same syntactic-semantic category.

A second distinction is that a code is a system of signs containing one basic syntactic-semantic category, whereas language is a system of signs with two basic syntactic-semantic categories, namely, names and sentences; in other words, to use Bühler's term, it is a two-class system. This distinction leaves among codes such systems of signs embracing an infinite number of signal types as analog systems with one basic syntactic-semantic category or systems of signs that are logical products of an infinite number of factors belonging to the same syntactic-semantic category. On the other hand, what remains in the group of languages in addition to natural language are all artificial systems of signs decomposable into two syntactic-semantic categories. Thus the division of systems of signs made by this distinction partly overlaps the previous one.

According to a third distinction, included among codes are all systems of signs produced or intentionally used by humans, but language is a code characterized by a double articulation. The first articulation is the segmentation of text into morphemes, termed also monemes (i.e., the smallest meaningful sound units—roots and affixes). The second articulation involves the segmentation of morphemes into phonemes, that is to say, minimal abstract constituents of the former. Thanks to first articulation an infinite number of meaningful morpheme combinations may be formed out of their finite number, and second articulation makes it possible to split every meaningful element into meaningless constituents. This distinction enables the separation of natural language among codes because it refers to notions characteristic of this language: morpheme and phoneme. The description of a natural language is sometimes augmented by the indication that the second articulation of this language is incomplete because elements of intonation cannot be split into constituents deprived of the semantic function, that the most relevant—and perhaps characteristic—feature of language is the fact that some linguistic signifieds are classes between which there occurs the relation of inclusion or intersection, that only in language may a given message be transmitted with different signs, and consequently that in languages there are synonyms as well as an identity of meaning between an individual word and a certain combination of words, which fact enables defining. Natural language is related with such codes—or, according to some opinions, languages—as the mimic, the gestural, the intonational, and so forth.

According to a fourth distinction, languages are seen to include systems of signs characterized by first articulation regardless of whether or not the second articulation belongs to them. It is only in the systems with first articulation that we find grammar. The systems of signs that are not articulated or those that are characterized by second articulation only are not regarded as languages because they lack grammar. In agreement with this distinction, the languages include (in addition to natural language), for example, the system of signs used by arithmetic or algebra enabling the formulation of an infinite number of propositions out of a finite number of signs.

Finally, according to a fifth distinction, every system of signs is regarded as a language, with the term *code* being reserved for the set of rules according to which in the given language signifieds are ascribed to their signifiers. The range of the term *language* depends in this case on the range of the term *system of signs* and indirectly on the range of the term *sign,* for the object of consideration may be only signs occurring in the process of communication between people, emitted intentionally or unintentionally; or those in communication between animals, both intentional and unintentional; or those in the process of information flow between parts of an animate organism; or, finally, between parts of a machine.

This is connected with the possible narrower or broader understanding of the word *communication,* in particular with whether in addition to exchange of messages we include in communication the COGNITION of reality with the use of signs, in the broadest sense of the latter word.

See also POETICS.

Bibliography. Kazimierz Ajdukiewicz, *The Scientific World-Perspective and Other Essays, 1931–1963,* ed. by Jerzy Giedymin, Dordrecht, The Netherlands, and Boston, 1978; Antoine Arnauld and Claude Lancelot, *General and Rational Grammar: The Port-Royal Grammar* (in French), ed. and trans. by Jacques Rieux and Bernard E. Rollin, The Hague, 1975; Karl Bühler, *Sprachtheorie: Die Darstellungsfunktion der Sprache* (1934), 2d ed., Stuttgart, 1965; Noam Chomsky, "Human Language and Other Semiotic Systems," *Semiotica* 25 (1979): 31–44; Jean-Louis Gardies, *Rational Grammar* (Esquisse d'une grammaire pure), trans. by Kevin Mulligan, Washington, D.C., and Munich, 1985; Louis Hjelmslev, *Prolegomena to a Theory of Language* (Omkring sprogteoriens grundlaeggelse), rev. ed., trans. by Francis J. Whitfield, Madison, Wis., 1961; Wilhelm von Humboldt, "Über die Kawi-Sprache auf der Insel Java" (Vols. 1–3, 1830–1835), in *Gesammelte Schriften,* 17 vols., ed. by Albert Leitzmann, Berlin, 1903–1936; Susanne K. Langer, *Philosophy in a New Key: A Study in the Symbolism of Reason, Rite, and Art,* 3d ed., Cambridge, Mass., 1967; Gottfried Wilhelm Leibniz, "Nouveaux essais sur l'entendement" (1698), in *Die philosophischen Schriften,* ed. by C. J. Gerhardt, Berlin, 1882, reprint Hildesheim, FRG, 1960–1961; Stanisław Leśniewski, "Über die Grundlagen der Ontologie," *Comptes rendus des séances de la Société des Sciences et des Lettres de Varsovie* 23 (1930): 111–154; André Martinet, *La linguistique synchronique,* Paris, 1970; Charles Morris, *Writings on the General Theory of Signs,* The Hague and Paris, 1971; Charles Sanders Peirce, *Collected Papers,* Vols. 1–6 ed. by Charles Hartshorne and Paul Weiss, Vols. 7–8 ed. by Arthur W. Burks, Cambridge, Mass., 1931–1960;

Figure 1. *(Signage)* Las Vegas, 1978. Courtesy of Venturi, Rauch, and Scott Brown.

Luis J. Prieto, *Messages et signaux,* Paris, 1966; Ferdinand de Saussure, *Cours de linguistique générale* (Course in General Linguistics, ed. by Charles Bally and Albert Sechehaye, London, 1959, reprint 1974), Paris, 1916.

JERZY PELC

SIGNAGE

Signs are an essential part of the modern urban and roadside environment. They inform, guide, and influence. Related to the messages conveyed explicitly through written and graphic signs are messages implicit in the appearance and location of buildings in the environment.

Urban Messages

In cities messages are communicated to people as they move about on the street. There are three message systems available for urban communication: (1) *heraldic,* written and graphic signs of all types (*see* HERALDRY); (2) *physiognomic,* messages implicit in the facades of buildings (e.g., columns and pediments on a neoclassical bank, evenly spaced windows and balconies on a modern high-rise hotel); and (3) *locational,* messages implicit in the location of urban landmarks (e.g., the corner store, the railroad station at the end of a main street, the monument overlooking a public square).

The three systems are closely related in the city. For example, the city hall may have broad stairs, a monumental entrance, a tower, and flags, to herald its importance and evoke associations with the past. The sign that says "City Hall" may evoke classical Rome through the style of its lettering. The city hall may be located on a public square, but it may as easily sit on a city block, cheek by jowl with small-scale, commercial concerns. In either case the city hall's civic importance is accentuated symbolically through the use of a "civic" architectural style and applied civic signs and symbolic decoration. Relations and combinations in most modern city streets among signs and buildings, ARCHITECTURE and symbolism, and civic pride and honky-tonk express the vitality and complexity of modern urban life.

Roadside Signs

In many countries the signs and billboards we see as we drive along streets and highways are mostly commercial advertisements (*see* ADVERTISING). Their words and symbols attempt to inform and persuade the potential customer in the automobile. These signs are designed to be seen across vast distances and at high speeds; the big roadside sign must leap out at the driver, directing him or her to a particular store. The products in the store are also advertised on the highway, on billboards sponsored by their national manufacturers. On the suburban strip, buildings are small and cheap, signs large and expensive. The graphic sign in space has become the architecture of the highway landscape.

Most strip signs are composed of "high readers," which communicate eye-catching and evocative images, and "low readers," which give specific information ("Over a billion sold") and directions ("Park here"). Seen from afar the high reader suggests we slow down; the low reader tells us why we should stop and where to go. The McDonald's arches on the strip and the wagon wheel on the suburban front lawn serve much the same purposes. Each identifies its owner and refers symbolically to the owner's aspirations, commercial in one case, personal and communal in the other. However, the glowing, soaring, parabolic arches of McDonald's have become an international symbol. They signify the same hamburger wherever you are and suggest a familiar location for fast food for the traveler in any town. Strip signs differ from city signs in that the latter are, with the exception of traffic signs, nearly always attached to buildings.

Historical Perspective and Recent Trends

Nineteenth- and early twentieth-century commercial signs were extravagant and abundant. They were placed in windows, above windows, and high on building facades, with little regard for structural niceties or relation to architectural decoration but with close attention to visibility from the sidewalk and the mass transit system. Victorian signs were cluttered and ornate. Ornate letter types, often gilded, crowded the available space. Signs were wordy. Extensive use was made of representational images: traditional striped barber's poles, eagles, clocks, faucets, eyeglasses, and store Indians. Most signs were made of painted wood or baked enamel.

Such famous emblems as the Coca-Cola sign and the Mobil flying red horse date from the first part of the twentieth century, as does the use of neon. Neon reached its highest artistic expression in Las Vegas, but thousands of brightly colored store-window signs remain as local souvenirs of this almost bygone art. Today commercial signs are frequently made of backlit plastic or metal. They are usually placed over store windows, perpendicular or parallel to the facade. The nineteenth-century practice of attaching signs high on the walls of buildings has stopped, except where occupants make decorative use of window lighting in tall buildings at night. Big signs may be placed on the tops of buildings, where they are visible from afar, but this form of advertising is restricted in most cities to the largest corporations.

Modern signs are less assertive in style than their

Figure 2. *(Signage)* Baker's shop, Switzerland. The Bettmann Archive, Inc.

Victorian counterparts. Modern taste dictates "Swiss" graphics, single words rather than complicated messages, and the use of abstractions rather than representational images (*see* TYPOGRAPHY). Some high-class stores have barely visible signs or no signs at all. These stores cater to "discriminating tastes" and also attract attention by looking different.

Architects in the past made more use of signs on buildings than do architects today. Building names figured prominently on facades and were incorporated into decorative panels. For important buildings, mottoes and hortatory texts might be extended across facades in the classical Roman manner—as, for example, on the Pantheon. Architects considered these inscriptions part of the decoration of buildings.

Architects continued to give signs pride of place on the facades of buildings into the 1930s. However, as public revulsion against the "vulgar" and commercial grew, building signs were often reduced in size until they were almost imperceptible, sometimes appearing to have been afterthoughts.

A half-century ago a driver could maintain a sense of orientation on the highway. At a crossroad a small arrow directed traffic right, left, or straight ahead.

Figure 3. *(Signage)* Sign at a gunsmith's shop. The Bettmann Archive, Inc.

Figure 4. *(Signage)* "Tail o' the Pup" hot dog stand, Los Angeles, 1975. Courtesy of Venturi, Rauch, and Scott Brown.

Figure 5. *(Signage)* Aquarium, Central Pier, Atlantic City, New Jersey, 1980. Courtesy of Venturi, Rauch, and Scott Brown.

Today the crossroad is a cloverleaf. To turn left, one must turn right. The driver has no time to ponder the paradox involved in this maneuver but must rely on signs for guidance—large signs seen at great distances and at high speeds.

Today as we drive the interstate we see signs that tell us where to eat, sleep, and get gas. Billboards and high readers tell us whose gas, food, and lodging is available. The false fronts of a nineteenth-century frontier main street in the United States performed much the same function. They were wider and taller than the stores behind to accommodate signs and signal the stores' importance. They also enhanced and unified the street front. False fronts were effective on a main street scaled to the horse and buggy. With the advent of the car, however, the need for parking forced buildings to separate and recede from the street. False fronts were disengaged and moved down the highway to the exit, where they became billboards.

The big sign—independent of the building and made up of three-dimensional sculptural or two-dimensional pictorial elements—calls attention to itself by its position, perpendicular to and at the edge of the highway, and by its scale and shape. Signs use mixed-media words, pictures, and SCULPTURE to persuade and inform.

Signs work as polychrome sculpture in the sun and as silhouette against it; at night they must reflect or become a source of light. A sign might revolve by day and become a play of light by night. It might contain six-inch-high words to be read close up and ten-foot-high words to be read at a distance.

Signs can communicate through the use of a representational image that stands for a trade or product—for example, a hammer for a hardware store, a spigot for a plumber, or a bib and tucker for a clothing store (*see* REPRESENTATION, PICTORIAL AND PHOTOGRAPHIC). They can also communicate in a purely descriptive, usually terse manner (e.g., "EAT," "GAS," "VACANCY"). The message can be evocative or humorous.

The representational signs of the recent past increasingly are being abandoned for abstract logos and "corporate identification systems." Signs that are a rich mixture of symbols, words, and pictures are becoming less fashionable than "modern" signs that sacrifice evocative imagery for the sake of "boldness," "clarity," and "good taste."

See also ICONOGRAPHY; POSTER; VISUAL IMAGE.

Bibliography. Paul Hirshorn and Steven Izenour, *White Towers,* Cambridge, Mass., 1979; Chester H. Liebs, *Main Street to Miracle Mile,* Boston, 1985; John S. Margolies (photos and text), *The End of the Road,* ed. by C. Ray Smith, New York, 1981; Robert Venturi, *Complexity and Contradiction in Architecture,* 2d ed., New York, 1977; Robert Venturi, Denise Scott Brown, and Steven Izenour, *Learning from Las Vegas,* 2d ed., Cambridge, Mass., 1977.

STEVEN IZENOUR

SILK ROAD

For nearly two thousand years the chief trade route between Europe and China. It was not known as the Silk Road until German geographer Ferdinand von Richthofen named it so in the nineteenth century, but the name was appropriate. The most prized goods that passed over the road were silks from Shantung and Honan. Silk was very popular in Greece and Rome. A chronicler of the times says that Cleopatra, to dazzle her banquet guests, "appeared in a silk gown." The Romans called the Chinese "Seres," which comes from the word for silk, and China was "Serica," the "silk country." Tiberius (42 B.C.E.–37 C.E.) prohibited Roman men from wearing silk so that there would be enough for the women who craved it. So Chinese silk, along with lacquer ware, rode westward, and in return gold and silver articles, precious stones, glassware, and wine rode back to China.

It was a very long and dangerous ride from Antioch, Alexandria, or other ports on the Mediterranean to Chang'an (modern Xian), the first great city that eastbound travelers reached in China. Much of the middle part of the journey was threatened by the Huns from Mongolia, bandits from both the deserts and the mountains, and the Parthians, who were determined not to yield sovereignty over the road to either Rome (i.e., Europe) or China. Therefore, before the Mediterranean travelers had gone very far they handed over their goods to Iranian merchants, later to Uighur traders from Turkestan. When the road reached the site of present Sinkiang (Xinjiang), China's farthest northwest province, travelers were most likely to be attacked or embattled. Here the road forked into northern and southern branches at the base of the mountain ranges, along a line of oases at the base of the northern mountains or another at the base of the southern mountains. Rich towns had been built on these oases, which were often the scene of hostilities between the Chinese and the Huns. Once through the Sinkiang region, the eastward travelers were in China and could advance beside the Great Wall as they made their way to Xian. The farther east they went, the lower the chances that their load would be taken away from them, though they still had a return trip to make.

West of Sinkiang another road branched off to the south. It was the route by which Alexander invaded India. More important, it was the road by which Buddhism came from India to China.

In the thirteenth century the Chinese emperors reestablished their power in Sinkiang. This enabled MARCO POLO, among others, to ride the Silk Road to China before sea travel between China and the West became more frequent.

See also EAST ASIA, ANCIENT; EXPLORATION; ROMAN EMPIRE.

Figure 1. *(Silk Road)* Major East-West trade routes by land and sea. Redrawn after J. E. Vollmer, E. J. Keall, and E. Nagai-Berthrong, *Silk Roads, China Ships,* Royal Ontario Museum exhibition catalog, Toronto, Ontario, 1984, p. 26.

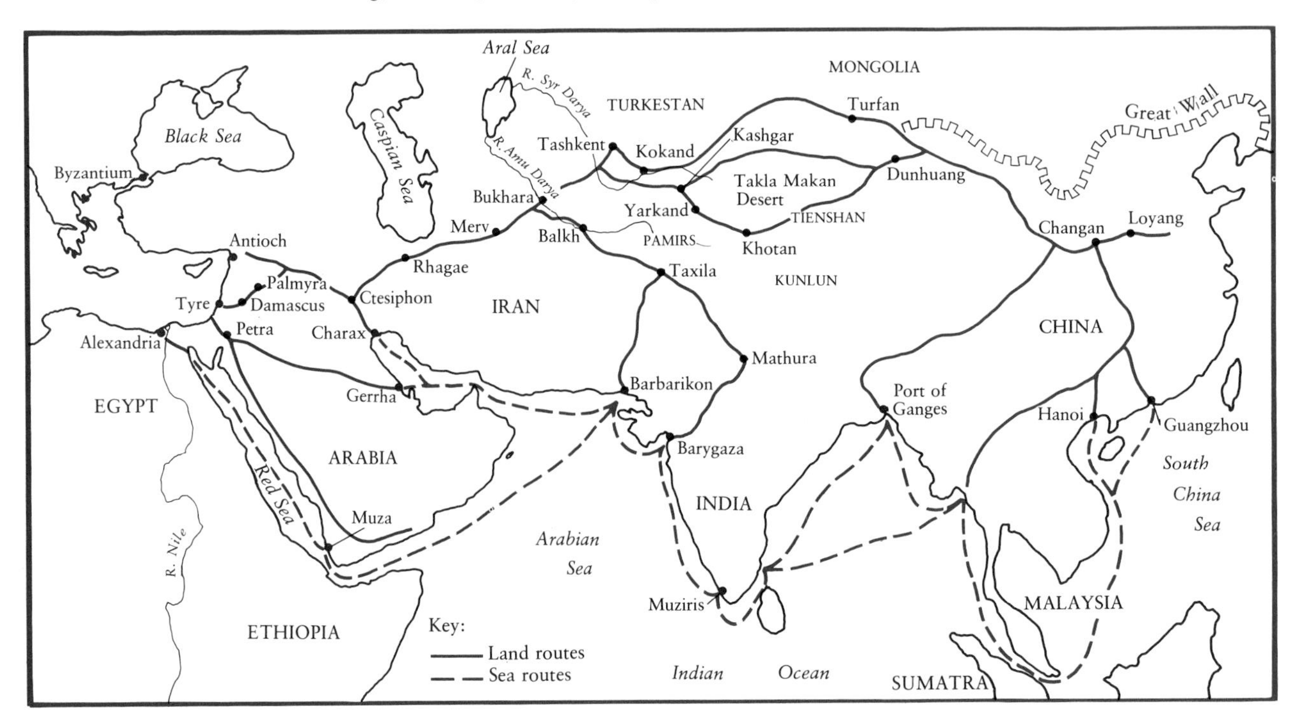

Bibliography. Ryōichi Hayashi, *The Silk Road and the Shoso-in* (Shiruku Rōdo to Shōsōin), trans. by Robert Ricketts, New York, 1975.

WILBUR SCHRAMM

SIMMEL, GEORG (1858–1918)

German sociologist and philosopher, analyst of small-group interaction and hierarchies. Georg Simmel was one of the founders of modern sociology. He declared that sociology could not pass judgment on the meaning of society as a whole but must describe and analyze individual forms of human interaction—those patterns of communication that constitute society in its most basic sense. He spent most of his career as a popular lecturer at the University of Berlin, but a combination of anti-Semitism at the university and suspicions of dilettantism kept him from any tenured academic rank until 1904, and a full professorship was not granted him until 1914, when he was already fatally ill. But through his many books and articles and widely publicized lecture series on such subjects as the outsider and the power of money, Simmel had an influence far beyond his academic circle. At the time of his death in 1918 Simmel was ranked alongside his most famous sociological contemporary, MAX WEBER.

Probably Simmel's most important contribution to the emerging study of society was his focus on the small group. He began his most famous study by asking, "What is needed for interaction to take place?" A dyad, or set of two people, constitutes a form of society that, Simmel believed, is not conducive to interaction. Between two people only limited forms of interaction are possible: they either agree, disagree, or do not communicate at all. In none of these cases does full social interaction take place. But the introduction of a third person creates conditions leading to complex social interaction: hierarchies (which Simmel was the first to study in depth), majority power, enforcement problems, unstable coalitions, and possibilities for SECRECY and fraud (*see also* DECEPTION). In the group of three, or triad, Simmel found all the same social phenomena that his contemporaries were analyzing in mass social settings.

Simmel's research into the group led him to study the possible victim of group dynamics, the outsider. Interaction between an established social group and an outsider who attempts to gain entrance into it constitutes one of the most fascinating topics in GROUP COMMUNICATION. Among the topics Simmel studied were strategies used by the outsider to gain acceptance, tests established by the group for admission, and the means by which the group signals the outsider's progress. He even extended his study, in *The Metropolis and Mental Life* (1903), to include the plight of those members of society who, unable to cope with the conflicts and demands of contemporary urban existence, become outsiders—what more recent observers call alienation.

Perhaps the most stimulating of Simmel's observations for later theorists was his idea that conflict was not necessarily a destructive force. Especially in modern societies, in which conflict is intellectual and verbal rather than emotional or physical, conflict can be an integrative force, ensuring that issues are not apathetically left to the dictates of the few but are resolved through the active engagement of society as a whole. Simmel's speculations on the place of conflict and the status of the outsider have formed the basis for a number of contemporary psychological and sociological theories, such as role analysis and behaviorism.

Bibliography. David Frisby, *Georg Simmel,* London and New York, 1984; Rudolph H. Weingartner, *Experience and Culture: The Philosophy of Georg Simmel,* Middletown, Conn., 1962.

HARTLEY S. SPATT

SLAVE TRADE, AFRICAN

The transatlantic slave trade effected one of the largest population movements in history, dispersing black peoples of Africa among European and Native American peoples of the New World and ultimately leading to the DIFFUSION of elements of African CULTURE. The 10 to 11 million victims of this forced MIGRATION were drawn mainly from western Africa, in the area extending from the Senegal River to the southern limits of Angola. Representing many groups and cultures of Africa, they became concentrated particularly in Portuguese Brazil, the multinational Caribbean, and the Spanish-settled areas of the mainland. About 6 percent landed in the present-day United States.

Interrelated with the commercial and industrial revolutions, the slave trade linked Africa with Europe and the Americas for three and a half centuries (*see* COLONIZATION). European nation-states and private venturers sought products for Europe—precious metals and tropical staples. Several considerations led to the resort to African labor. The cultivation of tropical staples, notably sugar, required many hands and hard labor over a long growing season. The hot climate deterred white workers, and the Native American population suffered huge losses from exposure to new diseases brought by the Europeans. From the beginning of the encounter between Europe and Africa whites held prejudicial attitudes toward black-skinned people that were used to justify enslavement.

Moreover, blacks had a high degree of immunity to tropical diseases. African officials and traders were willing to exchange laborers for European products, especially textiles, metal wares, liquor, and guns.

The conjunction of sugar and slaves goes far to explain the existence of the African slave trade. A luxury in the sixteenth century, sugar was a common household commodity by the nineteenth. Planters in tropical America wrung great fortunes from the sweat and mortality of a labor supply furnished by the African slave trade. Blacks also produced gold, tobacco, coffee, rice, indigo, and cotton, thereby contributing to the vast expansion of international commerce.

Reaching into the African interior from a long stretch of coastline, the slave trade drew into its network disparate peoples, divided in RELIGION, political organization, and social and economic arrangements (*see* AFRICA, PRECOLONIAL). The ethnic and geographic sources of slaves shifted over the long span of time, responding to variables in availability and national carriers. These factors complicated the pattern of cultural survival and diffusion in the Americas.

Evolution of the Trade

The African slave trade began with Portuguese EXPLORATION of Africa. At first Africans were imported into the Iberian Peninsula, where they intermingled with the white population. In early years drawing heavily on West Africa and the Guinea Coast, the Portuguese came to depend especially on Angola, where they established colonies and their agents married African women. The Portuguese provided slaves to Spanish America as well as to the Portuguese possessions in Brazil, where the trade responded in turn to the expansion of the sugar industry in Bahia, the discovery of gold in the Minas Gerais, and the development of coffee, sugar, and gold-mining operations in the hinterland of Rio.

The slave trade to Spanish America had its own character. The Spanish, owners of nearly all the New World except Brazil, were barred by a papal decree from owning the source of slaves—Africa. They therefore relied on others—first the Portuguese, then carriers of various other nations—to import slaves for their possessions in Mexico and later in the West Indies, as Puerto Rico and Cuba participated in sugar cultivation.

The Dutch broke the Portuguese monopoly and in the seventeenth century became the second most important carrier for other nations. Their sources in Africa shifted from a heavy dependence on the Slave Coast in the seventeenth century to the Ivory Coast and Angola in the eighteenth. In addition to providing slaves to others the Dutch established three major markets under their own flag in the Caribbean—Curaçao, Saint Eustatius, and Surinam—and these ultimately received the bulk of the African cargoes.

From small beginnings the French trade soared in the decade after the American Revolution, when departures from France averaged over a hundred vessels a year, and continued as a large illegal trade in the first half of the nineteenth century. In Africa, France early established an interest in Senegambia and later drew heavily from the Bight of Benin and Angola. In the Caribbean, after exploiting Guadeloupe and Martinique, France turned to developing the rich sugar potential of Saint Domingue.

The British trade rose to preeminence by the second third of the eighteenth century and became immense in the last two decades of the century. At first in the hands of a royally chartered monopoly, the trade passed to private merchants in London, Bristol, and Liverpool who plied the business with great efficiency, selling to all buyers. Until British abolition of the trade in 1807, the Bight of Biafra furnished the largest number of slaves, the Gold Coast the next largest, and the Congo-Angola region the third largest. The sugar islands of Barbados and Jamaica were the main markets in the British West Indies.

British North America was slow to be involved in the slave trade. Not until the 1730s did it take an active part, with Rhode Island dominating the colonial-based trade. The slaves came directly from Africa—not from the West Indies, as has been thought—and were imported mainly from Senegambia, Angola, the Bight of Biafra, and the Gold Coast. Four of the thirteen colonies were the destinations of most of these Africans: in 1780 Virginia led in the number of blacks, followed by South Carolina, North Carolina, and Maryland. The United States outlawed the foreign slave trade in 1807.

Effects of the Trade

In the diffusion and retention of African culture resulting from the transatlantic slave trade, four factors have had special significance: the African region from which the slaves came, the culture of the region to which they were taken, the persistence pattern of the slave trade with its effect of renewing the African heritage, and the density of the transplanted population.

The slave trade was a great diaspora, transporting millions to a doubly alien environment—another hemisphere dominated by another race. The trade made its impact on American regions in an uneven chronological pattern: for example, continuously in Brazil over several centuries, but in changing portions of the country; briefly in North America, for about one century and mainly in four colonies; and briefly also in Cuba, where three-quarters of the slaves arrived in the nineteenth century. Moreover, slaves formed differing proportions of American populations, comprising nearly the whole in some communities and small percentages in others. Blacks in Latin America, themselves from different African ethnic groups, often mixed with Indian and white races.

This kaleidoscope had its significance for the cultural legacy it left to the Americas. Survival of African culture appears to have been strongest among early generations, diminishing as creolization occurred and being reinforced as successive generations of Africans joined earlier arrivals. Survivals are more elusive in the United States than in the Caribbean and Latin America.

The Caribbean, holding no fewer than fifty insular societies, has a diversity that almost defies generalization. Each society has developed its own pattern. In the search for African survivals scholars have turned away from specific examples to an emphasis on the process by which African culture underwent change, responding to new circumstances and forming a new culture neither African nor American but Afro-American.

In Brazil the matter of African cultural survivals is complicated by the high degree of race mixing. Although Brazil imported nearly 4 million slaves over a span of three and a half centuries, in 1890 its black population numbered a little more than 2 million, and the mulatto population stood at twice that figure. Brazil practiced a less formal kind of segregation than did the United States, offering an escape hatch through intermarriage. For many Afro-Brazilians the goal was not to retain African culture but to cross racial barriers and pass as white.

Contrasting with miscegenation was the creation of Maroon societies in Brazil where African runaways lived apart from white domination. The most famous was Palmares, far in the interior of Pernambuco. Its government, a centralized kingdom, appears to have been modeled on several central African sources. For most of the seventeenth century Palmares demonstrated that an African political system could be successfully transplanted. It vigorously resisted efforts to subdue it until in 1694–1695 a force of Portuguese-Amerindian métis and frontier settlers destroyed Palmares in hand-to-hand combat.

Another form of assertion of African identity and unity was rebellion, particularly in the long series of rebellions in Bahia in the first third of the nineteenth century, initiated by newly arrived Africans with a common and uneradicated heritage. The high incidence of slave revolts in Brazil, in contrast to the low incidence in the United States, is partly attributable to the persistence of the Brazilian slave trade, which reinforced the African heritage generation by generation.

Africans imported into what is now the United States arrived over a short period of time and lived in a region where they were often a numerical minority. There was little race mixing or rebellion. In the nineteenth century African culture was threatened with near eradication. Many blacks in the United States and elsewhere sought to adopt white culture.

In the twentieth century black consciousness developed in the Americas as well as in Africa. Emerging black leaders made appeals for black consciousness and black unity. The search for African survivals quickened. The consensus has been that survivals are most clearly discernible in LANGUAGE, FOLKLORE, and music (*see* MUSIC, FOLK AND TRADITIONAL).

African language survivals are readily traceable in a few instances, such as the Twi language among Jamaican Maroons and Gullah among South Carolina Sea Islanders and some inhabitants of Caribbean and South American communities. More common has been the development of pidgin languages, mixing together West African and European languages. The Portuguese began this process, creating a trade pidgin; other nations made similar adaptations, with Africans inserting native words that were familiar and meaningful to them. A rich and varied pidgin grew because West Africans spoke many languages. *See* LANGUAGE VARIETIES.

Similarly, folklore represents an interaction between African and American sources. U.S. folklorist Richard M. Dorson found that only about 10 percent of over a thousand oral narratives told by Afro-Americans in the southern United States were known in West African folktales. African folklore had drawn on such sources as Aesop, whose influence—and the popularity of his animal fables—was widespread. *See* FOLKTALE.

In music the story has again been one of interaction of African and other elements. Afro-American spirituals and blues reflect the outlook of an oppressed people rather than an expression of African survivals. In jazz, which traveled back across oceans to become a part of world culture, traces of West African rhythms can be found, but also much else, echoing generations of interaction, creation, and renewal.

Bibliography. Roger Bastide, *African Civilizations in the New World* (Les Amériques noires, les civilisations africaines dans le nouveau monde), London, 1971; Margaret E. Crahan and Franklin W. Knight, eds., *Africa and the Caribbean,* Baltimore, Md., 1979; Philip D. Curtin, *The Atlantic Slave Trade: A Census,* Madison, Wis., 1969; Carl N. Degler, *Neither Black nor White: Slavery and Race Relations in Brazil and the United States,* New York, 1971; Sidney W. Mintz, ed., *Slavery, Colonialism, and Racism* (*Daedalus* [Spring 1974], Journal of the American Academy of Arts and Sciences), New York, 1975; Richard Price, ed., *Maroon Societies: Rebel Slave Communities in the Americas,* 2d ed., Baltimore, Md., 1979; James A. Rawley, *The Transatlantic Slave Trade: A History,* New York, 1981.

JAMES A. RAWLEY

SLEEPER EFFECT

An effect observed in social psychology experiments that suggests how ideas can eventually take hold, whatever their source. Tending to confirm more casual observations, the findings have important implications for communication generally, but especially in such areas as DISINFORMATION, PROPAGANDA, ADVERTISING, and media ethics (*see* ETHICS, MEDIA).

During World War II, and later at Yale University, CARL HOVLAND and his associates studied the effect of a communicator's perceived credibility or prestige on the persuasive power of a message (*see* PERSUASION). It had been demonstrated that when a message is attributed to a source considered untrustworthy, the message has little or no effect on the audience. After several weeks, however, the negative effect of the source's perceived lack of credibility seems to disappear and "positive" attitude changes occur; by that time there is actually little difference between the ATTITUDES of people who had been exposed to a message attributed to a high-credibility source and people exposed to the same message attributed to a low-credibility source. This unexpected change in the attitudes of persons who had been exposed to messages from low-credibility sources was called the "sleeper effect."

How did this change come about? Obviously, some kind of forgetting was involved. Hovland and his colleagues found that when the audience was reminded of the untrustworthy source of the message, the "sleeper effect" vanished and attitudes returned to their previous unfavorable level. By manipulating the research design Hovland was able to show that the audience had forgotten neither the message nor its attributed source, but rather the relationship between the two. It was all too easy to forget where the message had come from.

See also CONSUMER RESEARCH; MASS MEDIA EFFECTS; POLITICAL SOCIALIZATION; PUBLIC RELATIONS; RUMOR.

Bibliography. Carl I. Hovland, Irving L. Janis, and Harold H. Kelley, *Communication and Persuasion,* New Haven, Conn., 1953.

WILBUR SCHRAMM

SLIPS OF THE TONGUE

Normal (i.e., nonpathological) SPEECH errors characterized by a clear violation of the speaker's intention. Common categories of slips include phonemic reversals, or "spoonerisms" (e.g., *barn door* for *darn bore*), anticipations (*barn bore*), perseverations (*darn door*), additions (*darn blore*), and deletions (*dar bore*). Also included are word reversals (*ringing sirens and wailing bells*), blends (*splisters* for *splinters* and *blisters*), and malapropisms (*magician* for *musician*). Other categories have been identified as well. Definitions usually exclude common dysfluency phenomena (hesitations, false starts, vocalized pauses, etc.), as well as violations of intended receiver effects (ambiguity, impoliteness, social blunders, etc.).

Linguistic interest in slips began with Austrian psychologists Rudolf Meringer (around 1895) and SIGMUND FREUD (around 1901) but was generally dormant until the 1970s, when linguistic research began to focus on cognitive language-production processes. Research methods have included laboratory elicitation of slips as well as the collection of natural slip data. Research questions generally have concentrated on two areas: discovery of the cognitive operations for speech production and discovery or confirmation of the linguistic rules governing component operations.

Certain phonemic and morphemic patterns are common to slips, while others are unheard of. For example, of the many patterns allowed by a random phonological rearrangement of, say, *tongue slips,* those patterns found in verbal slips (e.g., *slung tips, tongue lisps*) are common to the English language. The fact that anomalous possibilities (e.g., *tlung sips*) never occur is taken as evidence that cognitive rules exist to indicate the allowable and/or disallowable phoneme patterns within the language. Similarly, evidence of morpheme rules is obtained by the fact that error morpheme segments, though accidentally rearranged, do maintain the common construction patterns found in legitimate utterances (e.g., *evidencingly* for *evidently*) but almost never manifest anomalous possibilities (e.g., *ingidencively*).

Findings from verbal slip research have increased our understanding of cognitive processes involved in speech production, providing evidence against one-word-at-a-time processing, evidence for a prearticulatory editing operation, and evidence that verbal slips may be caused by nonlinguistic factors independent of the impending speech message, as in "Freudian slips."

Of the theoretical accounts for the causes of verbal slips, the most precise hypotheses blame competition between viable alternative versions of the impending speech plan. For example, the error *motherpie and applehood* may be explained as the result of competition between, or indecision over, the message choices *motherhood and apple pie* versus *apple pie and motherhood.* In a variation of the competition hypothesis, the direction of the slip is seen as subject to influence from other kinds of associations. For example, greeting a competitor with *Pleased to beat* (for *meet*) *you* can be accounted for by recognizing that *beat* might be chosen both as a phonological associate of *meet* and as a semantic associate of the competitive context. Liberally interpreted, competition can account for most slips of the tongue.

See also HUMOR; SPEECH PLAY.

Bibliography. Victoria A. Fromkin, *Speech Errors as Linguistic Evidence,* The Hague, 1973; idem, ed., *Errors in Linguistic Performance,* New York, 1980.

MICHAEL T. MOTLEY

SMELL

The sense of smell is often considered a minor element in human communication, even though scents perceived as arising from other people may have significant interpersonal consequences. The conscious "meanings" or significance people attach to different scents varies depending on context, cultural values, and taboos. Students of NONVERBAL COMMUNICATION have been increasingly interested not only in conscious awareness of scents but also in the importance of nonconscious olfactory signaling.

The study of smell. The scientific study of the sense of smell has dealt largely with how individuals perceive test odorants and fragrances presented to them. Interpersonal communication through the sense of smell consists mainly of the signaling of sexual and social status by the use of perfumes and by culture-bound habits of personal hygiene. Throughout human history perfumes have had religious, medical, and hygienic uses. Nonetheless the main purpose of perfume has always been as an aphrodisiac acting through the sense of smell. The original species-propagating function of perfume materials in plants (insect attraction) and in animals (sexual attraction) is recapitulated in humans.

Odors continue to frustrate all attempts at chemical explanation, scientific classification, or correlation with other chemical properties. The smell of an individual odorant cannot be predicted from its chemical structure, nor can the attractiveness of a perfume be predicted from the individual scents that compose it. Perfumery remains more an art than a science.

Though perfumers have accumulated a large body of technical rules and scientific data on human responses to fragrant substances, no overall synthesis of these findings has emerged. It is clear that different perfumes, in different situations, have certain sexual and other interpersonal connotations. But whether responses to perfumes vary consistently with personality factors and the extent to which such variations are genetically or environmentally induced have not been determined. It would seem reasonable to assume, pending further evidence, that the response to any given blend of odorants is determined by an interaction of four elements: the composition of the perfume, the personality of the wearer, the personality of the perceiver, and the social circumstances in which the interaction occurs.

Smell in social communication. Failure to self-regulate olfactory emissions can lead to serious interpersonal problems. For example, some psychotic persons are described as emitting a cacophony of unusual or taboo nonverbal messages that the recipient does not consciously identify one by one but that on the whole produce a negative reaction, sometimes described as *Praecoxgefuehl.* Olfactory signals play an important role in evoking such rejections and counteraggressions.

In the rest of the animal kingdom the role of the sense of smell in social communication, particularly in eliciting attraction and revulsion, is much more clear-cut. It is obvious to any owner of a cat or a dog that these animals, at least, use olfactory cues to transmit to each other news on sexual status, aggressive mood, and territorial claim. Psychological data on such signals in pets remain anecdotal, but rodents in the laboratory have provided confirmation of the existence of these three types of signals. Chemical messengers in mice also transmit information on endocrine status, social status, and dominance as well as individual and group identity. Active substances serving as olfactory chemical messengers in these animals have been isolated. In addition, the following series of experimental discoveries has served to stretch our imagination concerning the possible range of olfactory messages:

1. Pregnancy block (Bruce effect): The rate of pregnancy failure in female rodents impregnated by one male increases sharply when they are exposed to olfactory stimuli from another male (this effect occurs at a distance and does not require the physical presence of the second male).
2. Adult male effect (Whitten effect): Puberty is slowed down in juvenile male mice when they are exposed to odors of adult males; in juvenile females, the same odor speeds up the development of puberty.
3. Genetic signals from lethal genes: About one in three wild house mice carries lethal alleles (half-genes). When males and females carrying the lethal alleles are mated, those offspring that receive lethal half-genes from both parents die during early fetal development. Carriers of the lethal allele are normal in appearance and behavior. They can be distinguished only retrospectively, by observing the outcome of matings. But female mice can recognize (and tend to avoid mating with) male carriers by odor alone.
4. Olfactory signals of genetic relatedness: Mice tend to select mates of different kinship genes from their own. This selection appears to be mediated

by olfactory chemical messengers that give information about the degree of similarity of the genetic makeup of the individuals. Such mate selection helps to improve the survival fitness of a mouse population by reducing inbreeding.
5. Olfactory signals from tranquilizer recipients: Male mice treated with diazepam are attacked more viciously by other mice because of an increased production of aggression-inciting urinary odors by the drug recipient's sex glands.
6. In groups of rhesus monkeys, mate selection is affected by chemical messengers (copulins) present in vaginal secretions. These substances provide the male with information about the hormonal status of the female.

Conscious and nonconscious perception of smell. Studies on rhesus copulins have served to stimulate research on analogous processes in humans. The nose and its brain connections, like all sense organs, accept some signals that are consciously perceived and others that are not. The entire system is best termed *olfaction,* divided into two functions: (1) the conscious sense of smell, and (2) out-of-awareness or nonconscious olfactory perception.

Humans possess a variety of secretory and excretory output systems and of brain circuits linked to olfactory input, which provide a rich substrate for olfactory emission and reception. These anatomical elements were formerly thought to be vestigial, but it is now understood that for us, as for our phylogenetic ancestors, meaningful olfactory communication may have a significant role to play.

Investigation of nonconscious human olfactory communication has been guided by two different but somewhat overlapping ideas: the pheromone hypothesis and the exohormone hypothesis. Experimental evidence tends to argue against the notion that humans emit species-specific substances that produce simple, clear-cut, reproducible behavioral responses (pheromones). But it is possible, though not proven, that there is a *complex* system of chemical emission and olfactory reception. These chemicals (exohormones or external chemical messengers) may be similar in nature and function to the many olfactory communicative substances found in lower animals.

Some phenomena have been observed in humans that are most simply explained by the presence of chemical-olfactory communication:

1. Menstrual synchrony. Groups of women living together at close quarters tend to show similar menstrual rhythms.
2. Alteration of menstrual timing by exposure to musk-type substances or to human armpit secretions.
3. Identification, on the basis of olfaction alone, of babies by their mothers and mothers by their babies.
4. The correct recognition of T-shirts of siblings and offspring on the basis of olfactory cues alone.
5. Mood changes. In young women olfactory exposure to the mammalian pheromone androstenol increases self-reports of irritability during menstrual periods and causes shifts in self-rating of moods from aggressive to submissive.

These phenomena are not, by themselves, of great moment. The auditory, visual, and motor channels carry interpersonal signals of far greater significance. What, then, explains the growing interest in research in olfactory signaling? Many important behavioral effects ascribable to olfactory communication have been identified in social mammals other than humans. If a number of these should in the future be discovered in our species as well, our understanding of human behavior and human communication could undergo profound change.

See also ANIMAL COMMUNICATION; ANIMAL SIGNALS.

Bibliography. Richard E. Brown and David W. McDonald, *Social Odours in Mammals,* 2 vols., New York, 1985; Richard L. Doty, "Olfactory Communication in Humans," *Chemical Senses* 6 (1981): 351–376; Trygg Engen, *The Perception of Odors,* New York, 1982; William McCartney, *Olfaction and Odours,* Berlin and New York, 1968; Harry Wiener, "Human Exocrinology: The Olfactory Component of Nonverbal Communication," in *Nonverbal Communication,* 2d ed., ed. by Shirley Weitz, New York, 1979.

HARRY WIENER

SOAP OPERA

Pejorative term coined in the United States in the 1930s for serialized DRAMA broadcast over RADIO in daytime hours, aimed at an audience of women, and in most cases sponsored by soap companies (*see* SPONSOR). The term was later applied to daytime television series and still later to prime-time serialized features such as "Peyton Place," "Dallas," and "Dynasty," although the GENRE underwent changes during these transitions. As the nighttime features won international distribution, the term acquired worldwide currency and was applied to programs in many countries, such as Britain's perennial "Coronation Street," India's "Hum Log" (We People), Italy's "Casa Cecilia," and Peru's "Simplemente María." *Soap opera* gradually lost its sardonic thrust and became merely the popular name for the genre, although networks and sponsors prefer to speak of "serial drama" in referring to their offerings. True soap operas, or "soaps," are designed to last as long as audiences and production budgets remain available. Thus they are distinguished from miniseries and from *telenovelas* that are serially presented but involve structured dramatic action leading to a final resolution.

History. Although SERIAL narrative has a long history in diverse media, early radio programmers tended to doubt its applicability to broadcasting on the ground that intermittent listening would negate the impact. The explosive success in the United States in the late 1920s of "Amos 'n' Andy" in a daily early evening spot on the NBC network scotched this notion. This series, which followed the tragicomic vicissitudes of two blacks on the south side of Chicago but was performed and written by two whites, not only proved the feasibility of radio serials but established techniques that became part of the genre. Its writers learned to devote weeks of programming to a single intensifying dilemma, such as a breach-of-promise suit brought by the Widow Parker against Andy. Day after day the impending trial was discussed, issues argued, advice given, daring stratagems weighed, perils assayed, threats made, lawyers consulted. Dramatic developments were few and could have been spanned in one half-hour drama. Far from losing listeners, the series showed that long sequences built around intractable dilemmas could actually increase audiences. They thus became a basic element in soap opera construction.

The success of "Amos 'n' Andy" precipitated daytime experiments, particularly by manufacturers of soap and other household products. Such sponsors favored time periods when many women were likely to be at home and in control of the radio dial. Several of these experiments, such as "Betty and Bob" and "Ma Perkins," soon won intensely loyal followers. By 1938 thirty-eight such offerings were on U.S. networks, all fifteen-minute serials broadcast five days a week.

Their merchandising function influenced soap operas from the start. Plots focused on human relations problems and glorified the woman's role. In this respect they paralleled and harmonized with the COMMERCIALS. Some of the series, such as "Ma Perkins," were built around helping-hand figures, towers of strength who saw other people through their problems. Other series, such as "Young Widder Brown," focused on characters who were themselves beset by afflictions but struggled through them. Still other series were built around relationships involving built-in, essentially insoluble tensions. "Backstage Wife" looked at marriage from the point of view of a woman whose husband moved in more glamorous circles than she did, always meeting women who represented potential threats. Would she remain interesting to him? In some series the dichotomy was a social one. The formula of "Our Gal Sunday" was articulated on each program. It asked, "Can a girl from a little mining town in the West find happiness as the wife of a wealthy and titled Englishman?"

Prominent among soap opera pioneers was Irna Phillips, a former schoolteacher who took up serial writing in the early 1930s and soon proved able to write several series simultaneously. In 1937 she started "The Guiding Light," which turned out to be almost indestructible. In 1941 it was discontinued but was then reinstated, reportedly in response to seventy-five thousand letters to its sponsor, Procter and Gamble. It remained on the radio until 1956, and meanwhile, in 1952, a television version was begun that proved even more durable than the radio series.

Of greater influence on soap opera production methods was the remarkable team of Frank and Ann Hummert, who at various times had twelve series on the air simultaneously. They outlined the action of each series in detail and hired free-lance writers, who remained uncredited, to "fill in the dialogue." The writers received their instructions in memorandums, by phone, or in meetings with assistants, but supervision was rigorous. These series were often called fantasy, but the Hummerts described them as true reflections of small-town American life and successful for that reason.

Impact on listeners. In the late 1930s researchers began to take an interest in soap operas and their audiences (*see* COMMUNICATIONS RESEARCH: ORIGINS AND DEVELOPMENT). Social psychologist Herta Herzog interviewed regular listeners to learn the kinds of satisfactions they derived from soap operas and was surprised at the number of listeners who spoke of the characters as though they were real people. The more complex a listener's own problems, the more serials she tended to follow. Many spoke of planning the day around their programs. Some looked to the series for guidance. An unmarried woman said, "I want to get an idea of how a wife should be to a husband." Other viewers offered help. Every series received letters addressed to the characters, giving advice or warning against other characters.

During World War II the U.S. government tried to channel soap opera loyalty into war needs. An envoy from the Office of War Information visited the Hummerts and discussed the anxieties of mothers who pictured their sons suffering under ruthless sergeants. The Hummerts cooperated by creating the series "Chaplain Jim," about a helping-hand figure in uniform ready to solve the problems of servicemen.

Transitions. There was widespread doubt that soap operas and their popularity could be transferred to television. Yet efforts began as television broadcasting resumed after World War II (*see* TELEVISION HISTORY). Early ventures seemed unpromising, but during the 1950s a number of series won a firm foothold in daytime schedules: "As the World Turns," "Search for Tomorrow," and "Love of Life," in addition to "The Guiding Light." By the mid-1960s television serials appeared to be an addiction comparable to the radio serial addiction at its zenith. An important step had been taken in the mid-1950s, when the fifteen-minute period of radio serials was expanded to a half hour. In the mid-1970s some serials shifted to a one-hour format, and most soon followed. These longer time periods necessitated more elaborate plotting and brought changes to the form. The serials also reflected the changing social milieu. Topics taboo in the puritanical world of prewar radio—divorce, illicit sex, illegitimacy—became staples of television soap opera.

In the complex hour-long serial, several interweaving sequences were constantly maintained, with the spotlight shifting from one to another. As one was resolved, another headed for a climax. In place of the small cluster of characters inhabiting a radio serial, the world of a television serial was likely to include as many as several dozen forming a community of innumerable relationships. A character might be husband to one, lover to a second, business rival to a third, threatened with blackmail by still another. Intrigue moved back and forth between home and business settings, with the serial seeming to proclaim the impermanence of all relationships. Business and professional occupations predominated in the often urban, primarily middle-class soap opera world (*see* PROFESSION).

The new complexity posed severe organizational challenges. A head writer was pivotal on most series, outlining action and commissioning further work from free-lance writers. Most series maintained a "bible" to keep track of the lives and interrelationships of characters. Occasional viewers were updated about important developments through information embedded in emotional passages of exhortation, recrimination, wooing, remorse, or threat. An additional device became available as soap operas switched from live broadcast to production on videotape, which became standard in the 1970s. This made it feasible to use flashbacks of key scenes, sometimes using shots with different camera angles. Another aid was provided by newspapers and magazines featuring summaries of soap opera events. Some periodicals were established solely for soap opera viewers, often including GOSSIP and profiles of soap STARS in addition to plot summaries.

With the soap opera invasion of the television evening, in most cases on a weekly basis, action moved into a milieu of still greater affluence, a world of power and family dynasties with sex and money as constant motifs. Vicious rivalries, blackmail, and double-dealing were pervading themes. A great diversity of products now sponsored the "soap" operas, reflecting advertiser awareness of their broader audience.

The adaptation of the soap opera format to prime time involved another significant shift, from videotape to production on film. This facilitated international distribution via dubbed versions in diverse languages, and many nations became familiar with U.S. prime-time soap operas. The wide distribution of these melodramatic, steamy depictions of U.S. life has had various ramifications. In the 1970s "Peyton Place" became one of the most popular series on Yugoslavia's state-controlled television. Its broadcast appeared to serve several Yugoslav purposes, indulging popular taste (*see* TASTE CULTURES) and at the same time permitting officials to point to the series as illustrative of the degradations produced by capitalism. A decade later "Dallas" won distribution and popularity in diverse cultures, including such places as Saudi Arabia.

Such developments have provided researchers with unique opportunities to study not only the effects of the genre (*see* MASS MEDIA EFFECTS) but also how mass media messages are translated across cultures (*see* INTERCULTURAL COMMUNICATION). The popularity and durability of the form has also drawn attention to the structure and function of soap opera NARRATIVE; to the genre's antecedents in nineteenth-century FICTION, particularly the so-called domestic novel (*see* LITERATURE, POPULAR); and to the relationship of soap opera themes and content to those of other fictional forms directed at female audiences, such as the romance (*see* FOTONOVELA; ROMANCE, THE).

Bibliography. Robert C. Allen, *Speaking of Soap Operas,* Chapel Hill, N.C., 1985; Erik Barnouw, *A History of Broadcasting in the United States,* 3 vols., New York, 1966–1970; Muriel G. Cantor and Suzanne Pingree, *The Soap Opera,* Beverly Hills, Calif., 1983.

ERIK BARNOUW

SOCIAL COGNITIVE THEORY (SOCIAL LEARNING THEORY)

Because of the influential role the mass media play in society, understanding the psychosocial mechanisms through which symbolic communication influences human thought, emotion, and action is of considerable import. Social cognitive theory explains psychosocial functioning in terms of triadic reciprocal causation. In this model of reciprocal determinism, behavior, cognitive and other personal factors, and environmental events all operate as interacting determinants of one another (Figure 1). Interacting factors work their mutual effects sequentially over variable time courses. Reciprocal causation provides people with opportunities to exercise some control over events in their lives, but also sets limits to self-direction.

Mediating mechanisms. In analyzing the personal determinants of psychosocial functioning, social cognitive theory accords a central role to cognitive,

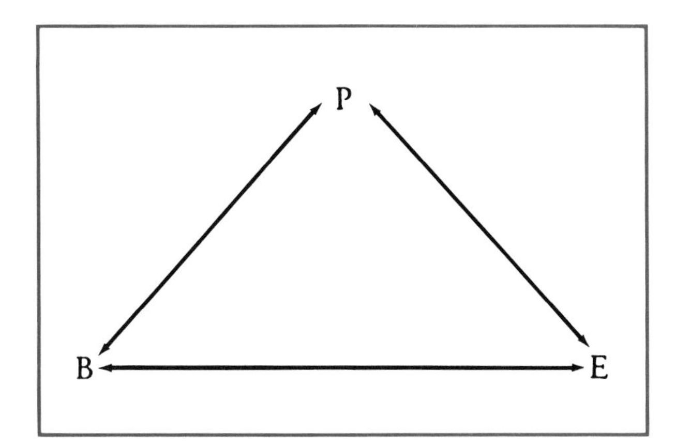

Figure 1. *(Social Cognitive Theory)* Schematic representation of reciprocal determinism. *B* signifies behavior, *P* the cognitive and other internal events that can affect perceptions and actions, and *E* the external environment.

vicarious, self-regulatory, and self-reflective processes. Symbolization provides people with a powerful instrument for comprehending their environment and for creating and regulating environmental events that touch virtually every aspect of their lives. It is with symbols that people process and transform transient experiences into internal models that serve as guides for future action. Through symbols people give meaning, form, and continuity to their past experiences. However, in keeping with the interactional perspective, social cognitive theory devotes much attention to the social origins of thought and the mechanisms through which social factors exert their influence.

People are not only knowers and performers. They are also self-reactors with a capacity for self-direction. The self-regulation of motivation and action operates partly through internal standards and evaluative reactions to one's own behavior. Discrepancies between behavior and personal standards generate evaluative reactions, which serve as motivators and guides for action. The capability of forethought adds another dimension to the process of self-regulation. Most human behavior is directed toward goals and outcomes projected into the future. Because future events have no actual existence, they cannot be causes of behavior. However, by being represented cognitively in the present, conceived futures can have causal impact on current behavior.

The capacity to reflect on one's own thinking and personal efficacy is another dimension that receives prominent attention in social cognitive theory. In verifying thought by introspection, people monitor their ideas, act on them, or predict occurrences from them; they then judge from the results the adequacy of their thoughts and change them accordingly. People's judgments of their efficacy to exert control over events that affect their lives play a central role in human agency. People's belief in their personal efficacy influences what courses of action they choose to pursue, how much effort they will invest, how long they will persevere in the face of difficulties, their thought patterns, and their emotional reactions in transactions with the environment.

Psychological theories have traditionally emphasized learning through the effects of one's actions. Humans have also evolved an advanced capacity for observational learning that is better suited for expeditious acquisition of competencies and survival than is learning solely from the consequences of trial and error. Numerous studies have shown that virtually all learning phenomena resulting from direct experience can occur vicariously by observing people's behavior and its consequences for them. The capacity to acquire by observation the conceptions and rules of behavior portrayed symbolically enables people to transcend the bounds of their immediate environment.

Processes governing observational learning. Observational learning is governed by four component processes, which are depicted in Figure 2. *Attentional processes* determine what is selectively observed in the profusion of modeling influences and what information is extracted from ongoing modeled events; people cannot be much influenced by observed events if they do not remember them. A second major subfunction governing observational learning concerns *retention processes.* Retention involves transforming and restructuring information about events for memory representation in the form of rules and conceptions. In the third subfunction in modeling—the *behavioral production process*—symbolic conceptions are translated into appropriate courses of action. This is achieved through a conception-matching process in which behavior patterns are altered until they reflect the internal conception.

The fourth subfunction in modeling concerns *motivational processes.* Social cognitive theory distinguishes between acquisition and performance because people do not enact everything they learn. Performance of observationally learned behavior is influenced by three major types of incentive motivators: direct, vicarious, and self-produced. People are more likely to exhibit modeled behavior if it results in valued outcomes than if it has unrewarding or punishing effects. The observed costs and benefits accruing to others influence the performance of modeled patterns in much the same way as do directly experienced consequences. Personal standards of conduct provide a further source of incentive motivation. The evaluative reactions people generate to their own behavior regulate which observationally learned activities they are most likely to pursue. They express what they find satisfying and reject what they personally disapprove of.

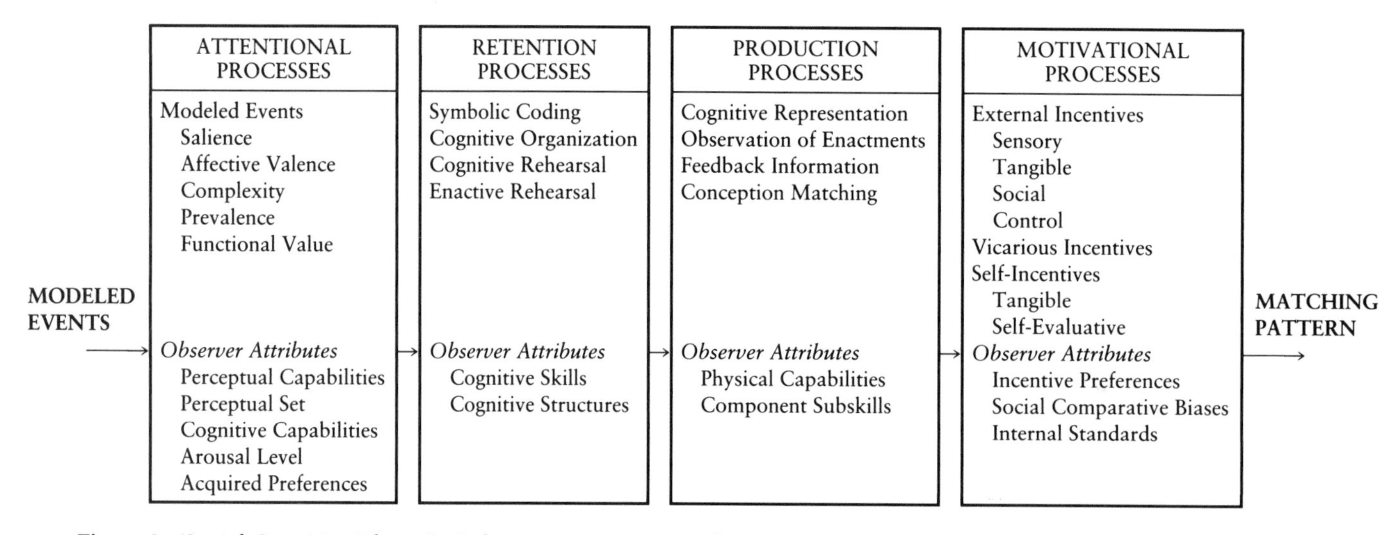

Figure 2. *(Social Cognitive Theory)* Subprocesses governing observational learning.

Modeling is not merely a process of behavioral mimicry. Highly functional patterns of behavior, which constitute the proven skills and established customs of a culture, may be adopted in essentially the same form as they are portrayed. However, modeling influences convey rules for generative and innovative behavior as well. Through the process of abstract modeling, observers extract the rules underlying specific activities for generating behavior that goes beyond what they have seen or heard. Acquiring rules from modeled information involves at least three processes: extracting relevant attributes from social exemplars, integrating the information into composite rules, and using the rules to produce new instances of behavior. By this means, people acquire, among other things, judgmental standards, linguistic rules, styles of inquiry, information-processing skills, and standards of self-evaluation. Evidence that generative rules of thought and conduct can be created through abstract modeling attests to the broad scope of observational learning.

Multiple functions of modeling. Social cognitive theory distinguishes among several modeling functions, each governed by different determinants and underlying mechanisms. In addition to cultivating new competencies, modeling influences can strengthen or weaken inhibitions over behavior that has been previously learned. The effects of modeling on behavioral restraint rely heavily on the information conveyed about the performability and probable consequences of modeled courses of action. The impact of such information on personal restraint depends on several factors: observers' judgments of their ability to accomplish the modeled behavior, their perception of the modeled actions as producing favorable or adverse consequences, and their inferences that similar or unlike consequences would result if they themselves were to engage in analogous activities. Inhibitory and disinhibitory effects of modeling have been studied most extensively in relation to transgressive, aggressive, and sexual behavior.

The actions of others can also serve as social prompts for previously learned behavior that observers can perform but have not done so because of insufficient inducements, rather than because of inhibition. One can get people to behave altruistically, to volunteer their services, to delay or seek gratification, to prefer certain foods and apparel, to converse on particular topics, to be inquisitive or passive, to think innovatively or conventionally, or to engage in almost any course of action by having such conduct exemplified. Such social facilitation effects are distinguished from observational learning and disinhibition because no new behavior has been acquired, and disinhibitory processes are not involved because the elicited behavior is socially acceptable and unencumbered by restraints. The actions of models acquire the power to activate, channel, and sustain behavior when they are good predictors for observers that positive results can be gained by similar conduct.

Social interactions commonly involve displays of emotion. Seeing models express emotional reactions tends to elicit emotional arousal in observers. If the emotional expressions of others aroused observers only fleetingly, it would be of some interest but of little psychological import. What gives significance to vicarious influence is that people can acquire enduring attitudes and emotional dispositions toward places, persons, and things associated with the model's arousal. They learn to fear the things that frightened the models, to dislike what repulsed them, and to enjoy what pleased them. Fears and intractable phobias are ameliorated by modeling influences that convey information about coping strategies for exercising control over threatening events. Values can be both developed and altered vicariously through the evaluative reactions modeled by persons who wield social influences.

Because of severe constraints of time, mobility, and resources, people have direct contact with only a small sector of the vast collection of physical and social environments. In their daily routines they travel the same limited routes, visit the same familiar places, and see the same groups of associates. As a result, people form impressions of many social realities, with which they have little or no contact, from symbolic representations of society, mainly by the mass media. To a large extent, people act on their images of reality. Because of its appeal and pervasiveness, televised modeling has become an influential acculturator (*see* CULTURAL INDICATORS).

In sum, modeling influences serve diverse functions: as tutors, inhibitors, disinhibitors, facilitators, emotion arousers, and shapers of values and images of reality. Although the different modeling functions can operate separately, they often work concurrently. Thus, for example, in the spread of new styles of aggression, models serve as both teachers and disinhibitors. When novel modeled conduct is punished, observers learn the conduct that was punished as well as the restraints. A novel example can both teach and prompt similar acts.

Social diffusion through symbolic modeling. Symbolic modeling can transmit knowledge of wide applicability to vast numbers of people simultaneously. Social cognitive theory analyzes social DIFFUSION of new behavior patterns in terms of three constituent processes and the psychosocial factors that govern them: the acquisition of knowledge about innovative behaviors, the adoption of these behaviors in practice, and the social networks through which they spread.

Symbolic modeling is often the principal conveyer of innovations to widely dispersed areas, especially in the early stages of diffusion. It has been commonly assumed in the theory of mass communication that modeling influences operate through a two-step diffusion process. Influential persons pick up new ideas from the media and pass them on to their followers through personal influence (*see* OPINION LEADER). Evidence reveals no single pattern of social diffusion. Analyses of the roles that the mass media play in social diffusion must distinguish between their effect on learning and on adoptive use, and examine how media and social influences affect these separable processes. In some instances the media both teach new forms of behavior and create motivators for action by altering people's value preferences, perceptions of personal efficacy, and outcome expectations. In other instances the media teach, but adopters provide the motivation for others to perform what has been learned observationally. In still other instances people who have had no exposure to the media can be influenced by adopters who have had the exposure and then, themselves, become the transmitters of the new ways. Within these various patterns of social diffusion, the media can serve as originating as well as reinforcing influences.

The acquisition of knowledge and skills regarding new forms of behavior is necessary but not sufficient for their adoption in practice. A number of factors determine whether people will act on what they have learned; environmental inducements serve as one set of regulators. Adoptive behavior is also highly susceptible to incentive motivators, which may involve social and monetary benefits or self-satisfactions derived from the new activity. Innovations spread at different rates and patterns because they differ in the skills and resources they require for successful adoption. Such prerequisites serve as additional determinants of the diffusion process.

The third major factor that affects the diffusion process concerns social network structures (*see* NETWORK ANALYSIS). People are linked to each other directly by personal relationships or indirectly by interconnected ties. Information regarding new ideas and social practices is often conveyed through multilinked relationships. People with many social ties are more apt to adopt innovations than those who have few ties to others. Adoption rates increase as more people in one's personal network adopt an innovation. The effects of social connectedness on adoptive behavior may be mediated through several processes. Multilinked relations can foster adoption of innovations because they convey more factual information and mobilize stronger social influences; or it may be that people with close ties are more receptive to new ideas than those who are socially estranged. Moreover, in social transactions people see their associates adopt innovations as well as talk about them. Multiple modeling alone can increase adoptive behavior.

The course of diffusion is best understood by considering the interactions among psychosocial determinants, properties of innovations, and network structures. While structural interconnectedness provides potential diffusion paths, psychosocial factors are likely to determine the fate of what diffuses through those paths. Structural and psychological determinants of adoptive behavior should be included as complementary factors in a theory of social diffusion, rather than be cast as rival theories of diffusion.

See also CHILDREN—MEDIA EFFECTS; MASS COMMUNICATIONS RESEARCH; MASS MEDIA EFFECTS; PERSUASION; VIOLENCE.

Bibliography. Albert Bandura, *Aggression: A Social Learning Analysis,* Englewood Cliffs, N.J., 1973; idem, *The Self and Mechanisms of Agency,* Englewood Cliffs, N.J., 1982; idem, *Social Foundations of Thought and Action: A Social Cognitive Theory,* Englewood Cliffs, N.J., 1986.

ALBERT BANDURA

SOCIAL INSECTS. *See* INSECTS, SOCIAL.

SOCIAL SKILLS

Those patterns or styles of social behavior that produce some degree of effectiveness in making friends or in achieving other social goals. Individuals vary in all aspects of social PERFORMANCE, but in particular they vary in effectiveness. While some are brilliant orators, therapists, or managers, others are lonely, shy, or have great difficulty in coping with some situations or relationships. The concept of social skill developed as an analogy with motor skill; in each case there is feedback leading to corrective action and to attainment of goals. The additional implication in the social skill model is that social performance could be made more effective by social skills training.

The Meaning and Assessment of Social Competence

By social competence is meant the ability to cope successfully with social situations and relationships. One's goals may be personal, such as making friends and influencing people, or professional, such as more effective TEACHING, selling, or interviewing. The best way of assessing social competence is in terms of results—patients cured, productivity of group, total sales, popularity—keeping in mind, of course, that the people being assessed may be in somewhat different situations (e.g., selling different kinds of goods). Role-played tests have been found to be rather unreliable. Some police departments have made use of reactions to videotaped vignettes. Ratings of one's own performance are useful, as are lists of situations that trainees rate for degree of difficulty or discomfort. These methods can be followed by interviews to find out more about the nature of the inadequacy. In social skills training in clinical settings it is usual to agree on goals for training, for example, to stop quarreling or to make a friend.

In order to carry out social skills training one must know what skills to teach. The traditional strategy has been to compare groups of effective and ineffective performers, discover how their social behavior differs, and teach effective skills to those who lack them. However, the differences may be quite subtle, and causes and effects may not be so obvious.

Research on Social Interaction Related to Social Skills

Several areas of social interaction research bear directly on issues of social competence and have implications for how social skills training should be done.

Handling difficult situations. Schemes of social skills training are often built around the range of situations found most difficult by the client involved. Some situations are quite commonly found difficult, such as making complaints or dealing with conflict, difficult superiors, or public performances. Situations can be analyzed using the analogy of games. In order to cope with them effectively, the necessary goals, rules, and other properties must be understood, and special skills must be learned.

The *rules* are behaviors that should or should not be performed. They are functional in relation to situational goals, as, for example, in the case of the rule of the road. Some rules are fairly general, such as "Be friendly"; others are specific to particular kinds of situations, such as "Keep to cheerful topics of CONVERSATION." The *goals* are central to situations, as are the relationships between them, how much they interfere with or enhance one another. People who undergo social skills training often do not understand what the goals of situations are. The *physical environment* is the aspect of situations that can be changed most easily.

Social skills training can be situationally focused if a group of clients finds the same situations difficult. This is done in intercultural learning; it often focuses on the main situations in the other culture that cause problems, such as shopping or dealing with women.

Nonverbal communication. Patients with social difficulties smile, look, and GESTURE less than others. In order to make friends it is necessary to send positive nonverbal signals. The FACE and the voice are the most important channels for signaling emotions and ATTITUDES to others. Studies of distressed marriages have found that it is usually husbands who are bad at sending positive signals. Teachers, nurses, and others in social service professions have to control their true emotional states and to avoid revealing their true emotions through voice or body. Training for INTERCULTURAL COMMUNICATION must take into account different gesture repertoires, INTERPERSONAL DISTANCE rules, and other nonverbal markers. For example, Arabs and Latin Americans stand closer, at a more direct angle, and talk and touch more in face-to-face interaction than northern and western Europeans do. *See also* BODY MOVEMENT; FACIAL EXPRES-

SION; INTERACTION, FACE-TO-FACE; NONVERBAL COMMUNICATION; PROXEMICS.

Conversational skills. Some socially unskilled people cannot sustain a conversation at all. Some have special ways of killing conversation, such as giving short answers to polite questions and not reciprocating or leading the conversation forward. One approach to learning these skills has been to point out principles on which good conversation is based, such as those put forward by the philosopher H. Paul Grice as conversational maxims. Some of these are "Be relevant to what has been said before," "Be responsive to previous speaker," and "Make your contribution no less and no more informative than is required." Others that can be suggested are "Don't monopolize the conversation," "Be polite," and—once again—"Be friendly."

Specialized conversation sequences can be learned, for example, for teaching, sales, and management-union negotiation (*see also* BARGAINING). HUMOR is an important conversational skill; it can avert conflict and soften criticism by discharging tension and redefining the situation as less serious or threatening.

Long-term relationships. Most social behavior takes place with friends, kin, and workmates, and many difficulties arise in connection with these relationships. They are important because happiness, health, mental health, and even length of life are improved by strong, supportive relationships. Relationships either buffer the effects of stress or have direct positive effects.

Generally accepted *informal rules* develop for each relationship to contain the main conflicts. For neighbors these can be about noise, fences, and pets, while for marriage there can be rules about faithfulness, creating a harmonious home atmosphere, engaging in sexual activity, and being tolerant of each other's friends. Collapse of friendship is attributed to the breaking of friendship rules, particularly those about rewardingness (see below), and third-party rules, like keeping confidences, standing up for the other in his or her absence, and not being jealous. The rules do not entirely include the *skills* of handling relationships.

A correct *understanding* of the basic properties of different kinds of relationships is important. Sometimes the problem is not a deficiency in social skills but unrealistic expectations about what a relationship will provide. For example, a high level of conflict can be normal in marriage and can be perfectly compatible with a high level of satisfaction. Friendship is not just about receiving rewards from others, as children and disturbed adolescents without friends think. Friendship involves loyalty, commitment, and concern for the other.

Men and women typically have different needs for social skills training. Women are usually more socially competent than men in a number of areas: they are more sensitive to nonverbal signals and more skilled in managing them, they are more rewarding and polite, they are likely to reveal more about themselves and form closer friendships, and they are better at reducing the loneliness of others. However, it is mostly women who seek assertiveness training. In addition many studies have shown that women like to form close friendships with equals but are less able or willing to cope with hierarchical, structured groups engaged in joint tasks and rarely emerge as leaders of such groups.

Self-presentation and self-disclosure. The sending of information about the self is done partly through words, though there is a taboo on making any positive claims too directly. It is also done through choice of CLOTHING, together with other aspects of appearance, speech style, and general social manner. Self-presentation can go wrong in various ways, especially by projecting an inappropriate image. *Self-disclosure*—revealing information about oneself to others—is normally gradual and reciprocated; the most common failure is not disclosing enough. Recent research suggests that some lonely people spend as much time with friends as do people who are not lonely; the difference is in their lower level of self-disclosure. They also lack other social skills; for example, they are less rewarding to others.

Rewardingness. Being rewarding to others is one of the main ways of influencing them during social interaction, such as showing interest and approval when a particular topic is mentioned. It is also one of the main sources of popularity.

Rewardingness is very important for friendship. The rewards that are needed include being affectionate, helpful, sympathetic, interested, cheerful, and fun to be with. One of the main problems in disturbed marriages is the lack of rewards and the high level of negative messages, such as criticism, which tends to be reciprocated. Rewardingness is important in all professional skills, including supervision of others.

Perception of nonverbal communication. In order to respond effectively to others it is necessary to perceive them correctly, including their emotions and attitudes. Socially skilled individuals are more accurate decoders, whereas anxious persons overestimate signs of rejection. Sensitivity can be measured by tests in which photographs, films, or audiotapes are presented, as in the PONS test developed by U.S. psychologist Robert Rosenthal. There can be problems detecting DECEPTION on the part of others; the face is particularly well controlled and can be misleading. Whereas women are somewhat more accurate decoders than men, they also attend more to faces and perceive what others intend them to; men attend to the "leakier" channels of voice and body. Training can be given in decoding by studying photographs and audio recordings of the voice.

In addition the socially unskilled are often very bad at assessing the thoughts or emotions of others. Training can include role-reversal exercises or simple interviewing to discover another's ideas and point of view.

Methods of social skills training. Social skills training has many applications. It is used with certain kinds of mental patients, and it is widely used in the training of teachers, managers, doctors, and others who have to deal with people. Some forms of training are becoming available to the general public, such as assertiveness training, marital therapy, and instruction in cross-cultural skills for those who are going to work abroad. The most widely used method at present is an elaborated version of role playing. There are three or four phases:

1. Explanation and modeling, live or from VIDEO
2. Role playing with other trainees or stooges
3. Comments from trainer and playback of videotape
4. Repeat performance (optional)

A serious problem is how to generalize from role playing to real-life situations. For those not inside institutions, homework is often used: trainees are asked to repeat the exercises (e.g., to make someone else talk more, or less) between sessions in real-life settings and to report back. However, for some professional skills, like those of managers and police officers, role-played sessions are too far removed from reality, so there has been a growth of on-the-job training.

Some of the research described has led to suggestions for specific forms of training apart from role playing. Examples are (1) nonverbal communication training using mirrors and audio and video recorders to train face and voice; (2) role reversal to improve ability to see others' viewpoints; (3) situation analysis to deal with specific difficult situations; (4) self-presentation to try to change appearance, accent, and the like; and (5) conversational analysis to correct errors by detailed observation of conversational style.

Lecture and discussion methods were abandoned long ago as methods of social skills training because they were found to be ineffective and also because motor skills cannot be learned this way. Conversational, intercultural, and relationship skills involve some understanding of the principles of conversational structure. In all these cases direct teaching may be the best method.

Bibliography. Michael Argyle, *The Psychology of Interpersonal Behaviour,* 4th ed., Harmondsworth, Eng., 1983; Michael Argyle and Monika Henderson, *The Anatomy of Relationships,* London, 1985; Stephen Bochner, ed., *Cultures in Contact,* Oxford, 1982; Paul Ekman and Wallace V. Friesen, *Unmasking the Face,* Englewood Cliffs, N.J., 1975; C. R. Hollin and P. Trower, *Handbook of Social Skills Training,* Oxford, 1986; Robert Rosenthal, ed., *Skill in Nonverbal Communication: Individual Differences,* Cambridge, Mass., 1979; William T. Singleton, P. Spurgeon, and R. B. Stammers, eds., *The Analysis of Social Skills,* New York, 1980; Sue Spence and Geoff Shepherd, *Developments in Social Skills Training,* London and New York, 1983.

MICHAEL ARGYLE

SONG

The term *song* is both elusive and enigmatic when considered cross-culturally. Birds, porpoises, and other animals have "songs"; does this mean that they are "singing"? And what of such creatures as the sirens of Greek mythology who were said to be able to lure sailors to their destruction through song? Is song, then, unlike spoken LANGUAGE, not a basically human activity, characteristic, and preoccupation? *See* ANIMAL SONG.

Do songs have to have music? There are numerous examples of books that have not one note of music in them yet are called *cancioneros, chansonniers,* or *canzonieri.* For the most part, however, it can be assumed that songs do have music and are usually intended to be sung. Singing can take place with or without instrumental accompaniment, alone or in groups, and with many different kinds of audience. *See* MUSIC PERFORMANCE; PERFORMANCE.

Language and song. It is axiomatic that both the SPEECH and the song of a society will be largely in the same language. That language, in turn, can logically be expected to have an effect on both types of vocal production.

Two major varieties of SOUND organization in language—pitch and tone—directly influence the nature of song. For example, aspects of song such as melodic contour, monotone (repetition at a single tonal level), vocable (the use of vocalized nonlexical syllables), scale type, and ambitus (pitch range) all vary according to whether the language is a tone language (e.g., Chinese) or a pitch language (e.g., English).

In speech, pitch languages may use any vocal frequency (fundamental) to generate the formants (resulting pitches) that create vowels in words. Although there are particular conventions for speaking, any pitches may be used in any sequence without altering the lexical MEANING of words. Pitch languages use variation of the fundamental to modify, clarify, or amplify the lexical content of sentences. This conventional pitch fluctuation is called intonation, and it comprises a complex system of speech melodies or intonation contours.

Tone languages, in contrast, use the fundamental frequency in two ways for speech. The fundamental generates the formants of which vowels are composed in both pitch and tone languages. However, the relative pitch of the fundamental is also varied in tone languages, so that the tone also assumes a phonemic (meaningful lexical) value. As described by U.S. linguist Kenneth Pike, some tone languages, the *register languages,* distinguish various high and low levels of tonemes (significant tonal levels). Others, the *contour languages,* employ tonemes with ascending and descending portamento (continuous gliding motion between tones).

The special language of song. Song melodies must at least partially reflect the tonemes of speech intonation in both pitch and tone languages. But the phonemic importance of tone may have a greater effect on melodic contour of songs in tone languages than it would in pitch-language songs, making cross-cultural comparison of vocal genres hazardous.

Thus the intonation patterns of the spoken language must be followed in song to a certain extent so that song texts may be understood by the audience. But music often requires alterations in normal speech patterns, or special language usage.

For example, Elsdon Best, writing about Maori music, notes the alteration of words in song texts for the sake of euphony: "Vowels may be inserted, elided, or altered, or an extra syllable may be added to a word. . . . not only do song makers employ archaic expressions and resurrect obsolete words, but they also sometimes coin a word." Another example is the Cherokee, who employ three main alterations from normal conversational speech: (1) aphesis, the loss of unstressed initial vowels or syllables; (2) syncope, contraction by omitting something from the middle of a word; and (3) apocope, the omission of the last part of a word. In addition, there is both prefixing and infixing of vocables, primarily the vowel *ah,* the use of archaic Cherokee word forms, and cryptic referents to generalized areas of meaning.

The use of archaic words and phrases in song might logically be expected in the context of religious music, especially when words are carefully retained over long periods of time and are thought to carry power. Although this is a common instance in which archaic words are found, they are equally likely in children's songs. Maltese children's songs, for example, seem to be retained over long periods of time. They may use styles and forms no longer current in adult music. In addition to using a special "children's language," texts often refer to archaic, historical systems of weight, measurement, or money. For example, one children's song refers to a *habba* (worth about one-twelfth of a penny), which has not been a Maltese coin in over a hundred years.

Boundaries and varieties of speech and song. Most cultures identify speaking and singing as two distinct forms of vocal production. Yet between these two terms can lie a multitude of indeterminate forms. Attention must be paid both to contextual, locally meaningful emic definitions and to aural commonalities in order to account for all the different forms of singing that occur.

U.S. ethnomusicologist George List's seminal 1963 article, "The Boundaries of Speech and Song," proposes a continuum for which the poles are speech and song. Recognizing all vocal production as musical, List attempts to establish a means of classifying those forms falling between the two polar boundaries. In Table 1, the top line represents speech intonation, which is gradually negated until a stabilized pitch is reached in the monotone zone of the continuum, followed by a gradual expansion of scale structure approaching song. The bottom line represents the gradual expansion of speech intonation toward the *Sprechstimme* zone of the continuum, followed by an increase of pitch stability as one moves toward song.

This continuum is useful, but it does not account for all types of song. List requires that any member of the song category have relatively stable pitches, a scalar structure at least as elaborate as the heptatonic (with seven notes), and little or no melodic influence from speech intonation (*see* MUSIC THEORIES—TUNING SYSTEMS). Further, he excludes all forms that are composed entirely of vocables and therefore lack "meaningful" text. These restrictions, if employed in a definition of song, would effectively eliminate much of what is recognized as song by societies throughout the world.

Perhaps more useful is a distinction between speech and song that examines intonational phenomena. Noting that speech melody must use a fundamental to produce the formants, or tone harmonics, that differentiate vowels, U.S. linguist Dwight Bolinger asserts that whereas in speech the fundamental communicates the notions of syntax and affect in pitch languages and defines one dimension of lexical meaning in tone languages, it is of secondary importance to the formants produced. Song melody, on the other hand, emphasizes the fundamental, whereas the formants produced—although important to understanding the text itself—are of secondary importance in song.

With this distinction it becomes possible analytically to account for the variety of vocal phenomena

Table 1. Chart for Classifying Forms Intermediate to Speech and Song

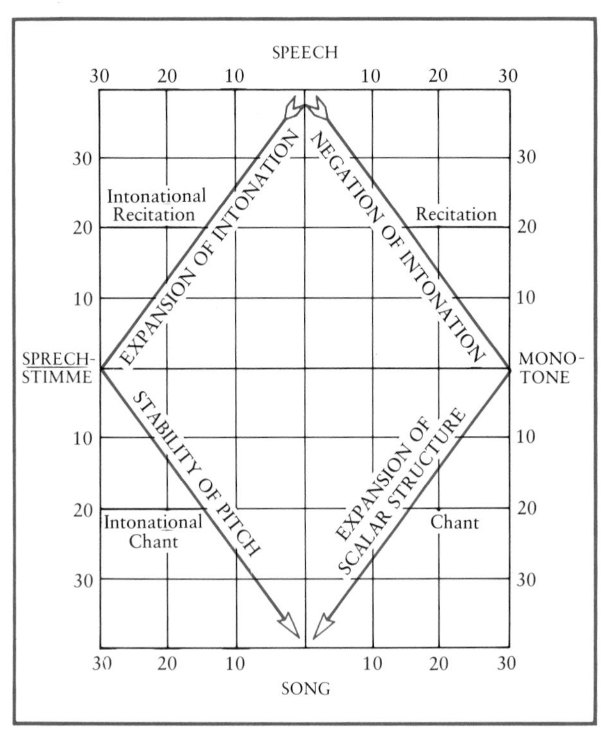

Redrawn after George List, "The Boundaries of Speech and Song," *Ethnomusicology* 7 (1963): 9.

that lie between speech and song based on the relative degree of emphasis on formant or fundamental. This is of primary importance if comparative work is being undertaken, but it is also useful in dealing with ambiguous or mixed forms.

For example, performers of country-and-western songs in the United States may use a technique of vocal production in which lyrics are recited, not sung, but which nevertheless feels more melodic than spoken, more intoned than enunciated. In this technique, in which an instrumental accompaniment plays the harmony and melody of the song, performers abandon the production of fundamental frequencies in a fixed sequence in favor of loose connection to the musical accompaniment. The result, analytically, is not quite song but is more clearly related to the French *diseuse* technique of vocal production.

Awareness of the varieties of vocal production is not limited to scholarly analysis. The Cherokee, for example, distinguish a continuum of four modes of communication: thinking, muttering, speaking, and singing. The sung form is thought to carry the greatest amount of power and is only used when a high degree of power is needed to balance a particular situation.

Verbal performance and cultural expression. The varieties of verbal performance, performance contexts, and modes of aesthetic evaluation are all context sensitive. Types of vocal expression have a central role in folk and popular culture.

Areas of conflict, for example, exist among all people and are often solved ritually (*see* RITUAL). Whether conflicts have arisen inadvertently or have been deliberately sought, song or other types of verbal performance are likely to be involved.

Patriotic songs are often used to get youths to join the cause of war. The Germans in World War I were enjoined to "Keep Watch on the Rhine." The United States at the same time sang about going "Over There" and knew that it was a "Long, Long Way to Tipperary." In World War II emotions in the United States were stirred by a song enjoining everyone to "Remember Pearl Harbor as We Did the Alamo." Indeed, war-oriented songs are commonplace in state-mobilized societies. In contrast, the absence of such songs in the United States during the Korean and Vietnamese conflicts may underscore reasons for lack of public support.

War cries heard in combat zones and commands shouted on military parade grounds, although not song, possess many of the characteristics of song. Often the words themselves are not distinguishable, but the interval patterns are sufficient for clarity.

Verbal combat is found in many parts of the world in the form of the song duel. Some societies use it for entertainment or for the release of aggression, but others use it to settle legal disputes. In most instances the song duel involves two people singing to each other within a formal system, each attempting to compose and perform a verse to INSULT, belittle, ridicule, or devastate the other.

Song may also be used to prepare individuals and groups for combat or conflict or to urge them on to greater efforts. The Cherokee, for example, make heavy use of songs to transform people who are headed for conflict from the "white" (everyday) to the "red" (aggressive) condition; after the conflict is over, songs are again used to reverse the transformation. In other tribal groups boasting songs may be used as an acceptable means of presenting information that otherwise would be taboo. A related form of verbal performance is the cheering at football games and other formalized conflicts.

Song is also heavily used in connection with ceremonies and ritual acts promoting well-being, restoring balance, or curing illness. This may be seen as yet another kind of conflict resolution because two opposing forces are usually thought to be at work.

These kinds of verbal performance range widely in length, complexity, and intention. In all cases, however, song may be said to sacralize time, space, and being, creating an atmosphere in which paranormal acts can be performed and opposing forces brought to a point of resolution.

Those points in the human life cycle that are

recognized as important in a given society will be marked by song and ceremony. In this instance song marks and gives protection in the liminal phase of a rite of passage.

As a form of cultural expression, song is associated with marked events, transformations, and the resolution of conflict. It serves to create special kinds of temporal-spatial continua as well as to signal the support of the social system. Those more ambiguous forms of verbal production falling in between speech and song serve similar but less marked purposes.

See also MUSIC, FOLK AND TRADITIONAL; MUSIC, POPULAR; MUSIC HISTORY.

Bibliography. Elsdon Best, *The Maori,* 2 vols. (Memoirs of the Polynesian Society, Vol. 5), Wellington, New Zealand, 1924; Dwight Bolinger, ed., *Intonation,* Baltimore, Md., and Harmondsworth, Eng., 1972; Marcia Herndon, "The Cherokee Ballgame Cycle: An Ethnomusicologist's View," *Ethnomusicology* 15 (1971): 339–352; idem, "Sound, Danger, and Balanced Response," in *Essays on Anthropology and Music,* ed. by Charlotte Frisbie (Detroit Monographs in Musicology, No. 9), Detroit, 1986; George List, "The Boundaries of Speech and Song," *Ethnomusicology* 7 (1963): 1–16; Alan P. Merriam, *The Anthropology of Music,* Evanston, Ill., 1964; Kenneth Pike, "General Characteristics of Intonation," in *Intonation,* ed. by Dwight Bolinger, Baltimore, Md., and Harmondsworth, Eng., 1972; idem, *Phonemics,* Ann Arbor, Mich., 1968.

MARCIA HERNDON

SOUND

The term *sound* suggests a wide range of related communications phenomena in natural and human history. Although *sound communications* is often used specifically with regard to audio technologies, the auditory channel, or the perceptual mechanism involving the ear and brain, one might better use the phrase to refer to the overall study of articulation, production, interpretation, and value judgments that relate sounds—natural and human, face-to-face or mass-mediated—to their social meanings. In this sense sound communications parallels the study of visual communications; each of these areas of communications research addresses a variety of contexts, cultures, media, and codes, and each builds data and theory on disciplinary perspectives from the physical, natural, and social sciences, the humanities, and the fine arts.

Traditional approaches to sound focus on the intertwined yet analytically separable facets of acoustic production and aural reception. Production and the material properties of any natural or human sound are generally studied from the standpoint of acoustics, physics, and engineering. In this domain emphasis is placed on the determination and measurement of patterned pressure waves and on the delimitation of frequency, intensity, and quality. Reception and the processes of auditory sensation, perception, and COGNITION are studied from the perspectives of physiology, psychology, and psychoacoustics (*see* PERCEPTION—MUSIC). Here emphasis is placed on the delimitation and measurement of auditory sensations of pitch, loudness, and timbre; on the physical mechanism of the ear; on hearing and auditory theory; on phenomena such as masking, echo and reverberation, Doppler and binaural effects, and localization; as well as on SPEECH and music learning, memory, and general cognitive processing.

Although these areas involve primary scientific research of a very significant nature, their centerpiece has been neither the question of communication per se nor of sound and social MEANING. The production and perception of sound tend to be described in ahistorical and culture-free terms, independent of issues of interpretation. Yet when a sound is made, and when it is heard, more than a chain (object → channel → sense organ → neural impulse → brain state → perception) is set into operation. A pair of ears connected to a brain, subjected to and perceiving stimuli, is a necessary but not a total model of the production and reception of sound. It is merely a skeletal model of human sound communications, because the enormous variety of adaptive and learned overlays that we call CULTURE provides the concepts through which humans transform, experience, and interpret perceptions as situated, historically and socially meaningful symbols; hence the rationale for studying acoustic production and aural reception in a broader biosocial, communicational framework.

Animal sound communication. Another significant component of this biosocial, communicational framework is zoological and evolutionary. Here we attempt to distinguish innate from learned abilities, species-specific from pan-species sound patterning, and sound signals and channels from olfactory, visual, and tactile-gestural ones. Research in evolutionary biology and psychology has greatly expanded our understanding of the evolution of the ear from a simpler organ of balance to a more complex one for information processing. And more recent ethological research has clarified how sound plays a very significant role in animal interaction (*see* ANIMAL COMMUNICATION; ANIMAL SIGNALS—AUDIBLE SIGNALS).

Studies of coordinated exchanges in the avian world, for example, have led to an understanding of functional differences between nonvocal and vocal sounds. Although nonvocal sounds may be either incidental (as in feeding, flying, or swimming) or deliberate and communicative (as in the different rates of tapping beats per second distinguishing species of woodpeckers or wing beats per second distinguishing species of hummingbirds), vocal sounds exhibit much more complex patterns. *See also* ANIMAL SONG.

Two delicate issues highlight potential differences between animal studies and similar behavioral-ethological approaches to human social interaction and communication. (1) The observer is an outsider to the system observed; researchers cannot ask questions of apes, birds, or other animals. It is therefore sometimes difficult to speak of animal communication at the level of intentional or meaningful articulation. (2) A related problem, anthropomorphism and the problem of "Clever Hans" effects (witting and unwitting cues and deceptions, expectation effects, and unconscious experimenter bias), may create other difficulties. Recent research with chimpanzee and ape vocalization and signing have produced cautionary tales about equating problem solving or task learning with "language" and operant conditioning with "communication."

Human sound communication. Human communication is transacted through modes of symbolic behavior, and these modes (visual, gestural, verbal, musical) provide culturally variable systems of codes and conventions through which objects and events can be perceived, conceived, and organized into forms that can be understood by others who possess knowledge of those codes and conventions (*see* CODE; MODE). The verbal and musical modes, both primary universal modeling systems, are each logically organized through symbols that pair sound and social meanings, and this factor suggests the fundamental importance of sonic-acoustic media, channels, and codes in human evolution.

In the case of languages, the general study of the variety of possible speech sounds is called phonetics. For any given LANGUAGE the subset of possible sounds that make up a regular inventory of systematically contrasting elements is called phonemes, and these are further analyzable in terms of their phonetic features. The branch of LINGUISTICS that describes the sounds of a language, their phonetic features, and the patterns governing their distribution and ordering is called PHONOLOGY. Those acoustic phenomena that accompany speech, such as voice set, quality, speed, rhythm, and intensity, are known as paralinguistic and prosodic features. In musical sound structure the general study of pitch inventories and tone systems is analogous to the realm of linguistic phonetics, and the relationship of tones, scales, modes, and tuning is more similar to the analysis of phonemes and phonetic features (*see* MUSIC THEORIES—TUNING SYSTEMS), whereas the analysis of timbre and texture has parallels with paralanguage and prosody.

Beyond this clear analogy in the realm of linguistic and musical sound organization is also an inevitable comparison of the variety of ways in which sonic media, channels, and codes are meaningfully interpreted. Both language and music can be approached along acoustic, psychoacoustic, and evolutionary lines, yet both clearly require a human-social, cross-cultural perspective, one that takes into account the forms and varieties of speaking and music making in human communities and the ways in which linguistic and musical means serve social ends, accomplishing real outcomes of personal and interpersonal meaning for participants.

The uniqueness of the verbal and musical modes goes beyond the notion that similar sensory apparatuses are involved or that production and reception of various stimuli characterize both. Although these two modes are unique and completely distinct from each other, they overlap considerably in communicative means and economies. Four dimensions of this overlap can be specified for acoustic and cultural comparison and contrast. (1) Throughout the world tunes are accompanied by texts, whether or not the society in question is characterized by adjacent or dominant traditions of instrumental music or verbal arts. Hence studies of *language in music* concern the fit between verbal artistry, musical melody and rhythm, and styles of sung vocalization, particularly as they contrast with other types of speech and oration. (2) In a complementary manner studies of *music in language* concern the melodic, metric, and timbral dimensions of speech varieties. Primary studies here concern dimensions of patterned sentence intonation, prosody, and vocal affect, as well as studies of how pitch and tonal patterns determine lexical meanings in some languages. All of this research on the overlaps between language and music contributes to our understanding of the boundaries of speech and SONG in acoustic, artistic, and cross-cultural perspective.

A parallel yet more abstract set of interrelations concerns cross-modal symbolization. (3) *Language about music* or, more generally, verbal discourse that prescribes or describes some dimension of musical experience points on the one hand to the systems and codifications of knowledge in culture-specific music theories (*see* MUSIC HISTORY) and on the other to the very fact that music is not linguistically translatable and that there are enormous cross-cultural and intracultural variations in discourse on musical experience and societal emphases on verbalization about music. Although both scientific and humanistic models of sound depend largely on visual recoding and notation systems for rational explication, they also depend on verbal descriptions of three types: (a) narrative of experience relating sound, source, and environment; (b) onomatopoeia/mimesis/imitative words; and (c) technicalized lexicon or metalanguage. The musicologist Charles Seeger wrote in detail about the "distortions" (overemphasis on space, underemphasis on time, overemphasis on event and product over process and tradition) produced by discussing the musical mode in these varieties of the verbal; in remembrance of his zeal researchers often use the phrase "Seeger's dilemma" to refer to the problem of using language to discuss music.

It is often said—as an admitted oversimplification—that in music sounds stand for nothing but sounds, and in language sounds stand for ideas, but the case of (4) *music about language,* or perhaps more accurately language through music, provides an interesting exception. Speech surrogates substituting for vocalizations are most commonly found when variations in linguistic tone level are a significant part of speech communication. In surrogate systems instrumental (commonly drum, gong, xylophone, or flute) or organic (commonly whistling, humming, or falsetto) sounds correspond to natural language sounds. In other words, linguistic tonal contours are directly transposed to other media in such a way that the sound patterns reflect sound patterns in the language.

Theodore Stern identified the two major kinds of speech surrogates: abridgment systems, in which a limited number of phonemic elements of the base language are evoked or imitated by the surrogate; and logograph or ideograph systems, in which the surrogate sound symbolizes a concept, making no reference at all to the phonemic structure of the base language. Moreover, at least throughout Africa, where "talking drums" are widespread as instrumental speech surrogates, it is possible to distinguish a signal mode (stereotypic texts and formulas) from a speech mode (creative and novel linguistic messages); sometimes these modes alternate with each other, or additionally alternate, even quite rapidly, with the use of the same instrument for purely musical PERFORMANCE bearing no referential or connotative message.

Sounds and meaning. Turning now to the question of how sounds relate to meaning, there are varying ways to approach the communicative properties and potentials of both language and music. Some traditional perspectives view languages as basically referential and predicative, denoting or reflecting objects or events in a nonlinguistic real world. Other perspectives, generally anthropological in orientation, view speaking as a more active construction and implementation of realities, placing more emphasis on the creative investments and pragmatic concerns of speakers and societies than on the formal linguistic code. A perspective associated with the linguist ROMAN JAKOBSON, later elaborated by others, mapped the communicative relationship among factors in a speech event (addresser, addressee, context, message, contact, code) and the multiplicity of functions and meanings (emotive, conative, contextual, referential, poetic, metalingual) that might be focused by shifts in emphasis or orientation to any one of those factors. This perspective has provided a sensible corrective to views of linguistic SEMANTICS more exclusively focused on the nature of denotation and reference.

Because musical sounds are not building blocks of word or sentence units, the patterns of musical sounds and rhythms are not interpreted as meaningful in reference to a nonmusical world. In various traditions composers express or depict emotions with materials that then come to have a conventional denotative character. Such is the case in the western European tradition with some of the devices of orchestral program music or with varieties of film music. At the same time, however, it is important to emphasize that such conventions are culturally grounded; they are not the result of an understanding by composers and listeners that a group of notes or chords or a rhythm in all cases and musical settings will represent a specific meaning or communicate a certain thought (*see* SOUND EFFECTS).

Some phenomena often labeled as musical reference or denotation are perhaps more like linguistic onomatopoeia, exploiting a variety of abstract principles of mimesis. The cuckoo calls of Ludwig van Beethoven's Sixth Symphony, the turtle dove of J. S. Bach's *Gott ist mein König,* the insects or water references by Béla Bartók and Maurice Ravel, or the birds of Olivier Messiaen's many works involve musical transformation to evoke the character of a natural sound. Such devices are transparent to listeners with knowledge of the natural sources but may be inaccessible or purely musical to other listeners. Similarly, the multiphonic growls and drones of an Aboriginal Australian didgeridoo may evoke the sounds and motions of animals such as a dingo, brolga, kookaburra, or emu to listeners with prepared ears; to others these sounds are perceived purely as structured pulsations of the music.

What, how, or whether music can communicate concepts or images is an old issue, often referred to as the absolutist/referentialist debate. The central problem here is whether, in addition to abstract intramusical meanings, music also refers to extramusical concepts or actions. Most contemporary treatments of musical meaning and communication build on this debate, tending to acknowledge that although referential meanings can and do exist, they are not strictly denotative, natural, or transparent. Moreover, as references can be apprehended only through a more thorough understanding of the historical and cultural contexts in which musical practices and ideas are situated, work on musical meaning at this level has fallen largely into the hands of anthropologists and ethnomusicologists, somewhat removed from formal musicological concerns with inherent musical structure (*see* ETHNOMUSICOLOGY).

No contemporary work on musical communication has more significantly extended this debate, or stimulated more general discussion and reflection on it, than Leonard B. Meyer's *Emotion and Meaning in Music* (1956). This important work argues that meaning is not uniquely a property of things, located in a stimulus, or a property of what a stimulus refers to; rather meaning is to be understood as a relationship between the interaction of these two and the conscious observer. Putting aside designative meanings, those meanings relating to nonmusical domains, Meyer concentrates on what he calls embodied meaning, namely, the meaning of musical activities in terms of the unfolding structure of a work. The implications of a work's structural features and the listener's developing expectations about them based on immediately and remotely past musical experiences provide the basis for Meyer's theory. Grounded in Gestalt psychology and JOHN DEWEY's theory that emotion is a product of frustration, Meyer shows how the delay or fulfillment of structural tensions creates patterns of suggestion and resolution and argues that emotional values and meanings are a result of the drama experienced in listening.

Recent researchers in the anthropology and sociology of musical communications have attempted to expand and develop Meyer's position to address a greater variety of musical traditions, processes, and performance practices and the more explicitly sociocultural dimensions of listening experience. Their work moves the emphasis from the specific structural features of drama and tension that might arouse the listener to the range and variety of musical feelings that are socially constituted through musical experiences. Common concerns in this new work on musical communication include the importance of texture and timbre in relation to melodic-rhythmic syntax; distinguishing the meaning of one musical piece from another; addressing the meaning of specific pieces and performances rather than music in general; exploring musically meaningful evocations not directly linked to drama and tension; and probing the varied meanings of pieces to different listeners as well as to the same listener over time. The communications epistemology that results enlarges the description of the musical encounter from the text-processing-interaction level to one relating the intertwined experiences that are drawn on in the listening process.

Sound technology. Given the universal importance of language and music it is not surprising that the proliferation of mass-mediated technologies for the transmission and reproduction of sound have been major forces in twentieth-century history. The TELEPHONE, RADIO, phonograph, and tape recorder and the sound systems of film (*see* MOTION PICTURES) and television have proliferated to become features of the daily life experiences of peoples all over the globe. These technologies continually create new patterns of listening, new listening communities, and new challenges to the conventions of recording realism and fantasy. They are also intimately connected to a history of mechanical-electric-electronic musical technologies from music boxes to digital sampling keyboards (*see* MUSIC MACHINES). In the last hundred years sound technology has gradually evolved to a point at which the entire range of human hearing can be fully recorded and reproduced (*see* SOUND RECORDING). Indeed, recording and reproduction have moved into a surreal dimension, presenting the possibility of ultrarealistic listening experiences with special phasing equipment, headphones, and digital delays—listening whose realism is impossible to experience with as much clarity in live settings. And in the latter part of the twentieth century almost every musical style in the world is available on radio, tape, or record virtually everywhere in the world. This fact has, particularly in the last thirty years, tended to increase world musical homogenization and the appropriation of musics. It has also certainly changed the nature of many oral traditions and the fixity of regional folk and traditional repertoires (*see* MUSIC, FOLK AND TRADITIONAL). At the same time, it has promoted an extraordinary creative synthesis among world musical traditions and has brought increasing varieties of musical knowledge and experience to ever-growing numbers of people. In many musical traditions it is no longer possible to analyze stylistic stability and change without examining the local circulation and consumption of recordings. On a mass scale urban Afro-American and Afro-Latin musics have become increasingly African, and urban popular African styles have become increasingly Afro-American and Afro-Latin. The circulation of recordings and radio broadcasts is largely responsible for this extensive set of new influences.

Music was once defined—for example, by the nineteenth-century German physicist Hermann von Helmholtz—in contrast to noise; Helmholtz meant to distinguish regular vibrations with harmonics proportionate to the fundamental frequency from nonperiodic or irregular oscillations. Similarly, many discussions of sound started with a diagram of the range of human audibility, in hertz (Hz) and decibels (db), bounded by the thresholds of hearing and pain (see Figure 1). Within this range several smaller circles were drawn, indicating the range of noises, speech, vocal music, and orchestral music. Language, music, and noise were thus conceived as overlapping subsets within the range of audibility. With the proliferation of sound technologies, the ranges of noise, music, speech, and audibility are potentially identical and entirely within the control of musicians and audio engineers. See Figure 2.

Current research. In the 1970s there was an increasing awareness of the importance of sound in human affairs, stimulated no doubt by the worldwide

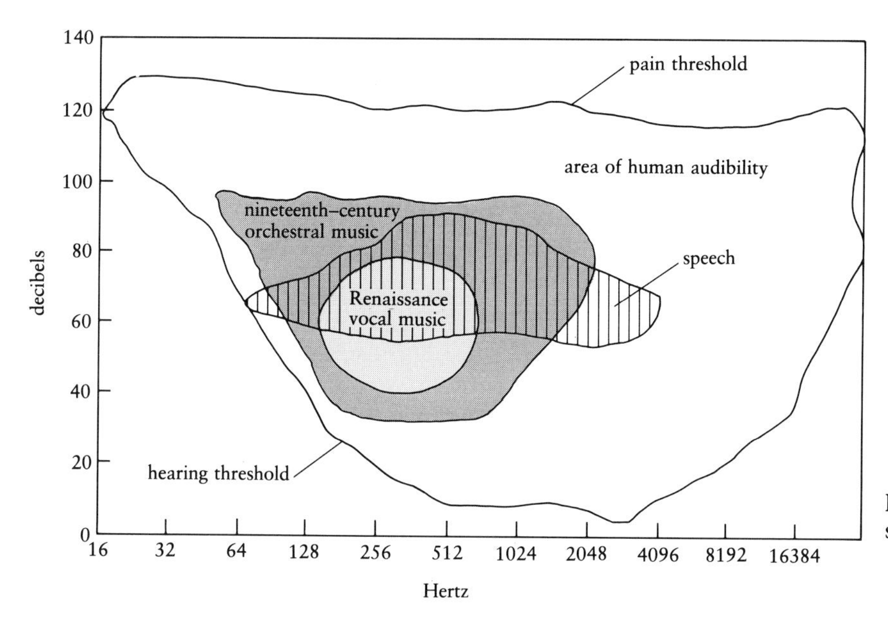

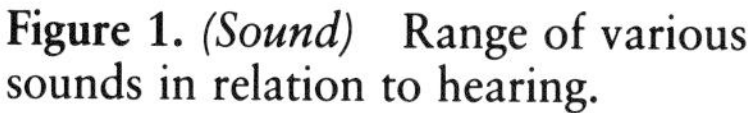

Figure 1. *(Sound)* Range of various sounds in relation to hearing.

Figure 2. *(Sound)* Decibel levels of some common sounds.

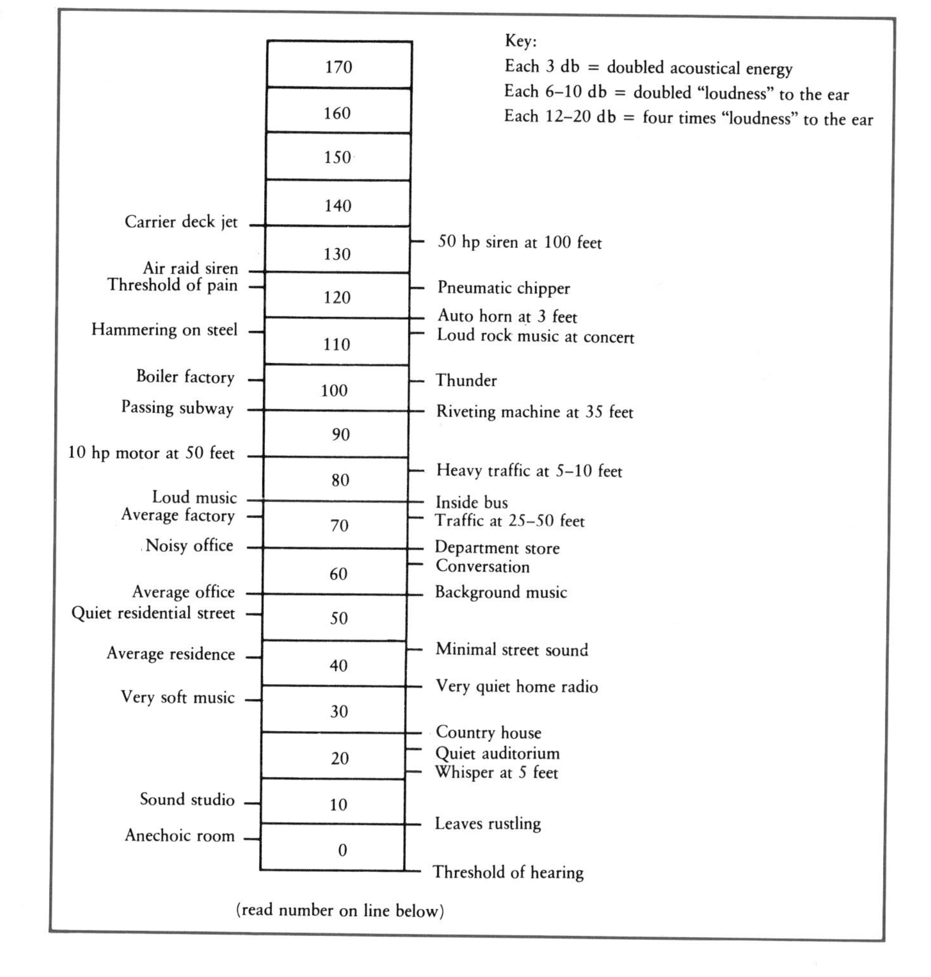

rise of popular musics and the rapid evolution of electronic technologies of music making and music reproduction. Two key synthetic books appeared and have since inspired a new generation of researchers: Peter F. Ostwald's *The Semiotics of Human Sound* (1973) and R. Murray Schafer's *The Tuning of the World* (1977).

Trained as both a psychiatrist and a musician, Ostwald studied a wide variety of noise, speech, and musical codes in terms of their communicative functions. For example, he developed diagnostic studies of speech for mood and personality assessment, studied schizophrenic speech pathologies, outlined the critical paralinguistic characteristics of the ways patients communicate with doctors, developed techniques for the analysis of newborn infant cries and sounds, enumerated the varieties and meanings of whistling, and investigated the relationship between physical and emotional disturbance and musical creativity, particularly in the case of the composer Robert Schumann. Major themes in Ostwald's work concern the uniqueness of sound as a resource in human emotional expression and the importance of a broadly biobehavioral approach to the physical and mental vicissitudes of sound making.

Schafer's writing builds on his background as educator and composer and as director of the World Soundscape Project, a research group devoted to community studies of soundscapes. Schafer coined the term *soundscape* to refer to the sound environment, and his work traces natural primitive, rural, town, city, industrial, and electric transformations in human history, showing how sounds and what he terms *schizophonia* (the splitting of an original sound from its source, brought about by electroacoustic reproduction) have played an important role in human invention. Some of his work in this area develops themes suggested by Edmund Carpenter and MARSHALL MCLUHAN, particularly concerning how electrically amplified sounds transform space to contain listeners. Schafer and his coworkers produced an elaborate series of notations, classifications, and measurements to describe the morphology and symbolism of sound environments. He also devoted particular attention to the study of noise; the nature of "hi-fi" and "lo-fi" soundscapes (environments with favorable and unfavorable signal-to-noise ratios); the problems of legislating the sound environment and devising creative approaches to what he terms *acoustic design,* namely, improvement of the aesthetic qualities of acoustic environments (*see* MUZAK); and acoustic ecology, that is, studies of the impact of soundscapes on the behaviors and outlooks of their inhabitants.

Another recent synthetic work about sound communications, integrating environmental, natural historical, linguistic, and musical concerns, is Steven Feld's *Sound and Sentiment* (1982). This anthropological study of sound as a symbolic system reports on the Kaluli, a remote rain-forest tribe in Papua New Guinea, and shows how patterns of adaptation to an environment in which sound is more important than vision permeates social and aesthetic communications. The Kaluli in good part encounter their world by sounds, reflected nowhere more importantly than in their classification of birds, which are believed to be their own spirit reflections. Bird sounds are transformed into the tonal materials of songs and weeping, two kinds of expression through which the Kaluli express sadness over death and loss. The texts of these are formed by special poetic codes called "bird sound words," and the songs are sung in a plaintive bird voice by a dancer costumed as a bird; the performance thereby moves an audience to cry, as if they had become birds as well. This symbolic circle linking birds, humans, death, life, nature, culture, language, and music is further rationalized in Kaluli mythology.

These works indicate that the study of sound communications in human social life increasingly integrates acoustic, psychological, cognitive, ecological, evolutionary, behavioral, historical, ethnographic, technological, institutional, humanistic, and artistic perspectives. That so many perspectives contribute to our understanding of sound communications is at once an indication of the extraordinary depth and complexity of sound phenomena in nature and culture and of the thoroughness with which they have captured human imagination.

Bibliography. Edmund Carpenter and Marshall McLuhan, "Acoustic Space," in *Explorations in Communication: An Anthology,* ed. by Edmund Carpenter and Marshall McLuhan, Boston, 1960; Robert Erickson, *Sound Structure in Music,* Berkeley, Calif., 1975; Steven Feld, "Communication, Music, and Speech about Music," *1984 Yearbook for Traditional Music* 16 (1984): 1–18; idem, *Sound and Sentiment: Birds, Weeping, Poetics, and Song in Kaluli Expression,* Philadelphia, 1982; Hermann von Helmholtz, *On the Sensations of Tone as a Physiological Basis for the Theory of Music* (4th German ed., 1877), 2d ed., rev. and trans. by A. J. Ellis, New York, 1954; Roman Jakobson, "Linguistics and Poetics," in *Style in Language,* ed. by Thomas A. Sebeok, Cambridge, Mass., 1960; Charles M. Keil, "Motion and Feeling through Music," *Journal of Aesthetics and Art Criticism* 24 (1966): 337–349; Leonard B. Meyer, *Emotion and Meaning in Music,* Chicago, 1956; Peter F. Ostwald, *The Semiotics of Human Sound,* The Hague, 1973; idem, *Soundmaking: The Acoustic Communication of Emotion,* Springfield, Ill., 1963; R. Murray Schafer, *The Tuning of the World,* New York, 1977; idem, ed., *The Vancouver Soundscape,* Vancouver, B.C., 1973; Charles Seeger, *Studies in Musicology, 1935–1975,* Berkeley, Calif., 1977; John Shepherd, Phil Virden, Graham Vulliamy, and Trevor Wishart, *Whose Music?: A Sociology* *of Musical Language,* New Brunswick, N.J., 1977; Theodore Stern, "Drum and Whistle 'Languages': An Analysis of Speech Surrogates," *American Anthropologist* 59 (1957): 487–506; Yoshihiko Tokumaru and Osamu Yamaguchi, eds., *The Oral and the Literate in Music,* Tokyo, 1986.

STEVEN FELD

SOUND EFFECTS

Sounds used by a storyteller to represent activity in a world created through a NARRATIVE presentation, or "story world." Their use exemplifies a form of SOUND symbolism in which a direct or metaphorical similarity is asserted between a sound effect and a story world sound. Sound effects can be used by the individual creator or collective creators of such narrative presentation forms as orally related tales, puppet shows, stage plays, films, and RADIO and television programs. *See also* MOTION PICTURES; ORAL CULTURE; PUPPETRY; THEATER.

Sound effects are distinct from other types of sound symbols in that they represent story world sounds considered nonlinguistic and nonmusical by storyteller and audience—so-called natural sounds—and they are modeled *in* natural sound. In the jargons of particular narrative presentation forms the term *sound effect* may be restricted depending on whether a sound is created live or played back from a recording, simulated or not, recorded synchronously with or separately from visual images, produced on- or offstage. However, *sound effect* is used here in a general sense to denote all natural sounds that are made available to an audience so that the term can be applied systematically in a discussion of how natural sounds are represented in a variety of storytelling forms.

Early history. The history of sound effects is part of the general history of DRAMA as a human communication mode. Some theorists, most notably ARISTOTLE in his *Poetics,* have identified the fundamental importance of imitation of reality, or mimesis, in dramatic art. Indeed, the human impulse to mimic the sounds of nature has figured in speculation on the origins of other communication modes such as LANGUAGE and music (*see* MODE).

The imitation of animal sounds as a hunting technique may have been one of the first impulses toward mimicry; it was incorporated into rituals during which spiritual aspects of the hunted animals were represented. Environmental sounds are also commonly associated with supernatural ritual. In many traditional cultures the sound made by a bullroarer, a small wooden object attached to a cord, when whirled is associated with thunder, perhaps the most universally awesome environmental sound. It has been thought that dramatic art forms may have developed from such imitative rituals.

The term *sound effect* was not coined until the silent film era, but the imitation of natural sounds has always been a potential part of narrative presentation. The first mention of a specialized sound effect device comes from the Greek scholar Pollux in the second century C.E., who counted the bronteum ("thunder machine") among the machinery used in Greco-Roman stage production. It produced a thunderlike sound, apparently by bouncing stones noisily against tightly stretched drum skins, and was used at appropriate points in the PERFORMANCE, such as the entrance of a god.

Sound effects were most certainly a part of prehistoric storytelling—in oral narratives (*see* ORAL POETRY), ventriloquism, and perhaps even puppetry—long before the appearance of human actors on stages. The human vocal tract is an extremely flexible sound effect device and is used to imitate sounds in many oral storytelling traditions, even in everyday informal conversation. A person may say, "Then the bomb exploded: (*sound effect*)!" to illustrate the sound of the impact. The hands may also be used to extend the range of vocal sounds, as in whistling, or to provide percussive sounds, such as clapping.

Ventriloquistic performances, like oral storytelling, can incorporate vocal sound effects. But although in the latter they are used primarily to illustrate and supplement verbal narration, they are often the sole means by which the story is presented in ventriloquism. The performer may create an illusion of reality, as when making an audience believe that there is a fly buzzing around the room by projecting, or "throwing," a vocally produced buzzing sound, usually while maintaining the appearance of noiselessness. Aural illusions of long, complex sequences of activity, such as the butchering of a calf accompanied by the shoptalk of butchers, the barking of a dog, and the sharpening of a knife, have been created by virtuoso ventriloquists.

In puppetry the audience's attention is drawn to the visual space in which the puppets move, and the puppeteer is commonly hidden from the audience by a screen. Sound effects can thus be provided offstage by the puppeteer or by an assistant or musician. In the Indonesian *wayang kulit* silhouette puppetry tradition the puppeteer, or *dalang,* operates both the puppets and a simple percussion instrument used to provide sound effects. In the Japanese Bunraku puppet theater, sound effects, including realistic rain and wind effects, are provided by the musician on an instrument called a samisen, in addition to nonrepresentational musical accompaniment. Vocal modification devices held in the puppeteer's mouth, such as the *swazzle* in Punch and Judy shows or the *boli* in the Rajasthani *Kathputli* string puppet tradition, are often also used to create sound effects.

Little is known of the use of sound effects on

Western stages until the late MIDDLE AGES, when popular mystery plays depicting biblical stories were presented through both puppetry and acted productions, at first in churches and later on both movable and permanent outdoor stages. These stages were typically large enough to permit teams of backstage technicians to operate the "secrets," or special effects machines. The elaborate visual effects that portrayed the descent of the Holy Ghost from heaven or that of the devil into hell were accompanied by appropriately loud and awesome sound effects, including earthquake and thunder noises produced by rolling a barrel half filled with stones, small gunpowder explosions that accompanied the appearance of a devil, and the metallic clashing of pots and pans to represent the aural environment of the nether regions.

During the European RENAISSANCE large permanent stages such as Shakespeare's Globe Theatre were built that could accommodate bulky sound effect machinery. The top story of the Globe, the "tiring house," provided an area for the musicians and sound effects operators to work. Thunder effects were most likely produced by the barrel and stones device or by the newer method of rolling a cannonball down an inclined wooden trough, called a "thunder run." Sound effect devices also included bells, loaded guns, drums, horns, and a machine for imitating galloping horses.

Increased control over the sound environment provided by indoor theaters allowed the modification of devices used in outdoor theaters to achieve more subtle and varied effects suited to the unique structures and acoustics of different playhouses. In order to add the realism of an overhead sound source, thunder runs were occasionally built into the ceiling spaces over the audience that caused the audience enclosure to vibrate. The thunder sheet, a thin sheet of iron and steel plate suspended and shaken to produce a thunderlike sound, was used in other theaters.

The trend toward illusionistic realism in eighteenth- and nineteenth-century Western stage productions in scenic design and visual effects was accompanied by the development of more realistic sound effects. Until this period a relatively limited number of stock effects had represented a wide range of offstage aural phenomena. Devices were now built to produce more of the unique sounds associated with particular kinds of activity, such as storms. The sound of wind could be produced with a hand-cranked paddlewheel device that rubbed against ribbed cloth stretched taut over the top of the wheel. The sound of rain was imitated by rotating a hollow wooden cylinder, fitted inside with rows of wooden cleats and partially filled with small pellets such as dried peas. Types of storms could be differentiated by adding the groaning sound of trees bending in a fierce windstorm or the clicking sound of freezing snow driving on walls and windows. Although sound effect technology remained relatively unchanged until the end of the nineteenth century, methods were developed to represent new sounds, such as railroad noises, that were continually being introduced into the Western soundscape.

During the nineteenth century slapstick COMEDY skits on vaudeville stages made use of exaggerated sound effects, a practice that had been characteristic of comedies and farces for centuries. The pit orchestra drummer, in addition to playing straight musical accompaniment, used a variety of drumrolls and cymbal crashes to accompany the blows and pratfalls of comedic performers. Slapstick comedy is named after a device used to produce an exaggerated slapping sound, made out of two strips of wood held parallel to each other by a handle or hinge at one end. It was operated by knocking the two strips together, and the loud effect was often augmented by placing a small percussion cap between them.

Early twentieth century. Silent films, introduced to the public as a new storytelling form at the turn of the century, were nearly always provided with music and sound effects as an aural accompaniment to the visual images. The first presentations were vaudeville theater attractions, so music and sound effects were added by the pit musicians, especially the drummer, whose "traps" included a large repertoire of sound devices. As special movie houses were developed for the presentation of silent films, some kept the vaudeville arrangement and others provided space for sound effects operators behind the screen. By the end of the first decade of the twentieth century equipment had been invented by which several such devices could be operated with levers or keys, a development that by the end of the 1920s had seen large pipe organs able to operate all sorts of sound effect devices from the keyboard and pedals via pneumatic connections. *See* MUSIC MACHINES.

Drama in radio offered sound effects a much more important role in storytelling than ever before. Unlike stage and screen presentations, radio provided no visual information to aid the understanding of a narrative. Sound effects had to help constitute the narrative, not merely illustrate or accompany it. Radio drama made use of sound effects from its very beginnings in the early 1920s, and their first documented use was in a simulation of the 1921 World Series. A SPORTS writer at the game telephoned a running description to a studio announcer, who relayed it over the air as if he were actually present in the ballpark. Two sound effects were used: the sound of the bat hitting the ball was simulated by snapping matches close to the microphone, and a group of people outside the studio window were signaled to cheer at appropriate moments.

In time it became clear that to help carry the action

Figure 1. *(Sound Effects)* "Fire!" The crackling of cellophane. Radio drama, 1930s. Courtesy of Erik Barnouw.

of a radio story a complex of sound effects needed to be performed simultaneously. To establish a location and thus take over the function of stage scenery, sound effects of the sea, barnyard, or traffic, for example, would be performed at a relatively low-volume level. To convey the specific activity of a character, rustling of clothing, footsteps, and gunshots would be provided at a higher level. The relative distances between objects and the listener could be represented by placing the sound sources closer to or farther from a microphone. Thus radio storytellers could represent activity in a story world through strictly aural means.

Radio drama brought sound effect production into the sound studio. Free from the necessity of working in a backstage area, sound effects operators took advantage of radio's microphone technology, which processed sound as electrical signals that could be increased or decreased in intensity or filtered to emphasize certain frequencies. By "mixing" signals from several microphones, dialogue, music, and sound effects could be subtly juxtaposed in volume as well as through time.

Because early microphones were highly susceptible to damage from extremely loud noises, sound production techniques had to be redesigned for the studio. Radio made the first wide use of electromechanical soundmakers such as buzzers, doorbells, and telephone bells, as well as the phonograph. Sound effect records were manufactured and sold to radio studios to make available thousands of sounds that were difficult to simulate, especially more complex ones like those of train crashes, orchestras tuning up, maternity wards, and bowling alleys.

Unrestricted as well by visual imagery, radio drama created fantasy sound effects to represent all kinds of unusual events. Arch Oboler's "Lights Out," a U.S. horror series of the late 1930s and early 1940s, was noted for its imaginative use of sound effects, such as that of a person being turned inside out that was created by slowly peeling a damp rubber glove off a hand close to the microphone while a berry basket was being crushed. Many of the fantasy sound effects familiar today in radio, television, and film have their origins in radio SCIENCE FICTION, fantasy, and horror programs (*see* HORROR FILM).

Early sound film production (ca. 1930) required that all dialogue, music, and sound effects be recorded simultaneously with the visual images. At first sound effect performers were stationed at off-camera microphones and worked much as they would in a radio studio. But within a few years the practice of optically recording sound effects on film separately from visual images allowed sound effects to be taken from both actual and simulated sources, edited together, or "dubbed," by rerecording onto a master sound track in a studio, and finally merged with the visual elements to produce a complete sound film. The use of magnetic tape as a recording medium began in the late 1940s; it permitted increased control over the collection and manipulation of sound effects by allowing immediate playback, erasure, and rerecording. *See* SOUND RECORDING.

The most recent development in studio-produced sound effect technology is digital sound synthesis, which received its initial impulse not from sound effect technicians but from Western avant-garde composers who wanted to use "nonmusical" noises as an extension of the sound palette at their disposal. In the early 1910s the Italian futurist painter and instrument maker Luigi Russolo designed various mechanical noise-producing devices called *intonarumori* ("noise intoners"), which were to be played by musicians positioned onstage like a traditional Western orchestra. Russolo's compositions were not accepted as music by the concertgoing public of the time, but he continued to develop his *intonarumori,* which were adopted by theaters as sound effects devices.

The interest in natural sounds as musical material taken up by the musique concrète tradition in the late 1940s, with concurrent developments in electronically generated music, led by the 1960s to the design and use of sound-synthesizing devices, called synthesizers, that could produce a wide range of unusual sounds for musical composition and performance (*see* ELECTRONIC MUSIC). In the mid-1970s computers able to store and manipulate digital representations of sound waveforms and convert them into acoustical signals were incorporated into synthesizers, enabling musicians to custom design the waveforms of interesting sounds. By the early 1980s

Figure 2. *(Sound Effects)* Walt Disney's sound men preparing a sound effect to accompany Dopey's movements in *Snow White and the Seven Dwarfs*. The Museum of Modern Art/Film Stills Archive.

digital synthesizers were built that could accept any acoustical signal for digital analysis and synthesis. Sound effect designers have begun to apply this new technology to the creation of a virtually infinitely graded continuum of realistic to nonrealistic sounds.

Conventions and genres. A storyteller must decide which story world sounds to represent, how they should be represented, and how they are to be juxtaposed to one another as well as to any SPEECH, music, and visual images. They can be simulated or prerecorded, realistic or fantastic, visually identified or unseen. A variety of narrative art form genres can be identified by their use of distinct sets of conventions for using sound effects.

Conventions of realism suggest a close relationship between sound effects and the everyday aural experiences of the audience. Realistic sound effects are desired in many fictional live action and nonfictional DOCUMENTARY genres, typically to further the presentation's illusion of reality. Nonrealistic sound effects may be motivated in a variety of ways. They may be exaggerated for comedic effect, as in slapstick comedy and cartoons. They may be designed realistically to represent sounds that are not available in everyday experience, such as dinosaur vocalizations, or are known not to exist at all, such as the "sound" of a spaceship traveling through the vacuum of outer space. Or they may be used to suggest metaphoric associations between visually represented activity and an accompanying sound effect, as when a cartoon character shown falling from a great height is provided with the sound of a slide whistle moving from a high pitch to a lower one.

The HOLLYWOOD storytelling conventions in radio, television, and motion picture fictional presentations mix realistic and nonrealistic sound effects. The majority are realistic, but certain classes of activity are typically portrayed by nonrealistic effects. In police and detective programs, for example, the sounds of gunfire, explosions, and fistfights are routinely exaggerated. Since these sound effects represent ritually important activities in these genres that are likely to be outside the everyday aural experience of many audience members, such nonrealism is perhaps easily accepted within the general realistic framework. The alternation between raising and lowering the intensity of environmental sounds, not to signal movement with respect to the audience but to refocus attention on simultaneously presented linguistic or musical material, is another example of nonrealism within Hollywood conventions of realism.

Another set of conventions relates the status of the sound effect to associated visual images on film or television. Two genres of documentary film can be distinguished on this basis. The NEWSREEL, which used location film footage with interviews and dramatizations, made heavy use of simulated or asynchronously recorded sound effects in its interpretive presentations of the "real world." The CINÉMA VÉRITÉ documentary genre, in order to depict reality in a "truer" fashion, often uses only sounds synchronously recorded with the visual images. Aural and visual elements are edited in tandem so that together they integrally constitute a record of the represented event.

A third set of conventions governs the representation of offstage and offscreen sounds. In the silent cinema the majority of sound effects were cued to the onscreen presence of the sound source, such as a bird. Bird-song effects would be halted as another image filled the screen even if the scene clearly remained in the vicinity of the bird. Radio drama developed the practice of allowing continuous sounds to go on as long as they were motivated by the activity in the story world, so that bird-song effects would continue as long as a bird in the story world kept singing. This practice was adopted by sound film, allowing sounds realistically expected in a given story world location to continue even though the image was not continuously onscreen. Indeed, one technique to build suspense in film is to cue the audience to the presence of a threatening object or activity by sound effects, such as the creak of a door accompanying the visual image of a frightened person in a dark room, and to delay revealing the source of the sound until an appropriate moment.

Knowledge of differences in sound effect conventions may serve to cue the audience to the genre of a narrative presentation. A cartoon is recognized aurally in part by the kind of sound effects that are used. The power of mixing genres was demonstrated by ORSON WELLES's 1938 "The War of the Worlds" broadcast in which realistic and fantasy sound effects, such as ray guns, were used in a program that conformed very closely to contemporary conventions of live radio news reporting from the scene of an unfolding disaster. Many listeners took the drama to be an actually occurring event, and the few fantasy sound effects were made plausible in the context of the otherwise realistically performed story.

Sound symbolism in language, music, and culture. Sound SYMBOLISM may be modeled in language and music as well as in natural sound. Program music,

Figure 3. *(Sound Effects)* Onomatopoeia in comic strip illustration. From Stan Lee, *Origins of Marvel Comics,* New York: Simon and Schuster, 1974, p. 173.

such as Ludwig van Beethoven's *Pastoral Symphony* and Paul-Abraham Dukas's *The Sorcerer's Apprentice,* is intended to suggest a narrative through the presentation of a series of musical images. Natural sound is symbolized in such works by representational music, which gives clues to the proper interpretation of the musical narrative; composers often provide other clues with suggestive titles or explanatory texts. Arthur Honegger's *Pacific 231,* which imitates the sounds of a locomotive, was originally used as representative music in the score to a silent film in the early 1920s. Composed in the same period, Ottorino Respighi's programmatic *Pines of Rome* incorporated a phonograph recording of nightingales in the orchestral performance, suggesting the close affinity of sound effects and representative music.

The representation of natural sound through language is called onomatopoeia, which in English includes words like *crash, boom,* and *hiss.* Such words are formed from the sounds of a given language arranged according to grammatically allowable sequences (*see* LINGUISTICS). In the sentence "Then the bomb exploded:______!" the onomatopoeic word *boom,* constructed out of the English-language sounds /b/, /u/, and /m/, could be used in the indicated position to imitate the sound of the explosion. Onomatopoeia is one of the most direct means to represent sounds in literature and is of particular importance in some comic book genres.

Sound symbolism through natural, linguistic, or musical sound usually asserts some similarity between the story world sound and its representation. But this similarity is not wholly intrinsic to the sounds themselves; it is a perception shared by storyteller and audience and is likely to reflect cultural specificity. This is clear in the cases of onomatopoeia and representative music, in which quite different iconic representations may be used around the world for the same class of natural sound. And because the perception and meaningful interpretation of natural sound is not an objective, acultural process, it is likely that cultures provide patterns for modeling story sounds in natural sound as well.

Since boundaries between sounds that are considered language, music, or natural sound may not be the same for every human community, the tripartite division of the aural elements of storytelling into language, music, and sound effects adopted here itself reflects a culture-specific way of understanding the kinds of sound that are available to storytellers and that exist in the story worlds they create. But regardless of the categories used for analysis, it appears that culture-specific storytelling practices for representing culture-specific perceptions of sound by imitation are universal in human communication.

See also MUSIC PERFORMANCE; MUSICAL INSTRUMENTS; SONG.

Bibliography. E. G. M. Alkin, *Sound with Vision: Sound Techniques for Television and Film,* London, 1973; Rudolf Arnheim, *Radio* (in German), trans. by Margaret Ludwig and Herbert Read, London, 1936, reprint New York, 1971; Raymond Chapman, *The Treatment of Sounds in Language and Literature,* Oxford, 1984; Mark Ensign Cory, *The Emergence of an Acoustical Art Form: An Analysis of the German Experimental Hörspiel of the 1960's,* Lincoln, Neb., 1974; Robert Ten Eyck Hanford, *The Complete Book of Puppets and Puppeteering,* New York, 1981; Allardyce Nicoll, *The Development of the Theatre: A Study of Theatrical Art from the Beginnings to the Present Day,* New York, 1966; Frances Ann Shirley, *Shakespeare's Use of Off-Stage Sounds,* Lincoln, Neb., 1963; Elisabeth Weis and John Belton, eds., *Film Sound: Theory and Practice,* New York, 1985.

MICHAEL WILLMORTH

SOUND RECORDING

This entry consists of the following articles:

1. **History**
2. **Industry**

1. HISTORY

Sound recording is widely used in mass communications. Its techniques are basic to the recording industry and also have many applications in MOTION PICTURES, RADIO, and television (*see* TELEVISION HISTORY). Furthermore, sound recording has applications to the TELEPHONE industry, business communications in general, and other forms of communication and information storage. There are three main techniques for recording and reproducing sound in analog form: mechanical, magnetic, and optical. Since the 1970s, digital (as opposed to analog) recording has also been developed.

Mechanical recording. In the simplest form of mechanical recording, sound vibrations are transformed directly into mechanical energy by means of a vibrating diaphragm and are then engraved with an attached stylus into a material support such as a wax cylinder or a disc. In order to reproduce the recorded sound, however, the engraved patterns must be transformed back to sound vibrations.

The principle of sound recording was first demonstrated in 1857 by Léon Scott de Martinville, the inventor of the phonautograph, but the first device that could actually record and reproduce sound was the phonograph, invented by THOMAS ALVA EDISON in 1877. In France, Charles Cros independently designed a somewhat different instrument the same year, but it was never actually constructed.

Edison's phonograph recorded sound on tin foil wrapped around a spirally grooved metal cylinder. The stylus embossed the vibrations perpendicular to the surface, producing a "hill-and-dale" groove. In 1885 Chichester A. Bell and Charles Sumner Tainter improved the phonograph by introducing wax as the recording medium. Other improvements were added by Edison and others, and in the 1890s the cylinder phonograph was marketed widely as a dictation machine, for home entertainment, and for other purposes. Most owners used the phonograph to make their own recordings, but prerecorded wax cylinders were also duplicated by a simple copying process.

Meanwhile, in Washington, D.C., in 1887, Emile Berliner modified the invention by using a disc with laterally etched grooves instead of a cylinder. Berliner also originated the idea of mass-producing sound recordings by using the original master recording to make a stamper to press records, first from hard rubber, later from shellac. Berliner's gramophones and discs were sold regularly after 1895. The sound was considerably improved after Berliner's partner, Eldridge Johnson, perfected the wax process for disc recording.

Around 1900 Edison and other cylinder manufacturers introduced a process of molding cylinders, thus making mass production possible, and the cylinder continued to compete with the disc for at least a decade. In 1906 the French company Pathé Frères (*see* PATHÉ, CHARLES) developed an alternative system of "hill-and-dale" disc recording that consisted of dubbing the recording from master cylinders. Edison himself introduced another vertical-cut disc in 1913, but Berliner's lateral-cut disc became the industry standard when Edison withdrew from the record business in 1928. But while Berliner's gramophone had prevailed, the word *phonograph* persisted and in many countries became the general term for a disc player.

All these recordings had been made acoustically, without any electrical amplification, which limited both the dynamic and the frequency range of the recordings. There had been experiments in electrical recording since 1919, and the method was finally perfected by Western Electric in 1925. Soon after that date all recordings were made electrically, using a microphone, amplifier, and recording head to record the sound. All-electric record players also became available, with magnetic or crystal pickups and amplifiers, although portable acoustic models continued to be used until the 1950s. Electrical reproduction also speeded the development of jukeboxes, coin-operated automatic record players.

After the introduction of electrical recording and reproduction, the main limitation of the disc was its short playing time, a maximum of five minutes per side for twelve-inch 78-RPM records. There had already been attempts to lengthen the playing time by reducing the speed or by using finer grooves in the late 1920s, but these long-playing discs were

DECEMBER 22, 1877.

THE TALKING PHONOGRAPH.

Mr. Thomas A. Edison recently came into this office, placed a little machine on our desk, turned a crank, and the machine inquired as to our health, asked how we liked the phonograph, informed us that *it* was very well, and bid us a cordial good night. These remarks were not only perfectly audible to ourselves, but to a dozen or more persons gathered around, and they were produced by the aid of no other mechanism than the simple little contrivance explained and illustrated below.

The principle on which the machine operates we recently explained quite fully in announcing the discovery. There is, first, a mouth piece, A, Fig. 1, across the inner orifice of which is a metal diaphragm, and to the center of this diaphragm is attached a point, also of metal. B is a brass cylinder supported on a shaft which is screw-threaded and turns in a nut for a bearing, so that when the cylinder is caused to revolve by the crank, C, it also has a horizontal travel in front of the mouthpiece, A. It will be clear that the point

Fig. 1.

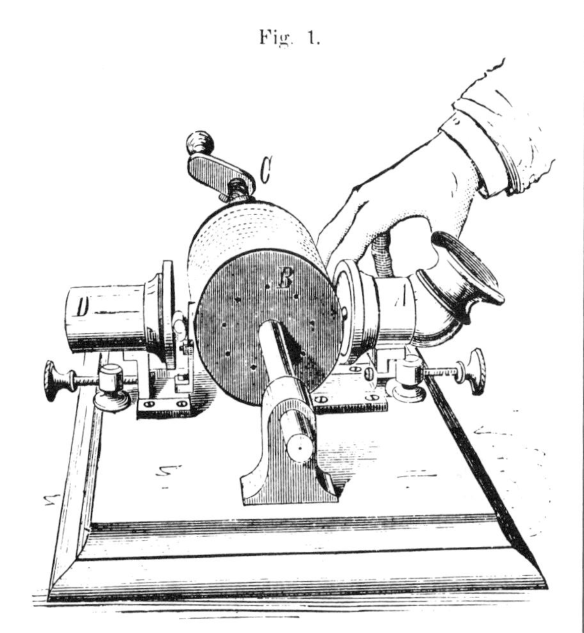

on the metal diaphragm must, therefore, describe a spiral trace over the surface of the cylinder. On the latter is cut a spiral groove of like pitch to that on the shaft, and around the cylinder is attached a strip of tinfoil. When sounds are uttered in the mouthpiece, A, the diaphragm is caused to vibrate and the point thereon is caused to make contacts with the tinfoil at the portion where the latter crosses the spiral groove. Hence, the foil, not being there backed by the solid metal of the cylinder, becomes indented, and these indentations are necessarily an exact record of the sounds which produced them.

Figure 1. *(Sound Recording—History)* "The Talking Phonograph." From *Scientific American*, December 22, 1877. Courtesy of the Library of Congress.

Figure 2. *(Sound Recording—History)* Emile Berliner, ca. 1875. Courtesy of the Library of Congress.

technical and commercial failures. The problem was finally solved by CBS engineers under the leadership of Peter Goldmark, who introduced the microgroove 33-RPM long-playing disc in 1948. A similar seven-inch disc using the 45-RPM speed was introduced by RCA in the following year, and both speeds soon became standard. The new records were basically similar to earlier discs, but owing to the use of vinyl instead of shellac, improved manufacturing processes, and soon also the use of magnetic tape to make the original recordings, the new records had a considerably improved sound.

Two-channel stereo recording was introduced in 1958. In this system, which was originally developed by A. D. Blumlein in 1931, two channels are engraved in the same groove at a forty-five-degree angle. Although there have been other improvements in the mechanical recording and reproduction of sound since then, the basic principle has remained the same.

Throughout its history mechanical recording was used mainly for the mass production of sound recordings; it became the basic technology of the recording industry. However, wax cylinders could be used for private recording, and cylinder phonographs continued to be manufactured for office dictation into the 1950s. (In the 1930s home disc-recording machines were also available.) Mechanical recording was also widely used in broadcasting in the 1930s and the 1940s. Acetate discs were used for the instantaneous recording of programs, while large pressed sixteen-inch discs were used to distribute syndicated radio programs to local stations. The first sound films also used mechanical recording processes: Kinetophone (ca. 1913) with cylinders; Vitaphone (1925–1927) with discs.

Magnetic recording. In magnetic recording, sound vibrations are first transformed into electrical impulses and then stored on tape or other material by means of magnetized particles. The principle was first demonstrated in 1898 by Danish engineer Val-

Figure 3. *(Sound Recording—History)* Early gramophone on a richly carved stand, 1903. The Bettmann Archive, Inc.

Figure 4. *(Sound Recording—History)* French musicians during a recording session, ca. 1905. The Bettmann Archive, Inc.

demar Poulsen. His telegraphone used steel wire to record sound magnetically. It was not practical because suitable amplifiers were not yet available, and the telegraphone fell into oblivion until the 1930s, when similar wire recorders were used mainly as dictating machines.

A magnetic recorder that used steel ribbon was invented in 1929, and it was used by some broadcasters and telephone companies. In 1935 the German company AEG (Allgemeine Elektricitäts-gesellschaft) introduced the magnetophon, a recorder that used paper or plastic tape coated by iron oxide as the recording medium. This recorder was used experimentally by several European radio stations. The sound quality was considerably improved by the invention of high-frequency bias during the war. The improved tape recorders were introduced in the United States in 1948, and they were soon adopted by radio stations and recording studios. Smaller units for home use became available in the 1950s, and they opened new uses for sound recording, such as FOLKLORE and ORAL HISTORY studies. There were some attempts to market prerecorded tapes, but owners of tape recorders used them mainly to make their own recordings.

In 1963 the Dutch company Philips introduced a new cheap tape recorder that used a tape encased in a cassette. A similar cartridge system was developed in the United States. Cassette and cartridge recorders became popular from the late 1960s. Cassettes were also successfully used to market prerecorded music, and soon record companies started publishing their new releases also on cassette or cartridge. In many developing countries cassettes practically replaced discs. For popular music devotees, the portable cassette player tended to become a constant companion. Cassette recorders brought the ability to record sound to practically everyone. In many industrialized countries the majority of homes have tape recorders. They are used not only to play prerecorded cassettes, but to record broadcasts, to make home recordings, to receive telephone messages, and so on. In business, cassette recorders and specially designed smaller tape recorders replaced stenographers.

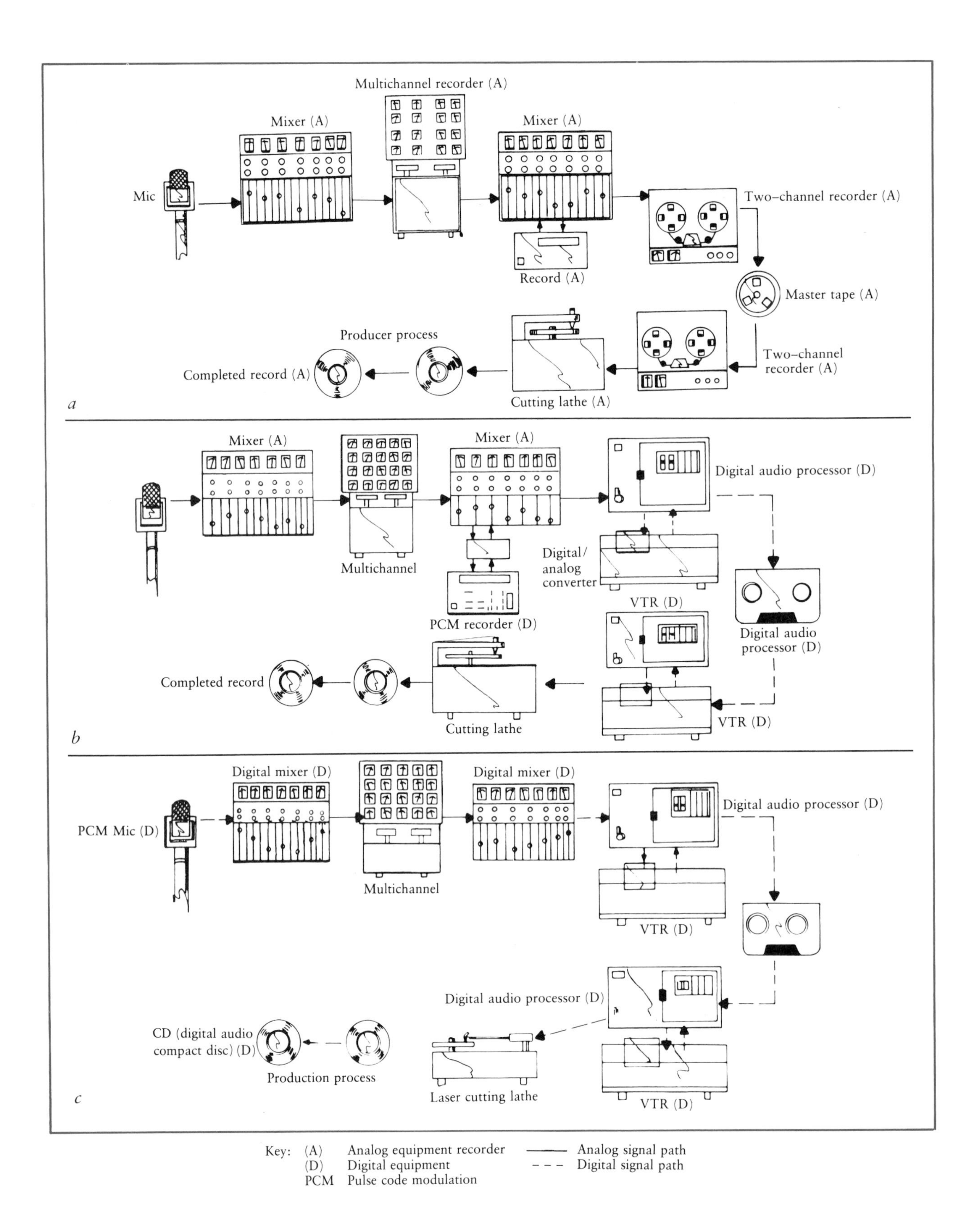

Figure 5. *(Sound Recording—History)* The record production chain. *(a)* Conventional system; *(b)* Mixed analog-digital system; *(c)* Full digital system. Redrawn after H. Nakajima, T. Doi, J. Fukuda, and A. Iga, *Digital Audio Technology,* Blue Ridge Summit, Pa.: Tab Books, 1983, pp. 42, 43, 44.

Meanwhile, other types of tape recorders were developed for professional sound recording. Tape had been introduced in recording studios in the late 1940s, and it soon changed the character of recording. Cutting, multiple recording, and complex sound editing became possible. Since the mid-1960s professional sound-recording equipment developed rapidly as a response to the expansion of the recording industry. "Hi-fi" became a focus of record enthusiasts. Multiple-track tape recorders, noise-reduction systems, and other new inventions expanded the possibilities of manipulating sound.

Magnetic recording in the form of a magnetic strip added to film was used for film sound, especially for 8- and 16-mm film. Magnetic recording is also used for VIDEO recording and for many computer information storage systems.

Optical recording. The first attempts to add sound to film were based on synchronized cylinders or discs, but the inadequacy of such systems directed research to optical sound recording. In 1919 Jo Engl, Joseph Massolle, and Hans Vogt of the German company Triergon developed a complete optical recording and reproducing system. In it sound waves were represented as varying degrees of black in the film soundtrack. A similar system was developed by LEE DE FOREST in 1923 in the United States. In 1927 the Triergon system was sold to Fox Movietone News, and the principle of optical recording soon became standard in the film industry.

Optical recording had few uses outside the film industry. In the late 1920s at least one record company used the method to make studio recordings, which were then transferred to disc masters. There was also an attempt in Europe in 1937 to introduce a home entertainment device based on optical sound. The cellophone played music recorded on film strips, but it was a commercial failure.

The Philips-Miller system was a hybrid system developed by Philips, based on an invention by J. A. Miller in the United States. Sound was recorded mechanically, using a cutting stylus to remove varying areas of a blackened filmstrip, which was subsequently read photoelectrically as in ordinary optical sound film. The system was used in broadcasting after 1935 until it was replaced by magnetic recording about 1950.

Digital recording. All techniques described above are based on analog recording, in which changes in the vibrations of sound are matched by analogous changes in the excursion or depth of a groove, in magnetism, or in light. Although these methods have proved satisfactory for a wide variety of uses, analog recording has certain limitations. Extremes of dynamics and frequency are difficult to reproduce, some background noise is almost inevitable, and the possibilities of manipulating the sound are limited.

In digital recording the sound is transferred into numerical symbols. The sound is typically sampled 44,100 times per second, and each sample is transformed to a sixteen-unit number. Extra bits (units) can be added to the encoded signal as an error-correction system. Thus it is possible to restore the original data even if some information is lost during the processing or reproduction of the recording. Digital recording makes possible an expanded frequency and dynamic range, and it is also possible to add other types of information, such as text or visual images, to the sound recording.

Digital recording can in principle use all three methods described above: mechanical, magnetic, and optical. The digitalized signal is usually first recorded on magnetic tape, for instance, by using an analog-digital converter and a videotape recorder. The first application of digital recording in mass production was the compact disc, which was introduced by leading record companies worldwide in 1983. In the compact disc the information is recorded with a laser beam on a glass disc coated with a photosensitive layer. The signal is stored in a series of pits, and in reproduction it is read with a laser beam. The original master is used to make stampers for the mass production of discs.

In recording studios digital recording encouraged the return to earlier ideals for realistic sound reproduction, away from multitrack recording. Digital recording also offers great possibilities for the manipulation of sound and for the restoration of historical recordings.

See also MUSIC, POPULAR; MUSIC MACHINES; MUSICAL INSTRUMENTS; MUZAK; PERCEPTION—MUSIC; SOUND; SOUND EFFECTS.

Bibliography. Paul Charbon, *La machine parlante,* Rosheim, France, 1981; V. K. Chew, *Talking Machines,* London, 1981; Journal of the Audio Engineering Society, *Centennial Issue: The Phonograph and Sound Recording after One-Hundred Years,* Vol. 25, nos. 10–11, 1977; Allen Koenigsberg, *Edison Cylinder Records, 1889–1912, with an Illustrated History of the Phonograph,* New York, 1969; Daniel Marty, *The Illustrated History of the Talking Machine,* Lausanne, Switzerland, 1981; Oliver Read and Walter L. Welch, *From Tin Foil to Stereo: Evolution of the Phonograph,* 2d ed., Indianapolis, Ind., 1976.

PEKKA GRONOW

2. INDUSTRY

After its invention in 1877, sound recording was initially viewed as a medium for personal communication such as dictation or recording TELEPHONE messages. However, in the 1890s demand gradually grew for sound recordings as a form of home entertainment. The mass production of sound recordings developed into an industry, and recordings became a medium of mass communication. By 1910 the recording industry had been established worldwide. By the 1980s, at least in the United States, the recording industry had approximately the same economic significance as RADIO and film (*see* HOLLYWOOD).

The early years. The recording industry was created mainly by companies that had played an active part in the development of sound recording. In the United States the three leading companies were Thomas A. Edison, Inc., founded by the inventor of the phonograph (*see* EDISON, THOMAS ALVA); the Victor Talking Machine Company, which held the patents of Emile Berliner, who had invented the gramophone, in which discs replaced the cylinders originally used by Edison and others; and the Columbia Phonograph Company, the outgrowth of a former Edison distributor. In Europe the leading companies were the British Gramophone Company, with close ties to Victor; the French Pathé Frères (*see* PATHÉ, CHARLES); and the German Lindstrom concern. There were some smaller companies, especially in the United Kingdom, Germany, and Russia, but the three major companies in the United States effectively limited competition through their control of the basic sound-recording patents until the late 1910s.

In the decade between 1900 and 1910 these companies grew into multinational enterprises. They built factories and studios at their home offices and in a few major markets. They established subsidiary companies or agencies in as many countries as possible. Traveling engineers were sent on recording expeditions around the world. These recordings were processed at the factories and the finished pressings and record players shipped to agents. Within a decade the industry was established worldwide, and in 1912 it was already suffering its first crisis from overproduction.

There are few statistics from the early years of the industry, but a rough picture can be reconstructed from various sources. In the United States the annual production of phonographs (cylinder and disc players) grew from 150,000 in 1899 to 500,000 in 1914; in 1910 at least 20 million records were sold. In Germany in the same year sales have been estimated at 10 million copies. In the United Kingdom, France, and Russia records also had a mass audience, and there was an established market for records in all industrialized countries. In the developing countries (then mainly colonies) only a privileged minority had access to sound recordings, but in India alone about one million records were sold annually.

In the 1890s the limitations of technology determined what could be recorded. Brass instruments and loud voices were preferred. By 1905 most sounds could be recorded reasonably well, although symphony orchestras still caused insurmountable difficulties. Record companies then tried to issue recordings by famous actors, authors, and politicians, but these recordings had little success. It was obvious that record buyers were interested mainly in music.

The best-known recording artists of this era were OPERA singers. Italian tenor Enrico Caruso became an internationally successful recording artist, and other illustrious singers helped to raise the image of the new invention. However, record companies recorded practically any type of music that showed commercial promise on the concert stage, in sheet music sales, or otherwise. They recorded well-known brass bands such as John Philip Sousa's band; stars of vaudeville, musical comedy, and minstrel shows; whistlers, accordionists, and banjo players; Gregorian chants; and hymns.

By World War I commercial recordings had been made in almost every part of the world. In such markets as the United States, Russia, and India, with ethnically mixed populations, the music of most ethnic minorities was issued on recordings. In the United States alone, more than a thousand new recordings were issued annually in the 1910s. The most popular recordings sold hundreds of thousands of copies, but to attract new audiences the companies were also willing to issue recordings selling only a thousand copies or less. Since few of the early recordings were collected in public ARCHIVES, many are probably lost forever.

The 1920s and 1930s. In the United States World War I did little harm to the recording industry. Wartime shortages curtailed production, but after the armistice sales took a sharp turn upward. In 1919, 2.2 million record players were produced. About 140 million records were sold in 1921, the first year for which we have such statistics. In the mid-1920s the industry was already suffering from a minor recession, but in the late 1920s sales picked up again.

Of the established companies, Victor and Columbia retained a strong position, but as the market grew many new companies entered the field. In the 1920s there were close to a hundred record companies in the United States, although many of them were short-lived. Some were one-person operations initiated by record-shop owners or individual performers, but several offered considerable competition to the established companies. Important new labels of the 1920s included Brunswick, Vocalion, Okeh, Cameo, Perfect, Banner, Grey Gull, Paramount, and Gennett.

In Europe the war had hurt the industry badly, and it took several years to recover, but after 1925 production increased rapidly. Not only in Europe but all over the world, 1928 and 1929 were boom years, and stock-market speculators invested heavily in record companies. The Gramophone Company, issuing records under the "His Master's Voice" trademark, retained a leading position. The British

Figure 1. *(Sound Recording—Industry)* "His Master's Voice": Emile Berliner's gramophone trademark. Courtesy of the Library of Congress.

branch of Columbia had become independent in 1922, and in 1925 it was able to acquire the German Lindstrom concern as a result of German inflation. Other important European companies that were active in several countries included Deutsche Grammophon-Polyphon, Pathé, and Ultraphon. But here, too, the expanding market encouraged the development of numerous smaller firms, and local record companies were also founded in several Asian and Latin American countries. As cheap, portable wind-up record players put recorded music within the reach of an increasing number of people, over 50 million records were sold in Britain in 1929 and nearly 30 million in Germany.

After the introduction of electrical recording in 1925 it became possible to record even symphony orchestras faithfully. Complete symphonies were soon routinely issued in album sets, but the most typical recordings of the late 1920s were made by dance orchestras and by popular vocalists who quickly learned to use the microphone to bring out the personal qualities of their voices. Gene Austin's "Ramona" sold more than a million copies. However, record companies continued to record practically any type of music that could conceivably attract a thousand buyers. In the United States record companies produced recordings for at least thirty ethnic minorities, and black music became an important market under the title "race records." Hillbilly music, the predecessor of country music, also emerged as a distinct market.

The economic depression of the early 1930s hit the recording industry harder than many other industries. Talking pictures had just become popular, and radio provided an inexpensive source of music. Record sales fell to one-tenth of 1929 levels. Companies were sold or went bankrupt. In a few years there were only two significant companies left in the United States: Victor, which was sold to RCA, and the Columbia-Brunswick-ARC (American Record Company) group. In Europe, Gramophone and Columbia merged as Electric and Musical Industries (EMI), and only a few local companies offered any competition. The number of new releases was drastically limited, and the future of the record industry looked bleak.

However, after 1935 sales increased again. Singing stars from radio and films, such as Bing Crosby, also became popular on records, and in the United States the swing bands of Benny Goodman, Artie Shaw, and others sold millions of records to youthful buyers. Decca (U.K. and U.S.A.) and Telefunken (Germany) emerged as new powers in the industry. Record-pressing plants were now opened in many smaller European countries, and new local companies were started. Even in the Soviet Union, where record production had remained insignificant for many years after the Revolution, the industry was reorganized and soon was reaching impressive production figures.

Postwar expansion: United States. In the United States record sales continued to grow slightly throughout World War II despite material shortages and industrial disputes. In 1946 sales doubled, and in 1947 about 300 million records were sold in the United States. In 1949 there was already a recession, which was probably deepened by the competition among new microgroove systems, "the war of the speeds," but in the mid-1950s sales turned upward again and continued to grow until the late 1970s.

New record companies had continued to enter the market from the late 1930s, and by the mid-1950s there were almost a thousand companies in the United States. Independent studios and pressing plants made it possible for almost anyone to start a record company. The growth of television had forced radio stations to rely more on recorded music in their programming. The smaller companies were quicker to adapt to new modes of production and promotion, and when black music ("rhythm and blues") was appropriated and modified to become a national trend under the name of rock and roll, established major companies lost a considerable share of the market. However, they regained much of their former position in the 1960s.

Record companies no longer attempted to produce recordings for all possible markets. The major companies concentrated on a number of nationally and internationally known artists in both the popular and the classical fields. They abandoned the production of record players and other related equipment and instead became part of multimedia communications and entertainment conglomerates.

It is an indication of the continuity in the recording industry that two of the three largest record companies in the United States in the 1970s were direct descendants of the founders of the industry: RCA Records, which had taken over Victor, and CBS Records, a successor of Columbia. The third was Warner, which had acquired a number of successful independent companies. Along with the industry leaders there existed a number of medium-sized companies and an indeterminable number of small enterprises. Most of the smaller companies focused on the production of popular music, hoping to create a hit record that would be played by radio stations and distributed by independent distributors or by one of the major companies. Some were satisfied to serve local or ethnic audiences such as the Mexican-American market in the Southwest. Others specialized in musical genres such as avant-garde concert music, historical jazz reissues, or polkas. Some small companies served simply as promotion vehicles for individual performers. In the 1970s more than ten thousand new records were issued annually in the United States, although the exact number is not documented anywhere. Average annual sales were about 600 million records and prerecorded tapes.

Worldwide expansion. The European record industry was again hurt badly by World War II, but by the mid-1950s it had fully recovered. Recording industries in Britain, the Federal Republic of Germany, and France entered a twenty-year period of expansion. By the 1960s other western European countries caught on. The introduction of cheap cassette players expanded the audience for recorded music, and although European radio broadcasting was still dominated by the public service ideal, there were more commercial stations and more programs based on recorded music. By the mid-1970s record sales in many European countries had grown three- or fourfold. The growth in Japan, Canada, and Latin America was equally rapid, and record production also increased considerably in eastern European countries, although the speed was slower.

EMI (U.K.) and Polygram (a Dutch-German company) became the leading European companies, with worldwide interests that rivaled the three leading U.S. companies. The general development of the industry also followed the U.S. model: in addition to a few major and medium-sized companies a large number of small companies also appeared on the market, ranging from successful regional companies to recordings published by individual performers.

In most parts of Asia and in the Arab countries the development took a different course. Here, too, cheap cassette recorders increased the market for recorded music dramatically in the 1970s. Since the duplication of cassettes is considerably easier than the pressing of discs, and many of these countries had not signed or were not able to enforce international COPYRIGHT conventions, the market was supplied with locally produced cassettes or imports from other noncopyright countries—often unauthorized copies of foreign products. As a result, multinational companies lost most of their foothold in these markets.

In the early 1950s half of all the recordings produced in the world had been sold in the United States; in the 1970s the U.S. share fell to one-fifth. Recorded music had become commonplace practically everywhere, and even small Third World countries like Papua New Guinea could develop local record industries that produced a hundred or more new cassettes annually. Although the United States still had the biggest record market in the world, many European countries sold as many or more recordings per capita. Exact figures are not available from many countries, but it can be estimated that about 2,500 million recordings were sold in the world annually in the late 1970s.

There had emerged a truly international music market, in which the dominant idiom was English-language popular music based on American idioms but often produced in Europe. A smaller but equally international market consisted of the standard classical repertoire recorded by internationally known conductors and soloists. In addition there were innumerable regional and local idioms. French recordings had a strong influence in the whole Mediterranean area. Latin America was another large regional market. Japan, Italy, the Soviet Union, and many smaller countries had strong national idioms, although the international idiom also had a strong influence. There were also smaller local, ethnic, or subcultural markets.

The 1980s. In the last years of the 1970s the sales of recordings were no longer increasing, and in many countries there was a slight recession. The reasons for this change are not clear. Youth unemployment and the economic recession, as well as the emergence of competing new media such as home VIDEO, are possible explanations. In some countries the illegal production of recordings continued to be a problem. The recording industry also blamed home taping, the practice of copying recorded music from radio or recordings for personal use.

In the early 1980s, however, there were signs that the industry was restructuring itself. Some of the new trends were the compact disc, new sources of income for the recording industry, and the growth of the music and home video markets. The compact disc was introduced in 1983, opening a way for further adaptations of digital technology. As sales of records stopped expanding, secondary sources of income became more important for the recording industry. In countries that had signed the Rome Convention for the Protection of Performers, Producers of Phonograms, and Broadcasting Organizations, record companies received royalties for the use of their recordings in broadcasts and public performances. Some countries introduced compensation for home taping. Income from music publishing subsidiaries also became increasingly important. Finally, as video became important as a medium for promoting recordings, many record companies entered video production, music television, and other new media. As a result, the largest record companies increasingly became multimedia companies. By the 1980s the recording industry had become one of the most important branches of mass communications worldwide.

See also MUSIC, FOLK AND TRADITIONAL; MUSIC, POPULAR; MUSICAL, FILM; MUZAK.

Bibliography. Kurt Blaukopf, ed., *The Phonogram in Cultural Communication,* Vienna and New York, 1982; Gillian Davies, *Piracy of Phonograms,* Oxford, 1981; R. Serge Denisoff, *Solid Gold: The Popular Record Industry,* New Brunswick, N.J., 1975; Roland Gelatt, *The Fabulous Phonograph, 1877–1977: The Story of the Gramophone from Tinfoil to High Fidelity,* 2d rev. ed., New York, 1977; Charlie Gillett, *The Sound of the City: The Rise of Rock and Roll,* New York, 1970; Pekka Gronow, "The Record Industry: The Growth of a Mass Medium," in *Popular Music 3: Production and Markets,* ed. by Richard Middleton and David Horn, Cambridge and New York, 1983; idem, "Sources for the History of the Record Industry," *Phonographic Bulletin* 34 (1982): 50–54; Oliver Read and Walter L. Welch, *From Tin Foil to Stereo: Evolution of the Phonograph,* 2d ed., Indianapolis, Ind., 1976; C. A. Schicke, *Revolution in Sound: A Biography of the Recording Industry,* Boston, 1974; Dietrich Schulz-Kohn, *Die Schallplatte auf dem Weltmarkt,* Berlin, 1940; Roger Wallis and Krister Malm, *Big Sounds from Small Peoples: The Music Industry in Small Countries,* London and Pendragon, N.Y., 1984.

PEKKA GRONOW

SOUTH ASIA, ANCIENT

Geographically the region of South Asia consists of the Indo-Gangetic Plain, peninsular India, and Sri Lanka. India, Pakistan, Nepal, Bhutan, Bangladesh, and Sri Lanka are within this region. The ethnic and linguistic diversity of South Asia is one of its most fascinating features and is partly the result of an accident of geography. Although the Central Asian mountain ranges, in particular the Himalayas, have in one sense inhibited MIGRATION into and out of the subcontinent, historically the primary direction of migration has been from the relatively arid regions of Central Asia through mountain passes into the fertile, subtropical Indo-Gangetic Plain. Within the subcontinent people have tended to migrate eastward and southward. There is some evidence to suggest that prehistoric migrations into the subcontinent may have been under way as early as thirty thousand years ago. More plentiful archaeological evidence from about 2500 B.C.E. on (supplemented by later textual, epigraphic, and other historical evidence) confirms that ethnic, linguistic, and cultural diversity are long-standing characteristics of South Asian societies. The Indian government, for example, officially recognizes fifteen regional languages, but the actual number of languages and dialects spoken on the subcontinent is well over one thousand. *See also* LANGUAGE; LINGUISTICS.

The vast and multifaceted topic of the flow of information and ideas in South Asia before 1500 C.E. can be divided into five broad categories: the Indian epics, the influence of the Indic (or Indo-Aryan) languages, the caste system, pilgrimage, and monastic and cultural institutions. These topics are designed to evoke general issues about how people communicate (through language, social codes, stories, and ceremonies), what they typically communicate (social, political, and religious ideas), and when they are likely to share the ideas that characterize their distinctive cultures (on pilgrimages, in schools, and during festivals).

Figure 1. *(South Asia, Ancient) Head of a Boddhisattva or Crowned Buddha,* ninth to tenth century. Indian, Bihar, Pāla Dynasty (730–1197). The Nelson-Atkins Museum of Art, Kansas City, Missouri (Nelson Fund).

The Indian epics. The circulation of the ethical, philosophical, religious, legal, and social ideas contained in the pan-Indian epics, the Mahabharata and Ramayana, attests to both significant media of communication in ancient South Asia (bardic storytelling, plastic and THEATER arts) and significant ideas (the epic tales) that have had an abiding impact at many levels of CULTURE throughout South Asia. *See also* MUSIC THEATER—ASIAN TRADITIONS.

The Mahabharata, familiar in modern times as the world's longest epic, is the product of eight centuries of compilation (ca. 400 B.C.E.–400 C.E.). Sometimes described as an encyclopedia of Indian civilization, its stories were circulated orally for centuries throughout the Indo-Pakistan subcontinent when recited by bards or performed in puppet shows, stage dramas, and folk dances (*see* DANCE; DRAMA; PUPPETRY). Professional reciters with distinctive repertoires, the bards are thought to have transmitted a vast store of ballads, tales, folk stories (*see* FOLKTALE; ORAL CULTURE; ORAL POETRY), and fables that were often interwoven in their accounts of the great Bharata war. The Mahabharata continues to provide a common store of myths, legends, and didactic tales that transcend religious boundaries of Hindu, Sikh, and Jain in India.

The Ramayana is a considerably shorter epic and a much more homogeneous one. It is thought to have been composed about 200 B.C.E.–200 C.E. by the author Valmiki. The Ramayana's story concerns the exiled prince Rama who engaged in heroic exploits to rescue his abducted wife, Sita. Told and retold for centuries in dance, theater, and puppet plays, its appeal throughout South Asia remains largely undiminished.

For many years historians generally agreed that commercial and economic interests were the main stimulus for contacts beyond the Indo-Pakistan subcontinent. The view holds that Buddhism, India's seminal contribution to China and Southeast Asia, was carried to China across overland trade routes through Central Asia. In recent years, however, opinion has become somewhat divided on the causes for Indian influence in Southeast Asia and the way it spread. Some have argued that perhaps traders were not the primary agents of Indian influence; missionaries may have been more instrumental in initiating the contacts.

By whatever means communications were established, the appeal of the Indian epics in ancient South Asia is amply documented and still very evident in modern times. Major scenes from both epics are magnificently carved in two seven-row panels in one of the Ellora caves, the Kailasa temple (of the Hindu god Śiva), which was excavated between the eighth and ninth centuries C.E. From about 100 to 1000 C.E. epic stories were widely represented in dance and drama throughout Southeast Asia, and epic themes were permanently assimilated into the subject matter of the performing arts. The Ramayana was the topic of shadow-puppet plays as well as dance. In Kampuchea the popularity of both the Ramayana and the Mahabharata is documented in ancient inscriptions. Stories from the Mahabharata are illustrated in bas-reliefs in the temple of Angkor Wat.

Influence of the Indic languages. Ideas communicated throughout South Asia before the thirteenth century C.E. were primarily transmitted through the medium of the Indic (or Indo-Aryan) languages, a branch of the Indo-European language family. Originally brought into the subcontinent from Central Asia by the Aryan invaders (ca. 1500 B.C.E.), Vedic Sanskrit (its earlier form as distinguished from classical Sanskrit) is the language of India's most ancient sacred literature, the Vedas, whose compilation began about 1300 B.C.E.

In subsequent centuries the language of the Aryan invaders developed into two branches—Sanskrit and Prakrit. The very meaning of the words helps to explain the distinction between them: Sanskrit ("cultured, refined") was the language of learning, and Prakrit ("uncultured, natural") the ordinary spoken language. A generic term for Middle Indic languages (usually excluding Apabhramsa), Prakrits were used to record inscriptions from the third century B.C.E. to the fourth century C.E.—including those of AŚOKA (d. 232 B.C.E.)—as well as literatures. The Buddhist and Jaina canons, themselves recorded in Prakrits,

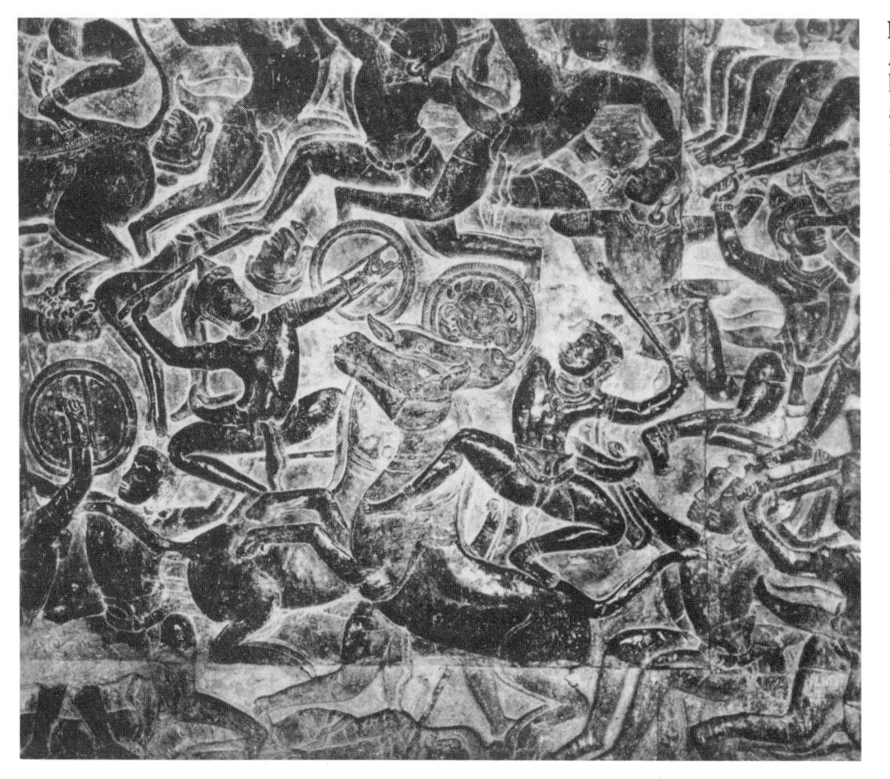

Figure 2. *(South Asia, Ancient)* Angkor Wat, Kampuchea: North gallery, western half; embattled gods and demons, from the Mahabharata. From Heinrich Zimmer, *The Art of Indian Asia: Its Mythology and Transformations,* ed. by Joseph Campbell, Bollingen Series 39. New York: Bollingen Foundation, 1955, vol. 2, plate 545. Copyright 1955, © 1960 by Princeton University Press.

Figure 3. *(South Asia, Ancient)* Figure of Vajragarbha Lokesvara: detail from the Prajnà Paramita sutra. Buddhist palm-leaf manuscript, Bengal or eastern Bihar, ca. 1085–1090 C.E. Ms. Sansk.a.7(R), fol.92v. The Bodleian Library, Oxford.

respectively recommend using the dialects to communicate the teachings of Buddha (ca. 563–ca. 483 B.C.E.) and his contemporary, the Jain leader Mahāvīra.

However, this branching of the language did not limit the use of Sanskrit, which has a preeminent position as the language of composition and transmission of the Hindu religious tradition. Before WRITING was introduced around the fourth century B.C.E. Vedic literature was communicated exclusively by oral means. Writing was only slowly adopted to record religious material, in part because of entrenched beliefs about the power of the words spoken during the Vedic sacrifice and in part because access to Vedic learning was by that time strictly regulated.

The priestly tradition of Vedic composition had a profound impact on Hindu South Asia. The separate bardic tradition of oral composition had an equally enduring but broader impact. India's epics were eventually written down in Sanskrit (and much later in India's regional languages), but as noted earlier their stories have been told in virtually every South Asian language to virtually anyone who cared to listen, regardless of class or RELIGION.

The composition of remembered and recorded religious literature in Sanskrit does not exhaust the significance of that language. In the early centuries of the common era a formidable corpus of scientific, technical, philosophical, medical, and political literature in Sanskrit began to be written. During that period in northern India Buddhists also began to use Sanskrit to compose their texts, just as the Jains would do much later. The evidence of inscriptions has enabled scholars to trace the history of Sanskrit as a medium of governmental administration. It became the official vehicle of administrative documents at different times in different regions of the Indo-Pakistan subcontinent, but by the Gupta period (fourth and fifth centuries) its use was widespread.

Why did the use of Sanskrit eventually so predominate over the Prakrits on the subcontinent? Scholars have suggested that there are two possible reasons. First, the close association of Sanskrit with Vedic religion is thought to have greatly benefited Sanskrit when Hindu orthodoxy, which had developed out of Vedic religion, gained influence in many parts of the subcontinent after the second century C.E. Second, the differences between local dialects steadily increased through the centuries, hampering local and regional communications. By contrast with the Prakrits, Sanskrit was a language codified (ca. fourth century B.C.E.) and therefore protected from excessive internal change. In this respect Sanskrit was both a convenient and a practical candidate for the subcontinent's "national" language.

The influence of Sanskrit and Prakrit in South India was more limited than in the central and northern regions because the native Dravidian languages dominated in the south. Nevertheless, these languages (except Tamil) tended to borrow heavily from the vocabulary of the Indic languages, and inscriptions document the use of Sanskrit and Prakrit by various dynasties for administrative purposes. For example, records of the influential Satavahana (or Andhras) dynasty, whose power waxed and waned from around the first to the third century C.E., are in Prakrit.

Buddhism was the primary vehicle by which the Indic languages spread across Central Asia along with other elements of Indian culture such as painting and SCULPTURE. In the early centuries C.E. vigorous trade between the Indo-Pakistan subcontinent and Southeast Asia facilitated the introduction of Buddhism and Hinduism there. Numerous Sanskrit inscriptions dating from the third century on have been found throughout Southeast Asia, extending as far as Campa in Indochina. South Indian kings sponsored much of the cultural expansion that left enduring traces on the literature, theater, and dance of Southeast Asia. Indigenous rulers adapted Indian

Figure 4. *(South Asia, Ancient)* Bathing pool and Hindu temple at Ramnagar. Banaras (Varanasi), India. The Bettmann Archive, Inc.

techniques of political organization, also spreading Indian notions of statecraft beyond the subcontinent.

The caste system. In order to understand how people communicate day to day in any age one must of course consider the language or languages they speak. However, when people talk with one another they do so within the context of a web of social rules that pattern the form, the content, and the occasions on which they communicate. Caste systems have pervaded societies throughout South Asia for much of its recorded history and are therefore a crucial aspect of INTERPERSONAL COMMUNICATION in the region. More than four-fifths of the people in South Asia are villagers; the outsider seeking to understand the network of communications within and among those villages could hardly find a better set of rules for the social, RITUAL, economic, and political relations than the caste system. Although most commonly associated with Hindus, caste and comparable hierarchical social systems can be observed among Nepalese Buddhists, Pakistani and Bangladeshi Muslims, Sikhs and Christians in India, and Sri Lankans.

The beginnings of the caste structure in India can be traced to the centuries following the close of the Vedic period (ca. 600 B.C.E.). The Greek ambassador Megasthenes observed some of the formative principles of social grouping in India about 300 B.C.E.: endogamy (marriage within one's group), occupational specialization, and hereditary membership. Although there has been a tendency to portray the Indian caste system as static, it was not until the tenth or eleventh century that the system familiar in later centuries had fully developed. The waves of ancient migration and conquest had a role in shaping social hierarchies and caste systems.

The rules and regulations of caste (*jati*) traditionally determined whom one could eat with, whom one could marry, and which occupations were permitted and which forbidden to an individual. Because the concept of hierarchy is basic to the system, Hindu groups were ranked by criteria of ritual pollution and purity determined by the group's practices. Con-

Figure 5. *(South Asia, Ancient)* Khasarpana. Chaduar, Orissa-Ganga dynasty, India, twelfth century. 41-23-1 Philadelphia Museum of Art: Purchased: Joseph E. Temple Fund.

temporary studies indicate that other criteria such as power and wealth were also taken into consideration in determining caste ranking. Important as the caste system was in structuring individual and group relations in South Asia, it never entirely determined with whom and how people communicated. *Jati* restrictions were often very much relaxed, for example, when villagers harvested crops and in certain recreational activities. However, the network of relations that extended from the joint family through local caste affiliations and beyond to the regional level was a primary mechanism through which cultural identity was fostered and maintained.

Pilgrimage. Pilgrimage has been a characteristic of religious practice among Hindus, Buddhists, and Jains in the region since the early stages of their self-definition. For Hindus in particular the length and breadth of the subcontinent is sacred territory demarcated by holy places of almost every imaginable kind: remote mountain temples, rivers, trees, caves, and city shrines. Whereas some pilgrimage sites are only locally known and frequented by members of one religious sect, others attract pilgrims from every corner of the subcontinent—every caste group, religious organization, and ascetic order. The sacred places at Banaras (now Varanasi), Brindavan, and Prayag are examples of the latter type.

A primary function of pilgrimages is to educate persons about theological, ritual, and mythological matters at the core of their religions. The urban centers of Banaras (Uttar Pradesh), Mithila (Bihar), and Taxila (Pakistan) were cherished sites of specialized education as well. Students from all over India lived there while enrolled in courses of Vedic study that might include logic, GRAMMAR, and astronomy as well as memorization of specific ritual material. However, introduction to new ideas was also likely to occur when pilgrims visited pan-Indian sites. Buddha, Mahāvīra, and the great Hindu philosopher-theologian Śankara (ca. 788–820 C.E.) all visited Banaras to teach. At such major pilgrimage centers individual Hindus, Buddhists, and Jains not only would encounter fellow believers from other regions in whom they might observe many differences of languages, dress, and behavior; they also were likely to meet a variety of religious specialists and believers previously unimagined who were nevertheless united in their acknowledgment of the sanctity of the place. Because it was common practice for pilgrims to travel long distances in groups, undoubtedly the journey also served to strengthen local and regional identities in the face of such great diversity. Once contacts were established between India and China and between India and Southeast Asia, the circulation of religious ideas was maintained in part by pilgrims, particularly Buddhists, who traveled from various regions to Indian religious centers.

Monastic and cultural institutions. The major pilgrimage sites of India are one model of centers for the communication of important ideas; monastic and cultural institutions are another. Buddhist monasteries (viharas) were established throughout the subcontinent over the centuries following Buddha's death and functioned, in the words of one scholar, as "networks of acculturation and contact within the Indian subcontinent." The Buddhist monastic community (sangha) initially dwelled in small groups in cave hermitages that tended to be on major trade

Figure 6. *(South Asia, Ancient)* Sāñcī, India: The Great Stūpa. North gate, early first century C.E. From Heinrich Zimmer, *The Art of Indian Asia: Its Mythology and Transformations,* ed. by Joseph Campbell, Bollingen Series 39. New York: Bollingen Foundation, 1955, vol. 2, plate 7. Copyright 1955, © 1960 by Princeton University Press.

routes or near towns rather than in isolated areas. One famous example of these communities is the Ajanta caves in Maharashtra. A complex of some thirty caves hollowed out of granite cliffs between the first century B.C.E. and the seventh century C.E., Ajanta is treasured for several reasons. It is a valuable record of Buddhist architecture, sculpture, and painting over many centuries and a particular example of places in ancient South Asia where commercial, artistic, and religious enterprises intersected. Reciprocal relations among monks, nuns, and the laity are at the heart of Buddhist ethics and practice; therefore, through study of the growth of Buddhist monasticism and the activities of its members one important dimension of communication in ancient South Asia emerges.

Eventually the monasteries developed into educational institutions as well as community centers of artistic and intellectual life. The Buddhist monastery at Nalanda in Bihar was perhaps the most widely renowned. Historians have described it as a thriving center of intellectual activity whose curriculum included philosophy, RHETORIC, and medicine. Most students at Nalanda were monks, some of whom had come from as far away as Java and China to study there.

Cultural relations between India and China from approximately the third to the eighth century C.E.

Figure 7. *(South Asia, Ancient)* Bhubaneswar, India: The Lingaraja Temple, ca. 1000 C.E. In the foreground are the gatehouse and assembly hall (Jagmohan), in the background a 180-foot tower (sikhara) over the shrine of the Tribhunavesvar. From Martin Hürlimann, *India,* New York: The Viking Press, 1967, plate 256. © Thames and Hudson, 1967.

were largely maintained by Chinese and Indian Buddhist monks. (Knowledge about the movements of Buddhist nuns during this period is too limited to allow historians to assert much about them.) Their spiritual and intellectual common interests carried them back and forth across overland trade routes through Central Asia and across sea routes between China's southeastern provinces via Indonesia and Sri Lanka to India's eastern coast. Records of travels kept by some of the Chinese pilgrims are invaluable sources of historical knowledge about ancient South Asia.

In a nation that is predominantly Hindu (about five hundred million in a 1983 population of some seven hundred million), Hindu temples have functioned as important cultural centers since about the fourth century. In addition to being a chief center of the performing arts, the temple grounds often served as a sort of community center. During religious festivals people would congregate for performances of well-known story cycles by itinerant bards. On a more regular basis people might spend their leisure evening hours listening to a local temple priest recite and expound popular religious stories. *See also* ARCHITECTURE; ART; FESTIVAL.

When construction of brick and stone Hindu temples began (earlier sanctuaries had presumably been built from perishable materials) there was a corresponding development in the production of sculptural representations of divine and semidivine beings for the shrines and exterior walls of the temples. As one scholar has noted, the images were both "visual theologies" and "visual scriptures" in which Hindus could read religious doctrines and myths.

Other art forms also flourished, in part through royal patronage. Acts of devotion, for example, might include music and dance performances to entertain a deity. Religious festivals remain the most important public occasions for the theatrical and dance performances that with each new performance ensure the continuity of these ancient means of communicating cultural values.

The art forms and stylistic conventions nurtured in the temples (and the courts) of ancient India spread throughout South and Southeast Asia in ancient times. Their creative stimulus precipitated the development of some of the world's artistic masterpieces; the architectural monuments at Borobudur (Java) and Angkor (Kampuchea) are only two spectacular examples among many of the worldwide impact of South Asian forms and concepts.

Bibliography. Brenda E. F. Beck, *The Three Twins: The Telling of a South Indian Epic,* Bloomington, Ind., 1982; Surinder Mohan Bhardwaj, *Hindu Places of Pilgrimage in India: A Study in Cultural Geography,* Berkeley, Calif., 1973; T. Burrow, *The Sanskrit Language,* 3d ed., London, 1973; Edward C. Dimock, Jr., et al., eds., *The Literatures of India: An Introduction,* Chicago, 1974; Diana L. Eck, *Banāras: City of Light,* New York, 1982; John S. Hawley, *At Play with Krishna: Pilgrimage Dramas from Brindavan* (trans. from Braj), Princeton, N.J., 1981; R. C. Majumdar, ed., *History and Culture of the Indian People,* 11 vols., London, 1952–1965; David G. Mandelbaum, *Society in India,* 2 vols., Berkeley, Calif., 1970.

BARBARA GOMBACH

SPACE, PERSONAL. *See* INTERPERSONAL DISTANCE.

SPATIAL ORGANIZATION

The influential work of U.S. psychologists Roger Barker and Herbert Wright, published in 1955, has inspired a considerable amount of theoretical, experimental, and observational research on relationships between the environment and behavior. These studies have been carried out within the frameworks of human ETHOLOGY, social and environmental psychology, PROXEMICS, and the sociology of face-to-face interaction (*see* INTERACTION, FACE-TO-FACE), as well as environmental design and ARCHITECTURE.

ERVING GOFFMAN observed that everyday social occasions involve a number of static and mobile participants and have a distinct spatial organization. These occasions can include such events as dinner parties, lectures, church services, court proceedings, weddings, demonstrations and riots, football matches, and parliamentary sessions. The spatial patterning observable at these events is a result of the intricate coordination of participants' placements, locomotory movements, interpersonal orientations and spacings, and postures and territorial claims. Individual and group spatial behaviors are not arbitrary or haphazard. They depend on the nature of the social occasion and the number of participants in it. In addition the spatial organization of social encounters reflects the spatial patterning of the physical context.

Hierarchical Structure of Spatial Contexts

Human affairs commence, unfold, and conclude in spaces with marked hierarchical organization. Whatever people do in one another's presence is always situated within an elaborate framework of nested environmental contexts. The most prominent of these is the *setting,* or that portion of the environment immediately accessible to its users' unaided senses and ordinary locomotory movement. Gardens, streets, supermarkets, airplane cabins, kitchens, and bedrooms are all examples. Settings usually acquire their own characteristic clientele and their own repertoire of usual behaviors. Thus parks in Australian cities tend to be entered by groups consisting mostly of females, whereas downtown pedestrian plazas tend to be frequented by individuals, the majority of whom are men. Further, roughly similar numbers of park users sit, stand, and walk, but over two-thirds of the people in plazas are walking, and the remainder consists of equal numbers of those sitting and standing.

Within a setting one can distinguish several *locations.* For instance, people at a swimming pool may place themselves around the pool or in the water, near its edges or away from them. The choice of a location within a setting often influences both the adopted INTERPERSONAL DISTANCE and the nature of the individual and group activities. Thus in Australian urban parks people on and around the benches tend to converse, eat, and drink, whereas those on the unfurnished lawns play games, sunbathe, and read. In both types of locations separate groups of people are usually distributed well apart, whereas in the parks' paths and roads—that is, locations used exclusively for walking—the space between groups of strangers is not as great.

Within each location a whole range of possible *placements* can be distinguished. For instance, a pair of students who decide to sit at a rectangular table in a library reading room may choose among chairs that provide different types of interpersonal orientation (face-to-face, side-by-side, corner, diagonal, distant). Again the choice of placement within a location is often highly significant. For example, U.S. psychologist Robert Sommer has found that people sitting side by side or at a diagonal or distant arrangement are less likely to enter a sustained CONVERSATION than ones in a corner or face-to-face arrangement. Furthermore, people who sit far apart from each other are less likely to initiate conversational exchanges than those who sit at a shorter distance.

Types of Environmental Features

The size, shape, and functional properties of settings, locations, and placements are delineated and signaled by three types of environmental features. Some of these features (e.g., trees, fences, curbs, walls) are *fixed.* They constitute a well-defined and rather unmovable boundary. Other environmental features, such as furniture, floor coverings, curtains, and screens, are *semifixed.* Usually they are left undisturbed, although they can be rearranged in the course of a given interaction. Finally, pools of light and darkness, the flow of passersby and vehicles, and the spatial claims and placements of gatherings and individuals represent *dynamic* and negotiable features of the environment.

Environmental features impose some form of sensory and locomotor restrictions: a theater curtain usually restricts visual contact between the stage and the audience, although it may allow some passage of sound. Other features, such as a garden fence, ha-ha (concealed) walls, and bushes, may permit a relatively easy flow of sensory data yet still limit a visitor's access. In other words, settings, locations, and placements are defined by various artificial and natural structures that restrict the flow of sensory data among the interacting parties and by the distances that render such a flow ineffective. Boundaries impervious to human senses form areas that can be used for separate occasions and activities. On the other hand, permeable boundaries allow gatherings to maintain separate integrity and yet retain communication with the surrounding environment.

Behavioral Properties of Environmental Features

Environments thus tend to differ in textures, firmness of boundaries, shape, and size as well as furnishings, ambience, and decor. These differences have consequences for the kinds of human activities that are preferred in such spaces.

Firm floor surfaces (e.g., pavements, parquet floors, concrete slabs) are viewed as congenial to walking, manual work, and sport exercises. Soft textures (e.g., carpets, grass, or beach sand) are preferred for sitting and lying down. Rough surfaces (e.g., rockeries, flower beds, or plowed fields) tend to act as obstacles to movement, though they are quite acceptable for manual work, play, or exploration.

In terms of shape, narrow spaces (e.g., doorways, corridors, staircases, paths, bridges, and pavements) are associated with passage. Broad areas, on the other hand (e.g., theater foyers, lecture rooms, and pedestrian plazas), are associated with stationary and relatively sustained gatherings. As Sommer pointed out, the shape of a setting can influence the way people orient themselves in it. Thus in round or squarish spaces (e.g., chapels, circuses, and sport arenas) people tend to place themselves around the perimeter and orient their bodies toward the center so that they create a joint focus of attention for all participants in the social occasion (sociopetal space). However, in irregular or rectangular spaces (e.g., lecture rooms, churches, or cinemas) people often occupy the center and orient themselves away from one another toward various objects placed throughout the area (as in a sculpture gallery) or structures (e.g., a rostrum, altar, screen) at one end of the setting (sociofugal space).

The size of a setting is significant. Small, confined spaces (e.g., telephone booths, toilets, and elevators) discourage both the movement of users and the formation of sustained face-to-face encounters. Social transactions initiated there tend to be transferred to more spacious places. However, very large areas are equally discouraging to social interactions. Thus people prefer places whose dimensions do not exceed the upper limits of comfortable and casual visual and acoustic monitoring of other people's presence. The attractiveness of a setting depends also on the relative number of people within a given area. One study has shown that pedestrians avoid outdoor spaces that, because of size or small number of users, offer more than three hundred square feet per person. Spaces with greater densities are entered on a frequent and regular basis.

The spatial arrangements of objects such as chairs and tables in restaurants; pews in a cathedral; and armchairs, coffee tables, and television set in a suburban living room are also influential. These fixed and semifixed arrangements of furniture act as templates that impose a definite spatial order on the occasionally spontaneous and thus unpredictable events that occur around them. For example, thick and meandering queues become straight and reduced to a single file as soon as they enter narrow passages formed by railings and walls. People who are equals in their interactional roles (e.g., those in conversational gatherings or card games) spontaneously create circular and square arrangements. Their equality may be reinforced by the presence of chairs spaced evenly around a square or round conference table, or, alternatively, it may be attenuated or destroyed by placing people at rectangular or horseshoe-shaped tables.

The impact of environmental features on people's spatial distribution within a place can be seen in less obvious situations. When people enter public settings, they usually cluster close to fixed features (no further away than a couple of feet) and avoid placing themselves in the middle of an open area or near other gatherings. Furthermore, features of the environment seem to affect the size of territorial claims. Stationary gatherings tend to appropriate larger interactional areas in places with relatively few users than in more densely occupied places or places close to fixed environmental features. It appears that walls, trees, and litter bins as well as stationary gatherings are used as indicators of the perimeter of the interactional territories people claim for the duration of a given social occasion. They seem to help people reach tacit agreement on how much of the setting is currently available for their use and movement, thus reducing stressful misunderstandings about the proxemic rules applicable to a given location and setting.

Transformations of the Spatial Contexts

Spatial contexts not only are complex but also change continuously. In the course of social occasions people have a tendency to modify, redecorate, and rearrange at least some of the physical features present. Even small children playing quietly in a schoolyard are capable of transforming that homogeneous space into an elaborate world of mazes and hopscotches created with ordinary chalk. This redefined space can enforce a tight control on the children's spacing and movement for the next hour or so.

Although fixed and semifixed environmental features are the most visible and tangible ones, the majority of transformations in the structure of the environment are caused by the way people distribute themselves within it. Thus at Sydney's Bondi Beach four occupancy zones are regularly established in the otherwise uniform expanse of sand. Young male surfers routinely occupy one of the ends of the beach. Next to them young to middle-age male and female swimmers sit, sunbathe, and enjoy the water. In the next area topless young women sunbathe. The remainder of the beach is populated by families with small children and the elderly.

In fact all environments are subject to explicit and implicit negotiation about their segmentation into bounded areas. Such subdivisions not only regulate patterns of human spacing within the setting and within the location but also serve an important communicational role. The various subdivisions of a setting and a location supply the interacting parties with a rich range of contextual and indexical information necessary for the smooth functioning of any social occasion.

Conclusions

Spatial contexts of human interactions are seldom inert, simple, or inflexible. They are influenced, structured, and defined by countless human actions through which some type of territorial and behavioral relationship between a given set of users and their physical and human context is claimed, marked, respected, challenged, defended, or otherwise acknowledged. Thus every place derives its unique appearance, layout, and character from patterns of events that occur there most often. Yet simultaneously, spaces invariably influence, structure, and define the anticipations, perceptions, and actions of people present there. Therefore, the spatial organization of interpersonal events is always anchored in the patterns of space surrounding those events. The extent to which there is congruity and scope for mutual support and reinforcement between the two is, according to Christopher Alexander, the ultimate measure of the environment's quality.

Bibliography. Christopher Alexander et al., *A Pattern Language: Town, Buildings, Construction,* New York, 1977; Roger G. Barker and Herbert F. Wright, *Midwest and Its Children,* New York, 1955, reprint Hamden, Conn., 1971; Erving Goffman, *Behavior in Public Places: Notes on the Social Organization of Gatherings,* New York, 1963; idem, *Relations in Public: Microstudies of the Public Order,* New York, 1971; Edward T. Hall, *The Hidden Dimension,* New York, 1966; Harold Proshansky, William H. Ittelson, and Leanne G. Rivlin, *Environmental Psychology: People and Their Physical Settings,* 2d ed., New York, 1976; Amos Rapoport, *Human Aspects of Urban Form: Towards a Man-Environment Approach to Urban Form and Design,* Oxford and New York, 1977; Albert E. Scheflen and Norman Ashcraft, *Human Territories: How We Behave in Space-Time,* Englewood Cliffs, N.J., 1975; Robert Sommer, *Personal Space: The Behavioral Basis of Design,* Englewood Cliffs, N.J., 1969.

T. MATTHEW CIOLEK

SPEAKING, ETHNOGRAPHY OF

An approach to the relationship among LANGUAGE, CULTURE, and society that includes both theoretical and methodological perspectives. It is a description in cultural terms of the patterned uses of language and SPEECH in a particular group, institution, community, or society that includes native theories and practices of speaking, both as overtly articulated by individuals and as enacted by them in a range of activities, situations, and interactions.

More specifically the ethnography of speaking is concerned with

1. The sociolinguistic resources available in particular communities. Such resources include not just GRAMMAR in the conventional sense but rather a complex of linguistic potentials for social use and social MEANING, among which are linguistic variables, styles, terms of reference and address, and words and word relations.
2. The use and exploitation of these resources in discourse (speech acts, events, and situations) and in social interaction (agreeing, disagreeing, showing deference or respect, greeting, cajoling).
3. The patterned interrelationships and organization of the various types of discourse and social interaction in the community.
4. The relationship of these patterns of speaking to other aspects and domains of the culture of the community, such as social organization, RELIGION, economics, and politics.

A complete ethnography of speaking would deal with each of these topics. Most research and publications, however, tend to focus on particular ones: the description of linguistic resources, organized as styles or ways of speaking (men's versus women's speech, baby talk); the analysis of particular speech events (greetings, drinking encounters); or the role of speaking in a particular segment of social or cultural life (politics, religion).

Origins. The ethnography of speaking as an approach began in the early 1960s when U.S. linguistic anthropologist Dell Hymes published a series of papers calling for ways to study language and speech that dealt with aspects of language use that fall between or otherwise escape established disciplines such as anthropology, LINGUISTICS, and sociology. Essentially his argument was that language and speech have a patterning of their own, as do social organization, politics, religion, and economics, and therefore merit attention by anthropologists. This patterning is not identical to the grammar of a language in the traditional sense, yet is linguistic as well as cultural in organization and thus merits attention by linguists.

Hymes introduced the notion of the speech event as central to the ethnography of speaking and argued that analysis of speech events requires study of the interrelationships among a number of components or factors: settings, participants, purposes, verbal or textual organization in terms of constituent acts, key or manner of delivery, linguistic varieties used, norms of interaction, and genres. The careful study of these components of speaking in their own terms, with regard to both terminology and patterned organization, and of the relationship between the functions of speech and these components leads to a description that captures each society's unique cultural organization of language and speech.

Collections of papers published in the middle and late 1960s and early 1970s helped to develop this field. These papers described aspects of language and speech typically overlooked or treated as secondary or marginal by anthropologists, sociologists, and linguists. Some of their titles are indicative of their focus: "Baby Talk in Six Languages," "How to Ask for a Drink in Subanun," "Sequencing in Conversational Openings," "Signifying and Marking: Two Afro-American Speech Acts," and "Social Meaning in Linguistic Structures: Code-Switching in Norway."

In the 1970s a new group of researchers focused their attention on particular societies around the world with the specific goal of conducting research in the ethnography of speaking. This research has led to a number of dissertations, articles, and books. Once again, some titles are illustrative: *A Musical View of the Universe: Kalapalo Myth and Ritual Performances, Kuna Ways of Speaking: An Ethnographic Perspective, Let Your Words Be Few: Symbolism of Speaking and Silence among Seventeenth-century Quakers, Portraits of "The Whiteman": Linguistic Play and Cultural Symbols among the Western Apache, Sound and Sentiment: Birds, Weeping, Poetics, and Song in Kaluli Expression,* and *The Invisible Culture: Communication in Classroom and Community on the Warm Springs Indian Reservation.*

Characteristics and foci of research. While research in the ethnography of speaking continues to be based on its original assumptions and goals, certain specialized foci have also emerged. These include intercultural and interethnic communication and miscommunication, the traditional verbal art of nonliterate peoples, the relationship between oral and written discourse, the acquisition of communicative competence, and language use within modern complex societies and in such institutional settings as education. *See also* LANGUAGE ACQUISITION; LANGUAGE VARIETIES; ORAL CULTURE; ORAL HISTORY.

The research methods of the ethnography of speaking integrate those of sociolinguistics and those of social and cultural anthropology. From sociolinguistics is borrowed the assumption of a heterogeneous speech community and the concern with collecting and analyzing a selection of representative forms of speech within this heterogeneity. From social and cultural anthropology is adopted the assumption of cultural relativity, the concern with discovering an *emic* or native insider's point of view, and the need to elicit and analyze native terms and concepts for ways of speaking. Also anthropological is the ethnographic method of constant INTERPRETATION, of relating ways of speaking to each other and situating them in social and cultural contexts from which they derive meaning and to which they contribute meaning.

One special feature of the ethnography of speaking is that it is discourse centered. It studies the speech acts, events, and situations—everyday and informal as well as formal and RITUAL—that constitute the social, cultural, and especially verbal life of particular societies. This involves attention to the relationship between text and context and among transcription, translation, analysis, and theory. Discourse is considered the focus of the language-culture-society-individual relationship, the place in which culture is conceived and transmitted, created and re-created.

The basic theoretical contribution of the ethnography of speaking is the demonstration that there are coherent and meaningful patterns in language use and speaking practices in societies around the world and that there are significant cross-cultural differences in these patterns. The role of language in society cannot be taken for granted, intuited on the basis of one's own experience, or projected from a single language, culture, or society onto others.

Bibliography. Ellen B. Basso, *A Musical View of the Universe: Kalapalo Myth and Ritual Performances,* Philadelphia, 1985; Keith H. Basso, *Portraits of "The Whiteman": Linguistic Play and Cultural Symbols among the Western Apache,* Cambridge and New York, 1979; Richard Bauman, *Let Your Words Be Few: Symbolism of Speaking and Silence among Seventeenth-Century Quakers,* Cambridge and New York, 1983; Richard Bauman and Joel Sherzer, eds., *Explorations in the Ethnography of Speaking,* Cambridge, 1974; Steven Feld, *Sound and Sentiment: Birds, Weeping, Poetics, and Song in Kaluli Expression,* Philadelphia, 1982; John J. Gumperz, *Discourse Strategies,* Cambridge, 1982; John J. Gumperz and Dell Hymes, eds., *Directions in Sociolinguistics: The Ethnography of Communication,* New York, 1972; idem, *The Ethnography of Communication* (special publication), *American Anthropologist* 66, no. 6, pt. 2 (1964); Dell Hymes, *Foundations in Sociolinguistics: An Ethnographic Approach,* Philadelphia, 1974; Susan U. Philips, *The Invisible Culture: Communication in Classroom and Community on the Warm Springs Indian Reservation,* New York, 1983; Joel Sherzer, *Kuna Ways of Speaking: An Ethnographic Perspective,* Austin, Tex., 1983.

JOEL SHERZER

SPECIAL EFFECTS

Nonroutine photographic and mechanical techniques used to produce motion picture images that are too costly, too difficult, too time-consuming, too dangerous, or simply impossible to achieve by means of conventional CINEMATOGRAPHY (Figure 1). Applications of these techniques are numerous and are lim-

Figure 1. *(Special Effects)* In the television-film production of *Cosmos* (1980) a locomotive seems to run directly into the camera but actually is driven into a large mirror positioned at a forty-five-degree angle to the train tracks and to the optical axis of the camera. Raymond Fielding Collection. Courtesy of *American Cinematographer.*

ited only by imagination and the requirements of a particular film production. The effects produced may be as simple as the fade-ins, fade-outs, dissolves, wipes, and other transitions that are used to indicate changes in time and place. Or they may be as complicated as the destruction of a building or of an entire city; the addition of a vaulted ceiling to a ballroom scene; the removal of trees, buildings, or other background detail from a cluttered picture; the addition of clouds or architectural detail to enhance a dull scene; the jigsawing of an actor who is photographed on the sound stage into a background scene that has been photographed many miles distant; the production of gunshot bullet hits, explosions, rain, fog, mist, snow, and ice; the creation of phantom images of people or objects; the sinking of a full-scale naval vessel during a storm at sea; the levitation of solid objects in defiance of the law of gravity; or the re-creation of seventeenth-century London. These and other kinds of assignments call for the use of so-called special effects, the general term embracing photographic effects (sometimes called visual effects, special cinematographic effects, or process photography), mechanical effects such as the use

Table 1. Visual Effects Techniques

In-the-Camera Techniques

Basic effects
- Changes in object speed, position, or direction
- Image distortions and degradations
- Optical transitions
- Superimpositions
- Day-for-night photography

Image replacement
- Split-screen photography
- In-the-camera matte shots
- Glass shots
- Mirror shots

Miniatures

Laboratory Processes

Bi-pack printing
Optical printing
Traveling mattes
Aerial-image printing

Combination Techniques

Background projection
- Rear projection
- Front projection

of reduced-scale models, and effects made possible by VIDEO and computer technology.

Visual Effects

Visual effects techniques can be classified as comprising (1) in-the-camera effects, whereby all the components of the final scene are photographed on the original camera negative; (2) laboratory processes, whereby duplication of the original negative through one or more generations is necessary before the final effect is produced; and (3) combinations of the two, some of the image components being photographed directly onto the final film composite while others are produced through duplication procedures (see Table 1).

Special effects cinematography has been employed since the earliest days of motion picture production. Some techniques, such as split-screen, photo-matte, and double-exposure, were adapted from nineteenth-century still PHOTOGRAPHY. Shots such as these appear in Edwin S. Porter's 1903 classic, *The Great Train Robbery,* in which, first, a locomotive train is seen through a window from the interior of a train station's office as the train pulls into the station, and, second, an exterior wooded scene is seen through an open door in a baggage car. In the language of the special effects worker, the images of the locomotive and wooded background were "matted into" the areas of the train station's window and the baggage car's door.

Other techniques, such as stop-motion photography, were intrinsic to the filmic process and were discovered by different workers throughout the world. Just before the turn of the century, Alfred Clark in the United States and Georges Méliès in France were among the first to discover that by alternately stopping and starting the camera they could achieve mysterious appearances and disappearances of people and objects in the frame, as well as to make inanimate objects move across the frame of their own volition, the objects being moved incrementally by the filmmakers between the exposure of individual frames of film. This technique, known as stop-motion or single-frame cinematography, was also the technique that would be employed after the turn of the century to produce the first animated cartoons. *See* ANIMATION; MOTION PHOTOGRAPHY; MOTION PICTURES.

Many early filmmakers photographed primitive miniature shots, employing reduced-scale models of ships, harbors, volcanoes, cities, buildings, and the like, for exciting, albeit crude, scenes of disaster and destruction. From the beginning special effects techniques were called upon to produce spectacular, fantastic, and obviously impossible scenes of the imagination. With the passing of time, however, they were just as often used to produce believable but difficult-to-photograph scenes at a lower cost or with less time and effort than would have been involved by conventional cinematographic techniques.

Modern high-quality special effects techniques can be said to have originated with the work of U.S. filmmaker Norman Dawn, who was the first known cinematographer to produce high-quality glass shots. This technique calls for certain aspects of the finished scene (such as the roof or upper stories of a building) to be painted onto a large sheet of glass that is positioned in front of the camera. The full-scale sets and the live-action performers seen *through* the glass and the painted elements on the *surface* of the glass are photographed simultaneously. If the painting is artfully executed, the two elements will fit as if they belong together. This technique was used by Dawn as early as 1907 for his production of *Missions of California.* Dawn also invented, patented, and popularized the so-called in-the-camera matte shot (also known as a painted matte), which requires successive exposures of matted-out areas of the image. He employed it for the first time in 1911 on his production of *Story of the Andes.*

Optical printing, the process of rephotographing a strip of film optically, frame by frame, did not become feasible until the introduction of modern fine-grain duplicating film stocks in the late 1920s and early 1930s. In time the optical printer became the most versatile of all special effects tools, allowing for an unlimited number and variety of image modifications and time-space distortions. Prominent in the development of this technology were engineers like Cecil Love and special effects supervisors such as Linwood Dunn, who created many of the astonishing special effects for *King Kong* in 1933 (Figure 2) and *Citizen Kane* in 1941.

The introduction of sound to film in the late 1920s placed a premium on special effects techniques that would allow one to photograph actors within an acoustically isolated sound stage and then to insert their images into background scenes that had been photographed elsewhere. The technique of rear projection, although used in crude fashion at least as early as 1913 by Dawn, could not be developed in any practical way until the introduction in the late 1920s and early 1930s of modern, relatively high-

Figure 2. *(Special Effects)* Merian C. Cooper and Ernest B. Schoedsack, *King Kong,* 1933. Courtesy of the Amos Vogel Collection/RKO Pictures, Inc. Copyright © 1933, renewed 1960 RKO Pictures, Inc. All rights reserved.

Figure 3. *(Special Effects)* A composite of miniatures and a rear-projected background. Raymond Fielding Collection/National Film Board of Canada.

speed panchromatic stocks and electrically interlocked motors. Over the years and through the efforts of workers such as Farciot Edouart at Paramount, the process was refined to the point that Technicolor film productions like *Dr. Cyclops* (1940) employed as many as three interlocked background projectors. After World War II a variation of the system called front projection was introduced by the Motion Picture Research Council in association with the Minnesota Mining and Manufacturing Corporation. Today both front- and rear-projection techniques are commonly used to solve a variety of production problems (Figure 3).

Still another technique for inserting actors into background scenes, the traveling matte, became available in crude form in the late teens and early twenties and has been continuously developed since that time. It requires photographing the actor in front of a white, black, or blue backing and the subsequent production of various strips of film that either obscure or reveal particular parts of the background and foreground images during successive duplications on an optical printer (Figure 4). The technique is extremely complicated but can produce filmic and dramatic effects that are impossible to produce by other means.

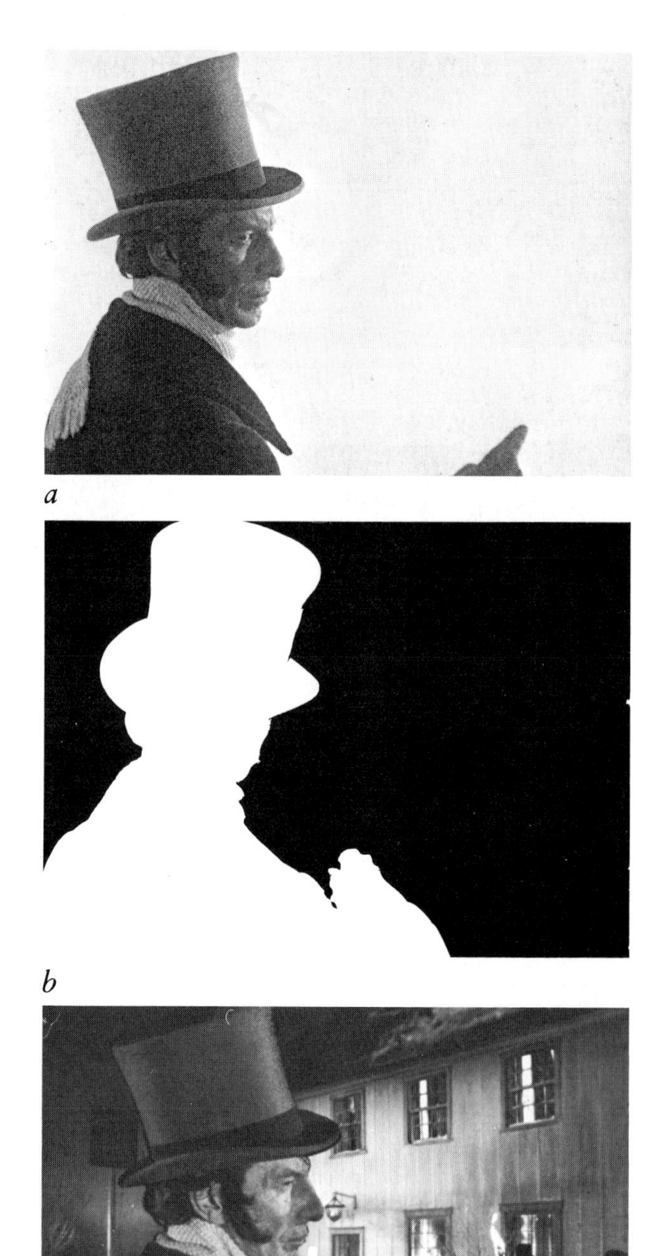

a

b

c

Figure 4. *(Special Effects)* The traveling-matte technique. *(a)* An actor is photographed so as to allow for production of a traveling matte of his figure. *(b)* A background printing mask, or countermatte, is prepared through step-contact or step-optical printing. *(c)* During composite optical, the separate foreground and background images are combined. This shot involves miniatures, a static matte-painting, a partially completed full-scale set, a foreground actor, and a traveling matte. Raymond Fielding Collection/National Film Board of Canada.

Electronic, Computerized Effects

The availability of sophisticated computer technology and the gradual marriage of film and video technique during the 1970s and 1980s have provided special effects workers with an entirely new set of techniques and tools. So-called motion-control systems allow for rephotographing, on separate strips of film, the various components of a composite image by a camera capable of being moved repeatedly through complicated maneuvers. The various camera movements are controlled by computers, and the separate strips of film are later composited through optical printing. Such equipment made feasible the production of immensely successful science fiction films such as *2001* (1968; Figure 5), *Star Wars* (1977), and *Close Encounters of the Third Kind* (1977).

A set of even more electronically sophisticated tools, which became available to filmmakers in the 1980s, enables filmmakers to combine computerized, animated graphic images with live-action scenes. Technologically important films of the 1980s, such as *Tron* and *The Last Starfighter,* incorporated hundreds of shots whose fantastic images were either partly or completely produced by computers. Television commercials and music videos soon began to make wide use of such techniques. By this time prototype electronic optical printers had begun to appear that were capable of achieving the high image quality associated with film production while offer-

Figure 5. *(Special Effects)* Stanley Kubrick, *2001: A Space Odyssey,* 1968. National Film Archive, London/Turner Entertainment.

ing the convenience, flexibility, and speed of operations associated with video production.

See also FILM EDITING.

Bibliography. Linwood Dunn and George Turner, *The ASC Treasury of Visual Effects,* Hollywood, Calif., 1983; Raymond Fielding, *The Technique of Special Effects Cinematography,* 4th ed., London and Stoneham, Mass., 1985; Christopher Finch, *Special Effects: Creating Movie Magic,* New York, 1984.

RAYMOND FIELDING

SPECTACLE

A large-scale, extravagant cultural production that is replete with striking visual imagery and dramatic action and that is watched by a mass audience. The spectacle is especially characteristic of modern societies, socialist and capitalist, but is also found in traditional societies significantly affected by modern influences. It is arguable that spectacle has surpassed religious RITUAL as the principal symbolic context in which contemporary societies enact and communicate their guiding beliefs, values, concerns, and self-understandings (*see also* RELIGION).

The repertoire of spectacles is vast, but the most familiar examples come from the field of SPORTS. The greatest of all spectacles is probably the Olympic Games, which attract tens of thousands of participants, live audiences of two to three million persons, and media audiences estimated to number a third of the world's total population. World Cup soccer matches also draw huge live and television audiences, as do, in the United States, championship and other "classic" games in professional baseball and football, college football, and various other sports ranging from golf through horse and stock car racing. When the magazine *Sports Illustrated* was started in 1954, it included a photographic section called "Spectacle," which in its prospectus stated, "Sport . . . is magic to the eye. It lingers in the life-long treasury of vision."

Other cultural productions commonly described as spectacle include various festivals (carnivals; *fastnachts;* saint's-day fiestas; ethnic, regional, and national celebrations), public entertainment extravaganzas (rock concerts, country music jamborees), exhibitions (national and world's fairs, action-centered theme and amusement parks), civic and political ceremonies (presidential inaugurations, royal coronations, party leadership conventions, opening of Parliament, Soviet May Day parade), and special religious events (papal visits, pilgrimages, large evangelical crusades). A common feature of these phenomena is that the central dramatic event is surrounded by other events and attractions that are seen as significant components of the total occasion: pomp and pageantry, parading and partying, sideshows of all kinds—including CROWD BEHAVIOR. It is for this reason that spectacles typically take place, in whole or in part, outdoors. Indoor settings are spatially too restrictive to allow sufficient ancillary activities. Notable exceptions include the three-ring circus, where the "stage" is designed to encompass a varied assortment of visual attractions. *See also* FESTIVAL.

Etymologically, the English word spectacle derives from the Latin *spectare,* "to look." In general, dictionaries define the term as (1) a sweeping, visually impressive public event, and (2) a person or thing

Figure 1. *(Spectacle)* Antoine Caron, *Festival at Bayonne, 1565, Catherine de' Medici's Water Fête.* Drawing. The Pierpont Morgan Library, New York.

Figure 2. *(Spectacle)* Dinagyang festival, Iloilo City, Philippines. Courtesy of the Philippine Ministry of Tourism—New York.

put on display that evokes responses ranging from admiration through curiosity and contempt. While the first definition most closely approximates the current meaning of spectacle in connection with cultural productions, the second reveals a basic ambivalence about the value and efficacy of spectacle. When spectacle was used in relation to THEATER—a meaning it acquired in the mid-eighteenth century—the negative valence prevailed. A theatrical spectacle was seen as "mere" stage display or pageantry, as contrasted with "real drama." The association of spectacle with conventional theater is now uncommon in English. In French, however, the cognate word *spectacle* is still used in connection with film, theater, and various other stage presentations, where its meaning is neutral, and in connection with "making a spectacle of oneself" (*se donner en spectacle*), where its meaning is derogatory. *See* DRAMA.

Spectacle as Performance Genre

The study of spectacle has been fostered by a growing interest in large-scale symbolic forms among a variety of social scientists and humanities scholars. Other contributing factors have been the diversification of anthropology to include the cultures of modern as well as traditional societies and the extension of concepts from literary and linguistic analysis to the analysis of popular performances. Among the more prominent influences are anthropologists Clifford Geertz and Victor Turner. Geertz, using Balinese cockfighting as an example, proposed the METAPHOR that this sort of PERFORMANCE (which, in Bali, is very much a spectacle) is a collectively authored "text" about Balinese society, a story the Balinese "tell themselves about themselves." Turner saw spectacles as one of the many performance genres in which modern peoples playfully but reflexively symbolize the assumptions, norms, and conventional roles that govern their ordinary lives. He claimed that these genres are the surrogates of religious ritual in traditional societies but emphasized that they have a greater potential for creativity and change. Whereas traditional ritual temporarily suspends but ultimately validates the principles of social structure, modern performance genres have the capacity to subvert the system and formulate alternatives. Such phenomena as spectacles impose their symbolism on social processes and often exert a major influence on the direction of those processes. Life follows performance.

U.S. anthropologist John MacAloon makes perhaps the first systematic attempt to examine spectacle as a distinct performance GENRE in his book *Rite, Drama, Festival, Spectacle* (1984). Using the Olympics as his main example, he argues that spectacle is a "megagenre" that encompasses other genres that are more limited in scope and more specific in meaning. The Olympics are simultaneously a game (an agonistic contest among national opponents), a rite (a solemn consecration of human unity aimed at symbolizing the ideal of world community), a festival (a joyous celebration of unity, cooperation, accomplishment, and excellence), and a spectacle (a grandiloquent display of imagery evoking a diffuse sense of wonderment and awe). These four genres are interconnected in the history, ideology, performance, and structural ordering of the Olympics, but each is separable and places its own semantic construction—its own "reading" in the semiotic sense—on the phenomenon.

Examining the spectacle genre as a communicative frame (in the sense meant by GREGORY BATESON and ERVING GOFFMAN), MacAloon sees its metamessage as one of entertainment and detachment. The spectator qua spectator remains individuated and uncommitted. But spectacle is also a "recruitment device" that opens access to the other genres it contains. Audiences are often induced to accept the deeper significance of the phenomenon, becoming not just watchers but celebrants, believers, and partisans as well.

For MacAloon, the profusion of spectacles is a

Figure 3. *(Spectacle)* The Olympic Games, Helsinki: Paavo Nurmi lighting the Olympic flame at the opening ceremony, 1952. The Bettmann Archive, Inc.

Figure 4. *(Spectacle)* Cockfighting: matching the cocks and making them angry. Batoean, October 5, 1937. From Gregory Bateson and Margaret Mead, *Balinese Character: A Photographic Analysis,* New York, 1942, plate 43, 3. The Institute for Intercultural Studies/Library of Congress.

Figure 5. *(Spectacle)* New York World's Fair of 1939: National Cash Register Building, Ely Jacques Kahn, architect. The numbers show daily attendance figures. The Museum of the City of New York.

popular response to the "master cultural confusion of the present era"—a profound ambivalence and concern about the relationship between appearing and being, image and reality. Contemporary thought is preoccupied with superficial forms—media stereotypes, opinion polls, advertising slogans, bureaucratic language, and so on. But it is also disturbed by the way these forms obscure deeper realities. Modern people enjoy the freedom of skeptically, even playfully, watching their social world, but they want the assurance that there are truths to be known and values to be practiced. Spectacle displays a modern quandary and serves further as a context for "thinking it out." *See* FACT AND FICTION.

A parallel argument is made by the British philosopher cum social scientist Ernest Gellner in his book *Spectacles and Predicaments* (1979). Gellner sees two major problems in the modern world: validation and enchantment. People seek both to verify bewildering complexity and to impose on it a decorous order. Spectacles offer decorum but ultimately transform themselves into predicaments by drawing audiences into the central action and enabling them to search experientially for verification. This epistemological process corroborates MacAloon's notion that spectacles have both an outer set of appearances that attract an audience and an inner sense of authenticity that is accessible through empathy and participation.

A contrary argument is put forth by the radical French social critic Guy Debord in his book *La société du spectacle* (1967). Debord sees all of modern life as spectacle, a pathological condition that preempts valid social discourse. *"Le spectacle n'est pas un ensemble d'images, mais un rapport social entre des personnes, médiatisé par des images"* (Spectacle is not a set of images, but social relations mediated by images). Spectacle in this view is a metaphor of modernity, not a performance genre that is nurtured by modernity and that, in turn, interprets it.

Spectacle as Tourist Attraction

Most spectacles are, among other things, tourist attractions, a factor that accounts for a great deal of their extravagance, publicity, and commercialism. When spectacles are movable (international athletic events, world's fairs), cities and countries compete intensely to host them. Motives typically include prestige, an envisioned stimulus to the economy, and the opportunity to acquire public facilities that will enhance the spectacle and remain after it. Montreal, for instance, built its subway system to provide for the transportation needs of Expo '67. *See* TOURISM.

In the case of spectacles that are fixed (carnivals, national ceremonies, some sports "classics"), promoters and public officials increasingly emphasize touristic appeal. The Trinidad Carnival, for example, was traditionally known as either "the creole bacchanal" (lower-class revelry) or "we ting" (an exclusivist celebration). But when the Trinidadian oil industry suffered reverses and the country adopted a policy of tourist development, carnival was vigorously advertised as "The Greatest Show on Earth." This newer emphasis has had a significant impact on the style and content of carnival and hence on the meaning it communicates within and beyond Trinidadian society.

In his seminal book *The Tourist* (1975), U.S. sociologist Dean MacCannell examines spectacle as a grandiloquent form of the myriad cultural productions that serve as focal points of tourist activity. As archetypal moderns, tourists view their own society as shallow and spurious. They seek deeper meaning in travel, which exposes them through cultural productions to enacted versions of their own heritage and to the lives of peoples less disturbed by the discontents of modernity. Tourists are "sightseers" (spectators), of course, but the entire semiotic ordering of tourist attractions is designed to create a sense of authenticity by drawing them "backstage," giving them an insider's understanding, and encouraging them to participate as well as observe. Like religious rites, tourist spectacles create and communicate a sense of reality, truth, and value. This argument supports the suggestion of many anthropologists—Turner, Edmund Leach, and Nelson Graburn among them—that tourism is a modern, secular version of pilgrimage.

Other factors contribute to the diffuse relationship among spectacle, modernity, and tourism. For one, visual codes generally have surpassed oral-aural codes in both aesthetic and epistemological importance, a process that probably originated in literacy and has been accelerated by film, television, and other visually oriented modern media. The visual nature of spectacles not only qualifies them as modern, but

Figure 6. *(Spectacle)* Nighttime view of Expo '70, Osaka, Japan. Courtesy of Japan Air Lines.

Figure 7. *(Spectacle)* May Day celebrations in Red Square, Moscow, May 1, 1970. UPI/Bettmann Newsphotos.

also enhances their transcultural portability and hence their touristic potential.

There is also the modern emphasis on LEISURE as free time, that is, time at an individual's disposal to spend in a manner of personal choice. Both tourism and spectacle are modern leisure pastimes. Subscription to them is voluntary and nonbinding, and one is free to leave at any time. No prior belief or commitment is entailed (even though these may be forthcoming later). The only predisposing reason for being there is to enjoy oneself.

Another important factor is the transition in Western societies from producer to consumer capitalism. The frugality and investment orientation of early capitalism—its ascetic rationalism, to use MAX WEBER's phrase—has been overshadowed by a standard that emphasizes the use of money to purchase commodities, services, and experience. Under the influence of the early Protestant ethic, spectacle was a flagrant taboo, a "deceptive bedazzlement" that lured people from moral purpose and, worse yet, distracted them from work. Contrastingly, in contemporary societies, spectacle is a showcase of popular culture's major assets and attractions.

Yet some Protestant influences undoubtedly persist, albeit in altered form. Distinguishing broadly between the spectacles and tourist attractions of Protestant and Catholic societies, it is readily apparent that the former are less licensed and socially invertive than the latter; that is, in Protestant societies spectacles are less likely to be used as an excuse to flout the normal social order. Within the Western hemisphere, for example, events such as the Calgary Stampede, the football "bowl" games, and the major national holiday celebrations of the United States' Protestant-oriented "civil religion" have but a small measure of the ludic illicitness and social parody found in the carnivals of New Orleans, Trinidad, and Brazil, as well as in many of the carnivalesque religious fiestas of Latin America.

Spectacle and Mass Culture

Spectacle is arguably the diagnostic performance form of modern mass culture. Like an amusement park, it is a setting where everything happens at once. Communication is dialogic, polyphonic, and polythematic. Spectacle is a phantasmagoric presentation of a phantasmagoric phenomenon—the modern world's pluralistic fragmentation. It unifies this fragmentation not by systematically ordering it, but simply by packaging it within a circumscribed performance context. It is precisely this sort of unification—in fact, an articulation of differences within a perceivable framework—that constitutes what MacCannell terms modernity's "unifying consciousness."

If spectacle is an appropriate depiction of the modern world—a form that both presents modernity and

GENERAL VIEW OF THE SOUTH NAVE OF MACHINERY HALL.

Figure 8. *(Spectacle)* Machinery Hall, dominated by two Krupp cannons from Germany, at the United States Centennial Exposition held in Philadelphia in 1876. From Frank H. Norton, *The Illustrated Historical Register of the United States Centennial Exposition, 1876,* New York, 1877, p. 241.

makes sense of it—it is also a summation of popular genres and cultural subsystems. Literary critics Julia Kristeva and MIKHAIL BAKHTIN and anthropologist Barbara Babcock point respectively to the "carnivalization" of the modern novel, the Rabelaisian cacophony and grotesqueness of our communications systems and social life, and the "surfeit of signifiers" in ludic literature and performance. Similarly, U.S. anthropologist James Boon asserts that modern entertainment forms are characterized by a "riot" of disconnected and disjunctive symbolic types. Spectacle is both an archetype of modern popular culture and, alternately, a comment on it.

The accommodative capacity of spectacle is perhaps its most distinctive modern feature. As a "super" genre, spectacle is a suitable form for mass culture. Spectacle does not obliterate or replace other genres; rather, it encompasses and frames them, situating them in a wider and more general communicative context. The semiotics of that enlargement process not only exemplify mass culture, but also provide a focus for a reflexive apprehension of it.

Bibliography. Paul Bouissac, *Circus and Culture,* Bloomington, Ind., 1976; Guy Debord, *La société du spectacle,* Paris, 1967, reprint *The Society of the Spectacle,* Detroit, Mich., 1983; Clifford Geertz, *The Interpretation of Cultures,* New York, 1973; Ernest Gellner, *Spectacles and Predicaments: Essays in Social Theory,* Cambridge, 1979; John MacAloon, ed., *Rite, Drama, Festival, Spectacle: Rehearsals towards a Theory of Cultural Performance,* Philadelphia, 1984; Dean MacCannell, *The Tourist: A New Theory of the Leisure Class,* New York, 1976; Frank E. Manning, ed., *The Celebration of Society: Perspectives* *on Contemporary Cultural Performance,* Bowling Green, Ohio, and London, Ont., 1983; Sally F. Moore and Barbara Myerhoff, eds., *Secular Ritual,* Assen/Amsterdam, 1977; Victor Turner, *From Ritual to Theater,* New York, 1982; Norton Wood, ed., *The Spectacle of Sport,* Englewood Cliffs, N.J., 1957.

FRANK E. MANNING

SPECTRUM

The RADIO spectrum is a unique resource that during the past century has become the basis of a global technical-industrial revolution. This revolution started when Great Britain, Germany, France, the United States, and Russia began in the 1890s to use the inventions of GUGLIELMO MARCONI and others to exchange information through the radio spectrum. The unique characteristics of the radio spectrum made it the first major example of worldwide common property as distinct from private property; its use by any group requires that all groups cooperate to minimize interference in its use. The structures and policies developed for its use were influenced by and in turn had consequences for all major global tensions and problems.

Characteristics. The electromagnetic spectrum consists of fields of magnetic and electrical force capable of transmitting electromagnetic energy in successive waves of different lengths. In addition to radio waves, the spectrum includes radiant heat, infrared light, visible and ultraviolet light, the X-ray spectrum, and, finally, cosmic rays. The presently usable radio spectrum ranges from about ten kilohertz to 300 million kilohertz per second. When energy waves are generated within these frequencies and information is imposed on them, it is decodable within limits. The limits are set by conditions that affect wave propagation, if natural and human-generated noise does not create intolerable interference.

The conditions that affect wave propagation depend basically on the conductivity characteristics of the environment. These characteristics are rooted in variable behavior of the ionosphere (magnetic and electrical fields of force as affected by sun and earth), geological and water formations, and weather. Other technical variables that affect wave propagation include the type of signal modulated (amplitude, frequency, pulse time, etc.), the width of the channel, antenna capacity at both the transmitting and the receiving ends, the power used in transmitting, the polarization of the signal (vertical or horizontal), the ability of the equipment to deliver the signals in desired directions, multiplex versus simplex capacity, and so on. Until the 1920s, electronic equipment was developed for the Low and Medium Frequencies, 30 kHz to 3 mHz. Development of the High Frequencies (3 mHz to 30 mHz) took place in the next decade. In the 1930s and 1940s, the art extended to the Very High Frequencies (30 mHz to 300 mHz), and in the late 1940s and the 1950s to the Ultra High Frequencies (300 mHz to 3 gHz). The Super High Frequencies (3 gHz to 30 gHz) were explored in the 1950s to 1970s. The frontier of development in the 1980s was in the Extremely High Frequencies (30 gHz to 300 gHz) and the Very Low Frequencies (10 kHz to 30 kHz). Because of the propagation factors mentioned above, the range of distance over which radio communication is possible differs greatly as between these sectors of the radio spectrum. The spur to development has been military research and development in the industrialized countries with civilian applications (e.g., radio and television broadcast) being spin-offs.

The radio spectrum differs from other natural resources in possessing the following characteristics. First, the radio spectrum's original and still principal use is the act of sharing information between transmitter and receiver; the principal function of both transmission and retention is characteristic of no other resource. Second, for one nation or one class of user to use the radio spectrum, all nations and classes of users must be able to use it. Therefore, worldwide cooperation is necessary in order for the radio spectrum to be used by anyone. Third, the radio spectrum is nondepletable and self-renewing. There is interference between users (minimized by international regulation), but this "pollution" disappears as soon as the interference ceases. Other natural resources such as soil, water, and air are depletable, and renewal may take millions of years. Finally, because the radio spectrum is used to transmit information and because control of the flow of information is the basis of political power, the allocation of the radio spectrum is essential in establishing and maintaining national sovereignty. Few other resources have this political, tactical, and strategic significance. At the same time, the very system on which this power rests is inherently and inescapably fragile and vulnerable to disruption. Natural forces (e.g., storms), technical factors, bureaucratic weaknesses, and deliberate actions span a wide range of causes of interference. Government studies (e.g., in Sweden and France) have warned of the fragility of modern telecommunications systems. Therefore joint decision making by all nations at the world level contributes to the practice of world sovereignty. This world regulation underlies the fact that, by international law, title to the radio spectrum does not rest with particular individuals or nations but with all humanity. *See* INTERNATIONAL ORGANIZATIONS.

Frequency allocation. For several millennia, Western law has recognized three types of relationships between people and environmental resources: private property, common property, and state property. The peculiar characteristics of the radio spectrum combine to place it partly in the category of common property on a world scale and partly in that of state property. It can never be private property because of the degree of regulation that it requires.

Radio frequency allocation is a process involving three mutually determining steps. The first step is to determine the specific classes of use for specific bands of frequencies, based on engineering STANDARDS that take account of environmental and technical parameters. For example, airlines require long-range frequencies for navigation and for long-distance communication (e.g., over oceans), but also short-range frequencies for communicating between air and ground (e.g., at airports). They must therefore have access to frequencies in different parts of the spectrum. Furthermore, because aircraft (and ships) move around the world, they must be able to use the same bands of frequencies wherever they move. Specific standards are necessary to assure them of maximum use and minimum interference. The second step is to determine the location of transmitting and receiving stations for use in a given hemisphere, region, or country, given a specific frequency band, a specific class of use, and the engineering standards that have been determined for that class (e.g., decisions determining how many television stations are assigned to particular locations). The third step is to determine the identity of the licensees who will use the specific locations for transmitters and receivers according to class of service and required engineering standards.

This allocation process became the responsibility of the International Telecommunications Union (ITU), the oldest functioning world-scale organization. The ITU originated in 1865 as the International Telegraph Union to deal with standards, service, and rate matters for TELEGRAPHY and cables. It was extended in the first quarter of the twentieth century to cover TELEPHONE and radio communications. The basic organization is the ITU Plenipotentiary Conference, at which every five to ten years the member countries meet to renegotiate the structure and policies of the ITU. These actions by the members when confirmed by their governments form the evolving constitution of the ITU. Technical, economic, and political negotiations prepare proposals for plenipotentiary conferences through work of the Consultative Committee for International Telegraph and Telephone (CCITT) and the Consultative Committee for International Radiocommunications (CCIR), which are elected by the ITU members. Administrative Conferences of members implement policies adopted at Plenipotentiary Conferences. This structure is served by the International Frequency Registration Board, an Executive Council (both elected by the members), an elected Secretary-General, and support staff.

In 1982, 157 countries, each with one vote, governed the allocation process. Enterprises that design and manufacture electronic equipment and each class of spectrum users (e.g., aeronautical, marine, broadcast) participate at every level of the process, as do their trade associations. Negotiation, lobbying, and compromise—in other words, politics—characterize the process.

Although the nations of the world have never departed from the basic "world property" concept of the right to use specific radio frequencies, in practice such rights have been allocated on a first-come, first-served basis. In the days of formal empires (*see* COLONIZATION) the imperial powers enjoyed colonial voting (i.e., major powers had as many as six votes each) in the ITU and its predecessor, the International Telegraph Union. After World War II, when formal empires were breaking up, and when the ITU became affiliated with the United Nations, the voting rule became one nation, one vote—as the result of a U.S. initiative.

A more subtle basis of maintaining imperial power was the priority allowed to the country that first notified the ITU of its intention to use a particular radio frequency. This principle was agreed to at the Berlin Conference in 1906, and it enabled the United States to lay the foundation for its dominance in world telecommunications after 1945. The policy came under attack by Third World countries in the 1970s, leading the dominant powers to deplore the "politicizing" of the ITU.

Third World. Through the 1980s, the great bulk of international communications using the radio spectrum flowed either to or from the United States. In comparison the lateral flow of information—as well as of real commodities—between Third World countries was very undeveloped. The dominant (industrialized) countries had 90 percent of the spectrum and 10 percent of the population. The Third World countries had 90 percent of the population and 10 percent of the spectrum. The domination by the industrialized countries is asserted conspicuously through the use of the radio spectrum by their military forces and national DIPLOMACY, and by transnational corporations including those that operate the worldwide network of transnational data teleprocessing.

About two-thirds of the members of the ITU were Third World countries. They varied greatly in size of population, natural resources, cultural character, and degree of commitment to goals of material progress. Yet these countries shared certain common interests.

If they were to change the asymmetrical power relations between themselves and the most industrialized countries, they needed to own, control, and operate their own communications systems. This was as vital to their independence as was their military capability. A communication system for them did not need to be highly sophisticated; the telephone, telegraph, radio broadcast, tape recorder, and photocopier would take them a long way.

Third World countries pressed their claims for equitable shares of world resources through a range of forums: the World Bank, GATT (General Agreement on Tariffs and Trade), the ITU, UNESCO and other UN organizations, the Club of Rome, and many ad hoc conferences. In the 1970s and 1980s their claims crystallized in demands for a New World Information Order and New World Economic Order. The Non-Aligned Movement, since its founding in Bandung in 1955, has been an increasingly cohesive and sophisticated coordinating agency for these struggles (*see* ASIA, TWENTIETH CENTURY). Two issues were sharply contested: the flow of information (one-way or balanced) and frequency allocation policy (planned or unplanned). *See* NEW INTERNATIONAL INFORMATION ORDER.

In the ITU the Third World countries rejected with increasing skill and determination the previous "first-come, first-served" basis of allocating frequency bands and station assignments. They sought positive, long-range planning for the use of the radio spectrum, with reservations of frequency assignments for countries not yet ready to make use of them. The United States, its capitalist allies, and the Soviet Union opposed such planning. They contended that fixed allotment plans that distributed frequencies and orbital slots for satellites to countries where there was no present demonstrated need and ability to use them would not permit optimal utilization of the spectrum or provide adequate incentives to adopt technologies that conserve the spectrum.

In 1974 the ITU Maritime Conference agreed to a plan that allotted frequency assignments according to a mathematical principle of fairness, and in 1977 the World Administrative Radio Conference (WARC) on direct broadcast satellites assigned specific orbital slots to all countries outside the Americas. For the latter, a Western Hemisphere WARC in 1983 assigned orbital slots to some countries and groups of countries that expected to use them immediately. *See* SATELLITE.

The 1982 ITU Plenipotentiary Conference was particularly stormy. Heated disagreements arose over the effort of Arab countries to exclude Israel from the conference. But the central issues were the initiatives of the Third World majority for ITU planning of frequency allocation and their insistence that the ITU provide technical assistance and cooperation. The United States opposed ITU technical aid and supported instead bilateral aid that could build markets for transnational corporation exports. Subsequently, the U.S. government considered refusing to pay its share of the ITU budget and withdrawing from the ITU altogether. However, a study by Georgetown University for the U.S. State Department in 1984 concluded that the ITU was indispensable and that the U.S. should continue to participate:

> Above all, the United States must recognize the absolute need for an ITU-type organization to allocate the electromagnetic spectrum, coordinate efforts to harmonize telecommunications facilities and equipment, allow collaboration on rates and tariffs and improve use of telecommunications in safety, rescue, air traffic, etc.

The study also approved the long-standing U.S. policy of favoring bilateral technical aid to developing countries rather than the ITU-administered aid, which the Third World countries preferred.

Future issues. At any given time the capacity of the radio spectrum is limited by the state of the electronic art. But because research and development make possible more efficient use of it, and there is always the possibility of increasing the capacity of the already-used portions of the spectrum (the intensive margin) and of the newly explored portions of the spectrum (the extensive margin), there is no *scarcity* of spectrum capacity over time. Because spectrum use produces economic rent, recovery of the cost of administering it through license fees would provide an incentive for licensees to economize in its use. Taxpayers' burdens could be reduced by raising license fees further to recover "unearned increment" received by broadcast licensees.

The mode of spectrum management within nation-states has generally been legislative and passive, leaving the initiative in steps two and three (above) to the potential licensees. A range of possible means of improving efficiency in the use of the spectrum depends on positive planning by national governments. New strategies in such planning include pressures for more research and development at both the intensive and extensive margins of spectrum development; requirements that licensees use newer, more efficient equipment; requirements that licensees make organizational innovations (e.g., undivided joint interest enterprises) that reduce spectrum demands; more insistence on circuit discipline and common-calling techniques.

As noted above, a unique characteristic of the radio spectrum is that it lies close to sovereign power where no market mechanism can exist. Indeed, in most if not all countries, the military is the largest single user of the spectrum. A large literature has grown since the 1950s by mostly U.S. neoclassical economists supporting the introduction of market forces into the frequency allocation process. This work assumes that perfect competition exists in the relevant markets. In the real world the necessary conditions are absent. For these reasons and because under international law radio frequencies cannot be private property, "deregulation" of radio spectrum management is not possible.

A number of developing countries have proposed recovery of revenue from the use by others of orbital slots allocated to them for geostationary satellites. And the MacBride Commission report to UNESCO, *Many Voices, One World* (1980), recommended consideration of an "international duty" on the use of the spectrum and orbital slots for the benefit of developing countries, and another "international duty" for the same purpose levied on "the profits of transnational corporations producing transmission facilities" to partially defray the costs of using international communication facilities.

In taking part in the allocation of the radio spectrum, the world's peoples are taking the first step toward determining the ends for which the spectrum may be used in the future. Cooperation to avoid unacceptable interference is the essence of radio spectrum management. Through the process of radio frequency allocation under the ITU, all countries have the possibility of setting the rules for its use. Through such rules and subsequent actions, all countries may obtain and secure control of their own resources.

Bibliography. George A. Codding, Jr., *The International Telecommunications Union,* Leiden, 1952; George A. Codding, Jr., and Anthony M. Rutkowski, *The International Telecommunications Union in a Changing World,* Dedham, Mass., 1982; Department of Communications, Canada, Telecommission Directing Committee, *Instant World,* Ottawa, 1971; Garrett Hardin, "The Tragedy of the Commons," *Science* 162 (1968): 1243–1248; IEEE-EIA Joint Technical Advisory Committee, *Spectrum Engineering: The Key to Progress,* New York, 1968; International Commission for the Study of Communication Problems (UNESCO), *Many Voices, One World: Communication and Society, Today and Tomorrow,* Paris and New York, 1980; Harvey J. Levin, *The Invisible Resource: Use and Regulation of the Radio Spectrum,* Baltimore, Md., 1971; C. B. MacPherson, *Property: Mainstream and Critical Positions,* Toronto, 1978; David Ricardo, *Principles of Political Economy and Taxation,* London, 1819, reprint New York, 1969; Dallas W. Smythe, *Dependency Road: Communications, Capitalism, Consciousness, and Canada,* Norwood, N.J., 1981; U.S. President's Task Force on Communications Policy, *Staff Papers,* Vol. 7, *The Use and Management of the Electro-Magnetic Spectrum,* Washington, D.C., 1969.

DALLAS W. SMYTHE

SPEECH

The form of communication used most frequently by human beings and the one that many would argue is characteristic of humans and no other species. Speech behavior is usually thought of in two distinct but interrelated ways.

From one perspective, the study of speech behavior concerns the actual process of generating and vocalizing sounds, with the sounds necessary for producing oral LANGUAGE assuming primary importance. This process involves a complex interaction and coordination of the brain, the nervous system, and various anatomical structures and organs (see Figure 1). The actions involved in sound production alone are respiration, phonation, resonation, and articulation. Although some languages use sounds produced while inhaling, most sounds are initiated by air exhaled from the lungs and sent up through the trachea. The air stream is made audible by the vibrations of the vocal folds in the larynx. Whispering occurs when the vibration of the vocal folds is not activated. By changing the shape of the oral and nasal cavities and by the various kinds of contact made between the mobile articulators (tongue, tongue tip, and lips) and the fixed articulators (hard and soft palates, alveolar ridge), different sounds are produced.

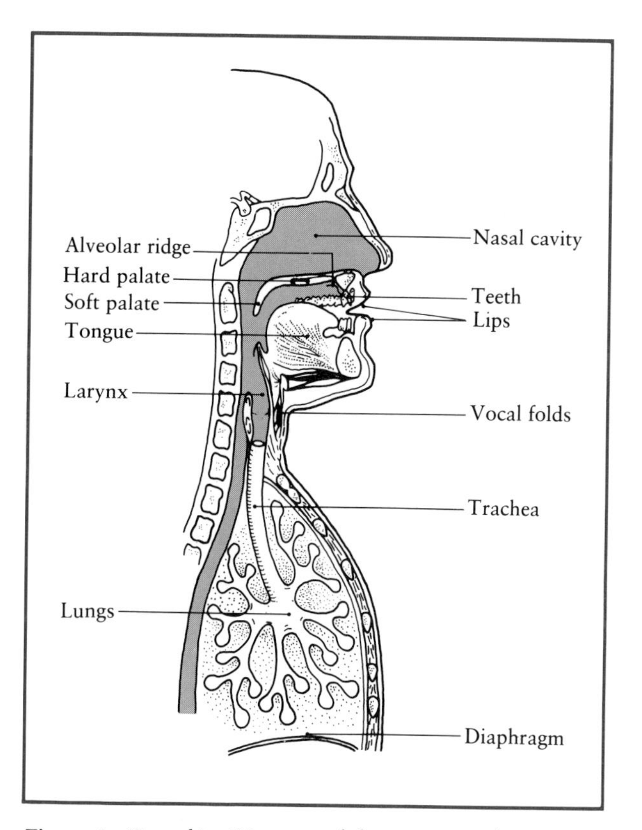

Figure 1. *(Speech)* Diagram of the organs and structures involved in speech.

Speech behavior is also viewed as an oral linguistic process used by human beings to communicate with others and with themselves. From this perspective, the emphasis is on spoken symbolic interaction. The cognitive processes involved in developing and planning spoken messages, the nature of the messages themselves, and the effects of spoken messages are all of interest to those who study speech from this perspective. *See also* LINGUISTICS.

The act of speaking has interdependent relationships with other important body processes. Most scholars acknowledge the existence of a mutual influence between thought and speech; that is, the way we speak about things affects how (and possibly whether) we think about them, and the way we think about things affects how we talk about them. The specific conditions that facilitate or inhibit this mutual influence are less clear and are subject to continued exploration. Human beings, like other animals, have thoughts that do not seem to be tied to speech behavior.

Speech has a close kinship to GESTURE as well. Several detailed examinations of gestures and speech have revealed a rhythmic coordination or synchrony between an individual's speech units and gesture units of varying sizes, suggesting a common controlling mechanism for these two separately produced systems. Speech and gestures work together in several ways. Sometimes gestures precede speech and act as a preface to the spoken message or even as a self-priming device for generating speech. Gestures may also be used to complete a spoken message after speech has ceased. For some messages, gestures can be used to replace speech entirely. But most gestures work in tandem with speech by providing different but simultaneous messages with speech or by providing emphasis, organization, and punctuation to speech. Furthermore, speech behavior also activates hearing (PERCEPTION) and listening (comprehension) processes of the speaker. Thus, a comprehensive study of speech behavior often requires close scrutiny of cognitive, gestural, and auditory processes as well.

Is Speech Unique to Human Beings?

For at least the last 2,300 years, humans have been wondering whether ARISTOTLE was correct when he described humans as the only animals "endowed with the gift of speech." Human beings are not the only animals that vocalize. Birds and other animals make sounds that closely resemble words used in human speech. Nor are human beings the only animals to use symbols to communicate. Nonhuman primates have been taught to use various forms of language to communicate. But humans seem to be the only animals capable of fusing vocalized sounds with symbolic language. Even when, in 1949, a psychologist and his wife raised Vicki, a three-day-old chimpanzee, in their home as they would a human infant, the chimpanzee did not learn and use symbolic speech. Prevailing opinions suggest that the chimpanzee's inability to learn spoken language is more than simply an inability to vocalize like human beings. The differences, it is argued, are in the capacity of the human brain for fusing, monitoring, and controlling the coordination of the sound-production equipment with the linguistic symbols. *See* ANIMAL COMMUNICATION; ANIMAL SIGNALS; COGNITION; COGNITION, ANIMAL.

For many scholars, the uniquely human ability to fuse vocalized sounds with symbolic language is significant because it results in a phenomenon quite different from either process alone. As anyone who has ever practiced a speech aloud knows, we perceive and react to spoken language much differently from when we read the same message. Also we perceive and react to spoken language very differently from when we "say" the same message to ourselves silently.

The Phylogenesis of Speech

Although human speech was being recorded graphically some five thousand years ago, it is likely that our ancestors of four hundred thousand years ago were already using spoken language to communicate. Determining exactly when humans began to use speech as their primary means of communication is very difficult. Despite their answers to many other questions about human evolution, skeletal remains have not yielded the necessary evidence. A few scholars once believed that the presence of geneal tubercles—bony protuberances on the inner side of the chin attached to the tongue muscles—were evidence of the presence of articulate speech, but this theory has not received widespread support. Paleoneurologists who have used the skulls of prehistoric humans to make brain casts can provide some indication about when speech may have evolved, but to date paleolaryngology seems to offer the most promising clues.

Paleolaryngology began by examining the development of the larynx in children. During the first eighteen months or so the position of the child's larynx is similar to that of living apes and monkeys. Then it begins to descend into the neck and alters the way the child breathes, swallows, and vocalizes. This unique position of the larynx is accompanied by a similarly unique skull shape. The base of the human skull accompanying the descended larynx is arched, while the skull base of other mammals that have larynges in a higher position is flat. Reasoning that a descended larynx was necessary in order to produce the range of sounds associated with human speech today, researchers are examining the basicraniums of our ancestors. Current evidence suggests that the earliest hominids had vocal tracts much like the apes and monkeys today. Some changes began to take place about one and a half million years ago, but the arched skull base of humans has not been found in skulls of humans who lived more than three hundred thousand to four hundred thousand years ago.

There is much speculation on how speech first emerged in the human species. Some believe the ability to speak had divine origins, but many theories are based on the emergence of the ability to make sounds. According to these theories, the origins of the sounds and sound combinations that eventually formed the structure of oral language came from the sounds early humans made mimicking those heard in nature, those used in emotional expressions (e.g., cries) or vocal play, and those made during physical exertion. Probably all these sources played a role as possible sources for sound groups that later became integral to the sounds used in spoken words. Other scholars point to the possible role of gestures in the phylogenetic development of speech. These theories generally assume that early human beings first developed a communicative system with gestures. According to these theories, sounds were often byproducts of this gestural communication system. Gradually, early humans sensed the advantages of using a system that was not dependent on visibility and that could be used while the hands were busy with other activities, and this then led to a refinement of the sound-making process.

The weight of scholarly opinion concerning the phylogenesis of speech can be summarized this way: most believe that the development of spoken language evolved slowly rather than quickly; most believe that the evolution of speech is closely linked to evolving increases in human brain size and the complexity of the nervous system; most believe that the evolution of speech was tied to matters involving the survival of the species; most believe that the process moved from an oral language of emotions and other here-and-now referents to one of more abstract symbolic ideas; and most agree that since children are today born into a world where people are already speaking, ontogeny is *not* a brief and rapid recapitulation of phylogeny.

The Ontogenesis of Speech

For the natural and timely development of speaking skills, human infants need a functional vocal apparatus for producing sounds, a healthy brain and neuromuscular system for monitoring and controlling speech, and a surrounding environment that provides the necessary stimulation and support for speech behavior. Before the child learns to use the arbitrary array of sounds as a symbol system, he or she goes through several preverbal, overlapping stages of sound production.

The birth cry is the neonate's first vocal activity. During the next two months, the infant reacts reflexively to a variety of stimuli such as heat and cold, thirst and hunger, pain and pleasure. These undifferentiated cries do not seem to be significantly altered by the nature of the stimuli. The cries do contain sounds that will later be used in speech. In English these are primarily vowel sounds.

Gradually, the infant's crying becomes differentiated, and during the second month of life special sounds refer to special needs, usually reflecting comfort and discomfort at first. Cries are primarily distinguished by pitch, rhythm, and intensity. Although these sounds are not made with the intention of having others respond to them, others do respond, marking the beginning of a sound-reaction pattern.

During the second three months, the child plays and experiments with sounds and his or her sound-making capabilities. This activity is commonly called babbling. Although babbling may provide some preliminary experiences and practice with speech sounds, children who do very little babbling also learn to make the necessary sounds for speaking. This form of vocal play seems to be largely instinctive, because nonhearing children have also been observed babbling. Some believe the apparent imitation of caregiver intonation patterns represents the most important foundation for learning during this phase.

During the second six months of life, the child continues his or her sound play and practices repeating sound complexes or syllables. This process, called lallation, is primarily self-imitation at first. But around the ninth or tenth month, the child gives more effort to repeating the sounds of others, often for the pleasure of the rewards given by those who have been imitated. Echolalia is the term used to refer to this process. During this time, the child also shows the first signs of verbal understanding by responding appropriately to words and/or phrases made by others.

Normally, the child produces his or her first words about the age of one year. First words are often monosyllabic nouns or duplicated monosyllables like "ma-ma." When the child utters a sound like mama, the mother may respond by attending to the child, repeating the sound so the child will say it again, and rewarding the child with a smile and a hug. The word "mama" comes to be associated with satisfaction for the child, and with a particular source of satisfaction, and soon the child says it in order to bring about that satisfaction. The development of human speech through the merger of sound making and language learning is now clearly manifest. By the time the child is two years of age, brain weight will have increased threefold, cerebral dominance will have begun, and the child's usage repertoire will be about two hundred words. By age six, the child's vocabulary is about twenty-five hundred words, and by seven or eight most children have reached the articulatory proficiency of adults. By puberty, the ability to initiate normal language learning is believed by many scholars to have passed. *See also* LANGUAGE ACQUISITION.

The Functions of Speech

Speech (which for most purposes here can be taken either as vocal language or as one of its surrogates, such as SIGN LANGUAGE) is central to the development of the person and the way that developing person is presented to and understood by others. Our individual identities and self-concepts are largely a result of speaking and listening to others and ourselves. We express our personalities by the way we talk about ourselves and, perhaps more important, by the way we talk about virtually anything. Our speech tells others who we are. In fact, speech patterns are often used as markers of mental and social pathologies—for example, talking too much or too little; talking to certain inanimate, nonhuman, or unobservable entities too frequently; or using language deemed inappropriate by one's social community.

Speech is also the primary vehicle for making contact with the human community. It enables us to establish social bonds with others of our species. On such occasions the content of our speech is often the act of speaking itself (or the potential for same) rather than the meanings associated with the specific words spoken. Speech in this sense acts as a means of identification with our species, with our humanness.

Speech also functions as a means of getting things done, of influencing ourselves and others in order to experience a sense of control over our environment. Even the way we describe our world affects our actions within it. We can talk ourselves into believing or doing things, and we can persuade others to believe or do things through speech; we can release emotions for self-gratification, for inflicting pain, or for obtaining comfort from others; we can verbalize written or silent ideas in order to make them more understandable to ourselves and to others; and we can speak to ourselves for pleasure and amusement, or we can use our speech to please others.

The Academic Study of Speech

Human speech behavior has been a subject of scholarly attention for over two thousand years. The treatises on practical public discussion in ancient Syracuse, Athens, and Rome launched a concern for oral RHETORIC that resulted in many learned volumes. Rhetoric also had a long tradition as a key part of the curriculum in higher education. *See also* PUBLIC SPEAKING.

Early in the twentieth century the study of speech began to broaden in a number of ways, particularly in the United States, where departments of speech had been organized in a number of colleges and universities. Continuing the focus on rhetoric and PERSUASION, these fostered a tradition of tournament debating that spread to secondary schools (*see* FORENSICS). In addition, the departments began to encompass scholars with interests in speech pathology and audiology (the description, etiology, diagnosis, and treatment of SPEECH AND LANGUAGE DISORDERS). Some departments extended speech studies to the study of THEATER and the new medium of RADIO.

Midcentury brought a new and significant development. In the rhetorical tradition the focus had always been on the process of persuasion as manifested by public speakers. Now research and teaching began to encompass informal, personal speech in ordinary social encounters, and the academic study of speech became known as speech communication.

The scope of research and teaching in the field of speech communication has come to encompass a number of interrelated areas.

Social cognitions. Here the focus is on information processing about a communicative event by an individual. These cognitions may occur prior to, during, or after a social encounter; they may be formal (as in creating and organizing a public speech) or informal; they may involve varying degrees of self-awareness or intent. Expectations, ATTITUDES, fantasies, plans, strategies, memories, and apprehensions related to a person's communicative behavior are of interest. Even though they may be studied separately, the ultimate goal for understanding social cognitions is to determine how they affect overt speaking and listening behavior.

Messages. Here the focus is on the nature of the messages produced. What linguistic, vocal, and gestural choices were made? What was the content of the message? How was the message manifested—the style as well as the timing in relation to other messages? The answers to these questions are of particular value for understanding the responses to the message.

Effects. Two approaches are usually used for understanding the effects of spoken messages. One examines the correspondence between speaker goals and listener reactions. Listener reactions may be overt (arguing with the speaker) or covert (changing one's attitude toward the speaker, the message, or both). To what extent, for example, is a speaker who wants to persuade a friend to do something distasteful, without losing the person's friendship, able to accomplish these goals? Another way of looking at effects is to concentrate on the developing interaction process. What is the nature of the process when a public speaker makes a statement that triggers a heckler's outburst from the audience, which in turn prompts an unrehearsed reply from the speaker? In a two-person CONVERSATION, process effects are commonly discussed as reciprocal (speaker and listener responses tend to be similar) and compensatory (speaker and listener responses tend to be offsetting or dissimilar). Process effects are scrutinized at one moment in time or over the course of an entire conversation. Explanations for the effects of spoken messages are derived from a knowledge of social cognitions, the nature of the messages produced, and an understanding of the context.

Context. The context within which human speech behavior occurs provides important clues concerning why certain messages occur and others do not, why messages occur in the manner they do, and why messages have the effects they do. Speech can be examined in different environments, such as hospitals, courtrooms, classrooms, and business organizations; in different communicator relationships, such as candidate-voter, friendships, marriages, supervisor-subordinate relationships, and family relationships; in encounters in which the communicators have different cognitive and behavioral backgrounds, such as age, GENDER, handicap, race, cultural heritage, and sexual preference; in encounters in which speech behavior is mediated by various kinds of auditory and visual technology; and in encounters in which speakers are members of different speech communities.

The unit of study in speech behavior varies in size, depending on the type of research. Dyadic or interpersonal analyses may focus on a formal job interview or small talk between two people on a coffee break; small-group behavior may involve a formal meeting or a social network; ORGANIZATIONAL COMMUNICATION may look at a large group like an entire organization or a smaller unit of the organization, such as a specific work group or a supervisor-subordinate dyad; public speaking and the oral interpretation of literature examine a single speaker and one or more audiences; and the study of speech in social movements usually involves many speakers and many audiences. *See also* GROUP COMMUNICATION; INTERPERSONAL COMMUNICATION.

Bibliography. Carroll C. Arnold, *Criticism of Oral Rhetoric,* Columbus, Ohio, 1974; Carroll C. Arnold and John Waite Bowers, eds., *Handbook of Rhetorical and Communication Theory,* Boston, 1984; Thomas W. Benson, ed., *Speech Communication in the Twentieth Century,* Carbondale, Ill., 1984; George A. Borden, Richard B. Gregg, and Theodore G. Grove, *Speech Behavior and Human Interaction,* Englewood Cliffs, N.J., 1969; Charles T. Brown and Charles Van Riper, *Speech and Man,* Englewood Cliffs, N.J., 1966; Frank E. X. Dance and Carl E. Larson, *Speech Communication: Concepts and Behavior,* New York, 1972; Giles Wilkeson Gray and Claude Merton Wise, *The Bases of Speech,* 3d ed., New York, 1959; Franklyn S. Haiman, *Speech and Law in a Free Society,* Chicago, 1981; Mark L. Knapp and Gerald R. Miller, eds., *Handbook of Interpersonal Communication,* Beverly Hills, Calif., 1985; Wilder Penfield and Lamar Roberts, *Speech and the Brain-Mechanisms,* Princeton, N.J., 1959, reprint New York, 1966; Lev Semenovich Vygotsky, *Thought and Language,* ed. and trans. by Eugenia Hanfmann and Gertrude Vakar, New York, 1962; Karl R. Wallace, ed., *History of Speech Education in America,* New York, 1954.

MARK L. KNAPP

SPEECH AND LANGUAGE DISORDERS

Disorders that can be classified behaviorally as disorders of language, articulation, phonation, and fluency. They can also be classified by type of disabling condition contributing to the disorder. The disabling effects of neurologic, auditory, laryngeal, craniofacial, learning, and emotional disturbances or pathologies on communication depend on the success with which compensatory coping strategies can be developed. Estimates of the number of people with SPEECH and LANGUAGE disorders range from 4 to 20 percent.

Diagnosis is determining the nature of the speech or language disorder and of any disabling condition contributing to it. Assessment is uncovering the abilities available with which the communication disorder can be ameliorated. Therapy is the process by which amelioration is effected.

Language disorders. In children, language disorders are manifestations of difficulties in mastering semantic, syntactic, phonologic, and pragmatic rules. These are the rules by which cognitive meaning is mapped in linguistic form for spoken expression. Types of developmental language difficulties for which different therapies are appropriate include specific language impairment (formerly called by several names, such as delayed language and childhood aphasia) and language problems associated with autism, mental retardation, learning disabilities, hearing loss, and head injury.

In adults impairment of acquired language is caused by brain injury that varies in type and severity with site and extent of neural lesion. Types of language impairment are numerous. Broca's aphasia is a nonfluent, agrammatic, expressive disorder. Wernicke's aphasia includes impaired attention as well as comprehension and production. Global aphasia is severe depression of all communicative abilities. Word retrieval is the chief problem in anomic aphasia. Speech is relatively normal in conduction aphasia except for paraphasic errors in which wrong "main" words are used. Right-hemisphere communication disorders include visuospatial deficits, linguistic processing deficits, and perceptual/cognitive deficits. Alexia and agraphia involve impairments of reading and writing. Transcortical motor aphasia is a disturbance of spontaneous speech. Subcortical aphasias, like global aphasia, show severe depression of all communicative abilities. Communicative deficits of traumatic head injury include cognitive impairment and confused language. Impaired memory, attention, and problem solving characterize general intellectual deficits.

Articulatory disorders. The term *phonologic disorder* has supplanted *articulatory disorder* as recognition has grown that deviant speech sound production, for whatever reason, is still a phonologic defect. What *articulation disorder* has come to mean is impaired ability to make the necessary movements to produce speech sounds normally. This impairment is generally attributed to oral, auditory, and neural dysfunctions.

Oral disabilities range from tongue thrust to cleft palate to velar paralysis to surgically removed portions of tongue, mouth, or throat. These disabilities impair vocal tract functions of speech. Auditory disabilities can involve the middle or inner ear or auditory neural paths in ways that interfere with the feedback that guides articulatory performances. Neural disabilities impairing articulatory development in children are cerebral palsy and developmental apraxia of speech (the nature of which is disputed). Apraxia of speech in adults, by contrast, is recognized widely as impaired ability to produce and sequence speech sounds automatically. Most neurally based articulatory disorders appear, as the motor system deteriorates with age, in the form of dysarthrias. They range from flaccid, spastic, and ataxic dysarthria to hypokinetic, hyperkinetic, and mixed dysarthria.

Phonatory disorders. Disorders of voice can be functional or organic. Regardless of cause, they are heard as pitch, loudness, or quality abnormalities. The most typical cause of functional problems is vocal abuse. It occurs frequently in childhood from screaming and yelling. In adulthood, it can result from excessive singing, shouting, and loud talking. When the vocal folds are fatigued or inflamed, vocal abuse tends to cause tissue damage in the form of nodules on the folds where they collide with greatest impact and sometimes cause contact ulcers. Other functional causes range from transsexual and postmutational voice problems (a particular problem of adolescent males whose voices "break") to aphonia and sometimes spastic dysphonia of psychogenic origin.

Organic causes of voice disorders typically involve laryngeal pathologies, such as tumors and paralyses. One or both vocal folds can be paralyzed in an adducted position, which makes phonation possible but breathing difficult, or in an abducted position, which facilitates breathing but precludes phonation. Tumors can be benign or malignant. If caused by vocal abuse, they can often be treated with vocal rest and voice therapy. Otherwise, surgical removal is required for benign tumors before the voice can be restored. With laryngeal malignancy, the prognosis is good if caught early; partial excision of the larynx may suffice. If cancer is advanced, total laryngectomy will be required, in which case some form of alaryngeal speech must be learned as a substitute for normal voice. These forms include esophageal speech (in which air is set in vibration at the neck of the esophagus), an artificial larynx (in which an electric vibrator or vibrating reed is substituted for the larynx), or a surgically implanted prosthesis (which permits voice generation with respiration).

Fluency disorders. Although fluency disorders can be associated with dysarthria and aphasia (and in children with language impairments are called "cluttering"), by far the greatest attention has been given to stuttering. Stuttering usually begins in early childhood. Despite half a century of extensive investigations of cortical, brain stem, auditory, laryngeal, respiratory, and vocal tract differences, firm evidence of genetic transmission is the only strong clue pointing to a constitutional predisposition to stutter. Although specific factors are unknown, environmental conditions, probably involving stress of some as yet undetermined form, appear to be necessary for the onset of stuttering. Spontaneous recovery of as high as 80 percent prior to adulthood has been reported.

More is known about effective treatment than about the nature of stuttering. Behavioral therapies can predictably replace stuttering with normal fluency, although maintenance of this fluency is still problematic. Fluctuations of confidence are probably a crucial factor in treatment.

See also SLIPS OF THE TONGUE.

Bibliography. Thomas J. Hixon, Lawrence Shriberg, and John Saxman, eds., *Introduction to Communication Disorders,* Englewood Cliffs, N.J., 1980; William H. Perkins, *Current Therapy of Communication Disorders,* New York, 1983–1984; idem, *Speech Pathology: An Applied Behavioral Science,* 2d ed., St. Louis, Mo., 1977; Paul H. Skinner and Ralph L. Shelton, *Speech, Language, and Hearing: Normal Processes and Disorders,* Reading, Mass., 1978; Charles Van Riper and Lon Emerick, *Speech Correction: An Introduction to Speech Pathology and Audiology,* Englewood Cliffs, N.J., 1984.

WILLIAM H. PERKINS

SPEECH ANXIETY

An individual's fear of actual or anticipated oral communication with another person or group of people. It is often referred to as communication apprehension or oral communication anxiety. One of its forms is popularly known as stage fright. Surveys seem to indicate that anxiety about oral communication is common in most cultures in the world. A common response to a high degree of such anxiety is withdrawal, frequently called shyness or reticence.

Types. There are three major types of SPEECH anxiety. The first is general in nature. Individuals who experience this type feel anxious about virtually all oral communication, regardless of its form, the nature of the receiver, or specific circumstances surrounding the communication.

A more common type is context specific. It is associated with communication in only one particular context, such as giving a speech to an audience, attending a job interview, or meeting new people.

Audience-specific anxiety is the third type, one based on a response to a specific person or group of people. A common example is a subordinate's reaction to communicating whenever a particular supervisor is present. It matters not whether the communication involves a CONVERSATION, a small-group conference, a large meeting, or a formal speech. What matters is whether the supervisor is present.

Causes. Two primary factors are believed to contribute to the development of speech anxiety in an individual. On the basis of research with identical and nonidentical twins, some investigators feel there is a genetic predisposition toward approaching or avoiding other people, which may in the course of time be reflected in speech behavior patterns. Others who have studied speech anxiety believe that most if not all such anxiety is learned as a result of an individual's communication experience. Such learning is believed to be rooted in the communication history of the individual and related to questions of whether early efforts to communicate met with success or failure, reward or punishment, gratification or pain, response or rejection. Particular childhood events, relating to a particular type of communication, may generate anxiety of a situation-specific type. If an individual has had negative experiences, mixed experiences, or no experience with a particular kind of communication in the past, it is likely the individual will suffer from anxiety if forced to engage in that kind of communication.

Effects. The only consistent effect of speech anxiety is an internally experienced feeling of discomfort and stress. It is important to recognize that this is a cognitive response of the individual and may or may not be associated with physiological arousal. Indicators of physiological arousal, such as increased heart rate or increased sweating, have no necessary relationship to the internal feeling of anxiety.

The most common effect of speech apprehension on behavior is a tendency to avoid or withdraw from communication. One might decline an invitation to give a speech, fail to appear for a job interview, avoid social functions or meetings, or even select an occupation that requires little interaction with others. However, such withdrawal behaviors are not necessarily associated with a high degree of anxiety about oral communication.

When avoidance of communication is impossible or the individual chooses not to withdraw, the communication behavior of the person experiencing high anxiety is likely to be disrupted. Such things as poor eye contact, inappropriate gestures, and vocal nonfluencies are likely to increase. It is important to note that such disturbances may not be present even for a communicator experiencing extremely high anxiety. Some individuals are able to control external manifestations of anxiety so that observers are unaware of the anxiety. A less common behavioral response to high anxiety is a tendency to overcommunicate. In an attempt to overcome their anxiety, some individuals become very talkative. In most cases the communication of such individuals also displays some of the disruptions noted above.

Overcoming speech anxiety. The level of oral communication anxiety experienced by most people in most communication situations is not a serious problem. The individual may be somewhat uncomfortable but is able to control the anxiety and communicate normally. Only when the level of anxiety is much higher, enough to produce change in communication behavior, is it considered serious by most people. Very few individuals are able to overcome extremely high speech anxiety satisfactorily without assistance from a trained professional. The three methods most commonly used by professionals are systematic desensitization, cognitive restructuring, and skills training.

Systematic desensitization, a behavior therapy, is the most effective approach for attacking the anxiety directly. In this method a person is taught how to relax the various muscle groups in the body and then is progressively conditioned to relax while visualizing increasingly threatening communication situations.

Cognitive restructuring, another behavior therapy, is directed toward changing how a person thinks about communication. The person is first taught to recognize the negative thoughts he or she has about communication and then trained to substitute positive thoughts for the negative ones.

The skills training approach assumes that the cause of the anxiety is lack of sufficient skill to ensure successful communication. The individual is taught specific skills to be used in specific situations. This approach is quite helpful for overcoming situation-specific speech anxiety when skills are truly deficient. However, its use for other purposes is severely limited. *See also* SOCIAL SKILLS.

Bibliography. Arnold H. Buss, *Self-Consciousness and Social Anxiety,* San Francisco, 1980; John A. Daly and James C. McCroskey, eds., *Avoiding Communication: Shyness, Reticence, and Communication Apprehension,* Beverly Hills, Calif., 1984; Mark R. Leary, *Understanding Social Anxiety,* Beverly Hills, Calif., 1983; James C. McCroskey and Virginia P. Richmond, *The Quiet Ones: Communication Apprehension and Shyness,* 2d ed., Dubuque, Iowa, 1982; Gerald M. Phillips, *Help for Shy People,* Englewood Cliffs, N.J., 1981; Virginia P. Richmond and James C. McCroskey, *Communication: Apprehension, Avoidance, and Effectiveness,* Scottsdale, Ariz., 1985.

JAMES C. MCCROSKEY

SPEECH PERCEPTION. *See* PERCEPTION—SPEECH.

SPEECH PLAY

The creative disposition of LANGUAGE resources; the manipulation of formal features and processes of language to achieve a striking restructuring of familiar discourse alignments. A great deal of conversational SPEECH play is essentially frivolous, yet it serves vital communicative needs, such as establishing a proper social bonding among participants in a speech event. Moreover, when it is used in connection with certain social and RITUAL enactments, speech play may acquire a profound or even exalted stature.

Speech play is a species of what ROMAN JAKOBSON refers to as "introversive semiosis," that is, language turned in on itself. Speech play highlights relationships among linguistic elements that tend to remain latent in the more reference-oriented uses of linguistic codes. It fastens on the "wrinkles" in the linguistic CODE, its points of overlap, inconsistency, ambiguity, and anomaly. It draws attention to inconvenient linguistic facts, such as the piling up of lexemes on a single phonetic unit, the close phonetic resemblance of contrasting lexical items (the French *poisson,* meaning "fish" and *poison,* meaning "poison"), or the ambiguity produced by optional deletions in a syntactic structure ("the shooting of the hunters was terrible"). Speech play draws attention to these nuances of the code, be it in finite, subversive episodes of wordplay or in the cadences of spoken POETRY.

Only those resources available in a given language's repertoire can be turned to playful ends. Speech play is inherently ecological. Each language is a medium, facilitating certain manipulations, ruling others out entirely. Consider the following instance of graffiti:

Con-gress Is the Opposite of Pro-gress

A technique of word formation based on autonomous roots and affixes makes possible this polemical juxtaposition of prefixes. Speech play dissects and analyzes the host linguistic environment.

Forms of speech play. The forms of speech play are legion, falling plausibly into four categories, with diverse representatives in the world's speech communities. The first might be called *wordplay,* consisting of isolated, discrete moments of speech play (puns, speech METAPHOR, graffiti).

Wordplay encompasses in pristine form all the conceivable permutations of the formal features of language. Wordplay, with its flashes of verbal creativity, occurs primarily in a conversational setting (*see* CONVERSATION). Its varieties can be charted in rhetorical figures of sound, schema, and trope or in the ethnic genres of specific speech communities. Classical RHETORIC abounds in atomistic formal devices of the sort likely to surface in playful speech, for many a witticism has been engineered on the basis of figures like (1) *antistasis,* repetition of a word in a different or contrary sense; (2) *metaplasm,* moving letters or syllables of a word from their place; (3) *hyperbaton,* departure from normal word order; and (4) *synecdoche,* substitution of part for whole, genus for species, or vice versa.

In the English language tradition, a number of wordplay varieties have been named:

- The *pun,* which substitutes one lexical item for another, where the two are phonetically related.
- The *Wellerism,* or quotation proverb, named for Sam Weller in Charles Dickens's *Pickwick Papers* (" 'My bark is on the sea' said the dog as he fell overboard").
- The *conundrum* with its riddlelike format resolving into a pun.
- The *spoonerism,* involving a switching of initial syllables, and named for the Reverend William A. Spooner (1844–1930) of Oxford University, who is credited with the following slip of the tongue in a speech to a group of farmers: "I have never before addressed so many tons of soil."
- The *malapropism,* named for a character in Richard Sheridan's comedy *The Rivals* (1775) with a tendency to misuse pretentious language.

The second form of speech play is *verbal games,* speech play harnessed to gaming structures (jokes, riddles, catches, verbal dueling). Verbal games harness speech play to a combative arena, where consensual rules specify the roles, moves, and goals of the game. At the informal end of the spectrum we encounter the RIDDLE, an interrogative ludic routine that sets the stage for launching episodes of speech play, challenging facile assumptions about linguistic and cultural codes. Verbal dueling lies at the more formal end of the spectrum, taking on the aura of public SPECTACLE, as participants attempt to outmaneuver their foes within the framework of well-established rule systems. *See also* HUMOR; INSULT.

The third form of speech play could be called *special linguistic codes.* This is speech play carried out systematically over an entire discourse segment to produce distinctive ways of speaking for special social purposes (adult baby talk, argots, play languages, glossolalia, ritual speech). Many play languages are created through a systematic reallocation of phonemes, as is pig latin, famous among North American schoolchildren. The technique is purely phonological:

Pig latin: igPay atinlay
Rule: Move the first phoneme of each word to the end of that word, and then tack on the vowel glide /ey/.

A simple phonological transformation of this sort produces speech that is quite difficult for the uninitiated to comprehend.

Special linguistic codes may also be created through transformations wrought on other language components. Argot and slang, for example, involve the process of lexeme substitution. The street language of Mexican-American youth, often referred to as *caló,* retains the standard PHONOLOGY of Spanish but introduces radical alterations in the lexicon. Its sources include the historical *caló,* an argot of the Spanish underworld with a strong Gypsy influence; the English language, which has loaned words like "chance" (*chansa*) and "dime" (*daime*); indigenous Mexican languages (the word *cuate,* "close pal," derives from a Nahuatl word meaning "twin"); and the Spanish language, the vocabulary of which is modified through metaphorical and vernacular processes.

Ceremonial codes are frequently generated from systematic speech play working simultaneously at various levels in the linguistic structure. They often display patterning of the aural texture of speech, along with grammatical parallelism and a special vocabulary. The ritual language of the Kamsa Indians of Andean Colombia exhibits all of these effects: a prosody composed of regular phrases shaped by isochronic meter and intonational contour; a complex type of word formation, creating ponderous lexical items; a syntactic structure producing high levels of grammatical parallelism; and a special lexicon composed of metaphorical equivalents to many ordinary words. Kamsa ritual language is a distinctive speech variety used to formulate speeches during ceremonial occasions. *See also* RELIGION.

The fourth category of speech play, *poetic forms,* is speech play harnessed to artistic expression in traditional genres (PROVERB, ballad, limerick). It lies at the foundation of all poetry, for poetic discourse achieves its artifice through the discrete moments of speech play that it weaves into global artistic patterns. What surfaces in wordplay as a fortuitous rhyme may emerge in verbal art as an instance of periodic end rhyme. Poetic forms are characterized by their prosodies, organizing the dimensions of time, stress, timbre, and intonation into the patterns we perceive as meter, rhyme, and speech melody. Within these prosodic vessels poetic forms display all the finite nuances of grammatical parallelism and lexical substitution endemic to speech play, but now harnessed to aesthetic forms concerned with issues like climax and closure. *See also* ORAL POETRY.

Speech play can run the gamut from the frivolous to the sublime, from conversational spice to poetic grace. Speech play, the creative disposition of language resources, is alternatively an amusement, a vocation, a mark of social standing, a religious obligation. It adds a note of levity to ordinary talk. It may be systematized to create special linguistic codes or harnessed to some institutional design, a game, or a poem. Whether incidental or prescribed, intended or unintended, orthodox or subversive, it attests to the indomitable spirit of human creativity, ever restless within the bounds of received cultural systems. Speech play opens a door to transcendence of sheer referentiality in verbal expression; in so doing, it promotes the many communicative uses of language, playful and affective, that are not strictly referential in scope.

See also SLIPS OF THE TONGUE.

Bibliography. Richard Bauman, *Verbal Art as Performance,* Rowley, Mass., 1977, reprint Prospect Heights, Ill., 1984; Peter Farb, *Word Play: What Happens When People Talk,* New York, 1973; Paul Garvin, ed. and trans., *A Prague School Reader on Esthetics, Literary Structure, and Style* (in Czech), Washington, D.C., 1964; Roman Jakobson, *Selected Writings,* Vol. 2, *Word and Language,* The Hague, 1971; Barbara Kirshenblatt-Gimblett, ed., *Speech Play: Research and Resources for the Study of Linguistic Creativity,* Philadelphia, 1976; Richard Lanham, *A Handlist of Rhetorical Terms,* Berkeley, Calif., 1968; John McDowell, *Children's Riddling,* Bloomington, Ind., 1979; Susan Stewart, *Nonsense: Aspects of Intertextuality in Folklore and Literature,* Baltimore, Md., 1979; Archer Taylor, *The Proverb, and An Index to the Proverb,* Hatboro, Pa., 1962.

JOHN HOLMES MCDOWELL

SPONSOR

The 1786 edition of the Chambers *Cyclopaedia* listed the term *sponsor* as follows: "*See* God-father." Later dictionaries defined it as "one who assumes the debts of another." In modern communications media, and especially in broadcasting, the term has come to mean a financial backer, usually of a special sort—the advertiser, a pivotal figure in many RADIO and television systems (*see* TELEVISION HISTORY).

Fees paid by advertisers for the presentation of their promotional messages provide most broadcasting systems with some part—in many cases all—of their operating funds. Sponsorship of this sort has given advertisers a unique role in ADVERTISING history as well as in social history. Like other forms of advertising, broadcast COMMERCIALS are a factor in the distribution of goods and services; at the same time, because of their importance in the economics of broadcasting, the sponsor has an influence (which may be exercised intentionally or unintentionally, directly or indirectly) on programming decisions and the values implicit in them. The significance of this is disputed. Sponsors have been described as a modern version of the ART patron of earlier times, but in societies served predominantly by sponsored television their influence may be far more pervasive. The mechanisms of sponsorship and of government policies relating to them have changed over time and have varied significantly from place to place.

Origins. When radio began its boom period after World War I, its use as an advertising medium was scarcely considered. Leaders in most countries looked on it as a means of public enlightenment comparable to the SCHOOL, LIBRARY, and MUSEUM, therefore meriting government funding—possibly defrayed in whole or in part by license fees to be levied on set owners. Arrangements of this sort prevailed in most European countries.

In the United States a more laissez-faire spirit took hold, which soon spread to Latin America and later elsewhere. The U.S. Department of Commerce authorized a large range of organizations to establish broadcasting stations; by the end of 1922 more than five hundred had gone on the air. They included electrical giants like Westinghouse and General Electric, which at first thought their revenues from the sale of radio sets would finance their broadcasting activities. Other licensees included universities, churches, newspapers, hotels, and department stores, which generally embarked on radio as an inexpensive prestige device. A public service approach was the keynote: colleges broadcast their lectures, hotels their string quartets, newspapers their news bulletins. People flocked to stations to make appearances, to take part in a moment of history; no one seemed to want payment. Within months, when artists began to ask for fees and authors for royalties, it became clear that other financial arrangements were needed.

In 1922 the American Telephone and Telegraph Company (AT&T) proposed a new kind of radio station, which it described as a historic extension of the TELEPHONE idea. Any person or corporation wishing to talk to the public at large would be able to do so for a fee: one hundred dollars for ten evening minutes, fifty dollars for ten daytime minutes. The idea was quickly denounced on both practical and philosophic grounds. The prospect of a new competitor for the advertising dollar alarmed publishers of periodicals. And besides, was it right for AT&T to be selling slices of the public domain for private profit? Secretary of Commerce Herbert Hoover declared it "inconceivable that we should allow so great a possibility for service . . . to be drowned in advertising chatter." Yet Hoover in his official capacity gave the go-ahead to the AT&T plan. The first commercial went on the air in the late afternoon of August 28, 1922, over WEAF New York; it promoted the sale of cooperative apartments in a New York City suburb. When it resulted in sales, the sponsor returned to "talk to the public" five more times and was followed by others—slowly at first, then in a rush. The messages soon took more theatrical forms. A 1923 program featuring actress Marion Davies on "How I Make Up for the Movies" led to encomiums on behalf of Mineralava soap. Listeners were offered an autographed photo of the actress, providing the sponsor with a merchandising hook as well as an audience-measurement device. An advertising agency had arranged the program. Scores of other stations decided to adopt the AT&T idea (for a time AT&T claimed they had no right to), and by the mid-1920s it dominated U.S. broadcasting.

A central element in the system was that a sponsor could buy airtime and decide how to use it—subject to the station's approval, which seemed to be a formality. This pattern governed both local and network broadcasting. Periods of fifteen, thirty, or sixty minutes (minus, in each case, a fraction of a minute for station identification, time signals, and other matters) in stretches of thirteen, twenty-six, thirty-nine, or fifty-two weeks came to be the main purchase units. The system gave sponsors considerable control over program schedules. This caused little public policy concern at first. If many hours were sponsor-controlled, others remained unsold and could be used for other, noncommercial purposes. There seemed to be something for everyone. But as commercial broadcasters sold more of their time, earned skyrocketing profits, and bought up most of the stations that had operated noncommercially, the system was increasingly questioned. Licensees, theoretically responsible for their schedules, had in effect sold control to advertisers. Key policy decisions seemed to be made by an advertising oligarchy. During the 1940s and 1950s U.S. broadcasting came under constant attack from critics inside and outside government as reforms were proposed and debated.

Other systems under pressure. While the U.S. system was increasingly involved in controversy, noncommercial systems in Europe and elsewhere were experiencing pressures of another sort, epitomized by the rise of Radio Luxembourg. Gaining attention in the 1930s as one of Europe's most powerful stations, it operated on the time-selling plan. Its power was irrelevant to the tiny area of Luxembourg itself, but the main target was Britain. Taking advantage of Britain's staid, intellectual programming and classical orientation, Radio Luxembourg featured U.S. jazz, winning a substantial audience among young Britons and support from advertisers—particularly multinational companies marketing food, drug, and tobacco products in Britain. The station also welcomed the U.S. SOAP OPERA, in many cases backed by the same companies that sponsored soap operas in the United States. The success of these maneuvers was irksome to Britain. It represented an erosion of audience as well as of advertising investments. It brought British Broadcasting Corporation (BBC) programming as well as its anti-advertising policy into question.

After World War II a similar confrontation developed in South Asia, precipitated by a station in Ceylon (later Sri Lanka) that, like Radio Luxembourg, was powerful and operated commercially. Under pressure in this case was All-India Radio (AIR), which had been created on the BBC model but which, after India won independence in 1947, became even more restrictive in its programming. Its emphasis was on instructional talks and on Indian classical and folk music. This music was a much-admired cultural treasure, but India's youth were addicted to another kind of music, the songs that were a key element in Indian feature films (*see* MUSICAL, FILM—BOMBAY GENRE). AIR's administrators considered it "hybrid music," contaminated by U.S., Latin American, and African rhythms and instrumentation, and they banned it from AIR schedules. Radio Ceylon took advantage of this, featuring Indian film songs and sometimes U.S. jazz. During the 1950s, operating with enough power to blanket India, it became the most popular station in the region and won support from many companies marketing consumer products in India. The leading program among young Indians was the weekly "Binaca Toothpaste Hour," which was modeled after the U.S. "Your Hit Parade" and revealed the top ten songs. The climactic moment, heralded by trumpet fanfares, when the new number one song was proclaimed, found young people in all parts of India clustered around radio shops. Here, too, the erosion of audience and advertising funds caused agitation, which was often leveled at AIR.

The same sort of pressure was continuing in Europe, where the French noncommercial system was harried by what it called peripheral stations, in this case advertising-supported stations operating from the independent enclaves of Monte Carlo and Andorra, directing French-language programs and commercials at French territory. In the 1960s such pressures were augmented by an eruption of pirate stations operating from ships and offshore islands in the Atlantic and the North Sea, often featuring rock and roll, amply supported by advertisers, and aiming at markets in various countries of western Europe served by noncommercial systems.

What finally brought such pressures to the breaking point was the advent of television and its rapid diffusion during the 1950s and 1960s. It soon became clear in many countries that license fees levied on set owners could not adequately support a television system unless fees were so high as to be beyond most homes. License fees were in any case increasingly difficult to collect, especially in developing countries (*see* DEVELOPMENT COMMUNICATION). A rapid change of policies began; most countries decided to welcome the sponsor, both to television and radio. Dual systems developed in some countries, such as Britain and Japan, with an advertising-supported television system operating alongside a license-supported system. In others, such as India and many other Asian and African countries, government monopolies remained in effect but sought revenue via commercials. Most socialist countries used advertising to channel the flow of goods, and the media carried messages to this end representing various industry sectors.

In many countries the advertiser as sponsor was welcomed with tight restrictions relating to length, frequency, taboo topics, and other matters. A plan initiated by Radiotelevisione Italiana (RAI) was to cluster commercials in time periods allocated to this purpose. The idea was to distance the advertiser from programming decisions. The sponsor was asked to sponsor the system, not a particular program or series. Each sponsor in such a cluster paid the same rate, as shown on a published rate schedule. To the surprise of many observers, periods of clustered commercials won a considerable following as leading directors became involved in their creation. A number of countries adopted the clustering plan.

Reforms in the United States. A time for reform came also to the United States. Scandals involving fixed television quiz programs brought matters to a head in the 1960s. Some QUIZ SHOW producers had devised means to make sure that popular contestants would remain victorious throughout a series of programs (thus increasing the ratings), and sponsors were found to have demanded such controls. The revelations brought national consternation. The networks resolved to "take charge in our own house." Network programming decisions would henceforth be made solely by the network, and all programs would be under its control. Advertisers would be invited to buy time slots (of thirty seconds, sixty seconds, or various other units) within the available program schedule. To some extent the major networks had already been attempting a shift to such a plan—which they called the magazine concept—but many advertisers had resisted. The scandals provided both the opportunity and the necessity for such a move.

This time the sponsors acquiesced—with significant reservations. Major sponsors took the position that they did not wish to influence programming but insisted on deciding with what programs their messages would be associated. In the U.S. system that now evolved (in contrast to the system that had been adopted in Italy) the sponsor bought slots in specific programs at prices determined by BARGAINING. A company preparing a campaign for one of its products might in one contract purchase slots in some two hundred different broadcasts scheduled for the following season, with a price specified for each slot. As the system developed, the prices for slots fluctuated wildly. Most sponsors wanted audiences with specific demographic characteristics. Because the Nielsen rating services provided such data about network audiences (*see* RATING SYSTEMS: RADIO AND TELEVISION), bargaining could readily proceed on this basis. Some sponsors defined their needs in precise terms: "We are ready to pay $8 per thousand women in the right age range." It meant that a single thirty-second slot in a prime-time series especially popular with young women (key purchasers of consumer goods) readily went for fifty thousand dollars or more. Many manufacturers of products sold in supermarkets were intent on reaching this same group, with resulting escalation in the price of appropriate slots. Other sponsors were after another, more elusive target. Luxury automobiles and computers were bought mainly by affluent men who could be counted on to watch major athletic contests (*see* SPORTS—SPORTS AND THE MEDIA). A single thirty-second slot in a U.S. Super Bowl football game could command a price of two hundred thousand dollars or more; indeed, a few sponsors found it worth twice that sum to talk to the public for thirty seconds in this context. A sponsor making such investments might also be ready to purchase a few spots in documentaries or newscasts, but at considerably lower prices.

The disparity of prices resulting from the bargaining system—along with its overall profitability—had a number of consequences. For commercial broadcasters elsewhere it posed the problem of whether to adopt such a system or at least to apply it to periods of widest interest. Within the U.S. networks the system had created strong internal pressures. It had given the networks financial incentives to match with their programming the demographics of the marketplace and to opt for programming that would yield the lucrative slots.

Network sponsors had been placed in a unique position. They could rightfully assert that they were not making programming decisions; the networks were. For this reason some major sponsors now insisted they should just be called advertisers. Yet their decisions in the buying of slots had come to exercise constant and powerful leverage over network decisions and thus over the selection of programs that would be featured in network schedules and go out into world markets.

Bibliography. Erik Barnouw, *The Sponsor: Notes on a Modern Potentate,* New York, 1978; Timothy Green, *The Universal Eye: The World of Television,* New York, 1972.

ERIK BARNOUW

SPORTS

This entry consists of three articles:

1. **Sports and Society**
2. **Sports and the Media**
3. **Psychology of Sports**

1. SPORTS AND SOCIETY

Sports belong in the world of PLAY and LEISURE, yet business elites, mass media, and government and political leaders recognize their potential for making profits, disseminating PROPAGANDA, and eliciting pride and solidarity. Organized sports prevail virtually everywhere and have developed over the past half-century into a major social institution.

Sports as International Culture

Sports promote connections from the broadest level to the momentary bonding of two strangers, whether as rival participants or as fans sharing the same passion. Organized sports parallel the intricate weave of government agencies in organizational structure: small towns, even rural areas, are linked to one another and to big cities for state and regional championships; major cities are knit together into national leagues and meet in regular competitions; and nations that play the same sports are drawn into relationships with one another through continental and worldwide federations that stage international contests between representative teams. Nationalistic feelings are fanned, and, simultaneously, people are united in a global folk CULTURE.

International sports have succeeded as a basis for global community by promoting common knowledge and shared symbols among people of different nations. Comparative data on audiences for SATELLITE-televised events show that major international sporting contests draw together more spectators than anything else. Sports provide a common frame of reference and rules that transcend cultural, political, and language barriers. A sports pantheon of STARS and a series of special events make up a set of universally recognized symbols that constitutes one of the elements of international culture.

The Fédération Internationale de Football Association (FIFA), established in 1904 as the controlling body for world soccer, is second only to the United Nations in number of members. Association football, called soccer in the United States and football everywhere else it is played, is the world's most popular participant and spectator sport. The quadrennial World Cup is the only global championship for professionals in a team sport. It is estimated that one of every two people in the world watches the final match of the month-long tournament.

Contests between professional athletes from different countries are common in individual sports like tennis, golf, boxing, and auto and bicycle racing, but contests in other team sports involve athletes officially ranked as amateurs. Basketball is followed by volleyball as the spectator team sport with the widest participation in international amateur tournaments. In terms of the number of players, both male and female, field hockey is one of the world's most popular participant sports. Played in more than seventy countries, it draws large crowds only in India and Pakistan.

At the local level, sports competitions have much older roots. Forms of ball-kicking games were played in ancient China, Rome, and Greece, and a riotous brand of soccer was played in the streets of medieval England during public holidays. At least since the intercity rivalry of the ancient Greek Olympic Games, glory has been shared by the townspeople of the victorious athletes. Across time and place, sports promoters, whether governments or management, have told fans that they can properly assume the victory as their own. Identification of fans with athletes—whether in terms of a common school, city, nation, race, or religion—is the foundation of every variety of spectator sport. Athletes and teams have served as important sources of collective identity. As objects of conversation, publicity, and mass media coverage, organized sports continue to focus community social life.

Sports and Social Structure

Whether one sees the consequences of sports as beneficial or harmful to society depends on which of two competing theoretical approaches—functionalist or conflict-oriented—is adopted. The functionalist perspective leads social scientists to examine the ways in which sports contribute to the smooth operation of society as a whole. The benefits of sports are seen to include the promotion of values such as the importance of rules, hard work, organization, and a defined authority structure; the legitimation of the goals of success and achievement; the social integration or reaffirmation of linkages of sports participants and also those they represent; and the development of physical skills and the promotion of the physical well-being of people who lead otherwise sedentary lives in industrial and postindustrial cities.

Conflict theorists do not disagree that widespread interest in commercialized sports leads to such consequences; rather, their perspective leads them to view those consequences as harmful. Critics of the status quo recognize the role of sports in socializing the young to fit into a regimented, bureaucratic work mold. Mass entertainment spectacles (*see* SPECTACLE), including organized sports contests, are viewed as providing escape and excitement and making participation in political or revolutionary organizations less likely.

Furthermore, conflict theorists argue that commercialized sports reduce players to material commodities exploited by others for the sake of profit, and the pressures to perform take their toll on athletes' bodies through injury or the inducement to take harmful drugs. The highly visible rewards given to athletes in turn publicize an IDEOLOGY of upward mobility. Conflict theorists point out that athletes' fame creates illusions about individualism by presenting a model in which success depends on hard work and perseverance, thus distracting attention from organizational bases for blocked mobility. Finally, fans' identification with athletes is used to sell a host of consumer goods, and the proliferation of participant sports has spawned a huge leisure industry in capitalist systems.

Functionalist theorists have been criticized for ignoring the possibility that sports may benefit some members of society more than others and for failing to note the exploitation found in organized sports. Conflict theorists have been criticized for overemphasizing the influence of capitalism when in fact contemporary sports function much the same way in socialist and Communist societies. Perceptive analysts have noted that theorists tend to apply the functionalist model to social systems they support and the conflict model to those they criticize.

The contours of sports specific to a culture shed light on its other institutions, values, myths, and inequalities. In the United States, for example, racial integration in team sports awaited the breakdown of societal segregation and hastened its demise by virtue of the attendant publicity. Yet blacks still are largely absent from elite sports and are excluded from many leadership positions in sports. Media attention to female athletes remains minimal despite women's increased participation in sports and sporting organizations. Changes in sports reflect and reinforce broader social changes in any society. Paradoxically,

Figure 1. *(Sports—Sports and Society)* A stadium wall collapsed, and twenty-eight people died after English soccer fans attacked Italians at the European Cup final, May 29, 1985. The sign reads, "Do not let the misconduct of a few spectators spoil the pleasure of the majority." Reuters/Bettmann Newsphotos.

club divisions, team colors, and fan rituals (*see* RITUAL) tend to stay the same as sports act as a force for social change.

Sports and Aggression

A different type of controversy surrounds one function of sports presumed to hold true across time and place, namely, that sports serve as a societal safety valve. Sporting rituals have long been thought to be cathartic. Roman elites believed that a diet of "bread and circuses" would keep workers from revolt. Neo-Freudians view the buildup of tension and frustration as inevitable and see violent sports as a healthy channel for the expression and control of aggression for participant and spectator alike (*see* VIOLENCE).

Contemporary empiricists raise two questions about these assumptions. First, they point out that games and sports are consistent with broader cultural patterns. Cooperative societies encourage noncompetitive sports; societies that stress individual achievement and success encourage competitive sports. Violent societies endorse violent sports. In U.S. football, for example, most of the violence is within the rules, or normative, and even violence outside the rules is often rewarded by coaches, communities, and the media. More than a reflection of societal values, sports also reinforce aggression because they condone and do not condemn it.

Second, it is clear that not all expressions of aggression by fans are harmless; rather, collective violence at sporting events has emerged as a major social problem for many nations. Do aggressive sports attract violence-prone fans, or do they create in them an inclination toward the display of violence? A decade of empirical research suggests that combative sports, as a mirror of cultural norms, teach and stimulate violence. It is not competition per se that increases hostility but rather the aggressive nature of that competition. Those who participate in combative sports show more aggression in response to anger and frustration than those who participate in noncontact sports. Athletes in combative sports are more likely than others to suffer from hypertension, a finding that further undermines the notion of sports as catharsis.

Emergence of Organized Sports

Sporting institutions cannot be understood in isolation from the prevailing social structure. They are inseparable from historical context, technological development, and shifting ideologies. An essential ingredient for the emergence of big-time sports was the development of mass leisure. Although play and games have been a part of every known society, the emergence of leisure institutions as a segregated part of life available to the masses required several changes.

The organizational change was the result of the Industrial Revolution and its concomitants, including the move from rural to urban life, the separation of the workplace from the home, and the emergence of routinized factory labor with shorter work schedules. A supportive value system was also essential. For example, in North America the Puritans took a dim view of recreation and emphasized work and religious worship. Not until the mid-nineteenth century did the old belief systems, with their prohibitions on sports and other amusements, begin to break down.

Another crucial ingredient for the emergence of sports as we know them was a system of mass communication. For sporting events to become parts of mass culture, mechanisms had to be found for reaching diverse audiences in distant places. At least since 1850 fans in Europe and the United States could get accounts of some events, particularly boxing and horse racing, through the growing telegraph system (*see* TELEGRAPHY). Journalistic accounts of angling, hunting, cricket, footracing, and boat racing were carried in magazines (*see* MAGAZINE). By the beginning of the twentieth century the newspaper sports page had arrived (*see* NEWSPAPER: HISTORY), some two decades later came RADIO, and by midcentury, television (*see* TELEVISION HISTORY).

Technological advances changed forever the way people relate to sports. The expansion of sporting news was related directly to instantaneous reporting made possible by the telegraph, and PHOTOGRAPHY introduced millions of readers to the visual form of sports. The invention of the electric light bulb stimulated the indoor sports of basketball and volleyball. Steamboats and railroads made possible regional competition, and trolleys facilitated intracity matches; fans as well as athletes utilized these mass transit systems. In geographically extensive countries like the United States and Brazil fully developed national championships had to await inexpensive, efficient air travel. Intercontinental matches were spurred by the advent of the jet plane. Television draws in regions with and without professional teams to the national sporting scene; satellites permit live transmission of televised events that unite audiences around the world.

Political and economic relations have played a significant role as well. Soccer is the world's most popular team sport because the height of the game's popularity in England coincided with the height of the British Empire's maritime, industrial, and diplomatic influence. The means of cultural DIFFUSION were many: students who studied at English schools brought the game home with them to the Continent and Latin America; the British Embassy staff displayed it in Scandinavia; sailors in the Royal Navy carried soccer to their port cities; British engineers and workers in local projects introduced it to Russia, Romania, Uruguay, and Argentina.

The emergence of sports as a major social institution is inextricably linked to general trends of modernization. The twentieth century especially has seen a progressive shift from informal, participant-oriented amateur sports to highly organized, spectator-oriented professional sports. The accompanying shifts from local or regional events to national and international events and from individual to team activities are part of the evolution of sports as big business, an expansion of their role to be expected in leisure-oriented mass societies.

Bibliography. John Arlott, ed., *The Oxford Companion to World Sports and Games,* London and New York, 1975; Jay J. Coakley, *Sport in Society: Issues and Controversies,* 3d ed., St. Louis, Mo., 1986; D. Stanley Eitzen, *Sport in Contemporary Society: An Anthology,* 2d ed., New York, 1984; Richard S. Gruneau, *Class, Sports, and Social Development,* Amherst, Mass., 1983; Janet Lever, *Soccer Madness,* Chicago, 1983; Michael D. Smith, *Violence and Sport,* Toronto, 1983.

JANET LEVER

2. SPORTS AND THE MEDIA

Examples of sports as a powerful currency of mass communication are not difficult to find. In the 1970s boxer Muhammad Ali was described as the most widely recognized person in the world. Since the 1960s the Olympic Games and soccer's World Cup have been among the most attention-getting nonmilitary international events. In most industrial countries and in a growing number of developing nations sports events constitute the single most popular media fare. The attachment to sports is so strong that people all over the world use athletes and sports teams as symbols of self-identification and community pride, and sometimes as sources of national pride.

Sports can be used to deliver a wide variety of messages. In the United States, for example, it is associated with competition and capitalism, while in the Soviet Union and the People's Republic of China it is seen as promoting cooperation and socialism. Sports may be used to teach such diverse values as achievement and pragmatism on the one hand and spontaneity and emotional expressiveness on the other. Regardless of the setting, the messages delivered by sports are likely to support the general cultural values of the people involved.

Interrelations

When the relationship between sports and the mass media is examined, there is a tendency to emphasize the impact of the media on sports. There is no question that this impact has been significant in the case of commercialized spectator sports. Commercial sports depend on the revenues produced by media coverage, they depend on the spectator interest generated by media-sponsored promotional campaigns, and they depend on the media to communicate scores and performance statistics to information-seeking fans. The impact of sports on the media has received less attention. Sports events have historically played important roles in promoting the debut of each of the modern media. For example, when Louis Lumière (*see* LUMIÈRE, LOUIS AND AUGUSTE) dispatched cameramen throughout the world in 1896 to demonstrate his amazing new invention, the cinematograph, the first things they filmed included a bullfight in Spain and the Melbourne Races in Australia. In 1899, when GUGLIELMO MARCONI came to the United States to demonstrate the wireless, his trip was sponsored by the *New York Herald,* which wanted him to report the America's Cup races so the *Herald* could have the news on the street before the ships reached shore. Marconi did it successfully, and the story made big headlines. In 1946, when NBC, introducing the new postwar television technology, telecast a Joe Louis–Billy Conn heavyweight prizefight, the *Washington Post* declared, "Television looks good for a thousand-year run." Taverns rushed to install television sets to attract crowds during boxing and wrestling events. The tavern prizefight showings were probably television's most effective promotion during that year. *See* TELEVISION HISTORY.

An analysis of newspapers and television in coun-

Figure 1. *(Sports—Sports and the Media)* California Angels baseball player Fred Lynn attempts to catch a long fly ball, which bounces off the television stand and comes back onto the field. UPI/Bettmann Newsphotos.

tries where the media are privately owned shows that they have come to depend on sports nearly as much as sports depends on them. Developments in the United States, though not entirely representative of the sports-media links in other countries, can be used to highlight the nature of the media's dependence on sports. In the United States, newspaper coverage of sports began in the late nineteenth century and grew steadily, eventually securing a substantial proportion of general news coverage in most major city papers. Many newspapers depend on sports both as a topic of news and as a basis for circulation. Furthermore, sports have provided incentives for some television companies to develop sophisticated technology to cover large spectator events. In general, the coverage of sports links television programming to an increasingly popular sphere of life in modern society; this link is crucial to its continued success.

Merchandising

Privately owned mass media use sports to attract ADVERTISING dollars. Businesses having products to sell to young and middle-aged consumers with average to above-average incomes often use the sports section for their ads. Similarly, television advertisers realize they can communicate with hard-to-reach audiences by buying commercial time on sports events. Even "elite" sports events with relatively low ratings—like golf and tennis—sell their commercial time at expensive rates because they are viewed by a high proportion of professionals and business executives. This is ideal for companies selling expensive items. *See* SPONSOR.

Advertisers like to associate their products with valued activities, and sports are highly valued in industrial societies. Sports and athletic models are used around the world to sell everything from cigarettes and alcohol to clothing and cars. College and professional teams alike are utilized as symbols in the marketing of products. There are few young people in industrial societies such as the United States, Japan, and western Europe who have not owned some piece of clothing or a toy displaying the logo of a sports team.

Top-level athletes in professional and amateur sports have been able to sell their names to companies looking for endorsements for their products. Some professional athletes have doubled their annual incomes with endorsements. Even many of the top "amateur" athletes around the world have been offered attractive cash rewards for endorsing products and winning medals in major international events while using those products. Of course, not all athletes make money on endorsements. But advertisers are well aware that people identify with popular athletes and use them as models for how to improve their physical and social skills. This identification is an important factor in successfully communicating messages about products.

Political Dimensions

Sports and politics are likewise linked to each other in important and subtle ways. As sports become more popular in a society, their potential as political tools increases. Sports have frequently been used to promote political socialization within countries and to establish prestige and power in international relationships. For instance, it is an accepted practice in many countries to display the national flag and play the national anthem at sports events. Political leaders have often found it useful to be publicly associated with sports, as both players and spectators. In fact, it has become a tradition for U.S. presidents to make congratulatory phone calls to the locker rooms of national championship teams and to individual athletes who have set noteworthy records.

Sports events may be used as scenes for patriotic displays emphasizing the superiority of particular political systems and ideologies. The impact of these displays is intensified both by the endorsement of sports by political leaders and by the fact that in some countries amateur sports programs are closely linked to the military. The influence of sports on the international level is significant enough to lead many countries, even those with serious economic problems, to invest vast sums of money in facilities and programs with the hope they will produce medal winners in major international sports events.

Of course, sports can also be used as a diplomatic tool in international relations. For example, when Commodore Matthew Perry of the United States negotiated the opening of Japan in 1854 after two centuries of Japanese seclusion, the signing of agreements was followed by festivities in which each side demonstrated some of its specialties. The Japanese began with a demonstration of sumo wrestling, a suggestion of their power. In the 1970s "Ping-Pong diplomacy" was used to pave the way for the establishment of political ties between the United States and the People's Republic of China. A touring Ping-Pong team followed by exchanges of other athletic teams was a "safe" way to initiate contact leading to political agreements. Under the right conditions, sports can be a playful, unthreatening medium for bringing people together and emphasizing their common interests.

The Olympic Games

The connection between the Olympic Games and politics has a long history. Even the ancient Greeks used the games at Olympia to enhance the prestige

Figure 2. *(Sports—Sports and the Media)* U.S. sprinters Tommie Smith *(center)* and John Carlos *(right)* make the "Black Power" salute during the playing of the national anthem at the awards ceremony, Olympic Games, Mexico City, 1968. UPI/Bettmann Newsphotos.

of their respective city-states and to gain public support for local political policies. Although the ancient Olympic Games were usually accompanied by temporary truces between warring city-states, they did not prevent wars from being fought. When the modern Olympic Games were revived by Baron Pierre de Coubertin, one of his purposes was to rejuvenate the spirit of young people in late-nineteenth-century France so that the French would be less vulnerable to military attack. Of course, he posed other goals as well, including the development through sports of international amity and goodwill, ultimately leading to world peace. Coubertin hoped and believed that peace would be furthered by the Olympic Games, and in fact he saw the foundation of political processes as resting in sports competition.

Even before the first of the modern Olympic Games was held in Athens in 1896, its organizing committee expressed numerous political concerns. Since then participation in the Olympics has become an issue of international diplomacy. The games became political showcases for host countries and for powerful nations that could use their economic resources to train medal-winning athletes. In the Olympiads following World War II the chauvinistic tendencies gave way to issues of domination and loyalty in international relationships. Participation in the Olympics became a symbol of political recognition and legitimacy. Between the 1948 games in London and the 1968 games in Mexico City, shifting political boundaries in Germany, Korea, and China presented the International Olympic Committee with difficult political decisions related to recognition. Starting with the 1968 Olympics, the German Democratic Republic and the Federal Republic of Germany competed separately. Political issues resulted in boycotts of the games by African countries in 1976, by the United States in 1980, and by the Soviet Union and other socialist countries in 1984.

Media coverage has increased the visibility of international sports events and made the Olympics an even more popular forum for political expression. Medal counts in the Olympic Games take on great political significance, and athletes are burdened with the responsibility of being "diplomats in track suits" for their respective countries.

Sports events are potentially powerful vehicles for the transmission of spirit and ideas. Like other forms of cultural expression such as drama, literature, art, and music, sports may serve to celebrate human skill and achievement. At the same time, unlike other currencies of communication, sports contains an overt element of competition that can destroy its potential for unity.

Bibliography. Jay J. Coakley, *Sport in Society: Issues and Controversies,* 3d ed., St. Louis, Mo., 1986; Richard Espy, *The Politics of the Olympic Games,* Berkeley, Calif., 1979; Leonard Koppett, *Sports Illusion, Sports Reality,* Boston, 1981; John W. Loy, Jr., *Sport, Culture, and Society,* 2d ed., rev., Philadelphia, 1981.

JAY J. COAKLEY

3. PSYCHOLOGY OF SPORTS

Sport, as the competitive exercise of physical skill, speed, strength, or endurance, organized and bound by rules, is one of many means for the communication and maintenance of cultural norms. Social scientists began to take a scholarly interest in sports at the end of the nineteenth century with psychological studies of the PERFORMANCE of athletes when competing against others or when performing alone. This area of research, known as *social facilitation,* is still pursued by sports psychologists. The formal discipline of sports psychology began in the 1920s when psychologist Coleman Roberts Griffith established a sports psychology laboratory at the University of Illinois, and Carl Diem established the Deutsche Hochschule für Leibesübungen in Berlin to study learning, psychomotor skills, and personality as they relate to athletic performance.

Contemporary sports psychology is concerned with athletic performance and in particular with the personality and motivational factors that maximize performance, with group dynamics as they pertain to the behavior of sports teams, and with the role of sports in psychosocial development and physical well-being (*see* GROUP COMMUNICATION; MOTIVATION RESEARCH). There is also interest in sports as a form of mass ENTERTAINMENT and in the relationship between sports and other social institutions. See sections 1 and 2, above.

Psychological Functions of Sports

Theories of the origins and purposes of sports may be grouped into two basic perspectives: the *excess energy* theory and the notion that sports and PLAY are forms of *socialization.* The excess energy perspective, which includes theories by Herbert Spencer in the mid-nineteenth century and SIGMUND FREUD at the turn of the twentieth, sees in sports a means of releasing energy that is superfluous to survival. Contemporary biological and social science theories derived from this notion conceive of sports as means of channeling aggressive and other forms of biological drives or psychic energy. The ethologist Konrad Lorenz, for example, viewed sports as a substitute for the aggressive drive that otherwise would result in warfare (*see* ETHOLOGY).

The second perspective can be traced to the nineteenth-century writer Karl Groos, who viewed play as a means of practicing roles and developing social and motor skills that would enable the individual to assume adult responsibilities. Modern versions of this approach stress the development of cognitive, psychomotor, and SOCIAL SKILLS, and the acquisition of cultural values through sports. This view of sports places emphasis on the social and cultural contexts in which play occurs and leads to the examination of how different cultures play the same game. For example, Japanese baseball differs in subtle but culturally meaningful ways from baseball in the United States. In Japan managers are rarely fired after a losing season, games may end in a tie, and there is an emphasis on team play rather than on individual achievement.

The types of games played in a culture may reflect its sociopolitical system. Research by U.S. anthropologist John Roberts and psychologist Brian Sutton-Smith indicates that games of physical skill are most often found in cultures that reward personal achievement and that games of strategy are prevalent in cultures with complex social structures and a focus on obedience in children. Games of chance are found primarily in cultures with high levels of anxiety and warfare and a harsh natural environment, and where religious beliefs stress the benevolence or coerciveness of supernatural beings. Some sports theorists have traced the development of modern sports to the rise of capitalism during the Industrial Revolution and to the spread of the Protestant ethic, with its emphasis on independence and individual achievement.

Contemporary sports differ in distinct ways from pre-nineteenth-century sports. Modern sports are largely secular, although many have origins in ancient religious festivals (*see* FESTIVAL). They place value on the equal opportunity to compete so that the conditions of competition are theoretically the same for all contestants. There is a greater specialization of roles or division of labor in modern team sports and a clearer distinction between the roles of spectator and participant.

The excess energy and the socialization perspectives are not mutually exclusive. Sports do not have only a single purpose, but serve a multitude of functions for both the individual and the society. One of these functions is to teach cultural lessons to participants. While sports and other forms of play have typically been thought to be a counterpoint to the serious adult world, more recent theories hold that the ways in which a society entertains itself are indicative of its values, beliefs, and ideals. LEISURE activities are not a counterpoint to culture but a reiteration of culture. Sports are means of TEACHING, communicating, and strengthening social values and are thus an instrument of socialization.

The socializing effects of sports have been noted by generations of social scientists, including GEORGE HERBERT MEAD, Freud, Johan Huizinga, JEAN PIAGET, and Erik Erikson. Traditionally it has been argued that participation in sports teaches youngsters competence, role-taking skills, self-control, goal-setting, appropriate attitudes toward cooperation and competition, and cognitive and motor skills, preparing the young for the nonplay business of adult social intercourse. Research conducted by clinical and developmental psychologists in the 1970s and 1980s supports the conclusion that children's play results in greater imagination, ability to cope with stress, and emotional control, and that these enhanced play-related activities carry over into adulthood.

The apparent relationship between sports and cultural values gives rise to the use of sports metaphors. In the United States, for example, many people speak of certain sports as a METAPHOR for society—football and baseball are widely used—and use certain features of these sports (aggressiveness, competition, and an emphasis on outcome) in their analogies. The selective use of sports as a metaphor tends to emphasize traditionally masculine values such as aggression, rugged individualism, and the equation of worthiness with victory. Sports, both as children are encouraged to play them and as they are presented to broadcast audiences, have also been viewed as teaching aggressive behavior and generally conservative political values.

Sports Violence

The two main theoretical positions differ in their interpretations and predictions of the effects of VIOLENCE in sports. The excess energy notion predicts that taking part in or witnessing sports violence should reduce residual aggression. In this way sports is presumed to serve as an outlet for aggression. This position is often called the *catharsis hypothesis.* It assumes that individuals possess a finite amount of aggressive energy that, like the hunger drive, requires periodic satisfaction or expression. On the other hand, the socialization perspective exemplified in SOCIAL COGNITIVE THEORY specifies that performing or witnessing violence is a means of learning and strengthening subsequent aggression. Research on the cathartic versus social learning perspectives is quite consistent: exposure to sports violence, whether as athlete or spectator, enhances the probability of subsequent aggression. However, nearly all the research on this issue has been conducted during a brief period, from the late 1960s to the mid-1980s, has examined only a limited number of sports, and has been conducted primarily in North America. Therefore the universality of such findings is open to question.

There are other interpretations of sports violence, particularly spectator violence. For example, spectator violence can be seen as a means of restoring equity. Many instances of group violence at athletic events follow what is perceived by the aggressors to be some unfair or inequitable action on the playing field, such as an unfair call by a referee. Because sports fans have few acceptable channels for expressing their disapproval, violence becomes a means of communication. Furthermore, the cathartic feelings reported by some fans may result from the restoration of justice or equity following the demonstration of this disapproval.

Spectatorship

Watching sports may relieve boredom, relax tension, provide for personal development, increase feelings of camaraderie and community solidarity, teach self-control of intense emotions, and enhance one's sense of achievement. Enjoyment is enhanced when the spectator identifies with the winner and believes that the opponents dislike each other. Sports fans are more likely to show overt signs of their identification, such as referring to the team as "we" or wearing the team's colors, after their preferred team wins a game. This is presumed to enhance the sports fan's self-esteem. Partisanship also influences the sports fan's perceptions of a game, leading to what has been called perceptual bias, in which an unfavorable outcome is seen as the result of external factors such as poor officiating, bad luck, or unfair play on the part of opponents.

The presence of partisan sports fans may influence the performance of athletes. This has been studied as social facilitation and as what is called the home team effect. As applied to the realm of sports, the presence of supportive fans tends to enhance the performance or play of skilled athletes. It is this enhanced performance that presumably gives the home team an advantage over a visiting team, though research suggests that this advantage is limited.

See also SPECTACLE; STARS—THE STAR PHENOMENON.

Bibliography. Mihaly Csikszentmihalyi, *Beyond Boredom and Anxiety,* San Francisco, 1975; Jeffrey H. Goldstein, ed., *Sports Violence,* New York and Berlin, 1983; Allen Guttmann, *From Ritual to Record: The Nature of Modern Sports,* New York, 1978; Johan Huizinga, *Homo Ludens: A Study of the Play-Element in Culture,* Leiden, 1938, reprint Boston (trans. by R. F. C. Hall from the German, 1944 ed.), 1955; Gunther Luschen and George H. Sage, eds., *Handbook of Social Science of Sport,* Champaign, Ill., 1981; John M. Silva and Robert S. Weinberg, eds., *Psychological Foundations of Sport,* Champaign, Ill., 1984; Paul Weiss, *Sport: A Philosophic Inquiry,* Carbondale, Ill., 1969.

JEFFREY H. GOLDSTEIN

SPY FICTION

This entry consists of two articles:

1. **History**
2. **Themes**

1. HISTORY

The term *spy* not only refers to one who gathers information but also embraces most foreign-dominated covert operations threatening state security: fifth columns, sabotage, assassination, liaison with regular or irregular troops (such as the European Resistance in World War II), and the activities of international criminal organizations. Spy stories often incorporate elements of such diverse genres (*see* GENRE) as crime, war, adventure, and romance (*see* ROMANCE, THE).

Much ESPIONAGE literature responds to current affairs. Particularly since World War II, innumerable memoirs, exposés, and histories have regaled an avid public with details of actual operations, from elaborate deceptions (like Ewen Montagu's *The Man Who Never Was*) to the burrowings of moles, double agents, and traitors. FACT AND FICTION have interacted with surprising frequency, involving events on all continents.

The ancestors of modern spy literature include the biblical Samson and Delilah story (anticipating the vamp theme), James Fenimore Cooper's *The Spy* (1821, military spying), Edgar Allan Poe's *The Purloined Letter* (1845, cryptography; *see* CRYPTOLOGY), and Charles Dickens's *A Tale of Two Cities* (1859, situating unsung heroism amid moral decay).

The modern spy story crystallized around 1895 as national rivalries intensified and governments systematized their secret services. At first Anglophone and especially British authors dominated the genre. Possibly Britain's special diplomatic-imperial position encouraged its early interest.

British novelists E. Phillips Oppenheim and William Le Queux devised two basic themes, both related to statecraft and indeed overlapping with each other. Oppenheim dwelt on diplomats and their amorous indiscretions. Le Queux told tall tales of dueling intelligence services—extravagant schemes, convoluted plots, and soot-and-whitewash heroics. Erskine Childers's *The Riddle of the Sands* (1903) and John Buchan's *The 39 Steps* (1915) introduced another perennial: innocent civilians stumbling onto foreign plots. Childers pioneered detailed REALISM in the spy novel, while Buchan initiated picaresque chases with a "pursuer pursued" through a variety of familiar or curious locations. ALFRED HITCHCOCK later refined Buchan's pattern for screen thrillers, beginning with his 1935 adaptation of *The 39 Steps.* Joseph Conrad's novel *The Secret Agent* (1907) elaborated the other side of espionage: the spy's family dramas, everyday experience, and psychology.

Early films displayed spy themes and reflected contemporary political concerns. *Mata Hari* (1932) popularized luxurious romances and the vamp-martyr nexus (Figure 1). *Nurse Edith Cavell* (1939) encouraged a British emphasis on nonchauvinistic duty. Austrian-born film director Fritz Lang bestowed V. I. Lenin's features on the arch-villain of his stylish pulp thriller, *Spione* (1928).

Somerset Maugham's *Ashenden* (1928) founded a new British school of spy fiction. Realistic descriptions of secret service operations portrayed tedium, terror, moral mediocrity, culpable errors, and sometimes even Machiavellian machinations victimizing innocents and allies. Successors to this tradition include Eric Ambler and Graham Greene.

With the onset of World War II depictions of Fascist-type spies multiplied. Lillian Hellman's play *Watch on the Rhine* (1941), for example, included passionate debates over divided loyalties in a German-American family, although it sacrificed complexity to the function of combating U.S. isolationism.

In 1949 Igor Gouzenko's revelations about Soviet espionage in the United States encouraged witchhunts by the House of Representatives' Committee on Un-American Activities (HUAC) and by Senator Joseph McCarthy in the U.S. Senate. Panicked by the rhetoric of these hearings and the systematic confusion of dissidence with subversion, the U.S. media were unwilling to allow "un-American" attitudes any rationale or emotional appeal. Graham Greene's *The Quiet American* (1955) and *Our Man in Havana*

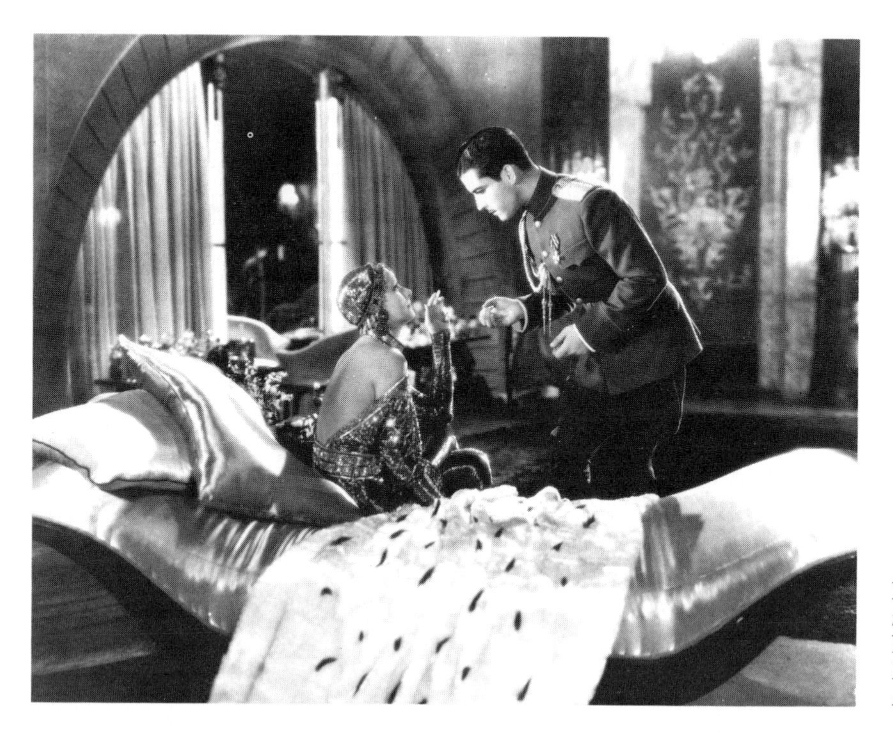

Figure 1. *(Spy Fiction—History)* Greta Garbo, with Ramon Novarro, in *Mata Hari,* 1932. The Museum of Modern Art/Film Stills Archive.

(1958) presciently criticized Western operations in Indochina and Cuba.

The cold war thaw around 1960 encouraged a new, apolitical interest in spying's privileges and pressures. British novelists adopted two contrasting emphases. In Ian Fleming's popular, eupeptic novels (1953–1966) James Bond was celebrated for his gadgetry, hedonism, and "license to kill." Sociological critics suggested that Bond's life-style was a METAPHOR for his readers' experience of the new affluence, which stressed expense accounts, social mobility, and sexual permissiveness. The film adaptations of Fleming's works were tongue-in-cheek—swashbucklers geared to modern "cool" (Figure 2). Among their many derivatives, a British television series, Patrick McGoohan's "The Prisoner" (1967), introduced a Kafkaesque ambivalence into the spy theme. A recalcitrant agent finds himself imprisoned in a strange, possibly hallucinatory village devised to brainwash him into conformity. U.S. television series of this period included "Mission: Impossible" (Figure 3) and "I Spy," both exhibiting enlightened racial attitudes (black and white spies working together in harmony) along with uninhibited cold war machinations. There was also "The Man from U.N.C.L.E.," which gave many viewers the impression that it pictured a United Nations spy agency. Enemy agents in such series generally represented unnamed "iron curtain countries" or "people's republics." Soviet television usually clothed capitalist spies in comparable ambiguity.

Fleming's popularity was rivaled by two British novelists of the more serious, saturnine school. In *The Ipcress File* (1962) author Len Deighton vindicated his lower-class agent's mistrust of his snobbish Establishment superiors. From 1961 on, an Establishment insider, John Le Carré, painted somber, exceptionally plausible depictions of British operations. Several, notably *Tinker, Tailor, Soldier, Spy* (1975), evoke an "old-boy network" of upper-class traitors (Guy Burgess, Donald Maclean, Kim Philby, Anthony Blunt).

The two decades following the cold war thaw appeared to be the golden age of espionage literature. Political attitudes covered the gamut. Alarm at U.S. volatility stimulated Deighton's startlingly revisionist *Billion-Dollar Brain* (1967), in which a mad U.S. oil tycoon masterminds a Bay of Pigs–style invasion of the Soviet Union. Leon Uris's roman à clef *Topaz* (1968) plausibly indicted French collaboration with the Soviet Union and Cuba. Anticommunism permeated Hitchcock's picaresque thrillers *Torn Curtain* (1966) and *Topaz* (1969). Conversely, a French film, Alain Resnais's *La guerre est finie* (1966), honored the lifetime devotion of Communists and fellow travelers to subverting Spain's durable Fascist regime (1939–1975).

A new U.S. theme developed in response to the 1960s assassinations of John F. Kennedy, Robert Kennedy, Martin Luther King, Jr., and Malcolm X; the disclosures of FBI and CIA autonomy; and the Watergate affair in the early 1970s. Journalists and novelists postulated conspiracies, too far-reaching to be fully clarified, between executives in security agen-

Figure 2. *(Spy Fiction—History)* Sean Connery as James Bond, with Daniela Bianchi, in *From Russia with Love,* 1963. The Museum of Modern Art/Film Stills Archive.

Figure 3. *(Spy Fiction—History)* Peter Graves in "Mission: Impossible." State Historical Society of Wisconsin, Erik Barnouw Collection/Paramount Pictures.

cies, multinational corporations, and reactionary political circles. This "literature of paranoia" might well be a metaphor for a painful loss of innocent optimism in the United States.

The spy theme has its echoes in literature, films, and television drama around the world. Regional as well as international conflicts and cold wars are echoed. Political shifts bring media shifts: diabolical Chinese agents, for example, common in U.S. productions of the 1950s and 1960s, vanished after the 1972 U.S.-Chinese rapprochement. However, producers and viewers alike downplay the significance of particular plots and stereotypes: the spy genre is commonly regarded as ENTERTAINMENT, not PROPAGANDA. Meanwhile, the media spy appears to be a lightning rod for diverse modern frustrations, fears, and enthusiasms.

See also MYSTERY AND DETECTIVE FICTION.

Bibliography. Raymond Durgnat, "Spies and Ideology," *Cinema* 2 (Mar. 1969): 5–13; Donald McCormick, *Who's Who in Spy Fiction,* New York and London, 1977; James Robert Parish and Michael R. Pitts, *The Great Spy Pictures,* Metuchen, N.J., 1974; Lenny Rubinstein, *The Great Spy Films,* Secaucus, N.J., 1979.

RAYMOND DURGNAT

2. THEMES

The GENRE of spy fiction appears to have ancient roots. For example, Chinese classical literature includes a novel, *San Kuo—The Romance of the Three Kingdoms,* that may be described as a spy story. However, there is general agreement that novels in which a spy's work is central to the NARRATIVE are a modern phenomenon. It is tempting to seek a sociological explanation; that is, that it is only the circumstance of warfare between nation-states that gives the work of the spy sufficient importance to serve as a meaningful symbol. Yet the themes raised by the nature of the spy—isolation, betrayal, moral ambiguity—are common in Western literature from the nineteenth century on. *See also* FICTION.

The defining feature of spy fiction is its focus on ESPIONAGE and on the spy or counterspy as the main character (*see* FICTION, PORTRAYAL OF CHARACTER IN). The type of activity most typical of such heroes is a mixture of deduction concerning the enemy's involvements and the action necessary to defeat the enemy's plans, with heavy emphasis on the professional ingenuity required to cope with extreme danger. On this basis it is clear that the spy story bears affinities both to MYSTERY AND DETECTIVE FICTION and to the adventure story.

The earliest commercially successful authors of spy fiction—William Le Queux, Erskine Childers, and John Buchan—were British, and their heroes were characterized by class snobbery, loyalty to the British Empire, and a sense of honor and patriotism expressed in ways that seem ridiculous, if not pernicious, to contemporary readers. In these early twentieth-century books patriotism is experienced as national superiority, and racist sentiments are common. It is no accident that these novelists also wrote traditional adventure stories; for them, and no doubt for their readers, spying was primarily the locus of adventure rather than a theme in its own right and implied no genre-based expectations on the part of the audience. One exception was the British writer Eric Ambler, who in *The Mask of Dimitrios* (1939) created a central character who is unsure of himself, becomes embroiled in espionage out of curiosity, and finally acts to frustrate unscrupulous international financial interests. In this novel the world of the spy serves as a powerful METAPHOR for the degradation of the modern world.

The first major contributor to post–World War II spy fiction was U.S. "tough guy" mystery writer Mickey Spillane, whose private eye hero, Mike Hammer, tackled Soviet spies and gangsters with the same righteous hatred. Mike Hammer also displayed a disregard for due legal procedure that reflected an aspect of cold war IDEOLOGY. The British novelist Ian Fleming borrowed aspects of Spillane's style—particularly his explicit portrayals of brutality and sexuality—when he invented James Bond, arguably the most successful fictional spy. Many theories have attempted to account for the Bond phenomenon—Fleming's eight novels as well as their successors and numerous imitations, constituting one of the most famous series in publishing history (*see* PUBLISHING—PUBLISHING INDUSTRY), and a string of popular films with several different actors incarnating James Bond—but perhaps the most convincing explanation for the character's enduring success is his ability over several decades to adapt to the prevailing Western social and political climate.

Among the most successful spy writers since the 1960s are John Le Carré and Frederick Forsyth. Le Carré's world-weary heroes embody themes drawn from novelists such as Graham Greene and the existentialists, and his later novels increasingly focus on the psychology and morality of spying's "secret world," as he calls it. The vision of the nation-state that emerges from Le Carré's books is diametrically opposed to that found in his predecessors': the earlier heroes' enthusiasm and belief in a mission is replaced by weary professionalism or cynical survivalism, their sense of solidarity by distrust or frank opportunism. Forsyth's novels are characterized by a disregard for character portrayal, painstaking research into the technical details of espionage and commandolike operations, and a cold brutality; the power of his novels lies in his control of suspense.

The central character in spy fiction is conventionally male—the rare heroines tend to be endowed with qualities traditionally considered masculine—and audience research suggests that the majority of the audience for these stories is male. Both facts indicate that one of the main sources of spy fiction's popular appeal is its portrayal of an idealized and stereotyped masculinity. The attributes composing this definition of masculinity derive in part from the tradition of heroic literature, in part from the events depicted in spy stories themselves.

These events are usually of two types: those involving risk or danger and those involving mystery. Spy fiction is fundamentally similar to mystery or detective fiction in that the reader's response is in large measure based on suspenseful curiosity, and the hero is the main or only source of relevant information. In some cases mystery arises because the source of a threat is unknown or the future course of events is uncertain. However, in many spy novels the element of mystery is secondary, and the reader's interest derives from the portrayal of spying as an exotic and perilous occupation.

Danger is central to the spy narrative. The risk is not necessarily physical, but the "Great Game" (as spying was first called in 1901 in British author Rudyard Kipling's *Kim*) is always played for high stakes. The hero must possess the qualities necessary to win: ruthlessness, cunning, decisiveness, and, frequently, skills of physical violence. The tradition of heroism generally places great premium on the isolation of the hero, the person who has exclusive right to our admiration, and the nature of spying makes this isolation all the more plausible. It is customary for the spy to practice his or her skills independently of those providing support, and the spy hero is admirable precisely because he or she possesses the skills to act alone and effectively in a dangerous world.

Central to the fictional world of the spy are the real-world features of the nation-state and the forms of action that its representatives can take without overstepping the legal boundaries on which the nation-state is founded. By definition the spy hero moves outside the realm of legality. Characters' skill in circumventing the law suggests that spy fiction implicitly validates disregard for legality when the survival of the state itself is concerned. The monstrous plots uncovered and thwarted by the spy show that the nation-state's continued existence is in constant jeopardy and that therefore the spy's actions are justified despite their dubious legality or morality.

In this ambiguous situation the pleasure the reader derives from the narrative itself contributes to the validation of illegality. The spy is admirable precisely because in a situation in which concern for lawfulness would be a shackle on effectiveness he or she has both the courage and the expertise necessary to ensure the survival of the nation-state. The world of the spy thriller posits constant menace to national survival and to the spy as the nation's representative; thus the spy and the reader are immersed in a world of threats and justified response to them. Accordingly, the emotional structure of this world is the structure of paranoia, for paranoia is the simultaneous sense of persecution and total self-justification.

Bibliography. John Atkins, *The British Spy Novel: Styles in Treachery,* London and Riverrun, N.Y., 1984; H. R. F. Keating, ed., *Whodunit? A Guide to Crime, Suspense, and Spy Fiction,* New York and London, 1982; Bruce Merry, *Anatomy of the Spy Novel,* Montreal and London, 1977; Jerry Palmer, *Thrillers: Genesis and Structure of a Popular Genre,* London and New York, 1978; Richard Usborne, *Clubland Heroes,* 2d ed., London, 1974.

JERRY PALMER

STAMPS

Postage stamps were first used in England in 1840. Until that time its POSTAL SERVICE had been financed by an expensive system involving fees paid partly by the sender, partly collected from the recipient, and based on complex distance calculations and other factors. The reform proposed in 1837 by Sir Rowland Hill called for modest fees paid solely by the sender and the use of a "bit of paper just large enough to bear the [ink] stamp, and covered at the back with a glutinous wash, which the bringer might, by the application of a little moisture, attach to the back of the letter." The first adhesive stamp carried the profile of young Queen Victoria and cost one penny. The system was adopted throughout the world and led to annual exchanges of billions of letters, postcards, packages, newspapers, and ADVERTISING matter. The postage stamps won a place on the front rather than on the back, as Hill had proposed. Many of the stamps bore an image of the head of state or other national icon. Stamps thus followed the precedent set by COINS in adding to their fiscal function a communications role. The image could serve as an assertion or reminder of the locus of power (*see* POLITICAL SYMBOLS).

Themes. Early stamps carried many designs other than portraits, but portraits remained common until World War II (*see* PORTRAITURE). After the war, with the breakup of colonial empires and the birth of new nations, other communication strategies came more often into play. Special stamp issues focused on cul-

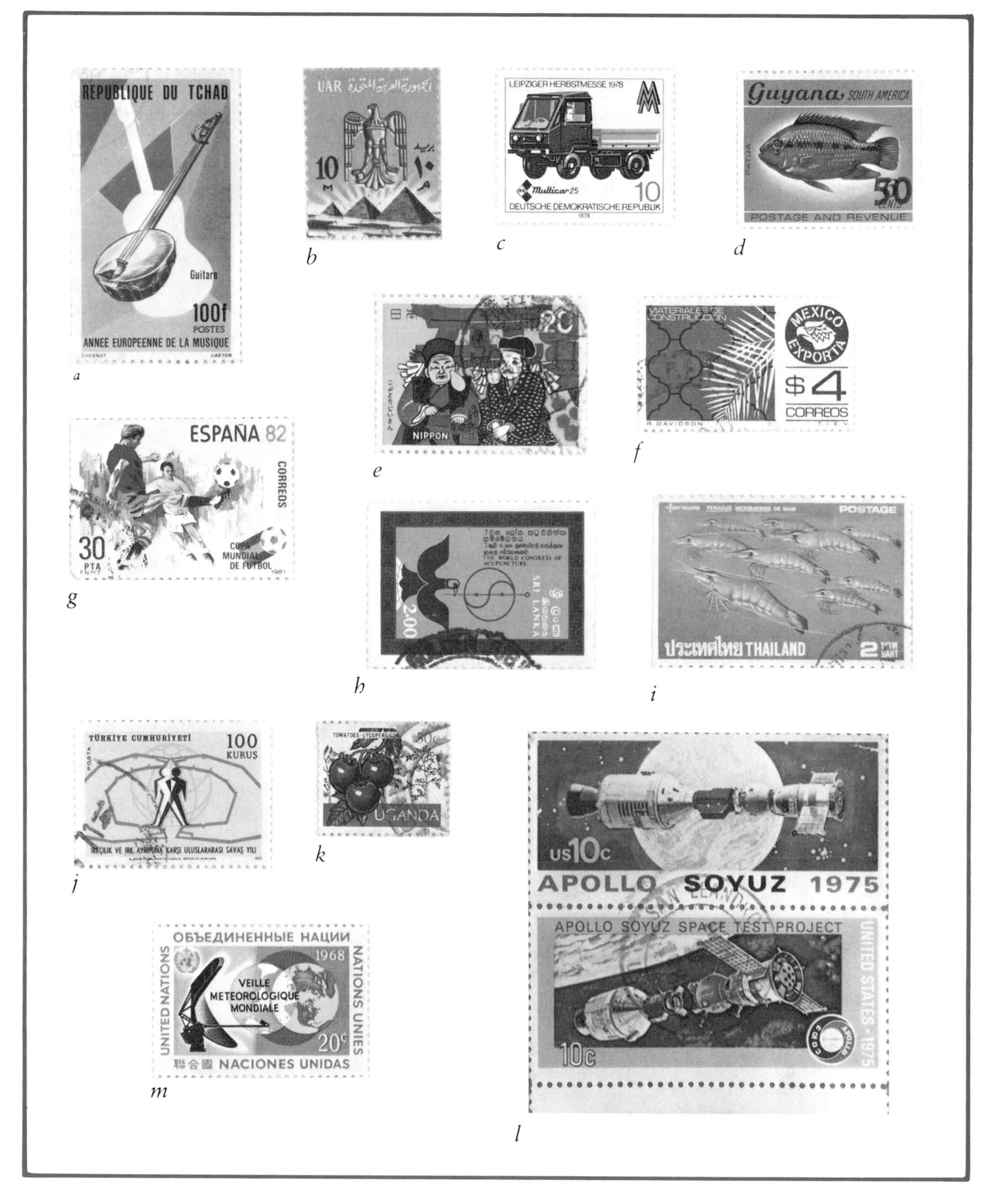

Figure 1. *(Stamps)* International examples of special stamp issues. Courtesy of Max Kenworthy.

ture, historic achievements, heritage, industries, resources, and scenic splendors. Thus, for example, (*a*) Chad proclaimed its musical tradition, (*b*) Egypt its antiquity, (*c*) the German Democratic Republic its manufactures, (*d*) Guyana its fauna, (*e*) Japan its performing arts, (*f*) Mexico its exports, (*g*) Spain its sports prowess, (*h*) Sri Lanka its medical work, including acupuncture, (*i*) Thailand its exotic fish, (*j*) Turkey its concern for human rights, and (*k*) Uganda its flora. The United States, at a time of détente, memorialized (*l*) joint U.S.-USSR space tests, while (*m*) the United Nations called attention to its meteorological services.

Fund-raising. Special-event stamps have won wide favor with stamp collectors, which has encouraged many nations to issue a steady stream of such "commemoratives" as a source of additional funds, quite aside from their postal functions. Stamps have also been used for other fund-raising purposes such as charity drives. These stamps usually bear two values linked by a plus sign, one value being the postal charge and the other the amount that goes to charity. New Zealand has issued stamps of this kind since 1929 for youth programs, called "stamps for camps." The Red Cross and its Muslim counterpart, the Red Crescent, receive sizable contributions from charity stamps issued in many countries. Argentina collected funds to combat polio ("Lucha contra la poliomielitis") through a stamp portraying a polio victim's face from Correggio's *Antiope*.

Postal history. Not surprisingly, stamp designs have often been used to chronicle the evolution of postal services. Every step in special delivery services, from the pony express to bicycle delivery to airmail, has been featured on stamps. Italy is credited with the first official airmail stamps, in 1917, for a regular service between Rome and Turin. The 1930s witnessed dramatic long-distance flights of giant German airships and occasioned stamps dedicated to the *Graf Zeppelin* and the *Hindenburg*. One of the most curious of all airmail stamps was a twenty-four-cent U.S. stamp of 1918 known as the "Upside-down Jenny," so named because one sheet of stamps was printed erroneously with an inverted airplane at the center.

Historical role. Stamps have not only reflected history; some have helped make it. A 1900 Nicaraguan stamp showing a volcano belching fire is reported to have been widely circulated in the U.S. Congress by a Panamanian lobbyist at a time when a decision on where to build the isthmus canal was about to be made. The stamp helped make the point that it would be safer to build in Panama than in Nicaragua. In wartime, countries have not been above making forgeries of one another's stamps, with propagandistic adjustments. German stamps forged by the United States in World War II portrayed Adolf Hitler's face as a skull. In return the Germans substituted, for the jewel in the crown of King George VI, a Star of David. Beyond that, both Great Britain and Germany counterfeited each other's stamps in wartime for use by their ESPIONAGE agents operating within enemy borders. But stamps have not often served hostile purposes. More often they have been celebratory, even while facilitating worldwide communications.

Bibliography. William W. Cummings, ed., *Scott Standard Postage Stamp Catalogue,* 4 vols., New York, 1984; David Lidman and John D. Apfelbaum, *The World of Stamps and Stamp Collecting,* New York, 1981; James A. Mackay, *Stamp Collecting,* New York and London, 1983.

MAX R. KENWORTHY

STANDARDS

There can be no communication without agreement on the symbols to be used and the meanings to be associated with them (*see* MEANING). Such agreements are called standards, or conventions, or codes. They are applied to a large range of matters from word usage to complex technological details. They are found in every facet of communications ranging from PUBLISHING, TELEGRAPHY, TELEPHONE, and RADIO to such twentieth-century developments as FIBER OPTICS, VIDEO, CABLE TELEVISION, and the SATELLITE. Even a dictionary is a standards document, recording the meanings associated with various words or strings of characters. The development of standards is a complex process—part political, part technological. It involves the efforts of firms, standards organizations, and governments. The existence or absence of a standard can affect the entire structure of an industry.

Historically national telecommunications and broadcast monopolies have been able to set domestic standards unilaterally. Negotiated, formal standards were needed primarily for international communications. With the convergence of computers and communications and increasing competition in communications products and services, cooperative standards processes have taken on new importance. *See* COMPUTER: IMPACT; TELECOMMUNICATIONS NETWORKS.

Functions of standards. Standards can be classified according to the economic role they play. *Compatibility* standards are necessary for products or systems from different manufacturers or carriers to work together. *Variety reduction* standards limit the number of different versions of a system in order to simplify training, maintenance, and inventory and to allow achievement of scale economies in manufacturing and operations. *Information* standards facilitate transactions involving complex goods by providing reliable ways of describing them. A standard definition of a "voice circuit" in terms of bandwidth, signal-to-noise ratio, distortion, and other characteristics provides a shorthand for describing a complex concept. *Testing* standards further specify how such attributes are to be measured. *Quality* standards set minimum performance levels that help the consumer to decide what characteristics are required for an application.

Standards can encourage entry and enhance competition by clearly defining what is required to serve a market. Compatibility standards give consumers access to a wide range of correspondents in the case of telephones, or programming in the case of broadcasting or tape cassettes. Standards—or the lack of them—can also serve to protect existing firms, stifle international trade, or inhibit innovation.

Development of a formal standard. While a standard can be thought of as a document, standardization describes a set of behaviors and a process. Firms may build compatible devices though what is required for compatibility may not be written down. Conversely, many written standards are ignored in the marketplace. Often one or more formal standards will coexist with de facto standards in the marketplace.

In the absence of a national MONOPOLY that sets standards unilaterally, formal standards development requires extensive negotiation among interested parties. Formal standards are developed by a wide range of organizations including international and national standards bodies, trade associations, professional associations, government regulatory agencies, and executive departments. Table 1 lists some of the most important groups involved in communications standards and some of the standards they have developed.

Standards bodies typically operate in small technical working groups through consensus procedures. Draft standards are then submitted for a formal vote to a larger membership or review committee. Representation in standards committees varies: in ISO and the ITU it is by country; in EIA and ECMA it is by firm; in IEEE participation is by individual professionals (see Table 1). In practice, vendor firms provide the financial support and personnel to develop standards. Standards adopted by national bodies or trade groups often are brought to the CCITT or ISO for international approval.

There are five distinct phases in the development of a formal standard. In the first phase agreement is reached on the functions to be performed by the standardized product or procedure. Failure to reach agreement on a standard often reflects differences in the perceived domain of application of the product. Beginning in the 1970s standards bodies began to use formal architectural models, which divide the standardization problem into "layers" corresponding to different levels of abstraction. Layering enables separate groups to work on the development of related standards in parallel.

In the second phase the standards body rigorously describes the specific methods used to accomplish each function. During the committee process parties in the industry are educated about the issues and trade-offs involved in choosing a standard, and the standard itself is written down in successively clearer and unambiguous drafts. Terms are defined, test methods are specified, and protocol specifications may be written in a formal, computerlike language. Firms often contest vigorously to have their own technology adopted as a standard, thus giving them a lead in the market.

Increasingly, standards agreements include numerous options in order to satisfy different participants. Consequently two products, both of which conform to a standard, may not work together or may work poorly if the vendors have implemented different options. Thus in phase three, user or government groups specify mandatory option sets for their procurements as a way of further reducing the diversity. Eventually in phase four, firms decide to develop products conforming to the standard and to bring them to market. Increasingly, however, a fifth phase, conformance testing—by vendors, users, an independent laboratory, or the government—is necessary to ensure that a complex standard has been fully implemented. Only then can buyers be confident that a purportedly standardized product will operate as expected.

Most formal standards are based on a product design that already exists as a de facto standard in the marketplace. However, starting in the late 1970s standards bodies increasingly were asked to develop standards in advance of marketplace introduction. For example, in 1984 the CCITT adopted a standard for 9,600-bit-per-second full-duplex modems before any such products had been manufactured. By agreeing to a standard in advance, firms eliminate the risk of backing a design that fails to become the standard. The telephone industry's development of standards for the Integrated Services Digital Network is perhaps the most prominent example. Unfortunately, a standard developed in advance of market experience is more likely to need revision and may fail to suit market needs. For these reasons, and because the complexity of communications systems is increasing, many standards must be viewed as moving targets rather than fixed points.

While adoption by a regulatory agency, or a PTT, may give a standard the force of law, most formal standards represent voluntary agreements. Thus mere codification does not ensure adoption by vendors or user.

Table 1. Organizations Concerned with Standardization

Organization	*Membership*	*Typical Standards*
International Organizations		
International Telecommunication Union	States	
International Consultative Committee for Telephone and Telegraph (CCITT)	PTTs, carrriers	modems, packet networks (X.25), telephone signaling
International Consultative Committee for Radio (CCIR)	Broadcast authorities	television format, channel spacing
International Organization for Standardization (ISO)	National standards bodies	HDLC, Open Systems Interconnection
National Standards Bodies		
American National Standards Institute (ANSI)	Corporations	character sets (ASCII), magnetic tape formats
British Standards Institute (BSI)	Trade associations	teletext standards
Association Française de Normalisation (AFNOR)	Corporations	videotex
Japan Industrial Standards Committee	Corporations	data communications
Trade Associations		
European Computer Manufacturers Association (ECMA)	Corporations	OSI, local area networks
Electronic Industries Association (EIA)	Corporations	DTE-DCE interface (RS-232)
Japan Electronic Industry Development Association	Corporations	consumer electronics
Professional Associations		
Institute of Electrical and Electronics Engineers (IEEE)	Individuals	local area networks
International Federation of Information Processing Societies (IFIPS)	Individuals	computer messaging
Government Agencies		
U.S. National Bureau of Standards (NBS)		Computer I/O standards
U.K. Information Technologies Standards Unit (ITSU)		U.K. subset of OSI standards
National Ministries of Post, Telephone, and Telegraph (PTT)		telephony standards

Theories of standards behavior. A manufacturer's decision to support a standard depends on numerous factors: the cost characteristics of the technology, the industry structure of both buyers and vendors, and the firm's position in the industry. Whether the industry in fact achieves a standard depends on the number and influence of the firms favoring it and the timing of the standards development process. Three aspects of this process are especially important: (1) the firm's decision to support standards, (2) the dynamics of standards at the industry level, and (3) the role of governments in standardization.

The decision by a manufacturer to support standards occurs for two basic reasons. First, the value of products such as telephones, facsimile, or electronic mail systems increases when other users have compatible products. Second, compatibility standards allow separate companies to manufacture complementary products (e.g., videocassette recorders and compatible cassettes). If the cost of translation is low a single standard may not be necessary to achieve these benefits. The benefits of specialization that flow from multiple standards can then be attained at modest cost.

In the presence of large networks of compatible products standards may increase dramatically the total size of a firm's market. However, standards can also lead to increased market entry, a lower market share, and ruinous price competition. A particular firm's decision to support or oppose standards depends on the combination of impacts on the firm's profits. Large, vertically integrated companies typically oppose interface standards that facilitate competitive entry. IBM has typically opposed standardization of computer-disk-drive interfaces. A dominant firm may oppose the development of formal standards that reduce its ability to alter de facto standards for competitive advantage, whereas the remaining firms in the industry are likely to support standards as a way of reducing the market power of the dominant firm. Concentrated buyers, such as the PTTs, national broadcasting authorities, and government agencies, tend to support standards and the price competition they engender.

The dynamics of standards at the industry level are also important. A standard will be adopted only when firms controlling a sufficient fraction of the market can be mobilized in its favor. Either a large number of smaller firms or a small number of very powerful firms may begin the process. If the industry is too fragmented it may be impossible to coordinate all the actors. If the industry is too concentrated the dominant firm may oppose attempts to undermine its de facto standard.

Successful standards are most often developed after early experience with a technology but before too many alternative designs have been established in the marketplace. For similar reasons it can be very difficult to persuade firms to abandon an existing standard in favor of an improved alternative. For this reason standards are sometimes cited as barriers to technical innovation, particularly in areas undergoing rapid technological change (*see* DEVELOPMENT COMMUNICATION).

When a standard is proposed initially, many firms may be skeptical of its success and unwilling to commit to its support. Eventually, as more firms adopt it, support accelerates in a chain reaction. Consequently the formation of an initial coalition is often critical to the success of a standard. J. Farrell describes two situations in which a standard may not be adopted: when all firms are moderately eager but no single firm is willing to take the risk of asserting a proposal that may fail, and when a few firms are eager but are too few in number to get the bandwagon moving. Support of large users through procurement specifications can be crucial in persuading firms actually to develop compatible products.

Governments play a crucial role in standards both directly and indirectly. Some standards are imposed nationally as a matter of law by government action. And governments indirectly influence the adoption of standards through their role as large buyers in the marketplace.

In many countries the PTT is the sole legal provider of telecommunications services. Thus a standard adopted by the PTT must be followed. Alternatively a regulatory agency may determine the standard. In the United States the Federal Communications Commission approves standards for connecting customer premises equipment to the telephone network. Broadcast standards are almost always set by government bodies. *See* TELECOMMUNICATIONS POLICY.

By acting as a concentrated buyer government can have a major impact on voluntary standards. Many countries have agencies in a ministry of defense, industry, or commerce that specify standards for government purchases of communications products (e.g., the U.S. National Bureau of Standards). As representatives of the larger consuming public, governments also act to encourage the adoption of standards viewed as helpful to the consumer.

Governments may use standards to aid national vendors in international markets. PTTs can set standards that favor the products of domestic firms. In addition government representatives can press international bodies to adopt standards based on the products of national firms. The French government played an aggressive role in attempting to swing European broadcasting authorities to back the French-developed SECAM standard for color television. The technology was licensed on extremely favorable terms to the Soviets in return for their support in the CCIR. However, attempts by the French developers to charge exorbitant rates for access to the SECAM patents led the German firm Telefunken to develop its own alternative, PAL, which was eventually adopted in northern Europe. Failure to agree on a single standard has meant extra costs for translation for such pan-European broadcasts as soccer and the Olympics and has made it more costly for viewers in border areas to receive both French and German programming.

In summary, when compatibility is a prerequisite to communication, standards are a major characteristic of communications products and services. Setting standards will continue to increase in importance as the number and range of communication technologies and applications multiply and the number of firms with a stake in the market grows.

See also COMPUTER: HISTORY.

Bibliography. Dorothy M. Cerni, *Standards in Process: Foundation and Profiles of ISDN and OSI Studies,* Washington, D.C., 1984; Rhonda J. Crane, *The Politics of International Standards: France and the Color TV War,* Norwood, N.J., 1979; J. Ryan, ed., *Telecommunications Standards* (special issue), *IEEE Communications Magazine* 23, no. 1, 1985; J. Farrell and G. Saloner, *Standardization, Compatibility, and Innovation,* Cambridge, Mass., 1984; Charles Kindleberger, "Standards as Public, Collective, and Private Goods," *Kyklos* 36 (1983): 377–396.

MARVIN A. SIRBU AND DEBORAH L. ESTRIN

STARS

This entry consists of two articles:

1. **The Star Phenomenon**
2. **Star System**

1. THE STAR PHENOMENON

Stars may be defined as performers in any medium who are highly successful, are widely recognized, and constitute the main attraction of whatever they appear in. Characteristically, however, stars exist as images extending beyond their performances to what are taken to be their personalities and ways of life. In modern entertainment industries the star is also

Figure 1. *(Stars—The Star Phenomenon)* Theda Bara in *Cleopatra,* 1917. The Museum of Modern Art/Film Stills Archive.

part of the labor that manufactures media images. He or she is first of all an image fashioned out of the raw material of a person's physiognomy, psychology, skills, and aptitudes. Many people in addition to the star may be involved in the manufacture of this image (photographers, publicists, agents, fashion designers, ACTING coaches, etc.). Stars are thus both labor and the image that this labor produces. The star image is then in turn used in the creation of performances—for example, in the making of MOTION PICTURES. By definition the star's image is already partly formed before a film is made or a PERFORMANCE given and to that extent constitutes a kind of congealed labor, a product of labor that, like machinery, can itself be used to make another product.

Stars are a characteristic feature of mainstream channels of communication in technologically developed capitalist societies. In tribal and feudal societies performance was not usually professionalized to the point that a person had a public identity based in performance; instead, people participated in performance on an occasional, amateur basis or as part of a RITUAL office in which the individual personality was subsumed. The star emerged with the gradual professionalization of performance, and then only slowly (*see* DRAMA—HISTORY). Performers in the

Figure 2. *(Stars—The Star Phenomenon)* Rudolph Valentino. The Museum of Modern Art/Film Stills Archive.

commedia dell'arte troupes, for example, were entirely identified with the stock characters they played—and the same was true of many traditional theatrical forms, such as clowns in the circus or the No and Kabuki theaters of Japan (*see* MUSIC THEATER—ASIAN TRADITIONS). By the late eighteenth century in the West stars were a feature of the dramatic THEATER and, to a lesser extent, the concert hall, but the development of the star system came with the growth of music hall and vaudeville entertainment as part of what is sometimes called the industrialization of CULTURE. *See* DRAMA—PERFORMANCE.

Star and audience. Attempts to explain the popularity of stars with audiences may be divided into those that use a broadly psychological model and those that use a broadly sociological model. The simplest psychological model contends that the star fulfills for audience members certain psychic needs. These needs can be expressed in familiar commonsense terms (such as "everyone needs someone to look up to" or "stars make up for what we lack in our lives"). Psychological analyses have explored these ideas, focusing particularly on the use of the star as a love or hate object and as a figure with whom the audience member identifies. Identification may involve a felt affinity with a star's temperament or situation ("he or she is like me" or "we're in the same position") or can go as far as actual imitation of the star in terms of physical features, dress, ATTITUDES, and perceived values.

Recent psychoanalytic work, influenced by developments in French psychoanalytic theory, has also focused on the question of identification. The appeal of such an approach, which has been greatly influential in academic FILM THEORY, is that it links conceptualization of psychic processes with what are taken to be intrinsic features of the film experience itself, suggesting a corollary at the level of the subconscious between primary psychic processes and the act of looking at images of people on film. *See* PSYCHOANALYSIS.

Sociological models of the relationship between

Figure 3. *(Stars—The Star Phenomenon)* Marlene Dietrich. The Museum of Modern Art/Film Stills Archive.

Figure 4. *(Stars—The Star Phenomenon)* John Wayne in *Hondo,* 1953. The Museum of Modern Art/Film Stills Archive.

Figure 5. *(Stars—The Star Phenomenon)* Robert Redford in *The Way We Were,* 1973. The Museum of Modern Art/Film Stills Archive.

star and audience are concerned with particular stars, or kinds of stars, and their link to other aspects of social meaning and value. Accounts of the way stars embody social values differ according to whether they are developed within a holistic model of society (emphasizing the attitudes and values held in common across a society) or within a conflict model (in which attitudes and values are seen to differ and to be in competition because of the disposition of power in society). Holistic accounts tend to see stars as reflecting consensual values already widespread in society—indeed, the star is a star precisely because she or he embodies widely shared values. On this view John Wayne was a star because he represented what Americans at that time wanted and valued: strength, independence, rugged individualism. Conflict-based accounts, on the other hand, tend to associate successful stars with the ideologies characteristic of ruling groups in society. Thus stars are seen to represent the myth of success necessary to competitive capitalism or as reinforcing the traditional GENDER roles of patriarchal society. From this perspective Wayne's HOLLYWOOD stardom would be related to his embodiment of the values held by those in power in U.S. society at that time.

More recent work in this tradition has introduced a far greater degree of complexity into this approach, on the one hand stressing the inherently unwieldy, nonuniform nature of IDEOLOGY itself, and on the other attempting to distinguish between the ideological implications carried by the star and what audiences themselves make of the star. The first emphasis examines the way stars may embody values that are not in any simple way supportive of dominant values (as with "independent women" stars like Barbra Streisand or "rebel" male stars like Marlon Brando). The second concerns the variety of ways of thinking and feeling that different groups in society may bring to their perception of the star, such that a star may be read in a variety of ways other than that intended by the dominant ideology. Of particular interest here has been the examination of feminist, lesbian, and gay male "readings" of star images ostensibly offered as patriarchal and heterosexual. *See* FEMINIST THEORIES OF COMMUNICATION.

Star and text. The presence of a star in a film, SPORTS event, or any performance generally will affect the shape and feel of that media "text." Certain elements may be used to make the structure of the performance fit the star image: plots that put the star in a characteristic situation or allow for the expression of the star's personality or create opportunities for the star's talents to be showcased. CINEMATOGRAPHY, mise-en-scène, and FILM EDITING can make the star the visual center of shots and scenes, thus encouraging the viewer to read everything else in terms of the star.

Even when the star's image has not markedly

influenced the shape of the text in which he or she appears, the star's presence may greatly affect how the text is read. Most media texts are in part read through what is already known about them in advance, and audiences may go to an event because of their interest in the star rather than any interest in story or outcome.

See also MUSICAL, FILM; TELEVISION HISTORY.

Bibliography. Richard Dyer, *Stars,* London, 1979; Christine Gledhill, ed., *Star Signs,* London, 1982; Alexander Walker, *The Celluloid Sacrifice: Aspects of Sex in the Movies,* London and New York, 1966.

RICHARD DYER

2. STAR SYSTEM

While the psychological and sociological ramifications of the star phenomenon have received wide attention (see section 1, above), its economic importance has been less carefully examined. Yet its place in the economics of motion picture production and distribution has been crucial and has involved many aspects. *See also* MOTION PICTURES.

Film production is at best a costly speculation in intangibles. Unpredictability governs every phase of the enterprise. Among the few elements that seem in a way to ensure success is the hold—or assumed hold—of a star over a segment of the audience. The star has thus been looked to in all major film industries as a stabilizing element, keyed to a particular pattern of distribution and an expected level of income, justifying a particular budget and scale of production. In the HOLLYWOOD of the big-studio era—the 1930s and 1940s, known as its golden age—stars were a central preoccupation in corporate planning.

Once the star system had acquired this status, stars were not so much discovered as created. Assigned to films by the production chief, the star was essentially an indentured employee, subservient to managerial decisions through a restrictive option contract. Entire studio departments functioned as components of the star-making machinery. The script department wrote vehicles for the star's persona, while the ADVERTISING and publicity departments constructed the uniqueness of the star by transforming his or her personal life to match the screen persona.

Evolution. In the early 1930s the major studios that had achieved dominance of the industry faced many marketing problems, including the problem of establishing rental prices for their products. *Sales Management,* a trade journal of the period, characterized the situation:

Picture a product distributed to thousands of dealers serving well over 50 million consumers weekly, a product without a fixed price because its value cannot be determined in advance. Imagine too that there is no preordained market for this product and that the product is not tangible at all, but a series of moving shadows.

The geographic location of the theater chains owned by the "Big Five" studios compounded this problem; for the most part these chains were regional rather than national. To achieve national distribution the majors had to play one another's pictures. In practice Warner Brothers' exhibitors would bargain with the distributor of a Paramount picture for a percentage of the box-office gross. But what percentage? One way of approaching the problem was through product differentiation, the creation of distinguishing marks that industry and consumer could recognize. If consumer demand could be stabilized by means of product differentiation, so could price.

But the creation of consumer demand accomplishes more than price stabilization; it actually allows a producer to raise prices. Demand, fixed through product differentiation, becomes less sensitive to increases in price. These concepts had effects at various levels of the industry. A distributor could exact a larger percentage of the box-office gross if a picture contained a successful star; at the level of exhibition, moviegoers readily purchased the higher-priced tickets of first-run theaters if the presence of the star was able to coax them into the theater soon after release. Hence the role of product differentiation was the star's most critical function.

In fact, the genesis of the star system can be seen in a series of experiments aimed at establishing marks of differentiation by which consumer demand could be stabilized. Between 1905 and 1910 film producers, searching for ways to create consumer loyalty, attempted to identify their own names in the public mind with a certain type of film. Thus Selig was known for outdoor pictures, Pathé (*see* PATHÉ, CHARLES) for theatrical imports. It was after 1910 that the rudiments of a star system began to fall into place. By that time NARRATIVE forms had supplanted the vaudeville acts and scenics that had typified the industry in its early days. The trend increased the public's interest in particular actresses and actors, and letters began to arrive at the production companies, inquiring who the actor was who jumped from a roof, who played the Indian maiden, and so on. As a result, actors began to receive screen credits, and in January 1910 Kalem, recognizing the value of star names, began sending to theaters posters and lobby cards promoting its stars, thus becoming one of the first companies to deliberately employ the star as a mark of differentiation.

Incontrovertible proof that audiences were focusing on film actors came when the fan magazine *Motion Picture Story* appeared in 1911. Bent on publicizing the plots of current films, the magazine queried its readers about what kinds of film stories were the best. Instead of the anticipated votes for stories, the magazine was deluged with ballots for stars, and the fact that audiences distinguished films by actors became inescapable.

Accordingly, producers began to use performers as a successful strategy for differentiation. With the cinematic and narrative components in place for an institutionalized star system, it seemed logical to recruit luminaries of the stage to work in motion pictures. The development of the multireel feature, with its promise of increased income—and potential for rereleases—made it economically feasible to hire the Mabel Taliaferros and Sarah Bernhardts and to exploit their fame in the service of product differentiation. But the fame of movie stars soon outdistanced that of stage stars, and the film industry began to develop its own.

The process. Star development began with the search for the correct character role. In practice, a player would be cast in a series of different roles. Audience response to these roles would be carefully monitored through fan mail, sneak preview questionnaires, box-office receipts, and exhibitor feedback. When the audience responded favorably to an actor in a particular role, the star persona would be built around that part.

The creation of the Bette Davis persona exemplifies this process at work. At the beginning of her tenure with the studio, Warners cast Davis in glamorous sex-goddess roles, with little success at the box office. Loaned to RKO to portray the vamp Mildred in *Of Human Bondage* (1934), Davis generated such a sensational response from the audience that Bette Davis the actress was to become the personification of the role that she played in this film. This transformation was accomplished through many channels, including the studio's legal department. Bound to the studio by the option contract, Davis could only appear in the films to which she was assigned. Eager to capitalize on her new popularity, Warners cast her again and again as the man-wrecking vamp, the woman without a soul, from her first successful starring feature, *Dangerous* (1935), to the last film she made for this studio, *Beyond the Forest* (1949).

The company supported the star-making process by fabricating a personal life that would make the artist the incarnation of his or her screen character. To accomplish this, the publicity department would provide a stream of articles, biographies, and photographs that created a unity of actor and role. Articles in the fan magazines portrayed Davis as fiery, independent, and hard-boiled, both on-screen and off. Physical traits were incorporated into the evolving persona. One story reported that the hallmark of her wicked, popping eyes had originated when her face was burned as a child, causing her eyes to bulge!

Figure 1. *(Stars—Star System)* Cover of *Modern Screen* magazine, featuring "Luise Rainer—The Rebel." From R. Griffith, *The Movie Stars,* New York: Doubleday & Company, 1970, p. 454.

Ultimately such a process belies the act of PERFORMANCE, as the actor "becomes" his or her screen persona. But this fusion of actor and character ensured the uniqueness of the star. Another performer might act the vamp, but only Davis *was* the vamp.

Star differentiation was carried through in communications addressed to exhibitors as well as to the public. It dominated promotional materials such as posters, lobby cards, and publicity items distributed to exhibitors and ads prepared for use in trade papers. Davis the vamp remained the central theme. Redundantly, ads promised that "man-wrecking Bette is on the manhunt again," and "Bette smacks 'em where it hurts!"

Implications. What is being marketed in such campaigns extends beyond the appearance of the star into a series of expectations about narrative structure associated with the star. Required to create vehicles for the star, the studio scriptwriters grafted the traits associated with star differentiation onto the film's protagonist. This had a profound effect on narrative structure. In the classical Hollywood cinema the goals and desires of the protagonist generally motivate the

Figure 2. *(Stars—Star System)* Bette Davis in *Of Human Bondage*, 1934. The Museum of Modern Art/Film Stills Archive.

causal logic of the action and consequently the structure and content of the narrative. Hence Davis's films repeatedly featured a triangle of characters consisting of Davis the vamp, her passive husband or fiancé, and another man. A "good" woman was often included as a passive counterpoint to "bad" Bette.

Structuring the narrative around the star performed a valuable function for the film industry by providing a framework by which the success of the star's pictures could be formularized and reproduced. It is in the role of structuring the narrative that the star can be analyzed as an auteur. For if the definition of AUTHORSHIP is the discernment of a coherent unity across the body of the auteur's work, then the star fits that definition. However, it is important to temper this assertion with the knowledge that in an industrial mode such as Hollywood, employing a high degree of division of labor, no one person has total control. Therefore, the star is but one of the voices of authorship. *See* ARTIST AND SOCIETY.

But the impact of the fusion of actor and character into the star image projects beyond the star's function of structuring the narrative or product differentiation. The star also operates as a social phenomenon. Cultural and sociological critics have asserted that the star delineates social types, thus presenting an idealized concept of how people are supposed to or at least expected to act.

Besides presenting models of behavior, the star presents models of appearance. Fashion designers have often utilized the star as arbiter of appearance to market their designs. Designers could differentiate their product through the association of apparel with the star image and popularity. Hence a woman who saw herself as strong and independent might want to attire herself à la Bette Davis.

In the contemporary film industry the complete control that yesterday's studios exercised over the image of the star has ceased to exist. Because of changes rendered by tax laws, by the antitrust decision that forced the divestiture of theaters, and by the concurrent rise in independent production, contemporary stars are not subject to the same image-making machinery as their earlier counterparts, and their roles are not mandated by a restrictive option contract. Yet the star is still a function of the economic imperatives of the film industry, for it is these imperatives that shape the very nature of the product itself.

Bibliography. Charles Affron, *Star Acting,* New York, 1977; Richard Griffith, *The Movie Stars,* Garden City, N.Y., 1970; Richard Schickel, *The Stars,* New York, 1962; Alexander Walker, *Stardom: The Hollywood Phenomenon,* New York and London, 1970.

CATHY ROOT

STRUCTURALISM

Broadly defined, the application of the methods of structural LINGUISTICS to any object or practice. The term thus designates less a definitive field of study than a distinctive approach applicable to a great variety of objects: myths, films, literary texts, wrestling matches, economic formations, and restaurant menus have all provided the materials for a structuralist analysis. In this sense structuralism differs from its near relation SEMIOTICS, which may be taken to denote the study of signifying systems and is to that extent a science defined by a particular kind of object. Structuralism may indeed take signifying systems, such as myth or literature, as its object of inquiry, but it also extends such an investigation to systems that are not strictly speaking significatory, such as economic activity or kinship structures. Its distinctiveness of approach in such areas is to treat the object or practice in question as though it were a signifying system, or "text"—to apply to it the kinds of concepts (CODE, SIGN, GRAMMAR, syntax, and the rest) that are essentially derived from the science of linguistics.

Structuralism is in this sense one of the clearest examples of what we might call the dominance of the linguistic paradigm in modern thought. It could be claimed that in any historical epoch one or more particular models or paradigms of thought will be assigned a privileged status, and the power of such models will be demonstrated by the fact that, though drawn from a specific field of intellectual inquiry, they will extend an imperial sway over surrounding realms. Thus in the MIDDLE AGES theological concepts governed not only the exploration of divine truth but also the discourses of politics, ethics, and AESTHETICS, whereas for the nineteenth century the natural sciences provided a framework within which, say, psychology and sociology could be addressed. In the twentieth century structuralism focuses on these and other fields and thinks them all through again, this time as LANGUAGE. Language becomes less a medium in which insights arising from such fields may be communicated than a METAPHOR for understanding their inner modes of operation. We can thus conceive, very broadly, of a tripartite historical movement from language as instrument of communication (the Age of Enlightenment) to language as a dense, enigmatic object in its own right (nineteenth-century philology) to language as a ruling model or metaphor for all social practices (twentieth-century structuralism).

More exactly, structuralism involves the application of the concepts of *structural* linguistics to adjacent domains, rather than just the idea of language as such. Just as the founder of structural linguistics, FERDINAND DE SAUSSURE, had "suspended" or "put in brackets" the actual message-contents (*parole*) of a language, in order to more efficiently extract its abstract underlying system of rules (*langue*), so a structuralist analysis will systematically set aside the specific content or meanings of a system in order to isolate and identify those deep codes, mechanisms, and conventions that generate such local, ephemeral significances (*see* MEANING). In the most basic sense, a structuralist analysis of a restaurant menu would concern itself not with the nature or quality of the particular dishes available but with the governing system of rules by which such dishes could be selected, permutated, and combined. Thus the Western culinary system will typically permit an initial selection of fish (but not chocolate), which might then be "syntactically" combined with steak or game (but not ice cream), which in turn could be coupled with wine (but not brandy). The meal, in other words, is determined by an invisible but orderly grammar whose operations may be quite absent from the consciousness of the participants at the actual point of eating and which are entirely conventional—they will not apply in, say, Beijing or Bombay (*see* FOOD). A structuralist analysis of a literary text will of course be incomparably more elaborate than this simple model, but it will nevertheless essentially obey the same methodological procedures, bracketing off the empirical significance of events, characters, and symbols in order to expose the hidden textual logic that permits such elements a certain determinate range of functions, combinations, contrasts, and equivalences.

Structuralism thus takes its place among the many twentieth-century formalisms, serenely indifferent to empirical content, attentive only to the highly abstract formal operations that bring such content into being. Indeed, one might claim that for structuralism the "content" of a poem, myth, or kinship system *is* the form: what such a text communicates is less an empirical referent or signified than its own significatory system. This is another way of saying that all such texts are fundamentally about themselves. Two such texts that could be revealed to display the same underlying system of rules, however different in theme, would be judged by structuralism to be in effect the same text. For a structuralist anthropologist like CLAUDE LÉVI-STRAUSS, all myths weave a set of local variations on a few constant, recurrent elements. These elements may be placed in binary opposition in one myth, made equivalent in a second, and inverted in a third, but it is to these formal operations of contrast, equivalence, exchange, inversion, and the like that the analyst's attention will be directed, not to a traditional INTERPRETATION of the contents of the text as (for example) symbolic, allegorical, or psychologically expressive. Just as, for Saussure, the meaning of any particular sign is a totally relational matter, a function of its arbitrary difference from other signs within the same SIGN SYSTEM, so for structuralism the meaning of a literary, mythological, or economic feature is wholly a question of its relations to other such features within the closed economy of a specific signifying structure. Elements of the structure do not first of all have meaning in themselves and then enter into mutual interaction; their meaning *is* their functional interaction. One element in the system may replace another, but if it retains the same structural function and location the system itself can be said to be unchanged.

Like its great modern philosophical predecessors, Marxism and Freudianism, structuralism insists on an essential discontinuity between appearances and reality. The "real" is not spontaneously available to our senses, as empiricism assumes; the true meaning, as for SIGMUND FREUD, is never the apparent one. Only by rejecting the empirical presence of a phenomenon, in order to decipher the submerged logic that brings it into existence, is true knowledge possible. To know truly thus involves suspending not only the signified or referent of a system but also the subjective experience of the knower. Like Marxism and Freudianism, structuralism is thus a form of antihumanism, deeply hostile to that privileging of the subjective experience of the individual that is the hallmark of Western bourgeois humanism. On the contrary, the human subject for structuralism is itself no more than the complex effect of a set of determining structures, the product of a signifying system. If structuralism dissolves any particular object into a more fundamental structural logic, it equally decenters the individual subject into an encompassing system, of which that subject is by definition unconscious. We would not be capable of acting effectively if we were continually conscious of the deep conventions and procedures that make such action possible. Such conventions are always in a sense artificial and culturally relative but will appear natural to those who are the bearers or exponents of them.

Structuralism's claim that even our most unique inward experience is the effect of a set of structures—social, biological, and linguistic—has provided a valuable antidote to the pieties of Western individualist humanism, in some ways parallel to LUDWIG WITTGENSTEIN's insistence on the sociality of even the most apparently "private" sign. To interpret, for structuralist theory, is less a question of consciously deploying certain techniques and procedures than being, so to speak, deployed by them. We would not even know what it was to interpret, or what counted as an object of interpretation, unless certain deeply unconscious assumptions were already securely in place. The act of READING is, for structuralism, less a lonely communion between a unique subject and a distinctive object (the text) than a suspension of both subject and object for a concentration on the structure of which both are simply local effects. This, however, leaves structuralist theory with the notable problem of the subject, which seems to have shed all transformative agency to become a mere prisoner of its signifying structures. Structuralism has a cognate difficulty with the whole question of historical change: its systems tend to be closed, synchronic, and self-reproducing, and the dynamics or dialectics by which one such system may be transformed into another are not on the whole adequately theorized.

Other criticisms have also been leveled at the structuralist method. It has been seen, for example, as a new kind of Platonism, which casts aside the particular material object in order to grasp it as no more than a reflection of some immanent Form (*see* PLATO). It is also perhaps questionable whether language has quite the centrality that structuralism would assign it: are not economic, political, and sexual production at least of equal importance in historical development, and is it not classically idealist to convert all material practices into forms of discourse? Structuralism has been powerfully challenged by its own poststructuralist progeny, which doubt whether codes, signs, and conventions are anything like as stable as classical structuralism would presume and which focus attention, as in the deconstructive theory of Jacques Derrida, on that within any given system that either escapes its governing logic or remains in some sense heterogeneous to it. It has also become clearer that structuralist methods must always be in some sense dependent on a preceding hermeneutical understanding: the structuralist may analyze the interaction of signifying units, but how does he or she determine what is to count as a signifying unit in the first place? For this, it would seem, we must look less to the rigors of structuralist logic than to our general hermeneutical grasp of the "life world," which can never be fully formalized. In its forceful subversion of the humanist subject, however, as well as in its scandalous exposure of even the most apparently natural operations as mere effects of convention, structuralism has made an abiding contribution to modern social theory.

See also AUTHORSHIP; LITERARY CRITICISM; POETICS; SYMBOLISM.

Bibliography. Jonathan Culler, *Structuralist Poetics: Structuralism, Linguistics, and the Study of Literature,* Ithaca, N.Y., 1975; Terence Hawkes, *Structuralism and Semiotics,* Berkeley, Calif., and London, 1977; Fredric Jameson, *The Prison-House of Language,* Princeton, N.J., 1972; Michael Lane, ed., *Structuralism: A Reader,* London, 1970; Richard Macksey and Eugenio Donato, eds., *The Structuralist Controversy: The Languages of Criticism and the Sciences of Man,* Baltimore, Md., 1972.

TERRY EAGLETON

STYLE, LITERARY

An aspect of LANGUAGE perceptible both in the form of a communication and in its effect on a receiver. Whether style resides in the language itself (GRAMMAR, vocabulary, RHETORIC), in the speaker/author, or in the context in which the communication takes place is a question that has stirred much discussion and much uncertainty.

The notion of style has a long history. The origin of the word is the Latin *stilus,* a pointed object (related to such words as *stigma, stimulus,* and *stick*) and specifically the metal tool used by the Romans for scratching on the wax tablets that served them for notebooks (*see* WRITING MATERIALS). *Stilus* came to mean WRITING itself and finally a manner of writing. In English *stile* or *style* developed further to mean the form as opposed to the substance of a message, then good form in writing, and eventually any manner of doing, being, or appearing that is characteristic of a group or individual. Thus English historian Edward Gibbon's style is his unique way of writing; the impressionist style is a way of painting like Henri Matisse or Claude Monet. But "dressing in style" or "a person with style" are expressions that imply approval as well as characteristic features.

Redundancy and information. The possibility of style in language derives from the fact that natural languages, unlike artificial codes (*see* CODE), have a structure containing substantial redundancy. Telephone numbers have zero redundancy and carry maximum information (*see* INFORMATION THEORY). Natural language, on the other hand, is about 50 percent redundant. If it were not, any interference with the transmission of a message would mutilate it beyond recovery, just as the loss of a single digit in a telephone number makes it useless. In any sentence only some of the material contains information; much of its grammar is duplicated. For example, in the sentence "In the past, colleges and universities were primarily religious institutions" the plural is indicated four times (by the endings on three of the nouns and the verb form *were*); the past tense is marked by the initial prepositional phrase and *were;* and the noun *institutions* includes *colleges and universities.* Redundancy can be defined as predictability. When a part of any communicative structure is predictable it fails to convey information. A telephone number is completely unpredictable and therefore completely informative. Knowing six of its seven digits will not help to predict the missing one. This predictability, which is not a defect but a valuable aspect of the structure of the language, can be observed in syntactic rules favoring certain constructions and disallowing others and thereby serves to protect the integrity of messages. Predictability or redundancy permits communication to take place even when part of the message is lost in transmission. Redundancy in language also makes it possible to convey a message in more than one form, according to the preference or disposition of the individual writer or speaker, whereas a nonredundant code, which provides only one form per message, makes no allowance for individual variation—that is, style.

Form and content. The concept of style requires a distinction between the form and the content of a message. Unless the content can be conveyed in a different form, content and form are indistinguishable, and there is no room for individual variation. This distinction is taken for granted in scientific, journalistic, and other forms of nonaesthetic communication. But in literary and aesthetic discussions it is argued that every change in form is invariably a change in MEANING. In some sense this argument is irrefutable. It is certainly true that Shakespeare's most famous line ("To be or not to be: that is the question") has a different effect on an audience than a PROSE paraphrase such as "Should one kill oneself?" The considerable difference between these two formulations may be viewed as a difference of emotional connotation, of emphasis, rather than of meaning. If it is insisted that all differences of emotional emphasis are differences of meaning, any discussion of style becomes impossible. For commenting on style in ordinary texts the heuristic assumption of synonymity is essential. For the discussion of POETRY and other aesthetic texts, style may be understood to include the emotional coloring and view of reality characteristic of an author and conveyed in his or her language.

Theories of style. The Greek and Roman rhetoricians established a hierarchy of styles (the low, the middle, and the high) based primarily on diction and suited to particular genres (*see* GENRE)—low for satire, high for epic. ARISTOTLE, for example, thought of style as the means of distancing a text from the ordinary use of language by means of unusual vocabulary or metaphors (*see* METAPHOR). Similarly, Quintilian considered style a feature that could be added to an existing text by the elaboration of figures, an exotic diction, or archaic syntax. This theory of ornate form held until the end of the eighteenth century. In the early nineteenth century the individualist theory, which holds that an individual will inevitably display a unique style, became prominent and has continued to be the basic explanation for the relation of writer and style (*see* AUTHORSHIP; ROMANTICISM). Early in the twentieth century, under the influence of the Italian philosopher Benedetto Croce, the organic theory of style arose; it insisted on the identity of form and content and claimed to abolish the notion of style as a distinct entity. This view became very popular among literary critics, aestheticians, and philosophers, and it has dominated the refined discourse of texts in many professional journals, but it has not displaced the individualist theory or, in fact, the theory of ornate form, which survives in the teaching of composition. *See* LITERARY CRITICISM.

The idiolect. A language is a collection of words subject to arrangement by means of rules called syntax and spoken by an assembly of people usually living in a certain geographical area. A variety of such a language used by a subgroup is a dialect (*see* LANGUAGE VARIETIES). An idiolect is that part of the total language known to an individual speaker of it. Although the speakers of a language hold the major portion of the language's resources in common, there are significant variations among individuals owing in part to the difference between active use and passive comprehension and in part to the process of LANGUAGE ACQUISITION itself. Except for the extremes of the educational range (a five-year-old child and a political orator of long experience, for example), most speakers can make sense of aspects of the language (e.g., complex rhetorical figures, technical vocabulary, complex syntax) that they do not use, that are not part of their active linguistic repertoire. Because of differences in upbringing, parents' LITERACY, schooling, READING preferences, work specialization, and place of residence, no two people have exactly the same linguistic resources available to them when they come to speak or write. It is a logical conclusion that each person will have a unique idiolect and an individual style of writing that does not change greatly once it is established.

The unconscious process of composition. Every speaker or writer is aware that the process of generating sentences is essentially beyond the reach of consciousness. The writer produces meanings and marshals them in an order that he or she believes will be effective or persuasive or attractive. The syntactic and lexical means for achieving this end operate below the surface of consciousness, in a manner not unlike the muscles of the leg in walking or the reflexes of the driver of a car. Like handwriting, which with small variations remains consistent throughout a person's lifetime and expresses, however uncertainly, that part of a personality under neuromuscular control, the production of language is controlled by the limits of the idiolect and by certain contextual requirements manifested as rhetorical variations. The speaker draws from a finite set of linguistic resources (idiolect) but can also adapt his or her SPEECH to particular circumstances (the social context), speaking in one way (register) to a group of children and another to an assembly of academics gathered for a convocation, regulating the level of the vocabulary, the complexity of the syntax, and the elaboration of the rhetorical figures to the expectations and understandings of the audience. To a great extent these adjustments in an impromptu speech are made without any considerable participation of the conscious language-generating machinery. In a writer the unconscious machinery is subordinated to the conscious editing procedure in the course of which the final version emerges. Much of what is called rhetoric and POETICS represents revision after the original thrust of the thought has been framed in language. This interaction differs significantly from the superimposition of ornate form on the literal meaning. The mark of the individual is the predominant fact about any piece of writing and the reason that readers prefer one writer to another who may be conveying the same message.

Stylistics

Stylistics is the study and analysis of style for any of three purposes: (1) the INTERPRETATION of a text, (2) the identification of an unknown author, and (3) the discovery of the process by which language becomes individualized. The study of individual style began in the late eighteenth century, when such rhetoricians as Hugh Blair criticized the style of Joseph Addison and Jonathan Swift in highly particular ways and Robert Burrowes noticed the unusual features of SAMUEL JOHNSON's prose. These early critics of style based their comments on the belief that any deviation from grammatical or syntactic norms, any singularity, was a deviation from correctness and required revision. This view soon gave way to a belief in individuality of style. Hence the primary goal of stylistics has been the description of the individual features of style of an author, sometimes for the eventual purpose of permitting unattributed work to be identified by internal evidence, sometimes merely to gain a better understanding of a writer's personality. (Although no firm link between style and personality has been established, there is a general belief in its existence.) In such a version of stylistics the emphasis may be placed on the writer's whole work or on a segment of it.

More recently, literary critics have used linguistic-stylistic approaches in the service of interpretation, that is, the attempt to better understand individual works of literature. Some linguists have tried to construct grammars of individual poems in order to explain the linguistic deviations of the poet in the work. Apart from these specific purposes (identification and interpretation) there is a more general purpose to stylistics, which can be described as a concern with the process of style, the transmutation of the material of thought into the apparent concreteness of language.

The earliest work in stylistics was impressionistic. The reader was struck by the language of an author and attempted to state this impression, usually with reference to the personality of the author. Such were the accounts of Swift's style as nervous or matter-of-fact, Gibbon's as flabby, and Ernest Hemingway's as muscular—adjectives factually unrelated to the phenomena they were describing.

With the development of LINGUISTICS and an increased belief in the power of science, a positivist tendency emerged that has led to an adoption of the methods not only of linguistics but also of statistics to testify to the significance of the results. Mathematicians and statisticians, primarily interested in identification problems, have done much of this work. Computers greatly increased the reach and popularity of this approach, especially after collections of machine-readable texts were formed. In 1964, for example, using computer statistical methods, U.S. scholars Frederick Mosteller and David L. Wallace asserted that James Madison had composed all the disputed *Federalist* papers. Large comparative norms such as the one-million-word Brown Corpus have been compiled for use as controls. Concordances and other reference works useful to those engaged in stylistic analysis have proliferated. *See also* CONTENT ANALYSIS.

The literary products of this approach, however, have been found meager and unsatisfactory. Some critics have cast doubt on the very existence of style. Others have ridiculed the pretensions to scientific objectivity asserted by the followers of linguistic methods. The difficulty they have identified is real: although it is possible to specify in considerable detail the linguistic features of style of a text or the work of an author and to show how these differ from the work of others, such a description provides no similarly certain means of interpreting the significance of the differences. To resolve this difficulty, stylisticians under the influence of reader-response critical theory have attempted to include the reader's reaction to the text as part of the analysis (*see* READING THEORY). This approach, because it is related to the effort to deny the text's objective existence, has also created uncertainties, one of which is the necessity of erecting a hypothetical ideal reader to protect against subjectivity. Such a reader invites equal skepticism. The branch of stylistics devoted to literary interpretation is likely to continue to be full of thorns.

See also AESTHETICS.

Bibliography. Alvar Ellegård, *A Statistical Method for Determining Authorship,* Göteborg, Sweden, 1962; Nils Erik Enkvist, *Linguistic Stylistics,* The Hague, 1973; Roger Fowler, ed., *Style and Structure in Literature: Essays in the New Stylistics,* Oxford, 1975; Gustav Herdan, *Language as Choice and Chance,* Groningen, The Netherlands, 1956; Anthony Kenny, *The Computation of Style,* Oxford,

1982; Louis T. Milic, *A Quantitative Approach to the Style of Jonathan Swift,* The Hague, 1967; Wolfgang Müller, *Topik des Stilbegriffs,* Darmstadt, FRG, 1981.

LOUIS T. MILIC

SULLIVAN, HARRY STACK (1892–1949)

U.S. psychiatrist and influential theorist of interpersonal relations. Harry Stack Sullivan attended Cornell University briefly and in 1911 enrolled in the Chicago College of Medicine and Surgery. In 1921 he settled in Washington, D.C., where he began formal investigations of schizophrenic states.

For about eight years, as assistant psychiatrist at the Sheppard and Enoch Pratt Hospital in Towson, Maryland, Sullivan established a clinical setting that enabled him to demonstrate the profound importance of the modalities of communication in the therapeutic treatment of schizophrenic patients. The therapeutic environment he promoted was first and foremost a social encounter. His early success in treating schizophrenic patients received wide recognition. Subsequent developments in milieu therapy had a significant impact on psychiatric social work and related fields.

Sullivan believed that schizophrenic states were far more common than imagined, and he argued that particularly during adolescence the powerful feelings of loneliness were symptomatic manifestations of these states. By adapting SIGMUND FREUD's "talking cure" to the treatment of mental states other than neuroses, Sullivan gave psychiatry a powerful impetus to view mental disease as biologically *and* socially given. Cure thus became a social recovery as much as a return to a physiological state of well-being. Throughout his professional career Sullivan eschewed chemical agents, shock treatment, and lobotomies in the treatment of psychosis.

Sullivan's commitment to a communicative model of mental health led him both professionally and intellectually beyond the specialized grounds of the psychiatric treatment of schizophrenia. In late 1930 he moved to New York City, where he opened a private practice. Sullivan's theory of interpersonal relations, grounded initially in his views of preadolescent and adolescent development and in his treatment of severely mentally disabled patients, was reformulated through his contact with a broader range of patients and his reading of the works of such social scientists as EDWARD SAPIR (with whom he formed a close friendship), Ruth Benedict, Bronisław Malinowski, GEORGE HERBERT MEAD, and CHARLES HORTON COOLEY. Sullivan elaborated his thinking in such books as *The Interpersonal Theory of Psychiatry* (1953) and *The Fusion of Psychiatry and Social Science* (1964).

Sullivan's deepest influence has undoubtedly been on that configuration of modern therapy beyond psychiatry proper that attempts to restore the individual to active participation in social life. Although he called for a fusion of psychiatry and social science, there is little evidence that this has occurred. Sullivan's hope to establish an ideal of interpersonal intimacy remains elusive, despite his efforts to universalize that ideal in the analysis of race relations and nuclear confrontation. Yet, in his postulate that "we are all much more simply human than otherwise, be we happy and successful, contented and detached, miserable and mentally disordered, or whatever," Sullivan expressed his hope for a form and content of communication that was, finally, true to a human nature capable of overcoming its fears of isolation in a complex and modern world.

See also INTERPERSONAL COMMUNICATION; PSYCHOANALYSIS.

Bibliography. Arthur Harry Chapman, *Harry Stack Sullivan: His Life and His Work,* New York, 1976; Helen Swick Perry, *Psychiatrist of America,* Cambridge, Mass., 1982.

JONATHAN B. IMBER

SURVEY RESEARCH. *See* EVALUATION RESEARCH; OPINION MEASUREMENT; POLL; PRINT-AUDIENCE MEASUREMENT; RATING SYSTEMS: RADIO AND TELEVISION. *See also* GALLUP, GEORGE; ROPER, ELMO.

SYMBOLIC LOGIC

Logic can help to formalize ways of thinking about a form of communication called *argumentation.* As we are constantly subjected to statements intended to persuade us, we may use logic to test the reasoning behind the arguments (*see* PERSUASION). Modern deductive logic is often called symbolic logic because it uses symbols to condense and formalize its representation of arguments. As the science of argumentation, logic cannot distinguish unerringly between true and false statements, but it can help us develop standards of validity and soundness in argumentation in general.

For example, logic explains why the first of the following two arguments is valid and why the second must be unsound:

> The merrier our party becomes, the noisier our songs will be.
> The noisier our songs are, the madder our neighbors will get.
> *Therefore,* the merrier our party is, the madder the neighbors will get.

> The person who forgets most is most ignorant.
> The person who knows most forgets most.
> *Therefore,* the person who knows most is most ignorant.

Arguments and Statements

Arguments are linguistic embodiments of pieces of reasoning. Their constituents are *statements* expressed by declarative sentences that are true or false, but not both. As the foregoing examples show, an *argument* is a string of statements, one of which, the conclusion, is said to follow from or be warranted by the others, the premises. A *valid* argument is one having a form such that if all its premises are true, then its conclusion must also be true. An argument is *sound* only if it is valid and has true premises. A statement is *true* if it corresponds to the way things really are. Thus while truth is a property of statements, validity and soundness are properties of an argument as a whole. Validity is the only condition that must be satisfied in a *hypothetical* use of arguments. In contrast, soundness is necessary in a *commitment* use: those who assent to the premises of an argument are committed to assenting also to its conclusion.

Deductive arguments are assessed in two complementary ways: content and form. We assess an argument's *content* by determining the truth or falsity of its premises. We evaluate the argument's *form* by establishing whether its conclusion follows from the premises. Why bother with the twofold assessment of arguments? Because it is rational to believe only what is true. The best way to establish the truth or falsity of our beliefs is to evaluate the arguments that can be advanced for or against them. And why is it rational to believe only truths? Because decisions based on false beliefs tend to be bad ones.

The difference between form and content of arguments is well illustrated by the story of a teacher of argumentation who made a peculiar contract with one of his pupils. The pupil would not have to pay for the lessons if he did not win his first case. After the lessons were completed, the student did not take any cases. In order to receive payment the angry teacher sued. The pupil defended himself with the following startling argument:

> Either I will win this case or I will lose it.
> If I win this case, I will not have to pay my teacher (because he will have lost his suit for payment).
> If I lose this case, I will not have to pay my teacher (because of the terms of our agreement).
> *Therefore,* I do not have to pay.

In response the teacher presented an equally impressive argument:

> Either I will win this case or I will lose it.
> If I win the case, the pupil must pay me (because I will have won my suit for payment).
> If I lose the case, the pupil must pay me (because he will have won his first case).
> *Therefore,* the pupil must pay me.

If we adopt the turnstile symbol $\vdash$ as shorthand for the frequently occurring expression "therefore" and let P and Q mark the gaps to be filled by appropriate statements, then the arguments by teacher and pupil are easily seen to share the following simple logical form:

$$P \text{ or not } P, \text{ if } P \text{ then } Q, \text{ if not } P \text{ then } Q \vdash Q.$$

The remaining English (in general, natural language) expressions are called logical statement *connectives.* Since the meanings of connectives are held constant, it is typical in logic to introduce the wedge $\vee$ as an abbreviation for the connective "or," the tilde $\sim$ as a symbol for "not," and the arrow $\rightarrow$ as a shorthand for the connective "if . . . then. . . ." On replacing the connectives by their symbolic abbreviations, we reach

$$P \vee \sim P, P \rightarrow Q, \sim P \rightarrow Q \vdash Q.$$

This is the final symbolic form of the arguments (both valid) by the teacher and his pupil. Although it is not known how the case was decided, what these formally identical valid arguments show is that the original contract between the teacher and the pupil contained a hidden self-referential contradiction and should not have been applied to their own case.

Symbols

Modern deductive logic is often called symbolic logic because it employs a symbolic apparatus much like that used above. Advantages of symbols are many: brevity, precision, perspicuity, parsimony, and generality. Logic owes its comprehensive range of application precisely to the fact that it is formal; arguments differing widely in content often have the same form.

The most basic and most frequently employed valid argument form is *modus ponens* (MP):

$$P \rightarrow Q, P \vdash Q.$$

This logical form is employed by every rational human being and has been recognized since antiquity. For example, Pope Paul VI used it in his famous message to world leaders:

> If peace is possible, then achieving peace is a duty.
> Peace is possible.
> *Therefore,* achieving peace is a duty.

MP may be used to explain the validity of more complex arguments. It is easy to confuse MP with the following invalid argument form, known as the *fallacy of affirming the consequent:*

$$P \rightarrow Q, Q \vdash P.$$

A typical argument that commits the fallacy is this:

> If the Bible is God's revelation, then it will withstand critical attack.
> It does withstand such attack.
> *Therefore,* it is revelation.

In general two kinds of error can be made when advancing an argument. In an unsound argument one makes a *factual* error by being mistaken in claiming that the premises are all true. In an invalid argument one makes a *formal* error by misinterpreting the deductive linkage between premises and conclusion.

Classical Logic

It is common to mean by classical logic the study of deductive arguments involving the usual connectives and quantifiers "all" and "some." With the resources of this logic it is possible to analyze and evaluate arguments of remarkable complexity and subtlety, far beyond any of the examples given above. Classical logic is completely safe because its body of admissible arguments is consistent, and it is at least as adequate (i.e., corresponds to the reality of argumentation) as any mature science. Logic stipulates the meanings of connectives, but these axiomatic meanings do not always correspond to the intuitive meanings of natural language expressions from which they have been originally abstracted. The following familiar argument about the existence of God elucidates the point:

> If I will have eternal life if I believe in God, then God must exist.
> I do not believe in God.
> *Therefore,* God exists.

While this natural language argument is clearly invalid, its symbolic translation most assuredly *is* valid. It is immediately evident that the formal version

$$(P \rightarrow Q) \rightarrow R, \sim P \vdash R$$

of the argument is not a wholly satisfactory translation of the natural argument. In this example the second premise does not entail the antecedent of the first premise, while formally $\sim P$ does entail $P \rightarrow Q$.

Because classical logic sometimes gives incorrect results even with arguments that seem to fall within its domain of applicability, logicians have proposed several *alternative* logics (including constructive, intuitionistic, strict, free, relevant, many-valued, and partial-valued logics) that accommodate many of the semantic peculiarities of natural language connectives and quantifiers. The question of which alternative logics are fact or fiction has not been properly resolved.

Applications to Communication

A natural habitat of arguments is human communication. Logic sets definite limits to communication situations. As a paradigm, consider the classic Wise Man Puzzle:

> A king, wishing to know which of his three advisers is the wisest, paints a dot on each of their foreheads, telling them that each man's dot is either black or white and that at least one of them has a white dot; he then asks them to tell him the color of their own spots. After a while the first replies that he does not know; the second, on hearing this, also says he does not know. After hearing both responses, the third man declares, "I know the color of my spot."

The puzzle is to generate the line of argument employed by the third wise man. The difficulty lies in the nature of the third wise man's reasoning about the knowledge of the first two. Not only must he pose a hypothetical situation, but then he must reason within that situation about what conclusions the second wise man would have to come to after hearing the first wise man's response.

Epistemic logic, based on conditional and common knowledge operators, provides a powerful framework for reasoning about knowledge in communication situations. In particular, it explains how the third wise man in the example above must reason: "Suppose my spot were black. Then the second of us would know that his own spot is white, since he would know that if it were black, the first of us would have seen two black spots and would have known his own spot's color. But since both answered that they did not know their own spot's color, my spot must be white."

In this example the communication situation is as follows. The agents communicate with each other via admissible channels. Each agent is at all times in some state of knowledge, and this state is a function of some earlier state and the messages received. Knowledge states contain not only facts about the world but also facts about the states of knowledge of others. From a logical standpoint each agent may be framed in terms of an algebra of statements (expressed in some fixed language) together with a string of admissible arguments (deduction rules) applicable to the statements in the algebra. Reasoning about the agents' knowledge is carried out in terms of a new logical operator, symbolized by square brackets [•]. So if P is a statement from the algebra of statements of wise man (agent) m, then the fact that "Wise man m knows that P" is conveniently symbolized by the expression $[m]P$. Iterations of the sort "Wise man m knows that wise man n knows that P" receive the obvious symbolization $[m][n]P$. Epistemic logic is based on classical logical argument forms and the following "knowledge" argument forms:

K_1 $[n](P \rightarrow Q), [n]P \vdash [n]Q$
K_2 $[n]P, [n]Q \vdash [n](P \wedge Q)$
K_3 $[n]P \vdash P$
K_4 $[n]P \vdash [n][n]P$
K_5 $[n]P \vdash [n]\sim[n]P$

Argument form K_1 says that each agent's body of knowledge is closed under MP (logical deduction). Simply, agents know the logical consequences of their own knowledge. Removal of this idealization of knowers has led to many alternative epistemic logics. Form K_2 legislates the fact that if agent n knows both P and Q, then n also knows their logical conjunction $P \wedge Q$ (the inverted wedge $\wedge$ is an abbreviation for the connective "and"). Principle K_3 suggests that an agent only knows things that are true, a condition that distinguishes knowledge from belief: one cannot know something that is false, although one may believe it. The last two conditions pertain to logical introspection. In particular, K_4 says that if agent n knows that P, then n knows that he or she knows that P. The last condition concerns negative introspection—the fact that one has knowledge about one's own lack of knowledge.

Common and implicit knowledge. A persistent theme in discourse understanding, convention, and coordinated action is *common knowledge.* In a logical model of communication we grant that when a social group has common knowledge of some statement P, then not only does everyone in the group know that P, but everyone knows that everyone knows that P, everyone knows that everyone knows that everyone knows that P, and so on ad infinitum. When the group consists of two agents, say m and n, then we may write $[m \wedge n]P$ as short for "It is common knowledge between m and n that P." As pointed out, common knowledge may be unfolded in terms of an infinite conjunction of iterated knowledge:

$$[m \wedge n]P =_{\text{def}} [m]P \wedge [n]P \wedge [m][n]P \wedge [n][m]P \wedge [m][n][m]P \wedge \ldots$$

It is not hard to show that the common knowledge operator $[m \wedge n]$ shares the properties expressed in K_1–K_5. For example, it is common knowledge among the three wise men (i.e., their "frames of reference" overlap to some extent) that at least one spot is white and that K_1–K_5 hold.

The next notion that is relevant in a logical model of communication is that of *implicit knowledge,* which is the knowledge that can be obtained by pooling together the knowledge of agents in a group. For example, suppose agent n knows that P and agent m knows that $P \rightarrow Q$. Then together agents n and m know that Q, implicitly, even if neither of them knows Q individually. If we adopt $[n \vee m]P$ as shorthand for the expression "Agents n and m have implicit knowledge of P," we have the rule

$$[n]P \vee [m]P \vdash [n \vee m]P.$$

Again, the operator $[n \vee m]$ satisfies K_1–K_5. No amount of communication in a closed social group can change the implicit knowledge about the world.

Since agents communicate with each other exclusively by exchanging messages of various sorts and through different channels, we need to know what states of knowledge are attainable via such communication. To this end we introduce a *conditional knowledge* operator $[m{:}M]$ such that for statements M and P the epistemic statement $[m{:}M]P$ expresses the fact that "Agent m knows that P, given the received message M." Here again, $[m{:}M]$ satisfies the deduction rules K_1–K_5 and the following argument forms:

M_1 $[m]P \vdash [m{:}M]P$ if $\sim[m]\sim M$
M_2 $[m]M \vdash [m{:}M]P \rightarrow [m]P$
M_3 $[m{:}M]N, [m{:}N]P \vdash [m{:}M]P$
M_4 $[(m{:}M){:}N]P \vdash [m{:}M \wedge N]P$ and $[m{:}M \wedge N]P \vdash [(m{:}M){:}N]P$
M_5 $\vdash [m{:}M]M$

Message axiom M_1 says that if agent m knows that P, then m continues to know that P even after having received message M so long as agent m does not know that $\sim M$. Condition M_2 expresses the fact that under the knowledge of M if an agent m knows that P, then m knows that P independently of receiving message M. Rule M_3 characterizes the transitivity of message reception. By contrast, rule M_4 captures the idea of composition of messages. First learning message M and then message N is the same as learning $M \wedge N$ in a single step. Finally, clause M_5 requires that whatever is received as a message must be known.

Deduction rules K_1–K_5, together with message principles M_1–M_5, provide an exact—albeit idealized—explanatory account of how the third wise man must have reasoned. This sort of logical methodology offers some distinct conceptual advantages over typical commonsense treatments, without the synergistic complexities so frequently encountered in studies of human communication. The logical model fits within the finely bounded region between formally tractable but oversimplified models and more realistic but less easily axiomatized views.

See also CYBERNETICS; INFORMATION THEORY; MODELS OF COMMUNICATION.

Bibliography. D. Harrah, *Communication: A Logical Model,* Cambridge, Mass., 1963; W. V. Quine, *Philosophy of Logic,* Englewood Cliffs, N.J., 1970.

ZOLTAN DOMOTOR

SYMBOLISM

Etymologically, *symbolism* derives from the Greek word *symballein,* meaning "to put together." A *symbolon* was half of a coin retained in lieu of a verbal agreement. Now symbolism is generally defined as the use of a SIGN to stand for something other than its usual signified. The symbol is both less precise than nonsymbolic terms and more explanatory: whereas the original Greek symbolic practice suggests that any coin would do, the modern "putting together" is often taken to reveal previously unthought-of affinities or likenesses, potentially codifiable but beyond the scope of discursive definitions. To this extent symbolic figurations can claim to be unique, neither translatable back into discourse like allegory nor infinitely expandable within discourse like METAPHOR and simile. This strong version of symbolism recurs in intellectual history but frequently gives way to a simpler one. The basic idea of the displacement of one MEANING by another is retained in both versions. Symbolism can occur within any SIGN SYSTEM, from PORTRAITURE to traffic lights. The color red, for example, can symbolize passion or danger as well as representing the color of a dress or giving an order to stop. In each case, if the symbolic function is dominant, a literal CODE of meaning is assumed to give way to one transferred from elsewhere.

However, theorists have often found it difficult to separate these supposedly different communicative acts. Some have taken symbolic LANGUAGE to be paradigmatic of how humans exchange information, making it unnecessary to distinguish a symbolic MODE. If all words are originally symbolic there can be no inherited background of literalness against which symbolic usage can appear divergent and innovatory. Others, usually assuming the strong version, have sharply differentiated symbolism from standard usage, often in defense of artistic privilege or a contrasting scientific objectivity. But although the scope of symbolism varies with the interests of different sciences of communication—linguistic, sociological, anthropological, aesthetic, psychological—all theories of meaning, from Platonism to poststructuralism, have had to provide an adequate account of symbolism (*see* AESTHETICS; COMMUNICATION, PHILOSOPHIES OF).

PLATO can be seen to have set the terms of this debate. In *The Republic* he ostensibly holds poets in disrepute, but as a result is able to adopt their techniques to describe the ideal reality behind the flux of appearance without fear of presumption. Ironically, Plato devalues ART only to employ myth and allegory to symbolize what science cannot represent. In reaction to Plato, but under his influence, ARISTOTLE's *Poetics* describes POETRY as the most philosophical of all kinds of WRITING, explicitly making its heuristic power dependent on its possession of a symbolic function distinct from that of scientific description. Subsequently this fragile dialectic between symbolism and science was frequently to collapse. For the later Greek philosopher Plotinus, art's power to figure the ideal reality simply *was* ultimate knowledge; and in the RENAISSANCE the esotericism resulting from the strong versions of symbolism in such doctrines as his came into open conflict with attempts to establish the foundations of modern empirical science. Political disputes, correlatable to the scientific debate, pitted the symbolic protocols of authoritarian regimes against the materialism of the rising commercial classes; the Reformation focused its attacks on the ecclesiastical establishment with reference to the way in which the priesthood appeared to exceed its symbolic function. In the broadest terms, then, theories of symbolism recapitulate basic philosophical and political disputes founded on disagreements about the proper distance to preserve between symbolic and scientific discourse.

Symbolism and romantic ideology. However, symbolism also has a more specialized history, beginning in the late eighteenth century with the romantic period in literature (*see* ROMANTICISM), in which the symbol becomes described as a particular trope and is used exclusively to legitimate art. In romantic IDEOLOGY the gap between the symbolic and the true is closed, and symbols merge with their meanings while still retaining their advantages over a bare scientific terminology. In the Kantian language out of which romantic theories of the symbol grew, the symbolic embodies an aspect of the intelligible or noumenal world (Plato's ideal reality) in unitary form; it is not, that is, restricted to representing through contradiction or antinomy—the modes in which ideas of Reason appear to the Understanding. Immanuel Kant held that symbols were noncognitive, but post-Kantians like the German philosopher Friedrich Schelling and his English follower Samuel Taylor Coleridge, at least in his theology, influentially advocated a strong version of symbolism as a kind of knowledge superior to allegory and metaphor. Johann Wolfgang von Goethe, too, thought it was in the nature of poetry to let its readers see immediately general truths that allegory could only report on as though from a spatial and temporal distance.

The romantic theorists for whom poetry was, in the words of the early nineteenth-century German aesthetician A. W. Schlegel, "an eternal symbolizing," were as influential for literature as they were for critical theory, and as a result almost all European literatures had their symbolist movements, most famously in France. There Charles Baudelaire revived the identification of essential reality with ideal aesthetic truth, often through sordid examples of reality that made his poetic appropriation of them appear all the more creative. Such conventionally unpromising situations concentrated attention on the symbolist consciousness, which could redeem from them a previously hidden residue. The poet Stéphane Mallarmé's endeavor "to paint, not the thing, but the effect it produces" continued to encourage a highly reflexive style, since the poem itself must be one of its subject's effects. Everything else is "chance," and later poets such as W. B. Yeats, Paul Valéry, and Rainer Maria Rilke inherited in their individual ways this basic confidence that ultimate truth lies behind poetry's own self-examination.

Developments in critical theory. Critiques of the romantic theory were foreshadowed in the 1820s in G. W. F. Hegel's *Aesthetics* but were developed in the twentieth century by European critical theorists such as WALTER BENJAMIN and THEODOR ADORNO, by the later structuralist and poststructuralist polemics of ROLAND BARTHES and Jacques Derrida (*see* STRUCTURALISM), and by U.S. deconstructive criticism, practiced most influentially by Paul de Man and Geoffrey Hartman (*see* AUTHORSHIP). With a growing appreciation of the force of these ideas there was once more an upsurge of interest in the communicative procedures poetic symbolism might share with other forms of thought. The gap between symbol and truth is reopened and the presence of meaning in the symbol made problematical, as in any other kind of discourse. In this process of assimilation a distinctively scientific discourse is as much at risk as romantic symbolism. If all linguistic functions are equally figurative there ceases to be room for literal, scientific description. Following philosopher of science Thomas Kuhn's arguments for the way in which scientific revolutions expediently abandon paradigms, many philosophers have taken a more pragmatic view of scientific truth, compatible with the simpler form of symbolism.

This development can be traced in a more radical and more visible form by considering relations since 1945 between critical and linguistic theory. W. K. Wimsatt spoke for the ascendant American New Criticism when, drawing on the semiotic distinctions of CHARLES S. PEIRCE (*see* SEMIOTICS), he described poetry as a "verbal image . . . an interpretation of reality in its metaphoric and symbolic dimension." For the New Critics a poem need not "mean" other than through its "being"; it is iconic of the reality whose features it symbolizes (*see* ICONOGRAPHY). Although it is iconic the poem still appears to allow for the open-endedness commonly attributed to symbolism, because it shares specific properties with what it denotes. Danish linguist Louis Hjelmslev explained this participation by describing symbols as being "isomorphic with their interpretation," when interpretation brings in all the other features that must remain constant if the iconic property is still to belong to what is denoted. Macbeth's "naked newborn babe" can only be a symbol of pity given a cultural background much too large to be denoted completely. The Italian semiotician Umberto Eco has objected that such a theory is still too restrictive because symbols are vaguer and our use of them less determined than Hjelmslev allows. The interpretive background may be invented along with the symbol rather than preexisting it. Many theorists have noted that poetry, and modern poetry in particular, can make a virtue of such novelty, challenging the reader to construct a viable interpretive model of its elements.

An icon is a determinate feature of an indeterminate background, but it is equally arguable that symbols are indeterminate tokens presenting determinate ideas. Conventionally we abstract from a range of possible qualities in order to see the image of a baby as primarily symbolizing pity rather than, say, softness, pinkness, or innocence. In that case the category of the natural that motivates the symbol is part of a wider, arbitrary relation between signifier and signified. The symbol contrasts explicitly with the unmotivated or arbitrary sign that is the basic unit of the LINGUISTICS of FERDINAND DE SAUSSURE. Structuralists and poststructuralists have therefore frequently criticized the pretensions of symbolism to preempt arbitrary interpretation and to anchor the purely differential structure of language in natural reality.

Since for Saussureans such an anchoring is impossible, the argument for it has been attributed to polemical motives. Barthes and others attacked the conservative politics they believed were implied by the naturalized symbolism of what Barthes called "mythologies." For Barthes a myth is "stolen language," a naturalization of what is in fact arbitrary and unlimited. Dream symbolism was similarly subjected to critique, and in LITERARY CRITICISM the archetypal interpretive codes of Northrop Frye were opposed by Harold Bloom's psychoanalytic theories (*see* PSYCHOANALYSIS) by which "the meaning of a poem is another poem." SIGMUND FREUD was reinterpreted to show that his analyses of dream-work and its mechanisms of psychic repression had unwittingly rediscovered the traditional figures of RHETORIC. For Jacques Lacan dream-work, when unraveled, uncovered neither the archetypal code that Freud often appeared to be searching for in his interpretation of dreams or his investigations into the psychopathology of everyday life nor a Jungian reservoir of instinctual drives (*see* JUNG, CARL), but the substitutive functions common to all linguistic operations, whereby words produce not extraverbal "origins" but more words.

Post-Lacanian French theorists, while still taking

their bearings from the Saussurean tradition, have felt the need to try to rediscover a symbolic function in which language registers the force of what exceeds its own linguistic economy. This recalls the disparity noted in the original Greek model between the *symbolon,* the half-coin, and the verbal contract it commemorated; for in the new theories the possibility of the figure for some extradiscursive assurance of intradiscursive agreement surfaces yet again. The experience of "jouissance" Barthes eventually sought for in READING; Julia Kristeva's detection of a feminist energy anterior to the patriarchal symbolic order of language (*see* LANGUAGE IDEOLOGY); the "figural" quality by which language, according to Jean-François Lyotard, can show the ways in which its object escapes discursive organization—all these are new names for a symbolic activity that once again is something more than a metaphorical or allegorical divergence from standard discourse. Its history suggests that symbolism answers a particular need that, though periodically effaced in fresh theories of language, will always recur.

See also POETICS.

Bibliography. Hazard Adams, *Philosophy of the Literary Symbol,* Tallahassee, Fla., 1983; Anna Balakian, ed., *The Symbolist Movement in the Literature of European Languages,* Vol. 2, *A Comparative History of Literatures in European Languages,* Budapest, 1982; Morton W. Bloomfield, ed., *Allegory, Myth, and Symbol,* Cambridge, Mass., 1981; Ernst Cassirer, *The Philosophy of Symbolic Forms,* 3 vols. (Philosophie der symbolischen Formen), trans. by Ralph Mannheim, New Haven, Conn., 1953; Umberto Eco, *Semiotics and the Philosophy of Language,* Bloomington, Ind., 1984; Mary LeCron Foster and Stanley H. Brandes, eds., *Symbol as Sense: New Approaches to the Analysis of Meaning,* New York and London, 1980; Tzvetan Todorov, *Theories of the Symbol* (Théories du symbole), trans. by Catherine Porter, Ithaca, N.Y., 1982.

PAUL HAMILTON

SYNDICATION

Distribution mechanism by which the cost of a newspaper feature or radio or television series is divided among diverse outlets. First used in the newspaper field, the term has been applied to news commentaries, comic strips, political cartoons, reviews and columns, and other special features as well as to a parallel range of radio and television offerings. Syndication may be done by an individual newspaper or broadcasting station (or a group of papers or stations) wishing to gain added revenue from its popular features or by an organization established specifically for syndication, offering items it has produced or has obtained by contract. An outlet acquiring an item via syndication is generally granted limited rights in a specific geographic area and within a specific time period. It pays a fee that may depend, in the case of a newspaper, on the paper's circulation, the population of its distribution area, or other criteria. In the case of a broadcasting station, such a fee may depend on the power of the station's transmitter or on its advertising rates.

In television, syndication is generally used as a supplement to commercial network distribution, usually after network distribution. It is sometimes used as a substitute for such distribution, particularly for programming keyed to specialized ethnic, linguistic, or other audience groups. Internationally, syndication emerges as the principal method for the marketing of rights in television series; actual delivery of programs can be done via prints or tapes or by satellite transmission. With the sophisticated development of dubbing and subtitling techniques, syndication has opened worldwide markets to the commercial programmer. *See* TELEVISION HISTORY.

ERIK BARNOUW

SYNTAX. *See* GRAMMAR.

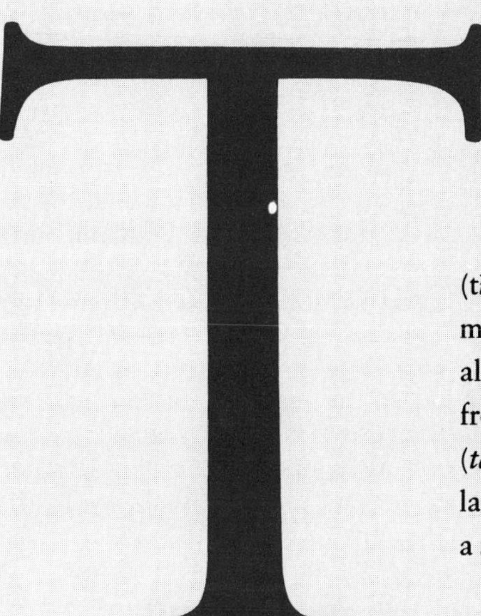

(*tī*), the twentieth letter of the English and other modern alphabets, the nineteenth of the ancient Roman alphabet, corresponding in form to the Greek Τ (*tau*), from the Phœnician (and ancient Semitic) + × × × (*tau*), in Phœnician, and originally also in Greek, the last letter of the alphabet. . . . Several varieties of a *t*-sound occur in different languages. . . .

TARDE, JEAN-GABRIEL DE (1843–1904)

French lawyer, criminologist, and sociologist. Often overshadowed by his compatriots Auguste Comte and ÉMILE DURKHEIM, Jean-Gabriel de Tarde ranks as one of the three most outstanding social thinkers of nineteenth-century France. Tarde's writings and thought have various implications for students of communications theory, but of particular interest is his scrutiny of collective behavior, mass communication, and PUBLIC OPINION.

Tarde was born and grew up in the small town of Sarlat in southern France, where his ancestors had resided since the eleventh century. This family tradition and historical background gave Tarde material for a number of books he later wrote about the town and his family. After a strict classical education and training in the law, Tarde practiced law in the Sarlat area for the next twenty-five years. He also read widely from the writings of the major philosophers and social theorists of his era, including G. W. F. Hegel, John Stuart Mill, and Herbert Spencer. This reading provided the basis for his most important theoretical volume, *The Laws of Imitation* (1890). Through his work in the courts Tarde also became interested in the causes of crime and deviance. He wrote extensively on criminology, emphasizing the need to examine socialization and imitation as social forces leading to crime. His work led to national recognition, an appointment as director of the criminal statistics bureau in the Ministry of Justice in Paris (1894–1900), and a professorship at the Collège de France (from 1900). Tarde and Durkheim were bitter rivals, and throughout their lifetimes they debated basic issues of sociological theory in their writings.

Some of Tarde's most important work comes from his interest in processes of communication. He wrote specifically on the role of TELEGRAPHY, the TELEPHONE, the mass-produced BOOK, and other printed materials (such as invitations and announcements) in the development of modern industrialized societies. He focused on the shift in social control from medieval towns and villages to large industrialized cities, which he related to the invention of various means of communication. Tarde contrasted the politics and currents of ideas before and after the beginning of newspapers and mass communication. He believed that before the mass media existed, communication was characterized by thousands of separate opinions providing no continuing ties among people. The advent of rapid communications via the telegraph, the telephone, and the means to distribute newspapers over a large territory brought a far greater efficiency. Tarde emphasized the power of newspapers as molders of public opinion in modern times (*see* NEWSPAPER: HISTORY). He wrote that a daily press permitted primary groups of highly similar individuals to form much larger secondary groups whose members were closely associated without ever seeing or knowing one another.

Tarde further projected at the close of the nineteenth century that it would be impossible to isolate the impact of the communications industry from the many other technological developments associated with modern societies. He realized that in order for international conflict to grow to the extent of arousing the passions and involvement of entire populations (as well as mobilizing national economies), it must be based on established communication networks. Although the social transformations associated with newspapers and other means of rapid communication enhanced the potential threat of large-scale conflicts, Tarde felt that in the long run mass communication would be a force contributing to rationality and movement toward world peace.

Bibliography. Jean-Gabriel de Tarde, *On Communication and Social Influence: Selected Papers,* ed. by Terry N. Clark, Chicago, 1969.

EDITH W. KING AND R. P. CUZZORT

TASTE CULTURES

Term coined in 1967 by U.S. sociologist Herbert J. Gans to refer to the cultural strata or subcultures in a society that parallel the strata of social class in that society. In 1949 Russell Lynes suggested a stratification of creators and consumers of U.S. CULTURE into "highbrows, upper middlebrows, lower middlebrows, and lowbrows." Gans married this concept to the more sociologically oriented social-class schema proposed by W. Lloyd Warner and Paul S. Lunt in their 1941 study of New Haven ("Yankee City"). Gans described five general taste cultures in the United States: high culture, upper-middle culture, lower-middle culture, low culture, and quasi-folk low culture.

In identifying these taste cultures Gans attempted to discard the value judgments traditionally associated with such rankings. A cultural relativist, he assumed that all human beings have cultural wants—possibly even needs—but that because of social class and class position people satisfy these needs in different ways. Thus high culture, in a functional sense, is neither a more nor a less valid form of expression than lower-middle or even quasi-folk low culture for those who create and consume it. By making this point Gans lodged the concept of taste culture solidly within the pluralist tradition in what is perhaps best known as the elite-mass culture debate that characterized much social science in the United States in the 1940s and 1950s.

Fearful of the effects of industrialization, urbanization, and the development of mass media, critics such as Dwight Macdonald, Bernard Rosenberg, and THEODOR ADORNO pointed to these social changes as major factors accounting for the destruction of cultural diversity in society and its replacement by a bland, homogeneous mass culture that was dangerous to political freedom. Deriving their ideological impetus from the cultural elitism of eighteenth- and nineteenth-century Europe, these critics turned their attention, in the United States, to the effects of commercial RADIO, MOTION PICTURES, and mass-circulation magazines, as well as to the PROPAGANDA uses made of these media by socialist governments during the post–World War II period. The tone of these critics was often strident in their warnings about the effects of mass culture on society. With this proliferation of mass culture, it was argued, taste levels would sink to the lowest common denominator, rendering citizens susceptible to the techniques of mass PERSUASION.

This concept of massification and its attendant dire effects did not long stand unchallenged in the social sciences. In 1957 Richard Hoggart published an empirical study of the British working class and the "full rich life" of this subculture. And in the United States, in 1959, Edward Shils asserted that mass culture enhanced individuality because of the increasing number of consumer choices that must be made by the individual. Talcott Parsons argued in 1960 that the mass media actually increased the diversity and quality of popular culture in the United States, a position seconded in 1964 by Harold Wilensky, who claimed that mass culture was in reality a plurality of cultures from which consumers selectively chose combinations that best suited their needs. This pluralist tradition was the bedrock upon which Gans built his concept of taste culture.

In addition to his relativistic position concerning the worth of various taste cultures, Gans made a second crucial distinction in developing this concept, a distinction between culture itself and those who consume it. This bifurcation of the concept into what he called "taste cultures" and "taste publics" follows Alfred L. Kroeber and Parsons's 1958 distinction between cultural systems as "symbolic-meaningful systems of values and ideas" and the artifacts produced to reflect them on the one hand and, on the other, social systems as the interaction of individuals and collectivities. Thus, for Gans, taste cultures are the array of arts, ENTERTAINMENT, information, and consumer goods available to different taste publics, while taste publics are aggregates of individuals who make similar choices for similar reasons.

This distinction is important in that culture does not always totally satisfy or meet the needs of those who consume it, a point obscured by the inseparability of culture and public. In addition, in a world dominated by large mass media networks and industries, in order to remain viable the media must serve several taste publics with a single cultural product, such as network television (*see* TELEVISION HISTORY). Gans's analytic distinction between culture and public allows investigation of these central concerns in communications and audience research (*see* COMMUNICATIONS RESEARCH: ORIGINS AND DEVELOPMENT).

Although there has been some empirical research in the United States (Paul DiMaggio, Paul Hirsch, Richard Peterson), Britain (Dick Hebdige, Hoggart, Michael Smith), and Sweden (Keith Roe, Karl-Erik Rosengren) to suggest that the concept of taste culture is valid and useful, the most important work, both theoretically and empirically, is that done in France in the 1970s and 1980s by Pierre Bourdieu.

Bourdieu argues that cultural artifacts have symbolic codes embedded in them that make sense only to those socialized in these codes. For those from different social strata cultural objects are viewed through inapplicable or misleading codes that cause a confusion of interpretation, while those from the same social stratum, who know the codes because they have been socialized in them, will interpret, understand, and appreciate the cultural object in question. *See* ARTIFACT; CODE.

One important implication of Bourdieu's position is that, if the dominant culture is a code into which some people are inducted from birth and which others must master, then debates over the value of cultural artifacts are highly political in nature, since they involve the argument that the worth of cultural objects is closely equated with the social worth of consumers, with respect to their position in the class structure.

MAX WEBER, the German sociologist, distinguished between social class (based on economic position) and social status (based on style of life), but Bourdieu sees them as overlapping markets—one fueled by economic capital, the other by cultural capital. Culture, then, has a central place in the power struggles of social classes and the perceived worth of individuals in society.

To some extent cultural capital can be used in a conscious and strategic way to better one's class position; however, a great deal of it lies even deeper, in the culture codes of early socialization. The reflexively felt sense of what is true, beautiful, natural, and/or good—the very sense of self-identity—is, in Bourdieu's eyes, an expression of that mix of cultural and economic capital that defines membership in social classes and, in many systems, allows the dominant classes in society the sort of hegemonic control proposed by Italian scholar ANTONIO GRAMSCI.

Although a focus on the correspondence between taste culture and social class has been an important and central thrust of the work surrounding this concept, there is more. Gans, in 1985, modified his five original taste cultures to include a middle culture that seems to cut across and blend upper- and lower-middle cultures in the United States. He has also pointed to age (youth culture), ethnicity (black U.S. culture), and GENDER (feminist movements) as discriminating variables, important in defining taste cultures and publics not necessarily constrained to one social class. In addition, private market researchers have developed complex mappings of the U.S. population, dividing people into taste publics on the basis of cultural consumption patterns, residential areas (defined by postal zip codes), and census demographic data for use by the media and cultural industries that have enough money to afford these complex and expensive analyses.

Finally, in the United States some researchers such as Peterson, DiMaggio, and James Davis have noted very loose correlations between cultural preference and class level. In examining the audience for country and western music in 1975, Peterson and DiMaggio found that the audience was more clearly distinguished by race and age than by social class and that many of the same stratum, race, and age did not like the music. They coined the term *culture class* to refer to that aggregate of individuals who seek out similar cultural forms, even as this aggregate is indefinable in the traditional socioeconomic terms of social class. Davis's 1982 analysis of a number of U.S. attitude surveys (an analysis contested by Gans) supports Peterson and DiMaggio in that Davis found so little correlation between social class and cultural consumption that he suggested the concept may no longer be valid, at least in the United States.

In highly industrialized societies, under conditions of relatively high social mobility, greater discretionary income, easy credit, efficient distribution of goods, high diffusion rate of cultural products, and a substantial amount of LEISURE time, the linkages between cultural consumption and social class are not automatically correlative but are contingent, problematic, and variable. The concept of taste culture, especially as it has been developed by Gans and elaborated on in other cultures and contexts, is primarily a helpful conceptual tool for studying culture, communication, and social class.

See also ART; ARTIST AND SOCIETY; LITERARY CANON; LITERATURE, POPULAR.

Bibliography. Pierre Bourdieu, *Distinction: A Social Critique of the Judgement of Taste* (La distinction: Critique sociale du judgement), trans. by Richard Nice, Cambridge, Mass., 1984; Herbert J. Gans, *Popular Culture and High Culture: An Analysis and Evaluation of Taste,* New York, 1974; idem, "Popular Culture in America," in *Social Problems: A Modern Approach,* ed. by Howard S. Becker, New York, 1966; Dick Hebdige, *Subculture: The Meaning of Style,* London, 1979; Richard Hoggart, *The Uses of Literacy,* London, 1957; George H. Lewis, "Taste Cultures and Their Composition: Towards a New Theoretical Perspective," in *Mass Media and Social Change,* ed. by Elihu Katz and Tamas Szecsko, Beverly Hills, Calif., 1980.

GEORGE H. LEWIS

TAXONOMY. *See* CLASSIFICATION.

TEACHING

The planned and organized attempts to facilitate the learning of others. *Learning* is the name given to the process of changing through experience. Through the cognitive and affective processes of learning people acquire relatively permanent changes in knowledge, skill, belief, ATTITUDES, and feelings, which give new meanings to experience that lead to changes in behavior.

Because of its social and individual importance, societies foster learning from infancy through adult life. Especially in modern complex societies, with their continually changing knowledge bases, an enormous amount of learning occurs in the SCHOOL and in daily life out of school. This learning includes and goes beyond the acquisition of facts, values, knowledge, attitudes, and beliefs to include learning strategies and self-control of one's abilities to learn (*see* SOCIAL COGNITIVE THEORY).

To promote these socially significant kinds of learning, people instruct and teach other people (a) by structuring experience that would otherwise be too diffuse; (b) by providing models whose activities, modes of thought, and general outlooks learners can copy or imitate, as was the case in preceding centuries when apprentices learned from models called "masters"; and (c) by providing symbolically coded information—LANGUAGE, numbers, pictures, and the like—to substitute for direct experience. Both teaching and instruction, in contrast to indoctrination or conditioning, imply learner awareness of the process of change (*see* PERSUASION).

Instruction, often used loosely as a synonym for teaching, denotes attempts to facilitate the learning of a limited area or domain by using either people or inanimate devices such as books, machines, and curricular materials as the facilitators. The primary objectives of instruction are to impart to students specific facts, skills, pieces of information, techniques, or strategies and to create in them an understanding of phenomena in limited domains.

The active roles of learners and teachers. In contrast, teaching implies greater primary concern for the long-term intellectual, personal, and social learning and development of the learner in harmony with the attainment of the more specific and immediate objectives of instruction. In addition, teaching means that at least two people, the teacher and one or more learners, actively engage in the learning activity, each with a distinctive responsibility. The teacher is responsible for designing and conducting the teaching activities that are appropriate for engaging the thought processes, learning strategies, and metacognition (awareness and control of one's thought processes) of the learner in attaining the short-term instructional objectives and in achieving the long-term, intellectual, social, and personal objectives of EDUCATION. The teacher is responsible for practicing techniques that reflect the current state of knowledge about teaching, including teaching learners how to learn.

The learner is responsible for learning, for engaging in the thought processes that will focus attention and generate relations between knowledge and experience, on the one hand, and the material, skill, or techniques to be learned, on the other. Learners are responsible also for becoming aware of their thought processes and learning strategies, for monitoring them, and for using them to enhance learning, memory, and comprehension.

These modern concepts of teaching and learning differ from their ancient counterparts (such as learning to memorize and teaching by recitation) and from behavioristic models developed in the first half of the twentieth century, when teaching was defined by the behavior that was learned. With the increased interest in cognitive psychological principles in education during the last twenty years, the meanings of teaching and learning have further evolved.

Modern conceptions of the causes of learning. Formerly teaching was thought to be the direct cause of learning. Good teaching meant good learning, and poor teaching meant poor learning. More recently the critical role of the learners' thought processes in influencing achievement has been studied and established. As a result, teaching is now thought to produce its effects by stimulating learners to construct new meanings for their experience. The engagement of these thought processes in turn facilitates learning.

As a result, teaching now includes giving students awareness of and control over their thought processes and learning strategies. Through this awareness and self-control students acquire new information, skills, and ideas in school, and they also learn how to learn in school and how to learn in other contexts later in life.

These cognitive and affective processes constitute an indispensable link between teaching activities and student achievement. They imply that teaching does not produce learning in the everyday sense of directly imparting information. Instead, teaching engages the learners' thoughts and strategies in the active process of constructing relations between new information and existing mental structures, which produces achievement.

Teaching is a two-way, interactive process. The teacher stimulates the students' thought processes. The students in turn respond and stimulate the teacher to invent the next, most appropriate teaching activity. This conception of teaching alters approaches to students. They are perceived not as passive recipients of one-way communication, from the teacher to the learner, but as having active responsibility for generating knowledge and for interacting with the teacher (*see* MODELS OF COMMUNICATION).

Advances in knowledge. This conception of teaching has led to new lines of research that have focused on the learner's thought processes as mediators of the effects of teaching. From this research have come the following findings, which provide new interpretations of earlier findings. First, learning in schools does not seem to be the process of practicing the appropriate behavior to receive rewards from teachers. Teachers give praise too infrequently to too few students to enhance their learning through principles of reinforcement. Instead, by observing a student receiving praise, many of the other students in the class learn the teacher's objectives and desires. The reward serves to focus their attention rather than to form an association between a stimulus, such as a question, and a response, such as an answer. Behavioral objectives given to learner and teacher questions also seem to direct students' attention to the teacher's goals. Again, teaching functions by influencing student thought processes—in this case, attention—which mediates achievement.

In another area of research, motivation, a related finding occurs. Reinforcement, such as the giving of rewards only when children give correct answers to questions in class, seems to motivate students to continue learning primarily when they attribute the reinforcement to their own effort rather than to luck, ability, or the ease of the task. In this case the way the student thinks about the cause of the reinforcement, not the teacher's act of giving it, increases motivation to learn the subject matter.

Last of all, in the area of comprehension, many teaching studies have shown that large gains in students' understanding can be achieved through the use of guided discovery, feedback, interactive images, and related techniques that teach learners to construct relations between their knowledge and the text they are learning. For example, by asking elementary school children to generate summaries or images as they read, comprehension can be increased by 50 to 75 percent. In these studies teaching produces its effects by stimulating learners' thought processes to generate meanings for experience (*see* MEANING). These new meanings result in measurable changes in behavior.

In sum, modern concepts of teaching emphasize the critical role the learner plays in interpreting the teacher's activities and in constructing meaning from them. The constructed meaning influences student learning and achievement.

See also AUDIOVISUAL EDUCATION; COGNITION; EDUCATIONAL TELEVISION.

Bibliography. Walter Doyle, "Paradigms for Research on Teacher Effectiveness," *Review of Research in Education* 5 (1977): 163–198; Michele Linden and Merlin C. Wittrock, "The Teaching of Reading Comprehension According to the Model of Generative Learning," *Reading Research Quarterly* 17 (1981): 44–57; Donald Meichenbaum and Joan Asarnow, "Cognitive-Behavior Modification and Metacognitive Development: Implications for the Classroom," in *Cognitive-Behavioral Interventions: Theory, Research, and Procedures,* ed. by Philip C. Kendall and Steven D. Hollon, New York, 1979; Greta Morine-Dershimer, "Pupil Perceptions of Teacher Praise," *Elementary School Journal* 82 (1982): 421–434; Merlin C. Wittrock, "The Cognitive Movement in Instruction," *Educational Psychologist* 13 (1978): 15–30; idem, "Learning as a Generative Process," *Educational Psychologist* 11 (1974): 87–95; idem, ed., *Handbook of Research on Teaching,* 3d ed., New York, 1986.

MERLIN C. WITTROCK

TELECOMMUNICATIONS NETWORKS

Telecommunication is the transmission of signals over long distances. The earliest form of telecommunication was visual signaling with smoke, flags, or lamps. However, in the nineteenth century a revolution in communications began with the development of TELEGRAPHY and the TELEPHONE and continued with the invention of the RADIO and related technologies near the turn of the century. By the second half of the twentieth century the development of cables with substantially increased capacities and the application of FIBER OPTICS, as well as the microwave transmission of television signals in connection with SATELLITE technology, meant that a wide variety of signals could be sent around the world instantaneously. These developments ushered in the modern telecommunications system.

System characteristics. The basic functional components of such a system are (1) the communication terminal, which today could be a telephone, a teletypewriter, a facsimile machine, a personal computer, or a large computer central processor; (2) the local loop (i.e., the network of wires, cables, poles, and related equipment that connects terminals to a local central office); (3) switching equipment in the central office that provides the necessary connections when calls are made and performs network management functions; (4) larger-capacity trunk cables or occasionally direct microwave links that connect central offices (e.g., a local end office with a long-distance toll office); and (5) transmission equipment that sends and receives signals over long distances, including higher-capacity coaxial or fiber optic cable, microwave radio, and satellites.

For signals to be communicated effectively over such a system there must be technical compatibility among all functional components, and each component must be capable of handling the signals of the highest-quality service that will be provided over the system. When telephone systems were upgraded to meet the requirements of national and international long distance it required technical improvements not only in the transmission function but in all other functions as well, including the telephone instrument.

Innovations in telecommunications technology in the second half of the twentieth century have expanded both the capabilities and the capacity of the facilities used to communicate. Telecommunications systems can now carry different types of messages, including not only telegraph, voice, and television signals but also facsimile, VIDEO, and computer data signals. Off-air broadcasting has been supplemented by CABLE TELEVISION and direct broadcast satellites.

Cellular radio has expanded the possibilities for mobile communication within cities. Telephone companies are upgrading their voice telephone systems with digital switching and fiber optic cable to facilitate computer data transfer and processing over telecommunications networks with greatly expanded capacity. Cable television companies have been upgrading their distribution cables to permit data transfer. Some business and residential subscribers may now select from an increasing variety of computer communication terminals to obtain access to computer data and information banks (*see* COMPUTER: IMPACT; DATA BASE). In addition, the quality of equipment used to record and transmit visual images (film, television) and SOUND (music, FM radio) continues to improve (*see* SOUND RECORDING; TELEVISION HISTORY).

The telecommunications system of interconnected facilities is now used to provide a wide variety of different communication services. Each service provides connection among a particular network of potential users, employing a particular type or quality of communication signal. Local telephone service provides public access to telephones in the local area at voice-grade technical standards. But the local telecommunications facilities also provide connections for voice, telegraph, video, and data signals that are separate from the local public telephone network. These may be either private communication lines connecting only a few locations or special networks such as a local data network. Some services require four-wire loop connections for higher-quality service rather than the two-wire loop required for voice telephone. The local facilities also provide access to the public long-distance network and, if the particular facilities have been upgraded, to national and international networks for video or data signals, such as airline reservation systems.

The telecommunications system was designed originally to meet the standards of voice communication. It employed the analog transmission method, which used signals that were exact reproductions of the pattern of sound waves being transmitted. But this restricted the speed with which digital data signals could be transmitted. In addition, signal distortions that did not significantly affect the quality of voice communication created errors in data transmission. A major thrust of research and development was therefore a search for new techniques that would improve accuracy in data communications.

Telephone companies and administrations began to convert their signal standards from analog to digital and to upgrade systems to the standards of digital computers. Progress was most rapid for the long-distance transmission function, and digital terminals were widely available by the 1980s. The conversions of local switching and loops were more costly and were implemented more slowly. POTS (the plain old telephone system) was in the process of being converted to an ISDN (integrated services digital network), a sophisticated multipurpose network used to provide a wide variety of communication and information services. This conversion process is likely to continue at least until the end of the twentieth century.

Industry structure and regulation. Traditionally telecommunications services have been supplied under the concept of end-to-end service by a MONOPOLY supplier. In most countries the primary and often exclusive supplier has been a department of the national government, usually part of the post office (the post, telephone, and telegraph administration, or PTT). In North America and a few other regions the dominant mode of supply has been by private corporations with geographically defined monopolies, subject to government regulation of investment, financing, services, and tariffs.

The telecommunications system was extended to less populated areas through cooperatives and municipal and provincial companies, often receiving direct government subsidies (e.g., the U.S. rural telephone program). In the United States the American Telephone and Telegraph Company (AT&T) until 1984 was the largest company in the world, a holding company with ownership of regional telephone companies serving the most populated regions of the country (82 percent of the telephones), the dominant telecommunications equipment supplier (Western Electric), the major research and development operation (Bell Laboratories), and a division that supplied almost all domestic and most U.S. international long-distance services.

Most PTTs set rates for public services at a relatively high level in order to subsidize postal service and make generous contributions to their respective national treasuries. Their expansion was slowed by investment limitations placed by governments with higher priorities for the use of public resources. In North America the private companies obtained their investment funds from the capital markets. Their rates for public services had to be approved by a state or federal government regulatory agency. Generally these regulatory agencies have attempted to limit the overall profit of the telephone companies to a reasonable level, but great flexibility has been allowed in setting individual rates for particular services.

From the early 1960s the concept of end-to-end monopoly came under increasing criticism in the United States, stemming primarily from the growing interaction between the telecommunications and computer industries. Other equipment manufacturers and potential suppliers of telecommunications services claimed that they could provide improvements to the system that would benefit consumers. This led to a gradual but substantial liberalization of traditional regulatory restrictions in the United States and the beginnings of similar changes in Britain, Japan, Canada, and several other countries.

In the mid-1960s the U.S. Federal Communications Commission (FCC) began an investigation into the growing demands to connect computers to the telephone network. In 1968 the commission ruled in its *Carterfone* decision that AT&T's restrictions against the attachment of terminals owned by others (called "foreign attachments" by AT&T) were unlawful. In 1969 the FCC approved an application by the MCI Corporation to supply long-distance services between Chicago and Saint Louis. In 1971 other applications to supply long-distance services were approved, and a policy allowing competition in domestic satellite services was adopted. In 1976 the commission adopted a policy of permitting the resale of communication services, allowing new competitors to offer public services using capacity they had leased from established telephone companies.

Throughout the 1960s and 1970s AT&T resisted the development of competition by restricting and impeding efficient interconnection, by selectively implementing deep price cuts in those segments of the market in which competitors appeared, and by creating costly and time-consuming delays for would-be competitors. Although these practices slowed down the development of competition, they did not stop it. On several occasions the FCC and/or the courts ordered AT&T to stop various anticompetitive practices, and a number of AT&T competitors filed court cases claiming that they had been damaged by AT&T's violation of the U.S. antitrust laws.

In November 1974 the U.S. Department of Justice charged that AT&T was engaging in the systematic destruction or prevention of competition for subscriber terminal equipment, long-distance telecommunications services, and telecommunications equipment manufacturing. It argued that only a breakup of the AT&T monopoly would allow effective competition to develop. By raising a variety of technical arguments AT&T was able to delay the trial until 1981. As the trial was reaching conclusion in 1982, AT&T and the Department of Justice agreed on a settlement that would restructure the AT&T monopoly by 1984.

The twenty-two Bell System telephone companies were grouped into seven regional holding companies. The new AT&T kept the backbone long-distance telecommunications system (including the international services), the manufacturing company, and the Bell Laboratories—about one-third of its former assets. Only AT&T's long-distance service was still subject to federal regulation, because AT&T retained over 90 percent of this market. The Bell telephone companies were to provide local telecommunications and some long-distance service in their geographical areas and connect AT&T, MCI, and the other long-distance companies to business and residential subscribers. The telephone companies remained subject to regulation by both state commissions and the FCC, and they were prohibited from offering information services over their monopoly local systems.

The merging of computer and telecommunications functions provided an avenue for incorporating the efficiencies of MICROELECTRONICS into telecommunications equipment and networks. The terminal equipment market was opened to international competition in most countries. Factories, offices, and "smart" buildings (buildings designed to provide access to a variety of telecommunications and information capabilities) were being transformed into centers of information movement and management. Telecommunications administrations throughout the world found it increasingly difficult to continue purchasing modern switching and transmission equipment from favored national suppliers in the face of superior equipment at substantially reduced prices from international competitors.

With respect to national long-distance facilities and services, as of 1987 only the United Kingdom and Japan, in addition to the United States, were experimenting with new competitive systems. In many countries the use of the telecommunications network is being liberalized so as to permit a wide range of data, information, and value-added network services. In the international market competitive fiber optic cable and satellite systems were planned for both the Atlantic and Pacific regions by the 1990s.

Public policy issues. The introduction of competition using new technologies in telecommunications networks raised important issues of public policy (*see* TELECOMMUNICATIONS POLICY). The imposition of market efficiency standards on monopoly carriers that heretofore had not been perceived as terribly efficient provided clear benefits to the economy. But if, at the same time, it precluded the continuation of social policy directed to the maintenance of universal telephone service, large benefits to one sector of society would be achieved at a cost to already disadvantaged sectors. Where universal telephone service has been achieved it has not been primarily a result of social cross-subsidies in telephone tariffs but rather through direct grants, low-interest loans, and similar approaches. Most PTTs have had relatively low subscriber penetration rates and have never attempted to provide universal service.

The monopoly telecommunications carriers claimed that competition for long-distance services meant that they would no longer be able to subsidize basic local telephone service. They claimed that local rates would have to increase dramatically and the universal telephone service objective would be seriously compromised. By the term *subsidy* the carriers meant the contributions from long-distance service revenues covering a share of the local facility costs that were used in common by both local and long-distance services. Yet, in the relatively few cases in which telephone companies supplied only local facilities and services, they claimed that the contribution from long-distance service was not sufficient to cover the costs imposed on local facilities by long-distance services. The costs of local telecommunications facilities were determined primarily by the requirements of long-distance service, not local service.

Of even greater significance was determining which services would be assigned the massive costs of the system upgrading to computer standards (i.e., the ISDN). Under prevalent industry accounting and regulatory practices the great majority of these costs would be allocated to local telephone service and could require dramatic local rate increases by threatening the universal telephone service objective. If these costs were to be assigned to the services causing their increase and benefiting from the system upgrading, more detailed accounting and rate regulatory standards would have to be adopted by the authorities. One possible scenario for telecommunications service pricing was a flat monthly charge for the right of access to the system and usage charges for all services actually used, including local telephone service. This approach was favored by commercial customers with high volumes of use for all services. However, consumer groups argued that high access charges might force low-income people desiring only telephone service to disconnect from the system.

It was doubtful that regulators and policymakers would need to enforce a massive program of social cross-subsidies in order to protect the public user of basic local telephone service. Rather, they needed only to prevent exploitive pricing of the monopoly local telephone service, that is, the subsidy of competitive services with revenues from monopoly services. But whether regulators and policymakers were capable of such a task in the face of the combined pressure from telecommunications carriers and large business users was questionable.

The telecommunications equipment and services market was enormous, valued in 1984 at $128 billion in the United States and more than double that in the rest of the world. It was growing at more than 12 percent per year, and there were vast opportunities for selling equipment and services in both developed and developing countries. The largest transnational corporations (TNCs) in the world economy were involved either as suppliers or as customers. The implications of these developments for the domestic economies of most nations were sufficiently large as to make telecommunications an important part of industrial policy. In addition, telecommunications issues were taking on a new significance for several INTERNATIONAL ORGANIZATIONS, including the ITU, the OECD, the GATT, UNESCO, and others. *See* NEW INTERNATIONAL INFORMATION ORDER.

The international competitive battle for the 1980s and 1990s revolves substantially around the issue of technical standards that ultimately would be adopted for the ISDN. International Business Machines (IBM) had already established a standard for connecting its own (as well as IBM-compatible) equipment, called Systems Network Architecture (SNA). Telecommunications carriers were working toward a different initial standard, open standards interconnection (OSI), but it took longer to be fully defined. In addition, the digitalization of the public telecommunications network made it possible for the increasing number of sophisticated "intelligent" functions to be located either in the network (and controlled by the telecommunications carriers) or in the terminal equipment purchased by the subscriber.

Implications. It has long been recognized that advanced communication techniques can provide enormous military, political, and economic advantages. Information is power, and communication techniques have had an important influence on the distribution of power within societies, as well as the rise and fall of empires. The major portion of research and development in telecommunications technology has been financed by the military budgets of the major powers. Military concerns included data encryption to protect against the interception of signals, techniques for more precise satellite surveillance, communication control over weapons in space, and techniques for jamming enemy communications.

The newest telecommunications technologies had significant influences on the way people lived and worked. Inevitably new opportunities were opened for some, but traditional ways of doing things were rendered impossible for others. Access to computerized information banks over telecommunications networks provided more and better information for large corporations, government agencies, and certain professions at a cost they were willing to pay. But with the availability of on-line information banks the collections and services of public libraries began to be reduced (*see* LIBRARY—TRENDS).

By overcoming the limits of time and space and expanding enormously the volume and variety of information that can be transmitted and processed, the new telecommunications system would provide substantial benefits and economies to very large users with substantial budgets for specialized computer communication equipment. The new information networks permitted an extension of the bounds of administrative control and offered increased productivity in large centralized organizations. Perhaps the primary beneficiaries were transnational corporations that were able to expand their scope, enlarge their markets, and transfer financial resources instantaneously around the world. But in many countries this created a major threat to domestic production and employment, national sovereignty, and local cultures, especially in developing countries. The vast majority of the world's population did not have access to a telephone, and in the 1980s 75 percent of the world's telephones were found in only eight of the world's 175 countries. Unfortunately this imbalance was not likely to be altered significantly without a major realignment of international telecommunication and economic policies.

Bibliography. John Brooks, *Telephone: The First Hundred Years,* New York, 1975; Harold A. Innis, *Empire and Communications* (1950), rev. by Mary Q. Innis, foreword by Marshall McLuhan, Toronto, 1972; Manley R. Irwin, *Telecommunication America: Markets without Boundaries,* London and Westport, Conn., 1985; W. H. Melody, ed., *The Information Society: Unveiling Some Contradictions* (special issue), *Media, Culture, and Society,* July 1985; Rita Cruise O'Brien, ed., *Information, Economics, and Power,* London, 1983; OECD, *Telecommunications, Pressures and Policies for Change,* Paris, 1983; Robert J. Saunders, Jeremy J. Warford, and Bjorn Wellenius, *Telecommunications and Economic Development,* Baltimore, Md., 1983; Herbert I. Schiller, *Information and the Crisis Economy,* Norwood, N.J., 1984; Dallas W. Smythe, *Dependency Road: Communications, Capitalism, Consciousness, and Canada,* Norwood, N.J., 1981.

WILLIAM H. MELODY

TELECOMMUNICATIONS POLICY

Policies that address the provision, organization, and control of networks for point-to-point transmission of information in electromagnetic or optical form and the services provided by such networks. As long as telecommunications involved a relatively simple and stable technology and a restricted range of simple services (telegraph, telex, and TELEPHONE), telecommunications policy remained the province of engineers and administrators and was relatively uncontroversial. However, from the 1960s on a range of related economic and technical developments forced telecommunications issues to the top of the policy agenda, both nationally and internationally.

The collection, manipulation, storage, and distribution of information became ever more central to the economic and social life of advanced industrial societies. According to some estimates, by the late 1970s more than 50 percent of the U.S. labor force was engaged in information processing, and the OECD (Organization for Economic Cooperation and Development) countries had either reached or were rapidly approaching that point. Moreover, the convergence of computing and telecommunications shifted these vital information flows increasingly into the electronic, digital mode. As far as government policies were concerned, this meant that not only was the provision of an efficient telecommunications infrastructure as important to the prosperity of national economies as railways and roads had once been, but the sectors of the economy supplying telecommunications and related information technologies became those with the highest growth rates and brightest future prospects. Thus many governments turned to this sector of their economies as the key to escape from the economic crisis in which they had found themselves by the late 1970s, and telecommunications policies became more crucial to industrial and economic policy.

Symptomatic of these pressures were the decisions by several countries in the early 1980s to dismantle telecommunications monopolies. Examples include the decision in the United States to break up American Telephone and Telegraph (AT&T) and to deregulate large sections of the telecommunications market, and similar actions in Great Britain and Japan to break the PTT (post, telegraph, and telephone) monopolies in the provision of networks, services, and terminals.

At the same time the shift to the electronic, digital mode began to dissolve the traditional demarcations between switched telecommunications and other communications media with differing institutional, legal, and regulatory frameworks. The end point of this development will be the installation of a worldwide Integrated Services Digital Network (ISDN) planned for the 1990s, which promises to create a single, integrated, broadband pathway down which all of society's information and entertainment will flow, even if this information is translated for consumers back into print, images, or sounds. How that pathway is provided, organized, and controlled has become an extremely important social policy question facing nations and the international community. The structure and regulation not just of the mass media but also of service industries such as banking and retailing have in turn become telecommunications policy issues.

Early monopolies. At the heart of the debates over telecommunications policy lies the issue of MONOPOLY versus competition. Since ALEXANDER GRAHAM BELL filed his basic telephone patents in 1876, switched telecommunications services have been developed by monopolies to a high but internationally very uneven level as tools of business and social communication. In most countries these monopolies have been direct arms of the governmental PTT ministries. In the United States the job was left to a regulated private monopoly, AT&T.

This arrangement was defended and can still be defended on the grounds of natural monopoly. A switched telecommunications network is a natural monopoly for two reasons. First, the high initial costs of establishing a telecommunications network, especially at the local level, make duplication highly inefficient. In addition, the value of a switched network to its users stems from its interconnectivity. This means that the value of the network rises exponentially with each additional subscriber and reaches its optimum capabilities with one universal service.

Within the richer industrialized nations, these monopolies, although operating in the market to sell goods and services to consumers, were used to pursue essentially sociopolitical ends, namely, the provision of low-cost service to all citizens throughout a particular nation. The service was universal in terms of both geographical location and price, and its services were provided at an average cost; that is, areas and routes of high density were priced at the same level as those of low density.

Monopoly control of the network was extended to encompass monopoly control of all terminal equipment attached to the network on technical grounds. In addition, telecommunications administrations developed a monopsonic relationship with their respective domestic equipment industries (i.e., each nation's telecommunications company was the sole buyer in the domestic equipment market). This relationship was defended on industrial policy grounds, but also and more importantly on the grounds that only the network controller could determine both the technical needs and the pace of development of the telecommunications network and thus required a close relationship with the industry supplying its equipment. This monopolistic structure produced telecommunications administrations that were among the largest economic organizations in their respective countries.

Trends supporting competition. Since the 1960s a number of interrelated economic and technical pressures influenced this traditional structure. The development of the multinational corporation as the dominant form of business organization made efficient and increasingly sophisticated telecommunications a strategic necessity for the corporate sector and in turn raised telecommunications costs. This trend was reinforced by the wider shift from manufacturing, a relatively low user of telecommunications, to services, a high user. Thus the cost, range, and efficiency of telecommunications services became a high corporate priority, and the business community became an advocate of competition in the telecommunications network, service, and equipment markets as a means of maximizing innovation and minimizing costs.

Parallel technical developments reinforced this trend. Largely as a result of military research, alternative transmission technologies (microwave, SATELLITE, coaxial, and optical fiber cables) were developed. Combined with the growing convergence of computing and telecommunications, these new technologies offered cheaper, more flexible networks and services than those provided by the existing monopoly supplier. The implementation of these new technologies also generated businesses with an interest in supplying these services as well as an economic base outside the traditional telecommunications industry. IBM's Satellite Business System was a classic example of this trend.

In other words, the convergence of computing and telecommunications created a major new corporate demand for data communications services, which existing telecommunications networks were not designed to meet. In addition, however, the ability to manipulate telecommunications traffic in complex ways (such as time-division multiplexing, packet switching, cellular radio, and store and forward) broke up the old homogeneity of the switched-voice telephone service. This made it increasingly difficult for telecommunications administrations to make choices among a bewildering range of possible service offerings and customer needs without using the mechanism of the market. Finally, the rising cost of research and development in the telecommunications equipment industry meant that no single national market produced large enough returns to justify the investment, thus undermining protectionist policies toward national equipment industries and pushing major manufacturers, backed by their governments, into intense competition for Third World export markets.

Monopoly versus competition. The policy issues raised by these developments were fundamental. Should competition be introduced in the provision of telecommunications networks and services at a national level, and, if so, to what extent and with what effect? What is the appropriate relationship between an industrial policy designed to foster the development of an internationally competitive equipment industry and a policy designed to foster the optimum development of domestic telecommunications services? Are economic and technical developments supportive of or antagonistic to the enhancement of human freedom, and thus will regulation or deregulation foster that freedom? What is the appropriate response at an international level to these questions? In particular, how should countries that have chosen to move in the direction of competition relate to those that have chosen to retain monopoly? Are national sovereignty and cultural plurality compatible with the free flow of information under free-market conditions?

In considering these policy issues it is important to stress that technology does not determine the outcome. The choices are not between desirable and undesirable technological solutions, but between solutions that represent the incompatible interests of various social groups, classes, and nations. For instance, the values of individual free expression and the free flow of information may clash with the values of communal solidarity, national culture, security, and prosperity; speed of development and innovation may conflict with the goal of maximizing access to their benefits; policies optimal for the production of information—such as COPYRIGHT and confidentiality—may clash with policies aimed at optimizing the DIFFUSION of information; policies aimed at the long-term maximization of human knowledge and prosperity may, in the medium term, increase inequalities between nations, classes, and social groups.

The crucial policy questions regarding the introduction of competition in the provision of telecommunications network services have been, first, whether the advantages that accrue from competition in terms of more efficient use of resources and higher rates of innovation outweigh the loss of advantages provided by a monopoly system; and, second, whether the costs and benefits will be equally borne by all sections of society. Competition in telecommunications raised particular problems because of the high level of shared costs and because of the value of universal interconnectivity. These factors produced a highly arbitrary relationship between costs for any given service or section of the network. This arbitrariness was enshrined in the principle of cost averaging and meant that telecommunications tariffs were determined politically rather than by the market. This in its turn meant that competition in the provision of basic service was only sustainable under certain conditions: (1) It was necessary to create regulations that forced the dominant network provider to subsidize competition. (Without such regulations market forces would always allow natural monopoly to reinstate itself.) (2) Competitive networks had to be protected by allowing them to compete only on low-cost, high-density routes without being obligated to provide universal service, but with the right to interconnect with the universal network and to benefit from the larger network's economies of scale, reliability, and carrying capacity. (3) Major bulk users had to be allowed to build private networks that bypassed the universal network, while themselves using that network when necessary.

The crucial policy question was not just how best to balance the conflicting benefits of competition or monopoly in general. The breakdown of the concept of a universal and homogeneous service began to create two distinct classes of users: the major corporations, which required an escalating range of sophisticated long-distance and international services at the lowest possible price, and the small, local business and domestic subscriber, who required cheap, reliable, mainly local voice telephony. Thus ways needed to be found to ensure that those gaining the benefits of competition did not do so at the expense of those suffering the loss of the benefits of monopoly.

The above arguments apply to basic services—those services that supply only end-to-end connection without manipulating the message. The provision of enhanced or value-added services, in which what is sold is message manipulation (e.g., from store and forward, or packet switching, to elaborate data management and information services), raises different policy issues. Here natural monopoly arguments do not generally apply. In fact, competition would seem desirable, especially since it is in these areas (such as CABLE TELEVISION and ELECTRONIC PUBLISHING) that telecommunications regulation increasingly involves the provision of entertainment and informational services, where considerations of freedom of expression are relevant.

Finally, at a national level there is the question of the balance between an industrial and a service-based policy in telecommunications. A service-based policy, on the one hand, might argue that opening the domestic equipment market to maximum international competition would maximize innovation and minimize cost, thus maximizing the efficiency of both network and service provision. An industrial policy, on the other hand, might argue that it was necessary to use the purchasing power of a national monopoly PTT, both to protect domestic employment and to ensure the survival of a national base for technological innovation and high-technology exports as well as the survival of national control over key strategic technologies.

A related policy issue is that of STANDARDS. Technical compatibility is an essential complement to interconnectivity. Traditionally PTTs imposed common standards within their national markets. Such standards can be and have been used as nontariff barriers to trade. Markets, to be fully competitive, require common standards. But competitive markets themselves militate against common standards. Thus such standards have had to be imposed, either by national governments unilaterally or internationally by negotiations between governments. This is difficult because decisions on standards may favor one national industry or firm over another and because decisions on standards may preempt policy options. For instance, decisions on international ISDN standards placed competitive and monopoly models of network and service provision against one another and made the extent to which control over network operations would remain at the national level highly contentious. However, if there is to be an international market in telecommunications and related information technology equipment and an international flow of telecommunications services, then either such international agreements must be reached or common standards will be imposed de facto by dominant multinational companies, reinforcing both oligopoly and national dependency.

International implications. All these policy issues have international ramifications, if only because the principle of interconnectivity does not stop at national boundaries. In the past, international relations in this field were regulated within the International Telecommunication Union (ITU) with little contention. This situation changed in the late 1970s for two reasons. First, the international market for telecommunications goods and services became an increasingly important and fiercely contested battleground between the industrialized nations. Second, Third World nations increased their voting strength in the ITU and made efforts to ensure their equitable access to world communications resources.

The central international issue was again that of competition versus monopoly. Those multinational corporate interests that had been pushing for the introduction of competition at a national level, especially in the United States, wanted the same privileges they had been granted in the United States to be made available to them in other countries. This was a contentious issue for two reasons. First, there remained deep philosophical and political differences among nations about how communications should be handled, in particular on the balance between free expression and economic competition on the one hand and social solidarity and public service on the other. Second, the future of national PTT monopolies had implications far beyond the borders of each country. The introduction of competition in a nation's communications ends its control not only over industrial policy in the telecommunications field but also over the flow of information across its borders. This has consequences for the future of the nation itself. For instance, all nations control a national currency and the banking system through which it flows. As money itself is increasingly transformed into an international flow of bits in a telecommunications network, the ability of a nation to control its economic destiny is gravely weakened. Similarly, if the vital economic and social intelligence about a country is held in data bases outside its borders and under the control of other national and economic entities, its ability to act independently is gravely threatened. A society's ability to protect and develop its own national culture is threatened by a free flow of words, sounds, and images under free-market conditions. Such flows favor the large nation over the small, the rich over the poor. For all these reasons, the appropriateness of competition as the norm for the operation of telecommunications networks lies at the heart of the international telecommunications policy debate.

Bibliography. Oswald H. Ganley and Gladys D. Ganley, *To Inform or to Control: The New Communication Networks,* New York, 1982; Cees J. Hamelink, *Transnational Data Flows in the Information Age,* Springfield, Va., 1984; International Commission for the Study of Communication Problems (UNESCO), *Many Voices, One World: Communication and Society, Today and Tomorrow,* Paris and New York, 1980; Leonard Lewin, ed., *Telecommunications: An Interdisciplinary Survey,* Dedham, Mass., 1979; OECD, *Telecommunications: Pressures and Policies for Change,* Paris, 1983; Ithiel de Sola Pool, *Technologies of Freedom: On Free Speech in an Electronic Age,* Cambridge, Mass., 1983; Dan Schiller, *Telematics and Government,* Norwood, N.J., 1982; Anthony Smith, *The Geopolitics of Information: How Western Culture Dominates the World,* New York, 1980; Christopher H. Sterling, ed., *International Telecommunications and Information Policy,* Washington, D.C., 1984.

NICHOLAS ROBERT GARNHAM

TELEGRAPHY

The modern era of communication, with its instantaneous contact over time and space, was inaugurated by the development of magnetic telegraphy. The introduction of this technology occurred with exceptional speed compared to that of earlier communication innovations, and its social repercussions were so profound that its ownership and operation became matters of public concern.

Invention and diffusion. The idea of telegraphy grew out of the Voltaic pile (1800), a device that converted chemical energy into electrical energy, thus providing a source of continuous electric current. This simple battery encouraged experimentation with electricity between 1820 and 1840 in England, France, the United States, and Denmark. As a result it was discovered that electric current flowing through a wire caused movement in a magnet suspended nearby. The invention of the telegraph still required the means for transmitting a signal at will and an effective device for receiving the message. That occurred with the invention of electromagnetic detectors in 1836–1837 by Sir William Cooke (1806–1879) and Sir Charles Wheatstone (1802–1875) in Britain and by SAMUEL F. B. MORSE (1791–1872) in the United States. Within forty years the technology of telegraphy grew to include high-speed printing, which culminated in ticker tapes and telexes, and duplex and quadruplex telegraphy, which allowed up to four messages to be sent over a wire simultaneously.

The first successful telegraph communications took place in Great Britain with the Paddington-West Drayton line of July 1839 and in the United States with Morse's Baltimore-Washington line of May 1844. The United States, Britain, and soon France began employing the telegraph almost immediately. In the United States, telegraph lines became commercially feasible in 1845–1846. By 1848 they had blanketed the east and west to Chicago and St. Louis, and had linked all major northern and southern cities by 1851. The line to California was completed in 1861, eight years before railroads spanned the continent. In Great Britain such major cities as London, Dublin, Liverpool, Manchester, Glasgow, Aberdeen, and others were connected by 1857, at which time nearly five hundred telegraph stations were open to the public. The telegraph was also rapidly adopted on the European continent: in Austria and Prussia in 1849, Belgium in 1850, the Netherlands and Switzerland in 1852, Sweden in 1853, and a number of other countries over the following ten years (see Figures 1 and 2).

Telegraph poles and lines sprang up quickly. In the United States there were thirty-two thousand miles of telegraph lines by 1860, when some 5 million messages were dispatched. In Great Britain at the same date there were about eight thousand miles of line and over 1 million messages were transmitted. On the European continent, forty-five thousand miles of lines had been erected by 1860, carrying 4.5 million messages compared with a quarter of a million messages eight years earlier. Lines and messages multiplied over the ensuing decades, but the best measure of the diffusion of telegraphy is the intensity of use between 1860 and 1910 (see Table 1). The slowdown in the years after 1890 reflected the grow-

Figure 1. *(Telegraphy)* An engraving of a telegraph key. The Bettmann Archive, Inc.

Figure 2. *(Telegraphy)* Erecting telegraph poles in 1889. The Bettmann Archive, Inc.

ing use of the TELEPHONE, especially in Great Britain and the United States.

Perhaps the most significant development in the expansion of telegraphy was the construction of submarine cables, first installed across the English Channel between Dover and Calais in 1851. A North Atlantic cable, proposed in 1847, was installed in 1858 but soon broke down. The next attempt, with the world's largest ship, the *Great Eastern,* as cable-layer, succeeded in establishing a permanent line between Newfoundland and Ireland in 1866 (see Figure 3). A burst of ocean cable projects followed, practically girdling the earth by 1872, when almost all the principal cities of the world were linked. One result of this expanded communications network was that large areas of Africa, Asia, the Middle East, and Latin America, already under the control of foreign powers, could be more rapidly and effectively colonized during the following years. In addition, telegraphy furthered the growth of a truly international economy governed by world prices and a single system of international payments.

Impact on business and government. The birth and diffusion of the telegraph was accompanied by extraordinary social optimism. In the United States a Cincinnati newspaper saw the telegraph in 1847 as "facilitating Human Intercourse and producing Harmony among Men and Nations. . . . it may be regarded as an important element in Moral Progress." A leading business publication in 1865 saw the nations of the world "brought into closer moral contact with each other. . . . The hand of progress beckons unceasingly to freedom, and whenever science achieves a victory, a rivet is loosened from the chains of the oppressed."

In the world of commerce and finance the telegraph was widely regarded as an agent for facilitating competition and perfecting markets over space and time; information on prices and quantities of goods would henceforth be available to everyone on an equal basis, so that MONOPOLY power would be

Table 1. Telegraph Messages per Hundred of Population (Including Ocean Cables), 1860–1910

	1860	*1870*	*1880*	*1890*	*1900*	*1910*
Australia	35	56	168	299	253	274
Austria	4	17	28	38	58	73
France	2	15	44	70	103	127
Germany	2	22	30	45	70	78
India	n	n	1	2	3	5
Italy	n	7	21	28	29	45
Japan	na	na	6	11	38	61
Russia	1	3	9	12	14	25
Sweden	4	14	22	37	49	71
United Kingdom	4	27	85	174	216	192
United States	16	29	63	94	114	117

n = negligible
na = not available
Sources: B. R. Mitchell, *European Historical Statistics 1750–1970,* New York, 1975; B. R. Mitchell, *International Historical Statistics, Africa and Asia,* New York, 1982; B. R. Mitchell, *International Historical Statistics, The Americas and Australasia,* Detroit, 1983; R. B. Du Boff, "The Telegraph and the Structure of Markets in the United States, 1845–1890," *Research in Economic History* 8 (1983): 253–277.

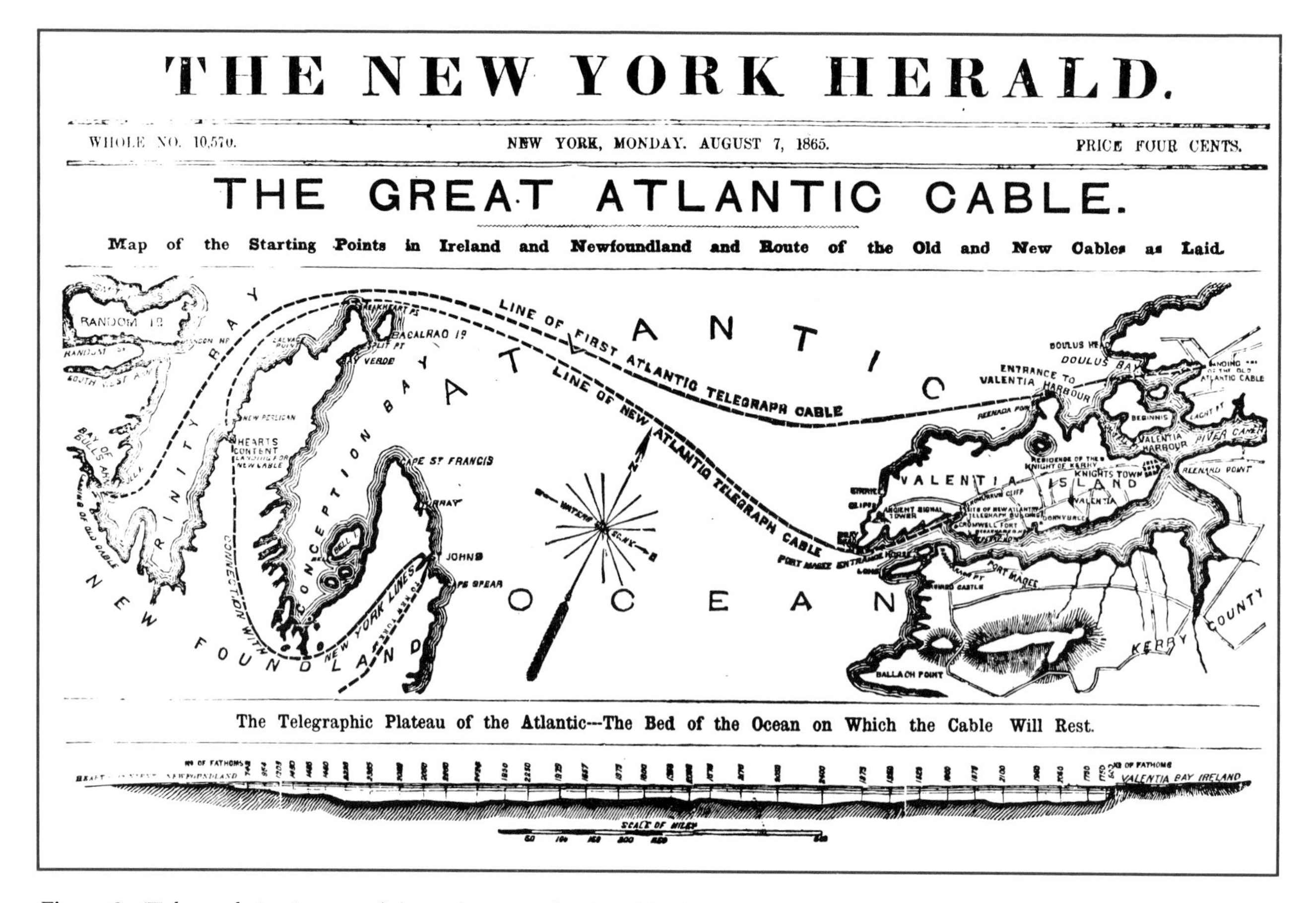

THE NEW YORK HERALD.

WHOLE NO. 10,570. NEW YORK, MONDAY, AUGUST 7, 1865. PRICE FOUR CENTS.

THE GREAT ATLANTIC CABLE.

Map of the Starting Points in Ireland and Newfoundland and Route of the Old and New Cables as Laid.

The Telegraphic Plateau of the Atlantic—The Bed of the Ocean on Which the Cable Will Rest.

Figure 3. *(Telegraphy)* A map of the early transatlantic cables between Newfoundland and Ireland. From the *New York Herald,* August 7, 1865. Courtesy Burndy Library, Connecticut.

weakened. In fact, the telegraph promoted both competition and monopoly. The telegraph did bring about sharp reductions in regional price differences and radically lowered the costs of obtaining and distributing information. For business firms it saved time, cut down the need for large inventories, decreased short-term financing requirements, and made it possible to eliminate many middlemen and wholesalers. In combination with railroads and steamships, the telegraph made possible the larger national and international markets that came into being between 1850 and 1900.

However, the effects of telegraphy on the conduct of business and government also included growth in the scale of enterprises, centralization of decision making, increased capacity for SECRECY, and centralization of information. Rather than increasing competition, these effects tended to encourage the development of monopoly power.

As a result of the telegraph and the accompanying plunge in the costs of communication, the overall scale of business enterprises increased rapidly. In the United States, for instance, by 1851 a ten-word message could be sent from New York to Boston for $0.20, to Chicago for $1.00, and to New Orleans for $2.40. The average cost of a message fell to $1.05 in 1868 and $0.39 in 1877 (even more in relative price terms, since the overall price level rose between 1850 and 1875). This raised scale thresholds: the size of manufacturing, wholesaling, and retailing firms grew because they could now carry on business outside their traditional market zones. Furthermore, business institutions that were actually created by telegraphy were inherently nationwide or international in scope—commodity exchanges and organized securities markets in particular.

The telegraph virtually invited centralization of decision making by drastically reducing the costs of gathering relevant information regarding prices; availability of raw materials, labor, and capital; and other data necessary for extending control over far-flung operations. All this applied especially to the control of colonies; the larger the territory, the more useful it was for authorities to have a rapid means for communicating with their most remote outposts. While Britain's colonial trade was to a large extent shaped by the ocean cable, much of the thinking of the Admiralty and the War Office revolved around the employment of the telegraph network as a vital component of imperial defense against external rivals and local political unrest alike. *See* COLONIZATION.

Speed and secrecy are the ingredients for success in many military, political, and economic endeavors. The advantages of the telegraph in this regard were recognized and employed in business operations from the start. Immediate transmission of orders and requests was assured, while secrecy for users of the wires was guaranteed by elaborate codes as well as strict telegraph company rules regarding confidentiality of messages. These intelligence dimensions were understood from the first days of the telegraph era; cipher systems and CODE language, replete with common commercial and financial phrases, were worked out as early as 1844–1845. In the United States the telegraph helped employers combat trade unions by allowing the swift transmission of information about known organizers. The value of having a direct telegraph line to factories and workplaces, one telegraph company official pointed out, was "evident: the master was felt to be among his men," even though physical distance intervened.

For governments, too, the new modes of intelligence inherent in telegraphic communication were quickly utilized. The "Ems Dispatch" of July 1870, precipitating the Franco-Prussian War, showed that the new technology could be used for purposes quite different from "producing Harmony among Men and Nations." In France the state-run telegraph began by giving priority to the police and the military. Telegraph lines existed there for six years before they were made available in 1851 to private citizens. The Vienna correspondent of the London *Chronicle* reported in 1854 that "Austria feels a greater degree of security against another rising of her subjects, in the fact that she possesses and controls an extensive system of telegraphy."

The telegraph also encouraged concentration of information sources. For example, the New York Associated Press was established in 1848 by six New York newspapers, which agreed to unite "for the purpose of collecting and receiving telegraphic and other intelligence" at common cost. Julius Reuter also understood the new capabilities of telegraphy when he set up his agency at Aachen in 1849 and began supplying foreign news to the English press in 1858. Wire services narrowed the base from which news was distributed. Telegraphic technology required fast news gathering at a single place; it placed a premium on fewer, standardized information sources that could be quickly sent out over the wires and cover wider geographic areas. This one-way, routinized version of news dispatching, essential for low-cost use of the telegraph, enlarged the area of news reception and dissemination but fostered monopolization in much the same way as growth of national and international markets promoted larger-sized business firms.

Organization. The most intensive use of telegraph systems, then, came from the worlds of commerce, finance, and government. Private citizens used the telegraph mainly for urgent communication with relatives and friends. But nowhere was telegraphy so dominated by business interests as in the United States, where the power of business to enforce its priorities appears to have been substantially greater than in Europe. Elsewhere inland telegraphy was or became state controlled. With the British Telegraph Act of 1868, which authorized the Post Office to purchase and operate all British telegraph companies, the United States and Canada became the only nations in which the telegraph remained private. In the United States the formation of the Western Union monopoly in 1866 stirred the proponents of government control of telegraphy into action. Agitation for a national telegraph system linking the nation's post offices went on until the 1890s, but its advocates never made any significant progress toward that goal. Submarine cables also remained almost entirely in the hands of the private enterprises that built them.

Both government and privately founded telegraph companies invested in telegraphy in foreign countries. Britain's Colonial Office showed a lively interest in both intra- and intercolonial communications. From 1879 to 1914, imperial telegraph subsidies totaled £1.9 million. Private U.S. investments in foreign telegraph systems were substantial for the same reasons. Western Union expanded into Canada in the 1850s, first by buying the Montreal Telegraph Company, then by pursuing plans to build a cable from British Columbia to Siberia (a plan later abandoned). From the 1860s through the 1880s, U.S. telegraph companies built lines to Cuba, Mexico, and the rest of Latin America, where large increases in telegraph traffic were recorded after 1900.

Since 1850 the communications sector of industrial nations has grown at a rapid rate, with the introduction of each technological innovation—telegraph, telephone, RADIO, computer, SATELLITE. The telegraph led the way, altering methods of production and exchange on a global scale. The outcome was a series of spectacular and unprecedented reductions in the cost and feasibility of sending and obtaining information.

See also COMPUTER: HISTORY.

Bibliography. Richard B. Du Boff, "The Rise of Communications Regulation: The Telegraph Industry, 1844–1880," *Journal of Communication* 34 (Summer 1984): 52–66; idem, "The Telegraph and the Structure of Markets in the United States, 1845–1890," *Research in Economic History* 8 (1983): 253–277; Alvin F. Harlow, *Old Wires and New Waves: The History of the Telegraph, Telephone, and*

Wireless, New York, 1936, reprint 1971; Jeffrey Kieve, *The Electric Telegraph in the U.K.: A Social and Economic History*, Newton Abbot, Eng., and New York, 1973; Lester Lindley, *The Constitution Faces Technology: The Relationship of the National Government to the Telegraph, 1866–1884*, New York, 1975; Robert L. Thompson, *Wiring a Continent: The History of the Telegraph Industry in the United States 1832–1866*, Princeton, N.J., 1947.

RICHARD B. DU BOFF

TELEPHONE

Since its invention by ALEXANDER GRAHAM BELL in 1876 the telephone has enjoyed remarkable success in Western industrialized economies. These nations have made telephone technology an integral part of their national communications systems. Indeed until the early 1960s approximately 90 percent of the world's telephones were found in North America and Europe and more than 60 percent in the United States alone.

The growth of national telephone networks proceeded differently in different countries. In the United States a private organization, the Bell Telephone Company, took charge of commercial development. Formed out of a patent association of Bell, Gardiner G. Hubbard, and Thomas Sanders, this firm initially tried to sell the Bell telephone patents to the Western Union Telegraph Company for one hundred thousand dollars, but the offer was refused. Possessing little capital, the fledgling Bell Company franchised the right to lease telephones to private agents scattered across the country.

In Europe telephone development fell under state direction almost from the start. Germany's telegraph administration oversaw telephones, producing a public MONOPOLY in the new industry (*see* TELEGRAPHY). Great Britain and France at first relied on mixed ventures, as government postal and telegraph bureaus leased the right to rent telephones to private firms in exchange for a percentage of the gross revenues. Only Sweden and a few other countries broke with this pattern, experimenting for a time with market competition.

Initially telephone growth proceeded slowly in all of these countries. Before the invention of the telephone exchange, telephony was strictly a point-to-point form of communications. Subscribers rented instruments and strung lines to the places with which they wished to communicate. But they were unable to talk directly with more than one or two other telephone users. The exchange revolutionized telephony by making multiple direct connections possible. Between 1878 and 1880 exchanges surpassed private lines as the main type of telephone service. Augmenting the utility of the telephone to subscribers by increasing the number of possible connections, the new technology fueled telephone expansion and led to important changes in the industry. In the United States and elsewhere scattered territorial agencies gave way to capitalized firms, because exchanges demanded greater capital than private lines and required maintenance and management.

United States. In the United States these changes took place at a time of important telephone industry reorganization. In 1878 Western Union had entered the business through its subsidiary, the Gold and Stock Company. Using a competing telephone developed by Elisha Gray and a telephone transmitter invented by THOMAS ALVA EDISON, the telegraph corporation quickly cut into National Bell's (the Bell Company's name in 1878) market share.

This brief flurry of competition ended quickly, however, as Bell and Western Union came to terms in 1880. Western Union agreed to give Bell a monopoly of the telephone business in exchange for Bell's promise not to start a message-for-hire service. As understood by Western Union this stipulation prevented Bell from engaging in long-distance message transmission. Bell willingly conceded this point, as commercial long-distance telephony was not profitable at the time. Western Union apparently believed that most long-distance messages would continue to be transmitted by telegraph. This assumption proved false, and the restriction in the contract provided no barrier to Bell's later entry into the long-distance communications market.

The Bell–Western Union accord set the structure of the U.S. telephone industry for the next fourteen years. American Bell (renamed again in 1880) used its patents on the telephone and related equipment to maintain an unbreachable private monopoly in the industry. The corporation also acquired Western Electric in 1882 to manufacture telephones and equipment for its licensed companies and began to acquire controlling interest in these regional (operating) companies. In 1885 Bell founded the American Telephone and Telegraph Company (AT&T) to develop long-distance telephone service. In all, Bell's monopoly enabled it to centralize telephone operations and to lay the foundations for an interconnected local and long-distance telephone network that would emerge as the Bell System in 1908.

Europe. European telephony also proceeded toward centralization, though more slowly than in the United States and by public rather than private efforts. France, Germany, and Great Britain all created postal, telegraph, and telephone administrations (PTTs) to oversee communications. Even Sweden ended its experimentation with competition and consolidated its telephone system under government control. By

Figure 1. *(Telephone)* "Weavers of Speech": an advertisement for the Bell Telephone System. Courtesy of AT&T Bell Laboratories.

1911 public ownership of telephone service was dominant in Europe. Some private systems remained, but gradually they too gave way to public monopoly.

The telephone systems of Europe differed markedly from that of the United States. Being public enterprises, they were shaped by bureaucratic rivalries, political considerations, and the limitations of public finance. In France and Germany, for example, a lack of capital slowed telephone expansion. Though the systems of these nations were under public control, subscribers themselves had to raise funds and demonstrate that adequate demand for service existed before authorities would provide lines. In Europe the drive to create an interconnected telephone network, which characterized Bell's efforts, was small. Instead the telephone was treated as one part of a combined communications system, and often its growth was sacrificed in the interest of other forms of communication. As a result no European nation approached the United States in telephone distribution per capita in this period.

Early twentieth-century developments. While European nations were creating their public telephone monopolies, the U.S. telephone industry underwent a sudden reorganization in 1894 with the reintroduction of competition. In that year the original Bell patents expired, and new firms, the independent (non-Bell) telephone carriers, entered the industry. They gained more than 50 percent of the market by 1902, and their presence rapidly increased the number of telephones in the nation and brought down prices by almost 75 percent.

Customers flocked to the independents in part because these new firms concentrated on inexpensive local service, something that most telephone users valued more than Bell's extensive but expensive long-distance system. These developments increased telephone distribution in the United States but also undermined Bell's goal of creating a single, unified telephone network.

Over time Bell regained its dominant place in the telephone industry and resumed its drive to create an interconnected network. Both private and public actions contributed to this result. AT&T, which took over ownership of the entire Bell enterprise in 1899, provided the private effort with its policy of "universal service." It expanded long-distance service, bringing a greater number of customers into the Bell System. Where demand for such service was weak, the corporation acquired competitors to gain market share. In other cases it compromised with its competitors by signing sublicense contracts with them. These agreements allowed the independents to connect with Bell lines, provided that they conformed to Bell standards and practices. In this way Bell drew more areas into its growing national network. Between 1900 and 1908 the percentage of non-Bell firms connected to Bell lines increased tenfold. By 1912 Bell commanded 58 percent of the telephone market.

Public sanctions helped to unify this new system. State legislatures took telephone regulation out of municipal hands and placed it in the hands of independent commissions. These commissions tended to side with Bell against local governments, which had used competition to tailor telephone service to local needs. Federal regulation, which had begun in 1910 with the Mann-Elkins Act, also played an important role. In 1913 the Justice Department, using the threat of an antitrust suit, got Bell to agree to allow noncompeting independent firms access to its lines. This accord, the Kingsbury Commitment, essentially conformed to the private policies Bell had devised earlier, but it removed the threat of antitrust enforcement.

By 1920 the telephone systems of Europe and the United States were centralized under their single administrations. These systems differed in important ways. The U.S. telephone industry was under the control of a single management, AT&T, but consisted of a number of different organizations. It grew rapidly under the stimulus of continued technological advances and a public policy that used revenues from long-distance service to subsidize local rates. European telephone systems were under public control, but they were less extensive and generally more expensive than the U.S. system, as European nations did not make the extension of the network their top priority.

Some of these differences disappeared over time. All countries faced a similar challenge: the creation of a single system that served a number of different regions within their economies. In both the United States and Europe public policy moved to incorporate more outlying areas into the national network. At the same time AT&T became increasingly dependent on GOVERNMENT REGULATION for its dominant position in the U.S. telephone industry, though it continued to remain a private corporation. By the late 1940s the United States began to lose its overwhelming lead in percentage of world telephones as European and other nations began to catch up.

After World War II. Japan in particular experienced rapid growth in telecommunications in these years. Like many European nations it had created a public telephone monopoly in the early twentieth century. But in 1949 it separated telecommunications from POSTAL SERVICE and placed it in a state-owned, privately run corporation, Nippon Telephone and Telegraph. This hybrid, halfway between the Bell System and the European PTTs, successfully expanded Japan's telephone network, so that by 1979 the country had more telephones per capita than any European nation except Sweden.

In the years following World War II less developed countries also began to establish national telecommunications systems, though with less success than industrialized countries. Underinvestment in telecommunications has characterized their economies despite efforts to promote the industry. In part these problems may reflect the special difficulty in applying the telephone to heavily rural and agrarian societies, a problem similar to that which existed in the early years of the Bell System. Yet newer technologies, such as RADIO and SATELLITE communications, have also offered new opportunities to shape telecommunications to fit less developed economies. Whether because the main benefit of telecommunications ac-

Figure 2. *(Telephone)* Early telephone switchboard. The Bettmann Archive, Inc.

Figure 3. *(Telephone)* An American Airlines employee uses a mobile phone at the crash site of a DC-10 at O'Hare International Airport, Chicago, May 25, 1979. Courtesy of AT&T Bell Laboratories.

crues to these nations' small urban sectors or because of misguided development policies, the distribution of telephones in Third World countries has remained below five per one hundred people into the 1980s.

Although the industrialized world has enjoyed rapid growth in telecommunications throughout the twentieth century, it underwent important and disruptive changes in the years following World War II. In the 1950s the era of stability and convergence came to an end as rapid technological change reshaped the boundaries of the industry. Seeking to take advantage of the opportunities these new technologies presented, large-business users of telecommunications services pressed to open the industry to competition. Demanding greater freedom to own and use telecommunications equipment and desiring lower rates, they created a wedge that opened the way for new competitors. These changes affected all telephone systems, but their impact was greatest in the United States, where they shattered the assumptions under which the Bell System had operated for nearly fifty years.

Increasing competition. The Bell System breakup began in 1956, when AT&T and the Justice Department signed a consent decree in an antitrust suit that had begun in the late 1940s. In this accord AT&T was allowed to retain its manufacturing subsidiary, Western Electric, in exchange for its agreement not to enter unregulated services or industries. Coming at a time of rapid change, this pact limited AT&T's ability to respond to new opportunities.

Only years later would the problems of the 1956 decision become apparent. More immediate developments, however, also called into question U.S. TELECOMMUNICATIONS POLICY. Using microwave technology, new long-distance carriers began to demand the right to furnish service, particularly over the profitable, heavily used routes between major cities. The Federal Communications Commission (FCC) slowly granted them licenses, but its caution was met with increasing demands from new entrants, which used the courts to gain greater access to the long-distance market. New firms such as Microwave Communications Incorporated (MCI) cut into AT&T's revenues. Using advances in switching technology, they offered both private-line and switched long-distance service, further threatening AT&T by undercutting its rates, which were set by regulatory policy.

AT&T tried to limit damage to its revenues by denying new carriers access to local distribution channels. Without interconnection privileges the new companies could not economically provide service. The FCC originally supported AT&T's efforts but was ordered by the courts to change its policy and allow all telecommunications common carriers access to the network. By 1977 the long-distance market was moving toward competition. In the years following, competing firms pressed for greater access, on more equal terms, to Bell's local distribution loops.

Similar changes took place in the terminal equipment market, which, like long-distance service, had been monopolized by Bell. Once again FCC policy was forced to change as new entrants demanded the right to make and market telecommunications devices that could be used on Bell lines. Court decisions forced the FCC and AT&T to end their absolute ban on such attachments and adopt standards for the use of non-Bell equipment in the network. This change effectively opened up the terminal equipment market to competition.

With the old monopoly structure under attack from several directions, the Justice Department began in 1974 another antitrust suit against AT&T. Bell operating companies, the government argued, refused to purchase telephone equipment from any supplier but Western Electric, preventing other equipment suppliers from competing in this market. More importantly, however, the suit also incorporated many of the issues raised by other corporations trying to gain entry into the telephone industry. Bringing together demands for greater competition voiced by the new long-distance carriers and large-business users, it was the most comprehensive reconsideration of U.S. telecommunications policy that had been undertaken in more than half a century.

The antitrust suit provided the means of reshaping that policy. In a 1982 consent decree AT&T was allowed to retain ownership of Western Electric, but it divested itself of its regional operating companies. These latter firms remained regulated providers of local telephone service, though they had to open their lines to all long-distance carriers. AT&T emerged as a smaller firm; though its long-distance business was still subject to regulation, it was free to enter new markets.

Most other nations have retained their postal, telegraph, and telephone public monopolies, and the growth of telecommunications in developing nations has generally proceeded with significant government assistance. Continued technological change, the merging of computer and telephone technologies, and the creation of new services such as electronic mail all suggest that the traditional boundaries of the telephone industry will continue to change (*see* COMPUTER: HISTORY; COMPUTER: IMPACT). New competition from U.S. telecommunications companies operating overseas may force a restructuring of European telecommunications systems as well.

See also AGENDA-SETTING; FIBER OPTICS; TELECOMMUNICATIONS NETWORKS.

Bibliography. Gerald W. Brock, *The Telecommunications Industry: The Dynamics of Market Structure,* Cambridge, Mass., 1981; Robert Bruce, *Alexander Graham Bell and the Conquest of Solitude,* Boston, 1973; Robert W. Garnet, *The Telephone Enterprise: The Evolution of the Bell System's Horizontal Structure, 1876–1909,* Baltimore, Md., 1985; A. N. Holcombe, *Public Ownership of Telephones on the Continent of Europe,* Cambridge, Mass., 1911; Kenneth Lipartito, "The Telephone in the South: A Comparative Analysis," Ph.D. diss., The Johns Hopkins University, Baltimore, Md., 1986; Dan Schiller, *Telematics and Government,* Norwood, N.J., 1982; George David Smith, *The Anatomy of a Business Strategy: Bell, Western Electric, and the Origins of the American Telephone Industry,* Baltimore, Md., 1985.

KENNETH J. LIPARTITO

TELEVISION. *See* CABLE TELEVISION; EDUCATIONAL TELEVISION; TELEVISION HISTORY; TELEVISION NEWS.

TELEVISION HISTORY

The evolution of television is here chronicled in three articles:

1. **Early Period**
2. **Global Development**
3. **World Market Struggles**

1. EARLY PERIOD

In the late nineteenth century the magic mirror of fantasy, through which faraway events could be glimpsed, began to seem not quite so fantastic but a likely development. The 1876 demonstrations of the TELEPHONE by ALEXANDER GRAHAM BELL brought this about. He had based his invention on study of the ear, and he referred to the telephone as an instrument for hearing telegraphically. If that was now feasible, why not also see telegraphically, by a device based on study of the eye? The ramifications of the idea were widely visualized. In 1879 in the British magazine *Punch,* artist and writer George Du Maurier pictured a couple watching a remote tennis match via a screen above the fireplace (Figure 1). Three years later French artist Robida presented more startling visions. In one drawing he envisioned a French family of the future watching a war on a home screen (reflecting France's overseas expansions of the time, it was a desert war, apparently in North Africa). In others he depicted a woman at home inspecting merchandise on display in a store and another watching a lecturer at a blackboard, again via a mirrorlike screen in the home.

The disk. A laboratory step toward such ideas followed with startling promptness. In 1884 Paul Nipkow of Germany devised the Nipkow disk—a round disk with perforations arranged in a spiral pattern. When the disk rotated, a beam of light passing through the perforations would cause pinpoints of light to perform a rapid scanning movement on some opposite surface, similar to the movement of eyes back and forth across a printed page. The device was at once seen as a key to transmission of pictures by wire, in the form of a series of dots of varying intensity. It became the main basis for ex-

Figure 1. *(Television History—Early Period)* George Du Maurier, an 1879 prediction: televised sports. From *Punch.* State Historical Society of Wisconsin, Erik Barnouw Collection.

periments in image transmission—still images and moving images, first by wire, later by radio waves. The Nipkow disk remained a central feature of such experimentation for half a century, involving activity in virtually every major industrialized nation (Figure 2).

But progress was slow. While other communication innovations—the phonograph, MOTION PICTURES, RADIO—made their appearance, set off entrepreneurial booms, and spread around the world, the Nipkow disk and its traveling dots of light remained a laboratory wonder, awaiting further technical breakthroughs. The array of names that people gave it—"distant electric vision," "telephonoscope," "seeing by wireless," "visual radio"—gradually gave way to a word used in 1907 by the magazine *Scientific American:* "television."

First start. In the mid-1920s, as radio broadcasting fever was spreading, some experimenters thought that television was finally ready. Among the most avid apostles was John Logie Baird of Scotland, who had experimented with television for some years but had been ignored by Britain's broadcasting establishment. Baird, skimpily financed, had to work on a makeshift basis. The Nipkow-style disk of his early demonstrations was made of cardboard cut from a hatbox, and a biscuit tin housed his projection lamp—but even with these means he impressed visitors. The British Broadcasting Corporation (BBC), which by charter controlled all broadcasting activities in Britain, was chastised by some critics for its inaction in regard to television, and specifically for not supporting Baird's explorations. In 1929 it finally agreed to joint experimentation with Baird, using BBC transmitters, at first in off-hours only. A year later "Baird televisors" were placed on sale—equipped, like the transmission equipment, with whirling disks—to retranslate the lines of dots back into sequences of images. The screen was the size of a saucer.

In the United States, at various locations, similar activities were in progress. At General Electric (GE) in Schenectady, New York, Ernst F. W. Alexanderson was in charge of television experiments and demonstrations. Here, too, various program forms

Figure 2. *(Television History—Early Period)* Scanner with Nipkow disk, as used by General Electric in experiments in the 1920s. Smithsonian Institution, Washington, D.C. Photo No. 60,005.

were tried and were observed by a scattering of viewers, some of whom made their own receiving sets. In 1928 some of them saw an adaptation of the stage melodrama *The Queen's Messenger,* announced by GE as television's first drama production (Figure 3). Only close-ups were used. Three cameras, all motionless, took part. The images, appearing on a postcard-size screen, were often little more than silhouettes.

All this offered the satisfactions of a pioneer experience. Yet none of it could be thought of as acceptable; clearly a mechanical system would not do in the long run. Gradually on both sides of the Atlantic the experimental effort subsided and collapsed. The stock-market crash and world economic depression contributed to this. Besides, the public was increasingly addicted to radio and did not seem to be demanding television. In 1934 the BBC discontinued its Baird telecasts; Baird televisors became museum pieces. In Germany, where the Nipkow disk had originated, its use persisted longer. In 1935 the regime of Adolf Hitler, intent on wide media impact, began the world's first regular television service, which operated for three years on a mechanical system. Then, in Germany as elsewhere, the disks stopped whirling. Television, in its first outing, had run into a dead end.

Second start. But a second lunge was in preparation. The keynote was electronic scanning. There would still be pinpoints of light in scanning movements, but they would be made by fusillades of electrons in a glass tube. The main impetus for the new effort came from the Radio Corporation of America (RCA), where the hard-driving DAVID SARNOFF became president in 1930. Using its powerful patent position and rapidly growing revenues from radio broadcasting and set manufacture, Sarnoff made the achievement of electronic television his top priority. Already VLADIMIR K. ZWORYKIN, who had experimented with television in Russia before the 1917 Revolution, had been given the task of solving the technical problems for RCA. All available resources were at his disposal.

RCA, formed in 1919 to create a patent pool of major communications companies (GE, Westinghouse, AT&T, and United Fruit), seemed to control almost all patents relevant to its coming task. Any other rights needed were bought outright by RCA. Under Sarnoff policy RCA did not pay royalties; it collected them. But some puzzling—and, to Sarnoff, infuriating—obstacles loomed. One was PHILO FARNSWORTH, a youth whose career had the quality of a legend. Raised on a farm near the upper Snake River in Idaho, he did not encounter electricity until he was fourteen and his family acquired a Delco system. But just six years later, set up in a San Francisco laboratory by West Coast backers, he demonstrated electronic television and applied for a patent on the basic tube, taking RCA totally by surprise (Figure 4). Its attorneys challenged Farnsworth's claims, grilling him for hours in patent hearings. Yet in 1930, as Sarnoff was taking over the RCA presidency and preparing his television plans, young Farnsworth got his patent. He refused to sell his rights on a lump-sum basis as RCA demanded; in the end it had to take a Farnsworth license on a royalty basis. A parallel dispute, which became a titanic feud, involved EDWIN H. ARMSTRONG, inventor of fre-

Figure 3. *(Television History—Early Period)* "The Queen's Messenger," the first television drama, WGY Schenectady, 1928. Courtesy Rosalind Greene. State Historical Society of Wisconsin, Erik Barnouw Collection.

Figure 4. *(Television History—Early Period)* Philo Farnsworth performing television experiments at Philco, Philadelphia, January 1932. State Historical Society of Wisconsin, Erik Barnouw Collection.

quency modulation (FM), the sound system chosen for RCA television, but without royalty payments to Armstrong. Lawsuits over this were not resolved until decades later, all in favor of the inventor's estate. Amid such legal disputes, impasses, and negotiations, along with problems over SPECTRUM allocations, electronic television gradually took shape. In 1936 program tests and demonstrations began. Sarnoff decided on a commercial debut at the 1939 New York World's Fair.

On April 30, 1939, Franklin D. Roosevelt, opening the RCA exhibit and inaugurating the age of electronic television, also became the first U.S. president to appear on the tube. Sets went on sale. Telecasting began in a number of U.S. cities, as well as in Britain and Germany. Experiments in linking stations via coaxial cable were also begun.

But suddenly it all evaporated. Resources were needed for defense production. Specialists with television experience were needed for a highly secret development—radar. As World War II began, television services were halted in Britain and Germany and gradually ground to a halt in the United States. NBC's New York television transmitter was put to use in the training of air-raid wardens via sets in police stations. Television, in its second outing, had reached another dead end.

In many ways it was just as well. Almost all weaponry developed during World War II involved electronic components, and they contributed to a vastly improved postwar television system, which would acquire a color option. Prewar black-and-white electronic television was never really satisfactory. The receivers, mostly with five-inch and nine-inch picture tubes, were flickery and balky. Studio cameras required extraordinarily intense lighting, and performers felt as if they were being fried. Around Radio City in New York, where NBC's studio experiments took place, actors were seen with yellow makeup and purple lipstick; unbalanced color responses by the cameras made such adjustments necessary. In retrospect it was all seen as valuable experience: they had found out what needed fixing.

Third start. In 1946, as RCA placed new sets on the market, stations erupted into action in a number of U.S. cities. Taverns hastened to install television sets; these attracted crowds, especially when boxing or wrestling was on the air (*see* SPORTS—SPORTS AND THE MEDIA). Other programming stirred euphoria: bits of OPERA, ambitious DRAMA, children's programs. In 1947 the opening of Congress was televised for the first time. A new "zoom lens," moving rapidly in on details, added excitement to sports. RCA introduced its new color system, and advertisers saw it at once as invaluable for COMMERCIALS. With color, surgeons began to see value in telecasts of surgical operations. In 1948 a new excitement galvanized the industry: millions watched television coverage of the Republican and Democratic parties' national conventions, both held in Philadelphia because it was linked by coaxial cable with New York, Washington, D.C., and a number of other cities where television was operative. Harry S. Truman, sitting in the White House, became the first U.S. president to see himself nominated on television.

But once again a roadblock appeared. The Federal Communications Commission, having licensed some hundred stations, called a freeze on station licensing and set manufacture. It wanted to review its policies and allocations. As it did so the Korean War broke out and became a reason for continuing the freeze, which lasted from 1948 to 1952. It seemed a catastrophic setback, but the freeze held unexpected implications for television.

The licensing of stations had been haphazard. By 1948 New York and Los Angeles, each with seven stations, saw television in full operation. But many other cities had no television. Thus there were television cities and nontelevision cities—a situation that constituted a laboratory for observing the impact of the new medium. In the nontelevision cities, radio listening, cinema attendance, LIBRARY usage, and other indexes of media use remained largely unchanged; not so in television cities. Here economic earthquakes took place. By 1951 most television cities reported a 20 to 40 percent drop in motion picture attendance. Areas well provided with television witnessed waves of movie theater closings: 70 closings in eastern Pennsylvania, 134 in southern California, 55 in metropolitan New York. Sports events saw a drop in attendance in most television cities. Public libraries reported a drop in BOOK circulation. A comedy series starring Sid Caesar and Imogene Coca, "Your Show of Shows," became a Saturday night terror to restaurateurs. Television had briefly drawn people to taverns; now it kept them at home.

What all this foreshadowed for television was that the lifting of the freeze, whenever it should come, would set off an extraordinary boom. It began in 1953 and soon involved much more than was anticipated. HOLLYWOOD had, since the beginnings of television, sought to exorcise it. In Hollywood films, television sets were never seen; the medium did not exist. The major studios had withheld their pictures and STARS from television. The few features that had appeared on the tube were largely of foreign origin or were westerns like those of Hopalong Cassidy or Gene Autry (*see* WESTERN, THE) from fringe companies outside the Hollywood oligopoly. A number of unemployed film actors had launched television projects of their own; the extraordinary success of one of these, Lucille Ball's "I Love Lucy" (Figure 5), was for studio heads a sobering phenomenon. Some began to feel that history was passing them by.

In 1954 Jack Warner, who earlier had led the motion picture industry into sound, again broke the united front by negotiating an agreement with the American Broadcasting Company under which his studio would produce filmed series for commercial television. His "Cheyenne" series brought a stampede of similar projects from other studios: "Wyatt Earp," "Gunsmoke," "Death Valley Days," and others. Along with these came detective series like "Perry Mason" and family series like "Father Knows Best." While embarking on series production the studios did more. Their backlogs of old features, once considered of dubious value, were suddenly unloaded for television use. In 1955 RKO released 740 of its old features to television, earning $25 million in the process. Similar

Figure 5. *(Television History—Early Period)* Desi Arnaz and Lucille Ball in a scene from the television show "I Love Lucy." The Bettmann Archive, Inc.

actions brought hundreds of Twentieth Century-Fox, Columbia Pictures, and Universal features into the television market, followed later by still others.

These actions brought upheaval to the young television industry. The schedules of most U.S. stations had been at least three-quarters live; suddenly they became three-quarters film. Station staffs, which had grown rapidly in size, were pared. Countless performers headed for Hollywood, hoping for a chance to survive. The industry had become centralized via film.

Commercial sponsors welcomed the shift. Hollywood telefilm series, based on continuing formulas, involved fewer controversial problems than the earlier live dramas, which were often social-problem plays in the Ibsen tradition. Hollywood favored action-adventure series, the pursuit of evildoers. Sponsorship of such a project linked a company with an attractive, continuing hero, who might also be available for the company's commercials. *See* SPONSOR.

But the ramifications were even wider. The Hollywood move took into account that television, firmly established in the United States and Britain, was about to begin in scores of other countries. All could be program markets.

Bibliography. Erik Barnouw, *Tube of Plenty: The Evolution of American Television,* New York, 1975; Asa Briggs, *The BBC: The First Fifty Years,* New York, 1985; Timothy Green, *The Universal Eye: The World of Television,* New York, 1972.

ERIK BARNOUW

2. GLOBAL DEVELOPMENT

In the mid-twentieth century television was poised for worldwide DIFFUSION. Having in two decades—the 1930s and 1940s—emerged from experimental beginnings to become a fixture in Britain and the United States, it would in two more decades become a world medium.

Developments came with startling speed. Industrial nations that had participated in prewar experiments could be expected to make early starts in postwar television; they included Japan, Canada, Australia, and a number of European nations. Less expected was a burst of activity from other nations.

In Latin America, Mexico, Cuba, and Brazil led the way, all launching television operations in 1950. They were followed rapidly by others. By the end of that decade eighteen Latin American nations had some form of television, with more on the verge. Asia virtually kept pace, with the Philippines starting in 1953. By the mid-1960s eighteen Asian nations had entered the television age; others were planning to. Africa was not far behind. Algeria began in 1956, Egypt in 1960. By the end of the 1960s fifteen African nations had made a start in television. Half the world's nations had by now joined the procession.

However modest the first step, it seemed momentous to many—especially the new nations—and also costly. Rationales pointed to television as a key to national development (*see* DEVELOPMENT COMMUNICATION) and public enlightenment. Television was often pictured as an electronic blackboard, creating a nationwide CLASSROOM. But the symbolism of the event was perhaps more crucial. The step into television seemed a leap into a new and better world. Meanwhile, those who took it had to face a further decision: what kind of television?

Issues. Inevitably they looked to the experience of those who had done the main pioneering: Great Britain and the United States (see section 1, above). Yet these had sharply contrasting broadcasting traditions. In Britain television had developed as a public service mission under unified control, financed from license fees levied on set owners. U.S. television had grown out of a free-market tradition, with stations privately owned, financed by ADVERTISING, and with minimal GOVERNMENT REGULATION.

Broadcasting authorities in most countries tended to look on the rapid growth of commercial television in the United States with a mixture of awe and disdain. Most—particularly in Asia and Africa—did not consider it a model for their own television development. They preferred a centralized system more along British lines, one that could be readily integrated into their existing RADIO broadcasting structures, which were in most cases government controlled. In 1954, however, the United States and Britain added confusion to the situation, each adjusting its system in the direction of the other. In the United States the first not-for-profit television station, KUHT in Houston, went on the air on one of the channels set aside by the Federal Communications Commission (FCC) for educational use. The new "ETV stations" had little immediate impact; plagued by money problems and unfavorable channel allocations, they needed more than a dozen years to organize themselves into the Public Broadcasting Service (PBS), linking a nationwide lineup of stations.

Also in 1954 Britain authorized a commercial system to operate alongside the British Broadcasting Corporation (BBC) television service. The step caused surprise. Three years earlier the BBC had received a new ten-year charter, reaffirming its MONOPOLY status. A legislative inquiry had considered alternatives, including a dual private/public system, but the committee was impressed with the BBC's record of service and passed over any idea of subjecting it to competition, which it was felt might lower standards.

Figure 1. *(Television History—Global Development)* Ladakh, India, 1985. © 1986 Rosalind Solomon.

The new charter was a vote of confidence in the BBC. Shortly thereafter, however, a determined campaign to authorize commercial television was mounted by British financial and industrial interests. The BBC monopoly was attacked on both philosophic and pragmatic grounds. The alleged tepid quality of the BBC's programs was stressed. It was even charged that they were used by mental hospitals to soothe patients. Commercial television, it was argued, would be livelier, more diverse. Whatever the merit of these arguments, the campaign succeeded. Legislation creating the Independent Broadcasting Authority was enacted by Parliament in July 1954. The new commercial stations soon won wide popularity, setting up a determined public/private competition.

The policy trail. This British decision had wide influence on the evolution of global television patterns during the next two decades. Dozens of countries moved toward mixed public/commercial systems of one sort or another. Some countries, such as Canada, modified their regulations to permit commercial competition with the governmental broadcasting system. In many others a government monopoly was retained, but time slots were made available for advertising, not only to defray mounting costs of television but also to accommodate commercial pressures. In Latin America commercial use of the medium had received strong backing from the start, as most governments proved willing to let private entrepreneurs develop nationwide systems; foreign corporate investments, especially U.S. investments, played a part in this, and rapid development was stimulated by it. In Mexico, which led the way, three companies were soon in strenuous competition. It brought all three close to bankruptcy, but they merged to form the profitable Telesistema Mexicano, which became the dominant national network. The government retained channels for public uses; it also held an option on time periods on the commercial system but did not attempt to compete with it. Comparable mixed systems evolved in other Latin American countries, as well as in several Asian and Middle Eastern countries, notably the Philippines and Iran, again stimulated by substantial foreign investments.

Many other governments, while accepting the role of advertising, were reluctant for both political and cultural reasons to give free rein to private entrepreneurs. In Italy television began as a monopoly under Radiotelevisione Italiana (RAI), a joint-stock company controlled by the government. It became one of the first European systems to experiment with limited advertising to supplement revenues from audience license fees, clustering the commercials in a prime-time period earmarked for the purpose—a practice later adopted by other national television systems. On this basis RAI, in spite of political attacks on the monopoly system, maintained control into the 1970s, when the nation's supreme court declared the RAI monopoly unconstitutional. This resulted in numerous private stations rushing to the air, in most cases for commercial operation. New legislation ratified the resulting mixed system.

France went through a somewhat similar evolution. In 1958 General Charles de Gaulle became head of state in an atmosphere of political strife. He found in television an ideal platform for promoting his own views and used it in bravura style. On one dramatic occasion, faced with a coup by dissident military officers, he went before the cameras to call for national unity and to warn against cooperation with the coup leaders. It was a unique demonstration of television's PROPAGANDA potential, and de Gaulle had no wish to yield control of it. But opposition to the monopoly was intense and grew more so. It was charged that between 1956 and 1959 French television had not carried a single program about the government's widely unpopular efforts to suppress the nationalist revolt in Algeria. Eventually, in the 1970s, France took steps toward a mixed system.

In Communist countries television policies were fully controlled by political and economic concerns. Like the press, television was seen as a means for guiding a nation toward an envisioned future. Even so, in the earliest television years neither of the Communist world's most powerful figures—Joseph Stalin and Mao Zedong—fully exploited the medium's political possibilities. For almost twenty years Chinese television was limited to a few experimental stations. Only after Mao's death was a concerted effort undertaken to develop a national network.

In the Soviet Union television's usefulness as a government information channel was recognized somewhat earlier. The 1959–1965 Seven-Year Plan gave priority to expanding the national network, setting a goal of 15 million receivers. Television soon won wide popularity, carrying SPORTS, ENTERTAINMENT, and cultural programs interspersed with political messages. Advertising was introduced in the 1960s basically as a form of public service announcement, but it also channeled the distribution of goods, relieving regional shortages as well as surpluses. By the 1970s satellites were being used to expand the network to the remotest parts of the country.

If various major powers were reluctant to give up government monopoly of television, most developing nations were even more so inclined. Leaders of new nations, such as KWAME NKRUMAH of Ghana, saw it as an essential resource in the difficult transition from colonial to national status. It helped to establish the legitimacy of new regimes and to win unity in the face of ethnic and tribal rivalries. For a number of Third World leaders—Gamal Abdel Nasser of Egypt, Fidel Castro of Cuba—it became an ideal platform for charismatic leadership.

Divergences. In a number of countries television developed under special circumstances. In Japan, Nippon Hosai Kyokai (NHK), the government-chartered broadcasting system financed from license fees, had held a monopoly until the U.S. occupation. In 1950 occupation authorities, aware of the role that centralized control had played in the rise of Japanese militarism and imperialist ventures, authorized a competing system based on advertising. Its operations began as the U.S. occupation departed. Vigorous competition followed, similar to that in Britain, with commercial and public systems both showing strength. Television developed with extraordinary speed.

In Germany, too, occupation policies played a formative role. Prevention of centralized control seemed the main issue to the Federal Republic of Germany's occupying powers—the United States, Great Britain, and France—but their solution was different from that adopted in Japan. They mandated a system of separate regional companies, each administered by a *Land,* or state. An impressive tradition of cultural programming developed, which often won viewers in the German Democratic Republic.

The German Democratic Republic, which began under Soviet occupation, developed television on Soviet lines, with the mission of providing an ideological counterweight to the popularity of readily available transmissions from the Federal Republic of Germany. The system became one of the most efficient in eastern Europe, with its own strong tradition of cultural programming. It occasionally broadcast charges against the Federal Republic of Germany's leaders, whom it accused of old links with nazism. A prickly relationship between the two television systems developed, especially in the early years.

In Africa the rush to television in the 1960s did not include South Africa, one of the few major countries holding back. Programming available from abroad—a crucial consideration in launching a new television system—tended to reflect racial customs seen as a threat to apartheid. Such programming would be, in the words of Albert Hertzog, minister of posts and telegraph, "a deadly weapon to undermine the morale of the white man and even to destroy great empires." Various solutions, such as a wired system, were under discussion, but action was still postponed.

The idea of beginning with a wired television system had been adopted in Hong Kong, which in 1957 launched such a system serving the colony's British population. Over-the-air television, with programs in

Chinese as well as English, did not begin until a decade later.

India began cautiously, afraid that television would divert the nation's focus from necessities to luxuries. When its first station was begun in New Delhi in 1959, much of its attention went to educational experiments directed toward villages of the surrounding area. Network operations catering to middle-class urban audiences were finally begun a decade later—with the knowledge that a vast program resource existed in the vaults of India's film industry, the world's most prolific. In the first network years one of the most popular series consisted of compilations of song-and-dance numbers from celebrated Indian film musicals (*see* MUSICAL, FILM—BOMBAY GENRE).

Homogenizing factors. Despite widespread discussion about television's potential for national development, little progress was made in using the medium to that end. A number of pressures propelled the medium in other directions. One was its audience, which was urban centered. Another was the kinds of programs—predominantly U.S. drama series made in HOLLYWOOD—available at low cost to fill hours of program schedules. The costs of maintaining a national television service were staggering for many countries, and such a staple was badly needed. The imports, dubbed into the principal world languages, tended to become the standard goods of television. They were welcomed by program managers, not only because they attracted audiences but also because they readily attracted advertising sponsorship (*see* SPONSOR) and came with gaps designed for COMMERCIALS. The commercials that became available to fill these gaps and bring in needed revenue were often those of international companies that sponsored similar programs elsewhere. The resulting standardization was often deplored and criticized, especially by those concerned with preserving ethnic and national identities, but the economic factor proved a powerful element in furthering a homogenization of television in many parts of the world.

See also AFRICA, TWENTIETH CENTURY; ASIA, TWENTIETH CENTURY; AUSTRALASIA, TWENTIETH CENTURY; ISLAMIC WORLD, TWENTIETH CENTURY; LATIN AMERICA, TWENTIETH CENTURY.

Bibliography. Erik Barnouw, *The Image Empire,* Vol. 3, *A History of Broadcasting in the United States,* New York, 1970; Asa Briggs, *Sound and Vision,* Vol. 4, *The History of Broadcasting in the United Kingdom,* Oxford and New York, 1979; Wilson P. Dizard, *Television: A World View,* Syracuse, N.Y., 1966; Sydney W. Head, *World Broadcasting: A Statistical Analysis,* Philadelphia, 1975; UNESCO, *World Communications: A 200-Country Survey of Press, Radio, Television, and Film,* 5th ed., New York and Paris, 1975.

WILSON P. DIZARD

3. WORLD MARKET STRUGGLES

Global marketing of television ENTERTAINMENT and information via filmed or taped programming represents one of the most significant forms of international communication. Other forms of transborder television communications include programs received across frontiers though not transmitted for that purpose; planned international or regional transmissions (such as Eurovision, Intervision, Nordvision) that provide simultaneous telecasts to participating countries; coverage of special events of all sorts; licensing of program concepts, such as quiz shows, which foreign companies purchase in order to produce their own versions (*see* QUIZ SHOW); and international PROPAGANDA telecasts. Among all these, the sale of filmed and taped programming has assumed a place of special economic and social significance.

The evolution of separate national television systems into an international market of programming consumers did not become important until the late 1950s, by which time all industrialized countries had television broadcasting. However, foreign SYNDICATION of programming is as old as the medium itself. Feature-length motion pictures that had long since completed their runs in cinemas were the earliest material available. Initially motion picture companies believed television would harm their business, and many hesitated to license films for televised exhibition in their own countries. But they did sell their pictures abroad, and consequently some British theatrical films found their way to North American television stations up to the early 1950s.

Another staple product in global syndication is programming made especially for television, such as the series. As late as 1953 three-quarters of network programs in the United States still were broadcast live, and it was not until widespread use of film (and later tape) that syndication could flourish as a global business. In the United States, at least, production shifted from television network studios to motion picture studios. There was a parallel shift in program ownership from commercial sponsors to networks and outside producers. *See* SPONSOR.

The interest of sponsors that owned programs was to persuade viewers to buy products. But the interest of networks and film companies that own programs also is to sell them widely. As in the case of theatrical films, the substantial expense of a television program is incurred in its initial production. A copy of the original represents little additional cost, so the producer has an incentive, especially in a profit-motivated economy, to distribute it broadly. In this way, and apart from aesthetic or cultural considerations, the program is introduced into the flow of trade and becomes a commodity. The program constitutes an investment of capital that the owner seeks to recoup and multiply.

This was a commanding reason to shift to prerecorded programming. It provided opportunities to amortize costs and recyle shows in many markets and to expand profit. The trend toward global centralization of production and distribution was one of the consequences.

Whereas in many countries the television system is structurally and administratively distinct from the theatrical film business, in the United States there is a considerable integration of function, finance, and ownership. Television program production and distribution is just one segment of the filmed entertainment industry, whose companies also have interests in CABLE TELEVISION, recorded music, PUBLISHING, and other fields.

The foreign sale of U.S. television programming followed a pattern established decades earlier for the exportation of U.S. theatrical films. In addition to their sales offices in major markets, the principal companies coordinated their efforts in an export cartel. The Television Program Export Association (TPEA) was incorporated in 1959 under the Webb-Pomerene Export Trade Act (1918), which provides limited antitrust immunity for companies selling overseas. Members were allowed collectively to set prices for foreign sales, allocate markets, and act jointly against foreign trade barriers. The television networks, some major film companies, and important independent producers of that time were TPEA members. The association was dissolved in 1970 for several reasons. The networks had relinquished their roles as program producers and owners; independent producers' shares of programming had diminished, giving them less to export; and the film companies already belonged to the Motion Picture Export Association of America (founded in 1945), whose functions duplicated those of TPEA. The film companies' overseas distribution systems also could handle television programming with little additional overhead cost. *See* MOTION PICTURES—SOUND FILM.

The commercial push by major producers to export exists in tandem with a need in most television systems to import. Original dramatic programs, for example, can be expensive for a television system to produce regularly. Most countries can import a series episode for considerably less than a twentieth of its production cost in the United States—in the case of small nations a minute fraction of production cost (see Table 1). An imported program also may have production values that lend prestige to a television schedule and cannot be readily duplicated with local resources. The comparatively low cost of imports can be an economical way to expand telecasting hours. Indeed, U.S. distributors occasionally have sold episodes at loss-leader prices so that some new foreign systems would be assured of programming. These distributors also were creating a market and establishing their presence in it. The purchase of a particular program (e.g., "Dallas") by television systems may respond to demands by a public whose appetite has been whetted by international publicity. Finally, commercially based systems seek to import programs having a proven ability to attract audiences with demographic characteristics that advertisers want. Proliferation of multinational advertising agencies and corporations selling consumer goods stimulates this practice (*see* ADVERTISING—ADVERTISING AGENCY).

Whereas economic motivations guide international program sales, cultural, political, religious, and linguistic concerns also shape the flow on a global or regional level. But they are of secondary importance when measured by volume or monetary value.

The global circulation of programming has particular characteristics. A UNESCO-sponsored study in 1972 and 1973 found that entertainment was by far the main content and that the flow was predominantly in one direction. A few industrialized capitalist countries were the largest exporters, with the United States the most important. Generally the rest of the world's nations were recipients. Some industrialized nations, such as Australia and Canada, also were net importers. Basically these findings also describe the international circulation of theatrical films. A follow-up study in 1983 revealed that the flow had not changed appreciably. The United States still accounted for most exports; Western Europe and Japan were distant followers. Regional exchange persisted, as among Arab states, and a few countries were important suppliers in other areas, such as Brazil and Mexico in Latin America.

There can be great differences in the kinds of programming selected by various nations. Profit-driven television systems primarily impose commercial criteria, whereas public and government systems can set cultural and social standards. Whatever the guidelines, there are political and ideological ramifications. On a different level, selection criteria may have to do with violence, family relations, divorce, nudity, sex, crime, treatment of the military, and so on.

In the early 1980s U.S. companies were receiving close to $500 million annually from foreign sales of television programming, whereas a decade earlier that market had been worth less than $100 million. Cinemas, however, provide twice as much foreign revenue for these companies as does television. About a quarter of the television program revenue of U.S. companies comes from abroad, but close to half of their cinema revenue is generated in foreign box offices. The worldwide growth of home VIDEO, cable television, and pay television is, however, increasing television earnings at a faster rate.

Although the United States is the leading exporter, its companies buy virtually no foreign material, and what is imported is almost exclusively from English-speaking countries. An exception is Spanish-language

Table 1. World Distribution of U.S. Television Programs

The production cost of a half-hour program (actually shorter by several minutes) is generally $100,000 or more. The U.S. producer hopes to recoup this via the first sponsored network showing in the United States. Revenue from network reruns and worldwide syndication will then represent profit, which can continue for years. Foreign broadcast rights are generally marketed on a country-by-country basis. The 1985–1986 range of prices for various countries, per half-hour episode, was reported as follows by the entertainment newspaper *Variety*. Australia purchases programs on a somewhat different basis and is omitted from *Variety*'s listings. The USSR rarely buys material on a dollar basis, seeking barter transactions. A one-hour program (actually shorter by several minutes) generally brings twice the half-hour price. Feature-film prices are substantially higher but represent a lesser part of the total revenue from television.

Purchaser	*Price range per half-hour episode (in U.S. dollars)*
Algeria	90–100
Argentina	1,000–1,500
Austria	900–1,400
Belgium	1,250–1,750
Bermuda	30–45
Brazil	4,000–6,000
Bulgaria	200–250
Canada	6,000–20,000
Chile	220–375
Colombia	800–1,500
Costa Rica	180–210
Cyprus	30–75
Czechoslovakia	400–600
Denmark	700–900
Dominican Republic	100–150
Ecuador	200–300
Egypt	400–600
El Salvador	75–90
Finland	900–1,000
France	8,500–10,000
German Democratic Republic	750–1,500
Germany, Federal Republic of	8,500–18,000
Gibraltar	40–94
Greece	700–750
Guatemala	100–125
Haiti	50–75
Honduras	85–90
Hong Kong	600–850
Hungary	200–300
India	500–600
Iran	500–750
Iraq	350–500
Ireland	300–350
Israel	400–500
Italy	6,000–18,000
Jamaica	80–95
Japan	6,000–7,000
Kenya	45–60
Kuwait	450–500
Lebanon	175–200
Luxembourg	1,200–1,500
Malta	45–50
Mexico	1,000–2,000
Monaco	400–450
Netherlands Antilles	55–85
Netherlands	2,000–2,250
Nicaragua	75–85
Nigeria	1,000–1,500
Norway	900–1,000
Panama	200–215
Peru	250–300
Poland	150–375
Portugal	215–500
Puerto Rico	1,100–1,250
Romania	200–450
Saudi Arabia	650–800
South Africa	1,250–1,800
Spain	1,500–2,500
Sweden	2,100–2,500
Switzerland	1,500–2,000
Syria	70–275
Trinidad and Tobago	130–140
United Kingdom	12,000–14,000
Uruguay	150–175
USSR	120–300
Venezuela	800–1,000
Yugoslavia	175–500
Zambia	100–115
Zimbabwe (Rhodesia)	100–125

programming, which is not directed to the Anglo audience. British commercial and public television companies aggressively market in the United States, but their sales successes have been limited to dramatic programs and documentaries—especially nature documentaries—whose acquisition for public television has been underwritten by major corporations. Still, British cash receipts, small as they are, depend heavily on sales in the United States. As a market for foreign producers and television systems, the United States is essentially closed. Although there are no government-imposed limitations on imports, the commercial system sets its own de facto quota of 100 percent U.S.-made.

Domination of the world's cinema markets by U.S. films prompted many nations to establish trade barriers against them. This pattern has been carried into television. Even though many restrictions apply to imported material regardless of nationality, the burden falls mainly on U.S. exports because they constitute the largest share of the international flow. Economic, social, political, and cultural reasons have been advanced to support these restraints.

Because U.S. companies do not reciprocate by purchasing foreign programming, some nations feel justified in limiting imports of U.S. material. The need to conserve critical supplies of hard currency for buying essential goods also can lead to restricting imports of television entertainment. Creative and technical workers claim they would have more employment if their national television systems imported less programming and devoted resources to original domestic production. Young people, too, would have an incentive to seek careers in television and motion pictures.

Some regulations favoring locally produced programs are based on the conviction that national culture needs to be preserved and that harnessing mass media can help. Furthermore, television is just one of many cultural vehicles, and indigenous productions are felt to deserve encouragement and subsidization just as do concert halls and live theater. Restrictions also are premised on the belief that without them control over television content, and particularly the use of new technology, would gravitate to foreign hands and decisions would be opposed to local needs. Restraints on foreign companies, then, serve to protect present and future prospects for domestic industries. Another justification is that foreign television material displays values and morality—for example, materialism, brutality, competitiveness—that conflict with those of the importing country. Finally, restrictions imposed by a government may stem directly from demands of its own private sector program producers who want a share of the home market.

These positions find expression in official and unofficial rules instituted by television systems themselves or the state. In Britain, for example, a longstanding benchmark is that foreign material should be limited to about 14 percent of hours telecast. Other major markets have similar guidelines. In Brazil imported television programming must be dubbed in local laboratories. Some countries restrict importations of finished goods so that the final assembly of videotape cassettes has to be done locally. Still other countries impose substantial duties on imported programming or regulate the exportation of revenue.

Problems associated with the international circulation of programs are part of a broader debate about national sovereignty, cultural domination, and media imperialism. They are expressed in calls for a NEW INTERNATIONAL INFORMATION ORDER. The complexities of positions are oversimplified by calling this a struggle between north and south, or developed and developing countries, or capitalist, socialist, and nonaligned states. As far as mass media, and particularly television, are concerned, there is desire to achieve a more balanced global circulation of material and to redress the unidirectional flow.

The U.S. exporters of television programming, speaking through the U.S. government, have urged a "free flow of communication," unimpeded by barriers to their business and unencumbered by quotas and subsidies, which they perceive as market distortions that favor foreign competitors. The U.S. industry's free-trade position obviously represents its own economic interests. The government's position on these matters is developed in consultation with major U.S. communication companies, including those in the television programming business.

A particular point for debate is new technology that feeds into the home television set. Some observers have said that introducing videocassettes, cable, and pay television into a country would offer indigenous companies and artists an opportunity to expand their audiences and to carve out a market separate from cinema and conventional television, which often are dominated by foreign material. What has happened, though, is that new media have become another outlet for imports, especially from the United States.

The use of satellites to transmit programs directly to homes (Direct Broadcast Satellite, or DBS), and thus to bypass a national television system, poses further threats to national sovereignty (*see* SATELLITE). The major suppliers of programming are eager to have this medium developed, particularly with advertiser support. In 1972, though, a UNESCO declaration established the principle that a state planning to start DBS service should receive permission from receiving states before transmitting programs to their peoples. A similar resolution was adopted by the United Nations General Assembly, with the United States casting the only negative vote.

Bibliography. Robin Day Glenn, *Legal Issues Affecting Licensing of TV Program Material in the European Economic Community,* Washington, D.C., 1983; Thomas Guback and Tapio Varis, *Transnational Communication and Cultural Industries,* Paris, 1982; Chin-Chuan Lee, *Media Imperialism Reconsidered,* Beverly Hills, Calif., 1980; Armand Mattelart, *Multinational Corporations and the Control of Culture: The Ideological Apparatuses of Imperialism* (Multinationales et systèmes de communication), trans. by Michael Chanan, Sussex, Eng., 1979; Kaarle Nordenstreng and Tapio Varis, *Television Traffic—A One-Way Street?* Paris, 1974; William H. Read, *America's Mass Media Merchants,* Baltimore, Md., 1976; Herbert Schiller, *Mass Communications and American Empire,* New York, 1969; Alan Wells, *Picture-Tube Imperialism?* Maryknoll, N.Y., 1972.

THOMAS GUBACK

TELEVISION NEWS

Programs designated as news but tending at the same time to serve entertainment, information, EDUCATION, promotion, and PROPAGANDA functions. News programs are included in the offerings of most television systems worldwide, generally on a daily scheduled basis. Scheduled programs may be superseded or supplemented for events considered of transcendent significance. Although news programs are broadcast under sharply contrasting economic arrangements and within diverse political systems and constraints (*see* TELEVISION HISTORY—GLOBAL DEVELOPMENT), they have assumed throughout the world surprisingly homogeneous formats.

Formats and Processes

In its early stage of development television news generally consisted of bulletins read by an announcer at a desk, but the trend has been to move rapidly toward more complex formats. News programs may be anywhere from fifteen minutes to an hour in length, with discrete "stories" illustrated by still or moving pictures, sometimes with background music, stitched together by an "anchor" person or persons (male or female or a duo) displayed in a specially designed studio setting. They may also call in reporters, whose reports may already be on edited videotape or film or who may report live from some scene of action. The called-in reports, whether taped, filmed, or live, may be products of the television system itself or of other television systems anywhere in the world and may have been relayed by transport, cable, or SATELLITE. A modern television news program can thus be considered the end product of international industrial processes involving innumerable manufacturers, distributors, and retail outlets buying, selling, and exchanging the raw materials of news and served by armies of personnel at every level.

Each morning camera and sound operators as well as reporters in places around the world swarm out to begin the process. Pictures of events, expected and unexpected, are trapped in the camera eye. Some are for local use, but quantities of pictures and related data also go to collecting centers or world bureaus, where they are edited, refined to suit the values and tastes of particular groups or regions, and then transmitted to the headquarters of subscribing networks or local stations on all continents. There they are further edited, polished, and assembled, together with material collected at national and local production centers, into news packages of requisite lengths for broadcast at designated time periods.

In this international traffic the final selection of program elements is made by a station or network presenting a newscast. Inevitably selections differ, reflecting divergent needs, tastes, taboos, pressures, and doctrines. Nations with very different interests may use the same footage for different purposes. But the process and formats are similar, although tone and style of presentation may differ. Television news in the United States tends to be snappy, sensational, crackling with electronic graphics. The style in most other countries is more formal and slower paced.

Dominant influences. The cost of television news is high, in personnel and especially in equipment, tending to give the richest nations a leading role in the global enterprise. Television networks in the United States, the United Kingdom, Japan, and other leading industrialized nations maintain bureaus in selected cities where news can be expected to happen or from which camera crews and correspondents can be quickly dispatched elsewhere. Events in or near these cities inevitably tend to get more detailed coverage than events in remote regions, such as areas of Africa or Latin America.

The dominant networks, in spite of their own coverage of news happenings through numerous foreign bureaus, also rely heavily on the four leading international NEWS AGENCIES, which supply news copy via wire and have a history antedating television: Associated Press (AP), United Press International (UPI), Reuters, and to a lesser extent Agence France-Presse (AFP). Night and day these major wire services periodically send out "budgets" or announcements of stories coming up; client editors and producers, depending on the wire editors to make newsworthy judgments, may choose to follow up the wire leads in their own television news formats. AP and UPI also monopolize the world Wirephoto market: the first still pictures of air crashes, floods, and other disasters reach most of the world's television screens via their Wirephoto services.

After World War II three major international organizations specializing in gathering television news came into being. Visnews, whose main shareholder is the British news agency Reuters, has headquarters in London. Worldwide Television News, whose principal shareholder is the ABC Television Network, is headquartered in the United States. CBS News, which gathers television news worldwide for its regular newscasts in the United States, also syndicates excess amounts to other broadcasters (*see* SYNDICATION).

The largest supplier is Visnews, which has its own staff of camera operators, reporters, and free-lance "stringers" distributed throughout the world. Visnews serves the NBC Television Network in the United States and several hundred other clients around the world; it provides pictures edited especially for individual customers. Because its national subscribers often have conflicting cultural attitudes and political values, Visnews asserts: "We don't take sides; we take pictures." The flow of news stories from Visnews to NBC is accompanied by a reverse flow: NBC provides pictures for Visnews, which the latter includes in its service to worldwide customers, along with material from the BBC and from the Japan Broadcasting Corporation (NHK). Visnews also has a two-way contract with Tass, the Soviet Union's news agency, for supplying and receiving pictorial material.

Format variations. The national evening newscasts in many countries are carried by a network of stations, but there may also be local news programs assembled by individual stations. These individual stations may draw on the same resources but are more likely to stress local accidents, crimes, fires, sports, weather, and reports of personal tragedies and triumphs. In the United States there is a trend, echoed in a number of other countries, toward "happy talk," empty badinage by the local news staff contributing little to the news but reinforcing the staff's familiar, cheery public images. By way of contrast the United States also has Cable News Network (CNN), a cable system that operates two all-news channels, one of which repeats headline news every half hour.

For extraordinary events—assassinations of heads of state, heroic funerals, royal weddings, coronations, and other occasions with mythic dimensions—normal time schedules are everywhere set aside. On such occasions television news may serve to give diverse audiences a common feeling of national identity and unity.

Staff. Playing a key role in television news packages, giving coherence to varied contents, are the anchorpersons. They are the visible messengers who bring the story to the public, their personalities acting as filters. Their inflections, gestures, and expressions can play a crucial part, intentionally or unintentionally, in cueing and channeling audience reactions to news items (*see* FACIAL EXPRESSION; GESTURE). They may become major celebrities, courted by politicians. In the early days of television, anchors generally had a journalism background, as did Walter Cronkite, whose dominance of CBS news programming lasted two and a half decades. Charisma appears to become an increasingly important consideration in the selection of anchors. Anchorpersons occasionally go into the field to cover a story so as to maintain credibility as reporters, but they often attract more attention than the events being covered.

Behind the anchor are the producer, the assignment editor, and the innumerable other functionaries needed to assemble the modern television news package. Preparing the day's work, they survey available news stories, and in a manner similar to that of the producer of a variety show they "routine" the structure of the coming program. As "lead" they choose the event best calculated to catch the viewer's attention. They end generally on a reassuring human-interest story. The final product is the result of the daily, hourly, and often minutes-before-airtime BARGAINING of decision makers working under pressure amid complex circumstances—harried "social historians in a hurry."

Issues

"The news," a perishable commodity, is extruded from the assembly line under the constraints of costs, cultural biases (conscious or unconscious), and numerous and diverse harassments. The need to fill prescheduled time periods, awareness of audience ratings (*see* RATING SYSTEMS: RADIO AND TELEVISION), uncertainties relating to the use of official information (*see* SECRECY), in commercial systems the shadow of sponsors (*see* SPONSOR), in the reporting of some disputes the possibility of LIBEL suits, and in all systems the pressures of GOVERNMENT REGULATION (in the form of licensing systems in some countries, of direct CENSORSHIP in others) further bedevil the manufacturer of the final product. The compression of the news into short bursts to capture and hold the fragile attention span of news consumers who absorb information night and day not only from television but from other sources as well, together with the competition for the viewer's eye and ear, compels reporters and editors of television news to dramatize, personalize, and fragment the happenings they are purporting to report objectively—in short, to shape the events they are reporting as much as to mirror them.

Television news is selective. It tells stories drawn from the real world, but in the selection process and in the narration it emphasizes conflict, officialdom, celebrity; it appeals to the senses, to feeling instead of analysis. All this is done in order to grasp and continue to hold the attention of television viewers, who frequently do not give their exclusive notice to the receiving set but engage in other actions such as eating, conversing, or reading while watching the screen.

In capitalist, Communist, and nonaligned nations alike television news tends to support and preserve the status quo, to ignore, suppress, downplay, or deflect dissident views except when these obtrude dramatically on the news horizon. Indeed there are social scientists who assert that in all countries, under all government authorities, television news (like all media) is a form of social management, a media construct, an illusion that meets little resistance as viewers are increasingly dependent on television for their view of the contemporary world.

That most viewers derive from television their picture of world events has been shown by many polls—for instance, in the United States since 1963 by the Roper polls. This influence is generally ascribed to television news, but television drama also deals with the contemporary world, often stressing international intrigue, ESPIONAGE, crime, TERRORISM, and covert war. Though classified as entertainment, such drama may also function for many viewers—particularly the young—as a kind of journalism. In most countries television fiction and nonfiction tend to give a unified impression, and their practitioners may consciously or unconsciously take cues from one another.

Television news professionals tend to reject, often heatedly, the criticisms leveled against them. They argue that a real, objective world is "out there," and though they make their selections of what they report on the basis of "gut instinct" or "the news perspective" and also admit to dramatizing the news, they nevertheless insist that they report the news of the world accurately, fairly, and with integrity. *See also* ETHICS, MEDIA.

A frequent observation made about television news is that it focuses on events mainly when they explode into crises. Festering problems are ignored until they burst into VIOLENCE. The stress is on results, which may be dramatic, and seldom on causes, which are less so. In consequence many major events take the public by surprise, and their meaning remains shadowy.

Historical Context

Television news scarcely existed in the 1920s and 1930s, when pioneer television ventures were conducted in a handful of countries (*see* TELEVISION HISTORY—EARLY PERIOD), with occasional experiments in news programming. Resuming after World War II, television news groped for its appropriate form. Radio-style bulletins read by announcers were clearly not a solution, so television turned for help to the theatrical NEWSREEL. During the 1950s newsreel staffs migrated rapidly into television, and most major theatrical newsreels passed out of existence, with remnants surviving in some countries as government services.

Television news became enormously influential during the late 1950s—in the United States, especially through the work of Edward R. Murrow in "See It Now" and, later, of Cronkite as perennial "CBS Evening News" anchor. When Cronkite called for an end to the war in Vietnam during one of his 1968 programs, it is said to have influenced President Lyndon Johnson not to run for reelection. An overt expression of this sort by a television anchor was rare, and the act therefore had unusual impact. Television journalists and politicians have come to live in a wary, symbiotic relationship. *See* GOVERNMENT-MEDIA RELATIONS.

The 1980s were a turbulent period for television news. Expanded satellite delivery systems, new forms of CABLE TELEVISION, the explosive rise of VIDEO, and the growing influence of the computer (*see* COMPUTER: IMPACT) created extraordinary new opportunities, which were complicated by new organizational alignments, corporate takeovers, privatization of government monopolies, and increased competition on a global scale. As news services continued to expand worldwide, developing countries shared the fruits via various forms of syndication. But the materials they received to fill their news programming reflected mainly the concerns of the suppliers and their world. This was one of the factors behind Third World demands, reiterated during the 1970s and 1980s in various forums, for a NEW INTERNATIONAL INFORMATION ORDER and for a new look at SPECTRUM allocations and procedures. Such issues seemed unlikely to be soon resolved.

Television news remains for social scientists a compelling, puzzling genre. Backed by global, transnational systems, it is flexible enough to yield endless national and local variations. Thought of as journalism, the final result seems rather a form of THEATER, enacted daily in hundreds of versions, each with a self-promoting momentum. Most viewers assess the validity of a news broadcast mainly by what they have learned from television itself via earlier broadcasts. And the newscasters, too, are by now a generation raised on television and imbued with its established performing standards. Television news has become, in effect, a PERFORMANCE genre.

See also DEVELOPMENT COMMUNICATION; MONOPOLY.

Bibliography. William Adams and Fay Schreibman, eds., *Television Network News,* Washington, D.C., 1978; David L. Altheide, *Creating Reality: How TV News Distorts Events,* New York, 1976; Robert M. Batscha, *Foreign Affairs News and the Broadcast Journalist,* New York, 1975; W. Lance Bennett, *News, the Politics of Illusion,* New York, 1983; W. Phillips Davison, *Mass Communications and Conflict Resolution: The Role of the Information Media in the Advancement of International Understanding,* New York, 1974; Anthony Smith, *The Shadow in the Cave,* Urbana, Ill., and London, 1973; Jeremy Tunstall, *The Media Are American,* New York and London, 1977.

ROBERT LEWIS SHAYON

TERRORISM

An attempt to bring about political change through VIOLENCE, usually in the form of bombings, assassinations, and kidnappings, directed at intimidating a population or government into granting demands. The violence is frequently perpetrated in an indiscriminate fashion, with the victims themselves having little or no connection to the political issues, all of which enhances the fear on which terrorism thrives. As a form of political violence, terrorism is unique in its reliance on the PROPAGANDA value of the act of violence itself. It can be said, then, that terrorists commit acts of violence as a means of communication. Through violence terrorists seek to create a climate of fear and simultaneously to direct international attention to their cause. Acts of terrorism are generally of limited military or strategic value and are best analyzed as political dramas organized for the purpose of getting publicity. The fact that terrorists seem to design their violence to attract media attention has made the role of the media one of the major controversies in the general study of terrorism.

Varieties of terrorism. *Terrorism* as a phenomenon is frequently confused with *state terrorism.* The latter generally refers to the use of violence by a government against its own people to create an atmosphere of fear and intimidation so that the government's rule and authority will not be challenged. Although there are similarities between terrorism and state terrorism, the intellectual, philosophical, and conceptual approaches to these two phenomena render them distinct subjects. This becomes readily apparent when the topic is approached from the perspective of communication. States that use terrorism to attain political acquiescence attempt to conceal such acts from the media. Not only is the act itself more important than the publicity generated about it, but the occurrence of the act is in fact something the state wants to conceal from the scrutiny of world opinion. In contrast, terrorism conducted by nonstate actors—groups out of power—is generally designed explicitly for its attention-getting effects.

State terrorism is not synonymous with *state-sponsored terrorism.* State-sponsored terrorism refers to the sponsorship of a terrorist group or action by a nation-state. The sponsorship is frequently difficult to prove and is almost always denied by the state involved. Even the seemingly obvious issue of what sponsorship means is itself controversial. Some states openly provide arms, training, and logistical support to groups that other states call terrorists. When the support is overt, the sponsoring state will deny that the support is anything other than legitimate military assistance to a group engaged in a war of national liberation. Most state sponsorship of terrorism is covert, and the media can rarely cut through the layers that separate sponsor from client.

As a type of political violence, terrorism is best understood by comparing it to other forms of political violence. The form of political violence any group chooses is a function of the amount of popular support and military power it possesses. A group with substantial popular support and with military power roughly equivalent to the group it wishes to dislodge will engage in civil war. A group with somewhat less power will engage in irregular or guerrilla warfare. A group with still less power will engage in sporadic riots and mass demonstrations (*see* DEMONSTRATION). The form of political violence found at the bottom of this power hierarchy is terrorism.

Terrorism is the political violence of the weak, of those who lack either the military strength or the popular support to engage in more intense forms of political violence. Terrorism is as much a manipulation of POLITICAL SYMBOLS as it is a form of political violence. Terrorists seek to compensate for their political weaknesses by creating the illusion of power through dramatic episodes that are designed to draw a disproportionate amount of attention on the part of the popular media. Thus terrorism is to a large extent a mixture of political propaganda and political THEATER. Terrorists want a lot of people watching, listening, and questioning.

Media coverage of terrorist acts. Because terrorist acts are frequently undertaken for dramatic effect, the media face difficult ethical and professional problems in deciding how to report these events. The media must report the news without becoming part of the news. Yet the terrorists have acted with the hope of using media exposure to influence both the public perception of the event and the climate of political opinion. The media must decide how to respond to what are legitimate, newsworthy events without becoming part of the process that encourages those events to occur. Some critics have argued that the events themselves should not be reported or should be reported differently. Defenders of the media reply that terrorism was practiced long before the existence of electronic or even print media. The Zealots and the Sicarii of Jerusalem in the first century C.E. and the Assassins (Ismailis Nizari) active in Persia and Syria from 1090 to 1275 committed acts of terrorism and gained wide attention. They made themselves known by murdering prominent people, usually on holy days, in public or sacred areas amid large numbers of onlookers. The events themselves were usually significant enough to generate reports and discussion of their occurrence. Even today, if the media ignored terrorism the terrorists could simply escalate their acts of terror until they could no longer be ignored.

In the reporting of ongoing terrorist events the media have at times become the eyes and ears of the terrorists by reporting in-progress police procedures, perhaps risking the safety of victims. Dramatic episodes have tempted the media to capture all the excitement of what is happening, sometimes without regard for the possible effects on victims. The other concern about media coverage of terrorism is the issue of whether the media are providing a forum for terrorist propaganda. Media interviews with terrorists have at times seemed less than newsworthy. A media interview with a terrorist has been described by critics as a situation ripe for exploitation and one in which blood is frequently spilled as payment for media access. For their part the media assert that terrorism is news and that journalists have a societal obligation to report the news. A media interview with a terrorist may provide the terrorist with a forum for propaganda, but this result, some argue, is no different from what is likely to occur in a media interview with a government official.

There is some consensus that the media's coverage of terrorism requires neither new ethical standards nor new guidelines but the adherence to well-known and proven professional procedures. When those procedures are questioned, most experts still agree that the media and not government should be the final arbiter of the role of the media in a free society. Nonetheless, in some democracies threatened by terrorism societal perceptions of media abuse coupled with concerns for public security have produced legislation severely limiting the media's access to news. The balancing of freedom of the press with freedom from fear is one of the difficulties that terrorists present to democratic societies.

See also ETHICS, MEDIA; RADIO, INTERNATIONAL; TELEVISION NEWS.

Bibliography. Richard Clutterbuck, *The Media and Political Violence,* London, 1981; Abraham H. Miller, *Terrorism and Hostage Negotiations,* Boulder, Colo., 1980; idem, ed., *Terrorism, the Media and the Law,* Dobbs Ferry, N.Y., 1982; Dan Nimmo and James E. Combs, *Nightly Horrors: Crisis Coverage by Television Network News,* Knoxville, Tenn., 1985; Philip Schlesinger, Graham Murdock, and Philip Elliot, *Televising "Terrorism": Political Violence in Popular Culture,* London, 1983; Alex P. Schmid, *Political Terrorism: A Research Guide to Concepts, Theories, Data Bases, and Literature,* Amsterdam and New Brunswick, N.J., 1983, 1984; Alex P. Schmid and Janny de Graff, *Violence as Communication: Insurgent Terrorism and the Western News Media,* Beverly Hills, Calif., 1982.

ABRAHAM H. MILLER

TESTIMONY

How people describe events they have observed plays a role in many communication processes. Testimony often serves as a basis for belief and action. In civil and criminal law cases, in which questions of liability or guilt often hinge on eyewitness testimony, its nature is a particularly crucial matter and is the focus of this discussion (*see* LAW AND COMMUNICATION).

Eyewitness Testimony

The term *eyewitness testimony* is not necessarily restricted to matters that have been observed visually. An eyewitness might testify about what words he or she heard another person utter or whether a telephone threat was in the voice of a particular person. Although the latter is often called earwitness testimony, the term eyewitness testimony applies generally to any testimony by a person who experienced an event directly through one of the five human senses. Having been an eyewitness to some event that has criminal or civil evidentiary implications, the eyewitness is likely to be asked explicitly to recount the event at least twice before the trial: once or more during police investigations and again at a preliminary hearing. At a preliminary hearing or any subsequent trial the eyewitness gives testimony under a sworn oath to tell the truth. Usually the matter of truth versus motivated DECEPTION is not at issue in eyewitness testimony, but issues of accuracy versus inaccuracy of the eyewitness's memory frequently are of concern.

Modern psychological theory describes memory as a process that involves the acquisition, storage, and retrieval of information. The human memory process operates differently from a videotape system in several respects. A VIDEO system can replay the recorded event in a relatively faithful manner. Unlike a video system, the human eye does not attend to all that appears in its view but instead is selective. This selectivity in human PERCEPTION is based on the interests and biases of the human observer and is influenced by the dynamic features of the event. In a human observer, unlike a video system, attention failure or common forgetting can result in gaps in memory, and these gaps may be filled in later by inferences, guesses, or externally provided information.

In criminal and civil cases courts of law depend heavily on eyewitness accounts of past events to help reconstruct the facts. When an eyewitness testifies that she or he saw a person commit a crime or cause an accident, the testimonial evidence is considered direct evidence. A witness's testimony that she or he saw a person in the neighborhood where a crime occurred earlier is considered circumstantial evidence in that the trier of fact (judge or jury) must make additional inferences in order to reach a judgment of guilt. In either case the trier of fact must decide how accurate the eyewitness's testimony is likely to be.

Historically courts have assumed that jurors are fully capable of deciding when to weight eyewitness testimony heavily and when to discount it. In the early 1900s, however, some experimental psychologists expressed their disagreement with this assumption. As early as 1903 German psychologist Louis William Stern was qualified by German courts to give expert testimony on the subject of eyewitness accuracy. In 1908 U.S. psychologist Hugo Münsterberg strongly attacked the assumption that the judge or juror is capable of judging eyewitness accuracy. Münsterberg's contention, expressed in his book *On the Witness Stand,* was sharply counterargued by U.S. legal scholar John H. Wigmore. The years from approximately 1920 to the mid-1970s resulted in little further development by experimental psychologists on the issue of eyewitness testimony.

In the mid-1970s psychologists began to reexamine the issue. The work was clearly needed. In Great Britain in 1976 a government-funded review of identification evidence headed and authored by the Honourable Lord Patrick Devlin concluded that the psychological literature was scant but that there were important issues of reliability. An explosion of research then emerged from laboratories around the world, primarily in the United States, Canada, and Great Britain. This research gave the study of eyewitness testimony a new respect and visibility within psychology. As the data base grew, many jurisdictions in the United States, Canada, and Australia began to allow eyewitness experts to testify in cases dealing with eyewitness testimony.

Psychological studies. Modern experimental research into the accuracy of eyewitness testimony involves presenting people with carefully controlled events using media such as slide sequences, videotapes, or live staged events for which the actual event characteristics are known in detail. In many cases these are simulated crimes, accidents, or other rich and complex events. Following exposure to such events people are tested for their memory. Witnessing and testing conditions are varied systematically to determine the extent to which testimony accuracy depends on characteristics of the event, characteristics of the interval between the event and later testing, and characteristics of the testing. Research experiments show clearly that the accuracy of eyewitness testimony cannot be described independently of the particular witnessing and testing conditions. Within this framework of considering the witnessing and testing conditions, some general conclusions can be reached.

In terms of witnessing factors, witnesses are more accurate under the following circumstances:

1. Their exposure time is longer rather than shorter.
2. The events they witness are less rather than more violent.
3. At the time of the event they were not undergoing extreme stress or fright.
4. They are generally free from biased expectations.
5. They are asked to report on salient aspects of an event rather than peripheral aspects.

In terms of testing conditions, witnesses are more accurate under the following circumstances:

1. They are tested after a short time has passed rather than a long time.
2. They have not been exposed to any biasing information after the event is over.
3. They are questioned in a way that does not suggest what answer is expected.

In the special domain of identification of previously seen people, psychologists have discovered a number of phenomena. An important one is called cross-racial identification, which refers to a situation in which a member of one race tries to identify a member of a different race. Witnesses have more difficulty recognizing individual members of a race different from their own.

Whether trying to recognize a previously seen person or simply testifying about the color of the traffic light or some other detail, witnesses will give their testimony with some degree of confidence. Some psychological studies have shown that there is little or no relationship between how confident witnesses are and how likely they are to be accurate. This means that inaccurate testimony is sometimes given with a high degree of confidence or certainty by an eyewitness. Thus one cannot assume that simply because a witness is confident, he or she is probably accurate.

Research on eyewitness testimony that is conducted under controlled conditions is considered an applied branch of experimental psychology or experimental social psychology. However, this research also has contributed to basic theoretical conceptions about the workings of human memory, especially with regard to the surprising degree to which memory reports are malleable and the controversial issue of whether or not memory is permanent. For example, one line of research, developed in the 1970s at the University of Washington at Seattle, indicates that people's testimony about an event they saw can be altered by information acquired after the event (usually called postevent information). Postevent information can be incorporated into the witness's testimony regardless of whether the information is true (i.e., reflects actual aspects of the event). In one widely replicated experiment, for example, people viewed a slide sequence of an auto-pedestrian accident. In one version of the slides the auto passed a stop sign; in another version, a yield sign. After viewing the slides some people were asked a leading question about whether or not another car passed the auto while it was at the stop sign; others were asked the same question with the word *yield* substituted for *stop*. Later, when asked whether they remembered the sign as being a stop sign or a yield sign, people tended to answer consistently with the leading question asked of them earlier—regardless of whether the sign in the original event was a stop sign or a yield sign. Similar phenomena have been observed in experiments involving a wide variety of stimuli, including faces. For example, after briefly observing a clean-shaven face, people who are asked a question like "What color was the man's mustache?" are later likely to describe the person they saw as having a mustache and are likely to incorrectly identify a mustached person from a set of photographs as the person they saw. The precise psychological processes by which postevent information alters testimony remain in doubt, but it is clear that postevent information has the greatest influence on testimony when the person's memory for the details of the original event is weak.

Research findings indicate that young children are influenced by postevent suggestions more than adolescents or adults are. In addition, young children generally provide less complete accounts of witnessed events in their free narrative statements than do adults. Although generally less complete, young children's accounts of witnessed events often are equal to adults' accounts in terms of the portion of the account that is accurate.

Credibility of eyewitness testimony. How jurors make decisions about the veracity of eyewitness accounts is not completely understood. The Devlin Report examined cases tried in England and Wales in 1973 and found that of 347 cases in which eyewitness testimony was the only evidence, 74 percent resulted in convictions. Experimental studies in which people read trial transcripts or view simulated court cases indicate that people are sensitive to a number of variations in eyewitness testimony that either augment or decrease its credibility. A series of studies begun in 1979 at the University of Alberta indicate that people evaluate the credibility of eyewitness accounts by attending to factors that are not particularly diagnostic of eyewitness accuracy. The confidence or certainty with which an individual proffers eyewitness testimony seems to be the most powerful determinant of whether or not people believe the testimony. Confident or certain eyewitnesses are much more credible to people in general and jurors in particular than are unconfident or uncertain eyewitnesses. Research indicates that the amount of detail and vivid elaboration an eyewitness provides during testimony also affects the credibility attributed to the witness, with greater detail and vividness being accorded greater credibility. A witness who says "I remember her; she was wearing blue shorts with Nike tennis shoes and pink socks" is likely to be perceived as more credible than a witness who says "I remember her; she wore casual summer clothing." Experiments on eyewitness accuracy, on the other hand, do not give strong support to the idea that either the eyewitness's confidence or the amount of detail provided by the eyewitness has a consistent relationship to eyewitness accuracy.

Bibliography. Frederic C. Bartlett, *Remembering: A Study in Experimental and Social Psychology,* New York and Cambridge, 1932; Brian R. Clifford and Ray Bull, *The Psychology of Person Identification,* London, 1978; Elizabeth F. Loftus, *Eyewitness Testimony,* Cambridge, Mass., 1979; Hugo Münsterberg, *On the Witness Stand: Essays on Psychology and Crime,* New York, 1908, reprint 1933; Patrick M. Wall, *Eyewitness Identification in Criminal Cases,* Springfield, Ill., 1965; Gary L. Wells and Elizabeth F. Loftus, eds., *Eyewitness Testimony: Psychological Perspectives,* New York, 1984; A. Daniel Yarmey, *The Psychology of Eyewitness Testimony,* New York, 1978.

GARY L. WELLS AND ELIZABETH F. LOFTUS

TEXTBOOK

A work written to facilitate the learning and TEACHING of a particular subject in SCHOOL, college, or UNIVERSITY. The textbook emerged as a significant educational tool during the eighteenth and early nineteenth centuries. Largely a result of the rise of state-supported EDUCATION, the textbook offered a way of coping with an increasing variety of pupils coupled with increasing dependence on less-skilled teachers, and by the mid-nineteenth century textbooks were numerous and diverse.

Texts of a sort had been used since the Roman and Egyptian civilizations, but until the last two hundred years teachers relied on traditional works such as the Bible or the writings of ARISTOTLE or Euclid. For beginning levels teachers first used wooden or stone tablets; later hornbooks, ABC books, or psalters; and then primers to present the ALPHABET, syllables, and the rudiments of moral and religious instruction. In many countries the first specially prepared textbooks dealt with the learning of the mother tongue, the inculcation of moral and religious beliefs, and the mastery of numbers (*see* NUMBER). Later textbooks were concerned with the acquisition of knowledge in basic academic subjects and salable skills in the less academic subjects.

One of the first textbooks widely used in Britain's North American colonies was the *New England Primer* (1683), presumably modeled on European examples. It was followed by Lyman Cobb's *North America Reader* and Caleb Bingham's *Readers* (1799–1832). NOAH WEBSTER's influential *American Spelling Book Containing the Rudiments of the American Language for Use of the Schools in the United States* (the famous "Blue-Backed Speller") appeared first in 1783 and during the next hundred years passed through at least 236 editions, selling millions of copies. The McGuffey *Readers* dominated early READING instruction (1836–1907).

In most countries today virtually any widely taught course at any educational level has a textbook, usually more than one. In many nations, including developing nations, textbooks are prepared to national specifications and are supplied by centralized ministries of education to reflect governmental policies. When control of the content and methodologies of education is not in the hands of the government, competing textbooks are prepared by various authors and publishers, and the schools select those that seem best to suit their purposes. At least forty publishers prepare textbooks for U.S. schools, ten being major (with annual revenues exceeding five to ten million dollars). However, educational PUBLISHING grows increasingly concentrated in the United States; during the mid-1980s five corporations accounted for 75 percent of all sales. In England, Canada, Australia, and other major English-speaking countries at least a half-dozen large publishers in each country vie for the textbook market.

Although an occasional textbook has been successfully adapted for use in various cultures, primarily at the tertiary or college level, the overwhelming majority of textbooks are indigenous to the CULTURE in which they are prepared and used and tend to reflect the values of particular societies. As the International Assessment of Education has made clear, the content taught, the degree of rigor, the pedagogy, and the emphasis on every subject vary from one national school system to another. Even a cursory study of textbooks on modern world history reflects sharp cultural differences in perception from country to country. Unlike trade titles prepared for general reading, textbooks seldom cross boundaries. Educational purpose is too closely allied to social and cultural priorities.

The largest market for textbooks in the world is in North America, where virtually universal schooling exists, at least through the secondary-school level, and where a substantial percentage of students engage in some form of higher education. In the mid-1980s U.S. schools spent about one and a half billion dollars annually for school textbooks, close to 1 percent of the annual expenditures for education, or about thirty-two dollars per pupil per year. Annual college textbook sales in the United States also exceeded one billion dollars. Of the total amount expended on textbooks by schools, about two-thirds went for elementary-school and one-third for secondary-school textbooks. Expenditures were greatest in the basic skill subjects (reading and basic mother-tongue books accounted for 40–45 percent of the total elementary-school expenditures; mathematics accounted for 20–22 percent).

Data are not easily available for other countries, but those checks that have been made yield strikingly similar patterns. In most countries textbooks are available in multiple-year series in all basic subjects, such as spelling, science, social studies, literature, composition, religion, and music, as well as in specific single-course subjects in high school and college, such as history, geography, economics, chemistry, biology, typing, and business education.

In many countries the more successful textbooks—those widely adopted and used by schools and colleges—tend to be revised every three to five years, sometimes more frequently. Thus some textbooks have a life cycle of two or three decades. Some distinguished textbooks—for instance, Samuel Eliot Morison and Henry Steele Commager's *The Growth of the American Republic,* Paul Samuelson's *Economics,* George Thomas's *Calculus and Analytic Geometry,* George Trevelyan's *History of England,* and James McCrimmon's *Writing with a Purpose*—have influenced generations of college students. Among the widely used English-language texts in the lower schools during the twentieth century have been the Scott Foresman Curriculum Foundations Series (the Dick and Jane readers, published 1930–1970), authored by William S. Gray; the Walter Rideout English-skill program in England, from Ginn Ltd. (1950–1980); the J. C. Tressler English programs of D. C. Heath (1930–1960); the Frank A. Magruder *American Government* program, published by Allyn and Bacon (from 1917); the six-year *Adventures in Literature,* published by Harcourt Brace Jovanovich (from 1930); *Modern Biology,* by James H. Otto and others, published by Holt, Rinehart, and Winston (from 1940); and the Mary Dolciani algebra programs of Houghton Mifflin (1960–1985). Each of these series has sold multiple millions of copies. The *Reading 360* program, authored by Theodore Clymer (Ginn and Company, 1969–1979), was a basal scheme separately adapted and widely accepted for a time in the four major English-speaking countries. But this phenomenon is an exception.

Textbooks frequently have been criticized for perpetuating a low standard of education, a criticism that gains some credence from CLASSROOM studies of the 1970s and 1980s, which reported that from 75 to 90 percent of all classroom decisions (in the United States, at least) were strongly influenced by the textbook used. Textbooks tended to limit not only the content covered but also the methods of teaching. Most textbooks are accompanied by a teacher's manual (extensive and prescriptive in the United States, Canada, and some other countries like Sweden and Japan; much less directive elsewhere); by tests that evaluate what pupils learn (and hence help to set the priorities of schooling); sometimes by workbooks that provide practice; and sometimes by supplementary materials such as print, visual, or auditory aids (*see* AUDIOVISUAL EDUCATION). An eight-year basal reading program in the United States or a multiple-year reading scheme in the United Kingdom could have as many as two hundred separate items.

Education reform efforts in various countries have frequently focused on developing new instructional material, such as the Nuffield mathematics and science materials in the United Kingdom or the instructional materials sponsored by the National Science Foundation in the United States during the academic reform movement of the early 1960s. Similarly, social and cultural groups committed to influencing the ATTITUDES and beliefs of children frequently attempt to influence what is included or excluded. In Nazi Germany, for example, textbooks were used to implant the social attitudes desired by the regime. In countries with nationally directed schools, textbooks are frequently changed when the central government changes. In the United States and Canada, state and regional pressure groups frequently try to influence the content of textbooks (*see* PRESSURE GROUP). However, when the proposed changes differ markedly from the content widely accepted and used, attempts to influence the ideas in texts tend to set off strong counterpressures. The textbook is part of a complex social system that involves teachers, parents, and total educational systems. It reflects the attitudes and values of the society in which it has been developed. It is one of the major tools used by societies to acculturate the young.

Bibliography. Hillel Black, *The American Schoolbook,* New York, 1967; John Y. Cole and Thomas G. Sticht, eds., *The Textbook in American Society,* Washington, D.C., 1981; Nila B. Smith, *American Reading Instruction* (1934), rev. ed., Newark, Del., 1986.

JAMES R. SQUIRE

THEATER

The term *theater* designates forms of communication based on mimetic activity. It differs from the closely related PERFORMANCE arts of film and television by its requirement that the enactment be physically present to its observers (*see* MOTION PICTURES; TELEVISION HISTORY). It also differs from most other communication acts involving physical presence by the very different expectations and communication roles of the two parties in the process—the performer and the spectator. Essentially the performer may be considered the sender of a message that the spectator receives and interprets, although in fact the process is considerably more complicated than this. In most forms of theater the message emitted by the performer is supplemented by a great variety of other visual and auditory messages provided by costume, scenery, lighting, music, SOUND EFFECTS, and so on, according to variously codified systems in different theater cultures. The contemporary French theorist Tadeusz Kowsan proposed thirteen such systems for the typical theatrical experience. The audience also is involved in this process in a more complex manner than simple reception of a message. It contributes to the communication process by such traditional overt methods as laughter or applause and by the subtler psychic interplay of the performance situation.

Theater, as the art that most closely imitates the ongoing processes of human society and CULTURE, has been used to communicate observations about almost every aspect of those processes—religious, historical, intellectual, emotional, political. It has served as a means of expressing the deepest emotional and spiritual intuitions of humanity as well as the lightest and most casual passing fancies. It has served to promulgate new ideas and attitudes and to confirm, celebrate, or challenge old ones. Its effectiveness in such matters has caused it to be, of all the arts, the most closely watched and regulated by civic and religious authorities.

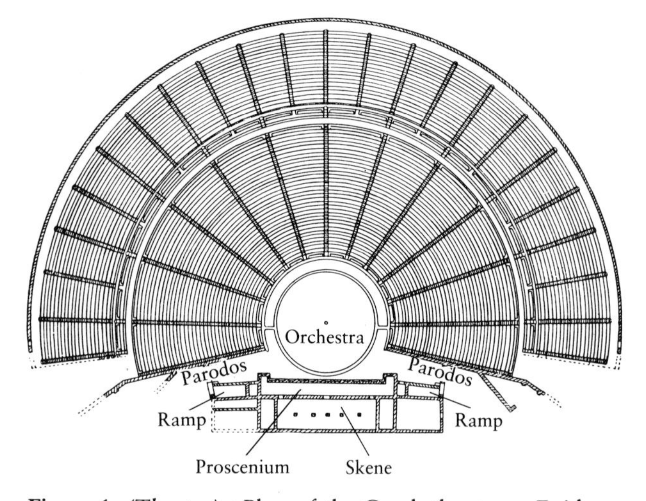

Figure 1. *(Theater)* Plan of the Greek theater at Epidaurus, ca. 350 B.C.E. From Allardyce Nicoll, *The Development of the Theatre: A Study of Theatrical Art from the Beginnings to the Present Day,* New York: Harcourt, Brace and World, 1966, p. 11.

A distinction is often made between theater and DRAMA, according to which drama refers to the written text that traditionally has served as the basis for the live enactment of theater. The proper relationship between the two has been a subject of controversy since the romantic period, when critics such as Charles Lamb (1775–1834) insisted that a drama, when placed onstage, necessarily communicated a different message. Modern semiotic theory regularly distinguishes between the written text and the spectacle text as different communicating structures, but controversy continues about their relative priority and autonomy. The primacy of the written text, generally accepted throughout most of the history of Western theater, has been challenged by many theorists and practitioners during the twentieth century. Some have suggested that the written text be considered only as a kind of preliminary outline, to be made complete by a potentially wide variety of interpretations in the theater. Some recent theorists, drawing on insights provided by anthropology, have urged that theater study and production move away even more radically

Figure 2. *(Theater)* Roman theater at Orange, France. Augustan period. Giraudon/Art Resource, New York.

Figure 3. *(Theater)* The stage for the Passion Play, Valenciennes, France, 1547. The mansions represented are *(from left to right)* Paradise, Nazareth, the Temple, Jerusalem, the palace, the Golden Door, and Hell's mouth. Painting by Hubert Cailleau. Phot. Bibl. Nat., Paris.

from the traditional association with drama and that theater be considered not a subdivision of or supplement to literature but a branch of performance.

Early history. Performance exists in all cultures, but theater, especially if it is thought of as the physical enactment of a preexisting literary text, is not nearly so widespread. Its first appearance was apparently in Greece in the fifth century B.C.E. (*see* HELLENIC WORLD). From there it spread to Rome, disappearing with the collapse of the empire (*see* ROMAN EMPIRE). Scholars disagree on whether some elements of this tradition remained alive through subsequent centuries, but the theater did not appear again as a significant element in Western culture until the late MIDDLE AGES. From the RENAISSANCE on, however, it spread gradually across Europe to become one of the major art forms and cultural expressions of Western civilization. Shakespeare in England, Goethe and Schiller in Germany, and Racine and Molière in France are regarded not only as preeminent creators of the drama and of theater in those countries but also as the leading figures in the heritage of their respective national cultures.

In East Asia, with the possible exception of Japan, drama, though widely found, has not been so central a form of cultural expression as it has been in the

Figure 4. *(Theater)* The commedia dell'arte stage. Jacques Callot, *Razullo and Cucurucu,* plate from *I Balli di Sfessania,* 1621. Courtesy of the Library of Congress.

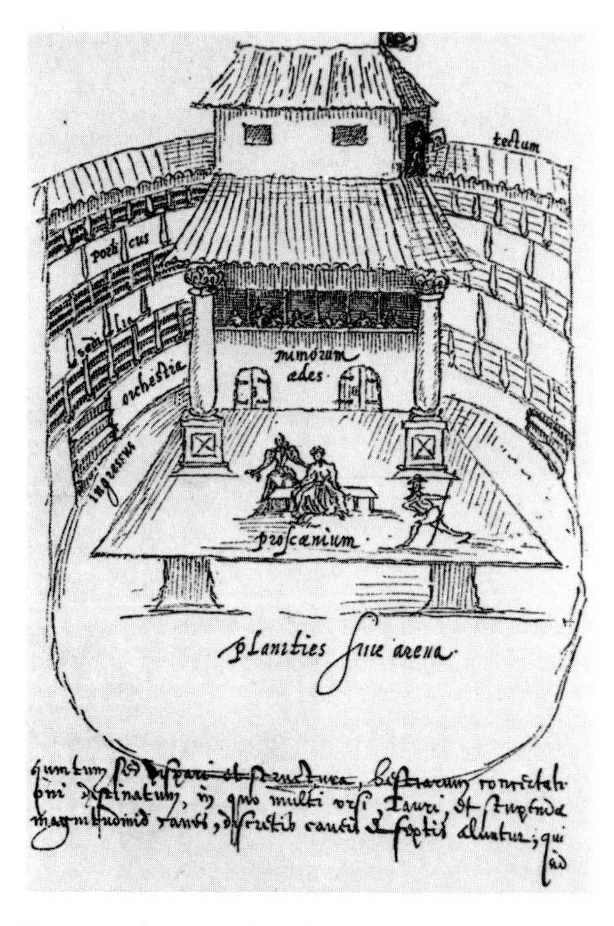

Figure 5. *(Theater)* The only extant contemporary representation of the interior of an Elizabethan playhouse. Arend van Buchell, copy of a sketch of the Swan Theatre, by Johann de Witt, 1596. From Marion Geisinger, *Plays, Players, and Playwrights: An Illustrated History of the Theatre,* New York: Hart Publishing Company, 1971, p. 95. © Bibliotheek der Rijksuniversiteit, Rijksuniversiteit te Utrecht.

West (*see* MUSIC THEATER—ASIAN TRADITIONS). Its earliest known appearance was in India, where Sanskrit dramas were created between the fourth and eighth centuries. In the latter part of this period drama appeared in China, possibly inspired by the Indian experience, and from China it spread into Korea and Japan. The classic Japanese theater, No, did not appear until the fourteenth century, and the more popular Kabuki not until three hundred years later.

Legend and myth often associate the origins of theater with communal religious observances. The god Brahma himself is said to have established the theater in India, and priestly dances associated with the Shinto RELIGION provided the basic performance modes for the Japanese No. The Greek philosopher ARISTOTLE traced the origins of COMEDY and TRAGEDY back to the phallic songs and chants and dances called dithyrambs celebrated in honor of the god Dionysius (*see* DANCE). The services of the medieval church provided the elements for the liturgical dramas of the late Middle Ages. Certain theorists of the early twentieth century, such as Gilbert Murray and F. M. Cornford, used evidence from anthropological research to argue that all theater and drama were descended ultimately from RITUAL observances of seasonal cycles.

Whatever its earliest relationship with religion and with ritual may have been, historically recorded theater has been, on the whole, much more devoted to secular than to religious concerns and has in fact frequently been viewed with suspicion or outright hostility by the church. Many of the church fathers, led by Tertullian (ca. 160–250) and St. Augustine (354–430), condemned the theater for its pagan associations and its concern with the arousal of the passions. English clerics from Thomas Wilcox in the 1570s to Jeremy Collier in the 1690s published widely

Figure 6. *(Theater)* Matthäus Merian's view of London in 1638. Detail showing the following playhouses: the Swan (39), the Hope (38), and the Globe (37), with St. Paul's Cathedral to the north. By permission of The Folger Shakespeare Library, Washington, D.C.

a

b

Figure 7. *(Theater)* Renaissance stage sets: (*a*) comic scene, (*b*) tragic scene. From Jehan Martin's Paris edition of Sebastiano Serlio's *De Architettura,* 1545. The Metropolitan Museum of Art, New York, Harris Brisbane Dick Fund, 1937. (37.56.2)

read pamphlets against the theater and its practitioners (*see* PAMPHLET). In pre-Revolutionary France actors were commonly deprived of civic rights as well as of the sacraments of the church. Only in the latter part of the nineteenth century did actors begin to obtain membership in the respectable classes of European society.

The relation of theater to public morality has thus been a matter of concern since classical times, and it has by no means been restricted to church writers. The Greek philosopher PLATO, like Tertullian and Augustine, condemned theater as being a stimulus to the passions and thus a hindrance to the clearer view of reality that the intellect can discover. His follower Aristotle admitted the potential ill effects of uncontrolled passions but argued that tragedy, through a process he called catharsis, could in fact contribute to this control. The Romans, and the poet Horace (68–5 B.C.E.) in particular, tended to take a rather more pragmatic approach to moral utility. Horace's observation that drama should both please and instruct became a central precept for all subsequent classically oriented theory.

New audiences and institutions. The great dramatic festivals of Athens and the great medieval cycles of religious drama were major annual events in the religious and cultural life of their respective communities, involving many members of those communities in the lengthy preparations and the performances themselves, which were spread over a period

Figure 8. *(Theater)* Ludovico Burnacini, scene from *La Zenobia di Rodamisto,* Vienna, 1662. Harvard Theatre Collection.

Figure 9. *(Theater)* A Chinese open-air theater. Detail of Chinese scroll no. 40. Reproduced by courtesy of the Trustees of The British Museum.

of several days and were attended by most of the community as well as a substantial number of visitors and guests. During the Renaissance the theater, so broadly based in earlier times, began to be fragmented into different forms for different levels of society, and although theorists continued to promulgate the Horatian formula, few of these forms were in fact much concerned with the instruction of their audience in the Horatian sense. The theater for the common people, probably owing much to the entertainment tradition of the wandering performers of the Middle Ages, was composed of such fare as folk farces and the beginnings of the commedia dell'arte—a highly popular form of largely improvised comedy built around stock characters, some wearing traditional masks, that eventually spread to all corners of Europe. Such performances were usually offered on temporary platform stages erected in such places of popular resort as markets and fairgrounds.

At the same time, a very different sort of theater was being developed by the aristocracy—a court entertainment often employing music, dance, allegorical figures, and lavish SPECTACLE, partially for entertainment but primarily as a display of the sponsor's power and wealth. Although magnificent princely entertainments were sometimes held in public spaces for a dazzled populace, the most common location was in rich theaters constructed within princely residences. Here the single-point perspective recently developed by Italian painters was used by court scenic designers in the construction of theatrical scenes so that the stage picture could be seen perfectly only from the sponsoring prince's seat, which was placed on a dais in the center of the auditorium or in an elaborately decorated box at the rear. The theatrical performance itself was in such surroundings largely a pretext for the political display of its prince.

By the end of the sixteenth century the popular street theater and the aristocratic private theater were supplemented in several parts of Europe by the first permanent commercial theaters, catering to a variety of social classes but tending to draw the major part of their audience from the emerging bourgeois population of merchants and tradespeople. Although popular, such theaters often experienced strong civic resistance. The private theaters of the Renaissance were protected from any external protest by the political power of their sponsors, and the temporary stages of wandering companies caused only occasional concern; they could be easily removed or even refused permission to enter a community if conditions were considered unfavorable. But permanent theater structures represented a continuing acceptance of theater within the social structure of a community, and many were opposed to this. In addition to religious leaders certain civic authorities resisted the development, fearing that the large crowds drawn to performances might prove a disturbance to public tranquillity.

Misgivings such as these were sufficient to keep the first public theaters in England, built at the time of Shakespeare, in physical locations clearly reflecting their social marginality. Across the Thames from the city proper and thus beyond the control of civic authorities, they shared their district with other establishments of public entertainment but questionable social status, such as bear-baiting arenas and bordellos. In Spain, on the other hand, where profits from the public theaters supported charitable institutions and where ties among theater, church, and state remained strong, major theaters were centrally located in cities like Madrid and Seville, often adjoining the elegant town houses of leading citizens.

Unlike Renaissance London and Madrid, Paris had only a single public theater, the Hôtel de Bourgogne. A special dispensation from the king not only protected it from civic authorities but also gave it a MONOPOLY on theatrical performances within the city. During the seventeenth century this royal protection of a particular troupe led to the founding of the first national theater, the Comédie Française. Similar official recognition was given to other theaters specializing in OPERA, comic opera, and Italian comedy (*see* MUSIC THEATER—WESTERN TRADITIONS). During this century France served as a cultural and political model for much of Europe, and the idea of national theaters spread widely. In some places, as in London after the Restoration of 1660, this idea meant little more than that certain individuals were given a more or less restricted monopoly on theatrical presentation within a major city (the two traditional "patent houses" of London—Drury Lane and Covent Garden—are descended from these first monopolies). Elsewhere, as in Vienna, the national theater remained closely tied to the court, which provided substantial financial support and often strong control over administration and policy. These national theaters became in many places the center of a country's theatrical life, the goal of the best actors and playwrights.

Eighteenth through twentieth centuries. During the eighteenth century the monopolies supposedly held by a number of the national theaters eroded, and the more typical arrangement of the nineteenth century began to appear. The most lavish and usually best-situated theater of the city became the opera house, supported by state or private funds, but in either case at least as important as a symbolic place of assembly and display for the upper classes as for any artistic function. The possession of a box at the opera came to serve as evidence of membership in the privileged classes, and attendance was compulsory for those claiming social distinction. Next in importance and centrality were the national theaters, devoted to the spoken word or to light opera and dedicated increasingly to performance of the nation's classic repertoire and less to the welcoming of new works. Then, usually gathered together in a developing theater district convenient to public transportation, hotels, and restaurants, came a collection of commercial theaters. By the late nineteenth century these theaters were for the most part concentrated in those districts still primarily associated with such activity—the Paris boulevards, New York's Broadway, London's West End.

Such theaters were democratic in the sense that anyone who could afford a ticket could sit anywhere in them (with the occasional exception of the still-reserved royal box), but the range of prices for different seats naturally imposed a general class pattern upon the audience, and poorer citizens would often not appear even in the relatively inexpensive gallery seats at the top of these theaters. The commercial houses appealed largely to the middle classes, while the lower-class public, if they attended theater at all, favored the more accessible and more congenial music halls, melodrama houses, and similar entertainments often located in their own sections of the city.

Thus in the course of the nineteenth century each of these types of theater became associated not only with a fairly consistent public but also with a fairly consistent repertoire. Opera and ballet, comic opera, classic revivals, new serious and comic works, and the great variety of popular forms such as melodrama, farce, vaudeville, and burletta each had a particular theater or theaters primarily concerned with its production. This system worked satisfactorily as long as no major changes occurred in the potential dramatic repertoire, but a crisis developed toward the end of the century when such dramatists as Henrik Ibsen, August Strindberg, Anton Chekhov, and George Bernard Shaw created a new sort of drama not easily assimilated by any of these theater organizations. Their work was not yet well enough established for the national theaters, and its radical form and content made it equally unacceptable for either middle- or lower-class popular theaters, where it faced the double enemy of possible CENSORSHIP and audience hostility.

To solve this problem a new sort of theater ap-

Figure 10. *(Theater)* Attributed to Okumura Masanobu, *Scene from Kanadehon Chushingura: A Play Given at the Nakamuraza Theater,* 1749. Japan, Edo period. William Sturgis Bigelow Collection. 11.19665. Courtesy, Museum of Fine Arts, Boston.

Figure 11. *(Theater)* Interior of Booth's Theatre, New York City, 1869. Harvard Theatre Collection.

peared—the experimental theater—a modest venture operating to a certain extent outside the established system and seeking to avoid that system's constraints on innovation in playwriting, staging, and performance in general. In the twentieth century such experimental theaters have become a significant part of theatrical culture, the favored location for the launching of new works or entire new movements. Sometimes they have been established as annexes to national theaters, but more often they are independent ventures, frequently found in sections of cities associated with artistic and bohemian culture. *See* AVANT-GARDE.

Theater is traditionally an urban art, often highly centralized. In some countries, most notably in England and France, the capital city has dominated national theater since the Renaissance. In these countries various governments, especially in modern times, have attempted to modify this pattern and to encourage decentralization of theater. Germany and Italy, probably because of their relatively late political unification, both entered the modern era with a decentralized theater system already in operation. The United States, although its theater has been centered since the beginning of the nineteenth century in New York, has not in fact followed the organizational model of any European country. Except for the brief experiment of the Federal Theatre in the 1930s, theater in the United States has received little official government recognition or support, and a national theater in the European style has never been established. This, along with the great size of the country, has worked as a counterforce to the concentration of theater activity in any one city. During the nineteenth century almost every town in the United States had its theater, sometimes called an opera house (less to indicate performances in that GENRE than to suggest a socially more elegant and respectable art form), and countless traveling companies toured among these theaters, uniting the nation in a web of theatrical offerings.

Although these ubiquitous opera houses were in

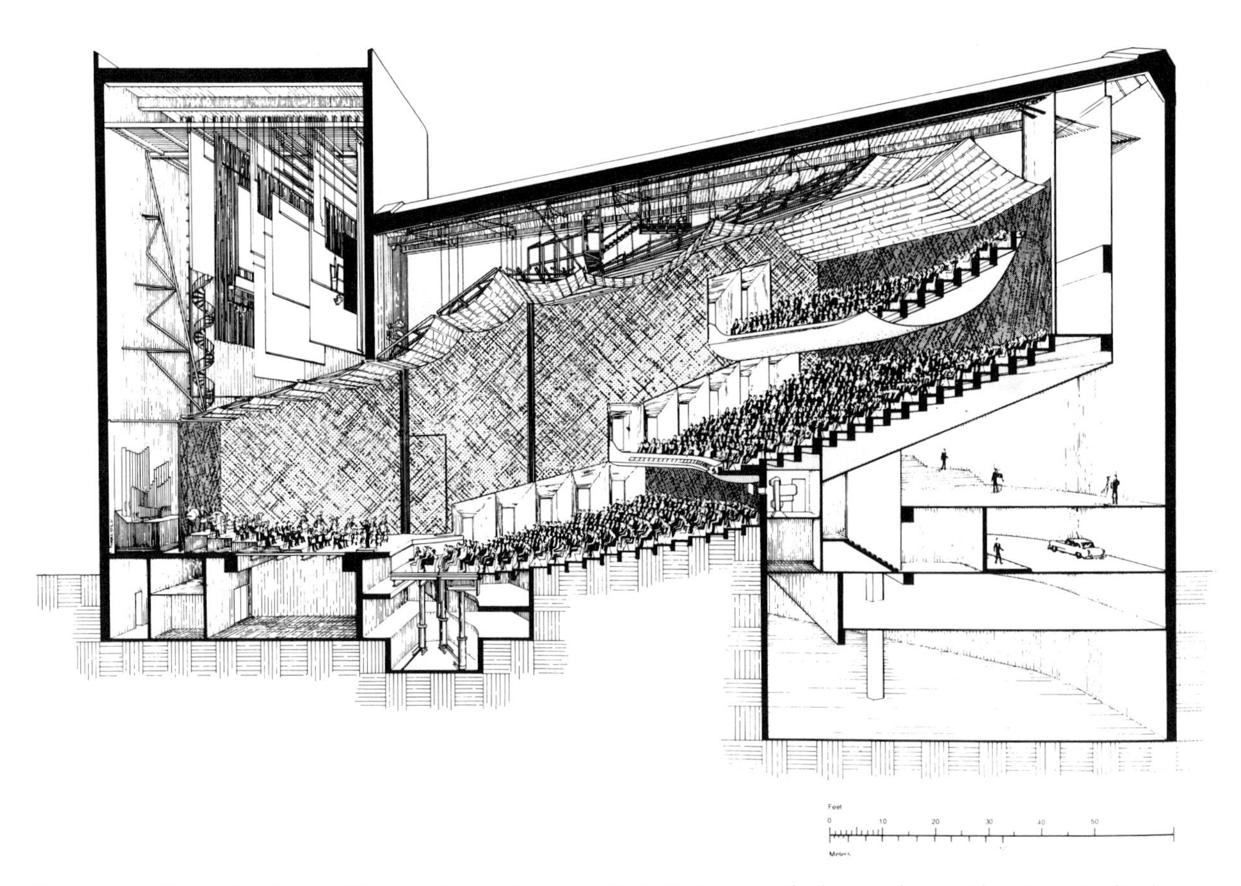

Figure 12. *(Theater)* Edward Thomas Performing Arts Hall, University of Akron, Akron, Ohio. Longitudinal perspective section, concert hall mode. From George C. Izenour, *Theater Design,* New York: McGraw-Hill Book Company, 1977, p. 376, fig. 7.75. George C. Izenour Archive.

time almost universally replaced by cinema theaters, the U.S. regional theater did not disappear with them. The traveling companies died out, but community theaters, drawing on local talent, began to appear in many parts of the country. These were supplemented by UNIVERSITY theaters, as U.S. universities began to exert more and more influence on the intellectual and cultural life of the nation. Theater studies, often originally developed in departments of English or ORATORY, became an independent discipline, a standard feature of U.S. university life as it rarely was in Europe. The production facilities of these programs often rival those of the best professional theaters, and the universities have become not only important regional cultural centers but also often the proving ground for new European and native works that more commercial theaters have been unwilling to attempt. More recently major regional theaters have also been established and have become important centers for classic revivals and the development of new works.

The arrival of cinema and subsequently of television has offered a major challenge to the theater, especially in one of its most important traditional roles as popular entertainment. A similar major challenge had appeared in the late nineteenth century with the rise of the novel when, as now, doubts were expressed about the future of theater. Despite their popularity, however, these newer arts lack the essential element of the theater experience—its physical presence—and the power of the relationship between living spectator and living performer has proven so durable across many cultures and many historical periods that theater in some form seems likely to remain an important element in the expression and transmission of human culture.

Bibliography. Jonas A. Barish, *The Antitheatrical Prejudice,* Berkeley, Calif., 1981; Oscar G. Brockett, *History of the Theater,* Boston, 1982; Oscar G. Brockett and Robert R. Findlay, *Century of Innovation: A History of European and American Theater and Drama since 1870,* Englewood Cliffs, N.J., 1973; Marvin A. Carlson, *Theories of the Theater,* Ithaca, N.Y., 1984; John Gassner and Edward Quinn, *The Reader's Encyclopedia of World Drama,* New York, 1969; Richard Southern, *The Seven Ages of Theatre,* New York, 1961.

MARVIN A. CARLSON

TOKUGAWA ERA: SECLUSION POLICY

When the Tokugawa shogunate (1600–1868) was established in Japan after long and bitter struggles, the newly born central government made every effort to fortify its authority and prestige vis-à-vis subjugated local lords and powerful religious sects. In 1639 it adopted a policy putting all contact with foreign countries under strict control of the shogunate. This policy came to be called *sakoku* ("national seclusion") in the early nineteenth century, but its real purpose had been to consolidate the power of the shogunate. In fact, throughout the Tokugawa period trade and DIPLOMACY with Korea and Ryukyu were sustained, and trade with Chinese and Dutch ships at Nagasaki flourished, though always under strict centralized authority.

In addition to limiting diplomatic relations, the shogunate prohibited any international trade except that directly controlled at Nagasaki with Chinese merchants and the Dutch East India Company (and its later equivalent) and that indirectly controlled with Korea and Ryukyu in a station in each country. The shogunate effectively erased the possible danger of free trade, which could have allowed rival domestic powers to emerge by taking advantage of the lucrative business.

Another main element of the "seclusion" policy was the proscription of Christianity. Since the middle of the sixteenth century Portuguese and Spanish missionaries had been very successful in the country. More than seven hundred thousand Japanese allegedly had become Christians by the early seventeenth century. However, they gradually came to be regarded by the government as a threat to its authority. The foreign mission was felt to be the first step toward a military invasion, following the pattern of Portuguese and Spanish COLONIZATION in many parts of the world. Also, this RELIGION of fervent believers in a deity demanding a higher respect than that due any earthly powers reminded the shogunate of the die-hard rebellions of the Ikko Buddhists in the sixteenth century. The Shimabara Rebellion (1637–1638) of Christian peasants confirmed their apprehension.

In order to implement the policy, the shogunate left no possible loopholes. Overseas travel was prohibited for all Japanese except a limited number of traders and officials to Korea and Ryukyu. The construction of ships that could easily voyage to China or Southeast Asia was also banned. Portuguese and Spanish, including those of mixed Japanese and other parentage, were expelled. Chinese and Dutch merchants were confined to separate small compounds in Nagasaki, and their contacts with the Japanese were closely watched. Special magistrates inspected imported books one by one for any reference to Christianity. Christians who refused to renounce their faith were executed, and informing against secret Christians was encouraged. Registries of commoners, recording each individual's affiliation with a Buddhist temple, were maintained.

Thus the "seclusion" policy coupled with rigid book CENSORSHIP and other controls effectively shielded Japan from any disturbing impact from abroad. This is one reason why the shogunate sustained its power and prestige for more than two centuries. Political and military institutions changed very little during the period. It was only after the forced "opening" of the country to the United States (in 1854 under the military threat of the squadron led by Commodore Matthew C. Perry) and to other Western countries that the shogunate lost its control over local lords and finally conceded its power in 1868 to the new government headed by the Meiji emperor.

The social and cultural effects of the policy were manifold. Before the implementation of the policy many Japanese traders had traveled to China, Southeast Asia, and even India. There had been prosperous settlements of Japanese ("Japan Towns") in Luzon, Annam, Cambodia, and Siam, but after the implementation of the policy no Japanese could go abroad (except to the above-mentioned stations in Korea and Ryukyu). Most Japan Towns vanished in a few decades. Christianity was completely swept away from the surface of society. Most of the Christians who had hidden in remote villages, mines, and other locations gradually died off. Only a few families in the Nagasaki area secretly continued as Christians for more than two hundred years. Some of them visited a newly built Catholic church in 1865 and declared their faith. However, some refused to return to the church because their views had been transformed while they were underground.

Within their clearly defined borders the Japanese were governed by the centralized political power in Edo (now Tokyo) and its subordinate local lords. Highways from Edo to local cities and towns were well arranged and well traveled. For example, there were fifty-three post towns on the 309-mile route from Edo to Kyoto. Commodities were sent and sold throughout the country. A member of a Dutch delegation to Edo in 1826 wrote that he had never seen a busier bay in the world than the bay of Osaka, the commercial center of the country with a population of three to four hundred thousand. Also, indigenous cultural activities like the Kabuki THEATER, the tea ceremony, flower arrangement, and the ukiyo-e art movement were popular nationwide. In sum, the communication network within the confined preindustrial archipelago developed very well. Under these circumstances the sense of unity among Japanese was further solidified, and insular self-complacence spread. On the other hand, the Japanese retained a keen curiosity about the outside world.

Since direct contact was limited to that involving sailors and merchants in Nagasaki, most information about China came in through books. Books about CONFUCIUS, literature, history, agriculture, and other topics were imported, and Confucianism became the mainstream philosophy among intellectuals. It was held to contain universally valid teachings on ethics and politics, and the ancient sages and some later scholars of China were highly respected. Many Japanese intellectuals wrote philosophical essays in classical Chinese. At the same time, the China-centered image of the world order was often rejected and pride in Japan's political independence maintained. The fact that contemporary China was governed by the Manchus, a tribe of northern "barbarians," and China's divergence from Confucian ideals were pointed out with increasing frequency. The defeat of China by Britain in the Opium War (1840–1842) further colored Japanese estimation of China. By the time of the "opening" of Japan to Western countries, scorn for the politics and military of contemporary China had become visible beneath the veil of traditional admiration for Chinese CULTURE.

As for Japanese ideas of Western countries, there were three main aspects. First, they were seen as Christian, which was something magical, mystical, and frightening; the "Evil Sect" (Jashumon) was the contemporary name for Christianity. Second, especially from the late eighteenth century on, Western countries came to be regarded as having detailed knowledge of medicine, chemistry, physics, and geography (*see* CARTOGRAPHY). Many Dutch books were imported and translated by Japanese scholars who were called *rangakusha* ("scholars of Dutch learning"). More than a hundred Dutch medical books were translated and printed during the period from 1774 to 1867. The new learning gradually acquired high prestige, and admiration for some aspects of Western civilization spread. Information about the West that trickled into the country from Dutch sources prepared the Japanese mentally for the period of westernization after the Meiji Restoration. Third, from the end of the eighteenth century Western countries were thought to be a military menace. The Russian government sent envoys to request commerce in 1792 and 1804. Various Western ships appeared from time to time off the coast of Japan. At the same time, the continued colonization of many parts of Asia by European countries became well known, and intellectuals called for preparedness for a possible Western invasion. Some asked for the introduction of new, Western military technology. However, the traditional political system resisted major military changes, and reform was minimal. Government leaders realized how hard it would be to resist a modern Western navy when the steamship squadron appeared in Edo Bay in 1853. This may be one reason why the shogunate succumbed rather quickly to demands of Commodore Perry, as if a long-anticipated inevitable catastrophe had finally arrived. *See also* NAKAHAMA MANJIRO.

The outside world had little knowledge of Japan during this period of "seclusion." The Chinese government knew that its merchants had substantial trade relations with Japan. In fact Japan was one of the main suppliers of the copper that China needed for its COINS. But Qing China had no formal contact with the shogunate and only a very vague knowledge of Japan.

Korea sent an envoy to Edo at the beginning of each shogun's reign, but no Japanese, to say nothing of a shogunate mission, traveled to Seoul. In Japan this was sometimes interpreted as proof of Japan's superiority to Korea. Koreans, however, thought it was a Korean precaution against ESPIONAGE by the Japanese, who had invaded Korea in the late sixteenth century. The literati-bureaucrats of Korea looked down on Japanese samurai rulers, and their interest in Japan was limited to the import of silver from Japan and the question of whether or not Japan would invade their country again. A Confucian scholar wrote in the early nineteenth century that since Japan seemed to have confucianized, or civilized, considerably in recent years, the possibility of a second invasion had diminished.

Members of the Dutch East India Company who lived in Nagasaki and paid regular visits to Edo "to show their gratitude to the shogun" represented the main information route between Japan and the Western world. Some of them, such as Engelbert Kämpfer, J. F. van Overmeer Fisscher, Hendrik Doeff, and Philipp Franz von Siebold, wrote books on Japan. But the flow of information was intermittent and slow. For instance, the book written by Kämpfer, who stayed in Japan from 1690 to 1692, was used as a source not only by Montesquieu in *The Spirit of Laws* (1748) but also by Townsend Harris, the first U.S. consul to serve in Japan, who arrived in 1856. Though exported Japanese pottery and "japanned" furniture were prized by nobility in Europe, information about Japan was extremely limited. This fact strengthened in the Western mind the image of Japan's "seclusion" and "strangeness," an image that lingered even into the twentieth century, making Japan a convenient mirror for European fancy, as in the OPERA *Madama Butterfly,* by Giacomo Puccini.

See also ASIA, TWENTIETH CENTURY; EAST ASIA, ANCIENT.

Bibliography. Naohiro Asao, *Sakoku,* Tokyo, 1975; Seiichi Iwao, *Sakoku,* Tokyo, 1971; Eiichi Katô et al., eds., *Sakoku,* Tokyo, 1981; Ronald P. Toby, *State and Diplomacy in Early Modern Japan: Asia in the Development of the Tokugawa Bakufu,* Princeton, N.J., 1984.

HIROSHI WATANABE

TOUCH

The largest organ of the human body is the skin, the organ of touch. It comprises about 17 percent of adult body weight and covers about eighteen thousand square centimeters, a vast surface to receive messages. At eight weeks after conception the embryo can respond to tactile stimulation, the earliest sensory system to develop. Four reflexive behaviors present at birth emphasize our biological disposition for physical social touch: (1) in the grasp reflex the fist clenches when the palm is touched and holds on with enough strength to sustain body weight, (2) in the Moro reflex the arms make a grasping-embracing reaction in response to loss of support, (3) in the rooting reflex the head turns when the cheek is touched by a stimulating object such as the nipple, and (4) in the sucking reflex the mouth begins to suck when it finds an object (thumb sucking can occur before birth).

Role of Touching in Social Interaction

Touch continues to play an important role in social communication throughout infancy and early childhood, especially for reassurance and calming. Holding a crying child tends to calm it rather than reinforce its crying. Holding and caressing serve as primary bonding mechanisms of mother-infant attachment; human and primate infants deprived of touch suffer retarded physical development and social-emotional disorders.

In Western societies, there is a progressive reduction of physical contact between parent and child, as well as among children, during middle childhood. Even between one and two years of age, touching between peers declines and is replaced increasingly by talking to get attention and to express interest and positive and negative feelings. By adolescence parent-child touch is virtually absent or takes ritualized adult forms. Same-sex touch is also ritualized into conventional forms, SPORTS, and horseplay, while opposite-sex touch becomes regulated by courtship rules.

Touch in adult social interaction can substitute

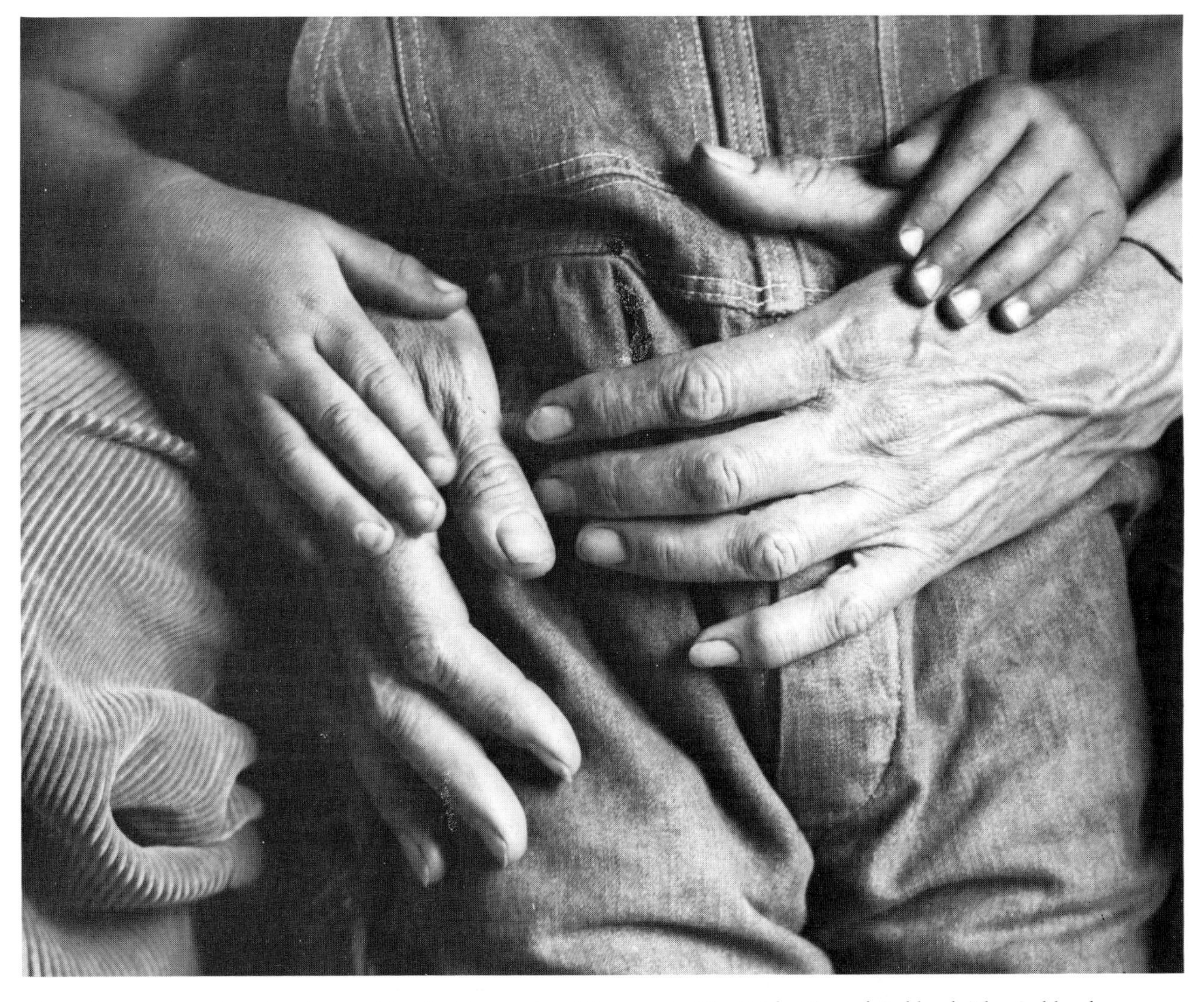

Figure 1. *(Touch)* Dorothea Lange, *Hands, Maynard and Dan,* ca. 1930. © The City of Oakland, The Oakland Museum, California.

for, emphasize, clarify, or contradict spoken words. How touch is interpreted depends on a number of features: location, duration, frequency, intensity, sequence, reciprocity, intention, setting, roles, and culture. Most important, the occasion, extent, and manner of touching in interaction closely reflect the nature of the social relationship between the participants.

Because of the association with sex, aggression, and status, occasions for physical contact in social interaction are carefully regulated in all cultures. The extent of its use may vary greatly, however. Thus, in friendly interactions in Middle Eastern, southern European, Latin American, and some African societies touching may be frequent. In contrast, touching in friendly interactions is quite infrequent in much of Asia, northern Europe, and North America.

Kinds of Touching

The communicative significance of touch may be classified into four categories depending on situation and relationship.

Task-oriented touch occurs when a professional function is being performed, such as the grooming touch of the barber or the diagnostic or treatment manipulations of the physician. Reciprocity of touch is not permitted, and patterns of touch are governed solely by the requirements of the task. Touch is also a part of faith healing and other spiritual and religious ceremonies. Individuals of special status, such as shamans and priests, heal by touching or what is called the laying on of hands. Medieval kings cured scrofula by a divine touch to the neck, and Eskimo shamans lick a wound as part of their healing ritual. Similarly, many aboriginal healers use touch as part of ceremonies for curing physical and spiritual problems. Medical and psychiatric research has documented the health-promoting and anxiety-reducing benefits of touch. Individuals undergoing physical or emotional trauma feel calmed and show concrete health gains (e.g., lowered blood pressure, enhanced postsurgical recovery) when touched by concerned professionals in a reassuring fashion.

Greeting-separation touch acknowledges and shows respect to casual friends, acquaintances, and strangers with special variation for people of rank. The handshake is the preferred mode in Western society. It is also used to express appreciation, congratulations, or the closing of a deal (e.g., palm touch among the Amhara of Ethiopia). Special (and sometimes secret) handshakes are used among members of fraternal organizations and ethnic groups (e.g., the palm slap or "soul" handshake among U.S. blacks) to express solidarity. Other cultures enact what Westerners might consider overintimate greetings by pressing the nose to the cheek and inhaling with a sniffing sound (e.g., Dasun of Borneo, Burmese, Lapp, Maori, Malay,

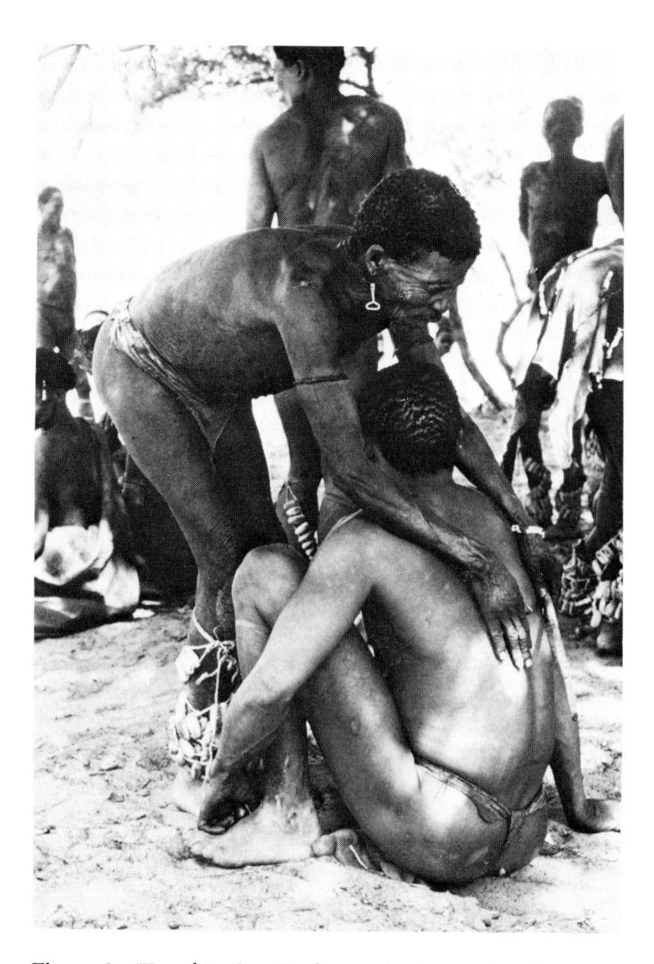

Figure 2. *(Touch)* San Bushmen: laying on hands, trance curing. Irven DeVore/Anthro-Photo.

Mongol, Tikopia of Melanesia) or kissing the ring, knee, or foot of a superior to acknowledge his elevated status as cardinal, king, or chieftain. In contrast, in East Asian, Indian, and Arab cultures, greeting or separation demands little or no physical contact, although other forms of respect are shown, such as bowing, holding the hands together, or the self-touching salaam.

Friendly touch occurs in relationships in which the individuals are familiar and like each other (i.e., close friends, family). Liking or camaraderie can be expressed by a hand on the shoulder for sincerity or a pat on the back for encouragement among adults or by hand holding among small children. Status differences within friendly relationships allow older, stronger, or more dominant individuals greater touch liberties with less dominant or lower-status individuals (e.g., man-woman, boss-secretary, teacher-student). In North America, females may greet with a cheek kiss, while a vigorous handshake expresses familiarity and warmth among males. Mediterranean, French, and Latin American males are more likely to embrace and cheek-kiss upon meeting close male friends and family and to use touch for getting attention or emphasis during conversation than are northern European and North American males.

Sport provides a special exception for touch taboos between men. Teammates may hug, kiss, and even pat buttocks in support or victory when such contact would otherwise be seen as homosexual displays. Similarly, rough-and-tumble play in childhood and mock fighting in adolescence are special settings where touch norms are suspended for affectionate or aggressive play. Social dancing, too, permits intimate physical contact between opposite-sex strangers, although there are cultures that consider such public contact even between husband and wife as too intimate (e.g., Orthodox Jews). Touch in opposite-sex friendships is regulated in all cultures. Misunderstandings can arise nevertheless, as when friendly touch gestures (e.g., hand on hand) are misinterpreted as erotic. Such gestures may, of course, be used intentionally to promote physical intimacy and move the relationship from friend to lover status.

Sexual intimacy, or love touch, is reserved for lovers and mates and involves a quality of touch far different from all other relationships. It allows a greater variety of reciprocal touch more responsive to emotion or passion than to social convention. Even so, each culture has its own emphasis on sensual and erotic practices, as shown, for example, by extensive Hindu and Taoist writings about spirituality and sexual touch. The need to touch or be touched and held may be exchanged for sexual favors because these occasions may provide the only opportunity to satisfy a "skin hunger" also suffered by isolated and elderly individuals.

The primitive message of not being alone that comes from touch and the immediate vulnerability of the body makes touch the most vigorously ritualized and regulated of all human communication channels.

See also GESTURE; INTERACTION, FACE-TO-FACE; INTERPERSONAL DISTANCE; NONVERBAL COMMUNICATION; PROXEMICS.

Bibliography. Ashley Montagu, *Touching: The Human Significance of the Skin,* 2d ed., New York, 1978; William Schiff and Emerson Foulke, eds., *Tactual Perception: A Sourcebook,* New York, 1982; John M. Wiemann and Randall P. Harrison, eds., *Nonverbal Interaction,* Beverly Hills, Calif., 1983.

STEPHEN THAYER

TOURISM

A form of travel for pleasure or edification that is also a particularly complex communicative system. Tourists take in tourist sites, not in isolation but as nodes in a network of attractions that constitute the tourist itinerary and recreational geography of a region. A vast, multinational tourist industry provides the infrastructure for developing tourist environments, moving millions of travelers from destination to destination and lodging and entertaining them at each place. The industry is global, and with the advent of space travel, tourism is potentially intergalactic. The consequences of tourism—processes of production and representation of CULTURE for outsiders, interactions between local people and more affluent visitors, and economic and social impacts—offer fertile areas for study.

History and development. Diverse in nature, tourism has a long history. In ancient Greece (*see* HELLENIC WORLD) and the ROMAN EMPIRE, the well-to-do sought edification and amusement when setting out on established itineraries in the Mediterranean basin. Pilgrims throughout the world have been making the rounds of sacred shrines for at least as long, journeying to Banaras (Varanasi), Jerusalem, or, at a later time, Mecca. By the seventeenth century the Grand Tour emerged: the European elite, especially the British, viewed travel on the Continent as an essential component in the education of a young man, and a somewhat standard itinerary persisted in various forms until fairly recently. By the eighteenth century the Japanese were touring various provinces of Japan and visiting hot spring resorts, as well as participating in the much older tradition of pilgrimage. With the advent of the railway and steamship by the mid-nineteenth century and the motor car during the first half of the twentieth, travel became less arduous and more accessible to more people, and the ground was prepared for the development of mass tourism. Inexpensive air travel and easier communication in the post–World War II period led to an unprecedented boom in international recreational travel.

Essential to the expansion of travel is the development of the tourist industry itself—travel agents, tour operators and guides, hotels and resorts, transportation networks and information and communications systems, mass media marketing, tourist regions and attractions, travel gear and souvenirs, travel literature and films, educational institutions that train industry personnel and foster scholarly research on tourism, regulatory and policy-making bodies, government agencies, professional associations, and international travel organizations and clubs. As the industry supports increasing numbers of tourists, particularly Westerners, in economically depressed areas such as Bali, Kenya, parts of the Caribbean, the South Pacific, and Southeast Asia, hosts come to depend on tourism as a major source of income and hard currency. In many regions tourism has become the number one source of foreign exchange.

Tourists, experiences, and productions. Tourists and tourist experiences are heterogeneous. Sociolo-

Figure 1. *(Tourism)* Duane Hanson, *Tourists,* 1970. Fiberglass with mixed media. National Galleries of Scotland, Edinburgh.

gist Erik Cohen distinguishes four tourist roles (organized mass tourist, individual mass tourist, explorer, and drifter) and five modes of tourist experience (recreational, diversionary, experiential, experimental, and existential) on a spectrum from "the experience of the tourist as the traveller in pursuit of 'mere' pleasure in the strange and novel to that of the modern pilgrim in quest of meaning at somebody else's centre." The tourist industry has become sufficiently diversified to accommodate this wide range of needs.

Tourist productions—the settings, events, and artifacts created for tourists—and their marketing constitute the most elaborated and expressive mode of communication in the entire tourism system. In tourist productions symbol takes precedence over information. Though tourist attractions are very diverse—natural wonders; distinctive neighborhoods, towns, regions, and life-styles; ARCHITECTURE and ART; historic landmarks, monuments, and museums; re-created villages and reenacted events; technology, work displays, and public works; expositions and amusement parks; gardens and zoos; sporting facilities; performances; sound-and-light shows; festivals and rituals; conferences and conventions—they share certain processes and structural features. *See also* ARTIFACT; FESTIVAL; MUSEUM; PERFORMANCE; RITUAL.

How does something become a tourist attraction? According to U.S. sociologist Dean MacCannell, the process of "site sacralization" involves *naming,* whereby the site is authenticated and then marked off as worthy of special attention by SIGNAGE or decree; *framing* and *elevation,* during which the site is protected and enhanced by special security measures, staging, or lighting; *enshrinement,* as structures are created over a special place (Dome of the Rock in Jerusalem) or to house objects of value (museums); *mechanical reproduction* of the site through postcards, miniatures, and souvenirs; and *social reproduction,* as groups of people elsewhere name themselves after the attraction.

MacCannell also analyzes the structure of tourist settings in terms of "staged authenticity." Building on ERVING GOFFMAN's notion of front and back regions in social life, MacCannell distinguishes front regions that are intended for tourists (hotels, shops, international food franchises), front regions with back-region elements for atmosphere (hotel lobbies decorated with local products), front regions that simulate back regions (re-creations of traditional architecture or villages), back regions that are open to outsiders (tours of the homes of celebrities), back regions that are minimally modified to accommodate outsiders (film sets, dress rehearsals, factories), and back regions to which outsiders rarely if ever have access but for which they yearn.

Some students of tourism have suggested that not all tourist situations are ones of staged authenticity. According to Cohen, *authentic* situations may be encountered by adventurous tourists who move off the beaten track. *Covert* tourist space is created when the industry conceals the staging of a setting in order to present it as "real." Once tourists become cynical, they may adopt an attitude of *staging suspicion* and deny the authenticity of sites that have not been staged. Finally, there are *overt* tourist settings that are blatantly contrived and accepted as such.

Authenticity and authentication. The issue of authenticity has stimulated much of the writing on tourism, which has been highly critical of tourists and tourist attractions. Daniel Boorstin's pseudo-events, Richard Dorson's fakelore, and MacCannell's staged authenticity all characterize tourism in ways that both idealize and take for granted notions of authenticity and culture. Alternative perspectives suggest that all culture is invented, not just tourist attractions, and that authenticity is not given in the event but is a social construction. The preoccupation with the authentic is a culturally and historically specific phenomenon: eighteenth-century lovers of ruins in England were rather permissive in the mingling of genuine and imitation antiques, whereas the makers of Plimoth Plantation in Massachusetts are fastidious about the historical accuracy of minute details of their re-creation of Pilgrim life frozen in the year 1627.

The issue is therefore less one of authenticity and more one of authentication: who has the power to represent whom and to determine which representation is authoritative? The representation of culture, what Richard Handler calls cultural objectification, is a complex ideological and political process. Edward Said, MICHEL FOUCAULT, James Clifford, George Marcus, and others have noted the relationship between knowledge and power and have suggested that the power to represent or to consume other cultures is a form of domination. One of the clearest instances is *orientalism,* defined by Said as the knowledge created by the West about the East and deployed ubiquitously in tourist productions. "Here history began . . . ," the sound-and-light show at the pyramids produced by a French team for the Egyptian Ministry of Culture, traces the history of Egypt from the pharaohs to the discovery of the Rosetta stone by Napoléon's officers to the French sound-and-light show itself. Indeed, orientalism is one of tourism's dominant modes.

Tourist art. In addition to settings and events, artifacts are produced for tourists. Variously known as tourist art, airport art, and the arts of acculturation, these objects are produced locally by one group for another. U.S. anthropologist Nelson Graburn classifies locally made artifacts along two axes: objects made for the local community versus those made for outsiders, and objects whose sources are traditional as opposed to "assimilated." Six categories emerge: the persistence of traditional objects for

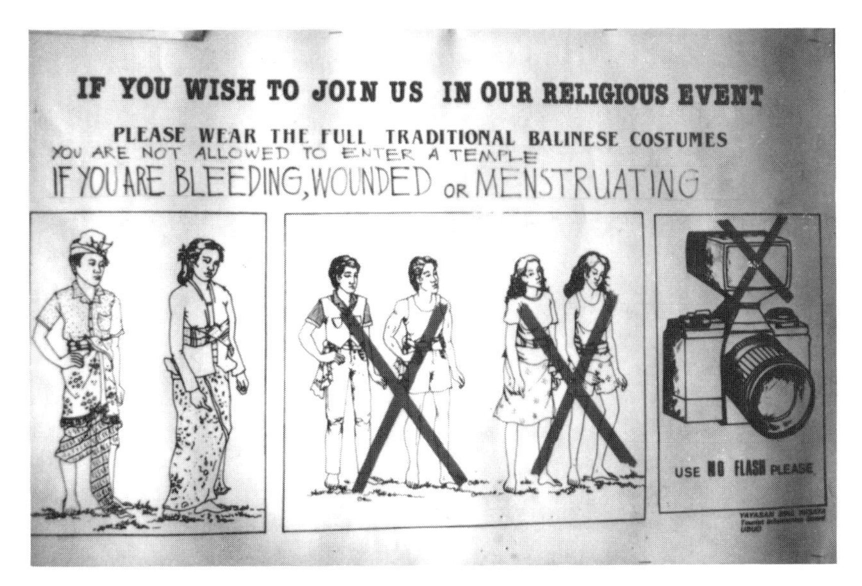

Figure 2. *(Tourism)* A sign from Bali, directing tourists to respect the local customs. Photograph by Edward M. Bruner.

Figure 3. *(Tourism)* Tourist making a purchase of Masai jewelry at Mayers' Ranch, Kenya. Photograph by Edward M. Bruner.

local use; pseudotraditional objects made for sale (Masai spears); souvenirs (Maori carved key chains); reintegrated arts, in which acculturated objects for local use also enter the tourist market (Cuna reverse-appliqué *molas*); assimilated fine arts for sale to tourists (European-influenced Balinese paintings); and popular arts, defined as acculturated objects for local consumption (Kenyan printed cotton *khanga* cloths).

Like authenticity, acculturation has its limits as a model for the study of tourist productions because changes are attributed to contact between what are presupposed to be autonomous, relatively isolated, and clearly identifiable cultures and the West. In contrast, Bennetta Jules-Rosette views tourist art not as a deviation from a traditional form but as an object emerging from a new social context. She suggests that "artists and consumers are joint producers of tourist art as a communicative process." Situated in a "complex international network of communication and economic exchange," these objects are interpreted in relation to the diverse markets in which they circulate. Whereas Graburn's scheme is based entirely on the producer's intended audience and sources, Jules-Rosette focuses on the malleable and multivocal nature of tourist objects in multiple contexts of exchange.

Controversies. Tourism is a mixed blessing. Anthropologist Philip McKean shows how tourism stimulates both traditional and innovative cultural activity in Bali. Florence Syme, a Rarotongan, complains: "Tourism is like a plague—it destroys people, their culture and heritage, and the environment. Rarotonga would be better off without the pilgrims and temples of their new religion." The Workshop on Tourism in Manila in 1980 condemned tourism as

Figure 4. *(Tourism)* Tourists at the Colosseum, Rome. Courtesy of the Italian Government Travel Office.

bringing economic exploitation, displacement of local populations, prostitution, crime, and deterioration of the social fabric of the Third World. Many have noted the economic benefits of tourism. For MacCannell the tourist is "one of the best models for modern-man-in-general." As tourism continues to expand and to take ever more inventive forms, the controversies regarding its nature, value, and dangers will command an ever greater share of our attention.

See also BAEDEKER, KARL; DEVELOPMENT COMMUNICATION; LEISURE; MIGRATION.

Bibliography. *Annals of Tourism Research,* Elmsford, N.Y., 1974–; Daniel J. Boorstin, *The Image: A Guide to Pseudo-Events in America,* New York, 1964; Erik Cohen, "The Sociology of Tourism," *Annual Review of Sociology* 10 (1984): 373–392; Emanuel de Kadt, ed., *Tourism, Passport to Development?: Perspectives on the Social and Cultural Effects of Tourism in Developing Countries,* Washington, D.C., and New York, 1979; Günther Dress, *Wirtschafts- und sozialgeographische Aspekte des Tourismus in Entwicklungsländern,* Munich, 1979; Michel Foucault, *Power/Knowledge: Selected Interviews and Other Writings, 1972–1977* (in French), ed. and trans. by Colin Gordon, Brighton, Eng., 1980; Nelson H. H. Graburn, ed., *Ethnic and Tourist Arts,* Berkeley, Calif., 1976; Bennetta Jules-Rosette, *The Messages of Tourist Art: An African Semiotic System in Comparative Perspective,* New York, 1984; Hans J. Knebel, *Soziologische Strukturwandlungen im modernen Tourismus,* Stuttgart, 1960; Jost Krippendorf, ed., *Fremdenverkehr im Wandel,* Frankfurt and Berlin, 1974; Dean MacCannell, *The Tourist: A New Theory of the Leisure Class,* New York, 1976; Valene L. Smith, ed., *Hosts and Guests: The Anthropology of Tourism,* Philadelphia, 1977; Jill D. Sweet, *Dances of the Tewa Pueblo Indians,* Sante Fe, N.Mex., 1985.

BARBARA KIRSHENBLATT-GIMBLETT
AND EDWARD M. BRUNER

TRAGEDY

One of the two great subdivisions of DRAMA in Western tradition, the other being COMEDY. Since the flowering of Greek drama in the fifth century B.C.E. works in the Western THEATER have generally been categorized as either tragedy or comedy. This has not been true in the Asian theater, in which tragedy as a GENRE has scarcely existed, although tragic ingredients are often used. Especially in South Asia there has been a conviction that drama, in keeping with its religious ritualistic origins, should culminate in a message of affirmation, not defeat. This overview of the genre of tragedy will thus focus on the Western cultural heritage.

The meaning of tragedy. Throughout the ages tragedy has been lodged at the center of human concern and interest. The writers of tragedy have felt the need to dramatize the terrible facts of death, determinism, suffering, failure, and mystery—the darker experiences of the human race. The forms used to express these experiences change with the passage of time, each age producing tragedies based on the beliefs and conventions of the age, but the substance of tragedy endures precisely because it touches what it means to be human, what it is that makes life a terrible puzzlement. Tragedy, emerging out of religious rituals (*see* RITUAL) of ancient Greece, has engaged the attention of audiences for a span of twenty-five hundred years. It is the most enduring and exalted of genres because it offers permanently valid truths about the human condition, affording pleasure even as it dramatizes the pain of life.

Classical traditions. How tragedy got its name is debatable. The Greek word *tragōidia* literally means "goat song," perhaps referring to the SONG sung by a chorus of goatlike satyrs, perhaps referring to the prize of a goat given to the chorus. Another explanation, touching the ritual origins of the genre and thereby directly related to the Greek religious festivals, posits the goat as a sacrifice, a scapegoat. Traditionally a virile animal, the goat, like the bull, was closely linked to Dionysus; in fact, Dionysiac ritual contained the symbolic dismemberment of the god with the goat serving as the god's substitute. This ritual connects Dionysus to Greek tragedy, supporting ARISTOTLE's view in his *Poetics* (ca. 330 B.C.E.) that tragedy developed from passionate choric songs honoring Dionysus, the god of fertility, connected with everything wet (blood, wine, sap, semen) and connected with vegetation—the dying *and* living god whose cycle of death and life paralleled the seasonal workings of nature. According to many scholars tragedy stemmed from this death-rebirth cycle, with the tragic protagonist representing both the god and the goat that had to be sacrificed, with the god's suffering and death expressed by the genre of tragedy and the god's resurrection expressed by the genre of comedy. (This is a pattern repeated in the later Christian story.)

The chorus is important to any discussion of Greek tragedy. Dancing and chanting, the chorus occupied the center of the theater that was erected as a shrine to Dionysus. The chorus celebrated a god as part of a ritual, and from ritual primitive drama was born. By the fifth century B.C.E., when the city-state of Athens witnessed its greatest tragedies, the chorus remained an intrinsic part of the PERFORMANCE of the play, not only providing background information but also responding philosophically and emotionally to what was happening in it. The chorus directed the larger response of the audience of approximately twenty thousand people who sat in the huge amphitheater, surrounding the orchestra or "dancing place"

Figure 1. *(Tragedy)* A scene from Euripides' *Alkmene* depicted on a Paestan bell-krater, third quarter of the fourth century B.C.E. The jealous husband, Amphitryon *(right)*, is shown attempting to burn his wife off an altar onto which she has jumped in order to escape from him. Zeus *(top left)* sends Clouds, who pour water from jars to quench the flames with rain, and Eros *(top right)* observes the entire scene. The elaborate costumes of the three principal characters reflect the influence of the stage. Reproduced by courtesy of the Trustees of The British Museum.

of the chorus. Performed in the open air, the choric odes were complex presentations, combining words and music and DANCE, appealing to both eye and ear, controlling the emotions of the audience that the chorus itself represented. The three great Athenian tragedians—Aeschylus (525–456 B.C.E.), Sophocles (496–406 B.C.E.), and Euripides (484–406 B.C.E.)—used the chorus in different ways, placing different emphases on the relationship of choral ode to dramatic enactment.

The Greek tragedians took their subject matter from traditional myths and legends, each playwright using them to offer his particular tragic vision. In the *Oresteia,* the only surviving trilogy in Greek drama, Aeschylus dramatizes three important events in the story of the House of Atreus—the murder of Agamemnon in *Agamemnon,* the murders of Clytemnestra and Aegisthus in *The Libation Bearers,* and the trial of Orestes in *The Eumenides*—in order to examine the relationship between the gods and human justice, thereby touching the large tragic issues of suffering, evil, death, man's responsibilities, and the workings of the gods. In *Oedipus Rex,* the highest achievement of Greek drama, Sophocles uses the Oedipus myth to reveal man's tragic recognition of the dark, irrational, demonic forces within him and the appalling mystery of the gods. In *Hippolytus* Euripides pushes his legendary characters Hippolytus, Phaedra, and Theseus along a destructive path, placing irrationality and contradiction at the core of human life. Only thirty-one plays of the three tragedians survive out of approximately three hundred written, but these are enough to secure for fifth-century Athens the distinction of having produced one of the two greatest periods of tragic drama.

The most significant critical document dealing with tragedy is the first one, also a product of Athens, the *Poetics* of Aristotle. It is a fragment, perhaps the lecture notes of the great philosopher, offering ideas and terms that are not closely explained and are therefore debatable. Aristotle was describing what he saw and what he knew, but his important ideas provide the basis for almost all discussions of tragedy. Aristotle defines tragedy as "an imitation of an action that is serious, complete, and of some magnitude, in language that is artistically varied, dramatic rather than narrative, through pity and fear effecting a purgation [*catharsis*] of these emotions." He considered plot, the imitation of the action, to be the most important element of tragedy, with character revealed through action, and he believed that the most exciting parts of the tragic action are the reversal (*peripeteia*) and the discovery or recognition (*anagnorisis*). After plot and character the important tragic elements are thought, LANGUAGE, song, and SPECTACLE. For the action of a tragedy to be "serious," Aristotle insisted that the protagonist be nobly born and more admirable than ordinary men, but he should not be morally perfect because his downfall should be the inevitable consequence of some defect in character, usually referred to as the tragic flaw (*hamartia*).

Each of Aristotle's ideas has been debated through the years, especially his notion of the purgation of the emotions of pity and fear, indicating that Aristotle considered the effect of tragedy to be purifying or exalting rather than depressing. His belief that an action should be complete led RENAISSANCE rhetoricians to insist on the famous classical unities of time, place, and action. The *Poetics* is a useful starting point for critical discussions of tragedy, but it was not meant to be a list of rules for writing tragedy; it was an empirical description of dramatic form.

Postclassical developments. The Greek tragedies provided the models for the most influential of Roman tragedians, Seneca (ca. 4 B.C.E.–65 C.E.), the Stoic philosopher who provides a bridge between the two most important periods of tragic drama, the ancient Greek and the Elizabethan. Seneca took his plots from the Greek legends, retained the chorus, observed the unities, and emphasized the theme of revenge and the power of necessity. He added passionate monologues, the ghost as a character, philosophical maxims, and a general sense of violence and horror. More melodrama than pure classical tragedy, Seneca's plays, not performed on a stage and therefore perhaps less sensational than they seem, did help to preserve the tragic tradition. Translated into English from the Latin in 1581, Seneca's *Tenne Tragedies* deeply affected Elizabethan tragic drama. The first English classical tragedy, *Gorboduc* (1561), written by Thomas Sackville and Thomas Norton, is heavily influenced by Seneca, as are the popular tragedies of Thomas Kyd (1558–1594), Christopher Marlowe (1564–1593), and William Shakespeare (1564–1616).

Before classical tragedy made itself felt in Elizabethan England, the term *tragedy* was applied to NARRATIVE rather than to drama. In the MIDDLE AGES any verse narrative describing the fall of a high-born man because of the turning of the wheel of fortune was a tragedy, ostensibly written to remind Christians of the frailty of human life. Geoffrey Chaucer's "The Monk's Tale" in *The Canterbury Tales* (1387–1400), John Lydgate's *The Fall of Princes* (ca. 1430–1438), and the popular Elizabethan miscellany of stories *The Mirror for Magistrates* (1559) are important works in the development of the tragic narrative. Medieval drama, the outgrowth of a religious ceremony of priests, with Jesus, like Dionysus, the starting point of the mimetic representation of death and life and resurrection, consisted of mystery or miracle plays (the dramatization of biblical stories) and morality plays (dramatized allegories of the battle of good and evil for the soul of man). The plays of the native medieval tradition offered REALISM and allegory, mingled mirth and seriousness, and provided unlocalized playing areas ranging from heaven to earth to hell.

These characteristics, mingling with Senecan characteristics and form and absorbing some of the ideas of the tragical verse narratives, resulted in the great

Figure 2. *(Tragedy)* Illustration from Giovanni Boccaccio's *De Mulieribus Claris*, 1473: "The fortunes of Portia, wife of Brutus: She dies by swallowing live coals." From William Farnham, *The Medieval Heritage of Elizabethan Tragedy*, New York: Barnes & Noble, 1956, p. 89.

Figure 3. *(Tragedy)* Sarah Bernhardt in the role of Phaedra. The Bettmann Archive/BBC Hulton.

flourishing of tragedy in the Elizabethan age. This heterogeneous blending, this Renaissance synthesis, did not produce classical tragedy, much to the disappointment of such exponents of CLASSICISM as Sir Philip Sidney and Ben Jonson. Closer to romantic tragedy—with its emphasis on character, its greater variety of style and mood, and its greater freedom of presentation—this form of tragedy, usually written in blank verse, reached its peak of excellence in the work of Shakespeare, whose *Hamlet, Othello, King Lear, Macbeth,* and *Antony and Cleopatra* are among the highest accomplishments of the genre.

The movement away from the free and complex tragic form of the Elizabethans and back toward the more austere classicism of ancient Greece produced its best results in France in the seventeenth century. The neoclassical tragedy of Pierre Corneille (1606–1684) and Jean Racine (1639–1699), influenced by critical writings based on Aristotle, observed the unities of time, place, and action and adhered to the neoclassical ideals of decorum. Racine's *Phèdre,* taking its story from the Hippolytus myth and its inspiration from Euripides, offers a terrifying study of passion within the strict confines of neoclassical art. Written in polished poetry, it represents French tragic drama at its best.

Reaction to the rigidities of neoclassical tragic form found its most effective spokesmen in England's SAMUEL JOHNSON and in Germany's first important critic of drama, Gotthold Lessing. Johnson, himself a neoclassicist, in his *Preface to Shakespeare* (1765), defended Shakespeare's supposed irregularities, asserting, for example, that the mingling of the tragic and the comic is close to what we find in nature. Johnson felt that too great an insistence on the unities indicates a confusion between art and life because it is based on the false idea that spectators in a theater do not realize that "the stage is only a stage, and that the players are only players." Lessing, in his *Hamburg Dramaturgy* (1769), attacked the French neoclassical models for tragedy, urging greater flexibility. In fact, Lessing not only advocated but also wrote a different kind of tragedy, middle-class or bourgeois tragedy, the most important example being *Miss Sara Sampson* (1755). (Earlier in England, in 1731, George Lillo had written the first influential middle-class tragedy, *The London Merchant.*) These bourgeois tragedies—affected by the growing romanticism of the eighteenth century, written in prose, and dealing with the supposedly realistic affairs of middle-class people—were often ludicrously sentimental and essentially unreal, but they clearly reflect the tastes of new middle-class audiences throughout Europe, who demanded fewer neoclassical rules and legendary heroes and more portrayals of everyday people. That is, the middle class wanted a theater that more directly reflected its own contemporary interests, a theater that rejected not only neoclassical rigidity of form but also the kind of romantic excess found in the work of Victor Hugo (1802–1885). This anticlassical and antiromantic attitude led eventually to the realism of the modern theater.

Realism and modern forms of tragedy. In the preface to his *Thérèse Raquin* (1873), Émile Zola clearly shouts out for a naturalistic drama, plays that adhere to the facts of heredity and environment, that offer a "slice of life," that are written in prose spoken by characters who do not "play, but rather live, before the audience." Four years later Henrik Ibsen, considered the father of modern realism, presented his first important realistic drama, *Pillars of Society* (1877). But the realism of Ibsen and the modern dramatists who come after him is not the limited photographic realism favored by Zola. It is a modified realism, more ambiguous, more imaginative, belonging to a dramatic art that seems more subjective, more self-conscious, and, because of the influence of Friedrich Nietzsche—who declared the death of traditional values and in *The Birth of Tragedy* (1872) celebrated the deeper, irrational, wilder side of humanity by claiming that Greek tragedy and all true tragedy was informed by the spirit of Dionysus—more rebellious and more romantic.

New ideas about humanity and the modern world, ideas clinging to no traditional frame of reference, fostered a wide variety of forms in the writing of tragedy. Biological determinism (CHARLES DARWIN), economic determinism (KARL MARX), psychological determinism (SIGMUND FREUD), and scientific determinism (Albert Einstein) helped to make modern tragedy seem less exalted than Greek and Elizabethan tragedy. In fact, many critics believe that tragedy is not possible in modern times. The title of George Steiner's book *The Death of Tragedy* (1961) represents the belief of many commentators who claim that modern humanity has become too insignificant for tragedy, lacking greatness of spirit, an organic worldview, and any meaningful ritualistic or mythological context—in short, that tragedy, like Nietzsche's God, is dead. Certainly the Greek and Elizabethan forms of tragedy can no longer serve modern dramatists, but the ambiguous condition of modern humanity—with its sense of aloneness, inability to explain the mystery of existence, confrontation with death, suffering and sense of terror, newly created myths and rituals—has given rise to new forms of tragedy, forms of unlimited variety. The tragic vision is authentic and enduring, and such different modern dramatists as Ibsen, August Strindberg, Anton Chekhov, Eugene O'Neill, Arthur Miller, Tennessee Williams, and Samuel Beckett have dramatized that vision in different forms, often mixed forms with strong doses of irony and comedy. Each of these dramatists touches the same dark experiences that fascinated Sophocles and Shakespeare and Racine. Each testifies to the fact that tragedy cannot be defined by any one age and cannot be captured in any one form, that tragedy may be forced to speak in new languages but that those languages will always communicate the darkly terrible facts of human existence.

Bibliography. Eric Bentley, *The Playwright as Thinker,* New York, 1946, reprint 1963; Normand Berlin, *The Secret Cause: A Discussion of Tragedy,* Amherst, Mass., 1981; Faubion Bowers, *Theater in the East: A Survey of Asian Dance and Drama,* New York, 1956, reprint 1969; Barrett H. Clark, ed., *European Theories of the Drama,* Cincinnati, Ohio, 1918, reprint (rev. by Henry Popkin) New York, 1947; Robert W. Corrigan, ed., *Tragedy: Vision and Form,* 2d ed., New York, 1981; Francis Fergusson, *The Idea of the Theater,* Princeton, N.J., 1949; Robert B. Heilman, *Tragedy and Melodrama,* Seattle, Wash., 1968; Laurence Michel and Richard B. Sewall, eds., *Tragedy: Modern Essays in Criticism,* Englewood Cliffs, N.J., 1963; Herbert J. Muller, *The Spirit of Tragedy,* New York, 1956; Richard B. Sewall, *The Vision of Tragedy,* new ed., enl., New Haven, Conn., 1980; George Steiner, *The Death of Tragedy,* New York, 1961.

NORMAND BERLIN

TRANSBORDER DATA FLOWS (TDF). *See* COMPUTER: IMPACT—IMPACT ON THE WORLD ECONOMY; DATA BASE; NEW INTERNATIONAL INFORMATION ORDER; SPECTRUM; TELECOMMUNICATIONS NETWORKS; TELECOMMUNICATIONS POLICY.

TRANSLATION, LITERARY

The translation of literature makes possible the preservation and transmission of cultural knowledge that might otherwise be unavailable to wide circles. Despite the extinction of the languages in which they were first written, such literary works as the epic of Gilgamesh or of the Trojan War can still be read as informative and enduring expressions of the cultures that produced them. We can refer to "Homer's Greece," "Dante's Italy," or "Chaucer's England" as naturally as if history and CULTURE were themselves by-products of their representations in literature rather than the other way around. READING these authors in translation can convey a sensation of cultural context to general audiences, not merely to specialists, historians, archaeologists, or philologists.

However, the process of literary translation remains one of the most problematic issues in LANGUAGE theory, still far from being adequately accounted for. Translating any type of text is an inordinately puzzling activity to explain, as the early disappointments of machine translation showed. The most decisive obstacle has been the lack of a realistic SEMANTICS to mediate between the potential meanings of words (as known to speakers of a language or recorded in a dictionary) and the actual meanings of texts (*see* MEANING). LINGUISTICS generally proposes the inclusion of large quantities of specifications in the listings of some dictionary or lexicon yet disregards the selection and specification occurring in actual communication, that is, the ways in which context decides what things mean from case to case. Discourse is thus left seeming strangely indeterminate, and the processes whereby determinacy is in fact established have barely been explored.

An additional obstacle is that literature both affirms and modifies the systems it uses and addresses. Literature is free to foreground possibilities that are normally backgrounded, marginalized, or excluded in ordinary discourse. Whereas an adequate theory of ordinary language has to focus on central, commonly used options, a theory of literary language requires a more expansive and creative scope. Linguistics has not yet been able to bridge the gap between the abstract system and its concrete literary realizations. Only some ostensibly deviant or ungrammatical usages in POETRY have received much attention.

Meanwhile, a venerable tradition in the practice of literary translating continues despite the lack of an adequate theory. The translator is obliged to proceed in a pragmatic, ad hoc fashion from context to context, often without overarching principles to arrange priorities and promote consistency in solving interrelated problems. As a consequence, the quality of available translations is remarkably uneven and the role of the translator poorly defined. PUBLISHING houses tend to consider standards of quality less urgent than cost and profit.

When theoretical positions are advanced, they typically belie the complexities of literary translating. A prime example is the long-standing polemics setting "literal," word-by-word translation against "free" translation focused on global effects of "literariness." The two positions demarcate extremes, which, if rigidly followed, promote unsatisfactory results. The skilled translator navigates between the two.

A more productive approach is the postulate that what should be translated is neither words nor literariness but an experience comparable to that sought or elicited by the original text. That experience should not include interfering signals of a divergence between language codes (*see* CODE), such as literal translations convey, but neither should it assimilate itself so completely to the reader's own cultural idioms and expectations that the foreign culture is totally transformed or erased. The reader should be able to sense unfamiliar possibilities, though in culture, not in GRAMMAR.

The literary translator should accordingly attempt to reconstruct a model response and to gauge the extent to which it depends on a margin between the individual work and readers' expectations based on the source language, both in ordinary discourse and in prevailing literary conventions. This margin should be preserved by using and adapting the resources of the target language and its literary conventions. The exactitude of reproducing this margin is promoted not by unduly literal or free methods but only by a detailed awareness of the various forces exerted on the reading process in two cultures.

Consequently, a theory of translating literature presupposes a workable theory of responding to literature. Recent decades have witnessed an impressive increase in efforts to develop such a READING THEORY. The net result so far, however, is more a sense of the vast perplexities involved than a consensus about the specifics of the process. The essence of literature is to elicit multiple ways of reading, each of which appears to be inspiring its own set of theories.

Nonetheless, some major points of convergence can be recognized. The main function of literature, as is generally acknowledged, is to reflect on any prevailing system of culture and discourse by treating it as one among other alternatives. FICTION is thus not the opposite of fact, nor set apart in some unrelated world, but a special MODE for examining and understanding how facts and worlds are constituted (*see* FACT AND FICTION). Literature is construed to convey not factual truths of circumstance so much as general truths about the human situation in all its richness and diversity. The aesthetic experience imposes a special framework for organizing and integrating knowledge of particularly diverse kinds. For the "great" work, many such frameworks can be provided, none of which exhausts the work or stabilizes its meaning once and for all.

Such theses suggest that what the literary translator should mediate is not a "message" but an open-ended problematics. The drive to solve problems and incorporate solutions or explanations into the translation must be strongly resisted so that the reader of the translation is not denied the opportunity to actualize the work and participate in its creativity. The translation should be a special act of reading and responding that makes possible a continuation and expansion of response beyond the confines of the original culture and language but that does not foreclose that response.

A theory of literary translating should accordingly try to model the ways in which the translator is interposed between author and reader. The translator should view his or her own response to the original as a partial actualization of materials to be rerendered in terms that will continue to allow many other responses. The translator should read the original numerous times from as many perspectives as possible, noting the aspects and sections that come to the foreground in each case. The task is then to generate coincidences in the target language that can elicit a similar range of responses. The major difference between PROSE and poetry is the greater dependence of poetry on coincidences between forms and meanings, between forms and other forms, or between meanings and other meanings. When parallel coincidences cannot be found, a commentary can be included to indicate what has been reduced, altered, or lost. This recourse splits up the aesthetic experience, but at least strives to keep the range of actualizable meanings in view.

Literary authors might seem to be the best qualified for such a task. And in fact they have produced many great translations, as when Alexander Pope exerted himself for Homer, Dante Gabriel Rossetti for François Villon, Stefan George for Charles-Pierre Baudelaire, T. S. Eliot for Saint-John Perse, and so on. But this requirement is not necessary. A translator may well be able to reconstruct a performance that he or she would not have initiated; Walter Arndt's translations of Aleksandr Pushkin or Michael Kandel's renditions of Stanisław Lem demonstrate a fortunate convergence of talents in which the translator seems to be carried by the author's inspiration. Conversely, literary AUTHORSHIP is no guarantee of skill as a translator. An author is likely to foreground whatever best fits his or her own style (*see* STYLE, LITERARY) and AESTHETICS, which are again only part of the total space offered by art. Hence, the ideal author-translator would be able to adapt to other stylistic possibilities and to maintain a balance with those of the original author.

No doubt literary translating is a utopian enterprise, as José Ortega y Gasset remarked. A work can no more be definitively translated than it can be definitively read or interpreted. Yet by the same token the task always leaves room for improvement. And its vital service in the transmission of culture renders it worthy of all the exacting effort it may demand.

See also INTERPRETATION; LANGUAGE REFERENCE BOOK; TRANSLATION, THEORIES OF.

Bibliography. Robert de Beaugrande, *Factors in a Theory of Poetic Translating,* Amsterdam, 1978; Andrei Fedorov, *Vvednie v teoriju perevoda,* Moscow, 1958; Jiři Levy, *Die literarische Übersetzung,* Frankfurt am Main, 1969; José Antonio Ortega y Gasset, "Miseria y esplendor de la traducción," in *Obras completas,* Vol. 5, Madrid, 1966, reprint 1983.

ROBERT DE BEAUGRANDE

TRANSLATION, THEORIES OF

Translation serves communal aspirations, for it has always been the basic means of communication across the barriers of LANGUAGE and the cultures they separate. Not only does translation reach every corner of the present, but it also maintains contact with the remote past and thus provides at least the basis for a greater understanding of what it is to be human.

The word *translation* itself contains an ambiguity; it denotes both the process and the product, both the attempt and the achievement of translating. The practice of translation is an art rather than a science, and its success is relative rather than absolute. Translations are neither true nor false but more or less faithful to an original. The process thus requires as much skill as knowledge to manage the right balance of effects. The variety of theories that converge on translation come from LINGUISTICS and SEMIOTICS, from psychology and anthropology, making any serious study of the subject interdisciplinary.

The translation field comprises a very important body of evidence for any study of language and communication. By almost every account communication involves some kind of representation and transmission, with a message that cannot be perceived or transmitted directly and a signal that can, the whole point being that the one should represent and transmit the other. That point is also the problem: the message itself cannot be observed but has to be inferred from the signal. The problem in practice is to find the right inference, the one that gets the message right. The problem in theory is to find the right explanation for the entire process, all its elements and operations, its success as well as its failure. In the case of verbal communication, that requires cogent answers to some basic questions about the nature of MEANING and its relation to form. Here is where translation helps. Though it cannot show or reveal meaning as such, independent of any form, translation can do the next best thing: it can produce another form with the same meaning and thus provide evidence for the correlation of meanings in different languages.

Language as code. Translation is supposed to preserve meaning in the passage from one language to another. There are bound to be differences in translation, differences in form or language, but there are not supposed to be any differences in meaning, in substance or content. How can that be? The traditional idea of language, which is at least as old as ARISTOTLE, offers an explanation that has great appeal. It assumes that words represent thoughts and thoughts in turn represent things. Verbal communication is seen as a process of encoding and decoding that moves back and forth between words and the corresponding thoughts or things. Translation would thus require only a method of transcription, the regular substitution of equivalent signals, much as it is done automatically by telegraph (*see* TELEGRAPHY) and TELEPHONE.

The old idea of language has a commonsense look but is hardly plausible. It has been discredited most notably by the dramatic failure of machine translation. The idea of devising an effective and fully automatic procedure for translation was obviously encouraged by the rapid development of the modern computer (*see* COMPUTER: HISTORY), and yet it also seems to have been inspired by the mystique of CRYPTOLOGY. U.S. mathematician WARREN WEAVER set the scene when he said that it was enough to consider an article in Russian as if it had really been written in English and then coded for protection. The rest would be ordinary cryptanalysis, difficult but not impossible, because there was a real solution. Though striking, the analogy did not hold; mistakes were simply too numerous and often quite ludicrous. As a result it seemed reasonable to conclude that Russian was not an encoding of English and, further, that no language was really a CODE in any strict sense. There lies the crux for any theory about translation: it has to explain why there is no strict correlation between form and meaning in verbal communication.

Language and thought. There could be no correlation whatsoever between form and meaning without the existence of both and a real difference between the two. Yet the most radical theories about language contend that the traditional correlation fails to hold precisely because those basic conditions fail to obtain.

Indeterminacy of translation is a negative thesis defended by the analytic philosopher W. V. Quine against claims about meanings, and other entities like thoughts and propositions, which he finds dubious for want of valid evidence. The argument relies heavily and rests finally on his objections to exhibits of translation as proof of synonymy. Before it can provide support for the identity of meaning and thus warrant the postulation of some such things, either mental or purely logical, translation must have evidence of its own. But in most cases Quine sees no reason, other than habit or convenience, to prefer one translation to another. He concludes that translation is indeterminate because meaning is not intersubjectively or even intrasubjectively verifiable. That is no fault or cause for change in practice, though it does argue for a change in thinking about what happens in translation. It argues specifically against the traditional notion that translation is the transfer of a determinate meaning from one language to another and argues generally against the very idea that language is the expression of thought. When faced with the question of what has been said in some other language, we readily assume there is a definite answer that can be given in translation. Quine would dismiss both question and reply; in his view there is nothing objective to be right or wrong about.

Linguistic relativity covers a whole range of hypotheses about the relations between language and thought. The strongest version is commonly attributed to EDWARD SAPIR and BENJAMIN LEE WHORF for their contrastive studies of American Indian languages. They claim that grammatical structures determine cognitive capacities: because one cannot say what the native says, one cannot think what the native thinks. The evidence remains equivocal. It is tendentious to assume that every difference in language has significance in CULTURE. Compare, for instance, sex and nominal GENDER, or time and verbal tense; they are not equivalent. Also, it is circular to adduce differences in talk alone as proof of differences in thought. The argument for a causal connection requires evidence, independent of language, of the effects of thought. More modest claims are made for simple correlations between lexical items and cultural interests. The standard example of the Eskimo with many words for snow can be matched by the skier or anyone else who needs a special terminology for a specific purpose. Vocabulary is the most responsive and therefore the least restrictive part of language. And as shown in the case of terms for color, humans already see and know more than they can say. New ideas have to find new words, as when languages borrow from each other and thus increase their means of expression, sometimes by direct translation.

Contributions of cognitive science. It may still be possible to explain the facts of translation with theories that see language as a correlation of form and meaning. A new discipline, cognitive science, seeks to understand the workings of the human mind much as if they were the operations of a powerful computer. Cognitive science explores and elaborates the idea that thinking and computing are essentially the same because they both involve the regular manipulation of symbols and thus require something like an internal code. The analogy works either way. If the mind is really a system of rules and representations, then any device with an equivalent program could also think or at least simulate COGNITION. Hence the attempt to develop ARTIFICIAL INTELLIGENCE as a form of experimental psychology. The results have been mixed, and the project itself remains controversial. Yet there is a growing consensus, if only about the main requirements for a theory of verbal communication in the cognitive MODE. Major contributors to that part of the enterprise include Noam Chomsky in linguistics, Jerry Fodor in psychology, and Dan Sperber in anthropology. Their work provides the outline for a comprehensive, composite theory of language that would also explain both the possibilities and difficulties of translation.

In this theory, meanings are once again the thoughts expressed by sentences, and they are independent as well as different from those sentences because they exist in a different language. Like all thoughts they exist in the mind as the formulas of an internal language that is neither English nor Japanese but a regular mentalese. Before a single word can be said or heard, communication needs translation in the form of an exchange between thought and expression.

See also INTERPRETATION.

Bibliography. Brent Berlin and Paul Kay, *Basic Color Terms: Their Universality and Evolution,* Berkeley, Calif., 1969; Noam Chomsky, *Reflections on Language,* New York, 1975; Jerry A. Fodor, *The Language of Thought,* New York, 1975; F. Guenthner and M. Guenthner-Reutter, eds., *Meaning and Translation: Philosophical and Linguistic Approaches,* London, 1978; W. V. Quine, *Word and Object,* New York and London, 1960; Dan Sperber and Deirdre Wilson, *Relevance: Communication and Cognition,* Cambridge, Mass., 1986.

JOSEPH F. GRAHAM

TYPOGRAPHY

The technical processes used to produce printed words; it also means the style, appearance, and arrangement of printed material. JOHANNES GUTENBERG invented typography, the letterpress PRINTING of books from movable types, around 1450 in Mainz, Germany (*see* BOOK). For 450 years of letterpress printing, typographic DESIGN was primarily handled by compositors who set type by hand. In contemporary society a graphic designer is an individual, usually with ART training, who plans and designs the visual aspects of printing and other graphic communications.

Development. During the Incunabula—the first fifty years of book printing in Europe—the design of the earliest typographic books imitated hand-lettered manuscript books as closely as possible. The first type styles were based on the traditional black letter of the medieval scribe (*see* MIDDLE AGES). An early practice of printing type, then manually adding ornaments, illustrations, and illuminated initials, declined after Venetian printers of the Italian RENAISSANCE made major innovations in the typographic book. The evolution of roman typefaces with capitals based on Roman inscriptions and lowercase letters patterned after the humanistic WRITING styles of Italian scribes reached full flower in the fifteenth century in the designs of Nicolas Jenson. In the earliest extant title page design for a typographic book (Figure 1), Erhard Ratdolt and his partners used roman letterforms, a large initial, and a decorative woodcut border design. Venetian scholar Al-

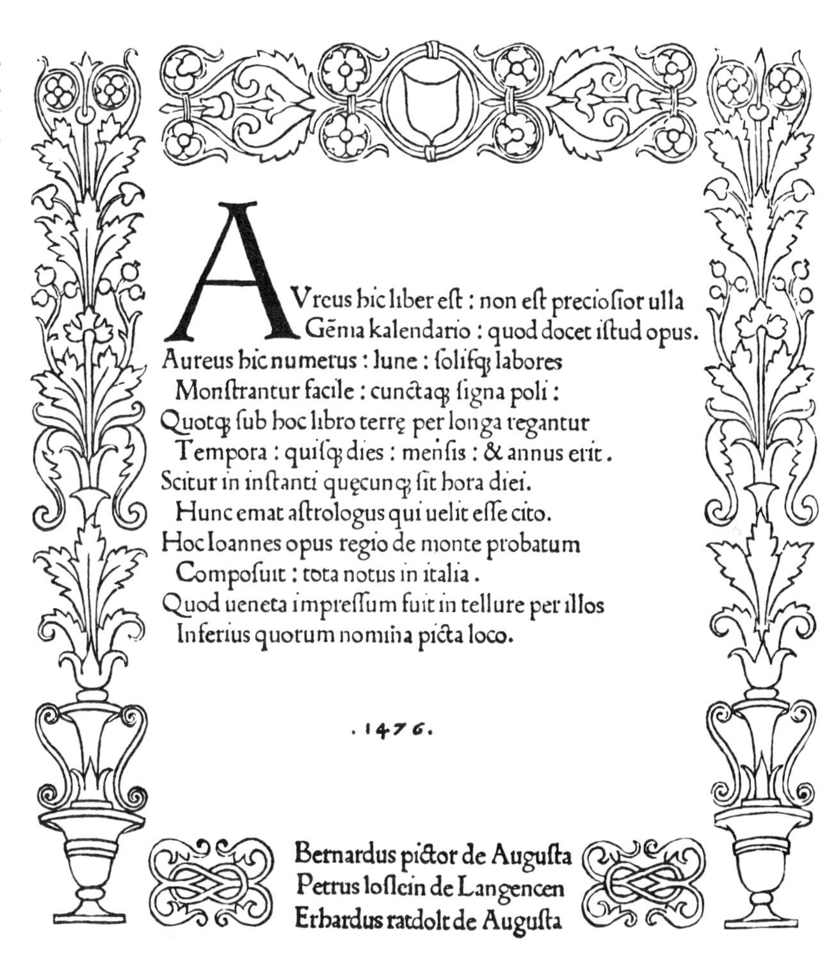
AVreus hic liber eſt : non eſt precioſior ulla
Gēma kalendario : quod docet iſtud opus.
Aureus hic numerus : lune : ſoliſq; labores
Monſtrantur facile : cunctaq; ſigna poli :
Quotq; ſub hoc libro terrę per longa regantur
Tempora : quiſq; dies : menſis : & annus erit .
Scitur in inſtanti quęcunq; ſit hora diei.
Hunc emat aſtrologus qui uelit eſſe cito.
Hoc Ioannes opus regio de monte probatum
Compoſuit : tota notus in italia .
Quod ueneta impreſſum fuit in tellure per illos
Inferius quorum nomina picta loco.

.1476.

Bernardus pictor de Auguſta
Petrus loſlein de Langencen
Erhardus ratdolt de Auguſta

Figure 1. *(Typography)* Erhard Ratdolt, Peter Loeslein, and Bernhard Maler, title page for *Calendarium,* by Regiomontanus, 1476. All artwork in this article appears courtesy of Philip Meggs.

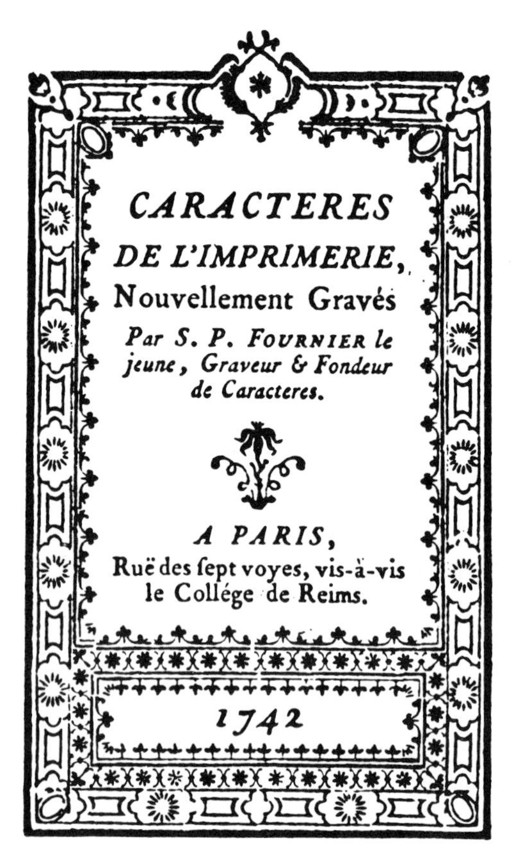

Figure 2. *(Typography)* Pierre-Simon Fournier le Jeune, title page from *Caractères de l'imprimerie,* 1742.

dus Manutius established a press in 1495 to print major works by the great thinkers of the Greco-Roman world. His typeface designer, Francesco da Bologna, surnamed Griffo, designed a major typeface, Bembo, which became a prototype for later developments and is still used in books today. In 1501 Manutius revolutionized PUBLISHING by producing the first "pocket book," a 3¾-by-6-inch edition of Virgil that could be carried easily in a pocket. To increase the number of words in each line of text, Griffo designed the first italic type style, which increased by 50 percent the characters per line. Together Manutius and Griffo achieved great elegance, legibility, and clarity. Other Italian innovations included printed page numbers, fine-line woodcut illustrations, cast-metal ornaments, and original approaches to the layout of type and illustrations. Italian Renaissance printers passed down the basic format of the typographic book, which has continued to the present. Further design refinement occurred in sixteenth-century France, where type designers including Claude Garamond created roman typefaces as we know them today, and printers in Paris and Lyons brought an unsurpassed elegance to book design. Contemporary typefaces based on these French designs are called Old Style.

Typographic innovation declined until the eighteenth century, when Paris typefounder Pierre-Simon Fournier le Jeune established a standard measurement system and pioneered the "type family" concept with a variety of compatible weights and widths that could be easily mixed in page designs. He designed florid ornamental letterforms and typographic flowers for richly garlanded pages paralleling the fanciful designs of decorative art and ARCHITECTURE of the French rococo era (Figure 2). Fournier's type designs evidence a tendency toward sharp, tapered serifs and increased weight contrast between thick and thin strokes that occurred during the 1700s. At midcentury John Baskerville designed transitional letterforms that articulated these qualities so beautifully that typefaces based on his designs and bearing his name are used today. Baskerville's book designs were free of ornamental treatments and relied on an exquisite typographic arrangement on smooth, hot-pressed paper for a refined design effect. Transitional type designs evolved into the Modern Style typeface designs (Figure 3) of Giambattista Bodoni and François-Ambroise Didot, characterized by geometric proportions, extreme contrast between thick and thin strokes, and hairline serifs. Closely related to the late-eighteenth-century classical revival in painting and architecture, book designs of this period featured simple, symmetrical page layout with severe proportions and meticulous engraved illustrations with classical motifs (*see* CLASSICISM).

Industrial Revolution. The Industrial Revolution radically altered typographic design. As Western civilization shifted from an agrarian base to factory and mass production, typographic expression was adapted to the needs of the new industrial culture. To meet the demand for bold posters (*see* POSTER), announcements, and ADVERTISING, an explosive production of typeface designs occurred: Fat Faces, roman styles whose strokes are bloated to a 1:2 stroke-width-to-capital-height ratio; Egyptians, with bold, slablike serifs; sans serifs, denuded of the serifs that had existed on ALPHABET forms since the ROMAN EMPIRE; and a Pandora's box of novelty and special-effect styles, including outlines, perspectives, and decorated faces. This design expansion was hastened in 1827, when U.S. printer Darius Wells invented a lateral router that enabled the economical manufacture of large wood types.

Nineteenth-century letterpress printers designed posters and other typographic matter by mixing a variety of type styles. A different typeface was generally used for each of the lines, which were then centered on a medial axis and often letterspaced to be flush with the left and right margins. Figure 4 combines decorative, sans serif, Fat Face, and Egyptian styles.

As the setting of type by hand was a slow and

costly process, numerous efforts were undertaken to perfect a typesetting machine. In 1886 OTTMAR MERGENTHALER perfected the Linotype machine, which cast lines of lead type from keyboard-controlled circulating matrices. The increased efficiency and economy of machine typesetting dramatically reduced the cost of newspapers (*see* NEWSPAPER: HISTORY), magazines (*see* MAGAZINE), and books, with a concomitant growth in circulation. *See* GRAPHIC REPRODUCTION.

During the nineteenth century the quality of book design and typography fell victim to the manufacturing expediencies of the Industrial Revolution. English artist and author William Morris rejected the mass-produced goods of the Victorian era and advocated a return to handicraft, respect for the nature of materials and production methods, a fitness of design to purpose, and individual expression by both designer and skilled worker. Morris led the English Arts and Crafts movement in a reaction against the social and aesthetic abuses of industrialism during the last quarter of the century. In 1888 Morris plunged into typeface design and printing in an attempt to reclaim the lost design and production qualities of Incunabula books. He established the Kelmscott Press, which used handmade paper, handpresses, hand-cut wood-block illustrations and decorations, and hand-cast types in three typefaces designed by Morris after Incunabula styles. The Kelmscott approach (Figure 5) inspired the private-press movement at the turn of the century, as designers and printers sought to produce limited-edition books of high quality. Even more important, it inspired a rejuvenation of typographic design encompassing the development of improved typefaces based on historical precedents and better design of mass-produced books and other commercial printing. The Arts and Crafts movement blended with the art nouveau style of the late nineteenth and early twentieth centuries to produce stunning typography and graphics. Original visual properties are found in the Parisian posters of Henri de Toulouse-Lautrec and Alphonse Mucha, book designs by Belgian architect Henri van de Velde, and posters and periodicals by Will Bradley in the United States.

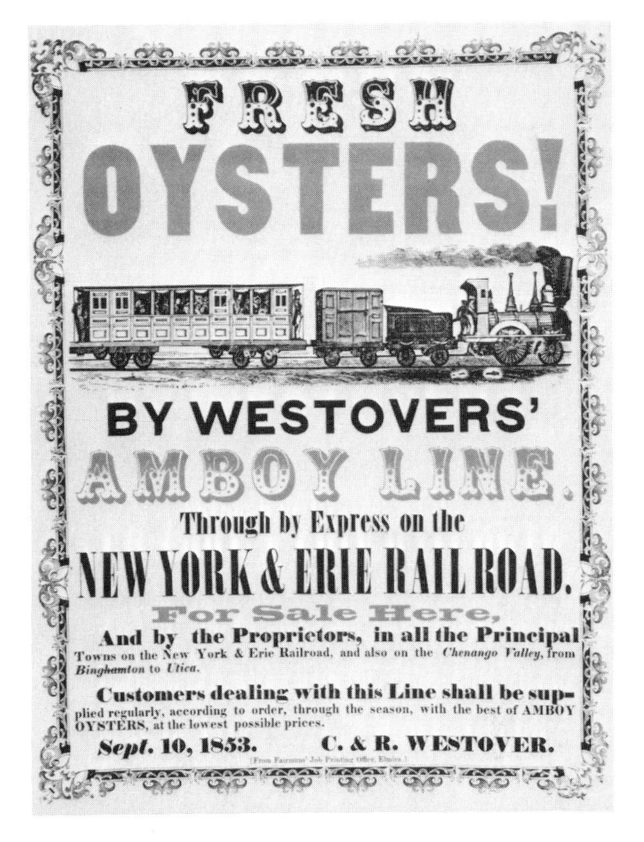

Figure 4. *(Typography)* Fairman's Job Printing Office, letterpress poster, 1853.

Figure 3. *(Typography)* Giambattista Bodoni, page from *Manuale tipografico,* 1818.

Influence of modern art movements. Technological innovation and political and social ferment in Europe before and during World War I profoundly influenced visual art, which in turn affected the course of

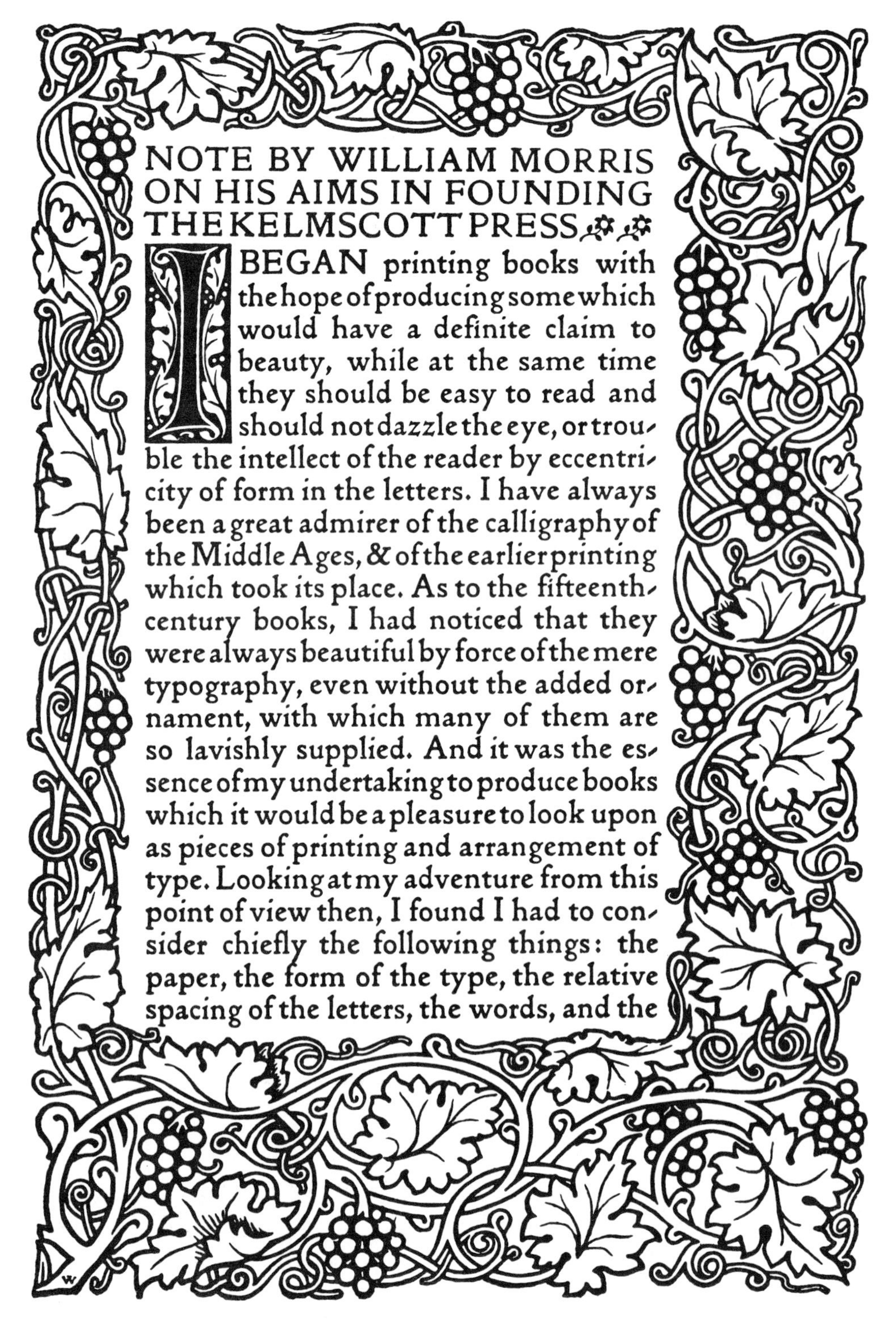
NOTE BY WILLIAM MORRIS ON HIS AIMS IN FOUNDING THE KELMSCOTT PRESS

I BEGAN printing books with the hope of producing some which would have a definite claim to beauty, while at the same time they should be easy to read and should not dazzle the eye, or trouble the intellect of the reader by eccentricity of form in the letters. I have always been a great admirer of the calligraphy of the Middle Ages, & of the earlier printing which took its place. As to the fifteenth-century books, I had noticed that they were always beautiful by force of the mere typography, even without the added ornament, with which many of them are so lavishly supplied. And it was the essence of my undertaking to produce books which it would be a pleasure to look upon as pieces of printing and arrangement of type. Looking at my adventure from this point of view then, I found I had to consider chiefly the following things: the paper, the form of the type, the relative spacing of the letters, the words, and the

Figure 5. *(Typography)* William Morris, last publication of the Kelmscott Press, 1898.

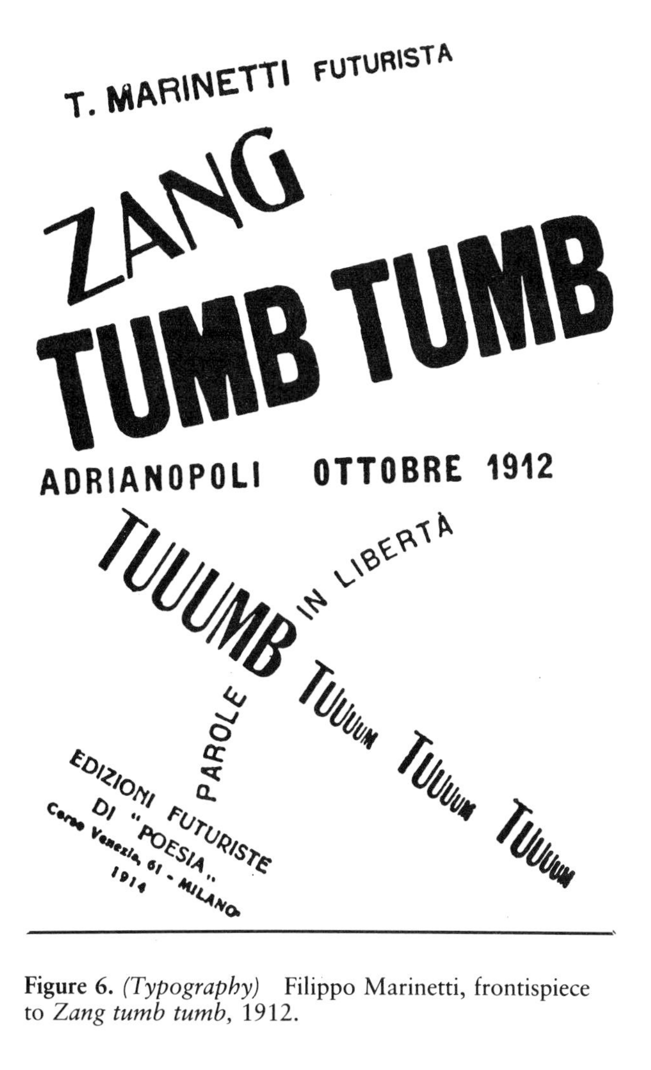

Figure 6. *(Typography)* Filippo Marinetti, frontispiece to *Zang tumb tumb,* 1912.

typographic design. Typography was freed of its traditional syntax and structural conventions as the futurist poets sought dynamic, nonlinear composition in an effort to express the circumstances of twentieth-century life (Figure 6). The cubist painters used letterforms in their paintings, calling attention to the optical and formal properties of type. The dada movement, spawned in Zurich by an international group of writers and artists protesting the war, further challenged conventional typographic precepts and continued cubism's concept of letterforms as both concrete visual shapes and phonetic symbols. The attitudes and experiments of these movements seeped into general typographic practice.

Geometric abstract painting, particularly the Russian suprematist and constructivist movements and the Dutch de Stijl movement, proved to be more directly influential on typographic design. The modernist typographic aesthetic that emerged from these influences coalesced at the Bauhaus, a German design school founded in 1919 and closed by the Nazis in 1933, which became a confluence for advanced applied art. Herbert Bayer became master of the printing and advertising workshop in 1925 and played a major role in developing the basic precepts in this new typography. Bayer's design of a Bauhaus catalog (Figure 7) displays major attributes of this modern typographic style that spread through Europe during the 1920s and 1930s, seeking to sweep the slate clean of "degenerate typefaces and arrangements" and create a typography that would capture the visual sensibility of a new technological age. Ornament was rejected absolutely, and sans serif typefaces were embraced as elemental alphabet forms that best expressed the spirit of the century. Symmetrical arrangements were shunned, for it was believed that dynamic, asymmetrical design best interpreted content and expressed the machine age. A young master calligrapher, Jan Tschichold, attended the 1923 Bauhaus exhibition and through his design work and writing disseminated the new typography to a broad audience of compositors and designers.

After World War II the new typography evolved into a cohesive movement called the International Typographic Style, or Swiss design, after the country of its origin. Josef Müller-Brockmann emerged as a leading Swiss theoretician and practitioner. Carlo Vivarelli's cover for the magazine *New Graphic Design* (Figure 8) shows major aspects of this style:

Figure 7. *(Typography)* Herbert Bayer, page from a Bauhaus catalog, 1925. Copyright Joella Bayer.

Neue Grafik
New Graphic Design
Graphisme actuel

Internationale Zeitschrift für Grafik und verwandte Gebiete
Erscheint in deutscher, englischer und französischer Sprache

International Review of graphic design and related subjects
Issued in German, English and French language

Revue internationale pour le graphisme et domaines annexes
Parution en langues allemande, anglaise et française

2

Richard P. Lohse, Zürich
Max Bill, Zürich

Gérard Ifert, Paris

Fritz Keller, Zürich

Hans Neuburg, Zürich
Emil Ruder, Basel,
Fachlehrer für Typografie
an der Gewerbeschule Basel
Ulrich Hitzig, Zürich,
Schweizer Fernsehdienst

Ausgabe Juli 1959

Inhalt

Expo 58
Kataloge für Kunstausstellungen 1936–1958
Grafiker der neuen Generation

Vorfabrizierte Elemente für Schaufenster und Ausstellungen
Italienische Gebrauchsgrafik
Univers,
eine neue Grotesk von Adrian Frutiger

Wettbewerb für ein neues Signet des Schweizer Fernsehdienstes

Einzelnummer Fr. 15.-

Issue for July 1959

Contents

Expo 58
Catalogues of Art Exhibitions 1936–1958
Graphic Designers of the new Generation
Prefabricated Parts for Showcases and Exhibitions
Italian Industrial Design
Univers,
a new sans-serif type by Adrian Frutiger
Competition for a New Symbol for Swiss Television

Single number Fr. 15.-

Juillet 1959

Table des matières

Expo 58
Catalogues pour expositions de beaux-arts 1936–1958
Graphistes de la génération nouvelle

Eléments préfabriqués pour vitrines et expositions
Graphisme italien appliqué
Univers,
une nouvelle grotesque d'Adrian Frutiger
Concours destiné à créer une marque distinctive de la Télévision suisse

Le numéro Fr. 15.-

Herausgeber und Redaktion
Editors and Managing Editors
Editeurs et rédaction

Richard P. Lohse SWB VSG, Zurich
J. Müller-Brockmann SWB VSG, Zürich
Hans Neuburg SWB VSG, Zürich
Carlo L. Vivarelli SWB/VSG, Zürich

Druck/Verlag
Printing/Publishing
Imprimerie/Edition

Verlag Otto Walter AG, Olten
Schweiz Switzerland Suisse

Figure 8. *(Typography)* Carlo L. Vivarelli, cover for *New Graphic Design,* 1958.

type and pictorial material are organized on a geometric grid system; the number of typefaces used in any instance is reduced, often to two sizes, one for display material and the other for text; and only sans serif typefaces are selected. Objectivity is stressed, and the designer's subjective interpretation is minimized. This approach found great favor worldwide, particularly in visual identity programs for multinational corporations, SIGNAGE and information systems for airports and international expositions, and other situations involving large international audiences.

New typesetting technologies. During the 1960s metal type was rapidly replaced by photographic typesetting systems for display material and keyboard-controlled, computer-driven photographic systems for text material (*see* PHOTOGRAPHY). This freed designers from the rigid size limitations and spatial constraints of metal type, enabling them to use an infinite variety of sizes, optically distort letterforms, and overlap characters at will. U.S. designer Herb Lubalin demonstrated an exceptional understanding of these new design freedoms, manipulating typographic material into original configurations that intensified messages in unexpected and imaginative ways (Figure 9). Another leading figure was English typographer and journalist Stanley Morison, who directed the design of the Times Roman typeface, wrote several influential books on type, and in 1945 became editor of *The Times Literary Supplement.*

The introduction of a new typeface once required a costly investment in hundreds of matrices and metal types in a range of sizes. The simple, inexpensive film fonts needed to introduce phototypesetting typefaces dramatically reduced their cost. The piracy of typeface designs, which are not protected by COPYRIGHT in many countries, seriously discouraged new designs; but establishment of the International Typeface Corporation in 1970 provided a mechanism for licensing new designs to all equipment manufacturers

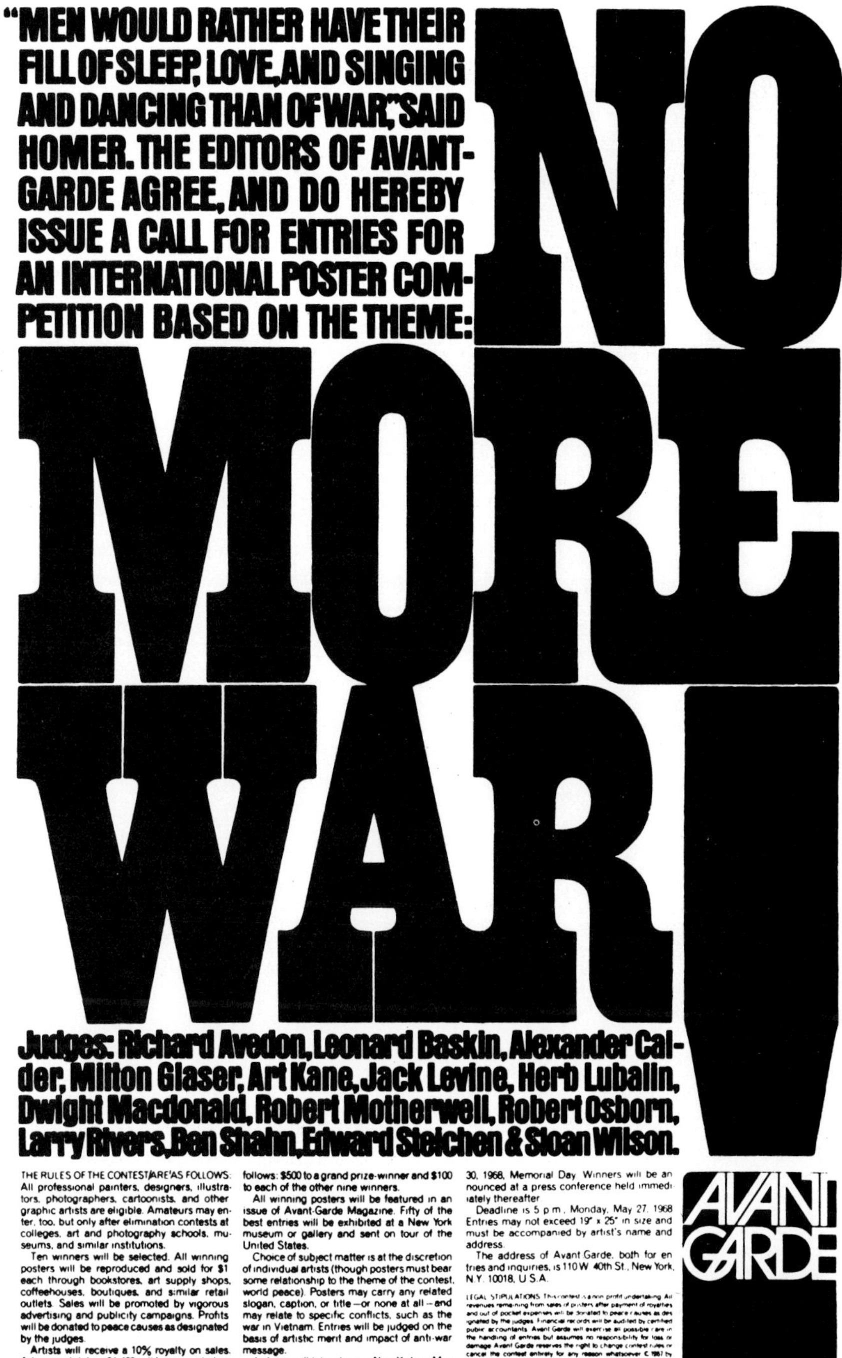

Figure 9. *(Typography)* Herb Lubalin, poster competition announcement for *Avant Garde* magazine, 1967.

while paying a royalty to designers. This innovative concept combined with the economy of film fonts to promote an outpouring of new typefaces.

At the same time the simplified geometric approach of the modern movement was rejected by a new generation of designers who introduced greater visual complexity and personal expression into their work. The postmodernist work of architects and graphic designers such as Swiss designer Wolfgang Weingart and U.S. designer April Greiman expanded and enriched the vocabulary of typographic design.

The rapid advance of digital computer technology opened a new era of typographic communication during the 1980s (*see* COMPUTER: IMPACT). Typesetting became an extension of word-processing systems, allowing improved quality of typographic output for routine business communications and more efficient production of newspapers and magazines. Electronic workstations afford designers the opportunity for an interactive design process. The unification of the design process and production of final reproduction proofs into one procedure is rapidly becoming a reality. *See* ELECTRONIC PUBLISHING.

Bibliography. Aaron Burns, *Typography,* New York, 1961; Rob Carter, Ben Day, and Philip B. Meggs, *Typographic Design: Form and Communications,* New York, 1985; Philip B. Meggs, *A History of Graphic Design,* New York, 1983; Emil Ruder, *Typography, A Manual of Design* (in German, French, and English), Teufen AR, Switzerland, 1967; Ruedi Rüegg and Godi Fröhlich, *Basic Typography* (in German, French, and English), Zurich, 1972; Herbert Spencer, *Pioneers of Modern Typography,* London, 1969; Daniel Updike, *Printing Types: Their History, Forms, and Use* (1922), 2 vols., 3d ed., Cambridge, Mass., 1962.

PHILIP B. MEGGS

(y*ū*), the twenty-first letter of the modern English and the twentieth of the ancient Roman alphabet, was in the latter identical in form and origin with V . . . , the same symbol being employed both as a vowel and a consonant. In Latin manuscripts written in capitals the form V is retained; but in uncial manuscripts, of which the earliest specimens belong to the third or fourth century, the modified form U appears, and is continued in [later manuscripts] as U.

UNITED NATIONS (UN). *See* INTERNATIONAL ORGANIZATIONS.

UNITED NATIONS EDUCATIONAL, SCIENTIFIC AND CULTURAL ORGANIZATION (UNESCO). *See* INTERNATIONAL ORGANIZATIONS.

UNIVERSITY

The emergence of the European universities in their traditional form would hardly have been possible without other developments of the late MIDDLE AGES, including especially an improved climate of communication within western Europe and between the Arabic and Christian worlds. Once firmly established, universities played at different periods major or minor roles in the communication of knowledge, ideas, and cultural ATTITUDES. As the economic and political power of Europe was imposed on other parts of the world, universities passed overseas their structure and organization.

Early history. Relative peace in Europe as a whole from the eleventh century on stimulated the growth of commerce and trade, enabling individuals to move in greater safety. As cities expanded, especially in northern France, the judicial and administrative work of their bishops increased, and the bishops' chancellors found it necessary to communicate with other ecclesiastics, the pope, and secular statesmen. To do this they needed educated clerics well trained in Latin. The schools they established were also attractive to those seeking EDUCATION, not in a monastery but in the less restricted social milieu of a French city. By the time of the death of the controversial French scholar Abelard in 1142 large numbers of students and masters were gathering in these centers in search of education.

Their studies were hampered, however, by a lack of scholarly materials. The legacy of the Greek and Latin world had been better received and sustained by the Arabs (*see* ISLAM, CLASSICAL AND MEDIEVAL ERAS). With the return of more peaceful times European scholars set out to recover their lost inheritance. Journeys to Muslim schools in Spain by scholars such as Gerard of Cremona and the encouragement of translations by King Roger in Sicily provided the West in the twelfth century with Latin versions of many Greek, Arabic, and Hebrew philosophical, medical, and scientific texts. It has also been suggested that the Arabic world communicated to the West some of the nomenclature that we associate today with the structure and organization of the medieval universities. At the same time scholars in northern Italy, especially at Bologna, were attempting to recover and comment on the corpus of Roman law. Canonists also codified ecclesiastical law, and theologians provided texts to be used for educational purposes. The schools of the late twelfth century now had usable advanced material to communicate to their students.

It was this subject matter that the universities spread and developed before the early sixteenth century. Expanding largely under the umbrella of ecclesiastical protection and using a common LANGUAGE (Latin), they were able to encourage intellectual communication among all parts of Christian Europe. From the early centers of Paris, Oxford, and Bologna scholars were sent to other cities able to provide resources for the establishment of a university. During the fifteenth century most populous areas of western Europe had reasonable access to a university. Teaching material spread quickly as it was carried by wandering scholars from place to place, even though books were still written by hand and therefore were expensive (*see* BOOK). By 1500 most universities had libraries, often created by teams of copiers employed for this purpose (*see* LIBRARY); the advent of PRINTING greatly eased this problem. Lines of intellectual communication varied according to the position and status of a particular university. Established centers such as Oxford, Paris, Vienna, Montpellier, Bologna, and Padua attracted many foreign students. Marsilius von Inghen, earlier rector of the University of Paris, was the first rector of Heidelberg University, founded, according to its statutes, "after the fashion of Paris." Other local, smaller

Figure 1. *(University)* Seal of the University of Paris, thirteenth century. The relationship between religion and medieval learning is illustrated: The Virgin and Child (divine source of wisdom) are at the top, flanked by a saint and a bishop. Below, two professors teach. Phot. Bibl. Nat., Paris.

universities, such as most of the German ones, attracted few foreign students. At the close of the medieval period the universities of Italy were enticing many wishing to gain acquaintance with the "new learning." These Italian universities trained many scholars who communicated the ideas of the Italian RENAISSANCE to their contemporaries north of the Alps.

The Reformation era. The conflicts of the Reformation seriously damaged this ease of communication among the various European universities. It was usually not possible for a Catholic to study in the universities of Protestant lands or vice versa. Divisions among Protestants further split Europe. Michael Servetus, the Spanish physician who denied the doctrine of the Trinity, escaped from Catholic persecution to be burnt in Calvin's Geneva in 1553. Some states, such as Venice, attempted to keep open lines of intellectual contact: the English and Scottish nations were represented at Padua University until 1738. Refugees from persecution played a major role in communicating their scholarship to countries that protected them. John Drusius, the Flemish biblical scholar who fled to Oxford and Cambridge during the reign of Elizabeth I, greatly encouraged the study of Hebrew in England; English Catholic refugees helped to establish the university of Douai; many Italian theologians, fleeing from the Inquisition, enrolled at the universities of Basel and Krakow.

Such Italian scholars were particularly at risk because their country had been well advanced in the early modern period in the application of scientific discovery to such areas as medicine and astronomy. The debt of Galileo to the works of fourteenth-century scientists from Oxford and Paris, made available in northern Italy especially by the printing presses of Venice, has been challenged, but there is no doubt that many Italian scientists were aware of earlier hypotheses and were interested in developing them. As the interests of academics during the sixteenth, seventeenth, and eighteenth centuries switched more to the natural sciences, attempts were made by the Catholic church to restrict the reception of new scientific theories. After the suppression of Galileo and the Accademia del Cimento in Florence most important scientific advances were made in northern Europe, especially in the rich commercial centers of England, Holland, and northern Germany.

However, much of this scientific work, especially the application of "useful knowledge" to the needs of society, was not communicated to the educated populace by the older universities but rather by academies and learned societies founded by concerned individuals, not all of whom had academic experience. The Lunar Society of Birmingham brought together individualists such as Josiah Wedgwood and scientists such as Joseph Priestley, the discoverer of oxygen. The Academy of St. Petersburg was responsible for the attempt to spread Newtonian science among the educated elite of Russia. The eighteenth century also saw an attempt to spread enlightened ideas in eastern Europe. As the Turkish threat receded and Poland and Russia established themselves as powerful states, educational reformers in such countries owed much to the support of graduates from the universities of Jena, Halle, and Leipzig, and their influence helped to stimulate the national educational reform movement in Poland and the founding of the Universities of Warsaw and Moscow.

Enlightenment reforms. The educational role of the eighteenth-century enlightened despot culminated in the reforms of Napoléon I. With the establishment of the University of France and through the influence of his educational policies in the European lands conquered by the French, we see the demand for efficient, practical, useful, and scientific TEACHING. In Italy and Spain Napoléon's satellite kingdoms introduced major reforms, but it was in Germany that his policies were especially influential. Although resenting French political dominance, the German states adopted many Napoleonic educational principles. About half of the German universities were suppressed; the new university of Berlin, the Humboldt University, emphasized the coordination of teaching and research. Following these reforms the German universities provided the stimulus for wider developments and reform. The role of the doctoral degree, the importance of the seminar, the encouragement of research into the natural sciences, and the division of the faculty of arts into its independent constituent parts owe much to the German example.

Colonization. Such developments came at a crucial time for the communication of ideas, attitudes, and concepts beyond Europe itself (*see* COLONIZATION). From the late fifteenth century on, European powers had been establishing their authority overseas. Especially in large settlements of people from any one country, there arose a demand for local educational facilities. As would be expected, this was first experienced in the overseas territories controlled by Spain: seven universities were established in South America under the influence of the University of Salamanca alone in the sixteenth century. As Britain and France followed the Spanish and Portuguese in the creation of overseas empires, so the spread of European ideas through new universities increased. Harvard, the first university in the United States, was established as a college in 1636–1638, influenced by Cambridge University; by 1776 there were nine colleges in the British colonies in North America. Movement between such colonial institutions and the home countries strengthened cultural links, especially as an

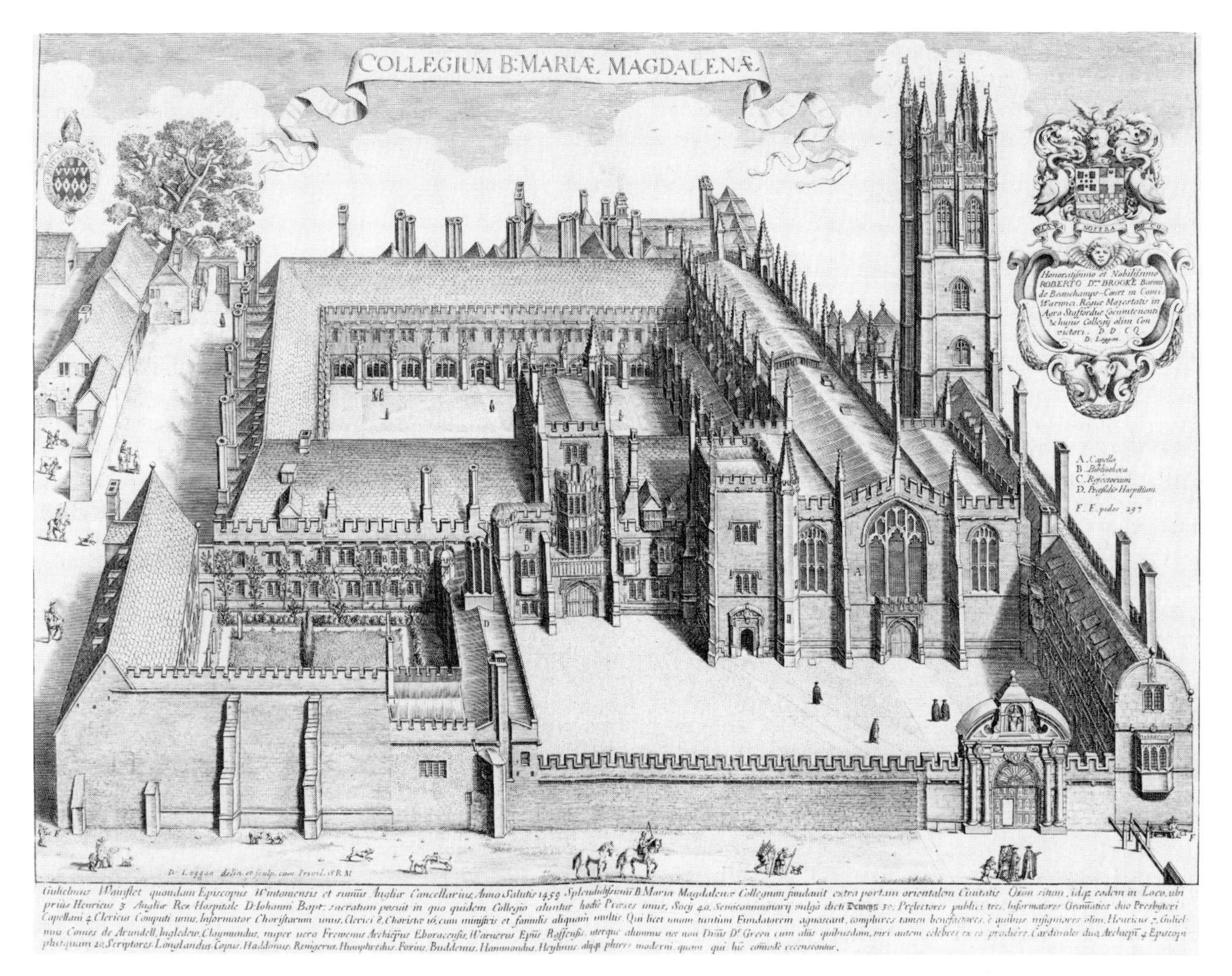

Figure 2. *(University)* Magdalen College, Oxford. From David Loggan, *Oxonia Illustrata,* Oxford, 1675. By permission of the Houghton Library, Harvard University.

overseas institution often relied on the recruitment of teaching staff from the colonizing country.

By the nineteenth century many older colonies had achieved their independence. Wishing to develop further their own universities, they were particularly influenced by the German models. Students, especially postgraduates wishing to benefit from German research methods and the possibility of obtaining the new doctoral degree, traveled to study in large numbers in the German universities. On their return they communicated to their contemporaries the achievements of the German system. Many universities founded in the nineteenth century owed much to the teaching methods and university structures developed in Germany; this is particularly true of the United States, where the spread of these ideas was encouraged by the movement of German immigrants into the country. Nor was this respect for German learning confined to former colonies of European powers. The new English universities were especially influenced by German scientific methods; by the early twentieth century Oxford was awarding the doctorate pioneered by the German universities. From England the German example was spread farther overseas as English colonies began to demand their own universities. Many of these were first satisfied, as had been the case in England, by the creation of "colleges" affiliated to the University of London and conforming to its academic standards. Universities established in parts of the former colonial empire of the European powers quickly became independent, but they often retained their links with their former associate universities through language and CULTURE.

The vocabulary of the earlier universities, with faculties, deans, lectures, degrees, and similar features, became common to universities everywhere. But much more than words was transmitted. What had begun as a western European movement in a few cities in the twelfth century had established its intellectual and cultural traditions in higher education throughout the world.

See also COMMUNICATIONS, STUDY OF.

Bibliography. Hans Daalder and Edward Shils, eds., *Universities, Politicians, and Bureaucrats: Europe and the United States,* Cambridge, 1982; Konrad H. Jarausch, ed., *The Transformation of Higher Learning 1860–1930: Expansion, Diversification, Social Opening, and Professionalization in England, Germany, Russia, and the United States,* Chicago, 1983; James M. Kittleson and Pamela J. Transue, eds., *Rebirth, Reform, and Resilience: Universities in Transition 1300–1700,* Columbus, Ohio, 1984; Hastings Rashdall, *The Universities of Europe in the Middle-Ages,* new ed., 3 vols., Oxford, 1936, reprint (ed. by F. M. Powicke and A. B. Emden) 1964; Agueda María Rodríguez Cruz, *Salmantica Docet: La proyecion de la Universidad de Salamanca en Hispanoamérica,* 2 vols., Salamanca, 1977; Helmut Rössler and Günther Franz, eds., *Universität und Gelehrtenstand 1400–1800,* Limburg, FRG, 1970; Lawrence Stone, ed., *The University in Society,* 2 vols., Princeton, N.J., 1974.

JOHN M. FLETCHER

USES AND GRATIFICATIONS. *See* MASS COMMUNICATIONS RESEARCH; MASS MEDIA EFFECTS.

UTOPIAS

The term *utopia* comes from the Greek and ambiguously combines two words: *topos,* meaning "place," and *eu,* meaning either "good" or "no." Literally, then, utopia means both the good place and nowhere. In the GENRE of utopian writing, the term was first used in its modern sense by English humanist Thomas More (1478–1535) in a small book entitled *The Best State of a Commonwealth and the New Island of Utopia,* which appeared in 1516 and is commonly referred to simply as *Utopia.* In that work More sketched a society that was both ideal and existed nowhere, thus satisfying both meanings of the Greek term. A literary piece in RENAISSANCE style, *Utopia* mocked contemporary customs and values, and proposed alternatives, but without any hint that these alternatives could serve as a realistic model for social practice.

Before More's *Utopia* there were many literary examples of the utopian genre in both the Judeo-Christian and Greco-Roman traditions. The Garden of Eden, the biblical millennium, the Golden Age, the Elysian Fields, the Blessed Isles, and the Land of Cokaygne are but a few of the many mythic images of a world without pain, sorrow, and strife, a perfect place beyond the reach of mortals. More extensive writings like PLATO's *Republic* and Lucian of Samosata's (ca. 117–ca. 180) *True Stories* also contain utopian elements and were certainly known to More and later writers. Yet there is agreement among scholars that not until More did a true utopian genre emerge. After More's *Utopia* there was a steady stream of writings that proposed to represent an ideal society, one that did not exist and could not be realized.

Visionary utopias. The Morean tradition of utopian writing, one that continued to the time of the French Revolution, is characterized by a static or atemporal quality. The ideal community depicted in these writings is remote, timeless, unchanging, and, most important, without any connection to the actual world; utopian writers restricted themselves to unattainable dreams of perfection. Oneiric (dream) worlds of the Renaissance were not plans for action, manifestos of revolution, or practical guides to remedy social ills. While they mocked and satirized the authority of the great, the kings, prelates, and aristocrats of the day, and called for economic and political justice, in general they assumed that the

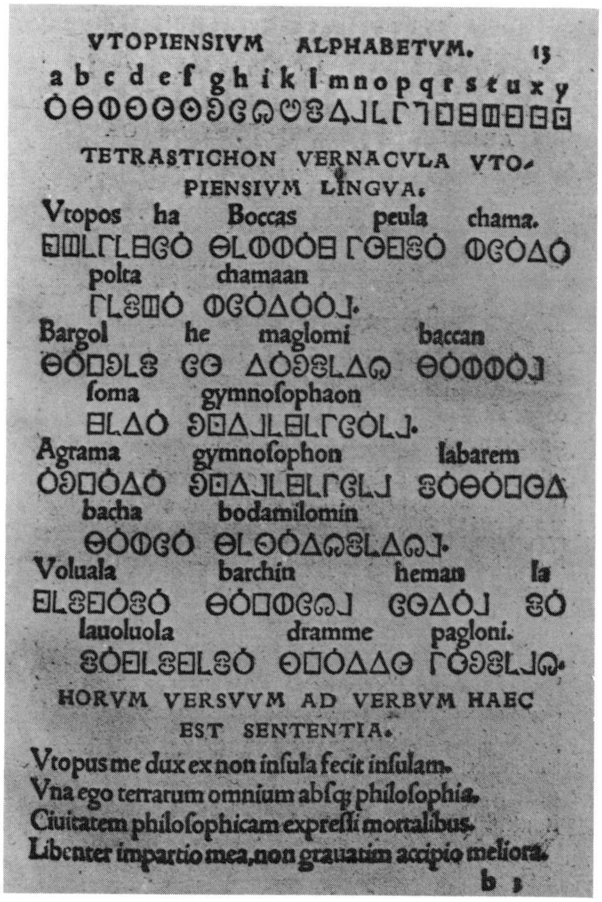
VTOPIENSIVM ALPHABETVM. 13
a b c d e f g h i k l m n o p q r s t u x y
TETRASTICHON VERNACVLA VTOPIENSIVM LINGVA.
Vtopos ha Boccas peula chama.
polta chamaan
Bargol he maglomi baccan
soma gymnosophaon
Agrama gymnosophon labarem
bacha bodamilomin
Voluala barchin heman la
lauoluola dramme pagloni.
HORVM VERSVVM AD VERBVM HAEC EST SENTENTIA.
Vtopus me dux ex non insula fecit insulam.
Vna ego terrarum omnium absque philosophia,
Ciuitatem philosophicam expressi mortalibus.
Libenter impartio mea, non grauatim accipio meliora.
b 3

Figure 1. *(Utopias)* The Utopian alphabet. Woodcut (facsimile). From J. H. Lupton, ed., *The Utopia of Sir Thomas More,* London and New York: The Clarendon Press, 1895, p. xciv.

THE CRISIS,

OR THE CHANGE FROM ERROR AND MISERY, TO TRUTH AND HAPPINESS.

1832.

EDITED BY
ROBERT OWEN AND ROBERT DALE OWEN.

London:
PRINTED AND PUBLISHED BY J. EAMONSON, 15, CHICHESTER PLACE,
GRAY'S INN ROAD.
STRANGE, PATERNOSTER ROW. PURKISS, OLD COMPTON STREET
AND MAY BE HAD OF ALL BOOKSELLERS.

Figure 2. *(Utopias)* Title page from *The Crisis, or the Change from Error and Misery, to Truth and Happiness,* ed. by Robert Owen and Robert Dale Owen, 1832. The Bettmann Archive, Inc.

powers of reason and imagination available to the writer were not potent enough to break the repetitious cycle of the rise and fall of nations or to dispel "the vale of tears" that was humanity's lot.

Explicit concern for problems of communication is largely absent from these early, visionary utopian writings. Even though the period is known for the PRINTING revolution in the reproduction of written texts, utopians tended to concentrate on institutional reforms and changes in the education of the self—the development of a more rational human being. Problems of transmitting knowledge and information were not emphasized in these utopian writings. In More and Francis Bacon (1561–1626) there is discussion of libraries that would be available to everyone (though women are generally not mentioned), and Bacon in *The New Atlantis* devotes some attention to the problem of institutionalizing scientific research and transmitting this knowledge (*see* LIBRARY). One may deduce that, until the nineteenth century, face-to-face interaction was so prominent in the minds of Europeans that the question of alternative forms of communication was not high on the agenda.

There was a body of writing, mostly at the turn of the eighteenth century, that sought to reshape LANGUAGE into a utopian form. Writers like John Wilkins (1614–1672), an English scientist, and, to a lesser extent, Gottfried Wilhelm Leibniz (1646–1716) proposed revisions to their native languages to excise all ambiguity, often meaning emotional tones, so that communication would become precise, clear, scientific. But such projects did not find their way into sketches for ideal societies.

Given the unreality of utopia in the Morean tradition it is not surprising that the period witnessed few efforts to build ideal communities. The only major exception to this assertion is found in the Puritan emigrants to the New World. Some of the charters written for the travelers to the Americas seem to express the intention to establish an ideal society or the New Jerusalem. With the Bible as their guide many of these Protestants conceived their venture as a practical utopia, an innovation that became widespread in the United States, particularly in the nineteenth century. *See* RELIGION.

Reformist utopias. Some movement toward bridging the gap between the utopian imagination and social change was made in the period before 1900. Renaissance architects, like Leon Battista Alberti (1404–1472), drew up plans for ideal cities that they hoped would be constructed by informed princes. During the Reformation utopian impulses grew still more insistent, as in the case of radical sects like the English Fifth-Monarchy Men, who boldly envisioned a Christian millennial society on earth that would fulfill the predictions in the Bible. The increase in utopian visions that were considered feasible was encouraged by reports of European explorers, whose contact with foreign cultures stimulated a vast body of travel and voyage literature, a great deal of which depicted ideal societies—perfect worlds that, the reader was led to believe, actually existed (*see* EXPLORATION). Examples of this version of utopia are Voltaire's (1694–1778) *Candide* with its land of El Dorado, the unrepressed sexuality of Tahitians in DENIS DIDEROT's (1713–1784) *Supplement to the Voyage of Bougainville,* and the wise oriental potentate of Baron de Montesquieu's (1689–1755) *Persian Letters.* In these instances the cloudy dreams of equality, wealth, and happiness found in More's utopia were transformed into vivid sketches of perfect worlds that were distant but not beyond reach.

Figure 3. *(Utopias)* Publicity poster for Welwyn Garden City, Hertfordshire, England. Early twentieth century. From I. Tod and M. Wheeler, *Utopia,* London: Orbis Publishing, 1978, p. 122.

At the end of the eighteenth century utopian writing abandoned the model of More entirely and followed new directions. The deep abyss between the ideal and the real was spanned by a new historical consciousness, in which ideal societies were considered fully attainable in the ensuing stages of history. Utopian fantasies had become linked to the dynamic of historical change, the evolution of humanity. A new sense of the malleability of institutions and the perfectibility of humanity characterized the new utopian imagination. A mood of urgency pervaded the literature, enhancing its importance in social and political movements. The new writers designed their dream worlds with a practical eye for the imminent realization of their utopias. The Marquis de Condorcet (1743–1794) wrote his *Sketch for an Historical Picture of the Progress of the Human Spirit* while in hiding from Robespierre's police, who had a warrant for his execution. In this tense atmosphere of revolution and personal danger, Condorcet gave shape to the modern utopian dream: the ideal society was the final epoch in the linear progress of humanity, and this epoch was not far off; humanity was perfectible; the process of improving the world was infinite; above all, the question of the future utopia was knowable with certainty. Reason, in particular mathematical reason, was the source of this knowledge and the basis for the rosy prospect of humanity.

Condorcet's utopia was that of the liberal philosophe, but the model he drew of the perfect society was applicable to all major utopian writers in the age of political and economic modernization. Given his assumptions, it is not surprising that Condorcet devoted little attention to the issue of communication. For him humanity's essence was reason, an attribute of consciousness that was transparent to others. Language was no more than a tool for the

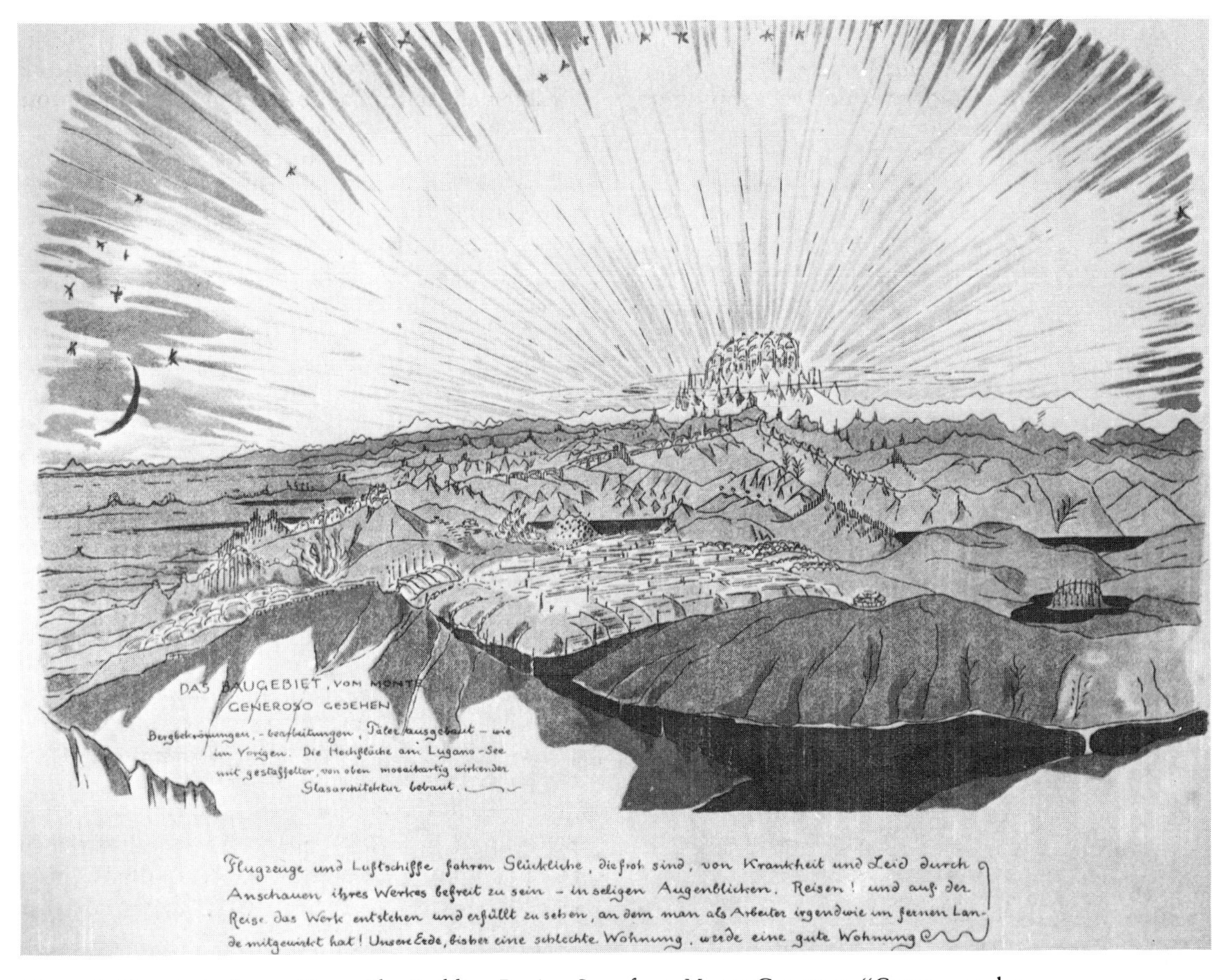

Figure 4. *(Utopias)* Bruno Taut, *The Building Region Seen from Monte Generoso.* "Crowns on the mountains—decorations, valleys transformed as in the foregoing. The plateau round the Lake of Lugano built over with graduated glass architecture, which gives the effect of mosaic when seen from above. Aircraft and airships transport their passengers on pleasure trips to find joy and release from sickness and sorrow through the contemplation of their own handiwork. To travel! And on the journey to see the growth and completion of the work to which one has in some measure contributed as a worker in a far-off country! Let our Earth, till now a poor habitation, become a pleasant place to live in." From *Alpine Architecture,* 1919–1920. British Architectural Library/RIBA, London.

perfect transmission of rational states of consciousness and, in its mathematical form, contained no ambiguity. The primary challenge to the fulfillment of utopia was to ensure that science had a strong institutional base and that nothing impeded the flow of scientific knowledge from one person to another. Social statistics, Condorcet predicted, would provide total knowledge of the state of society, and reason would direct the process of reform toward perfection. Here was the basis for a world without monarchs, a liberal, democratic world of complete freedom and equality.

In the next generation Claude-Henri de Saint-Simon (1760–1825) and Charles Fourier (1772–1837) refined and expanded the liberal utopian vision to account for different capacities of reason and for the emotions. In the context of a free and equal world Saint-Simon recognized a need for a division of labor. In addition to intellect, humans had will and emotion; individuals had these capacities in varying mixtures, and social organization had to reflect this fact. Thus each individual would contribute to society "according to his capacity." Such inequality would not lead to domination because it perfectly mirrored the souls of individuals. Fourier went further, insisting on the primacy of feeling and sensation. He imagined a world of countless varieties of people, based on their particular emotional configurations. Utopia would make possible the uninhibited expression of feeling and the expansion of the capacities for sensual and affective pleasure. With his romantic dream of emotional fulfillment, Fourier encountered a communications problem that Condorcet's rationalism had avoided. Fourier recognized that emotions are not transparent to the self or to others. He therefore envisioned a kind of proto-psychotherapy: people experienced in the ways of the feelings, usually older individuals, would advise the confused and distressed about the true nature of their desires. *See* ROMANTICISM.

For the rest of the nineteenth century and well into the twentieth, utopian writers revised and expanded the vision of Condorcet, choosing between Saint-Simonian and Fourierist varieties. KARL MARX (1818–1883) himself falls into this tradition with his motto: "From each according to his capacities, to each according to his needs." Like the liberals, Marx avoided the question of communication in utopia on the assumption that a classless society removed the walls between individuals. Once free individuals fulfilled themselves in work and love, they would become transparent to others. But Marx added a new element to the utopian tradition: he found agents in present-day society that would bring about the ideal world—the working class. By outlining the strategy and mechanisms for change he drew even closer the connection between the vision of perfection and its realization.

Countless experiments deriving from this Marxian impulse to realize utopia in practice were tried in the nineteenth century. From a castle in Romania to the wilds of Louisiana, groups set out bravely to build ideal communities. In the United States, where a majority of the utopias were attempted in the 1840s, the ideas of Fourier were popular, but so were those of Robert Owen and others. These communities were with few exceptions short-lived and ill conceived. One of the more enduring utopias was Oneida (1848–1881), which instituted a practice of public mutual criticism, one of the rare examples of an experiment in communication.

Twentieth century. After World War I utopian writing took yet another turn. In Yevgeny Ivanovich Zamyatin's (1884–1937) *We,* Aldous Huxley's (1894–1963) *Brave New World,* and George Orwell's (1903–1950) *1984* and *Animal Farm,* among others, the future was bleak. Dystopia, a perfectly evil society, was now a model, and for the first time the question of communication rose to prominence, especially in *1984.* In Orwell's dystopia totalitarianism was sustained by control of information. Information about the present was controlled with extensive surveillance techniques, and information about the past by means of the continuous rewriting of history. So important is the question of communications that the hero of the novel is an information worker who labors at revising history to reflect the official IDEOLOGY of the government. What makes the regime so repugnant is not so much the exercise of undemocratic authority but its capacity for total information control. The government in this dystopia has accurate knowledge of the innermost thoughts of individuals, even their dreams and nightmares. In the dystopian tradition advanced technology, once expected to benefit humanity by the elimination of toil, leads not to a rational and free community but to complete tyranny.

In the midst of the hopelessness of the 1930s experiments in utopia were continued by the kibbutz movement in Palestine. The kibbutzim were small agricultural communities based on democracy, free labor, and collective child rearing. They foreshadowed in many respects the flowering of "intentional communities" among hippies and radicals throughout Europe and North America in the late 1960s. In most cases the latter utopian experiments did not avail themselves of high technology and limited their reform of communication practices to an ethos of openness, emotional honesty, and love.

With the astonishing advance in information technology in the second half of the twentieth century, many writers addressed themselves to building an ideal society through the democratization of the means of communication. Countless schemes were devised in which radio, television, the computer, and communications satellites were employed to extend the ability of humanity to exchange ideas and facilitate life in general. Alvin Toffler's *The Third Wave* (1980) is one of the best expressions of this hope. The general principle of this communicational utopia is that through the mediation of information technology the needs of individuals can be more completely and directly realized.

Confronted by high-technology communications media, utopian thinkers have moved in two opposite directions: one toward the dystopia of tyranny enforced by centralized control, the other toward the dream of freedom enhanced by democratic and communal social organizations. In both cases, however, a significant erosion in the level of imaginative thinking is apparent in these writings: both camps simply translate the new technology into their dream mood. One finds little fundamental rethinking of the nature or significance of communications among the modern utopian writers, nor is there the deep recasting of this thinking into a utopian form that matches the creativity of More and Condorcet.

See also REALISM; SCIENCE FICTION.

Bibliography. Lawrence Foster, *Religion and Sexuality: Three American Communal Experiments,* New York, 1981; Frank E. Manuel and Fritzie P. Manuel, *Utopian Thought in the Western World,* Cambridge, Mass., 1979; Richard Ofshe, compl., *The Sociology of the Possible,* Englewood Cliffs, N.J., 1970; Melford E. Spiro, *Kibbutz: Venture in Utopia,* augmented ed. (Studies in the Libertarian and Utopian Tradition), New York, 1970; Sallie TeSelle, ed., *The Family, Communes, and Utopian Societies,* New York, 1972.

MARK POSTER

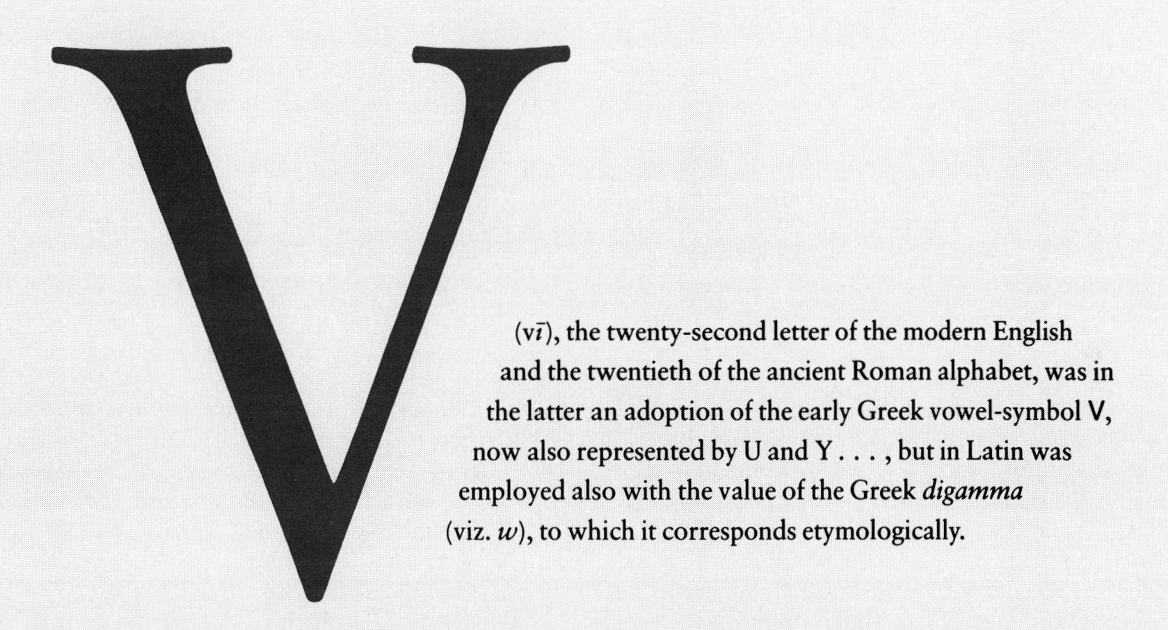

(vī), the twenty-second letter of the modern English and the twentieth of the ancient Roman alphabet, was in the latter an adoption of the early Greek vowel-symbol V, now also represented by U and Y . . . , but in Latin was employed also with the value of the Greek *digamma* (viz. *w*), to which it corresponds etymologically.

VERTOV, DZIGA (1896–1954)

Russian filmmaker, considered one of the pioneers of the DOCUMENTARY. Dziga Vertov was born in Bialystok, a city that was then part of the czarist empire and inhabited mostly by Russian-Polish Jewry. Born Denis Arkadyevitch Kaufman, he changed his name to a pseudonym that roughly means "restless spinning," suggesting the power packed into reels of film.

Vertov belonged to the generation of Soviet filmmakers of the 1920s who had a profound impact on world cinema. His films of everyday life played a major role in shaping the documentary movement of the 1930s, the CINÉMA VÉRITÉ school of the 1960s, anthropological cinema, and the Third World documentary. His metaphorical editing and contrapuntal use of sound have been a major source of inspiration for the AVANT-GARDE FILM movements of the twentieth century. Vertov is a filmmaker's filmmaker: SERGEI EISENSTEIN, JOHN GRIERSON, Jean Rouch, Santiago Álvarez, Peter Kubelka, Dušan Makavejev, and Jean-Luc Godard, among others, have considered his work essential to the development of their craft.

Vertov's practice of working with a regular team and in a collective fashion is also part of his legacy. His Cine-Eye group was formed in 1919 and survived until 1928. Its other leading members were his wife, Elizaveta Svilova, and his brother Mikhail Kaufman. Svilova edited almost all of Vertov's films, under his supervision. Kaufman was Vertov's cameraman throughout the 1920s and must be credited with the major SPECIAL EFFECTS and shooting techniques evolved by the group. However, Vertov remained the mind and mover behind every aspect of his films, as well as the author of the manifestos signed by "The Council of Three" and "The Cine-Eye." These manifestos were assembled posthumously in a collection of Vertov's writings titled *Stat'i, dnevniki, zamysly* (articles, diaries, notes, 1966) and were translated into many languages.

Life and work. During his childhood and adolescence in Bialystok, Vertov experimented with written and oral POETRY. As a medical student in Leningrad, he created a "Laboratory of Sound" and became fascinated by the poetry of Vladimir Mayakovsky and the futurists. The year 1917 found him in Moscow, where he discovered filmmaking and revolutionary politics at the same time. In 1918–1919 Vertov helped to organize the weekly film journal *Kinonedelia* (Film Weekly). Editing incoming footage from the civil war front, he went on to make a series of compilation films, *Istoriya grazhdenskoi voini* (A History of the Civil War, 1922). His experience of that period—in particular, his work for the agit-trains that showed films throughout the nascent Soviet Union—remained a major influence on him. Given a free hand by the film committees, Vertov and his Cine-Eye group then produced a thematic NEWSREEL series, *Kinopravda* (Film Truth, 1922–1925), and such feature documentaries as *Kinoglaz* (Cinema Eye, 1924), *Shagai, Soviet!* (Forward, Soviet!, 1926), and *Shestaya chast mira* (One-Sixth of the World, 1926).

By 1927 Vertov's increasingly experimental editing style and his vitriolic attacks on the acted cinema had alienated the film administration. He was sent away from Moscow to the Ukraine, where he made two masterpieces, *Chelovek s kinoapparatom* (The

Figure 1. *(Vertov, Dziga) Chelovek s kinoapparatom* (The Man with the Movie Camera), 1929. Courtesy of the Amos Vogel Collection.

Man with the Movie Camera, 1929) and his first sound film, *Entuziazm: Simphoniya Donbassa,* (Enthusiasm: Symphony of the Don Basin, 1930). Both were acclaimed in Paris, Berlin, and London, but not at home. Back in Moscow, Vertov came under increasing attacks from the Stalinist film bureaucrats for his formalist style and made his last great film, the lyrical *Tri pesni o Leninye* (Three Songs of Lenin, 1934). The last twenty years of Vertov's life were spent in shadow and frustration. Most of his projects were rejected; the few that were accepted were often reedited, such as *Kolibelnaya* (Lullaby, 1937). Largely ignored, he worked on newsreels until his death.

Theory and practice. Vertov wanted his films to demonstrate to millions of illiterate people that they were the owners of the land. Vertov felt that this goal could not be achieved by the acted cinema, which distracted rather than empowered the masses. As a result he relentlessly attacked FICTION films.

If the people were to see themselves on the screen, it followed that the camera had to be brought out from the world of the studio into the street. This became a cornerstone of Vertov's theory and practice. Instead of using a static camera to film STARS under heavy lights, Vertov's cameramen ran after people involved in everyday activities and photographed them in natural lighting. In order to film people at work and play without disturbing them, it became necessary to develop devices such as the candid camera. This ability of the camera to make people observe themselves in an unprecedented way led Vertov to contend that the "cine-eye" was superior to the human eye.

Vertov's theory was futurist in concept, yet in practice it was also subservient to his realist goal of showing "man, his behavior and emotions." This is precisely what makes Vertov's theories difficult to unravel: they often subscribe to two apparently opposite traditions, the realism of an objective observer and the idealism of a revolutionary. It was Vertov's peculiar genius to document "life as it is" with his camera and to turn these "pieces of truth" into fiction and poetry on the editing bench. *See* FILM EDITING.

Vertovian editing can be seen at its best in *The Man with the Movie Camera.* It organizes images not only according to a political theme but also metaphorically and rhythmically. Not until all the parts of the film fit with one another, as in a poem or a musical piece, does the work find its completed form. It is this interdependence of all the shots in his films, along with the skillful use of sound (in the sound films that followed), that distinguishes Vertov's editing from that of the other Soviet innovators of his time.

Vertov is an essential filmmaker, but he is also a paradoxical and elusive one. His writings on film show a rare poetic insight into the nature of the medium, but, like his films, they are often enigmatic. The paradox that perhaps best epitomizes Vertov is that his films are the work of a poet, a musician, and a storyteller who claimed, most of the time, that one should do away with art, music, and storytelling in the cinema. Yet it is precisely this turn of mind that led him to demonstrate, perhaps in spite of himself, that the nature of cinema is to turn newsreels into fairy tales.

See also FILM THEORY; MOTION PICTURES.

Bibliography. Seth R. Feldman, *Dziga Vertov: A Guide to References and Resources,* Boston, 1979; Annette Michelson, ed., *Kino-Eye: The Writings of Dziga Vertov,* trans. by Kevin O'Brien, Berkeley, Calif., 1984; Georges Sadoul, *Dziga Vertov,* Paris, 1971; Dziga Vertov, *Stat'i, dnevniki, zamysly* (articles, diaries, notes), Moscow, 1966.

BERTRAND SAUZIER

VIDEO

The term *video* is often used interchangeably with television, although video as a medium encompasses television and extends far beyond it. Video is both a production and a distribution medium, a vehicle for ART, ENTERTAINMENT, and information, used by broadcasters, cablecasters, visual artists, teachers, children, psychiatrists, businesspeople, musicians, and HOLLYWOOD filmmakers, among others. Linked with a computer, video can produce complex interactive programs, high-density storage of audiovisual information, astounding art, and intriguing games. It is one of the latest technological innovations for the recording of moving images and sound. *See* COMPUTER: HISTORY; TELEVISION HISTORY.

Unlike film, which consists of a series of still photographs, video is a series of messages, or magnetic patterns, on a field of oxide-coated plastic tape. Exposed film consists of actual pictures, visible to the naked eye, which when projected in rapid succession—usually at twenty-four frames per second—give the impression of a moving scene (*see* MOTION PHOTOGRAPHY). A strip of videotape reveals no images to the eye; it must first be scanned electromagnetically and its signal decoded before black-and-white or color pictures and sound emerge from a television monitor. These images and sounds can be played back immediately—no processing is required as in film—and because the electronic impulses virtually duplicate the live transmission, videotape creates the feeling of a live event.

Evolving technology. The development of video depended on progress in miniaturization, magnetic tape, assembly mechanisms, and electronics. Its first public appearance in the United States was in 1951, when the Electronics Division of Bing Crosby Enterprises demonstrated the features of videotape. Two years later DAVID SARNOFF demonstrated RCA's magnetic tape for recording both black-and-white and color television programs. By 1956 the Ampex Corporation had developed what would become the U.S. broadcast industry standard for nearly twenty years: two-inch "quadruplex" videotape, requiring big, expensive machines with four separate recording heads.

The quest was on to develop a format and equipment that would be lighter and more portable than the stationary Ampex prototype. During the mid-1960s helical scan video equipment was introduced. With tape running at a slant against the moving recording heads, information was condensed onto narrower tape, and narrower tape meant lower cost and greater portability. Half-inch helical scan equipment was initially aimed at the audiovisual market—industry, schools, libraries, hospitals, and other institutions—thus opening the video market beyond broadcast.

In 1966 Japan Broadcasting Corporation (NHK) introduced a lighter-weight camera using a vidicon tube for its more mobile TELEVISION NEWS coverage. By 1971 a new, one-inch broadcast format was developed for CBS. In 1972 Sony announced the three-quarter-inch U-matic cassette, which became the standard for both broadcasting and the burgeoning educational and industrial markets.

Electronic news gathering. The arrival of truly portable equipment coupled with the advent of mobile microwave transmission and electronic editing ushered in a revolutionary new approach to broadcast news reportage known variously as ENG—electronic news gathering—or EJ—electronic journalism. Prior to ENG, live television newscasts depended mainly on prearranged events such as an inauguration or a convention. ENG meant that spontaneous events could be covered live—and broadcast within hours or minutes. In 1974 St. Louis television station KMOX became the first to use ENG exclusively. At that time only 10 percent of U.S. television stations were using any ENG equipment, but seven years later only 8 percent still used news film. Even as some countries converted to ENG—in 1979 Israel began its first ENG operations—others, like Great Britain, lagged behind owing in part to stiff union resistance to the new technology. The advent of ENG equipment had an impact on both the style and the content of television news. Some critics accused "live" or "eyewitness" news programs of trivializing and sensationalizing the news, although others praised the new technology for increasing television's ability to cover unplanned newsworthy events. Though the availability of the technology made the reporting of live news possible, the quality of that news continued to depend on the journalists in front of and behind the cameras.

Video became known popularly not so much for the news but for coverage of SPORTS, where instant video replay and slow motion were pioneered. Television drama and comedy programs more slowly switched over from film to video, as did commercial television advertising.

A personal medium. The invention of movable type in the fifteenth century made books portable and private; video did the same for the televised image. By 1969 the Portapak—the first portable video recorder—was available throughout the United States, offering the first generation of viewers raised on television the tool to make it their own way while exploring the unique aesthetic properties of the medium. Artists, hippies, journalists, filmmakers, actors,

Figure 1. *(Video)* Dan Reeves on location shooting *Smothering Dreams,* 1981. Photograph by Debra Schweitzer. Courtesy of Electronic Arts Intermix, Inc.

Figure 2. *(Video)* Ant Farm's *Media Burn,* San Francisco, July 4, 1975. Photograph by Diane Andrews Hall, 1975.

students, and others picked up the Portapak to experiment with feedback, document a riot or a love-in, or simply turn the camera on themselves.

In the United States video groups sprang up all over—the Videofreex, Raindance Corporation, Video Free America, People's Video Theater, Global Village, Top Value Television (TVTV), and Optic Nerve were some of the better known. By 1971 they had their own magazine devoted to video, *Radical Software,* linking them and spreading information about technical developments, access to equipment, sources of funding, and distribution networks for their tapes. In Canada, the Satellite Video Exchange Network in Vancouver developed an annual directory of people working in video all around the world.

Sony Corporation, the company most responsible for developing the small-format video industry and its market, decided to focus its first marketing of the Portapak in the United States. As a result, European, Asian, and Latin American experiments with the medium came later, but proliferated rapidly when they did.

In time two camps emerged within the international video scene—the video artists, many of whom had crossed over from other media such as painting, sculpture, and music, bringing their established reputations and artistic credibility to the new form; and the video activists, who were more concerned with communications issues than with art per se.

Video art. Video art was largely influenced by the "happenings," performances, dance, theater, music, and painting of the late 1960s. With the international interest in popular culture celebrated by pop artists like Andy Warhol, not only television images but the medium itself became a source for creativity and experimentation. At the studio for ELECTRONIC MUSIC in Cologne, supported by the Federal Republic of Germany's broadcasting system and directed by Karlheinz Stockhausen, Korean Nam June Paik met Wolf Vostell. Together they, along with others, inaugurated the Fluxus movement and the first video art "happenings" of the early 1960s. Before the Portapak made tape available, Vostell hammered, painted, and even shot at a group of television sets in *Ereignisse für Millionen* (Happenings for Millions, 1963), and Paik used magnets to distort television images in *Electronic TV* (1963). In 1965 Paik, who by then was living in New York, bought one of Sony's first portable video recorders and taped Pope Paul's United Nations visit from the window of a

Fifth Avenue taxicab. That evening he showed the first independently produced videotape at the Café au Go-Go in Greenwich Village, launching portable video as a medium for personal artistic expression.

Some artists saw video as a means of integrating their art in popular culture via television; others saw it as a new and interesting way of making images and artistic statements; still others saw it as a means of documenting their performances and extending the audience for their work. PERFORMANCE art, conceptual art, and imagist art all flourished in the early days of video as new kinds of environments for viewing video and new tools such as the synthesizer and colorizer were invented. Sculptural environments utilizing large-screen video projections or multiple monitors as well as time-delayed cameras or recording decks permitted such artists as Bruce Nauman, Dan Graham, Peter Campus, and Keith Sonier to experiment with video space and time. *Wipe Cycle* (1969), by Frank Gillette and Ira Schneider, was one of the first multimonitor installations, presenting viewers with a pyramid of video monitors where they could see themselves in the present and then, wiping across the monitor bank, in time-delayed pasts. This "attempt to integrate the audience into the information" was shown at "TV as a Creative Medium" at the Howard Wise Gallery in New York, the first all-video art exhibition in the United States.

Artists concerned with more abstract art and the nature of electronic imagery collaborated with engineers and computer specialists to invent unique tools for manipulating the medium. Steina and Woody Vasulka developed the Digital Image Articulator; Dan Sandin invented the Sandin Image Processor; Paik collaborated with Japanese engineer Shuya Abe on the Paik/Abe synthesizer; and Tom DeFanti in the United States developed a personal-computer graphics system known as the ZGRASS. These video tools often contained the seeds of costly SPECIAL EFFECTS equipment like the Quantel or Mirage that were later developed commercially for broadcast and industrial use.

In 1967 San Francisco's public television station KCET began a short period of experimentation in video art—one of the first signs of interest by U.S. broadcasting in the video art movement. Not until the arrival in the 1970s of music videos—videotape recordings of popular music pioneered by the British—was the legacy of video art absorbed by commercial media and transformed into a popular art form.

The principal outlets for video art have been galleries, museums, and festivals. In the late 1960s Gerry Schum opened the first gallery of films and tapes, the Television Gallery, in Dusseldorf. In time, museums like the Whitney Museum of American Art and the Museum of Modern Art in New York, the Centre Pompidou in Paris, and the Stedelijk Museum in Amsterdam all began regular exhibition of video art. One of the most celebrated museum exhibitions of video art was the Nam June Paik retrospective at the Whitney in 1982, the first such retrospective of a video artist's work by a major American museum, followed in 1986 by the Museum of Modern Art's major exhibition of Bill Viola's work. The Kijkhuis in the Hague, the São Paulo Biennale in Brazil, the San Sebastian Film Festival in Spain, the American Film Institute's National Video Festival, and the Federal Republic of Germany's Documenta likewise recognized video as an art medium. Such festivals served as the meeting place for MonitEur, an association of video critics and programmers from Italy, Belgium, the Netherlands, France, England, and the Federal Republic of Germany. Started in 1982, MonitEur awarded prizes to outstanding video work and otherwise helped promote the exhibition and serious study of European video art.

In recent years, video art has taken off in new directions. Experimental NARRATIVE has become an important interest of international video artists along with increasing formal sophistication paralleling developments in the technology for producing and editing video work. With the accessibility of the SATELLITE, video artists have also created bicoastal and multinational media art events.

Guerrilla television. Just as the development of offset PRINTING launched an alternative press in the 1960s, video's introduction hailed the arrival of an alternative television movement in the 1970s. The technological radicalism of the video activists was articulated in a manifesto written by Michael Shamberg in 1971, titled *Guerrilla Television.* Video was the tool that would decentralize broadcast television and give ordinary people a chance to get their messages out via CABLE TELEVISION. Cable was on the rise in the United States during the early 1970s, and federal regulations mandating local programming on cable, and for a time mandating public access to one or more of cable's multiple channels, made the utopian dreams of the video guerrillas seem attainable. A new style of video journalism was popularized by the award-winning tapes of the U.S. group known as TVTV—Top Value Television. Capitalizing on the immediacy and intimacy of the video medium, TVTV avoided the "voice of God" narration familiar to television viewers and replaced it with imaginative graphics, irreverent humor, and outspoken interviews with ordinary people as well as people at the power centers of the United States. Because small-format video was so new and so "low-tech," subjects tended to be unintimidated by the equipment and the hippie journalists. And since the equipment did not whir like television film cameras, many did not even realize that tape was running, which encouraged outspoken, off-the-cuff comments. *Four More Years* (1972), TVTV's DOCUMENTARY coverage of the 1972 Republican convention, was shown on cable and later on public television to much critical acclaim, proving that the alternative media could beat the networks at their own game and for a fraction of the cost.

Video guerrillas proliferated, using video to explore cultural roots, give voice to groups of people ignored by the mass media, and stimulate communication between such groups. In Canada the National Film Board's Challenge for Change program pioneered early uses of video to stimulate community awareness. The film *VTR: St. Jacques* (1968) documented the catalytic use of the medium in a depressed Montreal neighborhood. Projects with a similar community focus sprang up in some western European countries. In the Federal Republic of Germany, the Telewissen group, dedicated to making community television, was formed in 1970 in Darmstadt, while Community Video Viewing Shops appeared in the Netherlands. In England, John Hopkins founded the Fantasy Factory in London and became a key figure in the British video movement.

An important new stimulus to the movement was provided by the development of the stand-alone time base corrector, a black box that stabilized helical scan tapes and made them broadcastable. This event led many independents in the United States to aim their work toward broadcast television, especially because cable systems were proving a disappointing market. A number of the independents won a foothold in public television. The commercial networks at first flirted with the video guerrillas, sometimes purchasing their tapes, particularly of news events the networks themselves had failed to cover.

In general, however, the networks broadcast only excerpts, which were narrated by network commentators, beyond the editorial reach of the originators. The video guerrillas had done much of the research and development in the video medium, of ultimate value to the networks. In various programming genres, the stylistic and content innovations of the guerrillas were absorbed into mainstream television. Video guerrillas having been significant pioneers, remained on the outside. The growing tide of conservatism in the 1980s slowed the video guerrilla movement but did not halt it.

Video and the movies. Video has had a significant impact on the motion picture industry. Used to rehearse a scene and frequently to record actual takes, video saves time and money in costly film production and has become common on most movie sets. Material shot on film has also been transferred to videotape and edited with all the computerized special effects of state-of-the-art video. George Lucas, famed for his *Star Wars* films, added a computer division to Lucasfilm, which pioneered the EditDroid, a sophisticated video editing system for motion pictures. High-definition video, which is closer to film in resolution and tonal range than to video, has been developed especially with the commercial film market in mind. It was thought that satellite distribution of movies made on tape to theaters with wide screens and high-definition video projection would further marry the two worlds of film and video while streamlining movie distribution to theaters.

Home video. In 1975 the introduction of half-inch cassettes for the home market brought still another boom to the video field. Consumers bought the equipment primarily to record television and cable programs off the air, a phenomenon known as time-

Figure 3. *(Video)* Nam June Paik during the installation of his video work *Fish Flies on Sky,* Galeria Bonino, New York, January 1976. © 1976 by Peter Moore.

Figure 4. *(Video)* Charlotte Moorman with *TV Cello* and *TV Glasses,* 1971. © 1971 by Peter Moore.

shift viewing. But when miniature cameras and recording decks became available, video began to encroach on the home movie as the preferred way to record baby's first steps, daughter's wedding, and other family rituals and rites of passage traditionally memorialized with images.

The home video boom offered the film industry an important, new subsidiary market, and thousands of films were transferred to tape cassettes for home video sales and rentals. Pornographic films on tape proved to be home video's first best-sellers. And with inflation, the traditional Saturday night date—a movie down at the Bijou—was often replaced by watching one at home on tape or on cable television. Although this presented a financially attractive alternative for movie lovers, it also brought a change to viewing habits and expectations. The ambience of television viewing—random, lighted, interruptable—was extended now to film viewing. Younger viewers behaved in movie theaters the way they did at home watching television, while films, made now with the home video market in mind, were often structured more as made-for-TV movies than as theatrical events.

Unexpected social uses. The availability and relatively low cost of video technology in the 1970s and 1980s occasioned many unanticipated social uses. When used for security surveillance in banks, stores, and homes, it evoked the Big Brother of Orwell's *1984.* Police departments used video to nab drunk drivers and document highway violations as well as to entrap criminals in the act. Videotapes became a means of applying for a job, recording a will, submitting evidence in a trial, documenting inventories for insurance records, and organizing a dating service. Video, able to go where the human eye could not, could be used to inspect for termites or troubleshoot clogged sewers. Industry seized upon video early as a way of communicating with far-flung branch offices, instructing salespeople, or pitching to potential customers. In education, video could supply canned lectures or a more convenient way of viewing films, but more innovative approaches were also used, in which students and teachers made their own tapes. For the training of dancers, gymnasts, machine operators, and others involved in movements requiring extreme precision, video proved a boon. In psychiatry, Dr. Milton M. Berger of Columbia University blazed a path in the therapeutic uses of video in psychoanalysis and group therapy. Video games, the electronic version of the pinball gallery and pool hall, became a youth craze in the late 1970s. In the 1980s video games for the elderly appeared; they were aimed at developing hand-eye coordination and manual dexterity while generally stimulating brain functioning.

The decades of the sixties, seventies, and eighties informed and were transformed by video. Once envisioned by some as a tool capable of creating a new society through the decentralization of television, video had by the eighties become an adjunct of mainstream broadcasting and Hollywood film, and a middle-class status symbol of conspicuous consumption. However, new and imaginative applications—unforeseen by the video pioneers—continued to proliferate.

See also AVANT-GARDE FILM.

Bibliography. Deirdre Boyle, *Subject to Change: Guerrilla Television Revisited,* New York, 1987; Douglas Davis and Allison Simmons, eds., *The New Television: A Public/Private Art,* Cambridge, Mass., 1977; Ira Schneider and Beryl Korot, eds., *Video Art: An Anthology,* New York, 1976; Michael Shamberg and Raindance Corporation, *Guerrilla Television,* New York, 1971.

DEIRDRE BOYLE

VIDEOTEX

Data transmission systems that bring text and graphic information to viewers through TELEPHONE and CABLE TELEVISION circuits and display it using modified television sets. Videotex systems provide businesses and homes with a range of informational,

a

b

Figure 1. *(Videotex)* Two Antiope teletext magazines on the air in France. *(a)* Courtesy of Antiope Antenne 2. *(b)* Courtesy of Antiope SNCF.

educational, and leisure services. Pioneered in Britain, videotex soon found its way into other European countries, North America, and Japan. But despite substantial investment by government and business, videotex services have not met with much market acceptance, particularly outside the area of business services. The development of videotex also raises a number of social concerns about PRIVACY, access to the service, and social isolation.

Videotex is not to be confused with teletext, a less sophisticated system, which is broadcast rather than transmitted by cable. It is a one-way system that supplies digital data on the normal broadcast channel by placing messages in the unused lines of the standard television signal or the *vertical blanking interval* (VBI). The VBI is the dark bar that sometimes appears when the television picture rolls, requiring the viewer to adjust a dial. A teletext subscriber uses a control keypad, typically resembling a hand calculator, to display desired frames, or "pages" of text and pictures. One ordinarily begins with an index that indicates what is available on different pages and proceeds to specific stories. Information is edited in a broadcast studio and coded in digital form for transmission at a rate commensurate with an ordinary television. Transmission rates are important because low rates mean a longer wait for pages. This digitized information is inserted into the television signal on the VBI or a full channel set aside solely for teletext use. Information is detected by a decoder built into the television receiver or wired as an accessory to an ordinary television. The decoder receives, stores, and ultimately displays the data on viewer command. A typical teletext subscriber pays a monthly fee to receive updated information roughly comparable in volume to a weekly NEWSMAGAZINE.

Videotex proper, or *viewdata* as it is sometimes called, makes use of telephone or cable for distributing information. This wire connection provides subscribers with the opportunity to use large amounts of information. Rather than simply selecting from the two hundred or so pages that the teletext service broadcasts, the videotex user can process thousands of pages of information, contribute to an existing data base, and communicate this action to other subscribers. Videotex analysts envision the service opening the way to new forms of learning, shopping, banking, communication, and working.

Videotex systems include information retrieval and display terminals. These may be ordinary color television sets equipped with a digital decoder or a modified computer terminal capable of color display. Retrieval-response devices range from the simple keypad to a typewriterlike unit that expands the range of commands. Systems also include transmission lines for interactive communication such as ordinary telephone lines, a coaxial cable television network, communications satellites, microwave facilities, and combinations of these. Finally, videotex systems require computer systems and software. Specific programs permit users rapid access to information and record subscriber activity for billing. In addition to paying for a connection (i.e., phone charges), users are charged by the month, by the amount of time they use the system, by the page, or by some combination of these.

Videotex enjoys a number of advantages over its major competitors, the print media. Foremost among the advantages is speed—the amount of time it takes for a page of information to go from writer to reader. The months it takes for a book page, the days or weeks for a magazine page, the hours for a newspaper are reduced to seconds with videotex. Videotex also offers the user wider choice among comprehensive collections of data. In essence, a user can choose the specific kind of information desired when the user wants it. Moreover, videotex is interactive; it allows the user to respond to material on the screen, an advantage in learning, shopping, and working at home.

Videotex also suffers from a number of disadvantages. The display terminal is not as convenient as the printed page for conveying information. The screen holds fewer than two hundred words, less than half the number on a paperback book page, and can display only a page at a time. It is not nearly as portable as a newspaper, magazine, or book. Moreover, the cost of using videotex is far higher than that of traditional print media. Though the trend is toward decreasing component costs, analysts doubt that anything more than a simple teletext service will attract widespread interest in the foreseeable future. Consequently, most videotex promoters see banks, large retailers, travel agencies, and other businesses, rather than individual households, as their major market.

Despite these drawbacks, videotex soon attracted developers in several countries. Among these were governments, which saw videotex as a way to promote their national information industries, particularly in international markets. The British government took the lead with its Prestel videotex and the BBC's Ceefax teletext. France followed with Teletel (videotex) and Antiope (teletext), Canada with Telidon, Japan with Captain, and the Federal Republic of Germany with Bildschirmtext. In the United States, several large businesses, including AT&T, the television networks, major publishers, banks, and retailers moved into videotex.

Analysts agree that videotex services offer potential advances in information distribution and use. Many question whether this potential will be fully realized. Considerable differences exist among national technical STANDARDS, particularly between Europe and North America. Standards influence the type and cost of videotex systems, and the lack of agreement limits the investment incentive. Agreement or not, there is concern that consumers will find the cost and effort of use to be substantial barriers. It is uncertain whether this can be overcome by decreases in component costs and the growing consumer education in interactive electronics through automatic teller machines, cable television, videocassette recorders, and personal computers.

Observers also raise questions about the social implications of videotex. They wonder about the gap that videotex may widen between those who can and cannot afford access to these services. Moreover, there is concern about the potential for encroachments on personal privacy. This arises from the ability of videotex systems to monitor user choices for billing, marketing surveys, and so on. Finally, there are questions about the social consequences of providing people with the ability to perform many activities normally conducted outside the home in the convenience—but also the isolation—of their individual homes.

See also TELECOMMUNICATIONS POLICY.

Bibliography. Vincent Mosco, *Pushbutton Fantasies: Critical Perspectives on Videotex and Information Technology,* Norwood, N.J., 1982; Richard M. Neustadt, *The Birth of Electronic Publishing,* White Plains, N.Y., 1982; Efrem Sigel, *The Future of Videotex,* White Plains, N.Y., 1983.

VINCENT MOSCO

VIOLENCE

Violence in the mass media has been the subject of continuing controversy, principally in the United States, since the end of World War II, although neither media violence nor concern over it has been confined to the United States. Japanese television drama is acknowledged as among the most violent in the world, yet in Japan there has been little controversy over it; in Sweden the portrayal of violence but not the portrayal of sexual encounters has been sharply restricted on television.

In the United States the focus has been primarily on television because of its rapid rise to prominence among ENTERTAINMENT media (*see* TELEVISION HISTORY) and because television has been very violent since early in its history, with a violent crime rate at least fifty times greater than in real life and with children's programming far exceeding general audience programming in violent episodes. However, no mass medium has escaped the controversy because none is without a substantial quantity or prominent instances of violent depictions, representations, and symbols. The possible negative influences of newspapers, magazines, comic books, theatrical films, radio, videocassettes, popular recordings (and their album covers), and music videos have all been and continue to be subjects of debate.

The controversy in the United States over violence in the mass media, especially television, may be divided into two periods:

1. *Growing attention* (1952–1967). The first congressional hearing concerned with television content was held in 1952 by the House Committee on Interstate and Foreign Commerce; the topics were "sex and violence." Widely discussed Senate hearings—in 1954, 1961–1962, and 1964–1965—examined the possibility that juvenile delinquency was encouraged by violent television entertainment. Meanwhile, between the mid-1950s and mid-1960s the medium itself became markedly more violent as

action-and-adventure series became a staple of prime-time television.

2. *Scrutiny, controversy, and confrontation* (after 1968). Between 1968 and 1972 the question of whether the media increase antisocial behavior was examined by three federal task forces. In 1969 the National Commission on the Causes and Prevention of Violence concluded that violence in television drama was a "contributing factor" to "violence in society." By contrast the Commission on Obscenity and Pornography in 1970 concluded that PORNOGRAPHY did *not* contribute to antisocial behavior. The Surgeon General's Scientific Advisory Committee on Television and Social Behavior in 1972 reached the conclusion that violent television entertainment increased the aggressive behavior of *some* young viewers.

The succeeding years have seen continuing controversy among social scientists, and between social scientists and citizen groups on the one hand and broadcasters on the other, over the way television violence should be measured and over its effects on viewers. There have also been repeated House and Senate hearings; an ex officio attempt by the Federal Communications Commission (FCC) to impose a "family viewing" period in early prime time, restricting violent and sexually provocative content (this was overturned by the courts); and several campaigns by such groups as the National Parent-Teachers Association and the American Medical Association to reduce violent programming. The confrontation between broadcasters and their critics continues.

Empirical Evidence

In 1963 two experiments conducted by psychologists, demonstrating that within the laboratory setting exposure to violent film portrayals increases subsequent aggressiveness, were published in the United States. Albert Bandura demonstrated that children of nursery-school age would imitate aggressive acts seen on a film screen as well as those performed for them firsthand. Imitated screen behaviors included those of a "Cat Lady" costumed like a character in children's entertainment. Leonard Berkowitz demonstrated that college-age subjects expressed greater hostility toward an experimenter (who had mildly provoked them) after they had seen a portrayal in which violent retribution seemed justified. By the time of the surgeon general's inquiry (early 1970s) more than forty published experiments had documented a cause-and-effect relationship in an experimental setting. However, many remained skeptical of this experimental evidence because of characteristics inherent in laboratory experiments, among them the short time span, the improbability of retaliation by a "victim," and the simulated and unreal qualities of viewing and behavior in that context.

The surgeon general's inquiry added, as inferential material, data from surveys of everyday viewing and everyday aggressive behavior by young people. Survey data are rarely compelling in regard to causation, but they can be called upon when addressing the issue of whether everyday events occur in ways consistent with a particular causal interpretation. In this instance the surveys documented small but definitely positive associations between the regular viewing of violent television entertainment and everyday aggressiveness not wholly attributable to any alternative explanations, such as more aggressive children preferring violent entertainment.

This is what the surgeon general's committee called a "convergence" between the findings of experiments and surveys. Experiments demonstrate increases in aggressiveness unambiguously attributable to media exposure in settings that arguably limit the real-world circumstances and settings to which these findings can be generalized. Surveys document an everyday association between violence viewing and aggressiveness, thereby increasing the credibility that may be ascribed to generalizations from the experimental evidence to the real world.

Nothing has occurred since the surgeon general's inquiry to alter this pattern, despite the many new experiments that have been conducted and the quantity of new survey data analyzed. There has been little support for the catharsis hypothesis, which holds that violent portrayals will drain off or diffuse aggressive impulses; such portrayals, however, have been shown to inhibit aggressiveness when they make the viewer anxious over such impulses. Although the survey evidence is stronger in regard to interpersonal aggression (stealing, hitting, name calling) than for more serious and harmful forms of antisocial behavior, it also supports the view that violence viewing is associated with seriously harmful as well as less serious antisocial behavior. Most persons familiar with the scientific evidence interpret it as supporting the hypothesis that exposure to violent television entertainment increases the likelihood of subsequent aggressive or antisocial behavior. This majority view is reflected in the passage in 1985 of a resolution by the American Psychological Association's council of representatives calling for ameliorative action by parents and the media.

Theory and Process

Since the 1963 experiments, three theoretical explanations for behavioral effects in connection with media violence have been advanced. These are complementary theories; experiments have demonstrated that each explains a different but interrelated way in which media effects occur.

Bandura's SOCIAL COGNITIVE THEORY posits that the capability of performing an act is enhanced by—and, if the act is wholly unfamiliar, may be attributed to—observing another perform it. The appropriateness and efficacy attributed to a particular act are said to be influenced by the observed setting and outcome of another's behavior. Firsthand observation and observation through television and film media are held to influence behavior analogously; visual media are thus said to teach the how, when, and why.

Berkowitz's disinhibition and cue theory posits that portrayals alter the meaning attached to internal and external experience by modifying either the restraint associated with an internal state, such as anger, or the response elicited by an external stimulus. This theory argues that visual media are able to inhibit or disinhibit behavior and to affect the degree to which it is influenced by cues in the environment. This perspective emphasized the singular incident. Later, under the label "cognitive neoassociationism," Berkowitz speculated that the media, by such means, may shape mental scenarios that serve as guides to behavior.

Arousal theory, developed by Dolf Zillmann and Percy Tannenbaum, posits that the excitation created by exposure to violent or otherwise stimulating portrayals may transfer to subsequent behavior, so that when behavioral inclinations are aggressive such portrayals will heighten aggression. Arousal almost certainly plays a greater role in effects recorded for children because of their greater impressionability and emotional volatility. Arousal does not fully explain the effects encompassed by social cognitive theory or cognitive-neoassociation, however, because it does not explain why televised models are emulated or why, when equally violent portrayals are viewed, those with particular features should more greatly influence subsequent behavior.

The experiments provide a catalog of the factors on which effects are contingent (Table 1). These represent four broad dimensions, although some factors arguably fit more than one dimension: (1) *efficacy* (is the violence effective?); (2) *pertinence* (does it apply to real-life circumstances?); (3) *normativeness* (is it ordinary and acceptable—i.e., for the behavior in question?); and (4) *susceptibility* of the viewer. This body of psychological research implies that whenever an individual's position on these dimensions is raised or lowered in conjunction with media exposure, so too is the likelihood of a media effect.

Because of the experimentally demonstrated influence of these factors and dimensions, they would retain a strong claim to validity were such media effects so rare that the social impact was judged to be insignificant; that is, they explain effects, whether bizarre and shocking or humdrum.

Table 1. Factors Experimentally Demonstrated to Enhance the Likelihood That Television Violence Will Heighten Antisocial or Aggressive Behavior

1. Reward or lack of punishment for the portrayed perpetrator of violence
2. Portrayal of violence as justified by the behavior of the victim
3. Cues in the portrayal likely to be encountered in real life, such as the victim resembling a real-life antagonist
4. Portrayal of the perpetrator of violence as similar to the viewer
5. Portrayal of violent behavior ambiguous in intent as motivated by the desire to inflict harm or injury
6. Violence portrayed so that its consequences do not stir distaste or arouse inhibitions over such behavior
7. Violence portrayed as representing real events rather than events concocted for a fictional representation
8. Portrayed violence that is not the subject of critical commentary
9. Portrayal of violence whose commission particularly pleases the viewer or whose perpetrator is particularly liked by the viewer
10. Portrayals in which the violence is not interrupted by violence in a light or humorous vein
11. Portrayed abuse that includes physical violence and aggression instead of or in addition to verbal abuse
12. Portrayals, violent or otherwise, that leave the viewer in an unresolved state of excitement
13. Viewers who are in a state of anger, frustration, or provocation *before* seeing a violent portrayal
14. Viewers who are in a state of anger, frustration, or provocation *after* seeing a violent portrayal

Other Effects

Effects of media violence other than those on aggression and antisocial behavior also have been investigated empirically. These include the following factors:

1. *Desensitization and habituation: Are sensitivity and responsiveness lessened?* Among males, continuing exposure in fairly ordinary viewing circumstances to films featuring extreme violence against women in a sexual context apparently reduces the likelihood that they will label a particular film scene as violent and increases their acceptance of the "rape myth" (i.e., the belief that women long for violently imposed sex). The evidence of several experiments

that used children as subjects suggests that violence in the media deadens response to media violence. It is a demonstrated principle of psychology that desensitized and habituated responses will approach and often return to their initial levels when the stimuli are removed for a period. The implication is that the prominence of media violence in modern society is itself fostering greater acceptance of the presence of such violence and that those individuals heavily exposed become even more accepting. The same argument appears valid for the rape myth and applies analogously to pornography. It is implausible that media violence would deaden responsiveness to violence in one's immediate vicinity, and there is no evidence to support this notion (although the readiness to intervene between a victim and an attacker arguably might be reduced by media accounts of the perils of intervention). However, in addition to the rape-myth data, the apparent effectiveness of the mass media in times of war in labeling a people or a country as deserving to be destroyed supports the view that the media can alter sensitivities regarding the fate of others.

2. *Aggression against women: Do the media make a difference?* Some experiments suggest that the Commission on Obscenity and Pornography may have erred in 1970. The commission focused on erotica and unlawful acts. The new research focuses on portrayals of violence against women in an erotic context and on aggression against women. The experiments find aggression increased by a portrayal of the physical abuse of a woman by a man with no apparent sexual motive, by a portrayal of a rape that the victim eventually enjoys, and by the portrayal of a rape in which the woman suffers when the male subjects have some reason to be antagonistic toward their victim. Although subject to the same skepticism as the laboratory-type experiments on television violence, these findings imply that "stalker" and "slasher" films (in which men brutalize, torture, and murder women), violence in erotica, and the popular theme in entertainment of the violent harassment with sexual overtones are problematic for sexual relations in general and for the well-being of women in particular.

3. *Public perceptions and beliefs about reality: What do the media contribute?* Obviously the media must at least occasionally make some contribution, because sometimes in entertainment and often in news they are the principal or sole sources of information. In regard to media violence the research focus has been on the possible influence of television exposure on "mean-world" beliefs about the integrity of public officials, the future of today's children, and safety when walking alone at night. George Gerbner and colleagues at the University of Pennsylvania have labeled any possible effects "cultivation" to connote a continuing facilitation of an outlook (*see* CULTIVATION ANALYSIS). In this instance the hypothesized cultivation is of a pessimistic and fearful outlook. Survey data on television exposure and mean-world beliefs give some support to this hypothesis, at least for North America, although data from other regions are not devoid of support. There seems to be little question that in North America such beliefs are positively associated with television exposure; the evidence for their being attributable to greater exposure is less strong than for association but not absent. The evidence for both association and causation is decidedly stronger for measures of pessimism than for measures of fearfulness. The distinction is made clearer when alternative labels are reviewed for "pessimism" (cognitions, societal-level beliefs, perceptions about the world) and "fearfulness" (affect, personal-level anxiety, perceptions about self). *See* CULTURAL INDICATORS.

4. *Events transiently prominent in the media: What is the impact?* These "flash effects" are the other side of the coin from cultivation: short-term public response to irregularly repetitive classes of media content. Social statistics analyzed by U.S. sociologist David Phillips suggest that media attention to events such as prominent suicides, televised boxing matches, and publicized executions temporarily increases suicides, increases homicides, and decreases homicides, respectively. These analyses have been the target of much criticism, primarily methodological. Although they cannot be faulted for failing to deal with real-life events, there is no way to specify the exact expected time lag between media attention and public response, so that increases or decreases in reported behavior (as collected by police and other public agencies) occurring by chance might be falsely attributed to the media attention. The sole safeguard is replication, and data other than that originally analyzed are often not available.

International Comparisons

There is no survey of media violence worldwide, although comparisons of the amount of violent programming on television suggest that it is typically more frequent when programming must be supported by ADVERTISING revenue. From the viewpoint of broadcasters the principal purpose of violent portrayals is to attract viewers, a particularly significant criterion when financial support for a broadcasting system is dependent on audience size and quality, the two determinants of the value of (or price to be charged for) advertising accompanying a program.

One would expect both the character and the influence of television to be culture contingent, although the general principles developed in social learning (or social cognition), disinhibition and cue (or cognitive-neoassociation), and arousal theories apply. For example, an examination of violence in Japanese television found that quantitatively there were scarcely discernible differences between Japanese and U.S. television but that qualitatively there were great differences. Much more frequently in Japanese than in U.S. television, violence befell a figure the audience would like and with whom it would identify; in U.S. television violence more frequently was used with success by the hero. This difference reflects the differing norms for entertainment that hold in the two societies. The theories developed in U.S. research would predict far less, if any, increase in aggressive or antisocial behavior as a consequence of exposure to television emphasizing the noninstrumental or tragic character of violence. Thus the lack of concern over media violence in Japan has some theoretical and empirical justification.

Audience Response

When people respond as members of an audience, they are extending conscious patronage to a medium. Audience response, then, is distinct from such incidental and unintended (but not necessarily unimportant) responses as aggressive and antisocial behavior or pessimistic or fearful outlooks. Audience response is exemplified by television research in the United States, where dependence of the medium on popularity makes the behavior of people acting as audience members important to broadcasters, advertisers, reformers, and critics alike.

CONTENT ANALYSIS of *TV Guide* plot synopses has documented that the proportion of synopses describing a violent story oscillates, peaking every four or five years, and that this proportion is positively associated with the average ratings for such programs the previous year. The rise and fall reflect the rush of the industry to imitate programs that have proved popular and the consequences of programming by GENRE, with program cancellations rising as the audience for violence becomes dispersed and satiated, a process furthered by the tendency of dramatic imitations to be inferior to their models. There is no sign of a sustained, long-term trend, and this oscillation implies a ceiling on the quantity of programs featuring violence imposed by limits in the magnitude of the audience for violence.

Violence is a staple of programming, however, because it meets certain industrial criteria of television and other media as well: ready-made formulas, dramatic conflicts, compelling narratives, vehicles for popular stars, and clear-cut denouements. Undeniably a sizable proportion of the audience responds favorably to such programming. This raises the issue of conflict and action versus interpersonal violence. Empirical data help provide an answer. Over a fall-winter prime-time season, television ratings by the A. C. Nielsen Company were not correlated with amount of interpersonal physical violence in the programs (*see* RATING SYSTEMS: RADIO AND TELEVISION). When versions of a popular police series high and low in interpersonal violence were created by editing an episode, there were no differences in the degree of liking expressed for the two versions. Thus violence that is interpersonal and physical does not heighten series popularity or elicit more favorable expressions of opinion. The implication is that programs containing violence are popular because of the characters and the conflict and action, not because of interpersonal physical violence.

The public also has decided opinions about television violence. Typically when adults in the United States are asked whether they agree or disagree with statements that there is too much violence on television or that television violence is a serious problem, about two-thirds of a representative national sample will agree. When similar queries are made in regard to sex, slightly fewer agree. Far fewer adults express concern over sex and violence when, instead of opinions about the medium in general, objections to sex and violence are sought on a program-by-program basis with no hint of the kind of objections that might be offered. In such cue-free circumstances only about one out of ten persons offers an objection relating to violence or sex for the program receiving the most objections on these grounds, and for most programs the proportion receiving objections over sex or violence is decidedly smaller. It is not illogical, of course, to object to the programming schedule as a whole without seriously objecting to any particular program, although some of the difference may represent the respondents' giving what is thought to be the normative opinion when asked to agree or disagree. The discrepancy implies that media violence is not really of much salience to the public; that is, it is not something that is foremost when respondents are asked to give their opinion about one or another television program.

Policy

If media violence has negative social consequences, should it not be constrained? The problem is how to do so without impinging on one or more important values, such as freedom of expression, artistic integrity, honesty, and truthfulness. This is the issue that must be dealt with in policy-making everywhere in regard to media violence.

In all societies the three principal actors in the making of public policy are the government, the media organizations, and the general public. Because of the limitations on SPECTRUM space, among other factors, broadcasting everywhere is a matter for some

GOVERNMENT REGULATION. In the United States, for example, regulatory guidelines for serving the public interest have been imposed in exchange for broadcast licenses, whose periodic renewal is theoretically contingent on adequate performance. Violent content, however, has not figured in such review.

Direct action by the FCC or by Congress against any class of content, which implies prior restraint of expression, although frequently proposed, almost certainly would be declared invalid by the courts on First Amendment grounds. The FCC could proceed by requiring programming inherently antithetical to violence, such as that for children and family viewing, but it has never done so formally beyond the issuance of policy statements that only threaten, and it is unlikely to impose any rules for any class of television content. Meanwhile, technology reduces the power of any regulatory authority by making available distribution and playback systems that do not qualify for control or that elude control. Thus CABLE TELEVISION, pay television, and satellite transmission do not share with broadcasting the same spectrum limitations and therefore are not subject to the same regulatory restraints as a broadcast licensee—although cable systems, being locally franchised, may be subject to local pressures. In-home playback devices elude all reception restraints; only distribution can be restrained, and in the United States there is very little that is not deemed acceptable for self-consenting consumption. Technology thus withers an already ineffectual force.

Economic incentives ensure the continuing production of violent television programs and theater films, disseminated by cable, pay television, videocassettes, and/or typically later broadcast on television, including violent entertainment arguably unredeemed by any claims to topical, political, aesthetic, moral, or dramatic importance. Many would say stalker and slasher films fall into this latter category.

In rich and free circumstances of dissemination, self-regulatory industry codes are imperiled internally because such circumstances fuel competition among the media; externally they constitute a useful defense against critics of regulatory intervention. Thus the entertainment industry cannot be expected to constrain violence voluntarily. By default, responsibility falls to the public and various institutions such as churches, schools, private foundations, and professional and voluntary associations. The two means open to them are public pressure and the financing of nonviolent programming, neither of which historically has much affected the degree, quantity, or character of violence in the television programming available to the public.

Conditions in the United States exemplify to some degree the factors affecting public policy in regard to media violence in many societies. They include the authority of the government over the media; statutory and constitutional rights, privileges, and restrictions of the media; the priorities given freedom of expression and the minimization of social harm; the control, ownership, and sources of financial support of the media; the cultural setting, including societal values and traditions in regard to violence in real life and storytelling; and the changes being brought about by new technology. When greater authority is extended to the government, statutes, and regulatory bodies, the role of nongovernmental bodies may be sharply reduced, and violence in entertainment—as well as other media content, including news reportage and editorial commentary—may be effectively constrained.

See also CHILDREN—MEDIA EFFECTS; MASS COMMUNICATIONS RESEARCH; MASS MEDIA EFFECTS; PERSUASION.

Bibliography. Albert Bandura, *Aggression: A Social Learning Analysis,* Englewood Cliffs, N.J., 1973; Leonard Berkowitz, "Some Effects of Thoughts on Anti- and Prosocial Influences of Media Events: A Cognitive-Neoassociation Analysis," *Psychological Bulletin* 95, no. 3 (1984): 410–427; George Comstock, "Media Influences on Aggression," in *Prevention and Control of Aggression,* ed. by Arnold P. Goldstein, New York, 1983; idem, "Television and Film Violence," in *Youth Violence: Programs and Prospects,* ed. by Steven J. Apter and Arnold P. Goldstein, New York, 1985; George Comstock, Steven Chaffee, Nathan Katzman, Maxwell McCombs, and Donald Roberts, *Television and Human Behavior,* New York, 1978; David Pearl, Lorraine Bouthilet, and Joyce B. Lazar, eds., *Television and Behavior: Ten Years of Scientific Progress and Implications for the Eighties,* 2 vols., Washington, D.C., 1982; Surgeon General's Scientific Advisory Committee on Television and Social Behavior, *Television and Growing Up: The Impact of Televised Violence,* Washington, D.C., 1972.

GEORGE COMSTOCK

VISUAL IMAGE

Discussion of the nature of visual images has always centered on the question of their relationship not so much to reality as to the perception or conception of reality, and questions of representation (*see* REPRESENTATION, PICTORIAL AND PHOTOGRAPHIC) in ART have therefore been closely related to questions of psychology and epistemology. Socrates said that the senses paint on the soul, PLATO compared the imitation of things by words to that of painting, and ARISTOTLE wrote that the images of memory are something like a picture—these comments setting a pattern followed to the present time.

Image and Reality

In everyday usage "imitation" in painting means not simply the replication of things but the replication of something like our first experience of them. When Leonardo da Vinci wrote of painting as a universal LANGUAGE, he based this on the assumption that painting corresponds to common visual experience, to which all have equal access. But this assumption raises familiar problems. For over two millennia it was more or less agreed in a generally Platonic way that the level of reality treated by simple imitation was not true reality, which suggested that what should be imitated was not perceptual but rather conceptual: the forms of the mind rather than the traces of external things. This in turn involved the question of the relation between the perceptual and the conceptual. The question of how we know the true (is it mathematical, universal, beautiful, or all three?) raised aesthetic issues that have had the most pervasive consequences in both the theory and practice of Western art (*see* AESTHETICS).

At the other, perceptual end of the scale, questions regarding the nature of perception itself also affected art and reflection about it. The tonal painting that began in the RENAISSANCE was based on the understanding that the sense of sight distinguished light and dark, a distinction that provided the framework within which color could be placed. This understanding was of course susceptible to changes in the theory of visual perception. The Newtonian definition of the prismatic nature of light demanded a revision of this scheme. Painting is more real, both of these formulations imply, as it makes use of the elements of perception itself. In such terms an art made up simply of visual elements could be conceived that, although "abstract," could be justified as "more real" because grounded in the foundations of visual sensation itself. At higher levels of perception (as opposed to mere sensation) art could also be justified on the basis of its conformity with the structures by means of which we make sense of sensation (*see* PERCEPTION—STILL AND MOVING PICTURES).

The same issues are raised in more recent discussions. The problem concerning the question of the "realism" of images arises in part from the false assumption that all images are completely defined by iconicity, that is, reference by resemblance. This only translates into another language the further assumption that all art is at base naturalistic. If we follow that assumption, then in the face of the variety of styles there must be as many ways of seeing as there are ways of representing the world. This point of view is apparently corroborated by the analogy of the visual arts to language. Styles become modes of arbitrary signification (*see* MODE). But if many things about images are not determined by resemblance, then it is easier to see how images are rooted in the usages, paths, rituals, and routines of which they are an integral part.

If we define style in a narrow sense, not as the general "visual character" of a group of artifacts but rather as the manner in which artifacts are presented, or forms are represented, as the peculiar character of contour and line, color, and modeling in the art of a place or period, then the differences among styles are less problematical (*see* ARTIFACT). There are, after all, characteristic differences among groups of artifacts of all kinds—among tools, objects of use and decoration—and in the case of such artifacts questions of vision need not come into play in attempts to explain them. There is no reason why all the features of a work of art should be reduced to MEANING apprehensible only through what might be called the uniform visual and aesthetic surface given to them by facture.

Style in this restricted sense of characteristic facture is the result of the activity of a specialized community of artisans, and its continuity is a consequence of technique and traditions of technique (*see* ARTIST AND SOCIETY). There are any number of particular ways of shaping and ornamenting a bowl, and the election of one is arbitrary in that any number of choices might have been made—and also arbitrary in the more positive sense of being subject to judgment. Once a style is established, it becomes naturalized; that is, characteristic facture shapes the expectation that artifacts done in that way simply *are* artifacts of that kind, and artifacts done in other ways are viewed as alien. Both traditions of craft and the naturalization of styles may thus encourage conservatism, although styles are easily changed and easily influence one another simply because they are radically arbitrary. The conservatism of styles is less strict than that of function or ICONOGRAPHY, which are rooted in other dimensions of meaning and value.

Defining the Image

Significant implications follow from the argument that images are not defined by iconicity. The face on an Olmec hand ax (Figure 1) does not simply refer by resemblance; rather, it anthropomorphizes a power given to the implement by the very addition of the image. In order to do so, of course, the face must also be recognizable (at least in reference to previous comparable images, which means that it may become recognizable primarily by placement in succeeding versions), but it need not refer in any direct way to a model. Still, it may be seen as referring in the most general sense of being "of" something, and from this example may be derived an important principle: to make an image of something implies (or may imply) its existence.

An important part of the language surrounding images might be called genetic. Images are by or of their makers and are also of their model, who is often also their patron. Both *pattern* and *patron* are from the Latin *pater,* the first term preserving the genetic relation between model and image, the sec-

Figure 1. *(Visual Image)* Jade hand ax, ca. 1000 B.C.E. Olmec. Reproduced by courtesy of the Trustees of The British Museum.

ond the genetic relation between an image and the person who caused it to be made. These relationships of image to model, artist, and patron are integral to the magical identification of images with what they represent.

The "of" in the phrase "image of" entails vital connection, but it also implies difference. The image is not that of which it is the image. Solutions to the problem posed by this difference may run the gamut from the identity of image and model (the image is what it is not; the statue *is* the god) to the complete disrelation of the two (the model cannot be imitated, and the image is worthless). The recurrent iconoclastic controversy in Christian art was not simply the result of the prohibition against graven images but also turned on questions of the difference between image and prototype and the nature of the relation between the two.

In Plato's *Cratylus* Socrates entertains the possibility that words imitate things the way pictures do. This can only be so, he says, if letters somehow have qualities matchable to things, as the colors of pigments may be matched to things by the painter. It has been argued that Plato meant to refer to painting as a natural SIGN or icon. However, he also insisted that an image is always different from and less than that of which it is an image; otherwise it would not be an image but a double, or the thing itself. Perhaps Plato meant to say that materials used by artists are like what is imitated in such ways that they are able to stand for them. For example, a color is like a thing not simply in possessing "redness" or "blueness" but in that it has extent on a surface, and it may be further like a thing in that this extent is circumscribed to give it definite and recognizable shape. Making an image of something, in other words, is a transference from one extent to another, from one colored surface to another, or, to move from painting to SCULPTURE, from volumes of flesh to volumes of stone. The important thing is not that stone is not flesh but rather that stone can take the place of flesh by virtue of certain qualities they share. In an image the qualities of stone may become meaningful in relation to what it stands for (the permanence and hardness of stone instead of the mortality and vulnerability of flesh).

This argument provides an important general definition: images are realized together with some specific extent, and this extent in itself constitutes a separate and irreducible realm of human meaning. Extent is spatial by definition, and the basis of images thus places them in the vast phenomenological and historical realm of significant space. The significance of extent also separates images at once from verbal signs, whether spoken or written. Spoken words have no extent at all, and one must only consider the severe limitations of extent required for written texts to be intelligible—the uniformity of size of letters, lines, columns, and paragraphs—to understand by contrast the endless possibilities of the spatiality of images. Extent also has implications for the question of the conventionality of visual images. Precisely because they are always spatial objects configured to human use, images (and works of art in general) are accessible in ways that texts are not. This is not to say that works of art are natural signs but rather that their interpretation entails not merely their decoding but the examination of their evident spatial character and the recovery of the significance of spaces either implied or stated by them.

The idea of extent might be reworded to say that images are always made of some material. Material is not simply that which is given form, however. It is rather specific and in some way envalued, and this envaluation is integral to the final significance of an image. Materials may be distinguished by some striking qualities (gold or jade, for example) usually associated with rarity and some difficulty in finding or extracting them. Some materials may also be thought to possess magical powers, and realization of an image in rare or magical materials distinguishes it and irreducibly states its own value.

A more complex envaluation is given to material by labor. As a result of its quarrying, the stone out of which the image of the pharaoh was carved already had a determinate configuration before the image began to be made. The stone was cut out of the earth with great expense of labor in a way defined both by the nature of stone and by the state of technology, and it was transported with similar effort, so that by the time the stone began to be carved it had been given a prismatic form and a value immediately evident as a record and sign of the pharaoh's power to command the dressing, moving, and working of stone. In general, such envaluation entails a certain decorum, and those of or for whom images are made are those with the power to bring about their creation.

Images are also given value by the display of skill. The same pharaoh who moves the stone also commands the services of specialists able to work it, and centers of artistic skill are usually centers of political power. The evidence of skilled facture and, beyond that, of ingenuity of facture or elaboration also in themselves indicate value. This is as true of modern art as it is of ancient or primitive art.

There is a continuous relationship between the decorum implied by envaluation and that to which ornament is subject. The cathedral is bigger than other buildings in a city, and it is also more ornate. Ornament thus provides embellishment, makes status visible, and provides an endless justification for formal invention and the display of virtuosity. The Mayan lord (Figure 2) is distinguished not only by his copious ornamentation but also by the skill with which it is conceived and executed. When simplicity is identified with such distinction, this presupposes the decorum of distinction by elaboration and is meaningful in opposition to it.

Freestanding sculpture identifies an image with the material out of which it is made. When an image is placed on a two-dimensional support, or surface, however, it is immediately related in significant ways to what of the support is not image. The image is of course distinguished from the rest of the support, but it is also related to it according to two fundamental modes, the *surficial* and the *planar*. These two modes tend to be fitted to subject matter and therefore to the uses to which images are put.

The element of surficiality is the *mark*, that is, the actual pigment added to the supporting surface to represent something. The characteristic order of these marks is random and therefore determinable by content, which is perceptual and descriptive. The significance of individual marks is determined not so much by resemblance as by context. It is in relation to

Figure 2. *(Visual Image)* Mayan stela, Copán, Honduras, ca. 500 C.E. Art Resource, New York.

Figure 3. *(Visual Image)* Marching warriors, Cingle de la Mola Remigia, Gasulla Gorge, Castellón. From Johannes Maringer and Hans-Georg Bandi, *Art in the Ice Age,* New York: Praeger Publishers, 1953, p. 130. Reprinted with permission.

other marks that each is meaningful. Figure 3 shows a scene made up of marks freely disposed to record or imagine what we see as an event. Here nonimage is significant as a visual field, and the substantial identity of image and nonimage is sustained in the concreteness of the surface itself, an implicitly optical surface on which things are placed before our gaze. Surficiality occurs with descriptiveness of proportion and movement and with the informal order of chronicling or showing. As a basic mode of presentation of images, surficiality appears early in the history of art and still underlies impressionist painting or PHOTOGRAPHY.

Image and Planarity

Most of what we usually consider to be pictorial arrangement presupposes the uniformity of an underlying flat surface. Axiality presupposes a surface sufficiently regular for lines drawn on it to be treated as geometric lines. The operations of rotation and translation also presuppose a surface sufficiently flat to be manipulated as if it were a conceptual plane. These two operations yield symmetry and repetition, which are basic not only to ornament but also to bilateral symmetry and the frieze as fundamental ways of organizing images. These operations also yield regular division of the plane. In fact there is a close connection between the appearance of planar surfaces in human artifacts and the appearance of these kinds of visual arrangements. Paleolithic art is strikingly lacking in such features as symmetry and repetition, and in the few instances in which they occur they may be viewed as steps toward the definition of the relations they display rather than instances of them. The definition of the plane as a set of uniform points was a conceptual triumph as great as the discovery of metals or the invention of simple machines: it is essential to the keeping of records, to WRITING and MATHEMATICS, to city planning and the division of land, to the deepest forms of civilized order.

In Paleolithic art, images are superimposed and placed in all manner of sizes and locations. Such images might be called preplanar, simply not subject to planar definition. The importance of planar order then becomes evident. It is in relation to the plane itself that images are equal or unequal in size, high and low, left and right, central or peripheral. Even the randomness associated with surficiality is clearest as a relation in the plane. Planes are also intrinsically coordinate. Regular surfaces appear together with the right angles of the walls of Neolithic towns, and planarity is necessary not only to axiality and division but also to framing, to the regular definition of extent.

This raises the simple and important question of the real plane. An ideal plane may be of any extent, but any actual plane is always of some particular extent, and this particular extent defines it as a format, as *that* canvas or *that* lunette. This particularity determines the conditions of the division, measurement, and organization fundamental to any image placed on it, and it also means that in any instance the plane underlying an image is in an absolutely definite relation to those who see and use the image.

Planarity as a fundamental mode of visual order is associated with definition by uniform outline, that is, by drawing that is in the plane and tends to have the uniformity of the plane itself. This outline encloses shapes, some of which may be iconic. Although these iconic shapes refer by resemblance, they are descriptive only to the degree that their presentation is consistent with the real plane; that is, they are shown full-face or profile and are not foreshortened. Just as uniform contour brings the definition of the varying contours of a real thing into a univocal relation to the plane (and to the space of the viewer), so conceptual images bring the defining elements of a thing into equivalence on the plane. The frontality of such an image stands for the wholeness of what it represents. Conceptual images may be so called because they are definitionlike (and thus like the reality of the plane itself) and not because they correspond in some way to a mental concept. The upper register of Figure 4 is a good example of a conceptual image.

Conceptual images are also subject to the order of the plane itself. An ideal plane is nowhere and of any extent, but a real plane is always somewhere and of some specific and measurable extent. A real plane is always of a certain size and oriented so that it is in a specific and concrete relationship to a larger space and to a viewer. This same specification is also the condition of the division of the plane and the relation of these divisions to the viewer. Most real planes are vertical, like walls or framed canvases, and face the viewer. If they are divided in half vertically, then the resulting axis is of a specific size in relation to the viewer, whose own verticality and orientation it mirrors. Vertical axial division of the plane both defines and articulates the facing relation of viewer and image. It also establishes basic semantic relations in the plane itself. The halves resulting from the division are equal, but they are different with respect to the axis, which is a unity in opposition to their duality. The axis is also fixed relative to the halves, which may be seen as having been translated or rotated relative to the axis, yielding series (essential to NARRATIVE) or bilateral symmetry.

Out of these relationships planar order may be defined. From orientation (assuming the real plane is vertical) arises, in addition to facing and the possible significance of left and right, the significance of relative height. Figures are more important the higher they are in the plane, when they are raised up either in relation to the viewer or in relation to other images in the same plane. Relative size also signifies relative importance. Size may have two kinds of significance. The simpler, which might be called sculptural, is based on the actual size relation between viewer and image; the second is properly planar and has to do with the size relation between one shape and another in the plane and establishes an abstract relation of proportion that holds regardless of the actual size of the image. Both figures and images may be subject to these rules. The typical large-headedness of conceptual images states the importance of the head in relation to other parts of the body, as in Figure 4. Finally, from the division of the plane arise significant relations of center and periphery, identity and difference, unity and multiplicity.

Planar order should be understood not simply as a set of related qualities of certain images but as a

Figure 4. *(Visual Image)* Reconstruction of the *Tlalocan* (Paradise of the Rain God), Tepantitla, Teotihuacán, Mexico, ca. 500 C.E. From Pedro Ramírez Vázquez, *The National Museum of Anthropology, Mexico: Art, Architecture, Archaeology, Anthropology,* New York: Harry N. Abrams, in association with Helvetica Press, 1968, p. 79.

Figure 5. *(Visual Image) Hesire,* from Saqqara, ca. 2750 B.C.E. Egyptian Museum, Cairo. Marburg/Art Resource, New York.

set of significant elements in an embracing RITUAL space. The same holds true when images governed by planar order are reduced in size. Then they may be reduced or abstracted from collective ritual space but bring the reality and the power of the image into the significant realms of the portable, manipulable, and possessable.

Taken together the characteristics of planar order constitute a decorum that governs the presentation of images in many cultures and must be supposed to inhere in real planarity, which thus provides a universal potential mode for the presentation of images. Consider Figure 4 as an example of a planar image. Differentiation of parts of the image is made by uniform outline. Color differences emphasize this differentiation. The image is defined by central vertical division, the unity and centrality of which the figure of the central deity is identified with. This figure is frontal and whole relative to the attendant figures, which are shown in a subordinate but still planar profile aspect. The central, frontal figure is also larger, higher, and more ornate (and more replete with the powers indicated by the various symbols the ornamentation contains). The same axial order holds throughout. In the interlace band beneath the large central deity an entire rain god MASK is shown frontally, flanked by the subordinate, half-profile masks at either side. In the bottom register a mountain is central to a scene of sporting figures and butterflies. Despite the outline contours of these little figures, this lower scene is essentially a surficial image, and its location is significant as the subordination of the human to the divine, the lower to the higher. In general, planar images bring hierarchical relations into real space.

Planar images may be said to be organized on the plane considered as a uniform limit of the viewer's space. *Virtual* images have their own fictive spatial dimension and seem to exist on the other side of the plane. Surficial images are virtual, but in limited ways, and in order for virtuality to develop fully it is necessary that planarity be developed into the virtual dimension.

The upper register of the *Tlalocan* is a strongly planar image, the meaning of which is elaborated in terms of the order of the plane itself. At the same time, it possesses certain characteristics that contradict this planarity. The flat areas of the color imply three-dimensional forms; the front of the central figure implies a back; the profile presentation of the attendant figures demands foreshortening and overlapping. In Figure 5 the pull of the plane is still strikingly evident in the figure, its head in sharp profile, the chest turned into full view; but the figure also displays descriptive rather than conceptual proportions, and close attention has been paid to the description of the surfaces of the body. Hesire stands on the inner edge of the frame of the relief, which serves as a ground line. His legs, one before the other, seem also to be one behind the other, and it is as if there were a plane upon which he stands, a development into the third dimension of the ground line, perpendicular to the plane of the relief itself. This is the virtual plane, the implicit depth of which may be extended by overlapping forms, as in Figure 6.

Figure 6. *(Visual Image)* "Battle of Gods and Giants." Detail from the north frieze of the Treasury of the Siphnians, Delphi, ca. 530 B.C.E. Archaeological Museum, Delphi. Marburg/Art Resource, New York.

Figure 7. *(Visual Image)* Detail of a frieze from the Villa of the Mysteries, Pompeii, ca. 50 B.C.E. Alinari/Art Resource, New York.

The Virtual Plane

By later classical times a fundamentally important change had taken place in the virtual plane, which came to be shown as if seen from an optical angle. The virtual plane now ends in a horizontal division of the original plane, which is understood to be the far edge of the receding virtual plane (Figure 7). When this occurs, a number of important, systematically related changes occur. In painting, shapes become forms: that is, as the image is located and clarified on the virtual plane, modeling begins to be placed within outlines that are understood as the boundaries of changing surfaces in light. Modeling in turn implies a source of light. The image thus becomes physical at the same time that it becomes optical. This cluster of characteristics forms the basis of the naturalism that has dominated Western art.

Figure 8. *(Visual Image)* Figures of prophets, Sant'Apollinare Nuovo, Ravenna, ca. 504 C.E. Alinari/Art Resource, New York.

Figure 9. *(Visual Image)* Lorenzo Ghiberti, "The Story of Jacob and Esau." Detail from the east doors *(Gates of Paradise)* of the Baptistery of S. Maria del Fiore, Florence, 1425–1452. Gilt bronze. Alinari/Art Resource, New York.

On the optical virtual plane—the *explicit* virtual plane—forms could be located with a new degree and kind of clarity, and the geometry of light could also be plotted. The application of the notion of the virtual plane to the ground of the real space of vision seems to have yielded the horizon, which appears late in the history of art.

The optical virtual plane persisted in Early Christian, Byzantine, and medieval art (*see* MIDDLE AGES) as a horizontal division of the format and, however purely ornamental it may have become, preserved a definite relation, or the possibility of a definite relation, between viewer and image (Figure 8). It also preserved the possibility of the translation of planar order into the virtual dimension. One-point perspective (Figure 9) projects the modular division of the real plane onto the virtual plane seen from a fixed visual angle. Figure 10 is a perspective construction whose viewpoint is lower than the line establishing the virtual plane; it displays a new accommodation of planar order to order on the virtual plane. Forms are both higher on the plane and deeper on the virtual plane as they are more sacred, making fictive depth into a powerful METAPHOR. The vanishing point, which coincides with the viewer's line of sight and with the horizon, realizes in the virtual dimension the possible infinity of a mathematical plane.

Figure 10. *(Visual Image)* Masaccio, *The Trinity, with the Virgin, St. John, and Donors,* ca. 1428. Fresco, Santa Maria Novella, Florence. Alinari/Art Resource, New York.

Figure 11. *(Visual Image)* Hubert and Jan van Eyck, altarpiece of Saint-Bavon Cathedral, Ghent, completed 1432. Open, center panel. Giraudon/Art Resource, New York.

In general, planar images make entities present in real space. They are understood as magical and as integral to the organization of ritual space that their configuration implies. Their axiality typically coincides with the axiality of the architectural space in which they are set (*see* ARCHITECTURE).

Virtual images imitate in a simple sense; they represent appearances or state all meaning insofar as it can be made into appearances—hence the perennial significance of allegory and personification in Western art. In most cases planarity and virtuality are intertwined. In Figure 11, for example, the overall significant order of the image, much like that of the *Tlalocan* (Figure 4), is planar and integral with the real space of worship. At the same time, the figures themselves are treated naturalistically, as if represented to the viewer.

Figure 12. *(Visual Image)* Claude Monet, *Impression, soleil levant* (Impression: Rising Sun), 1872. Musée Marmotton, Paris. Giraudon/Art Resource, New York.

Figure 13. *(Visual Image)* Pablo Picasso, *Ma jolie* (woman with a zither or a guitar), Paris, 1911–1912. Oil on canvas, 39 3/8 by 25 3/4 in. Collection, The Museum of Modern Art, New York. Acquired through the Lillie P. Bliss Bequest.

Virtual planarity and surficiality are closely related. When the virtual plane was made explicit and forms began to be modeled, marks representing light and dark became elements of the structure of images in a way they had not been before. Perspective, on the other hand, developed the potential descriptive modularity of the plane in the virtual dimension. In impressionist painting surficial treatment defines not just figures but the whole visual field, the configuration of which is determined by the descriptive modularity dependent on virtual planarity (Figure 12).

These categories, in one or another degree of purity or combination, account for the vast majority of the images in world art. All depend on the assumption that images may adequately present or represent, that the image is the god or may be seen as the god. The means of presentation and representation might therefore be called transparent over very long and broad traditions. But modernism has been premised on the opacity of the means of representation. In analytic cubism (Figure 13), for example, the elements of representation lift away from the image they ostensibly set forth to become themes for development in their own right. This signals the beginning of a kind of art in which problems of representation and of making and acting with respect to art in general become central and in which images may become secondary or of no concern.

Bibliography. Moshe Barasch, *Theories of Art: From Plato to Winckelmann,* New York, 1985; Ananda K. Coomaraswamy, "Ornament," in *Selected Papers,* Vol. 1, ed. by Roger Lipsey, Princeton, N.J., 1977; Umberto Eco, *A Theory of Semiotics,* Bloomington, Ind., 1976; Ernst H. Gombrich, *Art and Illusion: A Study in the Psychology of Pictorial Representation,* 4th ed., London, 1972; idem, "Visual Metaphors of Value in Art," in *Meditations on a Hobby Horse,* 4th ed., Chicago, 1985; Rosalind Krauss, "Photography's Discursive Spaces: Landscape/View," *Art*

Journal 42 (1982): 311–319; W. J. T. Mitchell, *Iconology: Image, Text, Ideology,* Chicago and London, 1986; Avigdor W. G. Poseq, *Format in Painting,* Tel Aviv, 1978; Meyer Schapiro, "On Some Problems in the Semiotics of Visual Art: Field and Vehicle in Image-Signs," *Semiotica* 1 (1969): 223–242; David Summers, "Conventions in the History of Art," *New Literary History* 13 (1981): 103–125; idem, "The 'Visual Arts' and the Problem of Art Historical Description," *Art Journal* 42 (1982): 301–310.

DAVID SUMMERS

VISUAL PERCEPTION. *See* PERCEPTION—STILL AND MOVING PICTURES.

VON NEUMANN, JOHN (1903–1957)

Hungarian-born U.S. mathematician. John von Neumann led the development and construction of the world's first electronic computer and was the principal architect of game theory, which provided a mathematical approach to many forms of social behavior and has had wide influence on communication theories. Born in Budapest into a prosperous banking family, the young von Neumann's mathematical precocity and intellectual talents were recognized and encouraged. While still a teenager he entered the University of Berlin, attending lectures by Albert Einstein on statistical mechanics. In 1925 he received a degree in chemical engineering from the Federal Institute of Technology in Zurich and a year later a doctorate in MATHEMATICS from the University of Budapest. At the age of twenty-four he became a lecturer in mathematics at the University of Berlin.

Although von Neumann's genius ranged over many areas within pure and applied mathematics, he achieved particular eminence in three major fields: mathematical formalizations of quantum theory, the design of electronic computers, and the development of game theory, which has had a lasting importance for theories of conflict and communication in organizations. His contributions in these and other seemingly diverse areas reflected his continuing interest in the use of mathematical formalisms to illuminate difficult empirical problems in both the social and physical sciences.

Stimulated by German mathematician David Hilbert's pioneering work on the logical description of an infinitely dimensional space ("Hilbert Space"), von Neumann's early work pushed toward the formalization of the empirical theories of quantum mechanics. In *Mathematical Foundations of Quantum Mechanics* (1932) he set forth a rigorous logical and axiomatic basis for atomic physics.

In the early 1930s growing political instabilities in Germany and in his native Hungary led von Neumann to emigrate to the United States. At Princeton University's Institute for Advanced Studies, where he became professor of mathematics, von Neumann developed the logical basis for electronic computer design and built the giant computer known as MANIAC (Mathematical Analyzer, Numerical Integrator and Computer), which in turn made possible the construction and testing of the first model of the hydrogen bomb in 1952. Throughout his career von Neumann's advice was sought on matters of U.S. scientific policy, and he served as a member of the U.S. Atomic Energy Commission from its inception. Von Neumann's fascination with computational methods and computer design raised further questions regarding the nature of COGNITION and PERCEPTION. His theory of automata, which established the logical possibility of self-reproducing machines, includes some of the first mathematical descriptions of cognitive processes. *See also* COMPUTER: HISTORY; COMPUTER: IMPACT.

Von Neumann's theory of games has had the greatest relevance for the social sciences. Conceptually, the primary achievement of game theory lay in its formulation of the purely logical scheme of the gamelike situation. The "zero-sum two-person game," as it was explicated in a 1928 treatise, provided a paradigm for a competitive situation involving two individuals: after each round of the game the loser pays some money or gives points to the winner, but the total pot or winnings available never changes (hence the name "zero-sum"). The model assumes complete rationality on the part of the participants, in the sense that they possess the ability to choose from alternatives and to calculate the ranges of consequences associated with each choice. It rests on the notion that there exists, for each player, an optimal strategy that enables the player to do the best he or she can against an opponent. This work was developed further in *Theory of Games and Economic Behavior* (1944), published with economist Oskar Morgenstern. The assumptions of game theory, particularly the notion of the rational player motivated by self-interest, have since been challenged as an adequate description of human social behavior. However, in calling attention to the nature of logical reasoning in situations of competition and conflict, game theory has been a useful model for many problems in economics, political science, and other fields.

A well-known simulation based on von Neumann's work is the Prisoner's Dilemma, which has provided theoretical insight into the nature of conflict and decision making in organizations. Many variations of the Prisoner's Dilemma have been devised; in a well-known version, two persons suspected of being partners in a crime are being questioned in separate rooms. Each is told either to confess or to remain silent. If only one confesses, he or she will be released and given a reward, but the other will receive a stiff sentence. If both confess, they will both be jailed with light sentences. If both remain silent, the police will have no case, and both will be released. In its delineation of outcomes, or "payoffs," the Prisoner's Dilemma illustrates the consequences of interpersonal collaboration in competitive situations. More generally, such extensions of the original model have been instrumental in focusing attention on the role of communication in group decision-making processes. *See also* GROUP COMMUNICATION.

Bibliography. Morton D. Davis, *Game Theory: A Nontechnical Introduction,* 2d ed., New York and London, 1983; Steve Heims, *John von Neumann and Norbert Wiener: From Mathematics to the Technologies of Life and Death,* Cambridge, Mass., 1980; Anatol Rapaport, *N-Person Game Theory,* Ann Arbor, Mich., 1970; S. Ulam, "John von Neumann, 1903–1957," *Bulletin of the American Mathematical Society* 64 (1958): 1–49.

JANE JORGENSON

VYGOTSKY, LEV (1896–1934)

Soviet psychologist and semiotician whose major interest was the relationship between communication and human consciousness. After receiving a university education in Moscow in law and philology, Lev Semenovich Vygotsky returned to provincial Belorussia, where he taught in a high school and a teachers college. His career as a major theoretician of psychology began in 1924 when a presentation he made at a psychoneurological conference brought him to the attention of the major figures in Soviet psychology. From that time until he died of tuberculosis in 1934 Vygotsky carried out his teaching and his theoretical and empirical research in major research centers in the USSR. During this period he produced about nine volumes of writings, most of which were collected and published in a six-volume series in the USSR in the early 1980s.

The ideas Vygotsky developed laid the foundation for a major school of psychology in the USSR and later were influential in the West. These ideas can be understood in terms of three general themes. The first of these—genetic, or developmental, analysis—provided Vygotsky's basic methodology. In accordance with this theme it is possible to understand human mental functioning only by understanding its origins and the transformations it undergoes. Vygotsky developed this theme by carrying out research in several genetic domains: in addition to the development of the individual, he examined phylogenetic and social-historical differences. The social-historical comparisons, which grew out of his desire to devise a Marxist psychology, played such a central role in his thinking that his ideas are often referred to in the USSR as the "cultural-historical" approach to mind.

The second theme that runs throughout Vygotsky's writings is the claim that higher (i.e., uniquely human) mental functions such as memory, thinking, attention, and PERCEPTION have their origins in social life. A basic formulation of this theme can be found in his "general genetic law of cultural development," in which he states that higher mental functions appear twice, or on two planes, in the development of the individual. They first appear on the social or "interpsychological" plane and then on the individual or "intrapsychological" plane. In his studies of interpsychological functioning Vygotsky was concerned primarily with the kind of dyadic or small-group communicative processes that occur in socialization contexts such as adult-child interaction in the classroom. He argued that various aspects of the structures and processes involved in this communication are mastered and internalized in the formation of mental functioning in the individual. *See also* STRUCTURALISM.

Vygotsky's third theme was that human activity, on both the social and the individual planes, is mediated by tools and signs (*see* SIGN). This "instrumental" theme, which became increasingly important in his later writings, was the area in which Vygotsky made his most important and unique contributions to the study of communication and mind. Drawing on ideas being developed in the USSR and the West during the 1920s and 1930s in literary analysis, philology, and philosophy, Vygotsky developed this theme in such a way that it is analytically prior to the other two in the sense that the other two are defined, at least in part, in terms of mediation. In the case of genetic analysis this precedence is manifested in his tendency to define developmental shifts in terms of the appearance of new forms of mediation. In the case of the social origins of individual mental functioning his point is that human interpsychological (and hence intrapsychological) functioning can be understood only by taking into consideration the forms of mediation, especially semiotic mediation, that are involved.

Vygotsky developed these themes in a wide range of empirical studies that he conducted on clinical, developmental, and cross-cultural issues. His research on the process whereby inner speech derives from the functional differentiation of "egocentric" from social speech and his studies of "complexes," "everyday concepts," and "scientific concepts" are particularly important in this connection.

See also CHILDREN; PIAGET, JEAN; SEMIOTICS.

Bibliography. Lev Semenovich Vygotsky, *Mind in Society,* ed. by Michael Cole, Cambridge, Mass., 1978; idem, *Thought and Language* (in Russian), newly rev. trans., ed. by A. Kozulin, Cambridge, Mass., 1986; James V. Wertsch, *Vygotsky and the Social Formation of Mind,* Cambridge, Mass., 1985.

JAMES V. WERTSCH

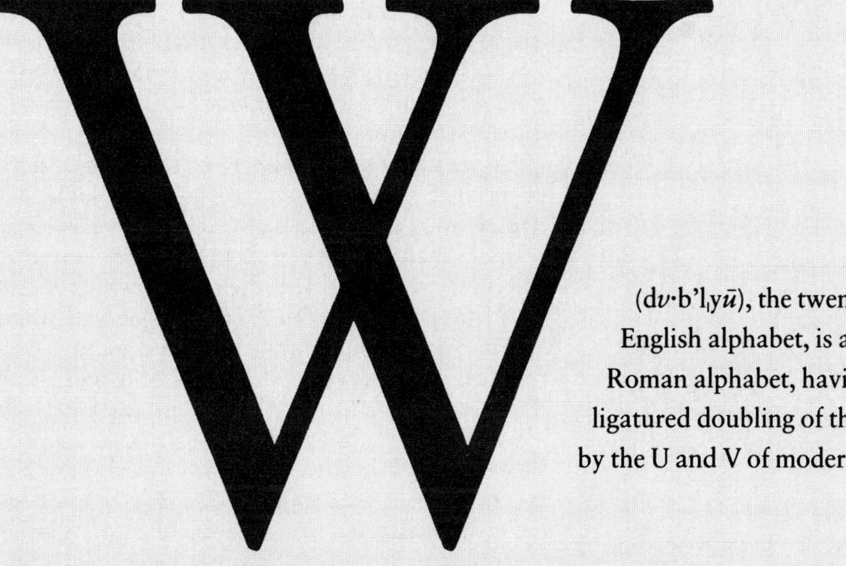

(d*v*·b'lˌy*ū*), the twenty-third letter of the modern English alphabet, is an addition to the ancient Roman alphabet, having originated from a ligatured doubling of the Roman letter represented by the U and V of modern alphabets.

WEAVER, WARREN (1894–1978)

U.S. mathematician who, with CLAUDE SHANNON, coauthored the foundational work on INFORMATION THEORY, *The Mathematical Theory of Communication.* After completing studies in civil engineering at the University of Wisconsin in 1917, Warren Weaver joined the Department of Mathematics at the California Institute of Technology. In 1920 he returned to the University of Wisconsin, where he remained as professor of MATHEMATICS for twelve years. During this period he collaborated with mathematician Max Mason in writing a book on electromagnetic field theory.

In 1932 Weaver was invited to join the Rockefeller Foundation as director of the Natural Sciences Division, a position he held until 1952. The well-known collaboration between Weaver and Shannon began in 1948, when Rockefeller Foundation president Chester Bernard invited Weaver to translate Shannon's mathematical theory of communication into less formidable language. Weaver's exposition of the theory was subsequently published, together with Shannon's original article, in *The Mathematical Theory of Communication* (1949).

Addressing engineering problems concerning the telegraphic encoding of messages (*see* TELEGRAPHY), Shannon had shown that there was a well-defined mathematical relationship between general properties of a physical system and the maximum rate at which information could be transmitted through it from a sender to a receiver, regardless of the specific nature of the information. Weaver argued that, in diagramming the basic system of relationships characteristic of the communication situation (i.e., an "information source" who selects a desired "message" out of a set of possible messages; a "transmitter" who changes the message into a "signal" that is sent over a "communication channel" to a "receiver"), Shannon had put forth a theory so powerful in its range of applications that it constituted a general theory of communication.

In his essay Weaver identified three levels of problems implicit in the communication process: (1) technical problems (i.e., how accurately can symbols be transmitted from sender to receiver?), (2) semantic problems (i.e., how precisely do the transmitted symbols convey the desired MEANING?), and (3) effectiveness problems (i.e., how effectively does the received meaning affect conduct in the desired way?). Shannon's theory of communication applied only to the first level, the technical problems associated with accurate transmission of signals from sender to receiver. However, Weaver was concerned with showing the interdependence among these levels, namely, that technical problems of accuracy in transmission have a critical importance for questions of SEMANTICS and effectiveness. Essentially, levels 2 and 3 make use only of those signal accuracies possible at the technical level of transmission.

Weaver was careful to point out the special sense in which the word *information* is used in this context. In its technical sense information refers to the freedom of choice available to one who constructs a message (i.e., the sender). When the range of possible messages is great, the amount of information associated with the selection of any one message is high. The concept of information in this sense applies not to the meaning of individual messages but rather to the freedom of choice that characterizes the situation as a whole.

The Shannon-Weaver model, as it came to be known, sparked a multitude of theoretical applications, not only to problems in communication engineering but also to many processes involving the transmission of messages with semantic content.

Weaver also made important contributions to systems theory and CYBERNETICS in a seminal paper, published in 1948, on the subject of *organized complexity.* In this paper he observed that social and biological phenomena had previously been viewed largely in terms of physical models based on the second law of thermodynamics. Such models were grounded in the notion of "unorganized complexity," exemplified in the random and individually untraceable movements of molecules in a gas. Weaver argued that many problems confronting the physical and social sciences required a shift from these classical scientific conceptualizations to models based on the notion of "organized complexity," in which phenomena are viewed systematically, as nondecomposable wholes.

See also MODELS OF COMMUNICATION.

JANE JORGENSON

WEBER, MAX (1864–1920)

German sociologist, a leading social thinker of the twentieth century whose theories have wide-ranging implications for the study of communications. Max Weber's father was a member of the Prussian House of Deputies (1868–1897), and Weber grew up in a suburban Berlin household that regularly entertained eminent politicians and scholars. He studied at Heidelberg, Berlin, and Göttingen, writing his doctoral dissertation on the agrarian history of ancient Rome and the evolution of medieval trading societies. His career was punctuated by prolonged bouts of depression, nervousness, and mental collapse, leading to his resignation from his professorship at Heidelberg. In 1907 an inheritance allowed him to pursue scholarly work at his leisure. All of his important work appeared during the later period of his life, from 1903 to 1920.

Weber's best-known and most controversial work is *The Protestant Ethic and the Spirit of Capitalism* (1904–1905), wherein he concluded that there was something within Protestant religious belief that encouraged the growth of the "spirit of capitalism." Weber examined the writings of such figures as John Calvin, MARTIN LUTHER, and Benjamin Franklin. In their writing he saw parallels between Protestant religious doctrine and capitalistic economic practices. In particular he noted two things. First, Protestantism emphasized that the individual stands alone before God; no one can function as an intermediary. Second, Protestantism—especially Calvinism—endorsed the belief that the future is predestined. One cannot know if one will go to heaven or hell after death, and one's individual actions have little to do with the matter. However, Protestantism also promoted the belief that work is a form of glorification of God. Through one's calling in this world, then, it is possible to glorify God and also to hope for signs of grace that will indicate that heaven rather than hell will be awaiting one after death.

These religious beliefs directed activity toward worldly efforts, hard work, and ascetic discipline. Capital accumulations were not used to promote hedonistic pleasures but were turned back into the enterprise, the capitalistic pyramid. Through the success of the enterprise early capitalists could hope for worldly signs of otherworldly salvation. The central thrust of Weber's argument is that economic systems are also moral systems. As such, any given economic system is influenced by the moral traditions that exist at the time of its development. This position made Weber a major critic of the materialistic doctrines of KARL MARX, who argued that moral systems are a product of the material economic process.

A second major theme running through the extensive historical and philosophical writings of Weber is the contrast between rational social systems and traditional systems. Rational systems are geared toward productivity and efficiency. They reject traditional procedures whenever tradition proves inferior in the quest for efficiency. The most rational form of social organization is the modern large-scale bureaucracy. Bureaucratic systems are characterized by hierarchy, rational evaluation of the means used to achieve goals, organization in terms of offices (rather than persons), the routinization of leadership, and the occupation of office through testing. Bureaucracies, in their pursuit of efficiency, generate less personal and less traditional interrelationships between people. They rely more on legal rules or written codes as a basis for evaluating the individual. A common characteristic of bureaucracies is that property is owned by the bureaucracy rather than by those individuals who occupy the offices of the bureaucracy.

Weber's writings are broadly relevant to any investigation of modern social practices, but his work on bureaucracy is especially relevant to students of communications. Communications take place through channels ranging from the elemental semiotic communications of insects and flowers to the elaborate institutionalized symbolic systems of modern corporate structures and nations. At the highest levels of communication we necessarily come face to face with bureaucratic structures.

Weber's work, then, raises questions for the student of communications: What happens when the means for human social communication are shifted from traditional to rational forms? What are the effects of the bureaucratization of communications? How do bureaucracies differ from other systems (e.g., the village) in communicating social knowledge? (What, for example, is the difference between the town-hall form of debate and news that is processed through a large media network?) Is it possible to penetrate bureaucratic systems to get at the truth of an issue? (The immediate cover-ups after mishaps at nuclear energy sites in the United States and the Soviet Union exemplify the interplay between bureaucratic control of information and the communities that rely on immediate information for effective action.)

Finally, Weber's work on the relationship between religious morality and economic ideology serves as a model for thinking about human communications in general. Communication takes place for human beings within moral contexts. There is certainly the suggestion in *The Protestant Ethic and the Spirit of Capitalism* that Protestant individualism has had a strong impact on communications as well as on economic morality.

See also COMMUNICATIONS RESEARCH: ORIGINS AND DEVELOPMENT.

Bibliography. Reinhard Bendix, *Max Weber: An Intellectual Portrait,* new ed., with an intro. by Guenther Roth, Berkeley, Calif., 1977; Hans H. Gerth and C. Wright Mills, eds., *From Max Weber: Essays in Sociology,* New York, 1946, reprint 1961; Max Weber, *The Protestant Ethic and the Spirit of Capitalism* (Gesammelte Aufsätze zur Religionssoziologie, Vol. 1), trans. by Talcott Parsons, New York, 1930, reprint 1974; idem, *The Theory of Social and Economic Organizations* (Wirtschaft und Gesellschaft, Part 1), trans. by A. M. Henderson and Talcott Parsons, New York, 1947, reprint 1964.

EDITH W. KING AND R. P. CUZZORT

WEBSTER, NOAH (1758–1843)

U.S. lexicographer who compiled the first comprehensive dictionary of English as spoken in the United

States. Noah Webster lived during the formation of the U.S. republic, participating in the REVOLUTION that won independence for the former British colonies. In addition to political independence Webster believed that the United States needed recognition for its own LANGUAGE and intellectual life. It became his life's work to establish and legitimize American English.

Born in West Hartford, Connecticut, Webster attended Yale University. After graduating in 1778 he continued to study law, meanwhile supporting himself by teaching. Finding only British schoolbooks available, Webster began to prepare his own texts (*see* TEXTBOOK). He published a speller (1783, the famous "Blue-Backed Speller"), a grammar (1784), and a reader (1785), the three called collectively *A Grammatical Institute of the English Language.* The speller, an instant success, introduced most of the current variations between British and U.S. orthography. Selling millions of copies, the "Blue-Backed Speller" has remained continuously in print for the past two centuries.

Webster gained admission to the bar in 1781 and eventually went into practice, but his other activities ranged widely. He engaged in politics and held local offices; produced numerous writings, including a defense of the U.S. Constitution ("Sketches of American Policy," 1795); founded *The American Magazine* plus daily and weekly newspapers in New York; and campaigned for a federal COPYRIGHT law (enacted in 1790). His interest in learning continued throughout his life: he edited the *Journal* of John Winthrop (first governor of Massachusetts), published a revised version of the Bible, and helped found Amherst College.

But Webster's central interest remained the English language. His *Compendious Dictionary of the English Language* (1806) was only a preliminary effort, but it was already more inclusive than SAMUEL JOHNSON's *Dictionary* (1755) and introduced several new features. In 1807 Webster undertook his masterwork, a comprehensive dictionary, hoping to finish it in three to five years. In 1812 he settled in Amherst, Massachusetts, where for ten years he worked around a large circular table, painstakingly consulting dictionaries and grammars in numerous languages. In 1824 he went to Europe to conduct additional research. At last, in 1828, after more than twenty years of labor, the seventy-year-old Webster published the two-volume *American Dictionary of the English Language.*

The first edition was a critical success. One of the dictionary's main features was its inclusion of thousands of technical terms among the seventy thousand or so entries, around half of which were new to any dictionary. The definitions themselves were models of lucidity, and Webster placed the etymologically primary MEANING first, an innovation followed by later lexicographers. But most important—and best reflecting the democratic spirit of the United States—Webster established (1) that a dictionary records the spoken rather than the written language and (2) that it records the language as it exists, not as an educated elite might wish it to be.

Webster's dictionary and its successors, especially the Merriam-Webster unabridged editions, have come to stand as the primary record of the English language as it is spoken in the United States, and Webster's name is used to lend authority to dictionaries published by many firms. Indeed, his name has come to be synonymous with dictionary, and every schooled person understands what is meant by "Look it up in Webster."

See also LANGUAGE IDEOLOGY; LANGUAGE REFERENCE BOOK; LANGUAGE VARIETIES; SEMANTICS.

Bibliography. Richard M. Rollins, *The Long Journey of Noah Webster,* Philadelphia, 1980; Ervin C. Shoemaker, *Noah Webster: Pioneer of Learning,* New York, 1936; Harry R. Warfel, *Noah Webster: Schoolmaster to America,* New York, 1936, reprint 1966.

ROBERT BALAY

WELLES, ORSON (1915–1985)

U.S. director-actor-producer-writer for stage, screen, and broadcasting—a maverick genius who shook up the world of media. Early in childhood George Orson Welles was already considered a prodigy, adept at cartooning, prestidigitation, and performing. He climaxed his high school years in Woodstock, Illinois, by collaborating with the principal, Roger Hill, on the book *Everybody's Shakespeare* (1934), a selection of Shakespeare plays crammed with sketches and production ideas by Welles. Graduating at fifteen, he launched on a zigzag career. During a landscape-painting tour of Ireland by donkey cart, he presented himself at the Gate Theatre in Dublin and asked for an audition. His resonant voice and assured presence won him major roles. In the United States the following year he appeared on tour and on Broadway with Katharine Cornell in productions of Shaw and Shakespeare. When the depression devastated the THEATER he moved to RADIO, portraying various world leaders on radio's "March of Time" series (*see* NEWSREEL) and delighting horror and mystery fans as "The Shadow." More significantly, he teamed with John Houseman to produce for the Federal Theatre, an ambitious New Deal unemployment relief project. The government favored plays with large casts; Welles and Houseman obliged with a tumultuous all-black version of *Macbeth* (1936) set in Haiti, with voodoo priestesses replacing the witches. Its spectacular success catapulted Welles as

Figure 1. *(Welles, Orson)* Orson Welles, sketches from the margins of an edition of Shakespeare's plays, annotated by Welles and his high school principal. From Roger Hill and Orson Welles, *Everybody's Shakespeare: Three Plays: Edited for Reading and Arranged for Staging,* Woodstock, Ill.: The Todd Press, 1934, pp. 50, 32, and 58. Copyright 1934 by Roger Hill and Orson Welles.

a director and Houseman as a producer into the Broadway spotlight. But a year later their plans for *The Cradle Will Rock,* Marc Blitzstein's politically radical musical, alarmed authorities, who sought to halt it. At the last moment the production was officially canceled by orders from Washington, but Houseman and Welles led an audience of hundreds to another theater where, performing from auditorium seats, the cast went on with the show.

The cause célèbre ended the team's Federal Theatre career but helped launch their own company, the Mercury Theatre. Hardly missing a stride, they staged *Caesar* (1937), a modern-dress version of Shakespeare's *Julius Caesar* in which Caesar and his followers wore quasi-Fascist uniforms. Another resounding success, it brought an offer from CBS—a weekly "Mercury Theatre on the Air" radio series. With no SPONSOR available, CBS looked on it as a bow to culture and was scarcely prepared for what followed. On Halloween 1938 Welles directed and narrated a free adaptation by Howard Koch of H. G. Wells's novel *The War of the Worlds.* News flashes that seemed to be program interruptions spoke of strange astronomical phenomena and then of landings in New Jersey, apparently by Martians, which were described by "eyewitnesses." In New Jersey and environs the program caused thousands to flee their homes in widespread panic (*see* RUMOR). This headline event was thought by some to have ruined Welles's career. Instead it brought in Campbell's Soups as sponsor, transforming "Mercury Theatre on the Air" into "The Campbell Playhouse." It also brought Welles a HOLLYWOOD offer to make MOTION PICTURES for RKO (Radio-Keith-Orpheum). At the age of twenty-three, Welles received one of the most liberal contracts ever offered a film director. With virtually a free hand, he led his Mercury troupe westward.

Welles's astonishing first feature for RKO, *Citizen Kane* (1941), is widely considered one of the finest films ever made. It is remarkable on many levels: its complex, fluidly constructed script by Welles and Herman J. Mankiewicz; the technical brilliance of the CINEMATOGRAPHY by Gregg Toland, utilizing deep-focus and wide-angle shooting; the stimulating, imaginative FILM EDITING; and the ACTING of a largely unknown cast, including Welles as Charles Kane, a newspaper tycoon. But, though *Citizen Kane* was a critical triumph and made Welles a world celebrity, it won him the deep enmity of WILLIAM RANDOLPH HEARST, on whose life the script was loosely based. The attacks Hearst was able to launch against the film through his newspapers and motion picture holdings hampered distribution and made *Citizen Kane* a financial loss for RKO. For Welles it had serious consequences. He was unable to maintain creative control over his subsequent RKO films. *The Magnificent Ambersons* (1942) and *Journey into Fear* (1943) were finished and altered by other hands after Welles had moved on to other projects. Mounting frustration marked his Hollywood sojourn.

During World War II, Welles, rejected for military service, staged occasional magic shows for troops. After the war he spent most of his life in Europe, working independently, scrambling for funds. A stream of projects followed, some successful and others not. His European Shakespeare films, *Othello* (1952) and

Figure 2. *(Welles, Orson)* Orson Welles in *Citizen Kane,* 1941. National Film Archive, London. © 1941 RKO Radio Pictures. Ren. 1968 RKO General, Inc.

Chimes at Midnight (1966; also titled *Falstaff*), had a limited success. He appeared as an actor in many films of other directors, notably *The Third Man* (1949), *Moby Dick* (1956), and *The Long Hot Summer* (1958). To raise funds he made television commercials. He produced for French and British television. He won some renown with his baroque thriller, *Touch of Evil* (1958), made for Hollywood, but he never again received the acclaim he had won with *Citizen Kane.*

Welles had made an impact on each medium he had essayed. To the Broadway theater he brought a zestful experimental spirit that had long been lacking. Radio drama before Welles had generally emulated all-dialogue theater, avoiding narration; Welles showed that radio drama could use NARRATIVE structures as free and varied as the printed page. He brought the same fluidity and dynamism to motion pictures.

Welles was perhaps trapped by his own virtuosity. To horror roles and wine commercials he could apply the same bravura resonance as to lines of Shakespeare. Increasingly style dominated substance. Yet he continued to be counted as one of the true auteurs of motion pictures. In 1975 he received the American Film Institute's Life Achievement Award.

See also COMMUNICATIONS RESEARCH: ORIGINS AND DEVELOPMENT.

Bibliography. Charles Higham, *Orson Welles: The Rise and Fall of an American Genius,* New York, 1985; Barbara Leaming, *Orson Welles: A Biography,* New York, 1985; Joseph McBride, *Orson Welles,* New York, 1972.

RICHARD PILCHER AND ERIK BARNOUW

WESTERN, THE

American popular GENRE with a long history of success in many media. The western traditionally narrates a fictional or quasi-historical episode of confrontation between civilization and savagery on the frontier. Civilization has usually been represented by pioneer settlers, while savagery is symbolized by Indians or outlaws. The traditional central figure in the genre is the western hero who is, at the beginning, torn between the ordered society of the pioneers and the freedom and spontaneity of the wilderness. The NARRATIVE often revolves around this conflict in the hero. In the final climactic combat or shoot-out he not only defends the ordered society but appears to resolve his own inner conflict.

The western has never been a static form but has constantly adjusted its repertoire of devices to shifting public attitudes toward social and other issues, such as VIOLENCE, ethnic minorities, the environment, and sex.

The origins of the western go back to conflicting European myths about America as moral utopia, as state of nature, and as new empire (*see* UTOPIAS). The first popular tales embodying these conflicting myths were the Indian captivity and settler-versus-Indian battle narratives of the seventeenth and eighteenth centuries. The genre apparently received major impetus from James Fenimore Cooper's "Leather-Stocking Tales," five novels published between 1823 and 1841. An important part of Cooper's contribution was the creation of the figure of Natty Bumppo, the "Leather-Stocking," a white man raised by the Indians and dedicated to life in the wilderness. Cooper based his character in part on legends of the historical frontiersman Daniel Boone.

Cooper's creation was immediately popular and widely imitated in novels like Robert Montgomery Bird's *Nick of the Woods* (1837). By midcentury in the United States the western hero had become a favorite mythical figure. Beginning with Edward S. Ellis's *Seth Jones,* he became one of the dominant figures in the widely popular dime novels and the first successful mass paperback publications. In addition to hundreds of dime novels about such actual or legendary western heroes as Buffalo Bill, Deadwood Dick, Wild Bill Hickok, Billy the Kid, Calamity Jane, and Jesse James, the western genre in the later nineteenth century also appeared in magazines, story paper weeklies, stage plays, and the Wild West shows (Figure 1). *See also* LITERATURE, POPULAR.

The Wild West show was a grand outdoor SPECTACLE combining feats of horsemanship, roping, and shooting with the enactment of mythical western episodes such as an Indian attack on a stagecoach or a shoot-out between cowboys and outlaws. Probably first put together by William F. Cody (Buffalo Bill) in the mid-1880s, the Wild West show flourished until the beginning of the twentieth century, when rising costs and the competition of the newly created western movie put most of the traveling troupes out of business. Many of the Wild West show's set pieces and a number of its actors and managers went on to play a part in the development of MOTION PICTURES.

Three events around the turn of the century influenced the twentieth-century development of the western. In 1893, historian Frederick Jackson Turner presented his famous "frontier thesis," which argued that cheap land on the frontier had shaped the American character. In effect, Turner's thesis gave the western myth historical respectability and an ideology that would heavily influence both the public's view of the westward movement and the creation of

Figure 1. *(Western, The)* Buffalo Bill and His Merry Men. From *Beadle's Dime Novel,* 1892. The Bettmann Archive, Inc.

western books and movies. Second, in 1902, the Eastern writer Owen Wister published his highly successful novel, *The Virginian*. Along with western novels by other popular writers like Emerson Hough, Harold Bell Wright, and Zane Grey, Wister's novel had a more sophisticated, "adult" appeal than the dime novels and Wild West shows. Finally, in 1903, Edwin S. Porter's film, *The Great Train Robbery*, created the western movie, which was to become *the* medium for the western genre in the twentieth century (Figure 2).

The earliest western films were largely one-reel and two-reel productions made cheaply and quickly in Eastern studios and lots. The film industry's gradual migration to California opened new possibilities for the movie western. California's spectacular desert and mountain landscape, with its bright and consistent sunshine, offered an epic backdrop against which the western theme of men on horseback in confrontation and pursuit could generate a new kind of movie excitement.

The period from 1915 to 1929 was the first great period of western filming. Westerns became full-length movies, and western STARS like W. S. Hart, Tom Mix, Buck Jones, Hoot Gibson, and Ken Maynard were among HOLLYWOOD's most popular figures (Figure 3). During this time the first high-budget, large-scale western epics were filmed. Such films as *The Covered Wagon* (1922), *The Iron Horse* (1923), *Tumbleweeds* (1925), and *The Flaming Frontier* (1926) reached new heights in spectacle, size of cast, and expenditure, as well as in film artistry.

The depression of the 1930s forced film studios to retrench. With a few exceptions, such as *The Virginian* (1929), *Law and Order* (1932), and *The Plainsman* (1937), the epic western was replaced by the inexpensively entertaining "B" western. The 1930s were a time of highly formulaic series westerns like

Figure 2. *(Western, The)* Edwin S. Porter, *The Great Train Robbery*, 1903. National Film Archive, London/MGM.

Figure 3. *(Western, The)* Tom Mix. National Film Archive, London.

those starring Buck Jones, William S. Boyd as Hopalong Cassidy, and the "Three Mesquiteers," a group in which John Wayne first rode to prominence. It was also, above all, the period of the singing cowboys, Gene Autry and Roy Rogers, and of the multipart serials cheered by young audiences at Saturday matinees (*see* SERIAL).

Late in the 1930s a combination of circumstances brought about a major revival of the western film. The approach of World War II not only generated increasing employment and more money for entertainment, but it gave a new ideological significance to the western myth of the lone hero who purges the town of the bad guys—for this was how propagandists were depicting the United States' intervention against the Axis powers. Beginning with John Ford's *Stagecoach* in 1939, the western film flourished as never before (Figure 4). Until the late 1940s, both A and B westerns were an important part of the Hollywood studio output. In the early 1950s the B westerns declined, but until the early 1960s the A western remained at the center of U.S. filmmaking.

The best of the westerns produced between 1939 and 1960 constitute a classic statement of the genre. An outstanding group of directors and performers, many of whom had been involved in moviemaking since the silent era, put together western after western of outstanding quality: *Jesse James* (1939), *Destry Rides Again* (1939), *The Return of Frank James*

Figure 4. *(Western, The)* John Ford, *Stagecoach,* 1939. National Film Archive, London/MGM/UA.

(1940), *The Dark Command* (1940), *They Died with Their Boots On* (1942), *The Ox-Bow Incident* (1943), *My Darling Clementine* (1946), *Duel in the Sun* (1947), *Red River* (1948), *Wagon Master* (1950), *High Noon* (1952), *Shane* (1953), *Hondo* (1954), *Rio Bravo* (1959), and many others. Many of the leading Hollywood directors worked on westerns during this period: John Ford, Howard Hawks, King Vidor, William Wellman, Raoul Walsh, Michael Curtiz, and Fritz Lang. And a number of the most popular male stars increased their popularity through western roles: John Wayne, Henry Fonda, James Stewart, Errol Flynn, Tyrone Power, Joel McCrea, Randolph Scott, Robert Mitchum, Alan Ladd, and Gary Cooper.

The new medium of television soon made westerns one of its major activities. The genre entered television in the late 1940s through reruns of B westerns. Their success prompted production of westerns for television, and the television day was soon filled with programs like "Hopalong Cassidy," "Roy Rogers," "The Lone Ranger," and "The Cisco Kid." By the mid-1950s, television was producing its own version of the A western in more sophisticated series like "Gunsmoke," "Cheyenne," "Wagon Train," "Maverick," "Have Gun—Will Travel," and "Bonanza." In the United States the television popularity of westerns reached its zenith in 1959 when eight of the ten most popular series were westerns. *See* TELEVISION HISTORY.

After 1960 the centrality of the western as a popular genre declined. By 1980 successful western films were rare, and television was stressing urban adventures in police, detective, and secret-agent thrillers. Ironically, while the western was losing its popularity in the United States, it was becoming something of an international phenomenon. In France and the Federal Republic of Germany entertainment parks and nightclubs began to use western motifs. Many of the most successful westerns of the late 1960s and 1970s were international productions, the "spaghetti westerns" made by Italian directors like Sergio Leone, often filmed in Spain with international casts. The western even had an impact in Asia, where the Japanese "samurai" film and the Chinese MARTIAL ARTS FILM produced in Hong Kong were strongly influenced by the U.S. western film. In the United States itself, however, while a sizable audience still followed paperback western novels and writers, the mass popularity of the western seemed to have disappeared. Perhaps in an age of nuclear terror, environmental deterioration, and worldwide violence, the dream of the western hero purging the town of its evil was no longer a match for the nightmare of reality.

Bibliography. John G. Cawelti, *The Six-Gun Mystique,* rev. ed., Bowling Green, Ohio, 1984; George N. Fenin and William K. Everson, *The Western: From Silents to the Seventies,* New York, 1973; Richard Slotkin, *Regeneration through Violence,* Middletown, Conn., 1973; Henry Nash Smith, *Virgin Land,* Cambridge, Mass., 1950; Jon Tuska, *The Filming of the West,* Garden City, N.Y., 1976.

JOHN G. CAWELTI

WHORF, BENJAMIN LEE (1897–1941)

U.S. linguist. Born in Winthrop, Massachusetts, Benjamin Lee Whorf received a bachelor's degree in chemical engineering from the Massachusetts Institute of Technology in 1919 and became a lifetime employee of the Hartford Fire Insurance Company, progressing from fire insurance investigator to special agent to assistant secretary of the company. His business provided perhaps the most powerful metaphor of the linguistic relativity theory (the so-called Sapir-Whorf hypothesis) with which his name is associated in communication-related disciplines: Unforeseen consequences may result, he pointed out, if a match is lit near a gasoline drum labeled "Empty" but still containing sufficient fuel to start a major fire; the reified label, in this case, is counter to fact in the "real" world (*see* LINGUISTICS; SAPIR, EDWARD).

Whorf never pursued a full-time academic career. Nonetheless, his private studies of American Indian languages, coupled with a childhood love of decoding exercises, led him into linguistics, particularly Central American hieroglyphics. In 1930 he traveled to Mexico under a Social Science Research Council fellowship, gathering data on an Aztec dialect and studying the Maya LANGUAGE and system of WRITING (*see also* AMERICAS, PRE-COLUMBIAN—WRITING SYSTEMS).

The turning point of Whorf's career, however, was the arrival at Yale University of Edward Sapir, North America's preeminent American Indian linguist. Whorf commuted to Yale to take Sapir's courses, became a core member of the research group that crystallized around him, and even taught Yale courses during Sapir's sabbatical and final illness in 1937–1938. Whorf himself died in 1941 at the age of forty-four.

Because of the popular controversy surrounding his ideas about the influence of grammatical form on human thought, Whorf has consistently been read—or misread—in simplistic terms (*see* GRAMMAR). His thought must be evaluated on three different levels in order to place his linguistic relativity hypothesis in its legitimate context.

First, Whorf's motives for the practice of linguistics were not professional or academic. Rather, he turned to language to support his theosophical principles, in a blend of religion and science that embarrassed later commentators. Moreover, many of his writings appeared in popular journals and were simply not intended for a scholarly audience. They have become available through the book *Language, Thought, and Reality: Selected Writings of Benjamin Lee Whorf,* which appeared in 1956 amid increasing interest in obtaining, from ethnographic evidence, scientific proof of the correlation between language, thought, and PERCEPTION of the external world.

Second, under the influence of Sapir, Whorf did a great deal of technical linguistic writing. He worked with a Hopi speaker in New York City in the early 1930s and visited the Hopi in the Southwest in 1938. He produced a grammar of Hopi and another of a dialect of Nahuatl, the language of the Aztec Empire. He also contributed to Sapir's development of the morphophonemics and grammar of English. His peers accepted him as a linguist.

Third, Whorf became increasingly interested in the differences in perception that result from speaking different languages. He argued not that the categories of grammar cannot be transcended but that "habitual thought" follows the grooves of linguistic categories. Several papers written toward the end of his life maintained that the Hopi worldview contrasts sharply with that of SAE (Standard Average European), that is, English and closely related languages. The repetition and nonlinearity of Hopi time categories, stressing aspect rather than tense, were his favorite examples. He argued that these attitudes toward time were reflected, essentially in a one-to-one correspondence, in Hopi RITUAL.

It was this last set of ideas that captured the imagination of a generation of American Indian linguists and spread to related disciplines, particularly anthropology and philosophy. Scholars were forced to address the apparent paradox that atomic physics can be elegantly expressed in Hopi although Hopi CULTURE lacks the scientific tradition to have invented it. Another concern was the possibility (or impossibility) of translating incommensurable worldviews. Anthropologists wanted cross-cultural evidence that linguistic categories correlated with cultural patterns.

Evaluation of Whorf's permanent contribution has fluctuated with scientific fashion. The influence of his work reached its apex in the 1950s, inspiring several conferences and research projects (particularly the Southwest Project of Harvard University). Subsequently, however, it became obvious that a simple correlation of language and culture was not forthcoming, and the immediate response was to discard the intuitive truth of Whorf's observations rather than to seek more concrete demonstrations of particular correlations. Linguistics and anthropology turned toward ethnosemantics and away from broad philosophical generalizations, excluding Whorf from the mainstream. However, Whorf undeniably focused interest in several disciplines on the importance of language in categorizing reality, and he is therefore the most eminent predecessor of such work in modern communicative sciences.

Bibliography. Harry Hoijer, ed., *Language in Culture: Conference on the Interrelations of Language and Other Aspects of Culture,* Chicago, 1954; Peter C. Rollins, *Benjamin Lee Whorf: Lost Generation Theories of Mind, Language, and Religion,* Ann Arbor, Mich., 1980; Benjamin Lee Whorf, *Language, Thought, and Reality: Selected Writings of Benjamin Lee Whorf,* ed. by John B. Carroll, Cambridge, Mass., 1956.

REGNA DARNELL

WIENER, NORBERT (1894–1964)

U.S. mathematician. Norbert Wiener is perhaps best known as the father and developer of the field of CYBERNETICS, which he defined as the study of control and communication in both the animal and the machine.

A child prodigy, he received his B.A. from Tufts College at age fourteen, his M.A. from Harvard University at age seventeen, and his Ph.D. from Harvard at age eighteen. His dissertation in mathematical logic and philosophy was followed by postgraduate work at Cambridge University, where he studied under the English mathematician and philosopher Bertrand Russell.

Wiener briefly held positions as lecturer and instructor at Harvard and the University of Maine, staff writer for the *Encyclopedia Americana* and the *Boston Herald,* and, during World War I, civilian computer at the Aberdeen Proving Ground in Maryland. In 1919 he joined the faculty of the Massachusetts Institute of Technology (MIT), where he remained until his retirement in 1960.

Early in his career at MIT, Wiener was introduced to the work of the U.S. physicist J. W. Gibbs. Gibbs's work in statistical mechanics, using probability and statistics as the basis for constructing an alternative to the Newtonian deterministic worldview, became a decisive influence on Wiener's intellectual development and a feature of the "contingent universe" perspective from which his theory of information and communication later arose.

Communication theory, which had long been an important background element in Wiener's more technical mathematical papers, was especially reflected in his concern with engineering communication problems of feedback control and electrical circuitry. However, his interest in communication theory rose to a central position in the 1940s, particularly through his work in weaponry applications during World War II, which included significant work on fire-control apparatuses for antiaircraft guns and noise filtration in radar systems as well as general work in tracking and gun-aiming devices. Through these projects Wiener began to recognize the importance of considering the operator as a "sender and receiver of messages" and thus as an integral part of a tracking or steering system. It was at this point that he made the key leap in seeing the analogy and then applying the concept of feedback from electrical engineering. He became aware of similar patterns, under the frame of communication, between the operations of systems from vastly different domains, such as computers and the human nervous system.

After the war Wiener continued these investigations, recognizing both the importance and ramifications of a "theory of messages," based on communication and feedback, of all forms. He was eager to move from a theory of communication and control in physical/mechanical settings to one in biological settings—and beyond. Wiener felt that a theory of transmission of messages, although fundamental to the development of scientific thought, fell into the cracks between scientific disciplines. In addition, there was no accepted term for the complexity of ideas in his theory of communication.

Wiener thus came to coin the term *cybernetics* (although he later came to recognize that others, including the French physicist André-Marie Ampère, had used the term previously) to embody this new science. He chose the term from the Greek *kybernētēs,* for "steersman." Wiener's book explicating his theory of the new science, *Cybernetics: Or, Control and Communication in the Animal and the Machine,* was published in 1948 and has been hailed as one of the most significant books of the twentieth century. In it he attempted to develop a field that "combines under one heading the study of what in a human context is sometimes loosely described as thinking and in engineering is known as control and communication." Wiener's cybernetics sets forth a theory to establish and cover the entire field of control and communication, both in machines and in living organisms—finding common elements in the functioning of automata, the human nervous system, and societies.

Wiener felt it important to classify control and communication together. He noted that communicating with another person involves imparting a message to the other, to which the other may respond with a related message. Controlling the actions of another involves a similar sequence of message and response, although the "controlling" message may be in the imperative mode, while the "return" message would indicate that the imperative has been understood and obeyed. Thus Wiener felt the theory of control (in engineering and elsewhere) to be "a chapter in the theory of messages."

Fundamental to Wiener's work was his concern with both human-human and human-machine interaction. He noted that in both processes a message or an order goes out, and a return message or a signal of compliance comes back. A complete cycle involving feedback is necessary in both instances. Wiener felt that whether the intermediary of a signal is a machine or a person may not greatly change one's relation to the signal. He observed that the similarities between human-human and human-machine interactions far outweigh their differences. Such a position in a theory of communication led him to be attacked, somewhat mistakenly, as an antivitalist. The complexity of Wiener's argument can be seen in

Figure 1. *(Wiener, Norbert)* Norbert Wiener, professor of mathematics at Massachusetts Institute of Technology, giving a lecture on Einstein's new theory, December 28, 1949. UPI/Bettmann Newsphotos.

his distinction between human and other ANIMAL COMMUNICATION; he stated that only in humans do we find that "this desire—or rather necessity—for communication is the guiding motive of their whole life."

These ideas were expressed in *Cybernetics* in a rather technical form. In response to what he felt was a demand to make them more accessible to the general public, Wiener wrote a less technical version that also extended his ideas more to social issues, in *The Human Use of Human Beings* (1950). The book's thesis is that "society can only be understood through a study of the communication facilities which belong to it." In it Wiener further developed his INFORMATION THEORY, which in his earlier work had been expressed mostly in mathematical-statistical terms, in parallel to the Shannon-Weaver "mathematical theory of communication" (*see* MODELS OF COMMUNICATION; SHANNON, CLAUDE; WEAVER, WARREN). Now Wiener described information as the medium of relationships in a communication system, no matter what physical form the communication system might take. Thus he came to claim the centrality of information, rather than energy or matter, as the fundament of any communication system.

Interestingly, many communication-systems technologies—especially ARTIFICIAL INTELLIGENCE, automata, and prosthetic devices for impaired human functions—trace their modern development to Wiener. In fact, he has been referred to as the "father of automation." Yet he became increasingly concerned with the human issues implicit in the development of communication machinery. He feared that the "second industrial revolution" might do to the human brain what the first had done to human muscle—make it a slave of technology. Such concerns led Wiener to apply his theory of communication and control to include an ethic with regard to his work; for example, he refused to allow the military access to some of his early mathematical papers (which had gone out of print) in order to prevent their use in the development of weaponry such as missiles. Wiener also became concerned with how cybernetics—particularly the development of machines that "learn" or that may "reproduce themselves"—impinged on religion. These ideas were expressed in *God and Golem, Inc.* (1964, published posthumously), a book for which he won the (U.S.) National Book Award in the area of science, philosophy, and religion. Two months before his death, Wiener was awarded the National Medal of Science by President Lyndon B. Johnson for his contributions to the fields of mathematics, engineering, and logical science.

Bibliography. Norbert Wiener, *Cybernetics: Or, Control and Communication in the Animal and the Machine,* 2d ed., Cambridge, Mass., 1961; idem, *God and Golem, Inc.,*

Cambridge, Mass., 1964; idem, *The Human Use of Human Beings: Cybernetics and Society,* 2d ed., rev., Garden City, N.Y., 1954, reprint 1967.

FREDERICK STEIER

WITTGENSTEIN, LUDWIG (1889–1951)

Austrian-British philosopher. Ludwig Josef Johann Wittgenstein has had an enormous influence on modern philosophical thought and on various fields related to it, such as communication, LINGUISTICS, psychology, and anthropology. Born in Vienna, the youngest of eight children, Wittgenstein was the son of a wealthy entrepreneur who organized the first cartel of the Austrian steel industry. He received his primary education at home and his secondary education at Linz, where he showed a great interest in MATHEMATICS and the physical sciences. Originally trained as an engineer in Berlin and Manchester, he turned his interest to pure mathematics and logic at Cambridge, where he worked under the direction of British philosopher Bertrand Russell. At Trinity College he applied himself intensively to logical studies and the ideas that eventually culminated in his first major philosophical work, the *Tractatus Logico-Philosophicus.* After five terms at Cambridge, he secluded himself in a self-made hut in Norway for several years and continued to consider logical problems. When World War I broke out Wittgenstein entered the Austrian army as a volunteer. During these years he continued to work on his book, which he finished in 1918 while he was held prisoner in an Italian camp. The German text of his book was published in 1921, and the English translation was published the following year in London.

After the publication of his book Wittgenstein became a schoolteacher in Lower Austria and an architect in Vienna. During these years (1920–1928) he gave little thought to logical or philosophical problems; however, he came in contact with the members of the Vienna Circle, a discussion group of scientists and philosophers who were profoundly influenced by the ideas in the *Tractatus.* In 1929 he returned to Cambridge to obtain his doctorate and to devote himself again to philosophy. He began lecturing in 1930 and in 1939 succeeded G. E. Moore in the chair of philosophy. During this period he began writing his second major philosophical work, *Philosophical Investigations* (1953). During World War II he held several jobs at a London hospital and the Royal Victoria Infirmary. In 1944 he resumed his lectures at Cambridge but was increasingly uneasy about his academic life. In 1947 he finally resigned his chair of philosophy. The following years he spent traveling and working when his health allowed it. In 1949 he was discovered to have cancer, and in 1951 he moved to the home of his doctor, where he died that same year.

Wittgenstein's philosophical thought is unified by a strong concern with the relationship between LANGUAGE, mind, and the real. But his thought divides into two different, and sometimes opposed, periods.

In the first period, the Wittgenstein of the *Tractatus,* he was trying to answer the question, What makes it possible for a set of words, namely, a sentence, to represent a fact in the world? In his own words his main task was to explain the nature of sentences. The result of this effort is known as "the picture theory of sentences." According to Wittgenstein, a direct logical correspondence exists among the configurations of objects in the world, words in a sentence, and thoughts in the mind. The nature of ideas in the mind and the relationship of words in a sentence are identical in formal structure with the structure of reality. The mental representation of objects, which creates both thought and language, works literally like a picture of the real. Wittgenstein's general answer to the problem was that when we assemble a sentence we are building a model or picture of reality. In his first period Wittgenstein also assumes that there is a universal form of language (though it may take different manifestations), which is basically this ability of language to picture the logical form of reality. This is also what confers MEANING to a sentence: the possibility that the words in the sentence are related to the objects in the real world. *See also* LÉVI-STRAUSS, CLAUDE; OSGOOD, CHARLES.

In the second period, the Wittgenstein of the *Philosophical Investigations,* he was concerned with the revision and sometimes rejection of the ideas in the *Tractatus.* In this book he stresses the conventional nature of language, opposing and rejecting the idea of a universal form of language that he had originally defended. He coined the term *language game* to refer to the conventional nature of language. According to him, every language is like a game with a particular set of rules and a limited number of elements. In the game the players learn how to use these elements by applying the given set of rules; through this process the players come to understand one another. There is nothing common to the various forms of language that he calls language games in his new view; there are just "family resemblances" among them and not a common essential nature. Hence the most basic presupposition of the *Tractatus* was mistaken. This presupposition was closely related to the picture theory of language, the notion that the correspondence with reality gives a proposition its meaning. In the *Investigations* Wittgenstein again rejects his previous conceptions and maintains that the meaning of a proposition or sentence is given by its "use." To understand the meaning of a sentence is to understand the special circumstances in which the sentence is actually used. "Circumstances" are essential to understand what language games are; without circumstances propositions are meaningless. *See also* JAMES, WILLIAM.

Wittgenstein's thought had a direct influence on at least two philosophical movements in the twentieth century. The Vienna Circle, influenced by the *Tractatus,* founded the movement known as logical positivism (later logical empiricism), which held that all meaningful statements can be verified by observation and experiment. Through his personal contacts, lectures, and writings Wittgenstein also influenced—particularly in his later period—the movement known as analytic and linguistic philosophy, originally called the Cambridge school and associated with such early figures as Russell, G. E. Moore, and Alfred North Whitehead. This school generally held that many philosophical problems can be solved through careful analysis of the language in which they are stated and through development of the ideal language, SYMBOLIC LOGIC. Other language-centered movements in the twentieth century, such as STRUCTURALISM, had a more distant relationship to Wittgenstein's thought. To a considerable extent Wittgenstein set the agenda and defined the terms of twentieth-century philosophical debate.

See also LOCKE, JOHN; PIAGET, JEAN; RICHARDS, I. A.; SAUSSURE, FERDINAND DE; VYGOTSKY, LEV.

Bibliography. Norman Malcolm, *Ludwig Wittgenstein: A Memoir,* London, 1958; Bertrand Russell, "Ludwig Wittgenstein," *Mind* 60 (1951): 297–298; Gilbert Ryle, "Ludwig Wittgenstein," *Analysis* 12 (1951): 1–9; Ludwig Wittgenstein, *The Blue and Brown Books,* New York and Oxford, 1958; idem, *Philosophical Investigations* (Philosophische Untersuchungen), trans. by G. E. M. Anscombe, New York, 1953, reprint Oxford, 1968; idem, *Tractatus Logico-Philosophicus* (1921), trans. by D. F. Pears and B. F. McGuinness, with an intro. by Bertrand Russell, London and New York, 1961, reprint 1971.

JAVIER A. ELGUEA S.

WOMEN. *See* FEMINIST THEORIES OF COMMUNICATION; GENDER; SEXISM.

WRITING

The expression of human LANGUAGE by means of visible signs. Although there are many semiotic systems that can be used to communicate simple notions and even rather complex messages, true writing differs from these in that it provides graphic notation of all the lexical, grammatical, and syntactic features of language (*see* GRAMMAR). Whatever can be represented by language can be put into writing. Writing is both more versatile and more specific than other semiotic systems, even if other systems function more efficiently and more effectively in the contexts for which they were designed. *See* SEMIOTICS; SIGN.

The international traffic SIGN SYSTEM, for example, communicates quite specific messages. The no-left-turn sign would be read just that way by nearly every speaker of the English language and has far greater efficacy than the signs spelling out "No Left Turn," which it has replaced. But the messages the traffic sign system can communicate are restricted in length and number and limited to one very narrow context. Certain Native American systems using both pictures and conventional markings can communicate longer messages with a wider range of subject matter. But whereas those conversant with such a system would interpret the ideas being communicated identically, individuals would "read" the message in many different ways. The system records ideas and notions but does not fix their linguistic expression. A written text will be read identically by all who know both the language and the writing system in which the text is recorded. Writing systems can represent language at the lexical level with word signs (logographic writing, such as Chinese) or at a phonetic level with syllabic or alphabetic signs. In practice most systems are mixed, so that there are phonetic elements even in a system as aggressively word-oriented as Chinese and word signs in a "purely" alphabetic system like the one used to write English (e.g., $, lb., &, @).

Origins. Figure 1 illustrates the widely accepted diffusionist view of the origin and spread of writing: invented only once by the Sumerians, the idea of writing spread from southern Mesopotamia westward to Egypt and, at a much later date and by questionable intermediaries, eastward to China. This view is no longer tenable. It is true that both Sumerian and Egyptian writing first appear a bit before 3000 B.C.E., in a period when there is some contact between the Nile Valley and Mesopotamia. But there is virtually no relationship whatsoever, formal or conceptual, between the two systems, and it can well be assumed that the chronological coincidence of their origins is just that, coincidence. At most the evidence might support the notion of some kind of stimulus DIFFUSION from Mesopotamia to Egypt. Certainly no positive evidence can be adduced for the diffusion of writing from the Near East to China, where the earliest Shang inscriptions are fifteen hundred years later than the oldest cuneiform and hieroglyphs. At a time when Chinese prehistory was poorly known, scholars, unwilling to imagine Shang and Chou China springing into being out of nothing, postulated a good deal of stimulus from the ancient Near East. Recent scholarly discussions of the subject

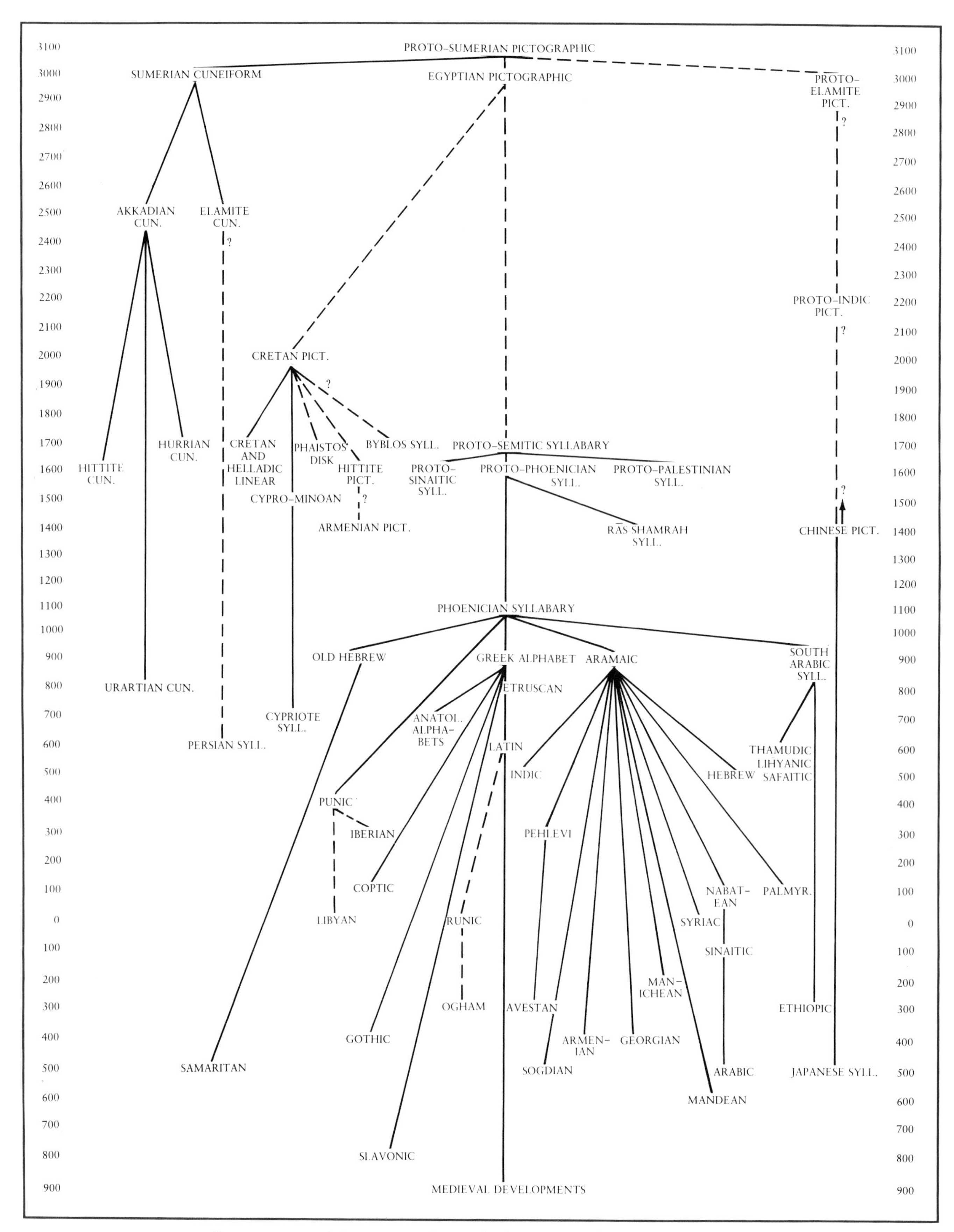

Figure 1. *(Writing)* Diffusionist view of the origin and spread of writing. Redrawn after I. J. Gelb, *A Study of Writing,* Chicago: University of Chicago Press, 1963, xi–xii.

minimize or reject entirely the possibility of substantive Near Eastern influence, stressing instead the continuities of a much-better-known early Chinese culture sequence from the Neolithic through the Shang period.

Thus it is possible now to think in terms of the independent origins of the hieroglyphic, cuneiform, and Chinese writing systems, and to these must be added a fourth, the Mesoamerican, best exemplified by Mayan. Mesoamerican systems do not even appear on the chart in Figure 1, because Mayan was not previously thought to be a true writing system, that is, a system capable of expressing both semantic and grammatical aspects of language. The phenomenal progress of Mayan studies since 1960, and especially since the mid-1970s, has established that Mayan is indeed a true writing system, and this fact, in turn, is fatal to the diffusionist argument. Writing, like metallurgy or agriculture, was invented at least twice, in the Old World and in the New, and if it could have been independently invented twice, then there is no reason to insist that it was not invented anew by the Egyptians and Chinese rather than borrowed from the Sumerians.

Cuneiform. The earliest true writing system originated in southern Mesopotamia, ancient Sumer, and there the origins of writing can now be traced very clearly. Whether or not one accepts completely the theories of Denise Schmandt-Besserat—which trace the origin of cuneiform to small CLAY TOKENS found at sites all over the Near East, spanning a period from the ninth to the second millennium B.C.E., when the chronological and geographical focus is narrowed to the time and place where CUNEIFORM writing first emerged—she has been able to reconstruct a remarkable and convincing sequence that leads from a crude system of numerical notation to the first written documents.

The sequence begins with hollow balls containing clay tokens of various shapes, which have been impressed on the balls before the balls were sealed, and passes to a stage when the tokens are dispensed with and the ball flattened to a cushion-shaped tablet onto which tokenlike shapes (probably numeric in meaning) are impressed, then rolled over with a seal (see Figure 2). These impressed tablets are found at the Sumerian site of Uruk, which experienced a period of sudden urban expansion, culminating there with the invention of the cuneiform writing system. But the other sites did not follow Uruk in that direction; writing was invented at Uruk and at first did not travel beyond the confines of ancient Sumer. Only in subsequent centuries did it extend to Iran, northern Mesopotamia, and Syria, borrowed directly from the Sumerian system, or, in the case of a short-lived system in southwestern Iran, created under stimulus from Sumer.

Figure 2. *(Writing)* Sealed impressed tablet, Susa, ca. 3200 B.C.E. From *Cahiers de la délégation archéologique française en Iran* 8 (1978): 47. Mission Archéologique de Suse.

Although the development from the tablet in Figure 2 to the archaic cuneiform tablet in Figure 3 may be clear in retrospect, there is nevertheless a world of difference between the two. They have the clay medium and numeric notation in common, but Figure 3 has, in addition, an array of complex signs that is infinitely more capable of signifying people and commodities than any system of tokens or tokenlike impressions. Archaic cuneiform tablets also manifest a highly sophisticated spatial organization, a kind of metasyntax that only partially overlaps with the syntax of the Sumerian language.

Two traditions have coalesced at Uruk. The first is the rude system of numerical notation represented by the impressed tablets. The second is a tradition of pictorial and symbolic representation whose development can be traced in the record of prehistoric Near Eastern art, especially glyptic. The wedding of these two traditions made it possible to supplement the information storage capacity of the impressed tablets with the semantic potential of humanity's most powerful semiotic system, language.

The primary stimulus for the development of a writing system at Uruk was the growth and increasing complexity of the bureaucratic state. The tablet in Figure 3 and tablets like it are accounts representing the transactions of a large administrative organization, as were the clay balls and impressed tablets they replaced. The advent of writing in Mesopotamia represents the appropriation by language of a hitherto nonlinguistic function, the recording of transactions. Far from mimicking SPEECH acts, writing created an entire province of language use that was unthinkable before its invention; accounts are never spoken, and if they are dictated or read aloud their manifestation as speech has been made possible only by their prior existence or potentiality as writing. From the first four hundred years of writing in Mes-

Figure 3. *(Writing)* Archaic tablet from Uruk, ca. 2900 B.C.E. From A. Falkenstein, *Archaische Texte aus Uruk,* Berlin and Leipzig, Deutsche Forschungsgemeinschaft in Uruk-Warka, Vol. 2 (1936), plate 60, no. 585.

opotamia primarily two kinds of written texts survive: accounts like the one in Figure 3 and lexical texts—long lists of words organized by subject matter, SOUND, or sign form that were used to teach the writing system and are unimaginable without it. Cuneiform, which in the long run proved to be the most flexible and adaptable of the four "original" writing systems, was not used to write continuous texts—historical inscriptions, literary compositions, administrative and legal records with full grammatical expression—until about 2600 B.C.E.

Egyptian hieroglyphs. The earliest evidence from Egypt is more complex. Nothing comparable to the commemorative palette in Figure 4 is known from archaic Sumer. Here the pictorial representation of a historical event is supplemented by captions identifying the protagonists. King Narmer (ca. 3000 B.C.E.), whose name is spelled out in the frame at the top center with the glyph for the *nar* ("catfish") and the glyph *mer* ("chisel"), is wearing the crown of upper Egypt, and he is symbolized by the falcon, who holds in tow a creature representing lower Egypt, symbolized by the papyrus patch. On the reverse Narmer is pictured wearing the combined crowns of upper and lower Egypt, a symbol of the united land. Various signs presumably identify the ruler's defeated foes, but the fact of their defeat, like the unification of the land, is conveyed pictorially and not through language. In this tentative insertion of writing into pictorial narrative, writing is not replacing or representing speech. Rather, it is appropriating for language a commemorative function once reserved solely for representational ART. *See* EGYPTIAN HIEROGLYPHS.

Already under Narmer's successor, Aha, we have the first of a series of wooden and ivory labels recording the contents of perfume and ointment jars delivered to royal tombs, adding the name of the year in which the offering was brought. These year names commemorated an important event, and unlike the palette, which depended on narrative art to relate the event, the labels have actual sentences with verbs. These are not yet lengthy, continuous texts, but the appropriate mechanisms are all in place. Another important early use of writing in Egypt is as an identity mark, just a personal name and perhaps a title, found on funerary stelae, vessels, and sealings. As such it replaces the emblematic ownership marks known universally in both literate and preliterate cultures.

No actual administrative accounts comparable to archaic Sumerian texts survive from archaic Egypt, but this is to be expected. Few records survive at all from Egypt that are not connected to funerary cults. This is because burials were in the desert, where dryness preserves the perishable materials used for recordkeeping. But the very fact that lists of commodities and dates of delivery were recorded in funerary contexts implies a concern in archaic Egypt with recordkeeping that certainly extended into other areas of administration. In Mesopotamia the primary medium for cursive writing, clay, is quite durable. In nearly every other literate culture, both writing surfaces—papyrus, leaves, bark, textiles—and the ink or paint used for writing are perishable and survive only in unusual contexts (*see* WRITING MATERIALS). This seriously distorts our perception of those early cultures, since the texts that survive are nearly always commemorative or RITUAL, having been laboriously inscribed on stone, metal, bone, or some similar durable surface.

Chinese writing. The earliest written records in China date from the Shang period, whose capital at Anyang has provided excavators with a wealth of artifacts that have revolutionized the study of early Chinese history (*see* EAST ASIA, ANCIENT). Shang records are of two types. A small minority of the well-known Shang bronze vessels contain inscriptions consisting of an emblem, probably of a clan, a kinship term, and the name of a day. The clan emblems are just that, and are not ancestral to any later sign forms in the Chinese writing system, just as city emblems on certain archaic Egyptian palettes have no correspondence in later hieroglyphs. A very small number of Shang bronzes have longer statements, none of more than fifty characters, concerning the circumstances that led to the vessel's casting.

a

b

Figure 4. *(Writing)* Palette of Narmer; (*a*) obverse, (*b*) reverse. Hierakonpolis, Egypt, Early Dynastic period, ca. 3000 B.C.E. Egyptian Museum, Cairo. Giraudon/Art Resource, New York.

But these bronze inscriptions are insignificant compared to the one hundred thousand or so inscriptions and fragments of inscriptions on specially prepared ox shoulder blades and turtle shells that record oracles taken for the king and other notables. The bones and shells were specially prepared so that when heated, characteristic cracks would appear, and the angles of these cracks would indicate whether the omen was positive or negative. Afterward the archivist would record the divination act on the bone or shell, sometimes adding a verification of whether or not the predicted event took place. In addition to information pertaining to the political history of the Shang, the subject matter of these oracles includes sacrificial rituals, hunting expeditions, weather, harvest, health, birth, dreams, and building activities. The inscriptions, though purporting to quote the words spoken during the divination inquiry, are not intended to replace or accompany those words. Rather, they are written down after the fact and are preserved apparently as records of the king's reign. A very small number of inscribed bones and shells are not oracular but contain calendrical records or accounts of tribute payments. These latter suggest that there may well have been an extensive administrative accounting system such as we know from Mesopotamia, but texts representing such a system have not survived. This is because, according to ancient tradition, they would have been written on wood or silk and hence have perished. Bronze, of course, could not have been a medium for such records, nor could bone or shell, whose preparation and inscription are very time consuming. Evidence that strongly points to the presence in the Shang period of records on perishable materials is provided by the observation that some of the oracle texts were first written on the bone or shell with ink and brush before they were incised. The brush, of course, is the traditional writing implement of the Chinese scribe, and its use on the oracle bones points to its probable use on other media, all of which would have been perishable.

The Shang texts do not antedate 1500 B.C.E. by very much and hence are fifteen hundred years later than the earliest writing in the Fertile Crescent. However, several scholars have proposed that pot marks going back to nearly 5000 B.C.E. are the direct ancestors of Chinese characters, thus making the Chinese writing system the oldest known by far. But most scholars seem to reject this view, and with good reason. At most, forty or fifty different marks have been identified, and the great majority of pots have inscriptions consisting of only a single mark; hardly any have as many as three. No writing system of the Chinese type can function with so few characters, and an inscription one character in length is inadequate to write even a personal name. The pot marks are best understood as clan emblems, much like those on Shang bronzes.

Mayan texts. The earliest datable Mayan texts go back to the first century B.C.E., though no more than the dates themselves can be understood on the very early inscriptions (*see* AMERICAS, PRE-COLUMBIAN—WRITING SYSTEMS). The monument in Figure 5, dated to 755 C.E., portrays the capture of Jewel-Skull and another enemy by Bird-Jaguar of Yaxchilan and his companion. The second glyph in the upper right is the name of Bird-Jaguar, followed by the Yaxchilan place emblem. In the upper left the first two rows of glyphs are the date, the third is the verb "to capture," followed by the name of Jewel-Skull, which is repeated on his thigh in the illustration. Most of the classical Mayan stelae are records of historical occurrences of this type; the inscriptions are dates and captions, supplements to the narrative art.

Painted Mayan inscriptions of a ritual or historical nature are found on pots and walls, but the bulk of Mayan literature is lost forever, because it was recorded on bark codices. Only four of these perishable texts have survived; they are postclassical and deal with ritual or astronomical-astrological matters (*see* CALENDAR). Such detailed recording and calculating of astronomical occurrences are completely outside the realm of spoken language use and are made possible only by writing.

Figure 5. *(Writing)* Bird-Jaguar captures Jewel-Skull, from a carved stone lintel at Yaxchilan, 755 C.E. From Michael D. Coe, *The Maya,* London: Thames and Hudson, 1984, p. 167.

Phoneticism. Three important aspects of all writing systems have often been misunderstood in discussions of writing's origins. The first is phoneticism; we often hear that the earliest writing used word-signs (logograms) only and that phonetic representation developed only gradually. In fact, phonetic writing was present to some degree in all writing systems from the beginning. You cannot easily draw a preposition or a pronoun, but even if you could, a system in which every word was represented by a different sign, and gave no clue to that sign's reading, would be quite unwieldy. And so the development of the writing system led almost immediately to—or was made possible by—the abstraction of sound from MEANING. This is accomplished by applying the well-known rebus principle: a sign with meaning *x* is used to write a homophonous (like-sounding) word with meaning *y*, or just to signify a phonetic sequence, that is, part of a word or a grammatical affix (e.g., writing "I see you" by drawing an eye, the sea, and a ewe). Thus the name of King Narmer is written with the signs for "catfish" (*nar*) and "chisel" (*mer*) (see Figure 4). Or, in Chinese, the sign for water as a semantic indicator is combined with the sign *lin'* ("forest") to write the word *lin'* ("drop") (see Figure 6). Over 90 percent of all Chinese characters are formed by this combination of semantic indicator and rebus, and words are often written by rebus alone. Both of these methods are already present in the Shang oracle inscriptions.

The ongoing decipherment of Mayan really took off only with the proper understanding of the use of phonetic writings in Mayan inscriptions, an understanding both delayed and resisted because of the misleading, but ultimately crucial, Mayan "alphabet" recorded by a sixteenth-century missionary. It is now recognized that Mayan words can be written (1) solely logographically, (2) logographically with one or more phonetic complements (such complements play important roles in both cuneiform and Egyptian as well as in the formation of Chinese characters), and (3) purely phonetically.

Curiously, cuneiform, which by 2500 B.C.E. was capable of purely phonetic writing, has a very much smaller amount of detectable phoneticism in its earliest stages than either Egyptian or Chinese, which never get as free from logograms and semantic indicators as certain kinds of cuneiform do. But the occasional early use of phonetic complements in the archaic texts from Uruk tell us that the principle was well understood from the beginning. After 2500 B.C.E.

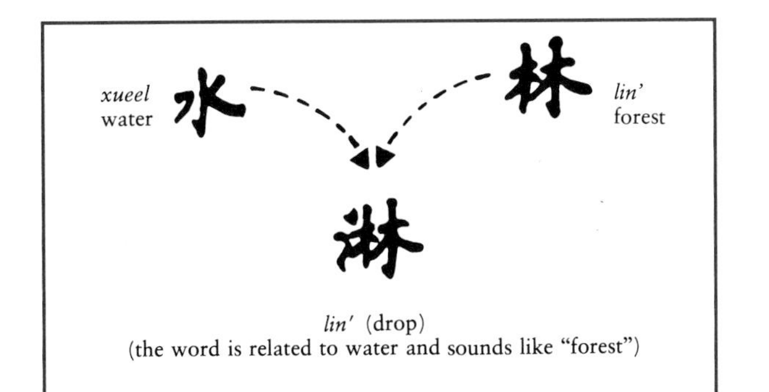

Figure 6. *(Writing)* Phonetic and semantic components in Chinese characters. Redrawn after Morris Swadesh, *The Origin and Diversification of Language,* Chicago: Aldine, Atherton, 1971, p. 69.

phonetically used cuneiform syllabograms were used to write Semitic languages in Mesopotamia proper and at Ebla, and ultimately they were employed for Indo-European Hittite as well as many other, lesser-known, languages of the ancient Near East.

In Egypt, where signs had primarily consonantal values—and to this day the vocalization of Egyptian is uncertain—a sign could be used phonetically to stand for one consonant or a series of two or three consonants. Already in the Old Kingdom the Egyptians had developed an ALPHABET, that is, a series of signs standing for each consonantal phoneme in the language, but this alphabet was never employed consistently. Even when an inscription was written with a high percentage of these alphabetic signs, semantic indicators and determinatives were not abandoned. Despite the Egyptians' unwillingness to use the alphabetic concept they themselves developed to simplify their writing system, it is this concept that was to be adopted by West Semites to create their alphabet, and eventually the Latin alphabet. This reluctance in ancient Egypt to simplify the writing system by abandoning logograms and determinatives in favor of purely phonetic representation was paralleled in Mesopotamia, where logograms continued to be used in primarily phonetic texts and where, in some text genres, the percentage of logographic writings increases dramatically in later periods. Similarly, although the Japanese have long had *kana* systems enabling them to write purely phonetically, they have steadfastly refused to abandon the logographic use of Chinese characters *(kanji);* with its combination of various kinds of *kana* and *kanji,* Japanese is perhaps the most complex and difficult writing system in use. In all of these cases any progressivist tendency toward simplification is resisted not only by cultural pressures favoring the retention of ancient forms but also by certain semiotic advantages inherent in a logographic system.

Pictorialness. The question of pictorialness is closely related to that of phoneticism. We learn that the earliest writing was pictographic, and only gradually did the pictograms become more schematic and finally lose their graphic relationship to the words they originally represented. In reality some of the earliest writing systems used abstract sign forms from the beginning. Originally pictorial cuneiform signs developed rapidly from pictogram to abstract bundles of wedges; by 2500 B.C.E. there was absolutely no pictorial content whatsoever in any cuneiform sign. But even the earliest forms of some signs have no pictorial content. The archaic Sumerian signs for livestock are shown in Figure 7. Remembering that the original orientation of the signs is ninety degrees to the right, the cattle signs do indeed look like schematic animal heads. But the sheep and goats look nothing at all like animals; rather, they consist of various combinations of circle, cross, and rectangle, with cross-hatching in the interior or exterior to mark the adult females and female kid, and lozenges to mark the males. Only the female lamb, like the female calf, is marked with the usual pictogram for female, which is the image of a pudendum. These signs are not representations of animals but, rather, abstract combinations of geometric elements.

	SHEEP		GOATS		CATTLE	
Adult female	U$_8$		UD$_5$		ÁB	
Adult male	UDUNITA		MÁŠ			
Young female	KIR$_{11}$		EŠGAR		AMAR-SAL	
Young male	SILANITA		MAŠ		AMAR-KUR	

Figure 7. *(Writing)* Archaic Sumerian livestock signs. Redrawn after M. W. Green, "Animal Husbandry at Uruk in the Archaic Period," *Journal of Near Eastern Studies* 39 (1980): 5.

Egyptian hieroglyphs are excruciatingly pictorial, but writing letters or accounts in beautiful pictures is very inefficient, and the Egyptians always had cursive hands for these mundane tasks. Significantly these cursive hands appear already on some of the earliest inscribed artifacts. But despite the existence of the more efficient cursive, pictorial hieroglyphic script remained in use throughout the history of ancient Egypt, so that, unlike the development of cuneiform in Mesopotamia, the link between the cursive forms and the underlying pictogram was never lost.

The pictorialness of Egyptian writing allowed an extraordinary interplay between texts and the illustrations they accompany. In Figure 8 it is difficult to know where the writing stops and the illustration begins. The objects above the offering table are all hieroglyphs for the foodstuffs being offered, and the arm interjected between them and the seated figure is the hieroglyph for "to offer." Yet there is neither grammar nor syntax in this juxtaposition of signs; it was not intended to be read. How different this resemblance and intermingling of script and art is from the appearance of inscribed Mesopotamian monuments, on which the cuneiform text appears as an indifferent band, cutting across but never entering into the bas-relief sculpture.

In China the Shang oracle characters are pictorial in a very schematic way, and Chinese characters quickly reach a state of complete abstraction, much like cuneiform signs. And, like cuneiform, Chinese characters, no matter how elegant their calligraphy, never entered into representational art in the way that Egyptian hieroglyphs did. Despite the similar brush technique used for both the calligraphy and the figure in Figure 9 (Japanese), there is never any blurring of the distinction between text and figure.

The Mayan situation is more like the Egyptian. Alongside more or less pictographic standard forms of Mayan signs there are highly abstract cursive forms, used mainly in codices, as well as superpictographic forms. These superpictographs, which begin to be used later rather than earlier than the normal sign forms, extend also to the writing of numerals, which in normal texts are composed simply of dots and bars. Even relatively cursive Mayan glyphs are closely related to the conventions of Mayan art, as can be seen from a folio of the Dresden Codex (see Figure 10), in which glyphs enter into the picture as offerings, much as they do in the Egyptian example in Figure 8.

All the early writing systems examined here used phonetic representation from their inception, and all either developed abstract cursive hands that were used contemporaneously with a pictographic script, like the Egyptian and Mayan, or quickly developed

Figure 8. *(Writing)* Painted stela of Nefertiabet. Egypt, Old Kingdom, fourth dynasty. Louvre, Paris. Giraudon/Art Resource, New York.

into systems of cursive characters that lost any apparent resemblance to their original pictographic shapes, like cuneiform and Chinese. Phoneticism means that a signifier, let us say the catfish hieroglyph, is wrenched from what it originally signified and is used instead to signify a sequence of phonemes. This intellectual feat presupposes the ability to break words down into phonetic strings, to abstract the phonetic from the semantic. The development of cursive hands can be described as the suppression of the iconicity of the written sign in favor of a purely symbolic representation. These processes of abstraction are concomitant with and essential to the creation of any writing system.

Full-blownness. One reads that the Sumerian or Egyptian or Chinese systems could not have originated in Sumer, Egypt, or China because they appear, in their earliest manifestations, as full-blown systems. In the first place, this is an exaggeration. In their initial centuries of use hieroglyphic and cuneiform undergo considerable refinement in their ability to represent language fully. But more to the point, a half-blown system is not very useful. For a writing system to have been adopted, its utility had to justify the establishment of an educational system and the submission to years of training for everyone who would use it. The fact, for instance, that all the systems we have looked at are phonetic from their inception means that systems that did not include the possibility of rebus phonetic writings were not considered useful enough to learn and thus did not spread beyond their creator or a circle of users so small that no traces have been left for us. There is nothing partway between the impressed tablets, with their small repertoire of numerical signs, and the archaic repertory of twelve hundred cuneiform signs. Full-blownness, far from pointing to external origins or stimulus, is rather the sine qua non for survival.

Writing, language, and speech. All early writing systems are complex and difficult to master. No society would allocate the resources necessary to adopt and propagate such systems unless the systems were meeting certain needs of the society, and meeting them well. In none of the instances examined, to the extent that evidence has survived, can it be shown that these needs included the representation of spoken language. Whether in accounting, the keeping of astronomical records, providing captions on commemorative monuments, or marking ownership, writing made it possible for language, the most versatile semiotic tool, to be applied to areas that were hitherto inaccessible to it. Certain categories of early documents, such as accounts and lexical lists, have no analogues in the realm of spoken language. And we have seen that the antecedents to recordkeeping in Mesopotamia and commemorative inscriptions in Egypt are to be sought not in oral discourse but in clay tokens and narrative art, respectively. The two primary functions of writing, as Jack Goody has so aptly put it, are storage and decontextualization, and this is how writing asserts its superiority over speech as a medium of communication.

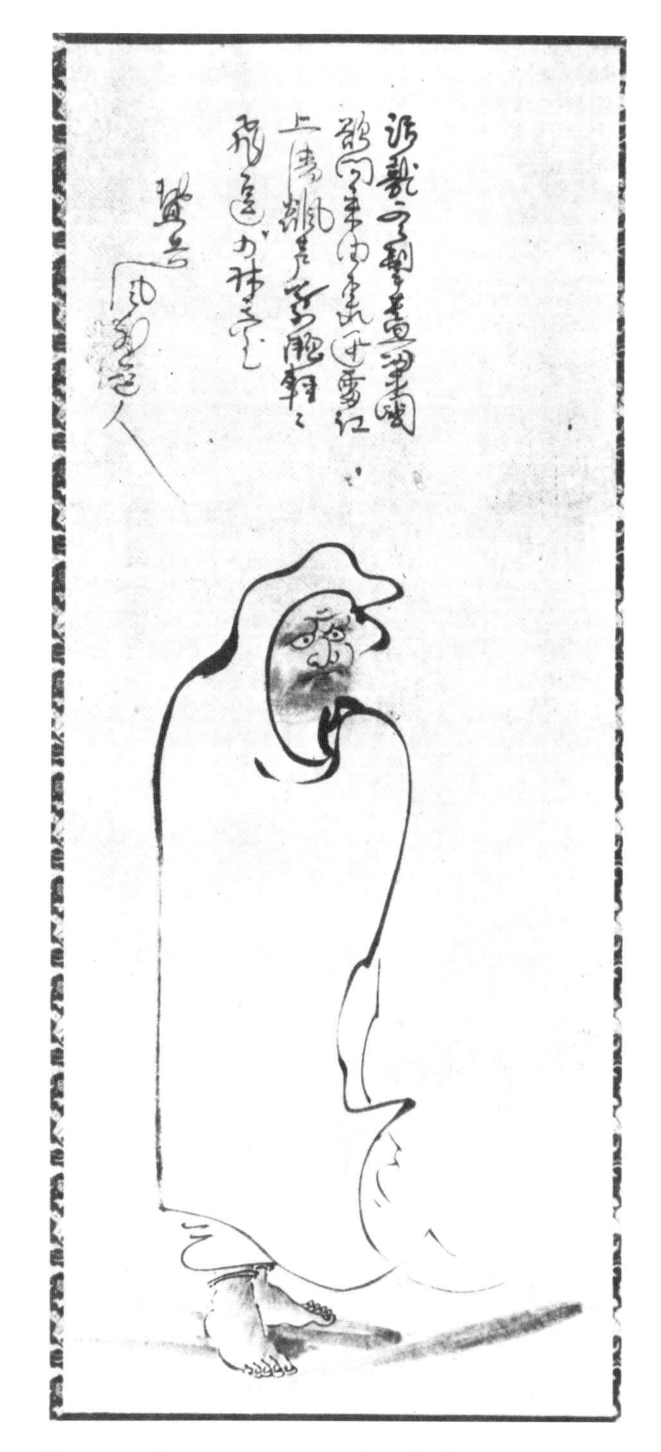

Figure 9. *(Writing)* Painting of Bodhidharma with poem by Fugai (1568–1650). Edo period. From J. Stevens, *Sacred Calligraphy of the East,* Boulder, Colo., and London: Shambhala Publications, 1981, p. 137.

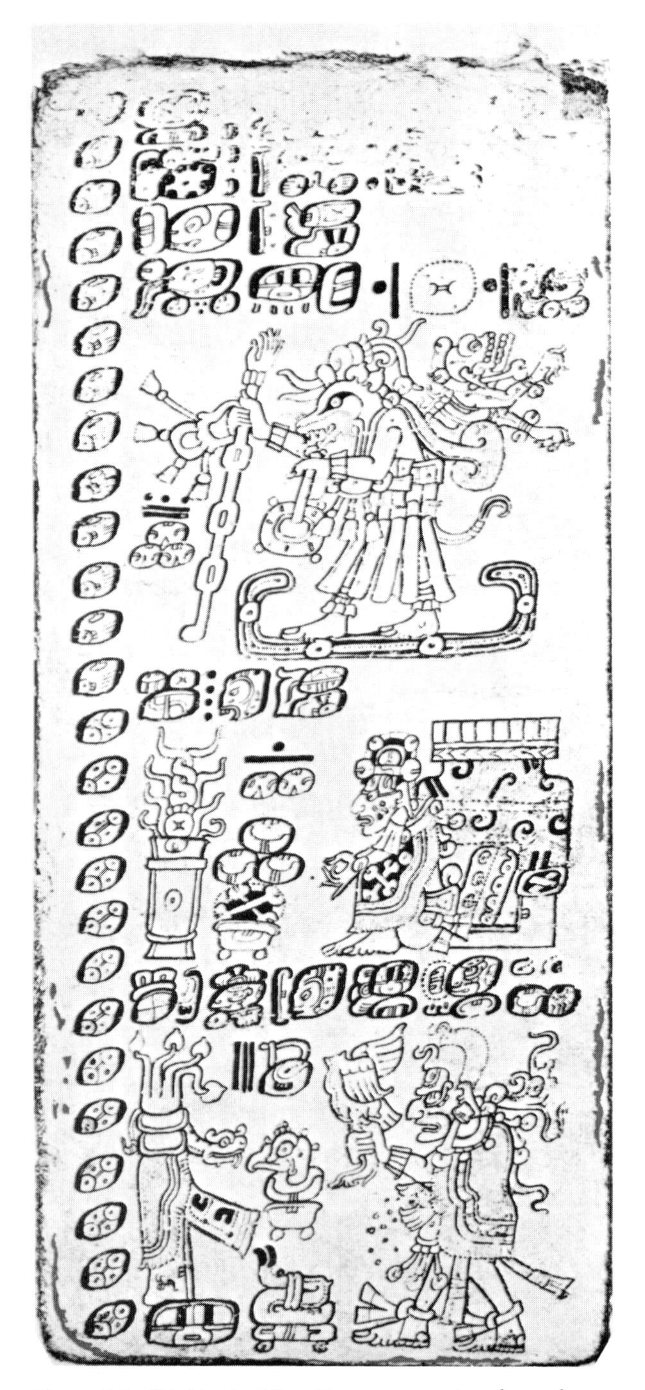

Figure 10. *(Writing)* New Year ceremonies, from the Dresden Codex, early second millennium C.E. From J. Eric S. Thompson, *A Commentary on the Dresden Codex: A Maya Hieroglyph Book, Memoirs of the American Philosophical Society* 93 (1972), Fig. 28.

Writing was invented because of a perceived lack in the possibilities of applying language in its spoken form to spheres of human endeavor to which the inventors of writing wished to apply language. Similarly it is not an inaccurate generalization to say that we use writing primarily when speaking is not sufficient. And even in those situations in which we do write when we could have spoken, or vice versa, our choice of oral or written medium can drastically affect the semiotic of the communicative act. This view of writing and speech as mutually complementary expressions of language has been most prominently represented by the Prague school linguist Josef Vachek as a reaction against the position of FERDINAND DE SAUSSURE that writing "exists for the sole purpose of representing" spoken language. Vachek's reaction was every bit as necessary as Saussure's extremism perhaps was in its time, and both models have their value, but Vachek's is more useful for studying and understanding the origins and early uses of writing.

Writing and literature. The earliest forms of both Egyptian and Mesopotamian writing were not used to record literary texts and probably were inadequate to do so. Over several centuries an expanded and systematic exploitation of the phonetic principle enabled writing to approach speech in its ability to fully represent morphological features of language, but writing's contact with speech is, with some important exceptions like letters and incantations, only tangential, as written literature veers away from spoken language and develops its own character as a written and to some extent academic enterprise.

In Mesopotamia the majority of the earliest literary texts are written cryptographically and, except for the occasional word or phrase, have not yet been deciphered. Large numbers of legible literary texts first appear at the end of the third and beginning of the second millennia, when Sumerian, the language nearly all are written in, was well on its way toward extinction. Many of these texts are royal praise-hymns that we know were written in the scribal academies heavily patronized by the ruler for just that purpose, and others commemorate specific historical events. There is good reason to believe that the Sumerian epics of legendary rulers like Enmerkar and Gilgamesh are also scribal products, at least in the version that we have them. The recent discovery of bilingual punning in early Akkadian epic poetry, generally thought to be somehow close to its oral origins, now situates this poetry firmly in the scribal academy. Our vision of the bard reciting the deeds of Gilgamesh or the tale of the Flood to the multitudes in the marketplace or at a festival becomes ever more fuzzy as our understanding of early Akkadian literature becomes more profound. Despite the frequent use of formulas, parallelism, and repetition in both Sumerian and Akkadian literary texts, there is no evidence that these texts were orally composed or part of an oral tradition. Any technique that facilitates composition for an oral poet facilitates composition for the scribal poet as well. *See* ORAL CULTURE; ORAL POETRY.

In Egypt the earliest literary texts were offering prayers and autobiographies, which grew out of lists of offices and titles inscribed in tombs. A scholar of archaic Chinese wrote recently that archaic Chinese was essentially a written language; it was not until the Han period, more than one thousand years after the Shang oracle bones, that Chinese characters were used to record the spoken language. The early literature that all of these most ancient civilizations have preserved belongs squarely in the camp of written language. In ancient Mesopotamia it is impossible to gauge what relationship, if any, the literary compositions passed on to us by Mesopotamian scribes have with the oral literature of the popular culture, which must have existed but has left no clear trace.

It is, then, both useful and apt to understand writing and speech as coordinate expressions of language rather than to view writing as a secondary representation of speech—speech that alone would be the true embodiment of language. Can one venture further and assert the priority of writing over speech? If one considers the relationship between graphic communication in general and speech, it is worth pondering that, according to some scholars, human speech depends on a very specific type of vocal tract, which can be shown to have existed in fossils only from the very same upper Paleolithic that produced the masterpieces of narrative painting found in the caves of southwestern Europe. Perhaps, then, the great eighteenth-century philosopher and historian Giambattista Vico was correct in asserting that "letters and languages were born twins and proceeded apace through all their three stages," that in their first stage communication was accomplished by "a mute language of signs and physical objects having natural relations to the ideas they wished to express," and that human language as we know it followed later.

See also INDUS SCRIPT; LITERACY.

Bibliography. Albertine Gaur, *A History of Writing,* London, 1984; I. J. Gelb, *A Study of Writing,* rev. ed., Chicago, 1963; Jack Goody, *The Domestication of the Savage Mind,* Cambridge, 1977; M. W. Green, "The Construction and Implementation of the Cuneiform Writing System," *Visible Language* 15 (1981): 345–372; Philip Lieberman, *The Biology and Evolution of Language,* Cambridge, Mass., 1984; Joan Oates, ed., *Early Writing Systems, World Archaeology* (special issue), Vol. 17, no. 3, 1986; Geoffrey Sampson, *Writing Systems: A Linguistic Introduction,* Stanford, Calif., and London, 1985; Ferdinand de Saussure, *Course in General Linguistics,* ed. by Charles Bally and Albert Sechehaye, London, 1959, reprint 1983; Josef Vachek, *Written Language,* The Hague, 1973; idem, "Zum Problem der geschriebenen Sprache," *Travaux du cercle linguistique de Prague* 8 (1939): 94–104; Leon Vandermeersch, "Écriture et langue écrite en Chine," in *Écritures,* compl. by Annie-Marie Christin, Paris, 1982; Giambattista Vico, *The New Science of Giambattista Vico* (Principi di una scienza nuova), trans. of 3d ed. by Thomas G. Bergin and Max H. Fisch, Ithaca, N.Y., 1948, reprint 1970.

JERROLD S. COOPER

WRITING MATERIALS

Surfaces, instruments, inks, and other equipment, which developed at various stages in the history of WRITING. Starting with cave drawings, the history of writing materials is characterized by creativity, ingenuity, and adaptation to available resources. Table 1 illustrates the dates and locations at which various writing materials originated.

Before writing. Drawings, engravings, and other markings that predate the earliest writing systems employed various materials. The earliest examples are prehistoric cave drawings and engravings on bones. The cave paintings used natural cracks and markings as part of the outlines of their subjects and employed pigments made from animal and vegetable substances. The colors were either applied with fingertips, sticks, or animal fur tufts or were blown onto the cave surfaces through hollow bones (see Figure 1). The bone engravings were apparently carved with a stylus made of quartzite.

Another example of markings that predate writing is represented by CLAY TOKENS—dating back to 8000 B.C.E.—that have been found in quantity in what was Mesopotamia. The tokens were fashioned with fingertips from clay into a multitude of shapes. They were marked with a stylus or a stick and were oven-

Figure 1. *(Writing Materials)* A hind, painting from the caves at Altamira, Spain. Magdalenian, ca. 15,000–10,000 B.C.E. SEF/Art Resource, New York.

Table 1. Origins of Writing Materials

Writing surfaces	*Year*	*Writing system*	*Places*	*Writing instruments*	*Inks, equipment*
Cave walls, bones	25,000 B.C.E.	Prewriting	S.W. Europe N. Africa	Feather, fur tuft, stylus	Paints
Clay tokens	8000	Prewriting	Mesopotamia	Stylus	—
Clay tablets, brick seals, stones	3000	Cuneiform	Mesopotamia	Stylus, chisel	—
Papyrus, stone	3000	Egyptian hieroglyphs	Egypt	Brush, chisel	Inks, scribal equipment
Leather	2500	Egyptian	Egypt	Brush, pen	Inks
Plaster	2500	Proto-Indic	India	Stamp seal	—
Animal bones, turtle shells	1400	Chinese	China	Chisel, stylus	—
Wooden tablets, leaves, textiles, bamboo, bark	500	Indic, Chinese	India, China	Brush, stylus	Inks
Parchment, leaves, bark, papyrus	300	Greek, Latin, Arabic	Mediterranean	Brush, pen, stylus	Inks
Paper	150	Chinese, Mediterranean	China, Mediterranean	Brush (rush and animal hair), pen (reed and quill)	
Bark paper, stone	300 C.E.	Maya hieroglyphs	Mesoamerica	Animal hair tuft, chisel	Inks

Other writing surfaces: Gold, silver, bronze, lead, copper; linen, cotton, canvas, silk; jade, wax and stucco coating, ivory; egg shells; ostraca, limestone flakes; wood chips; vessels, pottery, weapons.

fired for permanence. For shipment, tokens could be inserted in hollow clay balls that served as envelopes and were likewise marked with a stylus to indicate content.

Clay tablets. The abundance of clay and the deficiency of wood and stone in the Mesopotamian basin made it natural that clay tablets would be used for the early Sumerian pictograms and CUNEIFORM writings (see Figure 2). In addition, clay was used in bricks for building construction, and these clay bricks were also used as an early writing surface.

The writing tablets were made from local clay, which varied in color and consistency. A small amount of clay was kneaded in the hands to a suitable consistency and formed into a biscuit- or pillow-shaped tablet that was flat on one side. The tablets varied in size, shape, and color from site to site, so that the area of origin can sometimes be identified. The tablets, after inscription, were air- or sun-dried or baked for permanence.

The writing was inscribed on the wet clay surface with a stylus, fashioned from reeds, wood, bone, or, in some cases, metal (usually iron). In general, however, the stylus was made from the woody base of a reed, which had been shaped to a triangular tip to impart the wedge-shaped marks typical of cuneiform and related markings. The shape of the stylus and its application made the components of the symbols.

Stone monuments. Stone has been used through the ages for a permanent writing surface. In stone-scarce Mesopotamia writing on stone was generally limited to royal texts and cylinder seals. In Egypt countless inscriptions are found on stone walls of temples and tombs and other structures. A range of stone materials has been used: limestone, sandstone, basalt, granite, alabaster, and quartzite. The incising was performed with chisel and mallet. Similarly, in Central America stone (in this case limestone) provided the surface for writing the Maya hieroglyphs on temple walls and other structures in the early Classic Age (300–600 C.E.) (see Figure 3).

Egyptian writing materials. The major surface for writing EGYPTIAN HIEROGLYPHS was papyrus, although many other writing surfaces were sometimes used: ivory, bone, clay tablets (for correspondence in cuneiform with Mesopotamia), leather, parchment and vellum, metal (bronze and lead), pottery, reeds, and wax and plaster on wooden tablets. Writing, especially by students, was also done on fragments of limestone and on potsherds, called *ostraca*.

The original method of making papyrus, which was devised about 3000 B.C.E., is not known. A reasonably similar product has been developed in recent years in Egypt and Sicily. The modern Egyptian method involves harvesting the papyrus plant and slicing the stem into strips, cutting off the cortex but leaving the pith. The soaked pith strips are assembled into cross-laminated layers with overlapped edges, placed between blotters or cloth, and pressed until dry. Papyrus writing material became an important article of trade and commerce in Phoenician and Roman times and continued in use until the end of the first millennium C.E.

The main writing instrument used in Egypt for nearly three millennia was a rush brush. Lengths of ten to fifteen centimeters were cut at one end to a flat, chisel shape and chewed or beaten into a brush. The flat side was used to make coarse lines, and the fine edge was used for fine lines. Starting with the third century B.C.E. the brush was superseded by the split reed pen. In making the pen the end of the hollow reed was cut at an angle and a slit made opposite the cut section. A nib was then shaped on either side of the slit. The reed pen is still used by Islamic calligraphers.

The Egyptian scribe used only two colored inks, black and red. The black ink dates back to the First Dynasty. The pigments were soot from the bottoms of cooking vessels and red ocher (iron oxide), which were finely ground in the depression of a small, rectangular stone, using a cone-shaped stone pestle or a stone spatula. The pigment was mixed with water and a gum binder and dried in a cake form similar to modern watercolors. Painters used the additional colors of white, brown, blue, yellow, and green.

The scribe carried his brush and ink in a rectangular palette of ivory, wood, or alabaster. The brushes and pens were also carried in a special carrying case. The scribal equipment included a knife for reconditioning the writing instruments and a burnisher of ivory or metal to polish the papyrus.

Leather and parchment. Leather, a tanned animal skin, and incompletely tanned skins called parchments were used as writing surfaces in Egypt and elsewhere in the Middle East as early as 2500 B.C.E. Leather was the mandated writing surface for the Talmud and was the most used material in the Dead Sea Scrolls (see Figure 4). The first use of true parchment, an untanned animal skin, is traditionally credited to the reign of King Eumenes II of Pergamum (the origin of the word *parchment*) about 150 B.C.E. However, parchment had begun to replace leather as early as the third century B.C.E. The invention of parchment may have been associated with the shortage and cost of papyrus during the competition between the libraries at Pergamum and Alexandria (under

Figure 2. *(Writing Materials)* Cuneiform writing on a clay tablet from Nippur, Isin period. The University Museum, Philadelphia.

Ptolemy I). Parchment, remaining an important writing surface until the invention of the PRINTING press in the mid-1400s, was made from the skins of sheep, goats, and pigs. Vellum is a fine-grained parchment made from the skins of calves and kids.

Quill pen. The development of parchment, which was much smoother than papyrus, may have led to the evolution of the reed pen into the quill pen. The quill pen was introduced as a writing instrument in the sixth century B.C.E. It was used extensively for over a thousand years until the nineteenth century, when it was replaced by the steel pen, invented in 1800. The best quill pens were made from the first flight feathers of the goose, although feathers of other large birds were also used. The left wing feathers were generally chosen because the curvature best suited a right-handed scribe. The point was fashioned

Figure 3. *(Writing Materials)* Lintel 3 from Piedras Negras, Guatemala. Limestone. The University Museum, Philadelphia.

into a split pen point with nibs similar to those of the reed pen. The quill pen provided a finer line and required sharpening less often than the reed pen. The writing substance used with the quill pen was carbon-based ink.

Innovations in writing implements continued to appear. The use of graphite to make marks on paper was adopted widely only after the late eighteenth century, when graphite for writing was first encased in a wooden holder, the ancestor of the modern pencil. Pens were also continually improved. Several inventors in the late nineteenth and the twentieth centuries explored the possibilities of a rotating metal ball as the point of a pen, but the ballpoint pen was not marketed until immediately after World War II, and the new pen became firmly established as a popular writing implement.

Paper and other Eastern writing surfaces. The invention of paper has been traditionally attributed to Ts'ai Lun, an official in a Chinese court, in 105 C.E., although samples of protopaper dating to the second century B.C.E. have been discovered in recent excavations in central Asia. The earliest paper was made by macerating old rags of hemp and ramie, suspending the separated fibers in a vat of water, and forming a mat on a mesh screen and drying the paper mat. The separated fibers from the inner bark of the mulberry tree were soon introduced. They are used to this day in Japan, in paper known as *kozo* paper (see Figure 5).

Paper was first commercially produced in southeastern China in the early second century C.E. At this

Figure 4. *(Writing Materials)* One of the Dead Sea Scrolls. The partially rolled "Thanksgiving Scroll" contains forty psalmlike hymns all starting with the words, "I thank thee, O Lord." Courtesy of the Consulate General of Israel in New York.

Figure 5. *(Writing Materials)* A Japanese girl grinding mulberry leaves in preparation for making paper from the pulp—one of the oldest papermaking techniques. The Bettmann Archive, Inc.

time the Chinese writing surfaces included silk, bamboo strips, and wooden tablets, probably written on with a camel's-hair brush (invented ca. 250 B.C.E.) and a carbon-based ink. Excavations at watchtowers of the western end of the Great Wall of China have uncovered manuscripts from the eighth century written on paper, bamboo strips, wooden tablets and shavings, and palm leaves.

The technology of papermaking was limited to East Asia in the first half of the eighth century, after which it was introduced to Samarkand in central Asia. Paper manufacture spread south and west during the ensuing centuries, taking its place as the world's major writing surface (see Figure 6). The journey of paper-making techniques from China to the rest of the world is shown in Figure 7.

The papermaking process changed at Samarkand, where the use of cotton and flax fibers was introduced. The writing instrument also changed, with the Chinese animal-hair brush giving way to the split reed pen and quill pen. Cotton and flax remained the major papermaking fibers until the development of wood fibers in the middle of the nineteenth century. Paper gained momentum as a replacement for parchment during the expansion of papermaking in the Middle East in the last centuries of the first millennium C.E., and again after the invention of printing about 1440.

Bark, bark paper, and tapa cloth. Bark and bark products were used as writing surfaces by a wide variety of cultures. According to Indic manuscripts, the white bark of the Indian birch tree, growing in the Himalayas, was used as early as the fourth century B.C.E. The bark was first treated with oil and then polished. It was widely used by Buddhists and Hindus. The North American variety of white birch supplied the surface for drawings by some of the American Indians.

Bark paper, or *amate,* was produced in pre-Columbian America by the Mayas and the Aztecs. The bark was stripped from the fig tree, the inner and outer bark separated, and the former boiled in alkali, separated into strands, formed into a grid on

Figure 6. *(Writing Materials)* Papermaking in China. After Sung Ying Hsing. Paper sheets are dried on a wall heated by a stove (right-hand side). The Bettmann Archive, Inc.

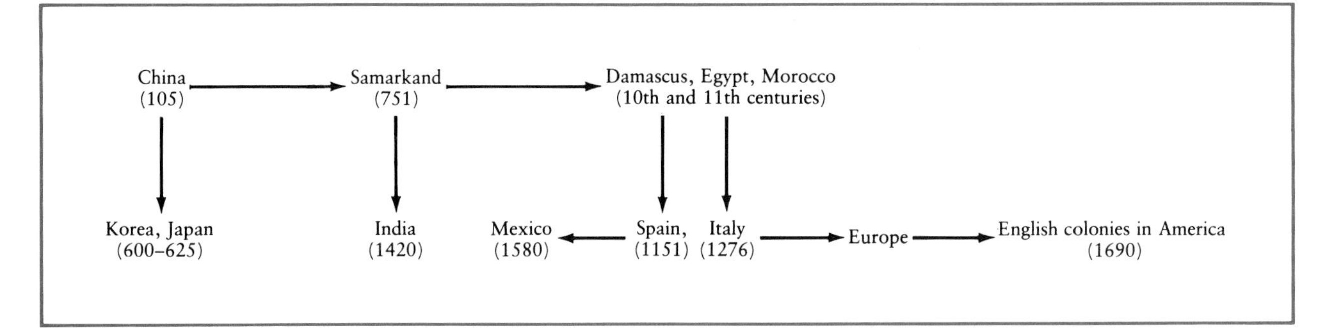

Figure 7. *(Writing Materials)* Spread of papermaking.

a board, beaten into a mat, dried, and covered. Writing implements were tufts of animal hair and an ink or paint made from carbon black and mineral pigments. Stone bark beaters, which have been excavated in various Central American sites, suggest that this paper was made as early as the second century B.C.E. The oldest preserved examples of bark paper date from the fourteenth century. Bark paper is still made from fig tree bark by the Otomi Indians.

Tapa cloth, a product of mulberry tree bark, was first made in the South Pacific islands during the second millennium B.C.E. However, it was originally used as clothing and only later as a writing surface.

Other writing surfaces. Cloth has sometimes been employed as a writing surface. Linen was used in Egypt in the third century B.C.E., as well as by the Etruscans and later the Romans. In India in the fourth century B.C.E., the Hindus used cotton for letters and documents. The cloth was first covered with plaster, then blackened with charcoal, and the marks were made with a white or yellow pigment.

Leaves have also provided a surface for writing. In India and neighboring countries the palm leaf and large leaves from other plants were scratched with a metal stylus. The indentations were then filled with a black pigment in oil. There is evidence that leaves were also employed by the early Egyptians (who used palm leaves), the Greeks about 800 B.C.E., and the Romans (who used olive tree leaves) in the first century B.C.E.

Metals were inscribed with an iron stylus in Sumerian cuneiform from about 1500 B.C.E. Later cuneiform writing systems in Mesopotamia continued this practice. The metals employed were gold, silver, bronze, and copper, which had been fashioned into tablets, figurines, and vessels. The Dead Sea Scrolls include a copper manuscript. Excavations have shown that elsewhere in the ancient world copper arrow and lance heads and buckles were incised. In addition, lead was sometimes used by the Greeks and Romans to fill inscriptions made on wood.

Bone, shell, and skin have also provided surfaces for writing. The earliest examples of Chinese writing, from about 1500 B.C.E., were oracle texts written on bones and on tortoise shells. Other examples include human and bird skins, and—in the case of seventh-century Arabic writings—ostrich shells. Writing paper has been made since 1830 in wood-deficient countries from nonwood plant fibers, including cereal and rice straws, sugar cane bagasse, bamboo reeds, grasses, Manila hemp, and others.

See also AMERICAS, PRE-COLUMBIAN—WRITING SYSTEMS.

Bibliography. George A. Buttrick and Keith R. Crim, eds., *The Interpreter's Dictionary of the Bible,* 5 vols., Nashville, Tenn., 1976; I. J. Gelb, *A Study of Writing,* rev. ed., Chicago, 1963; Dard Hunter, *Papermaking, The History and Technique of an Ancient Craft,* New York, 1943, reprint New York, 1978; Donald Jackson, *The Story of Writing,* New York, 1981; A. Lucas, *Ancient Egyptian Materials and Industries,* 4th ed., rev. and enl. by J. R. Harris, London, 1962; Alexander Marshack, *The Roots of Civilization,* New York, 1972; Ronald Reed, *The Nature and Making of Parchment,* Leeds, Eng., 1975; Keith N. Schoville and Martha L. Carter, eds., *Sign, Symbol, Script: An Exhibition on the Origins of Writing and the Alphabet,* Madison, Wis., 1984; Charles Singer, ed., *A History of Technology,* Vol. 1, Oxford, 1954.

J. N. MCGOVERN

Z (zed), the twenty-sixth and last letter of the English and other modern alphabets, derives its form, through the medium of the Latin and Greek alphabets, from the Phœnician and ancient Hebrew ⌶ Ƶ Z (Hebrew ז *zayin*); in the Phœnician, Greek, and earlier Roman alphabets it was the seventh letter, in the later Roman alphabet the twenty-third.

ZENGER, JOHN PETER (1697–1746)

Colonial New York printer who was the defendant in a trial popularly regarded as a landmark in the struggle for freedom of the press. Born in Germany, John Peter Zenger emigrated with his family to New York in 1710. His father died on shipboard, and his mother apprenticed the fourteen-year-old Zenger the following year to William Bradford, New York's first printer. After fulfilling his indentures Zenger followed his trade in Maryland. Returning to New York after the death of his first wife, Zenger was married a second time, to Anna Maulin, and in 1725 went into partnership with Bradford. Then in 1726 Zenger started his own PRINTING business. He subsisted principally on overflow from Bradford's press, but before long events overtook him.

In 1732 William Cosby was named governor of the colony and established an autocratic administration, alienating the assembly, the merchant class, and many of the city's attorneys. He took the interim governor who had preceded him, Rip Van Dam, to court to reclaim the wages Van Dam had been paid. When the court found for Van Dam, Cosby deposed its chief justice, Lewis Morris. Morris and two of his associates, James Alexander and William Smith, decided to publish a newspaper whose aim would be to attack the governor.

At that time Bradford published New York's only paper, the *Gazette,* the official organ of the government, controlled by Cosby and edited by one of his subordinates. Morris approached Zenger, who was pleased enough to have the business, and an opposition paper, the *New-York Weekly Journal,* began publication in November 1733. From the first the *Journal* took an independent, truculent tone, publishing accounts of Cosby's machinations, articles on LIBEL and freedom of the press, and attacks (sometimes disguised as advertisements) on Cosby's cronies. The anonymous editor and author of most of the *Journal* articles was Alexander, the intellectual leader of the colony. Although it was plain that the newspaper could not have been written by Zenger, whose English was poor, Cosby seized Zenger as the responsible publisher and had him thrown in jail.

Since the editor was still at large, the *Journal* continued to appear and to attack the governor. The printing was carried out by Zenger's wife, who took instructions from him through the door of his cell. When Zenger was arraigned for libel in April 1735 his attorneys challenged the jurisdiction of the court (whose justices had been appointed by Cosby) and were promptly disbarred. Zenger came to trial in August with other counsel, but when his case was called, Andrew Hamilton, at eighty the most famous attorney in the colonies, stood to announce that he would represent Zenger. His appearance had been arranged by Alexander.

By his Excellency

William Cosby, Captain General and Governour in Chief of the Provinces of *New-York*, *New-Jerſey*, and Territories thereon depending, in America, Vice-Admiral of the ſame, and Colonel in His Majeſty's Army.

A PROCLAMATION.

WHereas by the Contrivance of ſome evil Diſpoſed and Diſaffected Perſons, divers Journals or Printed News Papers, (entitled, *The New-York Weekly Journal, containing the freſheſt Advices, Foreign and Domeſtick*) have been cauſed to be Printed and Publiſhed by *John Peter Zenger*, in many of which Journals or Printed News-Papers (but more particularly thoſe Numbred 7, 47, 48, 49) are contained divers Scandalous, Virulent, Falſe and Seditious Reflections, not only upon the whole Legiſlature, in general, and upon the moſt conſiderable Perſons in the moſt diſtinguiſh'd Stations in this Province, but alſo upon His Majeſty's lawful and rightful Government, and juſt Prerogative. Which ſaid Reflections ſeem contrived by the wicked Authors of them, not only to create Jealouſies, Diſcontents and Animoſities in the Minds of his Majeſty's Leige People of this Province, to the Subverſion of the Peace & Tranquility thereof, but to alienate their Affections from the beſt of Kings, and raiſe *Factions, Tumults* and *Sedition* among them. *Wherefore* I have thought fit, by and with the Advice of His Majeſty's Council, to iſſue this Proclamation, hereby Promiſing a Reward of *Fifty Pounds* to ſuch Perſon or Perſons who ſhall diſcover the Author or Authors of the ſaid *Scandalous, Virulent* and *Seditious Reflections* contained in the ſaid *Journals* or *Printed News-Papers*, to be paid to the Perſon or Perſons diſcovering the ſame, as ſoon as ſuch Author or Authors ſhall be Convicted of having been the Author or Authors thereof.

GIVEN under My Hand and Seal at Fort-George *in* New-York *this Sixth Day of* November, *in the Eighth year of the Reign of Our Sovereign Lord* GEORGE *the Second, by the Grace of GOD, of* Great-Britain, France *and* Ireland, *KING Defender of the Faith, &c. and in the Year of Our LORD* 1734.

By his Excellency's Command, *Fred. Morris*, D. Cl. Conc. — *W. COSBY.*

GOD Save the KING

Figure 1. *(Zenger, John Peter)* Governor William Cosby's proclamation offering a reward for the conviction of the authors of scandalous articles appearing in John Peter Zenger's papers, 1734. Historical Pictures Service, Chicago.

Astonishing the court by granting that Zenger had indeed printed the offending passages, Hamilton based his case on the then novel notion that an attack on the government could not be libelous if it could be shown to be true. This defense was disallowed by the court, but Hamilton appealed directly to the jury, pleading with them to decide not only whether Zenger had printed the allegedly libelous numbers of the *Journal* but also whether they in fact constituted libel—in other words, to judge rather than merely to apply the existing law. His eloquence persuaded the jury, who returned a verdict of not guilty, and Zenger was set free to the acclaim of the spectators.

Despite its notoriety this case had little immediate effect either on the law concerning libel or on freedom of the press. The laws of libel that had been received from England continued until the end of the century, and those who criticized constituted officials could be convicted of libel without regard for whether the charges were true. But there can be no denying that a formidable symbolic value surrounds Zenger. He stands for freedom of the press to report events responsibly, whether or not the reportage criticizes the government; for the principle that truth is not libel; and for the right of the citizen to seek redress against a tyrannical government.

See also CENSORSHIP; GOVERNMENT-MEDIA RELATIONS; LAW AND COMMUNICATION; NEWSPAPER: HISTORY; POLITICAL COMMUNICATION.

Bibliography. James Alexander, *A Brief Narrative of the Case and Trial of John Peter Zenger, Printer of the "New York Weekly Journal,"* ed. by Stanley Nider Katz, Cambridge, Mass., 1963; Leonard W. Levy, ed., *Freedom of the Press from Zenger to Jefferson: Early American Libertarian Theories,* Indianapolis, Ind., 1966.

ROBERT BALAY

ZUKOR, ADOLPH (1873–1976)

Motion picture pioneer whose career, more than any other, symbolized the evolution of U.S. film enterprise from penny arcade beginnings to world dominion exercised from a new metropolis, HOLLYWOOD. Adolph Zukor was born in Hungary and entered the United States at sixteen amid the surge of immigrants at the turn of the century. Along with Carl Laemmle, William Fox, and Marcus Loew, among others, he wrested control of the fledgling film industry from the Motion Picture Patents Company and, within a few decades, transformed it into an oligopoly with virtual hegemony over the world's screens. *See* MOTION PICTURES.

Zukor entered the fur trade in New York. After acquiring a penny arcade in 1903, he plunged into motion picture exhibition during the nickelodeon craze, ultimately joining Marcus Loew Enterprises in 1910. In 1912 Zukor experimented with feature films by distributing *Queen Elizabeth,* a French import starring Sarah Bernhardt. The success of this venture led him to form a production company called Famous Players in Famous Plays in association with Broadway impresario Daniel Frohman. The goal was to produce filmed versions of theatrical hits.

To secure wider distribution for his pictures, in 1914 Zukor became aligned with Paramount Pictures, the industry's first national distributor of feature films. In 1916 he ousted Paramount chief W. W. Hodkinson, whose conservative business philosophy was not to Zukor's taste. Zukor thereupon merged Famous Players with Jesse L. Lasky's production company and other Paramount suppliers to form the Famous Players-Lasky Corporation. Paramount became the distribution arm of the new company. Zukor signed up top STARS, such as Mary Pickford, Douglas Fairbanks, Gloria Swanson, Fatty Arbuckle, and William S. Hart, and used their box-office power to raise film rentals and implement the practice of block booking. These tactics enabled Zukor to expand his production program and by 1918 to create the largest motion picture corporation in the world.

Exhibitor resistance to these tactics persuaded Zukor to branch out into the theater business. With backing from a Wall Street banking firm, he ignited the "battle for theaters" in 1919 by buying out important houses in New England, the South, and the Midwest. By 1926 Famous Players-Lasky controlled more than a thousand theaters, which Zukor consolidated under the name Publix Theaters Corporation. The alleged strong-arm tactics and freeze-out threats employed by Zukor's associates to acquire the chain led to an investigation by the Federal Trade Commission in 1927. Although nothing came of it, the seed of antitrust action that later resulted

Figure 1. *(Zukor, Adolph)* Adolph Zukor with Mary Pickford. The Museum of Modern Art/Film Stills Archive.

in the historic *United States* v. *Paramount Pictures, Inc., et al.* had been planted (*see* MONOPOLY).

The depression forced Paramount Pictures (as Famous Players-Lasky now called itself) into bankruptcy in 1933, and Zukor saw his company slip from his control. After the company was reorganized by the banks in 1935, he was promoted to board chairman. Although Zukor headed Paramount's studio operations for a while, the position became largely honorific. From 1964 until his death at the age of 103, he held the title of board chairman emeritus.

Bibliography. Will Irwin, *The House That Shadows Built,* New York, 1928, reprint 1970; Adolph Zukor and Dale Kramer, *The Public Is Never Wrong,* New York, 1953.

TINO BALIO

ZWORYKIN, VLADIMIR K. (1889–1982)

U.S. electrical engineer whose international career spanned the first half-century of television and contributed to its technical evolution at almost every stage (*see* TELEVISION HISTORY). Vladimir Kosma Zworykin's most significant work was done at the Radio Corporation of America (RCA), where, under the leadership of president DAVID SARNOFF, he played a major role in the advent of electronic television, the development of color television, and the application of television technology to numerous military projects.

Figure 1. *(Zworykin, Vladimir K.)* Vladimir K. Zworykin with the iconoscope tube. UPI/Bettmann Newsphotos.

Like Sarnoff, Zworykin was born in Russia. In 1912 he completed studies at the St. Petersburg Institute of Technology under Boris Rosing, who was already pursuing experiments toward an electronic (as opposed to mechanical) television system. After two years in France studying X rays under the physicist Paul Langevin, Zworykin returned to Russia at the outbreak of World War I to work on RADIO for the Russian Signal Corps. In 1919, after a period of travel, he settled in the United States, finding work the following year with the Westinghouse Electric Corporation. He hoped to experiment with television, but it was years before he was encouraged to do so.

In 1924 his demonstration for colleagues of what he called an iconoscope, a first attempt at a television camera, had a disastrous staff reception. But by November 1929 he had improved it and had developed the kinescope, a receiver for images sent by the iconoscope. At this point Sarnoff arranged for Zworykin to be transferred to RCA to head its electronic research staff in Camden, New Jersey. For Sarnoff, newly installed as president of RCA—which owned two radio networks and dominated both the broadcasting and set-manufacturing industries—television was the next step. RCA appeared to control almost all relevant patents, and in 1930 television was first mentioned in its annual report.

That was also the year that PHILO FARNSWORTH was granted a patent for an all-electronic television system. Sarnoff and Zworykin went to observe his achievement, including the image-dissector tube that corresponded to Zworykin's iconoscope, and announced that they would not need anything Farnsworth had done, but they apparently concluded otherwise. Years of patent challenges, hearings, and negotiations were finally resolved by a cross-licensing agreement. The television system that debuted at the 1939 New York World's Fair was an amalgam of Zworykin and Farnsworth contributions.

World War II halted telecasting and the manufacture of sets, and the new wonder disappeared for a number of years from public view. Yet the war years were among the most important of Zworykin's career, as military contracts poured billions of dollars into electronic development, revolutionizing television technology. When the medium reappeared after the war, the difference was at once visible in the sharper images that came from Zworykin's new image orthicon pickup tube.

In 1946 public interest was already focusing on color television issues, as the Columbia Broadcasting System (CBS) sought the approval of the Federal Communications Commission (FCC) for a vivid color system it had developed. But this used a revolving "color wheel" and was incompatible with existing sets, bringing scornful denunciation from Sarnoff. RCA, he said, would never allow such a "counterfeit scheme" to be foisted on the public. To block approval he told the FCC that within six months RCA engineers would demonstrate an electronic color system compatible with existing black-and-white sets. Asked how he knew they could have it ready, Sarnoff said, "I told them to." It was Sarnoff's style of leadership—and Zworykin's staff made good the boast.

The quantum leap in electronics that had made the home television boom possible had also revolutionized military technology. RCA's involvement in this had begun as early as 1934, when Zworykin prepared a monograph on a "flying torpedo with an electric eye," capable of being guided to its target from land or sea. Sarnoff and Zworykin began meeting with naval personnel, presenting RCA as the organization best able to solve problems of communication, reconnaissance, detection, and missile guidance. Early in the war Zworykin developed for the U.S. Army an infrared device that was attached to rifles to enable snipers to find targets in the dark. RCA equipment began to guide pilotless planes, to survey enemy terrain, and, after the war, to monitor atomic tests. In the postwar decade such innovations continued in profusion, as military revenue became the chief source of RCA income and television electronics became the "eyes and ears of the battlefield."

Bibliography. Kenneth Bilby, *The General: David Sarnoff and the Rise of the Communications Industry,* New York, 1986; Robert Sobel, *RCA,* New York, 1986; Vladimir K. Zworykin, "The Early Days: Some Recollections," *Television Quarterly* 1 (1962): 69–73; Vladimir K. Zworykin and Earl D. Wilson, *Photocells and Their Application,* 2d ed., New York, 1930, reprint 1937; Vladimir K. Zworykin, E. G. Ramberg, and L. E. Flory, *Television in Science and Industry,* New York, 1958.

JEANNE THOMAS ALLEN

Directory of Contributors

YEHIA ABOUBAKR
President, International Information and Communications Consultants, Cairo, Egypt, and West Windsor, N.J.
ISLAMIC WORLD, TWENTIETH CENTURY

ROGER D. ABRAHAMS
Professor of Folklore and Folklife, University of Pennsylvania
INSULT

JAMES S. ACKERMAN
Arthur Kingsley Porter Professor of Fine Arts, Harvard University
RENAISSANCE

HAZARD ADAMS
Professor of English and Comparative Literature, University of Washington
LITERARY CRITICISM

JEANNE THOMAS ALLEN
Associate Professor of Communications, Temple University
SARNOFF, DAVID; ZWORYKIN, VLADIMIR K.

DUDLEY ANDREW
Professor of Comparative Literature and Director, Institute for Cinema and Culture, University of Iowa
FILM THEORY

PAUL A. V. ANSAH
Associate Professor and Director, School of Communication Studies, University of Ghana
AFRICA, TWENTIETH CENTURY

VALENTINE APPEL
Senior Vice-President, Backer Spielvogel Bates Inc., New York
MOTIVATION RESEARCH

MAHADEV L. APTE
Professor of Anthropology, Duke University
HUMOR

MICHAEL ARGYLE
Reader in Social Psychology and Fellow of Wolfson College, University of Oxford
SOCIAL SKILLS

RUDOLF ARNHEIM
Professor Emeritus of the Psychology of Art, Harvard University
SCULPTURE

CARROLL C. ARNOLD
Professor Emeritus of Speech Communication, Pennsylvania State University
RHETORIC

PETER D. ARNOTT
Professor of Drama, Tufts University
PUPPETRY

PERRY J. ASHLEY
Professor of Journalism, University of South Carolina
BENNETT, JAMES GORDON; GREELEY, HORACE

DEREK ATTRIDGE
Professor of English, Rutgers University, New Brunswick
POETRY

RALPH A. AUSTEN
Professor of African History, University of Chicago
AFRICA, PRECOLONIAL

BARBARA A. BABCOCK
Professor of English, University of Arizona
ARTIFACT

EUGEN BAER
Professor of Philosophy, Hobart and William Smith Colleges
COMMUNICATION, PHILOSOPHIES OF

BEN H. BAGDIKIAN
Dean, Graduate School of Journalism, University of California, Berkeley
MONOPOLY

RICHARD P. BAGOZZI
Dwight F. Benton Professor of Marketing and Professor of Behavioral Science in Management, University of Michigan, Ann Arbor
ATTITUDES

BISHARA A. BAHBAH
Adjunct Professor of Political Science, Brigham Young University; former Editor in Chief, *Al-Fajr,* Jerusalem
NEWSPAPER: TRENDS—TRENDS IN THE MIDDLE EAST

ROBERT BALAY
Reference Editor, *Choice Magazine,* New York
BABBAGE, CHARLES; KELLER, HELEN; LAND, EDWIN; MORSE, SAMUEL F. B.; OCHS, ADOLPH S.; WEBSTER, NOAH; ZENGER, JOHN PETER

TINO BALIO
Professor of Communication Arts, University of Wisconsin–Madison
HOLLYWOOD; ZUKOR, ADOLPH

ALBERT BANDURA
David Starr Jordan Professor of Social Science in Psychology, Stanford University
SOCIAL COGNITIVE THEORY

ALAN W. BARNETT
Professor of Humanities, San Jose State University
MURAL

JOHN BARNICOAT
Pro-Rector, London Institute, and Head, Chelsea School of Art, London
POSTER

ERIK BARNOUW
Professor Emeritus of Dramatic Arts, Columbia University
DOCUMENTARY; ENTERTAINMENT; LASKER, ALBERT; LUMIÈRE, LOUIS AND AUGUSTE; MUSICAL, FILM—BOMBAY GENRE; SOAP OPERA; SPONSOR; SYNDICATION; TELEVISION HISTORY—EARLY PERIOD; WELLES, ORSON

DENNIS BARON
Professor of English and Linguistics, University of Illinois at Urbana-Champaign
LANGUAGE REFERENCE BOOK

RICHARD BAUMAN
Professor of Folklore and Anthropology and Chair, Folklore Institute, Indiana University
FOLKLORE; PERFORMANCE

JOHN BAYLEY
Thomas Warton Professor of English Literature, Saint Catherine's College, University of Oxford
FICTION, PORTRAYAL OF CHARACTER IN

ALAN M. BECK
Director, Center for the Interaction of Animals and Society, School of Veterinary Medicine, University of Pennsylvania
HUMAN-ANIMAL COMMUNICATION

HOWARD S. BECKER
MacArthur Professor of Arts and Sciences, Northwestern University
ARTIST AND SOCIETY

KARIN E. BECKER
Associate Professor of Journalism and Mass Communication, University of Iowa
PHOTOJOURNALISM

COLIN G. BEER
Professor of Psychology, Institute of Animal Behavior, Rutgers University, Newark
DARWIN, CHARLES; ETHOLOGY

GERARD HENRI BÉHAGUE
Professor of Ethnomusicology and Chair, Department of Music, University of Texas at Austin
MUSIC PERFORMANCE

LUIS RAMIRO BELTRÁN S.
Bolivian communication specialist and scholar, Quito
DEVELOPMENT COMMUNICATION—ALTERNATIVE SYSTEMS

DAN BEN-AMOS
Professor of Folklore and Folklife, University of Pennsylvania
FOLKTALE

ARTHUR ASA BERGER
Professor of Broadcast Communication Arts, San Francisco State University
COMMERCIALS

NORMAND BERLIN
Professor of English, University of Massachusetts at Amherst
TRAGEDY

JERRY J. BERMAN
Chief Legislative Counsel, American Civil Liberties Union, Washington, D.C.
PRIVACY

JACQUES BERTIN
Director, Laboratoire de Graphique, École des Hautes Études en Sciences Sociales
GRAPHICS

RAYMOND F. BETTS
Professor of History, University of Kentucky
COLONIZATION

JOHN BLACKING
Professor of Social Anthropology, Queen's University of Belfast
ETHNOMUSICOLOGY

STEPHEN BLUM
Professor of Ethnomusicology, Graduate Center, City University of New York
MUSIC HISTORY

JAY G. BLUMLER
Director, Centre for Television Research, University of Leeds; Associate Director, Center for Research in Public Communication, University of Maryland at College Park
PRESSURE GROUP

S. T. KWAME BOAFO
Lecturer, School of Communication Studies, University of Ghana
KENYATTA, JOMO; NKRUMAH, KWAME

ARTHUR P. BOCHNER
Professor of Communication, University of South Florida
INTERPERSONAL COMMUNICATION

LEO BOGART
Executive Vice-President and General Manager, Newspaper Advertising Bureau, New York
ADVERTISING—OVERVIEW

PETER BONDANELLA
Professor of Italian Studies, Indiana University
NEOREALISM

GERALD BORDMAN
Writer, Nottingham, Pa.
MUSIC THEATER—WESTERN TRADITIONS

DAVID BORDWELL
Professor of Communication Arts, University of Wisconsin–Madison
CINEMATOGRAPHY

TOM BOTTOMORE
Professor Emeritus of Sociology, University of Sussex
ADORNO, THEODOR; GRAMSCI, ANTONIO; MARX, KARL; MARXIST THEORIES OF COMMUNICATION—ORIGINS AND DEVELOPMENT

FAUBION BOWERS
Writer, New York
MUSIC THEATER—ASIAN TRADITIONS

DEIRDRE BOYLE
Senior Faculty Member in Media Studies, New School for Social Research, New York; Adjunct Lecturer, Fordham University, College at Lincoln Center
VIDEO

JOHN G. BRAINERD
University Professor Emeritus and former Director, Moore School of Electrical Engineering, University of Pennsylvania
FARADAY, MICHAEL; FARNSWORTH, PHILO; MAXWELL, JAMES

LEO BRAUDY
Leo S. Bing Professor of English, University of Southern California
SERIAL

ERNEST BRAUN
Professor Emeritus, Aston University
MICROELECTRONICS

MARTA BRAUN
Professor of Film and Photography, Ryerson Polytechnical Institute
MOTION PHOTOGRAPHY

JACK W. BREHM
Professor of Psychology, University of Kansas
COGNITIVE CONSISTENCY THEORIES

ERNST BREISACH
Professor of History, Western Michigan University
HISTORIOGRAPHY

DONALD BRENNEIS
Professor of Anthropology, Pitzer College
GOSSIP

ASA BRIGGS
Provost, Worcester College, University of Oxford
CULTURE; PUBLISHING—HISTORY OF PUBLISHING

GLEN DAVID BRIN
Associate, California Space Institute and Scripps Institution of Oceanography, University of California, San Diego
CETI

VIRGINIA L. BROOKS
Associate Professor of Film, Brooklyn College, City University of New York
PERCEPTION—STILL AND MOVING PICTURES

MARILYN A. BROWN
Group Leader, Evaluation and Technology Transfer, Oak Ridge National Laboratory, Oak Ridge, Tenn.
DIFFUSION

DONALD R. BROWNE
Professor of Speech Communication, University of Minnesota, Twin Cities
RADIO, INTERNATIONAL

EDWARD M. BRUNER
Professor of Anthropology, University of Illinois at Urbana-Champaign
TOURISM

DAYNA E. BUCK
Assistant to the Director, Library Programs, Office of Educational Research and Improvement, U.S. Department of Education, Washington, D.C.
LIBRARY—TRENDS

PETER BURKE
Reader in Cultural History and Fellow of Emmanuel College, University of Cambridge
PORTRAITURE

JOSEPH CADY
Member of the Faculty, New School for Social Research, New York
GALLAUDET, THOMAS; JAMES, WILLIAM; LUTHER, MARTIN; RICHARDS, I. A.

JAMES W. CAREY
Dean, College of Communications, University of Illinois at Urbana-Champaign
INNIS, HAROLD

JOHN CAREY
Director, Greystone Communications, Dobbs Ferry, N.Y.
INTERACTIVE MEDIA

MARVIN A. CARLSON
Sidney E. Cohen Professor of Theatre Studies and Distinguished Professor of Theatre and Comparative Literature, Graduate Center, City University of New York
THEATER

ROBERT OSKAR CARLSON
Associate Professor of Management and Business Policy, Adelphi University
PUBLIC RELATIONS

NOËL CARROLL
Associate Professor of Philosophy, Cornell University
FILM EDITING

JOHN G. CAWELTI
Professor of English, University of Kentucky
WESTERN, THE

COURTNEY BORDEN CAZDEN
Professor of Education, Harvard University
CLASSROOM

JANET SALTZMAN CHAFETZ
Professor of Sociology, University of Houston
SEXISM—OVERVIEW; SEXISM—SEXISM IN INTERPERSONAL COMMUNICATION

C. DAVID CHAFFEE
Executive Editor, *Superconductor Week*, Atlantic Information Services, Inc., Washington, D.C.
FIBER OPTICS

STEVEN H. CHAFFEE
Janet M. Peck Professor of International Communication and Chair, Department of Communication, Stanford University
ELECTION

RICHARD M. CHALFEN
Associate Professor of Anthropology, Temple University
PHOTOGRAPHY, AMATEUR

JEANNE S. CHALL
Professor of Education and Director, Reading Laboratory, Harvard University
READING

DAVID CHANEY
Senior Lecturer in Sociology, University of Durham
MASS OBSERVATION

MAURICE CHARNEY
Distinguished Professor of English, Rutgers University, New Brunswick
COMEDY

JACK CHEN (CHEN I-WAN)
President, The Pear Garden in the West, San Francisco; former Consultant Editor, *Peking Review,* Beijing
CONFUCIUS; SHIHUANG DI

MILTON CHEN
Director of Instructional Television, KQED-San Francisco
COMPUTER: IMPACT—IMPACT ON EDUCATION

CLIFFORD G. CHRISTIANS
Research Professor of Communications, University of Illinois at Urbana-Champaign
ETHICS, MEDIA

GODWIN C. CHU
Assistant Director, Institute of Culture and Communication, East-West Center, Honolulu
SCHRAMM, WILBUR

T. MATTHEW CIOLEK
Programmer, Computing Services Unit, Research School of Social Sciences, Australian National University
PROXEMICS; SPATIAL ORGANIZATION

JAY J. COAKLEY
Professor of Sociology, University of Colorado at Colorado Springs
SPORTS—SPORTS AND THE MEDIA

JEREMY COHEN
Assistant Professor of Communication, Stanford University
LIBEL

TED COHEN
Professor of Philosophy, University of Chicago
REPRESENTATION, PICTORIAL AND PHOTOGRAPHIC

GEORGE COMSTOCK
S. I. Newhouse Professor of Public Communication, Syracuse University
VIOLENCE

JOHN CONDON
Professor of Communication, University of New Mexico
SEMANTICS, GENERAL

DAVID A. COOK
Professor of Theater and Film Studies, Emory University
MOTION PICTURES—SOUND FILM

JERROLD S. COOPER
Professor of Near Eastern Studies, Johns Hopkins University
CUNEIFORM; NINEVEH; WRITING

IRVING CRESPI
Consultant, Irving Crespi and Associates, Princeton, N.J.
POLL

JAMES STEVENS CURL
Architectural historian, School of Architecture, Leicester Polytechnic
ART, FUNERARY

ALEXANDER CUTHBERT
Assistant Professor of Education, Virginia Polytechnic Institute
EDUCATION

R. P. CUZZORT
Professor of Sociology, University of Colorado at Boulder
DURKHEIM, ÉMILE; SCHUTZ, ALFRED; TARDE, JEAN-GABRIEL DE; WEBER, MAX

DANIEL J. CZITROM
Associate Professor of History, Mount Holyoke College
DEWEY, JOHN

JOHN H. D'ARMS
G. F. Else Professor of Classical Studies, Professor of History, and Dean, H. H. Rackham School of Graduate Studies, University of Michigan, Ann Arbor
ROMAN EMPIRE

REGNA DARNELL
Professor of Anthropology, University of Alberta
SAPIR, EDWARD; WHORF, BENJAMIN LEE

CHIDANANDA DAS GUPTA
Arts Editor, *The Telegraph,* Calcutta
AŚOKA; GANDHI, MOHANDAS; PHALKE, DHUNDIRAJ GOVIND

DENNIS K. DAVIS
Professor of Speech Communication, Southern Illinois University at Carbondale
OPINION LEADER

LENNARD J. DAVIS
Associate Professor of English, Brandeis University
FICTION

W. PHILLIPS DAVISON
Professor Emeritus of Journalism and Sociology, Columbia University
CANTRIL, HADLEY; LIPPMANN, WALTER; PUBLIC OPINION

ROBERT DE BEAUGRANDE
Professor of Linguistics and English, Institute for the Psychological Study of the Arts, University of Florida
TRANSLATION, LITERARY

JACK DENNIS
Hawkins Professor of Political Science, University of Wisconsin–Madison
POLITICAL SOCIALIZATION

DIANA DEUTSCH
Research Psychologist, University of California, San Diego
PERCEPTION—MUSIC

WILSON P. DIZARD
Senior Fellow, Center for Strategic and International Studies, Washington, D.C.
TELEVISION HISTORY—GLOBAL DEVELOPMENT

LUBOMIR DOLEŽEL
Professor of Slavic and Comparative Literature, University of Toronto
POETICS

ZOLTAN DOMOTOR
Professor of Philosophy, University of Pennsylvania
SYMBOLIC LOGIC

LEONARD W. DOOB
Sterling Professor Emeritus of Psychology, Yale University
PROPAGANDA

MARGARET ANNE DOODY
Professor of English, Princeton University
REALISM

R. G. DOTY
Curator, National Numismatic Collection, National Museum of American History, Smithsonian Institution, Washington, D.C.
COINS

RICHARD B. DU BOFF
Professor of Economics, Bryn Mawr College
TELEGRAPHY

STARKEY DUNCAN, JR.
Professor of Behavioral Sciences, University of Chicago
INTERACTION, FACE-TO-FACE

DONALD A. DUNN
Professor of Engineering-Economic Systems, Stanford University
COMPUTER: HISTORY

ALESSANDRO DURANTI
Assistant Professor of Anthropology, University of California, Los Angeles
ORATORY

RAYMOND DURGNAT
Tutor in Cultural History, Royal College of Art, London
SPY FICTION—HISTORY

WILLIAM H. DUTTON
Associate Professor of Communications and Public Administration, University of Southern California
COMPUTER: IMPACT—IMPACT ON GOVERNMENT; POLITICAL COMMUNICATION—IMPACT OF NEW MEDIA

RICHARD DYER
Senior Lecturer in Film Studies, University of Warwick
STARS—THE STAR PHENOMENON

TERRY EAGLETON
Fellow and Tutor in English, Wadham College, University of Oxford
BARTHES, ROLAND; BENJAMIN, WALTER; FOUCAULT, MICHEL; READING THEORY; STRUCTURALISM

VICTORIA EBIN
Équipe de Recherche en Anthropologie Urbaine et Industrielle, École des Hautes Études en Sciences Sociales
BODY DECORATION

HEYWARD EHRLICH
Associate Professor of English, Rutgers University, Newark
ROPER, ELMO

ELIZABETH L. EISENSTEIN
Alice Freeman Palmer Professor of History, University of Michigan, Ann Arbor
PRINTING—CULTURAL IMPACT OF PRINTING

PAUL EKMAN
Professor of Psychology, University of California, San Francisco
FACIAL EXPRESSION

JAVIER A. ELGUEA S.
Associate Professor of Sociology, Colegio de México
WITTGENSTEIN, LUDWIG

PHOEBE C. ELLSWORTH
Professor of Psychology and Professor of Law, University of Michigan, Ann Arbor
EYES

WERNER ENNINGER
Professor of English (Linguistics), Universität Essen
CLOTHING

MARTIN L. ERNST
Vice-President, Arthur D. Little, Inc., Cambridge, Mass.
COMPUTER: IMPACT—IMPACT ON COMMERCE

DEBORAH L. ESTRIN
Assistant Professor of Computer Science, University of Southern California
STANDARDS

FRANK B. EVANS
Deputy Assistant Archivist for Records Administration, National Archives and Records Administration, Washington, D.C.
ARCHIVES

STUART B. EWEN
Professor of Media Studies and Chair, Communications Department, Hunter College; Professor of Sociology, Graduate Center, City University of New York
ADVERTISING—HISTORY OF ADVERTISING

BRENDA FARNELL
Research Assistant, American Indian Studies Research Institute, Indiana University
BODY MOVEMENT NOTATION

STEVEN FELD
Associate Professor of Anthropology and Music and Director, Center for Intercultural Studies in Folklore and Ethnomusicology, University of Texas at Austin
MUSIC THEORIES—TUNING SYSTEMS; SOUND

JOHN L. FELL
Professor Emeritus of Film, San Francisco State University
MOTION PICTURES—PREHISTORY

GARY D. FENSTERMACHER
Dean, College of Education, University of Arizona
EDUCATION

JANE FEUER
Associate Professor of English, University of Pittsburgh
MUSICAL, FILM—HOLLYWOOD GENRE

RAYMOND FIELDING
Professor of Communication, University of Houston
NEWSREEL; SPECIAL EFFECTS

GARY ALAN FINE
Professor of Sociology, University of Minnesota, Twin Cities
FORGERY, ART

MOSES I. FINLEY
Professor Emeritus of Ancient History and Honorary Fellow of Darwin College, University of Cambridge
HELLENIC WORLD

RUTH FINNEGAN
Reader in Comparative Social Institutions, Open University, Milton Keynes, England
ORAL POETRY

CHARLES M. FIRESTONE
Adjunct Professor of Law, University of California, Los Angeles; attorney, Mitchell, Silberberg & Knupp, Los Angeles
MILTON, JOHN

B. AUBREY FISHER
Professor of Communication, University of Utah
GROUP COMMUNICATION

PHILIP FISHER
Professor of English and American Literature, Brandeis University
MUSEUM

JOHN FISKE
Professor of Communication Arts, University of Wisconsin–Madison
CODE

JOHN M. FLETCHER
Reader in the History of European Universities, Aston University
UNIVERSITY

CORNELIA BUTLER FLORA
Professor of Sociology, Kansas State University
FOTONOVELA

WILLIAM F. FORE
Assistant General Secretary for Communication, National Council of Churches in the U.S.A., New York
RELIGIOUS BROADCASTING

ADRIAN FORTY
Lecturer, Bartlett School of Architecture and Planning, University College London
DESIGN

ROBERT A. FOTHERGILL
Associate Professor of English, Atkinson College, York University
DIARY

JOHN G. FOUGHT
Associate Professor of Linguistics and Director, Language Analysis Project, University of Pennsylvania
LANGUAGE

MARIOS FOURAKIS
Research Scientist, Central Institute for the Deaf, Saint Louis, Mo.
PERCEPTION—SPEECH

ALASTAIR FOWLER
Regius Professor Emeritus of Rhetoric and English Language, University of Edinburgh; Visiting Professor, University of Virginia
GENRE

ROBERT A. FRADKIN
Assistant Professor of Hebrew, Brown University
JAKOBSON, ROMAN

ALAN J. FRIDLUND
Assistant Professor of Psychology, University of California, Santa Barbara
FACIAL EXPRESSION

MICHAEL G. FRY
Director, School of International Relations, University of Southern California
DIPLOMACY

HANS G. FURTH
Professor of Psychology, Catholic University of America
PIAGET, JEAN

ITZHAK GALNOOR
Professor of Political Science, Hebrew University of Jerusalem
SECRECY

HOWARD E. GARDNER
Professor of Education and Co-Director, Project Zero, Harvard University; Research Psychologist, Veterans Administration Medical Center, Boston
CHILDREN—DEVELOPMENT OF SYMBOLIZATION

NICHOLAS GARNHAM
Professor of Media Studies and Director, Centre for Communication and Information Studies, Polytechnic of Central London
TELECOMMUNICATIONS POLICY

HENRY GEDDES
Associate Researcher, Centro de Estudios sobre Cultura Transnacional, Lima
LATIN AMERICA, TWENTIETH CENTURY

GEORGE GERBNER
Professor of Communications and Dean, The Annenberg School of Communications, University of Pennsylvania
COMMUNICATIONS, STUDY OF

TOMASZ GOBAN-KLAS
Associate Professor of Communications, Uniwersytet Jagielloński
MINORITY MEDIA

JEFFREY H. GOLDSTEIN
Professor of Psychology, Temple University
SPORTS—PSYCHOLOGY OF SPORTS

BARBARA GOMBACH
Former Preceptor, Department of Religion, Columbia University
SOUTH ASIA, ANCIENT

JUDITH GOODE
Professor of Anthropology, Temple University
FOOD

MARK GOODSON
President, Goodson-Todman Productions, New York
QUIZ SHOW

JACK GOODY
Fellow of Saint John's College, University of Cambridge
ORAL CULTURE

ROBERT GORALSKI
Writer, McLean, Va.
ESPIONAGE

MARTIN GORIN
Associate Member, Laboratoire de Psychologie Sociale, École des Hautes Études en Sciences Sociales
CROWD BEHAVIOR

JAMES L. GOULD
Professor of Biology, Princeton University
INSECTS, SOCIAL

HENRY F. GRAFF
Professor of History, Columbia University
NAKAHAMA MANJIRO

JOSEPH F. GRAHAM
Assistant Professor of French, Tulane University
TRANSLATION, THEORIES OF

CHANDLER B. GRANNIS
Contributing Editor, *Publishers Weekly*, New York
BAEDEKER, KARL; GUTENBERG, JOHANNES; LUCE, HENRY; MERGENTHALER, OTTMAR

THOMAS A. GREEN
Associate Professor of Anthropology and English, Texas A&M University
RIDDLE

DONALD GREENE
Professor Emeritus of English, University of Southern California
BIOGRAPHY

PEKKA GRONOW
Director, Suomen Äänitearkisto (Finnish Institute of Recorded Sound), Helsinki
SOUND RECORDING—HISTORY; SOUND RECORDING—INDUSTRY

LARRY GROSS
Professor of Communications, The Annenberg School of Communications, University of Pennsylvania
ART; LÉVI-STRAUSS, CLAUDE; MODE

THOMAS GUBACK
Research Professor of Communication, University of Illinois at Urbana-Champaign
TELEVISION HISTORY—WORLD MARKET STRUGGLES

MICHAEL A. GUILLEN
Instructor in Mathematics and Physics in the Core Curriculum Program, Harvard University
MATHEMATICS

WILLIAM A. HACHTEN
Professor of Journalism and Mass Communication, University of Wisconsin–Madison
NEWSPAPER: TRENDS—TRENDS IN AFRICA

PATRICIA HAGOOD
President and Publisher, Oxbridge Communications, Inc., New York
NEWSLETTER

JACK P. HAILMAN
Professor of Zoology, University of Wisconsin–Madison
ANIMAL SIGNALS—VISIBLE SIGNALS

STUART HALL
Professor of Sociology, Open University, Milton Keynes, England
IDEOLOGY

JAMES D. HALLORAN
Professor and Director, Centre for Mass Communication Research, University of Leicester
DEMONSTRATION

PAUL HAMILTON
Lecturer in English and Fellow of Exeter College, University of Oxford
SYMBOLISM

JOHN G. HANHARDT
Curator of Film and Video, Whitney Museum of American Art, New York
BUÑUEL, LUIS

PHIL HARRIS
Communication Consultant, International Association for Mass Communication Research, Rome
NEWS AGENCIES

GALIT HASAN-ROKEM
Senior Lecturer in Hebrew Literature, Hebrew University of Jerusalem
PROVERB

TERENCE HAWKES
Professor of English, University of Wales, College of Cardiff
AUTHORSHIP

ROBERT P. HAWKINS
Professor of Journalism and Mass Communication, University of Wisconsin–Madison
SELECTIVE RECEPTION

SHIRLEY BRICE HEATH
Professor of English and Linguistics, Stanford University
LANGUAGE IDEOLOGY

PERTTI HEMÁNUS
Professor of Journalism and Mass Communication, Tampereen Yliopisto
NEWSPAPER: TRENDS—TRENDS IN EUROPE

STUART HENRY
Associate Professor of Sociology, Eastern Michigan University
DECEPTION

EDWARD S. HERMAN
Professor of Finance, Wharton School, University of Pennsylvania
DISINFORMATION

PEDRO F. HERNÁNDEZ-RAMOS
Lecturer, The Annenberg School of Communications, University of Pennsylvania
DEVELOPMENT COMMUNICATION—HISTORY AND THEORIES

MARCIA HERNDON
Executive Director, Music Research Institute, Hercules, Calif.
SONG

ROBERT D. HESS
Lee L. Jacks Professor Emeritus of Child Education, Stanford University
FAMILY

GORDON W. HEWES
Professor of Anthropology, University of Colorado at Boulder
BODY MOVEMENT

DELBERT R. HILLERS
Professor of Semitic Languages, Johns Hopkins University
BYBLOS

HILDE T. HIMMELWEIT
Professor Emeritus of Social Psychology, London School of Economics and Political Science, University of London
POLITICAL COMMUNICATION—BROADCAST DEBATES

JERRY R. HOBBS
Senior Computer Scientist, SRI International, Menlo Park, Calif.
ARTIFICIAL INTELLIGENCE

JULIAN HOCHBERG
Professor of Psychology, Columbia University
PERCEPTION—STILL AND MOVING PICTURES

DONALD HOKE
Executive Director, Outagamie County Historical Society, Inc., Appleton, Wisc.
CLOCK

THOMAS B. HOLMES
Director, Music Systems Research, Cherry Hill, N.J.
ELECTRONIC MUSIC; MUSIC MACHINES

MICHAEL HOLQUIST
Professor of Comparative and Russian Literature, Yale University
BAKHTIN, MIKHAIL

MANTLE HOOD
Senior Distinguished Professor of Ethnomusicology, University of Maryland, Baltimore County
MUSIC COMPOSITION AND IMPROVISATION

MAURICE HORN
Writer and editor, New York
COMICS

ROBERT C. HORNIK
Professor of Communications, The Annenberg School of Communications, University of Pennsylvania
DEVELOPMENT COMMUNICATION—PROJECTS

JANE HULTING
Artistic Director and Conductor, Anna Crusis Choir, Philadelphia
MUZAK

LINDA HUTCHEON
Professor of English and Comparative Literature, University of Toronto
INTERTEXTUALITY

HERBERT H. HYMAN
Crowell University Professor Emeritus of the Social Sciences, Wesleyan University
OPINION MEASUREMENT

JONATHAN B. IMBER
Associate Professor of Sociology, Wellesley College
PSYCHOANALYSIS; SULLIVAN, HARRY STACK

STEVEN IZENOUR
Senior Associate, Venturi Rauch & Scott Brown, Philadelphia; Lecturer, School of Architecture, University of Pennsylvania
SIGNAGE

PETER P. JACOBI
Professor of Journalism, Indiana University
NEWSMAGAZINE

DIANE JACOBS
Writer, New York
HITCHCOCK, ALFRED

SUE CURRY JANSEN
Assistant Professor of Communications Studies, Cedar Crest College and Muhlenberg College
CENSORSHIP—NONGOVERNMENT CENSORSHIP

IAN JARVIE
Professor of Philosophy, York University
MARTIAL ARTS FILM

ROBERT E. JOHNSTON
Professor of Psychology, Cornell University
ANIMAL SIGNALS—CHEMICAL SIGNALS

D. B. JONES
Professor of Communication, Drexel University
GRIERSON, JOHN

JANE JORGENSON
Assistant Professor of Communications, Norfolk State University
CHERRY, COLIN; VON NEUMANN, JOHN; WEAVER, WARREN

ESTELLE JUSSIM
Professor for Visual Communication, Graduate School of Library and Information Science, Simmons College
GRAPHIC REPRODUCTION

JOHN S. JUSTESON
Lecturer, Department of Anthropology, Stanford University
AMERICAS, PRE-COLUMBIAN—WRITING SYSTEMS

ADRIENNE L. KAEPPLER
Curator of Oceanic Ethnology, National Museum of Natural History, Smithsonian Institution, Washington, D.C.
DANCE

FRANK A. KAFKER
Professor of History, University of Cincinnati
ENCYCLOPEDIA

CHARLES H. KAHN
Professor of Philosophy, University of Pennsylvania
ARISTOTLE; PLATO

DAVID KAHN
Great Neck, N.Y.
CRYPTOLOGY

AARON H. KATCHER
Associate Professor of Psychiatry, University of Pennsylvania
HUMAN-ANIMAL COMMUNICATION

ELIHU KATZ
Professor of Sociology and Communications, Hebrew University of Jerusalem; Distinguished Visiting Professor, The Annenberg School of Communications, University of Southern California
MASS MEDIA EFFECTS

ADAM KENDON
Anthropologist
GESTURE; KINESICS; NONVERBAL COMMUNICATION; SIGN LANGUAGE—OVERVIEW; SIGN LANGUAGE—ALTERNATE SIGN LANGUAGES

MAX R. KENWORTHY
Philatelic Research Assistant, American Philatelic Research Library, State College, Pa.
POSTAL SERVICE; STAMPS

EDITH W. KING
Professor of Education, University of Denver
DURKHEIM, ÉMILE; SCHUTZ, ALFRED; TARDE, JEAN-GABRIEL DE; WEBER, MAX

CATHERINE E. KIRKLAND
Philadelphia, Pa.
ENTERTAINMENT

BARBARA KIRSHENBLATT-GIMBLETT
Professor of Performance Studies, Tisch School of the Arts, New York University
TOURISM

EVA FEDER KITTAY
Associate Professor of Philosophy, State University of New York at Stony Brook
METAPHOR

JEFFREY KITTAY
Visiting Scholar in French, New York University
PROSE

MICHAEL J. KLEIN
Project Manager, SETI Project, Jet Propulsion Laboratory, California Institute of Technology
CETI

HANNAH KLIGER
Assistant Professor of Judaic and Near Eastern Studies and Assistant Professor of Communication, University of Massachusetts at Amherst
JUDAISM

PETER H. KLOPFER
Professor of Zoology, Duke University
BATESON, GREGORY; MEAD, MARGARET

MARK L. KNAPP
Professor of Speech Communication, University of Texas at Austin
SPEECH

PAUL J. KORSHIN
Professor of English, University of Pennsylvania
JOHNSON, SAMUEL

CHERIS KRAMARAE
Professor of Speech Communication, University of Illinois at Urbana-Champaign
FEMINIST THEORIES OF COMMUNICATION

KLAUS KRIPPENDORFF
Professor of Communications, The Annenberg School of Communications, University of Pennsylvania
CONTENT ANALYSIS; CYBERNETICS; INFORMATION THEORY; SHANNON, CLAUDE

S. KRISHNASWAMY
Film and television producer-director, Madras
MUSICAL, FILM—BOMBAY GENRE; MYTHOLOGICAL FILM, ASIAN

DONALD E. KROODSMA
Professor of Zoology, University of Massachusetts at Amherst
ANIMAL SONG

JOHN B. KUIPER
Chair, Division of Radio/Television/Film, University of North Texas
ARCHIVES, FILM

WILLIAM A. LADUSAW
Assistant Professor of Linguistics, Cowell College, University of California, Santa Cruz
SEMANTICS

PNINA LAHAV
Professor of Law, Boston University
CENSORSHIP—GOVERNMENT CENSORSHIP

ZVI LAMM
Professor of Education, Hebrew University of Jerusalem
SCHOOL

DAN LANDIS
Professor of Psychology, University of Mississippi
INTERCULTURAL COMMUNICATION

GLADYS ENGEL LANG
Professor of Communications and Political Science, University of Washington
PLEBISCITE; POLITICAL SYMBOLS

KURT LANG
Professor of Communications, University of Washington
COMMUNICATIONS RESEARCH: ORIGINS AND DEVELOPMENT; POLITICAL SYMBOLS

RALPH W. LARKIN
Research consultant, Academic Research Consulting Service, New York
REVOLUTION

MAGALI SARFATTI LARSON
Professor of Sociology, Temple University
PROFESSION

D. L. LEMAHIEU
Professor of History, Lake Forest College
PALEY, WILLIAM

JOHN A. LENT
Professor of Communications, Temple University
NEWSPAPER: TRENDS—TRENDS IN ASIA

JANET LEVER
Pew Memorial Trust Fellow, RAND/UCLA Center for Health Policy Study, Santa Monica, Calif.
SPORTS—SPORTS AND SOCIETY

STEPHEN C. LEVINSON
Lecturer in Linguistics, King's College, University of Cambridge
CONVERSATION

GEORGE H. LEWIS
Professor of Sociology, University of the Pacific
TASTE CULTURES

JAY LEYDA
Pinewood Professor of Cinema Studies, Tisch School of the Arts, New York University
EISENSTEIN, SERGEI

LAWRENCE LICHTY
Professor of Radio, Television, and Film, Northwestern University
RADIO

JOHN LIGGETT
Senior Lecturer in Psychology, University of Wales, College of Cardiff
FACE

KENNETH J. LIPARTITO
Assistant Professor of History, University of Houston
TELEPHONE

ELIZABETH F. LOFTUS
Professor of Psychology, University of Washington
TESTIMONY

ALAN LOMAX
Director, Cantometrics and Choreometrics Project, Department of Anthropology, and Director, Center for the Social Sciences, Columbia University
CANTOMETRICS; CHOREOMETRICS

TREVOR LUMMIS
Historian and writer, London
ORAL HISTORY

SEAN MACBRIDE
President Emeritus, International Peace Bureau, Geneva; former Chair, UNESCO International Commission for the Study of Communication Problems
NEW INTERNATIONAL INFORMATION ORDER

MAXWELL E. MCCOMBS
Jesse H. Jones Centennial Professor in Communication, University of Texas at Austin
AGENDA-SETTING

THELMA MCCORMACK
Professor of Sociology, York University
PORNOGRAPHY

JAMES C. MCCROSKEY
Professor of Communication Studies, West Virginia University
SPEECH ANXIETY

TERESA M. MCDEVITT
Assistant Professor of Educational Psychology, University of Northern Colorado
FAMILY

JOHN HOLMES MCDOWELL
Associate Professor of Folklore, Indiana University
SPEECH PLAY

J. N. MCGOVERN
Professor Emeritus of Forestry, University of Wisconsin–Madison
WRITING MATERIALS

WILLIAM J. MCGUIRE
Professor of Psychology, Yale University
PERSUASION

DENIS MCQUAIL
Professor of Mass Communications, Universiteit van Amsterdam
MASS COMMUNICATIONS RESEARCH; MODELS OF COMMUNICATION

FRANK E. MANNING
Professor of Anthropology, University of Western Ontario
SPECTACLE

JOSEPH MARGOLIS
Professor of Philosophy, Temple University
AESTHETICS

CAROLYN MARVIN
Associate Professor of Communications, The Annenberg School of Communications, University of Pennsylvania
CITIZENS BAND RADIO; LITERACY

ANNE J. MATHEWS
Director, Library Programs, Office of Educational Research and Improvement, U.S. Department of Education, Washington, D.C.
LIBRARY—TRENDS

MYRON MATLAW
Professor Emeritus of English, Queens College, City University of New York
DRAMA—HISTORY

ARMAND MATTELART
Professor of Information and Communication Sciences, Université de Rennes II (Université de Haute Bretagne)
MARXIST THEORIES OF COMMUNICATION—THIRD WORLD APPROACHES

PHILIP B. MEGGS
Professor of Communication Arts and Design, Virginia Commonwealth University
TYPOGRAPHY

WILLIAM H. MELODY
Director, Communication and Information Technologies Programme, Economic and Social Research Council of Great Britain, London
TELECOMMUNICATIONS NETWORKS

SHELDON MEYER
Senior Vice-President, Editorial, Oxford University Press, New York
RENOIR, JEAN

LOUIS T. MILIC
Professor of English, Cleveland State University
STYLE, LITERARY

ABRAHAM H. MILLER
Professor of Political Science, University of Cincinnati
TERRORISM

JAMES MILLER
Associate Professor of Communications, Hampshire College, Amherst, Mass.
CABLE TELEVISION

JAMES D. MILLER
Director of Research, Central Institute for the Deaf, Saint Louis, Mo.
PERCEPTION—SPEECH

ANDREW W. MIRACLE
Professor of Anthropology, Texas Christian University
PLAY

MICHAEL MORGAN
Associate Professor of Communication, University of Massachusetts at Amherst
CULTIVATION ANALYSIS

TESSA MORRIS-SUZUKI
Senior Lecturer in Economic History, University of New England, Armidale, N.S.W., Australia
COMPUTER: IMPACT—IMPACT ON THE WORK FORCE

VINCENT MOSCO
Professor of Sociology, Queen's University at Kingston
COMPUTER: IMPACT—IMPACT ON MILITARY AFFAIRS; VIDEOTEX

SERGE MOSCOVICI
Professor of Social Psychology, École des Hautes Études en Sciences Sociales
CROWD BEHAVIOR

MICHAEL T. MOTLEY
Professor of Rhetoric and Communication, University of California, Davis
SLIPS OF THE TONGUE

HAMID MOWLANA
Professor and Director, International Communication Program, School of International Service, American University, Washington, D.C.
INTERNATIONAL ORGANIZATIONS

WILLIAM ARTHUR MUNFORD
Librarian Emeritus, National Library for the Blind, Stockport, England
LIBRARY—HISTORY

WILLIAM T. MURPHY
Chief, Motion Picture, Sound, and Video Branch, National Archives and Records Administration, Washington, D.C.
FLAHERTY, ROBERT

KAY MUSSELL
Professor of Literature and American Studies, American University, Washington, D.C.
ROMANCE, THE

JOSEPH NAVEH
Professor of West Semitic Epigraphy and Palaeography, Hebrew University of Jerusalem
ALPHABET

RICHARD ALAN NELSON
Associate Professor of Communication, University of Houston
PATHÉ, CHARLES

OTTFRIED NEUBECKER
President, Wappen-HEROLD, Deutsche Heraldische Gesellschaft, Stuttgart
HERALDRY

DAN D. NIMMO
Professor of Communication, University of Oklahoma
LOBBYING

CHRISTIAN NORBERG-SCHULZ
Professor of Architecture, Arkitekthøgskolen Oslo
ARCHITECTURE

ABRAHAM NOSNIK
Lecturer, Instituto Tecnológico Autónomo de México, Mexico City
COOLEY, CHARLES HORTON; MEAD, GEORGE HERBERT; MORRIS, CHARLES; PEIRCE, CHARLES S.

ELINOR OCHS
Professor of Linguistics, University of Southern California
LANGUAGE ACQUISITION

JOHN J. OHALA
Professor of Linguistics, University of California, Berkeley
PHONOLOGY

WILLIAM M. O'NEIL
Professor Emeritus of Psychology, University of Sydney
CALENDAR

HARRIET OSTER
Associate Professor of Psychology, Derner Institute, Adelphi University
FACIAL EXPRESSION

DAN O'SULLIVAN
Head, History Department, Prior Pursglove College, Guisborough, England
EXPLORATION

DAVID L. PALETZ
Professor of Political Science, Duke University
POLITICIZATION

EDWARD L. PALMER
Senior Research Fellow, Children's Television Workshop, New York
EDUCATIONAL TELEVISION

JERRY PALMER
Senior Lecturer, Faculty of Art, City of London Polytechnic
MYSTERY AND DETECTIVE FICTION; SPY FICTION—THEMES

DAVID A. PARISER
Associate Professor of Art Education, Concordia University
CHILD ART

BARBARA PARKER
Adjunct Lecturer and Assistant Research Scientist in Anthropology, University of Michigan, Ann Arbor
GENDER

ASKO PARPOLA
Professor of South Asian Studies, Helsingen Yliopisto
INDUS SCRIPT

RAPHAEL PATAI
Professor Emeritus of Anthropology, Fairleigh Dickinson University
DIASPORA

MILES L. PATTERSON
Professor of Psychology, University of Missouri–Saint Louis
INTERPERSONAL DISTANCE

JOHN ALLEN PAULOS
Professor of Mathematics, Temple University
NUMBER

MORSE PECKHAM
Professor Emeritus of English and Comparative Literature, University of South Carolina
ROMANTICISM

JERZY PELC
Professor of Logical Semiotics, Uniwersytet Warszawski
SIGN; SIGN SYSTEM

W. KEITH PERCIVAL
Professor of Linguistics, University of Kansas
SAUSSURE, FERDINAND DE

WILLIAM H. PERKINS
Professor of Communication Arts and Sciences, Otolaryngology, and Speech Science and Technology, University of Southern California
SPEECH AND LANGUAGE DISORDERS

STEPHEN PERLOFF
Editor, *Photo Review,* Langhorne, Pa.
NIEPCE, JOSEPH-NICÉPHORE

THEODORE B. PETERSON
Professor Emeritus of Journalism and Research Professor Emeritus of Communications, University of Illinois at Urbana-Champaign
MAGAZINE

RICHARD PILCHER
Instructor in Theater, Baltimore School for the Arts
BARNUM, PHINEAS T.; BERGMAN, INGMAR; CHAPLIN, CHARLES; DISNEY, WALT; WELLES, ORSON

EDWARD W. PLOMAN
Program Director, United Nations University, Paris
SATELLITE

DAVID F. POLTRACK
Vice-President of Marketing, CBS Television Network, New York
RATING SYSTEMS: RADIO AND TELEVISION

JEREMY D. POPKIN
Professor of History, University of Kentucky
PAMPHLET

MARK POSTER
Professor of History, University of California, Irvine
UTOPIAS

SIEGBERT S. PRAWER
Taylor Professor Emeritus of the German Language and Literature, Queen's College, University of Oxford
HORROR FILM

DAVID PREMACK
Professor of Psychology, University of Pennsylvania
COGNITION, ANIMAL

GERALD PRINCE
Professor of Romance Languages, University of Pennsylvania
NARRATIVE

LINDA L. PUTNAM
Professor of Communication, Purdue University
BARGAINING

ERIC RABKIN
Professor of English Language and Literature, University of Michigan, Ann Arbor
SCIENCE FICTION

ROY A. RAPPAPORT
Leslie A. White Collegiate Professor of Anthropology, University of Michigan, Ann Arbor
RITUAL

JAMES A. RAWLEY
Professor of History, University of Nebraska, Lincoln
SLAVE TRADE, AFRICAN

MICHAEL L. RAY
Professor of Marketing and Communication, Stanford University
CONSUMER RESEARCH

W. CHARLES REDDING
Professor Emeritus of Communication, Purdue University
ORGANIZATIONAL COMMUNICATION

FERNANDO REYES MATTA
Director of Communication Research, Instituto Latinoamericano de Estudios Transnacionales, Santiago
NEWSPAPER: TRENDS—TRENDS IN LATIN AMERICA

TIMOTHY RICE
Associate Professor of Music, University of Toronto
MUSIC THEORIES—OVERVIEW

DONALD RICHIE
Film historian, Tokyo
BENSHI; KUROSAWA, AKIRA; OZU, YASUJIRŌ

BERTHOLD RIESE
Professor of American Anthropology, Freie Universität Berlin
AMERICAS, PRE-COLUMBIAN—COMMUNICATIONS

BARBARA RINGER
Former Register of Copyrights and Assistant Librarian of Congress for Copyright Services, Washington, D.C.
COPYRIGHT—THE EVOLUTION OF AUTHORSHIP RIGHTS; COPYRIGHT—INTERNATIONAL ARENA; COPYRIGHT—CHALLENGE OF THE COMMUNICATIONS REVOLUTION

COLLEEN ROACH
Assistant Professor of Communications, Fordham University
NEW INTERNATIONAL INFORMATION ORDER

JOSEPH R. ROACH
Associate Professor of Drama and English, Washington University
ACTING

DONALD F. ROBERTS
Professor of Communication and Director, Institute for Communication Research, Stanford University
CHILDREN—MEDIA EFFECTS

ARTHUR H. ROBINSON
Lawrence Martin Professor Emeritus of Cartography, University of Wisconsin–Madison
CARTOGRAPHY; MAP PROJECTION

JOHN P. ROBINSON
Professor of Sociology, University of Maryland at College Park
LEISURE; OPINION LEADER

MICHAEL J. ROBINSON
Associate Professor of Government, Georgetown University
GOVERNMENT-MEDIA RELATIONS

EVERETT M. ROGERS
Walter H. Annenberg Professor of Communications, The Annenberg School of Communications, University of Southern California
NETWORK ANALYSIS

PAT ROGERS
De Bartolo Professor in the Liberal Arts, University of South Florida
LETTER

SUZANNE ROMAINE
Merton Professor of the English Language, Merton College, University of Oxford
LANGUAGE VARIETIES

RAFAEL RONCAGLIOLO
Director, Centro de Estudios sobre Cultura Transnacional, Lima; Vice-President, International Association for Mass Communication Research, Lima
LATIN AMERICA, TWENTIETH CENTURY

CATHY ROOT
Researcher, American Film Institute, Los Angeles
STARS—STAR SYSTEM

KARL ERIK ROSENGREN
Professor of Sociology, Lunds Universitet
CULTURAL INDICATORS

ALAN ROSENTHAL
Filmmaker; Communications Institute, Hebrew University of Jerusalem
CINÉMA VÉRITÉ

FRANZ ROSENTHAL
Sterling Professor Emeritus of Near Eastern Languages, Yale University
ISLAM, CLASSICAL AND MEDIEVAL ERAS

MARK W. ROSKILL
Professor of the History of Modern Art, University of Massachusetts at Amherst
ICONOGRAPHY

BILLY I. ROSS
Professor of Mass Communications, Texas Tech University
CLASSIFIED ADVERTISING

ANYA PETERSON ROYCE
Professor of Anthropology and Music, Indiana University
MIME

BERNARD RUBIN
Professor of Governmental Affairs and Communication, Boston University
MINORITIES IN THE MEDIA

JAY RUBY
Associate Professor of Anthropology, Temple University
ETHNOGRAPHIC FILM

WILLIAM H. RUECKERT
Professor of English, State University of New York College at Geneseo
BURKE, KENNETH

GAVRIEL SALOMON
Professor of Education and Communication, Tel-Aviv University and the University of Arizona
CHILDREN—USE OF MEDIA

BERTRAND SAUZIER
Filmmaker, Calcutta
VERTOV, DZIGA

MARIANNE SAWICKI
Alexander Campbell Hopkins Chair of Religious Education, Lexington Theological Seminary, Lexington, Ky.
HOMILETICS

RICHARD SCHECHNER
Professor of Performance Studies, Tisch School of the Arts, New York University
DRAMA—PERFORMANCE

DAN SCHILLER
Associate Professor of Library and Information Science, University of California, Los Angeles
COMPUTER: IMPACT—OVERVIEW; NEWSPAPER: TRENDS—TRENDS IN NORTH AMERICA

HERBERT I. SCHILLER
Professor of Communication, University of California, San Diego
COMPUTER: IMPACT—IMPACT ON THE WORLD ECONOMY

DENISE SCHMANDT-BESSERAT
Professor of Middle Eastern Studies, University of Texas at Austin
CLAY TOKENS

WILBUR SCHRAMM
Director Emeritus, Institute for Communications Research, Stanford University; Distinguished Center Researcher Emeritus, East-West Center, Honolulu
AUDIOVISUAL EDUCATION; COMMUNICATIONS, STUDY OF; DEVELOPMENT COMMUNICATION—HISTORY AND THEORIES; GALLUP, GEORGE; HOVLAND, CARL; LASSWELL, HAROLD D.; LEWIN, KURT; PALIMPSEST; PARK, ROBERT; SILK ROAD; SLEEPER EFFECT

ROBERT J. SCHREIBER
Research consultant, Stamford, Conn.
PRINT-AUDIENCE MEASUREMENT

MICHAEL SCHUDSON
Professor of Sociology and Communication, University of California, San Diego
POLITICAL COMMUNICATION—HISTORY

JOCHEN SCHULTE-SASSE
Professor of Comparative Literature, University of Minnesota, Twin Cities
AVANT-GARDE

BARBARA W. SEARLE
Education specialist, World Bank, Washington, D.C.
EVALUATION RESEARCH

JOHN W. SEYBOLD
Publisher, Seybold Publications, Inc., Media, Pa.
ELECTRONIC PUBLISHING

ROBERT LEWIS SHAYON
Professor Emeritus of Communications, The Annenberg School of Communications, University of Pennsylvania
TELEVISION NEWS

JOHN SHEPHERD
Professor of Music and Sociology, Carleton University
MUSIC, POPULAR

JOEL SHERZER
Professor of Anthropology and Linguistics, University of Texas at Austin
SPEAKING, ETHNOGRAPHY OF

MARSHA SIEFERT
Editor, *Journal of Communication,* University of Pennsylvania
OPERA

MALCOLM O. SILLARS
Professor of Communication, University of Utah
PUBLIC SPEAKING

DAVID L. SILLS
Executive Associate, Social Science Research Council, New York; Editor, *International Encyclopedia of the Social Sciences*
LAZARSFELD, PAUL F.

SCOTT SIMMON
Curator, Mary Pickford Theater, Library of Congress, Washington, D.C.
GRIFFITH, D. W.

ELEANOR SINGER
Senior Research Scholar, Center for the Social Sciences, Columbia University
BANDWAGON EFFECTS; RUMOR

MARVIN A. SIRBU
Associate Professor of Engineering and Public Policy and Industrial Administration, Carnegie-Mellon University
STANDARDS

NATHAN SIVIN
Professor of Chinese Culture and of the History of Science, University of Pennsylvania
EAST ASIA, ANCIENT

STEPHEN M. SLAWEK
Assistant Professor of Music, University of Texas at Austin
MUSICAL INSTRUMENTS

R. C. SMAIL
Fellow of Sidney Sussex College, University of Cambridge
CRUSADES, THE

NINIAN SMART
Professor of Religious Studies, University of Lancaster and University of California, Santa Barbara
RELIGION

ANTHONY SMITH
President, Magdalen College, University of Oxford
GOVERNMENT REGULATION

W. JOHN SMITH
Professor of Biology and Psychology, University of Pennsylvania
ANIMAL COMMUNICATION; ANIMAL SIGNALS—OVERVIEW

DALLAS W. SMYTHE
Professor Emeritus of Communications, Simon Fraser University
SPECTRUM

CATHERINE E. SNOW
Professor of Human Development and Psychology, Harvard University
CHILDREN—DEVELOPMENT OF COMMUNICATION

JOEL SNYDER
Professor of Humanities, University of Chicago
PHOTOGRAPHY

LOUIS L. SNYDER
Professor Emeritus of History, City University of New York
GOEBBELS, JOSEPH

CHARLES SOLOMON
Animation historian, Santa Monica, Calif.
ANIMATION

PETER L. SPAIN
Operations Officer, Academy for Educational Development, Washington, D.C.
EVALUATION RESEARCH

HARTLEY S. SPATT
Associate Professor of English, Maritime College, State University of New York
ARMSTRONG, EDWIN H.; BELL, ALEXANDER GRAHAM; DAGUERRE, LOUIS; DE FOREST, LEE; EASTMAN, GEORGE; EDISON, THOMAS ALVA; FESSENDEN, REGINALD; LOCKE, JOHN; MARCONI, GUGLIELMO; REITH, JOHN; SIMMEL, GEORG

JAMES R. SQUIRE
Former Senior Vice-President, Silver Burdett & Ginn, Lexington, Mass.
TEXTBOOK

STEVEN A. STAHL
Associate Professor of Elementary Education and Reading, Western Illinois University
READING

FREDERICK STEIER
Associate Professor of Engineering Management and Associate Director, Center for Cybernetics Studies in Complex Systems, Old Dominion University
WIENER, NORBERT

SUSAN J. STEINBERG
American and Commonwealth Studies Bibliographer, Sterling Memorial Library, Yale University
DIDEROT, DENIS

PETER STEINER
Associate Professor of Slavic Languages and Chair, Comparative Literature and Literary Theory Program, University of Pennsylvania
SEMIOTICS

BRIAN STOCK
Senior Fellow, Pontifical Institute of Mediaeval Studies, Toronto
MIDDLE AGES

BEVERLY J. STOELTJE
Associate Professor of Folklore, Indiana University
FESTIVAL

WILLIAM C. STOKOE
Editor, *Sign Language Studies,* Silver Spring, Md.
SIGN LANGUAGE—PRIMARY SIGN LANGUAGES

GEORGE C. STONEY
Professor of Film and Television, Tisch School of the Arts, New York University
CITIZEN ACCESS

LAWRENCE H. STREICHER
Director, Lawrence Streicher Associates, Chicago
CARICATURE

JOHN STURROCK
Editor, *Times Literary Supplement,* London
AUTOBIOGRAPHY

DAVID SUMMERS
William R. Kenan, Jr., Professor of the History of Art, University of Virginia
VISUAL IMAGE

FREDERICK SUPPE
Professor of Philosophy, University of Maryland at College Park
CLASSIFICATION

JOHN SUTHERLAND
Professor of Literature, California Institute of Technology
LITERATURE, POPULAR

PIERRE SWIGGERS
Research Fellow, Fonds National de la Recherche Scientifique, Brussels
LINGUISTICS

YASUMASA TANAKA
Professor of Social Psychology and Communications, Gakushuin University; Director, Gakushuin University Computer Center
OSGOOD, CHARLES; SEMANTIC DIFFERENTIAL

JOHN TEBBEL
Professor Emeritus of Journalism, New York University
BEAVERBROOK, 1ST BARON; DAY, BENJAMIN H.; HEARST, WILLIAM RANDOLPH; NEWSPAPER: HISTORY; NORTHCLIFFE, ALFRED; PULITZER, JOSEPH; SCRIPPS, E. W.

DENNIS TEDLOCK
McNulty Professor of English, State University of New York at Buffalo
ETHNOPOETICS

STEPHEN THAYER
Professor of Psychology, City College and Graduate Center, City University of New York
TOUCH

KRISTIN THOMPSON
Honorary Fellow, Department of Communication Arts, University of Wisconsin–Madison
MOTION PICTURES—SILENT ERA

JEFF TODD TITON
Professor of Music, Brown University
MUSIC, FOLK AND TRADITIONAL

YOSHIHIKO TOKUMARU
Professor of Musicology and Comparative Arts Studies, Ochanomizu University
MUSIC THEORIES—NOTATIONS AND LITERACY

JANE TOMPKINS
Professor of English, Duke University
LITERARY CANON

ELIZABETH TONKIN
Senior Lecturer in Social Anthropology, Centre of West African Studies, University of Birmingham
MASK

DAVID TRACY
Distinguished Service Professor and Greely Chair in Catholic Studies, Divinity School, University of Chicago
INTERPRETATION

DANIEL H. TRAISTER
Assistant Director of Libraries for Special Collections, Van Pelt Library, University of Pennsylvania
BOOK

TRAN VAN DINH
Professor of International Politics and Communications, Temple University
ASIA, TWENTIETH CENTURY

ANDREW F. TUDOR
Senior Lecturer in Sociology, University of York
EXPRESSIONISM

DAVID G. TUERCK
Professor and Chair, Department of Economics, Suffolk University, Boston
ADVERTISING—ADVERTISING ECONOMICS

JOSEPH G. TUROW
Associate Professor of Communications, The Annenberg School of Communications, University of Pennsylvania
PUBLISHING—PUBLISHING INDUSTRY

MICHAEL TWYMAN
Professor of Typography & Graphic Communication, University of Reading
PRINTING—HISTORY OF PRINTING

ZENO VENDLER
Professor of Philosophy, University of California, San Diego
MEANING

PASCAL VERNUS
Professor of Philology, École Pratique des Hautes Études
EGYPTIAN HIEROGLYPHS

BRIAN VICKERS
Professor of English and Renaissance Literature, Eidgenössische Technische Hochschule Zürich
CLASSICISM

AMOS VOGEL
Professor of Communications, The Annenberg School of Communications, University of Pennsylvania
AVANT-GARDE FILM

THOMAS WASOW
Professor of Linguistics and Philosophy, Stanford University
GRAMMAR

HIROSHI WATANABE
Professor of Law, University of Tokyo
TOKUGAWA ERA: SECLUSION POLICY

ALAN WATSON
University Professor of Law, University of Pennsylvania
LAW AND COMMUNICATION

THOMAS WAUGH
Associate Professor of Film Studies, Concordia University
IVENS, JORIS

WILLIAM M. WEILBACHER
President, Bismark Corporation, New York
ADVERTISING—ADVERTISING AGENCY

GARY L. WELLS
Professor of Psychology, University of Alberta
TESTIMONY

JAMES M. WELLS
Custodian Emeritus, John M. Wing Foundation on the History of Printing, Newberry Library, Chicago
CAXTON, WILLIAM

R. J. ZWI WERBLOWSKY
Martin Buber Professor of Comparative Religion, Hebrew University of Jerusalem
SCRIPTURE

JAMES V. WERTSCH
Professor of Communication, University of California, San Diego
COGNITION; LURIA, ALEKSANDR; VYGOTSKY, LEV

DAVID MANNING WHITE
Professor Emeritus of Mass Communication, Virginia Commonwealth University
LOWENTHAL, LEO

PAUL WHITE
Senior Lecturer in Geography and Sub-Dean, Faculty of Social Sciences, University of Sheffield
MIGRATION

PETER B. WHITE
Senior Lecturer and Chair, Centre for the Study of Educational Communication and Media, La Trobe University, Bundoora, Vic., Australia
AUSTRALASIA, TWENTIETH CENTURY

HARRY WIENER
Director of Professional Information, Pfizer Pharmaceuticals, New York
SMELL

RONNIE B. WILBUR
Professor of Linguistics, Department of Audiology and Speech Sciences, Purdue University
SIGN LANGUAGE—MANUAL LANGUAGE CODES

R. HAVEN WILEY
Professor of Biology, University of North Carolina at Chapel Hill
ANIMAL SIGNALS—AUDIBLE SIGNALS

ALAN WILLIAMS
Associate Professor of French and Cinema Studies, Rutgers University, New Brunswick
NEW WAVE FILM

MARTHA E. WILLIAMS
Professor of Information Science, University of Illinois at Urbana-Champaign
DATA BASE

RAYMOND H. WILLIAMS
Professor Emeritus of Drama and Fellow of Jesus College, University of Cambridge
FACT AND FICTION

MICHAEL WILLMORTH
Lecturer, The Annenberg School of Communications, University of Pennsylvania
SOUND EFFECTS

SVEN WINDAHL
Associate Professor of Information Techniques, Lunds Universitet and Högskolan i Växjö
MODELS OF COMMUNICATION

YVES WINKIN
Associate Professor of Communication, Université de l'État à Liège
GOFFMAN, ERVING

BRIAN WINSTON
Dean, School of Communications, Pennsylvania State University
MCLUHAN, MARSHALL

MERLIN C. WITTROCK
Professor of Education and Head, Division of Educational Psychology, University of California, Los Angeles
TEACHING

ROBERT WOODS
Senior Lecturer in Geography, University of Sheffield
MIGRATION

ALAN N. WOOLFOLK
Assistant Professor of Sociology and Anthropology, University of Southern Mississippi
FREUD, SIGMUND; JUNG, CARL

CHARLES R. WRIGHT
Professor of Communications and Sociology, The Annenberg School of Communications, University of Pennsylvania
FUNCTIONAL ANALYSIS; HYMAN, HERBERT H.; MERTON, ROBERT K.

LESTER WUNDERMAN
Chairman, Wunderman Worldwide, New York
DIRECT RESPONSE MARKETING

DAVID ZAREFSKY
Professor of Communication Studies and Dean, School of Speech, Northwestern University
FORENSICS

YASSEN NIKOLAEVICH ZASSOURSKY
Professor of American Literature and Dean, Faculty of Journalism, Moscow M. V. Lomonosov State University
NEWSPAPER: TRENDS—TRENDS IN THE SOVIET PRESS

Topical Guide

Titles of the 569 articles in the *International Encyclopedia of Communications* are here grouped under the following headings, each of which represents a major field of interest in the evolving communications discipline:

Articles relevant to more than one field may be listed under several headings. Titles of articles that offer a comprehensive view of a field or an important segment of it are shown in italics.

ADVERTISING AND PUBLIC RELATIONS

ANCIENT WORLD

ANIMAL COMMUNICATION

Animal Communication
Animal Signals
Animal Song
Cognition, Animal
Darwin, Charles
Ethology
Human-Animal Communication
Insects, Social
Other relevant articles under COMMUNICATIONS RESEARCH; NONVERBAL COMMUNICATION

AREA STUDIES

Africa, Precolonial
Africa, Twentieth Century
Americas, Pre-Columbian
Asia, Twentieth Century
Australasia, Twentieth Century
East Asia, Ancient
Hellenic World
Islam, Classical and Medieval Eras
Islamic World, Twentieth Century
Latin America, Twentieth Century
Marxist Theories of Communication
2. Third World Approaches
Middle Ages
Music Theater
1. Western Traditions
2. Asian Traditions
Mythological Film, Asian
Newspaper: Trends
1. Trends in Africa
2. Trends in Asia
3. Trends in Europe
4. Trends in Latin America
5. Trends in the Middle East
6. Trends in North America
7. Trends in the Soviet Press
Roman Empire
South Asia, Ancient
Television History
2. Global Development

ARTS

Aesthetics
Architecture
Art
Art, Funerary
Artifact
Artist and Society
Avant-Garde
Body Decoration
Caricature
Child Art
Classicism
Code
Comics
Dance
Design
Expressionism
Forgery, Art
Genre
Graphic Reproduction
Graphics
Heraldry
Iconography
Mask
Mode
Mural
Museum
Narrative
Opera
Oral Poetry
Perception
Photography
Poetry
Portraiture
Poster
Realism
Religion
Renaissance
Representation, Pictorial and Photographic
Ritual
Romanticism
Sculpture
Signage
Spectacle
Symbolism
Taste Cultures
Typography
Video
Visual Image
Other relevant articles under LITERATURE; MEDIA; MOTION PICTURES; MUSIC; PHOTOGRAPHY; TELEVISION; THEATER

COMMUNICATIONS RESEARCH

Agenda-Setting
Attitudes
Bandwagon Effects
Cantometrics
Choreometrics
Classification
Cognition
Communications Research: Origins and Development
Consumer Research
Content Analysis
Conversation
Crowd Behavior
Cultivation Analysis
Cultural Indicators
Diffusion
Evaluation Research
Functional Analysis
Gender
Group Communication
Human-Animal Communication
Interaction, Face-to-Face
Interactive Media
Intercultural Communication
Interpersonal Communication
Leisure
Literacy
Mass Communications Research
Mass Media Effects
Mass Observation
Models of Communication
Motivation Research
Network Analysis
Opinion Leader
Opinion Measurement
Oral History
Organizational Communication
Perception
Performance
Persuasion
Play
Poll
Pornography
Profession
Propaganda
Public Opinion
Revolution
Rumor
Selective Reception
Sexism
Sleeper Effect
Sound
Testimony
Tourism
Violence
Other relevant articles under ANIMAL COMMUNICATION; LANGUAGE AND LINGUISTICS; NONVERBAL COMMUNICATION; POLITICAL COMMUNICATION; THEORIES OF COMMUNICATION; THEORISTS

COMPUTER ERA

Artificial Intelligence
CETI
Computer: History
Computer: Impact
Copyright

EDUCATION

FOLKLORE

GOVERNMENT REGULATION

INSTITUTIONS

INTERNATIONAL COMMUNICATION

Coins
Colonization
Computer: Impact
Crusades, The
Cryptology
Deception
Development Communication
Diaspora
Diplomacy
Disinformation
Espionage
Exploration
Gandhi, Mohandas
International Organizations
Map Projection
Marconi, Guglielmo
Migration
Nakahama Manjiro
New International Information Order
News Agencies
Polo, Marco
Radio, International
Reith, John
Religion
Silk Road
Slave Trade, African
South Asia, Ancient
Spectrum
Telegraphy
Television History
  2. Global Development
  3. World Market Struggles
Television News
Tokugawa Era: Seclusion Policy
Tourism
Translation, Literary
Writing
Writing Materials
Other relevant articles under ANCIENT WORLD; AREA STUDIES; JOURNALISM; LANGUAGE AND LINGUISTICS

JOURNALISM

Beaverbrook, 1st Baron
Bennett, James Gordon
Comics
Day, Benjamin H.
Electronic Publishing
Gallup, George
Goebbels, Joseph
Government-Media Relations
Greeley, Horace
Hearst, William Randolph
Kenyatta, Jomo
Lippmann, Walter
Luce, Henry
Magazine
Mergenthaler, Ottmar
Minorities in the Media
Minority Media
Monopoly
News Agencies
Newsletter
Newsmagazine
Newspaper: History
Newspaper: Trends
Newsreel
Nkrumah, Kwame
Northcliffe, Alfred
Ochs, Adolph S.
Pathé, Charles
Photojournalism
Poll
Print-Audience Measurement
Printing
Publishing
Pulitzer, Joseph
Radio
Reith, John
Roper, Elmo
Scripps, E. W.
Sports
  2. Sports and the Media
Syndication
Television News
Zenger, John Peter
Other relevant articles under ADVERTISING AND PUBLIC RELATIONS; GOVERNMENT REGULATION; INTERNATIONAL COMMUNICATION; POLITICAL COMMUNICATION

LANGUAGE AND LINGUISTICS

Alphabet
Barthes, Roland
Bateson, Gregory
Burke, Kenneth
Children
  1. Development of Communication
  2. Development of Symbolization
Classification
Code
Cognition
Conversation
Ethnopoetics
Feminist Theories of Communication
Foucault, Michel
Grammar
Interpretation
Jakobson, Roman
Johnson, Samuel
Language
Language Acquisition
Language Ideology
Language Reference Book
Language Varieties
Lévi-Strauss, Claude
Linguistics
Luria, Aleksandr
Meaning
Metaphor
Mode
Morris, Charles
Oral Culture
Phonology
Piaget, Jean
Prose
Richards, I. A.
Sapir, Edward
Saussure, Ferdinand de
Semantic Differential
Semantics
Semantics, General
Semiotics
Sexism
Sign
Sign System
Sign Language
Speaking, Ethnography of
Structuralism
Symbolism
Vygotsky, Lev
Webster, Noah
Whorf, Benjamin Lee
Wittgenstein, Ludwig
Other relevant articles under LITERATURE; SPEECH

LITERATURE

Authorship
Autobiography
Barthes, Roland
Biography
Book
Caxton, William
Classicism
Copyright
Culture
Diary
Diderot, Denis
Encyclopedia
Ethnopoetics
Fact and Fiction
Fiction
Fiction, Portrayal of Character in
Folktale
Fotonovela
Genre
Gutenberg, Johannes
Interpretation
Intertextuality
Johnson, Samuel

MEDIA

MIDDLE AGES

MOTION PICTURES

MUSIC

Radio
Song
Sound
Sound Recording

NONVERBAL COMMUNICATION

Acting
Bateson, Gregory
Boas, Franz
Body Decoration
Body Movement
Body Movement Notation
Children
1. Development of Communication
2. Development of Symbolization
Choreometrics
Clothing
Code
Dance
Darwin, Charles
Deception
Eyes
Face
Facial Expression
Food
Freud, Sigmund
Gallaudet, Thomas
Gandhi, Mohandas
Gesture
Goffman, Erving
Heraldry
Interaction, Face-to-Face
Interpersonal Distance
Keller, Helen
Kinesics
Mask
Mead, Margaret
Nonverbal Communication
Proxemics
Sign Language
Smell
Spatial Organization
Touch
Other relevant articles under ANIMAL COMMUNICATION; ARTS; COMMUNICATIONS RESEARCH; MUSIC

PHOTOGRAPHY

Art
Audiovisual Education
Bateson, Gregory
Choreometrics
Cinéma Vérité
Cinematography
Daguerre, Louis
Documentary
Eastman, George
Ethnographic Film
Fotonovela
Graphic Reproduction
Land, Edwin
Luce, Henry
Lumière, Louis and Auguste
Mead, Margaret
Morse, Samuel F. B.
Motion Photography
Motion Pictures
Niepce, Joseph-Nicéphore
Photography
Photography, Amateur
Photojournalism
Pornography
Portraiture
Representation, Pictorial and Photographic
Television News
Video
Visual Image

POLITICAL COMMUNICATION

Agenda-Setting
Bandwagon Effects
Bargaining
Citizen Access
Demonstration
Diplomacy
Disinformation
Election
Forensics
Goebbels, Joseph
Government-Media Relations
Government Regulation
Ideology
Lobbying
Pamphlet
Plebiscite
Political Communication
Political Socialization
Political Symbols
Politicization
Poll
Poster
Pressure Group
Propaganda
Revolution
Spectacle
Terrorism
Other relevant articles under ADVERTISING AND PUBLIC RELATIONS; INTERNATIONAL COMMUNICATION; SPEECH

PRINT MEDIA

Beaverbrook, 1st Baron
Bennett, James Gordon
Book
Caricature
Cartography
Caxton, William
Classified Advertising
Comics
Copyright
Day, Benjamin H.
Electronic Publishing
Encyclopedia
Fotonovela
Graphic Reproduction
Graphics
Greeley, Horace
Gutenberg, Johannes
Hearst, William Randolph
Lippmann, Walter
Luce, Henry
Magazine
Mergenthaler, Ottmar
Minorities in the Media
Minority Media
News Agencies
Newsletter
Newsmagazine
Newspaper: History
Newspaper: Trends
Northcliffe, Alfred
Ochs, Adolph S.
Pamphlet
Park, Robert
Photojournalism
Print-Audience Measurement
Printing
Publishing
Pulitzer, Joseph
Scripps, E. W.
Textbook
Typography

RADIO

Advertising
Armstrong, Edwin H.
Cantril, Hadley
CETI
Citizen Access
Citizens Band Radio
Commercials
De Forest, Lee
Development Communication
3. Projects
Faraday, Michael
Fessenden, Reginald
Grierson, John

RELIGION

SPEECH

TELEVISION

THEATER

THEORIES OF COMMUNICATION

Sign System
Social Cognitive Theory
Structuralism
Symbolic Logic
Utopias
Other relevant articles under COMMUNICATIONS RESEARCH; THEORISTS

THEORISTS

Adorno, Theodor
Aristotle
Babbage, Charles
Bakhtin, Mikhail
Barthes, Roland
Bateson, Gregory
Benjamin, Walter
Boas, Franz
Burke, Kenneth
Cantril, Hadley
Cherry, Colin
Cooley, Charles Horton
Darwin, Charles
Dewey, John
Durkheim, Émile
Foucault, Michel
Freud, Sigmund
Goffman, Erving
Gramsci, Antonio
Hovland, Carl
Hyman, Herbert H.
Innis, Harold
Jakobson, Roman
James, William
Jung, Carl
Lasswell, Harold D.
Lazarsfeld, Paul F.
Lévi-Strauss, Claude
Lewin, Kurt
Lippmann, Walter
Locke, John
Lowenthal, Leo
Luria, Aleksandr
McLuhan, Marshall
Marx, Karl
Mead, George Herbert
Mead, Margaret
Merton, Robert K.
Milton, John
Morris, Charles
Osgood, Charles
Park, Robert
Peirce, Charles S.
Piaget, Jean
Plato
Richards, I. A.
Sapir, Edward
Saussure, Ferdinand de
Schramm, Wilbur
Schutz, Alfred
Shannon, Claude
Simmel, Georg
Sullivan, Harry Stack
Tarde, Jean-Gabriel de
Von Neumann, John
Vygotsky, Lev
Weaver, Warren
Weber, Max
Whorf, Benjamin Lee
Wiener, Norbert
Wittgenstein, Ludwig

Index

Boldface numbers followed by a colon indicate the volume in which index entries can be found. Multiple page numbers within a given volume are separated by commas; volumes are separated by semicolons. When main entries in the index are also article titles in the text, they reflect capitalization practice for titles. An asterisk following a page number or a range of page numbers indicates the location of the article in the encyclopedia.

A

B

C

D

F

H

I

K

L

N

P

T

U

V

W

X

Y

Z